Basic Law and the Legal Environment of Business

IRWIN LEGAL STUDIES IN BUSINESS SERIES

Basic Law and the Legal Environment of Business

John E. Adamson

Southwest Missouri State University

IRWIN

Chicago • Bogota • Boston
Buenos Aires • Caracas • London • Madrid
Mexico City • Sydney • Toronto

Senior sponsoring editor:	Craig Beytien
Senior developmental editor:	Laura Hurst-Spell
Marketing manager:	Cindy Ledwith
Project editor:	Karen J. Nelson
Production manager:	Laurie Kersch
Designer:	Larry J. Cope
Interior designer:	David Lansdon—Lansdon Design
Cover designer:	Andrew Curtis
Art studio:	Precision Graphics
Art coordinator:	Heather Burbridge
Compositor:	J.M. Post Graphics, A Division of Cardinal Communications Group, Inc.
Typeface:	10.5/13 Times Roman
Printer:	Von Hoffman Press, Inc.

Library of Congress Cataloging-in-Publication Data

Adamson, John E.
    Basic law and the legal environment of business / John E. Adamson.
      p.   cm.—(Irwin legal studies in business series)
    Includes index.
    ISBN 0-256-11302-5
    1. Commercial law—United States.   2. Business enterprises—United
States.   3. Trade regulation—United States.   I. Title.
II. Series.
KF889.A723   1995
346.73'07—dc20
[347.3067]   94–12327

Printed in the United States of America
1 2 3 4 5 6 7 8 9 0 VH 1 0 9 8 7 6 5 4

To my family, whom I hold dearer than all else, and to those who cherish and share the steadily disappearing way of life inherent in small town America. Non iam refugium.

PREFACE

First of all, for taking the time to read this, my congratulations and thanks. A preface is all too often ignored even by those who perhaps should know better (including myself). So, I'll try to make it as concise and rewarding as possible.

This text is intended to provide a thorough basic, working knowledge of the law and, perhaps more importantly, train the student to observe both potential and actual events from a legal perspective. These two goals are especially pursued in Part I, entitled THE BASIC LEGAL FOUNDATION, which includes materials on ethics, the legal system, torts, and the criminal law. Thereafter, in Parts II through IX, the focus narrows to a detailed study of traditional business law topics. The subjects for these Parts include Contracts, Sales, Commercial Paper, Bankruptcy, Business Organizations, Agency and Employment, Property, Insurance, and others. Finally, Part X deals with peripheral areas of the law that, nonetheless, may have a significant impact on the well being of a business.

Some *unique features* of *Basic Law and the Legal Environment of Business* include several practical *Insight* sections on topics such as **how to choose an attorney, how to compensate an attorney, how to enter the legal profession,** and others. Also, every chapter is written in a conversational tone that tries to impart not only the rules but the logic behind the rules that ties them together. In the same vein, where inconsistencies and gaps appear in the law, I have tried to openly note them so as not to leave the student with the feeling that she or he has missed something. Finally, every chapter begins with an outline that incorporates the objectives of the chapter and gives the student a basis on which to organize notetaking. The chapters also typically contain charts summarizing important topics and condensed definitions of all significant terms in the margins for quick reference.

Cases selected for their involving nature highlight the end of chapter materials. Also included in these materials are vocabulary studies and problems. Some of the problems are meant to be open-ended and capable of being answered in many ways.

A more detailed review of each chapter is provided in the separate publication *Study Guide for Use with Basic Law and the Legal Environment of Business.* Finally, an instructor's manual that includes detailed chapter outlines as well as a test manual with unit and book tests is available. The outlines in the manual incorporate references to end-of-chapter problems that provide the best example of a particular outline topic as well as the answers to those problems.

I would like to express my thanks to the reviewers of the manuscript:

Theodore M. Dinges
Longview Community College

Era Boone Ferguson
Sullivan College

Jean Ann Gallegos
Albuquerque Technical Vocational Institute

Steve Garlick
DeVry Institute of Technology

John Gubbay
Moraine Valley Community College

Karen Brown Gattozzi
Palm Beach Community College

Gardiner M. Haight
Commonwealth College

Harold Hickock
Western Business College

Robert Inama
Ricks College

M. Christine Kern
Sanford-Brown College

Susan C. McKnight
Sanford-Brown College

David E. Roos
Allen County Community College

Sanford Searleman
Adirondack Community College

Gwen Seaquist
Ithaca College

David J. Smith
Bryant & Stratton Business Institute

Mick Stahler
Stautzenberger College

Judith I. White
Heald Business College

Joseph M. Woodland
Capitol Business College

Well, that's about the whole package. I think it provides the student with the maximum chance of developing a true and balanced appreciation of our laws. As an old professor of mine was fond of saying, "the law is a record of life and how humanity chooses to live it. . . . In a sense it is the only true to life entertainment." I hope you will, as I have, come to agree with and relish the truth in his observation.

John A.

CONTENTS

| PART X

Other Legal Areas with a Significant Impact on Business   491

The Basic Legal Foundation

CHAPTERS

What Is Law, and How Have Our Historical and Ethical Backgrounds Contributed to Its Development?

CHAPTER OUTLINE AND OBJECTIVES

After studying this chapter, the student will be able to:

I. Explain why the law should be studied and what is included in that study.
   a. The definition of law
   b. The definition of business law
II. Describe the historical development of our laws and legal system.
   a. The establishment of the courts of law and the appellate court system
   b. The origin of the jury
   c. The use of precedent
   d. The development of courts of equity
III. Describe how our ethical systems contribute to the growth of our laws.
   a. The Judeo-Christian ethical system
   b. Egoism
   c. Utilitarianism
   d. Other ethical systems
IV. Analyze how the common law continues to develop, using *Marvin* v. *Marvin*, a case involving movie stars, sex, and money.

COUNTY
BUILDING

A CASE TO TEST
YOUR WISDOM

Then came two women . . . before King Solomon.

And the first woman said, O my lord, I and this woman live in the same house; and I was delivered of a child with her in the house.

And it came to pass the third day after that I was delivered, that this woman was delivered also: and we were together: there was no stranger with us in the house, save we two in the house.

And this woman's child died in the night; because she overlaid it [smothered the child with her body].

And she arose at midnight, and took my son from beside me, while thine handmaid slept, and laid it in her bosom, and laid her dead child in my bosom.

And when I rose in the morning to give my child suck, behold it was dead: but when I had considered it in the morning, behold it was not my son, which I did bear. And the other woman said, Nay; but the living is my son, and the dead is thy son.

And the women spoke no more save each to demand the child for herself, but those in the king's court that day shook their heads saying, "No greater test of wisdom shall befall Solomon. What judgment will he render?"

And what judgment would you render? Before you decide, consider the following questions: Why is the king responsible for deciding this case? What possible remedies to the situation can the king choose from? Can the king decide not to decide? Now, which remedy would you choose? Why? For King Solomon's decision, read on.

Why Study the Law, and What Is Included in That Study?

You and other business-oriented people must deal with the law every day. You may meet it firsthand, in the form of a highway patrol officer personalizing a ticket for you. You may feel its watchful eye on you as it regulates your workplace, product, and profit. Your response to it may be frustration, resentment, or gratitude, depending on the circumstances. Regardless, you must realize that a stable environment within which business can flourish is maintained by the law and the legal system that imposes it. Without the law, you would have to contend with a level of chaos that would make profitable trade improbable, if not impossible. Because of all this, knowledge of the law and how it works is crucial to your success. As a first step in acquiring that knowledge, you need to realize exactly what the law is.

Frankly, however, over the centuries, there have been as many answers to the question of what law is as there have been people who asked it. The answers varied so much because each answer was a product of the background and insight of the person who framed it. Although such philosophers as Aristotle and Hobbes posed formal definitions, you can be certain that the common people of their times offered their share of very practical ones. For the purposes of this book on business law, we need to favor the approach of the common people and pick an accurate but very practical definition.

The Definition of Law

For our purposes, therefore, the **law** is best defined as those rules of conduct that a central political authority will enforce. To be sure, we all obey many rules that lack the force of law. Religions suggest their codes of conduct to us, our communities and ethnic heritages have their customs, and even our social groups tell us what behaviors and styles are acceptable, but all of these lack the power to imprison or fine to enforce their rules. That power is what sets the law apart.

Law: rules authority will enforce

The Definition of Business Law

The first two parts of this book and most of the third are meant to give you a background in the law in general. Then, from Chapter 7 on, we will concentrate on business law, the aspect of the law that you doubtless expected to study in detail in this book. **Business law** is the relatively specific group of laws that regulates the establishment, operation, and termination of commercial enterprises. Don't skimp on your study of these first chapters, however. If you don't have the background that Chapters 1–6 are meant to give you, relying on a knowledge of the law obtained without them will be as dangerous as walking on thin ice over the waters of a deep, fast current.

Business Law: legal rules specifically applying to commercial enterprise

What Did Our Historical Background Contribute to the Development of Our Laws and Legal System?

Although the historical and ethnic backgrounds of the citizens of the United States are diverse, the roots of the vast majority of our laws and legal systems lie in England. There, over the course of centuries, the power to make, interpret, and apply the law was slowly transferred from the monarchy to legal institutions very similar to those of this country. So, for a better understanding of how the law works today, we have to go back to the middle of the 12th century.

The Establishment of the Courts of Law and the Appellate Court System

At that time, almost a century after their conquest of England, the Normans remained culturally separate from the people they had conquered. The Norman king, worried about the potential danger that this division posed to his rule, sought to bring about unity. As one means of achieving this end, he set up a system of circuit riding judges, selected from the Norman nobility. These judges would ride from village to village along a particular "circuit" and, using the power the king had given them, make decisions that settled disputes among the people.

The power to settle disputes had always been held by monarchs. Throughout history, a king or queen who held "court" was not conducting a social event but making the nitty-gritty decisions that kept his or her realm together. If a king decided wisely and fairly, his power and reputation grew. If he decided poorly and with obvious favoritism, he created long-standing grudges that often came back to haunt him in the form of revolt. In the case that begins this chapter, King Solomon followed the path of wisdom and fairness, as follows:

And the king said, "Divide the living child in two, and give half to the one, and half to the other."

Then spake the woman who was the living child's real mother, for her bowels yearned upon her son, "Oh my lord, give her the living child and in no wise slay it."

But the mother of the dead child said, "Let it [the living baby] be neither hers nor mine. Divide it with the sword."

Then the king answered and said, "Give her [the woman who did not want the surviving baby slain] the living child, and in no wise slay it: she is the mother thereof."

And all Israel heard of the judgment which the king had judged; and they feared the king.

Courts of Law: formal proceedings to resolve disputes

Appellate Courts: higher courts given authority over lower courts in order to maintain fairness and uniformity in decisions

So it was very important to the king of England that his judges act wisely when they held **courts of law.** These courts were formal proceedings in which the judges were to apply powers that the king had given them to resolve the disputes of the people. To be as certain as possible that his judges decided cases fairly, the king of England created a system of **appellate courts.** These higher courts were established to maintain fairness and uniformity in the decisions reached in the lower courts. Individuals disgruntled with the decisions reached in a court presided over by a circuit riding judge could then appeal to a higher court for review. In such cases, the appellate court would determine whether the lower court had acted properly. The king formed the appellate courts by having the circuit riding judges return to London for approximately half of each year and sit together in groups to hear cases brought on appeal. The highest of these appellate courts became known as the King's (or Queen's) Bench.

The Origin of the Jury

However, just having a reasonably fair structure for resolving disputes did not ensure that the Norman and older English cultures would draw together as one. To achieve that result within the legal system he created, the king had to utilize other devices that are very important to our law. To explain these, we need to follow a sample case through the system that the king set up.

his produce to London in his oxcart. It is the first time he has made the trip, and he has been on the road for two days. Worried that his goods might spoil, James is in a bit of a rush. As he approaches a four-way intersection, he sees another cart that could enter the intersection from his right at the same time that his oxcart will. Does James rein in his ox, which is lumbering along at maximum speed? No, because he knows that it is the custom around Northshire for the right-of-way at an intersection to go to the person on the left. He is that person, so on rumbles his cart. To James's surprise, the driver of the other cart, Ben of the Walnut Grove, does not rein in either. As a consequence, both carts collide in the middle of the intersection. James and Ben are injured, their property is destroyed, and James's ox is gored.

Upon hearing that a circuit riding judge is coming to the nearby town of Binghamton. James decides to bring a case against Ben. When the judge arrives and opens court, James appears before him, accuses Ben of being careless in not allowing him the right-of-way, and asks the court to have Ben pay for the damage. To James's surprise, Ben appears and accuses him of being the truly careless one and asks that he pay instead.

The Norman judge hears the case but is unable to decide it fairly because he does not know the custom of the region as to who has the right-of-way at an intersection. To find out, he inquires of several local citizens as to whom, in fact, would be to blame for the crash according to the commonly held rules of the road. These citizens advise him that, as in this area the right-of-way goes to the person on the right, James was to blame. The judge then enters a judgment that, as the customary or **common law** of the area grants the right-of-way to the person on the right, James was, in fact, to blame and owes Ben for the damages.

Common Law: customary law of an area

James is angered by the decision because he knows that if the judge had asked Northshire citizens instead of Binghamton citizens the same question, he would have won the case. He, therefore, decides to appeal.

Four months later, in London, James's and Ben's case is heard on appeal before the King's Bench, the highest court in the land. The judges, just back from riding circuit throughout the realm, consider whether as a matter of law for the entire kingdom the right-of-way should go to the person on the left or to the person on the right. Drawing on their experiences on circuit with the customs of the kingdom's various regions, they determine that in most areas the right-of-way should go to the person on the left.

The court then announces its decision:

> In the case of *James of Northshire* v. *Ben of the Walnut Grove* and from this day forward in the realm, we have determined that as a matter of law the right-of-way shall fall to the person on the left. Consequently, the decision in the lower court is overturned, and we direct that the lower court reconsider the case to determine the amount of damages to be paid to James of Northshire.

The Use of Precedent

A few months later, when the circuit judge again returned to Binghamton, the court determined how much money Ben was to pay James. The long-term significance of the case was that, after the final decision on appeal, it became law throughout the nation that the right-of-way belonged to the person on the left. If a lower court decided differently, the person who lost could always appeal and have the decision overturned because the **precedent** or rule of law to be applied to this particular legal issue had been set in the case of *James of Northshire* v. *Ben of Walnut Grove*. The policy of enforcing such established precedents so as to ensure fairness to all similarly situated parties is known as **stare decisis.** More details about the workings of the appellate courts within our state and federal court systems are contained in Chapters 3 and 4.

Precedent: set rule of law to be applied to a particular legal issue

Stare decisis: policy of enforcing settled precedents

As you probably suspected, the panel of citizens on which the Norman judge relied to interpret the local customs evolved into what we know as the jury. Today the **jury** maintains that same role of assessing evidence and advising the judge on the actual facts of the case. The judge's job is to identify and apply the appropriate law so as to ensure that the trial is conducted properly. In particular, the judge must determine what evidence the jury should hear (excluding hearsay, for example), ensure that proper legal procedure is followed, and, using the facts provided by the jury, reach a judgment in the case. This division of labor in the courtroom (i.e., the jury determines the facts, the judge determines and applies the law) is exceptionally important to the common law system. In the *James of Northshire* v. *Ben of the Walnut Grove* case, the judges ultimately determined the law to be that in England the right-of-way at intersections belongs to the person on the left. Since the facts, as determined by the jury, were that James had been on Ben's left and that Ben's failure to yield the right-of-way had resulted in the infliction of a certain amount of damages on James, the judge ruled that by law Ben must pay James that amount.

Jury: select panel of citizens who determine facts of case

The Development of Courts of Equity

As is often the case when an authority tries to treat everyone fairly through a detailed system of regulation, the rules of the king's courts of law became more and more inflexible. Thus, as the body of laws grew, the king's courts became prisoners of their own legal system. Unless everything was done just as it had been done before, nothing could be accomplished by these courts. As a consequence, many problems arose for which the courts of law simply could not provide a remedy. For example, if your cattle were watered solely from one stream and your neighbor dammed it up, you would have to wait until your cattle died and then sue for the damages that the law would provide. Such situations led to great waste. However, if you had the ear of the king, you could simply complain to him, and he would order the dam torn down. Few, of course, were in a position to plead for such an order. Therefore, in response to problems that the courts of law could not solve, the king created a new system of courts called the **courts of equity.** To these courts he gave some of his own power to issue orders. Within bounds these courts could fashion a remedy unavailable to the courts of law and then issue an order to enforce that remedy on the parties involved. Although separate for centuries in England, courts of equity and courts of law have been merged in the great majority of our states. Thus, you can now seek damages or,

Courts of Equity: courts with power to issue orders

that remedy is not satisfactory, a court order to remedy your problem from the same court. Remedies will be discussed further in Chapter 13.

This system that the king of England set up centuries ago ultimately molded English culture by producing a uniform common law for all of England, a common law based on the customs practiced by most of the realm's people and applicable to all of its subjects. Building on success, all but one of our states have adopted the English common law system as their own (Louisiana's law is based on the French legal system due to that state's historic heritage).

What Does Our Ethical Background Contribute to the Growth of Our Laws?

Although many of us never go so far as to study or even recognize the existence of the **ethical systems** we use, these codes of conduct exert a great deal of influence over our behavior. This influence is reflected in our customs and ultimately, since the common law is based on customary ways of behaving, in our laws.

Ethical Systems: codes of conduct

The Judeo-Christian Ethical System

Judeo-Christian ethics are well known in this country. This ethical system requires that in dealing with other human beings, a person behave in certain ways regardless of the consequences. "Thou shalt not steal" is not qualified by "unless your children will starve if you do not steal and the person you are stealing from is rich and fat." Because of this approach, our laws punish the Robin Hood who steals to save the poor as harshly as it punishes the thief who steals only for his or her own advantage.

Judeo-Christian Ethics: religion-based ethical system requiring certain behavior regardless of consequences

A person who follows the Judeo-Christian ethical system is called on to love others, to honor his or her mother and father, to refrain from killing, and to work hard so as to be able to help others rather than to satisfy personal greed. Such a person is to do all of this without consideration of worldly consequences but with an eye to a heavenly reward. Our legal system reflects the Judeo-Christian ethical system in part by making crimes out of certain acts that violate its standards, such as theft and murder.

Egoism

An ethical system that contrasts sharply with the Judeo-Christian system is **egoism.** Under this system a person's actions are determined by their consequences for his or her self-interest. Many laws take into account the fact that people are strongly motivated by the greed of egoism instead of the altruism of Judeo-Christian ethics. For example, our tax laws provide tax relief (popularly called loopholes) for those who tailor their investment or other behavioral patterns in a certain way.

Egoism: ethical system in which actions are determined by consequences for self-interest

The two main types of egoism are hedonism and psychological egoism. Under **hedonism** a person acts to satisfy or please his or her senses of taste, touch, smell, sight, and hearing. In the alternative, under **psychological egoism** a person acts primarily because of the impact that her or his behavior will have on others. Buying expensive cars or fashions to attract the esteem or envy of others is an example of behavior sparked by psychological egoism.

Hedonism: ethical system based on sensory gratification

Psychological Egoism: ethical system in which acts are based on their effect on others

Utilitarianism

Another ethical system that emphasizes worldly consequences in judging behavior is **utilitarianism.** Under this system an action is proper if it produces the greatest good for the greatest number of those people affected by it. In the law utilitarian analysis can lead both to programs mandating public education and to programs that ignore the educational requirements of minorities, such as persons of certain ethnic backgrounds and the handicapped.

Utilitarianism: ethical system based on an act's potential for good

Other Ethical Systems

Finally, there are ethical systems that, like the Judeo-Christian system, do not analyze an action by its worldly consequences. The most notable of these is the **Kantian ethical system.** This system was developed by Immanuel Kant in the late 1700s. It concluded that every potential action should be analyzed to see whether the principle behind it could be made a universal law without producing an illogical or self-defeating situation. For example, let us say that we are considering falsely yelling "Fire" in a crowded nightclub. The underlying principle here is whether or not freedom of speech should be an absolute right. If it were an absolute right no speech would be believable or reliable. No matter what you say, no one would believe it. This would make freedom of speech useless. Therefore, absolute freedom of speech is self-defeating and should not be permitted.

Kantian ethical system: ethical system based on analysis of potential for universal application of the principles behind acts

All of the ethical systems discussed above have affected and continue to affect the development and application of our laws. As with historical developments, changes in our ethical standards cause the law to follow suit and change accordingly.

Philosophers who study such evolution in the law explain the changes by using either or two popular such schools of thought. Aristotle and Aquinas, for example, saw the law as moving toward the achievement of a superethical moral standard higher than any that humans in their current state could determine or generate. They were adherents of the **natural law school,** which believes that an ideal legal system was implanted in the reason of human beings before they were ruined by passion, greed, and so forth. Other philosophers, in reaction to such views, saw the law as developing according to a nation's historical experiences. These philosophers adhered to the **historical school** of legal philosophy. (A term that you may hear in place of the term *legal philosophy* is **jurisprudence.**)

Natural Law School: explanation of legal principles as stemming from unspoiled human reason and ideals

Historical School: explanation of legal principles as stemming from historical experience

Jurisprudence: legal philosophy

Recognizing that philosophical differences on why the law changes will always be with us, in the next chapter, we will turn our attention to the more important questions of how legal change occurs and what institutions bring it about.

Vocabulary Development

Fill in the blanks with the appropriate term.

Appellate Courts	**Egoism**
Business Law	**Ethical Systems**
Common Law	**Hedonism**
Courts of Equity	**Historical School**
Courts of Law	**Judeo-Christian Ethics**

Jurisprudence	**Precedent**
Jury	**Psychological Egoism**
Kantian Ethics	**Stare Decisis**
Law	**Utilitarianism**
Natural Law	

1. The _____ has the responsibility of determining the facts of a case.

2. Barton Stonely, voted most likely loser by his high school class of 1992, turned to me one day and said, "Why'd I buy a Porsche 911, you ask? I'll tell you why. It makes people think you have money." Considering ethical systems, in buying the Porsche, Stonely was acting out his _____.

3. _____ requires the use of established precedents to decide current cases.

4. As our legal system was developing, damages as a remedy were available in courts of law. Alternatively, however, a court order to cease doing something or to do it was available in the _____.

5. _____ philosophers thought that the best legal system was hidden in the hearts of human beings unaffected by the corruption of the world.

6. The greatest good for the greatest number is the principle of the ethical system called _____.

7. "In our area the first vehicle to reach the four-way-stop intersection goes first, regardless of whether that vehicle is going straight, left, or right" is an example of a customary or _____.

Problems

1. According to the chapter material, which of the following should be considered law?

   a. The Old Testament's prohibition "Thou shalt not kill."

   b. A sign on the shoulder of the state highway that reads, "$50 to $500 fine for littering."

   c. A 20-mph speed zone past a grade school.

2. The courtrooms of this country still maintain the division of labor that was set in the English system, in which the judge decided the law to be applied and the jury decided the facts of the case. In some cases, however, a jury is either not required or not requested. In such cases, the judge determines the facts by evaluating the evidence. Can you think of reasons why a defendant in a criminal case, for example, would not request a jury?

3. If, after the case of *James of Northshire* v. *Ben of the Walnut Grove* was decided on appeal before the King's Bench, another case involving right-of-way at an intersection came before the Binghamton court, how would that case be decided?

   a. In favor of the person on the right, as the customs of the region have not had time to change.

b. In favor of the person on the left, as that is now the law.

c. In favor of the person on the left unless the other person can prove that she or he has not heard of the King's Bench decision.

4. You are late for work for the third time in the last two weeks. Ahead of you on the four-lane divided highway, a station wagon brushes up against the concrete median. It swerves sharply across the lanes of traffic and slams into a light pole on the right-hand side of the road. The force of the impact carries it over the shoulder and out of sight. Other drivers ignore the situation and go on. You are coming up to the accident site . . . How would you react if you subscribed to the utilitarian ethic? To the Judeo-Christian ethic? To the hedonistic ethic?

ACTUAL CASE STUDY

Marvin v. Marvin

Supreme Court of California
134 Cal. Rptr. (California Reporter) 815 (1976)

Read through this actual case study on how the common law continues to develop in response to society's needs in modern day America.

Actor Lee Marvin, famous for his movie roles in the *Dirty Dozen* and *Cat Ballou,* lived with Michelle Triola for several years. After their relationship ended, Ms. Triola sued Mr. Marvin for what she claimed was her share of the income and property he received during the time they were cohabiting. She claimed that she and Mr. Marvin had made an express agreement to that effect and that, as a consequence of the agreement, she had given up a promising career as an actress to be a homemaker and companion to him. The lower court threw out the case by ruling that the state's Family Law Act did not allow the enforcement of such private agreements. The case was appealed to the Supreme Court of California.

Justice Tobriner wrote this deciding opinion in the case:

During the past 15 years, there has been a substantial increase in the number of couples living together without marrying. Such nonmarital relationships lead to legal controversy when one partner dies or the couple separates.

We conclude: (1) The provisions of the Family Law Act do not govern the distribution of property acquired during a nonmarital relationship. Such a relationship remains subject solely to judicial decision. (2) The courts should enforce express contracts between nonmarital partners except to the extent that the contract is explicitly founded on the consideration of meretricious sexual services.

Defendant (Lee Marvin) first and principally relies on the contention that the alleged contract is so closely related to the supposed "immoral" character of the relationship between plaintiff and himself that the enforcement of the contract would violate public policy. He points to cases asserting that a contract between nonmarital partners is unenforceable if it is "involved in" an illicit relationship . . . , or made in contemplation of such a relationship. A review of the numerous California decisions concerning contracts between nonmarital partners, however, reveals that the courts have not employed such broad and uncertain standards to strike down contracts. The decisions instead disclose a narrower and more precise standard: a contract between nonmarital partners is unenforceable only to the extent that it explicitly rests upon the immoral and illicit consideration of meretricious sexual services.

In summary, we base our opinion on the principle that adults who voluntarily live together and engage in sexual relations are nonetheless as competent as any other persons to contract respecting their earnings and property rights. Of course, they cannot lawfully contract to pay for the performance of sexual services, for such a contract is, in essence, an agreement for prostitution and unlawful for that reason. But they may agree to pool their earnings and to hold all property acquired during the relationship in accord with the law governing community property; conversely, they may agree that each partner's earnings and the property acquired from those earnings remain the separate property of the earning partner. So long as the agreement does not rest upon illicit meretricious consideration, the parties may order their economic affairs as they choose, and no policy precludes the courts from enforcing such agreements.

In the present instance, plaintiff alleges that the parties agreed to pool their earnings, that they contracted to share equally in all property acquired, and that defendant agreed to support plaintiff. The terms of the contract as alleged do not rest upon any unlawful consideration. We therefore conclude that

the complaint furnishes a suitable basis upon which the trial court can render declaratory relief. The trial court consequently erred in granting defendant's motion for judgment on the pleadings.

Questions

1. What is the basis for the court's decision to uphold contracts between unmarried consenting adults such as the one at issue in this case?

2. Does this decision mean that Ms. Triola will receive one-half of the property in question?

3. Could two or more parties of the same sex enter into such a contract according to the precedent established in this case?

4. Which of the following ethical systems does this decision reflect most closely—the Judeo-Christian system, the utilitarian system, the Kantian system, or the egoistic system? Why?

How Are Laws Made?

CHAPTER OUTLINE AND OBJECTIVES

After studying this chapter, the student will be able to:

I. Explain where the power to make laws comes from.
    a. The people
    b. A constitution
    c. The branches of government

II. Describe how the lawmaking power is exercised and applied.
    a. The creation of a statute by Congress or a state legislature
    b. The utilization of the statute by a prosecutor
    c. The application and review of the statute by the courts

III. Explain the necessity for lawmaking by administrative agencies.
    a. The rationale for empowering agencies
    b. The extent of an agency's lawmaking power

IV. Analyze how conflicts between lawmaking bodies are resolved, by reading, at the end of the chapter, the *Silkwood* v. *Kerr-McGee* case, which was based on the factual situation behind the movie *Silkwood*.

Where Does the Power to Make Laws Come From?

The People

In a democracy such as ours, the ultimate lawmaking power is in the hands of the people who are governed by the laws that are made. However, the ways in which this power is transferred to an authority willing to put it into use vary greatly.

In some societies, the people allow the power to be seized or to reside in a dictator, monarch, or strongman simply because they are unwilling or unable to pay the price of recapturing it. In other societies, the people jealously guard the power with their very lives and only sparingly yield control over themselves to a central authority. For the latter, Patrick Henry, a leader of the American Revolution, put it best:

Why stand we here idle?
What is it that gentlemen wish?
What would they have?
Is life so dear, or peace so sweet, as to be purchased at the price of chains and slavery.
Forbid it, Almighty God!
I know not what course others may take, but as for me,
give me liberty, or give me death.
Address to the Virginia Convention, 1775

A Constitution

Constitution: fundamental law of the land

Regardless of their origin or current form, most governments today legitimize their powers by a constitution. That **constitution,** however arrived at, then becomes the fundamental law of the land. It is important to note that even the federal Constitution of the United States was written by a constitutional convention composed of appointed, not elected, delegates and ratified, not by a direct vote of the people, but by the state legislatures.

Constitutional Law: the Constitution and the laws and judicial rulings that interpret and apply it

The text of this document and the laws and judicial rulings that interpret and apply it are known as **constitutional law.** Whenever there is a conflict between the federal Constitution and federal law, for example, the federal Constitution prevails. In the same manner, all federal law, including the federal Constitution, preempts (supersedes) directly conflicting state laws and state constitutional passages. The states agreed to this by ratifying the federal Constitution, which in Article VI, Clause 2, provides that the Constitution itself as well as the laws and treaties of the federal government "shall be the supreme Law of the Land, and the Judges in every State shall be bound thereby." Given the volume and scope of federal laws, the constraints placed on state laws and actions by this "supremacy clause" of the Constitution are numerous and pervasive. To see how this clause works in practice, read the case at the end of the chapter. It involves a lawsuit by the estate of Karen Silkwood (remember the movie *Silkwood*) against Kerr-McGee, her employer at a nuclear plant.

The Branches of Government

The structure of government and the allocation of powers embodied in the US Constitution reflect the application of several principles thought to be vital to the continued freedom of the people. Chief among those principles are separation of powers and checks and balances. In accordance with the former, the power to make laws is given to the **legislative branch** (Article I, Sections 1 and 8). The powers to investigate violations and prosecute alleged violators are given to the **executive branch** (Article II, Section 1). Finally, the powers to conduct **trials** (formal proceedings for the examination and determination of legal issues) and pronounce judgment are placed with the **judicial branch** (Article III, Sections 1 and 2). This separation of powers is enhanced by allowing each governmental branch to check or balance out the potential misuse of power by another branch. For example, the judicial branch can declare invalid the laws passed by the legislative branch or can declare void executive actions, such as the use of improperly collected evidence in the prosecution of a criminal law case. By the same token, the very composition of the judicial branch is left to the legislative branch by Article III of the Constitution. As a result, the US Supreme Court was not created until the Federal Judiciary Act was passed by Congress in September 1789, over six months after the Constitution went into effect.

In a manner similar to that of the federal Constitution, the various state constitutions create and empower the various branches of state government. On the state level, legislatures make the laws. Those laws must be within the parameters established by the constitution of the given state. The governors and the rest of the executive branch of the state are charged with carrying out the laws. The state courts judge and sentence violators. Finally, the ultimate authority to interpret the state constitution is left to the highest state court, be it named a "supreme court" or a "court of appeals."

Legislative Branch: part of government empowered to make laws

Executive Branch: part of government empowered to carry out laws

Trials: formal proceedings for examination and determination of legal issues

Judicial Branch: part of government empowered to conduct trials and pass judgment

How Is the Lawmaking Power Exercised and Applied?

It is important to consider that in making laws in a free society, we must begin with the idea that all behavior is permissible unless it has been made illegal. The opposite approach, that all behavior is impermissible until the authorities specifi-

The Branches of the Government and Their Relative Powers in Making and Carrying Out Our laws

Figure 2–1

Legislative	Makes the laws
Executive	Investigates and prosecutes alleged violators
Judicial	Sits in judgment of alleged violators

cally allow it, is both frightening and, as shown by the recent disintegration of the communist bloc, self-defeating.

The amount of wisdom displayed in choosing what behavior to outlaw and what behavior to encourage is the measure of a democracy. In our society, such choices usually take the form of legislatively created laws called **statutes.** Care in drafting, interpreting, and applying specific statutes, especially those making certain behavior illegal, is vital to maintaining freedom. The various branches of the federal and state governments must act in partnership to wisely create and fairly enforce such statutes.

Statutes: legislatively created laws

The Creation of a Statute by Congress or a State Legislature

To see what this idea of partnership entails, let's consider an example at the state level. Suppose that for several months the legislators have been receiving reports from voters around the state about break-ins into homes at night while the occupants are asleep. Money and other property have been stolen, people have been injured or killed upon interrupting the intruders, and some homes have even been set afire.

To help stop this wave of violence against people when they are so vulnerable, the legislature creates or **drafts** a statute that makes the specific act involved an offense against the public good. The commission of such an act is then punishable by the government. In other words, the lawmakers define the act as a **crime.** Because there are already statutes that make it illegal to steal, to do physical harm to individuals, and to set fire to structures under such conditions, the legislature realizes that to be effective the penalty for this crime must be more severe.

Drafts: creates

Crime: offense against public good whose commission is punishable by government

As a consequence, the legislature creates the crime of burglary and defines it as "the breaking and entering of the dwelling house of another at night with the intent to commit a felony therein." ("Felony" is a more serious crime and penalized more severely than most other crimes. It is defined in full in Chapter 3.)

Because of the scrutiny it will receive from the courts, the wording of the statute creating the crime of burglary is extremely important. State legislatures and Congress occasionally make glaring mistakes in the drafting of statutes. A few years ago, the legislature of a state passed a law that specified the procedure for obtaining a divorce in that state. The law had been reviewed by committees, debated by both houses of the legislature, and signed by the governor of the state. Almost a year after the law was passed, an attorney read it closely and found that it clearly ordered all property accumulated during the marriage to go to the wife. As a consequence, a lengthy court battle ensued that was finally ended when the supreme court of the state struck down the statute as being in violation of the state constitution.

In the situation we're considering, however, the statute seems well drafted and clear on its face. The legislature has done its part. Now the statute must stand the test of real life.

A week after the statute goes into effect, in a small town in the southwestern part of the state, Aristottel B. Nasty, who was just released from the state penitentiary after serving three years for grand theft, is stopped at 3 AM while driving a brand-new, $3,500 lawn mower down a back street. The lawn mower has been hot-wired. As Aristottel is assuring the police officer who pulled him over that he has gone straight and is now mowing yards for a living (even after dark, there being an enormous demand for his services), a report over the police radio announces the theft of just such a lawn mower from the garage of a nearby home. Aristottel is arrested.

The Utilization of the Statute by a Prosecutor

The next day the state prosecutor, Euwell Burn, reviews the evidence and decides to charge Aristottel with burglary under the new statute rather than the lesser offenses of larceny or breaking and entering. Burn is certain that a conviction of a repeat offender and the greater length of sentence likely to be awarded by the court under the more severe guidelines for burglary sentences will serve potential violators with notice not to attempt similar crimes.

The Application and Review of the Statute by the Courts

At Trial. At the trial the prosecutor is able to prove that a lock on the closed front door of the home was broken to allow access to the garage, that the break-in occurred at night, and that a felony—the theft of the $3,500 lawn mower—was committed afterwards. The police officer then testifies that Aristottel was apprehended less than 15 minutes later as he proudly guided the same lawn mower along a darkened suburban street. The only problem for Prosecutor Burn comes when Aristottel's attorney, public defender Ann Issu, claims that a garage is not a "dwelling house," and that Aristottel is therefore not guilty. She puts into evidence the fact that the garage was built onto the side of the house years after the house itself had been constructed and that it was intended for storage and not as a dwelling place. Prosecutor Burn replies that extra rooms and closets for storage added to a dwelling house are protected by the burglary statute. Just because an area is labeled a garage does not mean that it should not be protected in the same way as these are.

On Appeal. The trial judge decides in favor of the prosecutor's interpretation of the law. Aristottel is found guilty and sentenced to 20 years without the possibility of parole for the first 10. Aristottel appeals the guilty verdict, maintaining that the judge erred in ruling in favor of Burn's interpretation of what a dwelling house includes. Five months later, the case is argued before the state court of appeals. Two more months pass before the court of appeals issues its ruling. In the opinion of the judge writing for the majority of that court, a garage is held to be a part of a dwelling house if it is permanently attached to the house.

If, instead, a garage is freestanding, it is not part of a dwelling house. As the garage in the case was attached to the house, Aristottel's conviction is upheld. Shortly thereafter he tries to appeal to the state supreme court, but that body declines to hear the case. Aristottel is then committed to the state penitentiary to serve his time.

If the prosecutor had lost his argument over what a dwelling house was, Aristottel would have been set free and could not have been tried again on charges arising out of the incident. Instead, the prosecutor, acting as part of the executive branch, properly investigated the case and brought it to trial. Then the courts interpreted and applied the statute to reach a fair result. The appellate court decision in the case helped by establishing a precedent that clarified the definition of burglary.

Through procedures similar to those used in this case involving burglary, repeated over and over again, the branches of a state or federal government play their roles in creating and enforcing our laws.

Why Are Administrative Agencies Needed to Make Law?

Interstate Commerce: trade and other commercial intercourse among the states

As the pace and complexity of life in this country increased, the ability of the federal government or state governments to make timely and proper laws regulating commerce declined markedly. This was especially true for the federal government, which had been given the responsibility for regulating **interstate commerce** (trade and other commercial intercourse between or among the states) in Article I, Section 8, of the US Constitution. For example, it took over 40 years for the federal government to recognize the problems posed by the "trusts," which were nearly complete monopolies of such areas of commerce as oil, sugar, and even whiskey, and then to pass and apply corrective legislation. By the time Congress acted, an irreversible and very detrimental consolidation of vast economic power had occurred. Many experts have identified this consolidation as one of the main factors in causing the Great Depression of the 1930s.

The Rationale for Empowering Agencies

In response to that depression and, by implication, to the failure of Congress to properly regulate interstate commerce, that body created a large number of federal administrative agencies to act in its stead. Congress delegated to each of these agencies the power to regulate a specific area of interstate commerce. The staff of each agency, consisting of people with considerable expertise in the area they were empowered to regulate, was expected to respond to developing problems with the required speed and specificity. This response was most often in the form of rules and regulations.

Up to the time of the Great Depression, however, the US Supreme Court defined interstate commerce as involving only commerce that actually flowed across state lines (such as a shipment of tires from an Illinois plant to a Michigan plant). All other domestic commerce was considered **intrastate commerce** (conducted wholly within one state), and the Constitution left the regulation of intrastate commerce to the individual states. Unfortunately, this division of labor produced uneven and often ineffective regulation.

The degree of uniform regulation that the new federal agencies felt necessary to counter the problems of the economy caused them to interfere in what had been previously defined as intrastate commerce. This in turn resulted in the US Supreme Court's invalidation of many of the agencies and their activities as unconstitutional. Finally, in 1937, the Supreme Court changed its mind and, in cases involving Social Security and minimum wages for women and children, yielded to pressure and allowed interstate commerce to be redefined to include not just goods actually transported over state lines but any activity within the states that might affect such commerce.

This redefinition greatly enlarged the job of the federal government and had the long-term effect of creating and empowering even more agencies at the federal level. As the Supreme Court has since held that the rules and regulations passed by an agency acting with the powers Congress delegated to it have the force and effect of federal law, the regulation of our economy by agencies has probably worked a greater change in the way we live than did the Declaration of Independence or the Constitution.

The Interstate Commerce Commission, the Food and Drug Administration, the Federal Trade Commission, the Securities and Exchange Commission, the National Labor Relations Board, the Federal Communications Commission, the Environmental Protection Agency, the Consumer Product Safety Commission, the Equal Employment Opportunity Commission, and many other agencies are the result. (The areas of responsibility of these agencies are covered near the end of Chapter 3.) Many of the state governments have since followed the federal government's example by setting up their own extensive system of agencies.

The Extent of an Agency's Lawmaking Power

Significantly, the courts have held that the rules and regulations made by agencies have the force of law. Thus, our body of laws is being constantly added to, not only by Congress and the state legislatures, but by the multitude of state and federal agencies exercising the legislative powers delegated to them. Realize that, as mentioned above, all federal laws, even those made by agencies, are constitutionally supreme when in conflict with state laws.

Intrastate Commerce: trade and other commercial intercourse conducted wholly within one state

APPLICATIONS OF
WHAT YOU'VE LEARNED

Vocabulary Development

Fill in the blanks with the appropriate term.

Constitution	**Draft**	**Intrastate**	**Statutes**
Constitutional Law	**Executive Branch**	**Judicial Branch**	**Trials**
Crime	**Interstate**	**Legislative Branch**	

1. A lawmaking body will create or _____ a statute.

2. The power to investigate and prosecute violations of statutes belongs to the _____ branch of government.

3. The power to judge and sentence violators of statutes belongs to the _____ branch of government.

4. Under the US Constitution the federal government has the power to regulate _____ commerce.

5. The fundamental law of the land is the _____.

[Now, do you remember the Chapter 1 terms to answer these last three questions? The answers are not in the above list.]

6. "In our area the first vehicle to reach the four-way-stop intersection goes first, regardless of whether that vehicle is going straight, left, or right" is an example of a customary or _____.

7. The _____ has the responsibility of determining the facts of a case.

8. _____ requires the use of established precedents to decide current cases.

Problems

1. According to Article II, Section 2, of the US Constitution, the president, with the concurrence of two-thirds of the Senate, has the power to make treaties binding the United States. Do these treaties have the force of law within this country? If so, should they be superior to state laws?

2. In the case involving Aristottel B. Nasty, assume that instead of being arrested escaping on a lawn mower, he was caught by the security guard when he tried to leave an apartment building with a solid gold canary cage hidden under his overcoat. The cage and the rare cockatoo inside it, whose whistling Aristottel could not stop, had just been taken from an apartment in the building. The incident occurred at night, and there was evidence of breaking and forced entry.

   a. Assume that you are prosecutor Burn. What issues are crucial to you if you are going to charge Aristottel with burglary in this case?

   What arguments will you make before the court to support your position on those issues?

   b. Assume that you are public defender Issu. What arguments will you make in defending Aristottel from the burglary charge?

3. Assume that you are an attorney and have just been appointed prosecutor for your area. Since high school, you have dreamed of going into politics. Now your name is going to be in the news frequently and you will become widely known for your success or failure at your job. There are two strategies that you can choose as prosecutor: first, to prosecute violators to the fullest extent of the law, perhaps breaking new ground in applying statutes to criminal behavior, but also running the risk of losing high-visibility cases; or second, to prosecute only cases in which you are sure of victory and to plea-bargain away the cases that you might lose. The latter choice would produce an

extremely high conviction rate that you could boast of in your political advertising. Which strategy would you choose, and why?

4. In the last 15 years, the area of consumer electronics has grown phenomenally. With that growth have come a myriad of legal problems, such as copyright violations from rerecorded audiotapes and videotapes, pirated computer programs, and photocopied books; patent violations from shared hardware; and antitrust problems associated with cable access. Should the government create an agency to regulate consumer electronics? What are the advantages and disadvantages of this course of action? If such an agency were created, how should the empowering statute be phrased? What alternatives are there to this course of action?

5. In late 1991, a California state lawmaker proposed that over 25 of the state's 50-plus counties form a new state, Northern California. The lawmaker made this proposal because many citizens of these counties were angered over the state government's orders that the counties be responsible for providing health and welfare services to their citizenry. However, although mandating that the counties make these services available, the state did not provide the money to pay for them. Instead, it gave the counties the power to finance any resulting budget shortfalls by raising taxes. For many decades, being a part of the state of California had made the same 25 counties vulnerable to state programs that used their resources, mainly water, to support the growing southern region of the state, a region that dominated the state government due to its large population. What document(s) would determine the right of the 25 counties to secede from the state of California and form their own state? What part of the California government would have primary responsibility for interpreting such document(s) to decide the issue?

Our Declaration of Independence reads in part: "But when a long train of abuses and usurpations, pursuing invariably the same object, evinces a design to reduce them [the people] under absolute Despotism, it is their right, it is their duty, to throw off such Government, and to provide new Guards for their future security." Does this attitude of our country's founders justify the secession of "Northern California"?

ACTUAL CASE STUDY

Silkwood v. Kerr-McGee Corporation

US Supreme Court
464 U.S. 238

Finally, read this actual case involving a potential conflict of federal law with Oklahoma state law in conjunction with Karen Silkwood's alleged plutonium contamination.

Acting for the estate of his deceased daughter, Bill Silkwood brought a successful lawsuit against her former employer, Kerr-McGee. The lawsuit was to recover for injuries to Karen Silkwood from plutonium poisoning sustained as a result of her employment at the Kerr-McGee plutonium fuel production facility near Crescent, Oklahoma. Kerr-McGee appealed the $10 million jury award in favor of Karen's estate.

The appeal stated that since the facility was regulated by the federal Nuclear Regulatory Commission (NRC), the Oklahoma laws under which the $10 million recovery was allowed were preempted by the NRC's rules and regulations. Neither these rules and regulations nor the empowering congressional statute contained anything on the subject of recovery by a private person injured by violation of NRC standards.

The appeal was ultimately decided by the US Supreme Court, in 1984. In its opinion the Court noted that Congress had probably omitted any mention of judicial recourse for persons injured in situations such as Silkwood's because it considered those parties free to bring lawsuits under state law. It then stated:

Preemption should not be judged on the basis that the Federal Government has so completely occupied the field of safety that state remedies are foreclosed, but on whether there is an irreconcilable conflict between the federal and state standards or whether the imposition of a State standard in a damages action would frustrate the objectives of the federal law. We perceive no such conflict or frustration in the circumstances of this case ...

We conclude that the award of ... damages in this case is not preempted by federal law.

Questions

1. Who won?
2. Would a provision in the Oklahoma state constitution allowing such lawsuits supersede an NRC rule that prohibited them?
3. Are you personally comfortable with the balance of power between the federal and state governments? Can you think of any way to improve the situation?

How Does the Federal Legal System Work?

CHAPTER OUTLINE AND OBJECTIVES

After studying this chapter, the student will be able to:

I. Identify the powers of the various federal courts.

   a. Source of the powers of the federal courts

   b. Extent of a federal district court's original jurisdiction

   c. Jurisdiction of federal courts of appeal

   d. Jurisdiction of US Supreme Court

II. Identify the jurisdiction of the federal administrative agencies.

III. Discuss the extent of court review of agency decisions.

   a. Due process

   b. Decisions within agency powers

   c. Decisions not arbitrary and capricious

IV. Analyze how the use of the agency safeguards might have determined the fate of Coach Tarkanian during the NCAA's recent two-year probation of the UNLV basketball program.

What Powers Do the Various Federal Courts Have?

Civil Case: lawsuit between private citizens or entities

To begin with, realize that courts must decide two basic types of cases. The first type is the **civil case,** in which private citizens resolve disputes by placing them before the courts in the form of lawsuits. So important is the ability to bring a civil case before the courts for resolution that, over the years, businesses and governmental bodies such as agencies have also been given the right to do so.

Criminal Case: prosecution for an offense against society

The second type of case that courts must decide is the **criminal case.** Such a case involves an offense against society as defined in its law code. Note that because the offense is considered as having been committed against society, the actual victim or victims cannot decide whether or not to prosecute those accused of it. That decision belongs to the attorney general, the district attorney, or the local prosecutor, depending on the nature of the case. The court procedures used in resolving criminal and civil cases will be discussed in Chapters 5 and 6, respectively.

Source of the Powers of the Federal Courts

Through Article III of the US Constitution, the people of this country conferred the power to judge certain criminal and civil matters on a system of federal courts:

> Section 1. The judicial Power of the United States shall be vested in one supreme Court, and in such inferior Courts as the Congress may from time to time ordain and establish.

Since the country had not even had a supreme court under the Articles of Confederation, some citizens thought that one was not needed under the Constitution. As a result, it wasn't until nearly six months after George Washington's inauguration as our first president that Congress passed the Federal Judiciary Act. This act "ordained and established" the US Supreme Court (USSC) and the circuit courts of appeal. Approximately a century later Congress acted in a similar fashion by creating the federal district courts. Certain specialized courts, such as those concerned primarily with tax and bankruptcy matters, have also been created as the need for them has arisen. (In working your way through the following description of the federal judicial system, it will be a good idea to keep yourself properly oriented by referring to Figure 3–1.)

Jurisdiction: power to hear and decide cases

Currently there are three levels of federal courts with what, for the federal system, approximates general jurisdiction. **Jurisdiction** means the power to hear and decide cases. A court with general jurisdiction can hear almost any kind of case. A court with special jurisdiction, such as the US Tax Court, hears only a specific type of case.

Trial Court: court in which case is first heard

At the lowest level of federal courts with general jurisdiction is the US district court. It is the trial court of the federal system. A **trial court** is basically a court in which a case is heard for the first time. The power to determine the facts of the matter and to make the initial determination of the law that is to be used in

The Federal Court System—Arrows denote appellate routes. Federal bankruptcy courts take their appeals to the court of appeals with jurisdiction over their state.) **Figure 3–1**

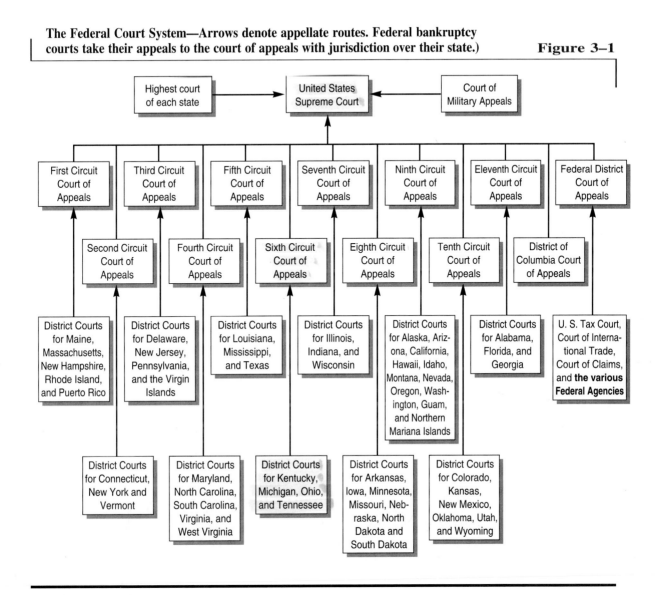

deciding such a case is called **original jurisdiction.** The district courts have that power for the federal system.

Original Jurisdiction: power to determine facts and initially select law used to decide case.

Extent of a Federal District Court's Original Jurisdiction

In general, district courts have original jurisdiction over (*a*) "federal questions," which are cases that arise under the Constitution, US law, and US treaties; and (*b*) lawsuits between parties with diversity of citizenship, which in this instance means between citizens of different states or between a US citizen and a foreign nation or between a US citizen and a citizen of a foreign nation. In all the lawsuits in the latter category, more than $50,000 has to be in dispute or the district courts will not handle the case, instead assigning it to a state court with appropriate jurisdiction.

Jurisdiction of Federal Courts of Appeal

The federal courts of appeal have appellate jurisdiction over the district courts, certain specialized federal courts, and many federal administrative agencies. **Appellate jurisdiction** is the power to review cases for errors of law. Such power is exercised when the result of a case in a lower court is appealed by one or more of the parties to the case. It is important to understand that appellate courts do not accept any new evidence or call witnesses. Instead, they may review the **transcript** (a verbatim record of what went on at trial) and the written and oral arguments of the opposing attorneys to reach a decision. It is a tribute to the power of our citizen juries to note that no appellate court, not even the US Supreme Court, can change the factual determinations of a jury. (However, if the appellate court detects significant errors in the original trial, it can order that a new trial be conducted. Thereby a new determination of facts would be made by a new jury.)

There are 13 federal courts of appeal. Twelve of these are circuit courts, each of which is responsible for an assigned geographic area. The 13th is dedicated to the "Federal Circuit." As such, it handles patent and claims cases appealed out of the district courts as well as appeals from specialized federal courts and from such bodies as the Court of International Trade and the International Trade Commission.

Jurisdiction of US Supreme Court

The US Supreme Court has both original and appellate jurisdiction. Although far less frequently used than its appellate jurisdiction, its original jurisdiction according to the Constitution is over "Cases affecting Ambassadors, other public Ministers and Consuls and those in which a State shall be Party."

The most indispensable function of the US Supreme Court, however, is the application of its appellate jurisdiction. This jurisdiction is exercised over cases on appeal from the US courts of appeal or from the highest courts of the various states. If, after a cursory review, the Supreme Court believes that a case contains a constitutional issue sufficiently important to be decided, it will issue a **writ of certiorari** to the last court that heard the case. This "writ" or order compels the lower court to turn over the record of the case to the Supreme Court for review. Note that the USSC's appellate jurisdiction over state supreme court cases is limited to those in which a federal law has been invalidated or whose issues center on the US Constitution. The decisions of the USSC that interpret or apply the Constitution are final and can only be overturned by the USSC itself or by a constitutional amendment. Without the USSC's firm hand as the ultimate interpreter of the Constitution, our system of government could not function.

Appellate Jurisdiction: power to review lower court cases for errors of law

Transcript: verbatim record of what went on at trial

Writ of Certiorari: order compelling a lower court to produce case records

What Is the Jurisdiction of the Federal Administrative Agencies?

As important as the courts are the many regulatory agencies at the federal level. As mentioned in the preceding chapter, Congress delegated to each agency the power to regulate a specific area. For example, the Federal Trade Commission (FTC) was given the broad power to "prevent persons, partnerships, or corporations from using unfair methods of competition in or affecting commerce and [from using] unfair or deceptive acts or practices in or affecting commerce."

Congress left it up to the newly formed FTC to set down rules and regulations that specifically defined what these methods, acts, and practices were. The FTC, like other federal agencies, was also given the power to investigate and prosecute violators in proceedings in which the agency personnel act as the equivalent of judge and jury. In effect, the executive, legislative, and judicial powers of government, which are usually held separately under the checks and balances system of the Constitution, were all given to the FTC in the interest of expediency.

Although this consolidation of powers may result in some abuses, appeals can be taken from initial agency decisions. Generally, however, appeals of this kind cannot be placed before a federal court until they have made their way through regional and national agency review boards. As mentioned, the federal courts of appeal handle such appeals.

What Is the Extent of Court Review of Agency Decisions?

Because of the high degree of expertise possessed by agency personnel and because of the heavy caseloads of the courts of appeal, court reviews of agency decisions are generally limited to three areas.

Due Process

First, the reviewing Court of Appeals checks to be sure that due process has been given to the parties involved. Notifying those parties of the charges and of the upcoming hearing or trial and providing them with an opportunity to appear at the proceeding to present evidence, confront witnesses, and otherwise defend themselves are the essence of **due process.**

Due Process: notice of changes and hearing and opportunity to appear, present evidence, and confront witnesses.

Decisions within Agency Powers

Second, the court checks to make sure that the action causing the appeal is within the powers of the agency as granted by Congress. See Figure 3–2 for a problem-oriented approach to the statutorily designated areas of responsibility of the various federal agencies.

Figure 3–2   **Problem Areas and Which Agencies to Contact for Help at the Federal Level**

Problem Area	Contact Agency
Air pollution	EPA
Air travel	FAA
Bank robbery	FBI
Chemical spill	EPA
Civil rights violations	CCR
Consumer goods	CPSC
Cosmetics quality	FDA
Drug quality	FDA
Drug trafficking	DEA
Espionage	FBI
False advertising	FTC
Federal law violations	FBI
Food quality	FDA
Hazardous wastes	EPA
Job discrimination	EEOC
Job safety	OSHA
Kidnapping	FBI
Mail fraud	USPS
Shipments of goods	ICC
Stocks and bonds	SEC
Unions	NLRB
Water pollution	EPA

ACRONYMS DECIPHERED by "REVEAL"
  (Recognize Even Vague and Evasive Agency Logos)
CCR—Commission on Civil Rights
CPSC—Consumer Product Safety Commission
DEA—Drug Enforcement Agency
EEOC—Equal Employment Opportunity Commission
EPA—Environmental Protection Agency
FAA—Federal Aviation Administration
FBI—Federal Bureau of Investigation
FDA—Food and Drug Administration
FTC—Federal Trade Commission
ICC—Interstate Commerce Commission
NLRB—National Labor Relations Board
OSHA—Occupational Safety and Health Administration
SEC—Security Exchange Commission
USPS—United States Post Office

Decisions Not Arbitrary and Capricious

Finally, the court reviews the record of the agency proceedings to ensure that the agency has not acted in an arbitrary or capricious fashion. In other words, the court checks to be sure that there is a reliable basis in the record for the agency action.

If the agency action passes the three tests, (due process, within the agency's powers, and not arbitrary and capricious), and the great majority of agency actions do, the action stands.

Of course, there are still the alternatives of appealing to the US Supreme Court or of getting Congress to change the statute that empowered the agency. However, these alternatives are seldom successful.

APPLICATIONS OF WHAT YOU'VE LEARNED

Vocabulary Development

Fill in the blanks with the appropriate term.

Appellate	**Due Process**	**Transcript**
Civil	**Jurisdiction**	**Trial Court**
Criminal	**Original**	**Writ of Certiorari**

1. Required of the federal government in the Fifth Amendment to the Constitution and of the state governments in the Fourteenth Amendment, this protection against governmental power requires at a minimum notice and a hearing before a person is deprived of "life, liberty, or property." It is referred to as _____ of law.

2. A _____ case is brought to prosecute a violation of the state or federal law code.

3. Required for any appeal, the verbatim (word for word) record of what went on at a trial is called a _____.

4. A verbatim record mentioned in Question 3 is a record of the proceedings in the court exercising _____ jurisdiction over the case.

5. A _____ hears a case for the first time.

6. The power to hear and decide cases is termed _____.

   [Now, do you remember the Chapters 1 and 2 terms to answer these last three questions? The answers are not in the above list.]

7. The power to judge and sentence violators of statutes belongs to the _____ branch of government.

8. The fundamental law of the land is the _____.

9. _____ philosophers thought that the best legal system was hidden in the hearts of human beings far apart from the corruption of the world.

Problems

1. Decide which of the following would result in a criminal case and which would result in a civil case:

   a. Lou Serre is clocked at 73 mph by a patrol officer on an interstate highway where the speed limit is 55 mph.

   b. As he pulls over, Lou accidentally runs into the front fender of the brand-new patrol car, spilling hot coffee onto the patrol officer's lap.

   c. The impact of the collision knocks off Lou's back right hubcap, causing the kilo of cocaine he had cleverly stashed there to fall onto the roadway in full view of the patrol officer.

    d. Lou's attorney forgets about Lou's case and fails to appear to earn the $5,000 fee Lou has already paid him.

2. Which of the following cases would fall under the original jurisdiction of the US district courts?

    a. A car accident involves a driver from Arkansas and another from Missouri. Damage claims from the accident exceed $140,000.

    b. A state supreme court strikes down a federal law.

    c. A Los Angeles man sues a citizen of Taiwan for violation of a contract worth more than $40,000.

    d. A Florida woman claims that, according to federal law, her employer is guilty of sex discrimination and she consequently seeks $30,000 in damages.

3. The sheer volume of cases that the US Supreme Court must administer borders on the overwhelming. Between 6,000 and 10,000 cases come before the Court each year. Each of these cases must be reviewed to see whether it contains issues that the USSC should resolve. Over 500 of the cases are then presented to the Court for its consideration. Most of them require detailed study and research before they can be decided. Lengthy written discussions of the complex legal issues in each case must be read, and often oral arguments by the representatives of the opposing parties must be heard as well. As a result, the USSC's ability to render decisions of the necessary quality has been placed in question. Suggestions on ways to reduce its oppressive workload include:

    a. Putting court in between the courts of appeals and the USSC.

    b. Increasing the number of justices (which has been as high as 10 and as low as 5) over the 9 currently on the Court.

    c. Increasing emphasis on alternative means of dispute resolution.
    What do you recommend?

4. Do you think Congress is justified in delegating so much of its regulatory power to administrative agencies such as the FTC? Why can't Congress do the job itself?

5. Finally, consider the Death of Commercial TV:

    The voice ripped the dream apart. The South Seas island, white sands, beaches beyond compare, and very, very friendly natives yielded to reality. You awoke and sat up on the couch. Pat, your best friend, was shrieking in your ear. "They've stopped WrestleBania XV. I can't believe it. Just as John ('Sears') Tower was about to use his 'coma clamp' to beat the Burbank Tank, they announced that network commercial TV was being banned by the FTC. Then they put on the test pattern."

    Pat stands up and points at you. "You're taking the law class. How could they do that? How do we stop them?"

    You shake your head. Since starting school, what with working and all, you haven't kept up with your sleep, much less the news. You promise Pat that you'll hit the library and research the whole thing as soon as possible. Just then the TV comes back to life with a syndicated children's show from the 50s. "Who's Princess SummerFallWinterSpring?" Pat asks.

    Later that evening, you enter the periodical section of the library and grab a newsmagazine. Its cover story is on the FTC action. Evidently, some months ago the agency decided to hold hearings to determine whether or not advertising on network television was an unfair method of competition under Section 5 of the FTC Act. To do so, it provided direct notice of the hearings by mail to all interested and concerned parties that it could identify. It also published notices of the hearings in newspapers and magazines. Anyone could appear and offer evidence. The hearings were held around the country. According to the magazine, the major TV networks hired expert witnesses, economists, and financial analysts to appear. These witnesses argued that TV fostered competition and offered vast amounts of statistical data to support their position. Professional sports figures, the heads of America's largest corporations, and leaders of the major political parties appeared in support of commercial TV. But you also read that a small group of academics presented contrary evidence. They maintained that the high cost of ads on network TV kept many small companies from using it and that American culture had been skewed as a result. Regional breweries, bakeries, dairies, and restaurants and countless other regional concerns with quality products had been forced out of business due to the financial ability of only the largest corporations to use TV. Real diversity in America had been franchised out of existence. School systems had been altered to foster the athletes and cheerleaders idolized on network TV rather than the engineers and scientists the country needed. The academics also documented their claims with statistical data. At the conclusion of the hearings, the FTC official in charge issued her findings. Her main factual determination was that commercial TV in its current form was an unfair method of competition. She then issued a cease and desist order directing the commercial networks to stop operating. Soap operas, professional sporting events, and Saturday morning TV were all to be replaced by locally originated and supportable shows and live talent presentations.

Your mind reels as you think of what you can tell Pat. To help you in that regard, consider the following questions:

a. What is the appellate route that must be taken if the decision is appealed?

b. If the appeal reaches the courts, which court will handle it first?

c. What standards of review will the courts use?

d. Given the facts of this case, is the decision likely to be overturned?

e. If the courts allow the decision to stand, do the networks have any further recourse?

ACTUAL CASE STUDY

National Collegiate Athletic Association v. Jerry Tarkanian

US Supreme Court
Reporter 454

Consider the importance of the guarantee of due process in a case involving big time college basketball and a very well paid coach.

Coach Tarkanian took over a mediocre basketball program at the University of Nevada at Las Vegas. Within four years his team was in the "Final Four" of the NCAA Tourney. His salary bordered on the fabulous. In lieu of the approximately $53,000 per year he would have made as a tenured professor, "Tark the Shark" had a contract for $125,000 and 10 percent of the net proceeds received by the university from its team's participation in NCAA postseason events as well as fees from endorsements, camps, clinics, newspaper columns, and his own radio and TV shows. Then the NCAA struck. After a lengthy investigatory process, it detailed 38 violations of its rules by UNLV personnel, mainly concerning player recruitment; 10 of the violations involved Coach Tarkanian. The NCAA placed UNLV on probation for two years, which meant that its basketball team could not appear on TV or in postseason games. The NCAA also required UNLV to show cause why it should not be further disciplined for not removing Tarkanian from its program during the probationary period. Ultimately, UNLV responded to this threat by doing just that. Faced with a drastic cut in salary, Coach Tarkanian brought suit, alleging that his disciplining was an action of the state government and that his right to due process guaranteed under the fourteenth

Amendment of the US Constitution had been denied him since the university administration had accepted the NCAA determination without giving him notice and a hearing. The university and the NCAA responded that no such due process was required as the NCAA was a private body and therefore not subject to the requirements of the Fourteenth Amendment. When the Nevada Supreme Court rejected this view, the NCAA appealed to the US Supreme Court.

In a 5–4 decision, the Supreme Court concluded as follows:

Embedded in our Fourteenth Amendment jurisprudence is a dichotomy between state action, which is subject to scrutiny under the Amendment's Due Process Clause, and private conduct, against which the Amendment affords no shield, no matter how unfair that conduct may be . . . As a general matter, the protections of the Fourteenth Amendment do not extend to private conduct abridging individual rights.

Careful adherence to the state action requirement preserves an area of individual freedom by limiting the reach of federal law and avoids the imposition of responsibility on a State for conduct it could not control . . .

In this case Tarkanian argues that the NCAA was a state actor because it misused power that it possessed by virtue of state law. He claims specifically that UNLV delegated its own functions to the NCAA, clothing the Association with authority both to adopt rules governing UNLV's athletic programs and to enforce those rules on behalf of UNLV.

These contentions fundamentally misconstrue the facts of this case . . . the NCAA's several hundred other public and private member institutions each similarly affected those policies . . . [They] did not act under color of Nevada law. It necessarily follows that the source of the legislation adopted by the NCAA is not Nevada but the collective membership. . . . UNLV retained the authority to withdraw from the NCAA and establish its own standards. The University alternatively could have stayed in the Association and worked through the Association's legislative process to amend rules or standards it deemed harsh, unfair, or unwieldy.

(The Court then concluded that the NCAA actions were not state actions and, therefore, that Tarkanian could not sue the NCAA for violation of his Fourteenth Amendment rights. The Court, however, did concede that UNLV's decision to suspend the coach was such a state action.)

Questions

1. Does the Fourteenth Amendment require that a private employer afford you due process (notice and a hearing of your side of the story) before firing you? What if your employer is a state government?

2. Was due process in such instances required of state governments before the passage of the Fourteenth Amendment?

3. Assume that your employer is a private guard company that hires you out to the state to do security work at a state installation. At the installation, you have the power to issue citations for violation of the state's laws. Can you claim a right to due process under the Fourteenth Amendment before being fired from this position?

4

How Do State and Local Legal Systems Work?

CHAPTER OUTLINE AND OBJECTIVES

After studying this chapter, the student will be able to:

I. Describe the powers of the state trial courts with general jurisdiction.

   a. State courts of appeal

   b. State supreme courts

II. Identify the functions of the specialized state courts.

   a. Associate circuit (county) courts

   b. Municipal courts

   c. Small claims courts

   d. Juvenile courts

   e. Probate courts

   f. Other courts

III. Analyze the case of *Texas v. Johnson*, in which the state and federal legal systems resolve the issue of flag burning.

What Are the Powers of the State Trial Courts with General Jurisdiction?

The typical state legal system mirrors the federal system in most instances. The state legislature makes the laws. The state executive branch enforces them before the courts of the state judicial branch. There are also state administrative agencies with powers given them by the state legislature. These agencies, for example, the Missouri Department of Natural Resources, often complement their counterparts at the federal level (in this case, the Environmental Protection Agency). However, the variations in these branches and agencies preclude a detailed description that holds true for all of them. Nonetheless, it is important that we give you some idea of what a typical state court system entails. The main part of this chapter is devoted to that end. We begin with the court of general original jurisdiction.

The State Trial Courts with General Jurisdiction

Court of Record: court in which documentary record of a case is formed

In most states the courts with general original jurisdiction over both criminal and civil matters are known as circuit courts. In some states, however, they are named superior courts, district courts, or courts of common pleas. Regardless of their title, they are the courts of record of the state system. In a **court of record** an exact account of what went on at trial is kept so as to allow appeals. This account may include a transcript of what was said, the evidence that was submitted, statements and determinations of the court officials, and the judgment of the court.

Courts of record will at times review the decisions of or handle appeals from courts of inferior jurisdiction (these will be discussed later in the chapter). When this occurs, however, they actually retry the cases in full so as to make the proper record, again for the purpose of potential appeals. Since it has original jurisdiction over a case before it, a court of record will make determinations of the facts in the case by using a jury or, if a jury is not requested for the case, by having the presiding judge determine the facts. Then the court of record will select and apply the law to the facts to reach a verdict in the case.

State Courts of Appeal

In approximately half of our states, an appeal from the determination of a case in a court of record is reviewed by a panel of judges from a state court of appeal. (In states where this intermediate level of appellate court does not exist, the appeal goes directly to the highest state court, usually referred to as the state supreme court. (State supreme courts will be discussed in the next section.) The panel of judges from the state court of appeal, usually consisting of no more than three judges, evaluates the record of the case and then hears the attorneys' oral and written arguments. It is important to note that no new evidence can be introduced at this level, as this can only be done at the lower trial court level, so the facts remain unchanged. The judges instead check to be sure that the correct law was used to resolve the case.

The court of appeals panel of judges may conclude that the trial court used the wrong law. If so, the panel may enter the correct judgment or send the case back down for a new trial. On the other hand, the judges may conclude the lower court used the correct law in the proper way and, consequently, let the lower court's judgment stand.

State Supreme Courts

Generally, we are all entitled to a trial and, if it is filed in a timely manner and in the proper form, to one appeal. As mentioned above, an intermediate state court of appeal handles that appeal in about half of our states. Otherwise, it is handled by the state supreme court.

In states with the intermediate level of courts of appeal, only cases that involve the most complex legal issues are taken to the justices of the state supreme court. (**Justice** is the title given to judges who sit on state supreme courts and the federal Supreme Court.) At the state supreme court level a panel of three or more justices reviews the legal issues and listens to the attorneys' oral arguments.

Justice: title of judges on state and federal supreme courts

State supreme courts issue the final decision on matters of law appealed to them unless the US Constitution or other federal issues are involved. In that case, as mentioned in Chapter 3, a further appeal can go to the US Supreme Court.

In addition to its appellate jurisdiction, in several states the state supreme court has original jurisdiction over most state impeachment cases. **Impeachment cases** involve the trial of governmental officials for misconduct in office. Finally, note that some states name their court of final authority something other than "supreme court." For example, the Court of Appeals is New York State's highest court.

Impeachment Cases: trials of officials for misconduct in office

What Are the Functions of the Specialized State Courts?

As indicated in Figure 4–1, a number of courts with specialized jurisdiction or jurisdiction inferior to that of the courts of record exist in every state. These courts include the associate circuit, municipal, small claims, juvenile, and probate courts.

Associate Circuit (County) Courts

Many states have a layer of courts below their courts of general original jurisdiction. These lower courts are referred to as associate circuit courts or county courts. Such courts hear minor criminal cases, state traffic offenses, and lawsuits in which relatively small amounts are in contention (usually no more than $25,000). Generally, these courts are not courts of record. However, they take a significant burden off the higher courts, even though appeals from their decisions can be taken to the circuit courts for a trial on the record.

Figure 4–1   **A Typical State Court System**

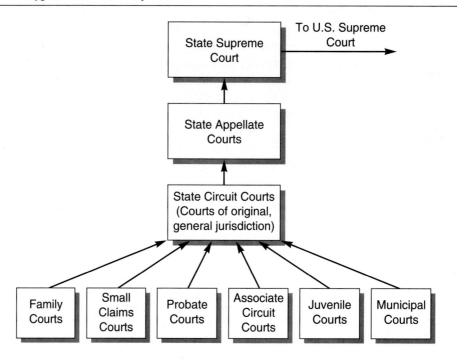

Municipal Courts

Cities typically have courts that administer their ordinances. These municipal courts are usually divided into traffic and criminal divisions. As city ordinances often overlap or duplicate state laws, less serious violations occurring within city limits end up before such municipal courts for their first trial. The result can then be appealed to the circuit court level if necessary.

Small Claims Courts

Many relatively minor individual suits would not be heard if not for the small claims courts. These courts handle cases in which small amounts, generally $2,500 or less, are in contention. The cases are handled informally before a judge and without a jury. The costs of filing such cases are held to a minimum. Often attorneys are not allowed or are allowed only if they're acting for themselves or for a corporation of which they are salaried employees. The decisions of the small claims court can be appealed to the circuit court level.

Juvenile Courts

Juveniles: youths not held fully responsible for criminal acts

Individuals under the age of full responsibility for their criminal acts (generally set at 18 years) are known as **juveniles.** To protect such individuals from the full consequences of their criminal acts, special courts have been set up. These courts ensure that most of the criminal cases involving juveniles do not become public knowledge. The courtroom is closed while an informal hearing into the charges is conducted. Any records made are not open to the public. The juvenile is entitled to his or her full constitutional rights, including the right of representation by an attorney. Should the juvenile be adjudged guilty of the charges brought, the court has wide powers in determining what should be done for rehabilitation. Possibilities open to the court include release into the supervision of parents, guardians, or governmental officials; placement in foster homes; and detention in correctional facilities.

Note that most states also provide that a juvenile, usually at least 16 years old, can be tried and punished as an adult. This occurs only in cases in which a very serious offense was allegedly committed by the juvenile. For example, murder and certain other crimes may bring about such treatment. Appeals from actions of the juvenile courts are directed to the circuit courts.

Probate Courts

The **probate court,** a very specialized court, is charged with administering wills and estates. When an individual dies, the interests that the deceased had in various assets must be allocated according to the deceased's wishes and the appropriate laws. The procedure to accomplish this is formal and complex. The probate court (referred to as the surrogate court in some states), is therefore, staffed with experienced professionals, so as to properly settle the deceased's affairs.

Probate Court: special court for wills and estates

Other Courts

Other courts of inferior jurisdiction that are found in some states include domestic relations (family) courts (for divorce and child custody cases) and justice of the peace courts (for traffic violations and some ceremonial duties). The justice of the peace courts, which usually employ nonlawyers as judges, are being phased out.

APPLICATIONS OF
WHAT YOU'VE LEARNED

Vocabulary Development

Fill in the blanks with the appropriate term.

Appellate Court	**Justice**
Court of Record	**Juveniles**
Courtus de Historicus	**Probate Court**
Honor	**Youth**
Impeachment Cases	

1. A court that keeps an accurate history of trials is a _____.

2. In a lower court, this person would be referred to as "just" a judge. _____.

3. The legal title of an individual under the age of criminal responsibility. _____.
[The following terms are from previous chapters. The answers are not in the above list.]

4. _____ is an ethical system in which actions are determined by their consequences for self-interest.

5. Courts of _____ have the power of the order.

6. Commerce wholly within one state is _____ commerce.

7. A _____ is a verbatim record of what was said at trial.

Problems

Match the legal issue with the court that will decide it by putting the letter of the court most likely to decide the issue in the blank after each one.

The courts:

a. State supreme court
b. State court of appeals
c. Circuit court
d. Associate circuit court
e. Municipal court
f. Juvenile court
g. Small claims court
h. Probate court
i. Federal district court
j. Federal courts of appeal
k. US Supreme Court

The legal issues:

At 9:13 AM on Friday, March 13, Norman Bates III, an Addamsville, California, resident, is ticketed by a policeman of that city for driving 39 mph in a 20-mph school zone. Mr. Bates protests that he was driving too fast to see the school zone sign. He must appear before the Addamsville _____.

Later in the morning of March 13, Mr. Bates is ticketed by a California patrol officer for driving 78 mph on an interstate highway. Mr. Bates must appear before the _____.

That afternoon, Hy Biscus, an avid gardener, files suit against Norman Bates III for $275 in damages done when Norman allegedly cut down Mr. Biscus's rare roses while employed to mow Mr. Biscus's yard. Neither party wants to hire an attorney. The ideal court to hear their case is the _____.

Just after school is out, Norman Bates III's 13-year-old son is charged with attempting to steal a Seeing Eye dog. The attempted theft failed because the dog slowed young Bates's getaway by waiting for the streets to clear before crossing. The court that will try young Bates's case will be the _____.

As he is leaving the jail after visiting his son, Norman Bates III unexpectedly meets his 17-year-old daughter, Lala. She informs him that she is about to turn herself in for stabbing her boyfriend to death. The court likely to hold her trial is the _____.

That evening Mr. Bates meets with the attorney handling the division of the property of his grandfather, who recently died. The attorney informs him that his sisters Rhea and Dee will receive almost everything. The court overseeing the division of the deceased's property is the _____.

The same attorney informs Mr. Bates that it will cost almost $20,000 to further appeal his father's convictions on embezzlement and fraud charges. A noted televangelist, Norman Bates II made himself famous by proclaiming that there was a pet heaven in which he could guarantee Fido or Fifi a place in return for an appropriate contribution. The California Supreme Court ruled against him last month, but the attorney is confident that victory is around the corner due to the federal constitutional issue in the case. The court to which the appeal will be directed is the _____.

Texas v. Johnson

109 S. Ct. 2533

Read this case to see if you, like Voltaire, would defend to the death Gregory Lee Johnson's right to "speak" by way of the burning of an American flag. (It also shows the working relationship between federal and state court systems.)

The protest march swirled through downtown Dallas during the Republican National Convention in 1984. One of the marchers pulled an American flag from a flagpole and handed it to Gregory Johnson. The march ended in a prolonged demonstration in front of Dallas City Hall. There Johnson unfurled Old Glory, drenched it in kerosene, and set it on fire.

As the American flag burned, the demonstrators chanted, "America the red, white, and blue, we spit on you." Although no one was threatened or injured physically by Johnson's actions, many witnesses later testified that seeing the flag in flames had offended them deeply.

Johnson was charged with violating a Texas Penal Code provision relating to "desecration of a venerated object," tried and sentenced to one year in prison, and fined $2,000. After this trial and conviction in the state court with original criminal jurisdiction, he appealed the conviction to a Texas intermediate appellate court. That court affirmed the conviction. Johnson then appealed to the Texas Court of Criminal Appeals, the highest state court with appellate jurisdiction over his case. That court reversed his conviction on First Amendment grounds, namely that Johnson should not be punished for symbolically exercising his freedom of speech.

The state of Texas then petitioned the US Supreme Court to review the case. Justice Brennan wrote the deciding opinion:

"The act for which appellant [Johnson] was convicted was clearly "speech" contemplated by the First Amendment. To justify Johnson's conviction for engaging in symbolic speech, the State asserted two interests: preserving the flag as a symbol of national unity and preventing breaches of the peace.

"The Texas court [Texas Court of Criminal Appeals] concluded that furthering this interest by curtailing speech was impermissible. The Texas court also decided that the flag's special status was not endangered by Johnson's conduct. As to the State's goal of preventing breaches of the peace, the court concluded that the flag-desecration statute was not drawn narrowly enough to encompass only those flag-burnings that were likely to result in a serious disturbance of the peace. And, in fact, the court emphasized, the flag burning in this particular case did not threaten such a reaction . . .

"Johnson was convicted for engaging in expressive conduct. The State's interest in preventing breaches of the peace does not support his conviction because Johnson's conduct did not threaten to disturb the peace. Nor does the State's interest in preserving the flag as a symbol of nationhood and national unity justify his criminal conviction for engaging in political expression. The judgment of the Texas Court of Criminal Appeals is therefore affirmed."

Questions

1. Who won? Will Johnson have to serve his time and pay his fine?

2. Are the rights "guaranteed" by the Bill of Rights absolute? What part of the opinion supports your answer?

3. Assume that Johnson burned his draft registration card. Is there a state or federal interest that might overcome his right to freedom of speech so as to allow his punishment for that act?

4. The holding in this case provoked the US Congress to pass the Flag Protection Act, which prohibited anyone from knowingly desecrating Old Glory. The act was quickly put to a court test, and the case was appealed to the US Supreme Court. How do you think the Court held?

How Is Criminal Behavior Handled by Our Legal System?

CHAPTER OUTLINE AND OBJECTIVES

After studying this chapter, the student will be able to:

I. Define a crime and apply that definition to actual facts.
  - a. The elements of a crime
  - b. Strict construction of statutes
  - c. Classification of crimes

II. State the purposes of the different stages of criminal procedure.
  - a. The arrest
  - b. Pretrial procedure
  - c. The trial
  - d. Posttrial procedure

III. Identify the constitutional protections and defenses available to those suspected or accused of crimes.
  - a. Miranda warning
  - b. Other significant constitutional protections
  - c. Defenses to the showing of the criminal act
  - d. Defenses relating to the required mental state

IV. Analyze the *United States of America v. John W. Hinckley, Jr.* case which pays tribute to the ability of counsel to argue constitutional protections and available defenses even in the interests of a man accused of attempting to assassinate the President of the United States.

How are Crimes Defined?

As we discussed in Chapter 2, crimes must be carefully defined in a free society. A crime too vaguely or too broadly defined may cause some citizens to stop doing legitimate productive work for fear of being prosecuted. In addition, such a statute may be used for purposes not intended by the legislature. For example, recently enacted statutes have created severe penalties for using lethal weapons in committing a crime. These statutes were intended to be employed against individuals using guns, knives, and the like in committing robberies or other serious crimes. Some prosecutors, arguing that a car is a lethal weapon, have employed the statutes against reckless or drunken drivers. Although the result may be commendable, the effect is to improperly place the legislative power in the hands of prosecutors and courts.

The Elements of a Crime

Actus reus: physical element of a crime

Mens rea: evil intent element of a crime

To stand the best chance of avoiding such unintended results, the definition of a crime should include at least two elements: the physical act (referred to at law as the **actus reus**) and the mental state (the **mens rea**).

The Physical Act

> Oh, you can't be put in jail for what you're thinking.
> Matter of fact, neither can I.

Act: movement directed by the actor's will

This lyric from a classic song reflects some commonsense wisdom about our criminal laws. A properly worded criminal statute should prohibit a specific **act** (defined as a movement directed by the actor's will). Generally, thoughts without overt acts should not be prosecutable. However, a few statutes wisely make it criminal to refuse to act when a person has a legal duty to do so. For example, a lifeguard who refuses to try to rescue a drowning person may be charged with manslaughter if the person drowns.

Note that involuntary acts, such as movements while asleep, while hypnotized, or during convulsions, do not bring on criminal liability.

The Mental State (Intent).   To be prosecutable as a crime, the act must be accompanied by the specific state of mind required in the statute defining the crime. For example, some statutes require that the alleged criminal act be performed **"knowingly,"** that is, with the knowledge that a particular harm is likely to result from it. A person who, seeing a loved one suffering without hope of recovery, cuts off the power to the loved one's life-support system does so knowing that the loved one will probably die as a result. Other mental states often used to define criminal behavior include **recklessness,** which is acting without consideration of the high risk that harm will result from the action, and **negligence,** which is acting in a way that violates the due care a reasonable person owes to others. Driving the wrong way on a one-way street would be reckless conduct, whereas exceeding the posted speed limit by 5 miles or so per hour would be negligent conduct.

Knowingly: with knowledge of likely result

Recklessness: acting regardless of high risk of harm from action

Negligence: acting in violation of duty of due care to others

Too often the mental state used to define criminal behavior is referred to as "criminal" or "evil" intent. Such phrasing causes uninformed persons to incorrectly assume that there is a moral character to this part of a crime's definition. This, in turn, leads to focusing on the actor's **motive** or reason as an excuse for committing the crime. The law does not allow such analysis. For society to rest on the stabilizing pillars of fairness and justice, we must conclude that those who steal food and money to help the starving, who burn draft cards, or who bribe legislators to vote one way or another on abortion issues are common criminals and deserve to be prosecuted as such.

Motive: reason for committing crime

Strict Construction of Statutes

As previously indicated, a free society presumes that all forms of behavior not specifically prohibited by the law are permissible. The possession and use of cocaine, opium, and heroin were legal a century or more ago. Alcohol has been on and off the list of illegal drugs during the past century. However, regardless of how permissive society is toward an activity at a particular time, it is vital that if the activity is prohibited, it be defined as clearly and restrictively as possible. In legal terms, this means that it is vital that a crime be "strictly construed."

As a detailed example, consider the crime of burglary, which we initially discussed in Chapter 2. The definition we used, "the breaking and entering of the dwelling house of another at night with the intent to commit a felony therein," actually originated centuries ago in the English common law. It seems pretty definite and specific, doesn't it? Even so, from the time of its origination to the present, the crime has been subject to more and more definition. Why? Because the definition has been tested repeatedly in court. With each test, each application of the definition to a new set of facts, the definition has become clearer. The question of when a garage is a part of a dwelling house was one such test. The answer, "when it is permanently attached to the main structure," sets the precedent for future cases in which a similar question might arise.

Other elements of burglary required clarification as well. For example, has a person broken into a house if he or she found the door unlocked and just turned the handle and walked in? The precedents say yes. Any time force is used, even to turn a handle, to gain unauthorized entry, there has been a "breaking." If the door or window is open wide enough for the intruder to gain entry without moving it, then there is no "breaking." According to some cases, "entering" requires that a part of the intruder's body penetrate the plane of the house. The courts have held that it was not an entry if a thief standing in the darkness outside a dwelling house picks up a stick off the ground and pokes it through a window that she or he had forced open in order to take a $10,000 pearl necklace lying on a nearby dressing table. No part of the thief's body penetrated the plane of the house. Therefore, if a prosecutor mistakenly charged and tried the thief solely for burglary, the thief would be found not guilty and could not be retried for the same offense. (This prohibition of retrial for the same offense after being found not guilty, referred to as "double jeopardy," is a protection afforded by the Fifth Amendment to the US Constitution.) For the common law definitions of other crimes see Figure 5–1.

Figure 5–1

Common Law Definitions of Crimes

Burglary	Breaking and entering the dwelling house of another at night, with the intent to commit a felony therein.
Arson	The malicious burning of the house of another.
Forgery	The false making or the material altering of a document with the intent to defraud.
Fraud	An intentional perversion of truth for the purpose of inducing another to part with some valuable thing belonging to her or him or to surrender a legal right.
Murder	The unlawful killing of a human being by another with malice aforethought, either express or implied.
Rape	Unlawful sexual intercourse with a person of the opposite sex without the latter's consent.

Note: Definitions of the specific terms used to define crimes can be obtained from the case law or from such publications as *Black's Law Dictionary.* Typical sentencing ranges for most of these crimes and others can be found in Figure 7–1.

Is an apartment a "dwelling house"? When is it nighttime (defense attorneys have been quick to point out that it is still light for some time after the sun goes down, so "after sundown" can't be the answer)? Can a married person legally separated from his or her spouse burglarize the family home if both parties own it?

All of these questions and many, many more had to be answered by the courts to thoroughly define the crime of burglary, a crime that originally had been defined more clearly than most. In general, these questions could not have been anticipated by the authority that drafted the crime's definition. The same is true for all of the hundreds of other crimes that dot our statute books. Crimes become fully defined by being applied to actual behavior. As a result, alleged criminals often do not know whether or not they have violated a law until a court reaches a decision like those mentioned above. This element of uncertainty rightfully causes the courts to strictly construe crimes so as to protect the citizenry from the misapplication of laws, if nothing else.

Classification of Crimes

Felony: crime punishable by death or imprisonment for a year or longer.

The last element of the definition of burglary, "with the intent to commit a felony therein," brings us to the subject of the classification of crimes. Crimes are classified by their degree of severity and according to their origin. A **felony** is a crime severe enough to be punishable by death or by imprisonment for a year or longer. Examples of felonies include murder, arson, burglary, robbery, and rape. So, in accordance with the definition of burglary, breaking and entering the dwelling house of another at night with the intent to commit arson would be burglary.

A **misdemeanor** is a crime punishable by a relatively minor fine and/or imprisonment for less than a year. Shoplifting, disorderly conduct, and most traffic offenses are examples of misdemeanors.

Criminal statutes can be drafted by either a state or the federal government. However, whereas the definition or punishment of a crime may vary greatly from state to state, the federal government's criminal code remains the same throughout the country. Note that the federal government adds treason as a special category of crime. **Treason** is the levying of war against the United States or adhering to the enemies of this country by giving them aid and comfort. Some states add minor offenses called **infractions** (such as littering and parking offenses) to the categories of crimes.

Finally, crimes are considered to be either mala prohibita or mala in se. **Mala in se** crimes are inherently and essentially evil in their nature and consequences. They include murder, arson, larceny, and acts that have been defined as crimes by the common law. A **Mala prohibita** crime is not inherently evil but is considered wrong only because it has been defined as such by the legislature or Congress. Speeding, jaywalking, and other minor offenses fall into this category.

> **Misdemeanor:** crime punishable by minor fine and/or imprisonment for less than a year
>
> **Treason:** levying war or giving aid and comfort to enemies of United States
>
> **Infractions:** very minor offenses
>
> **Mala in Se:** Crimes with evil intent
>
> **Mala Prohibita:** crimes without evil intent

What Are the Different Stages of the Criminal Procedure?

Criminal procedure begins with the violation of a criminal statute. At that time, according to our laws, an offense has been committed against the governmental body that drafted the statute. This is because almost all criminal offenses involve an actual or constructive **breach of the peace.** Such a breach is a violation or disturbance of the public tranquillity and order. Realize that the offense is not considered to be against the victim of the crime and that it therefore becomes the duty of the citizen to report such incidents to the proper authorities as the first step in criminal procedure. Realize also that those authorities, as representatives of the government that made the behavior criminal in the first place, have the power to decide whether to prosecute the person who allegedly committed the crime. It is not up to the victim, although whether the victim will aid in the investigation and prosecution is a significant factor in the decision to go forward with such efforts.

> **Breach of the Peace:** disturbance of public order

The Arrest

Upon the reporting of a crime by a private citizen or the observation or discovery of a crime by the police, an investigation is conducted. This investigation may result in an immediate **arrest,** which is the taking into custody of a suspect to answer a criminal charge. It may also result in the development of facts indicating that a certain person was responsible for the crime. At the state level, if the facts are conclusive enough, the responsible public officer (the state attorney general or the local prosecutor) will swear out an accusation based on his or her oath of office. This accusation is known as an **information.** At the federal level, where only a grand jury (see next paragraph) can issue an indictment, the decision to

> **Arrest:** taking of a suspect into custody to answer criminal charge
>
> **Information:** criminal accusation on oath of public officer

put the matter before such a jury belongs to such individuals as the US attorney general and his or her assistants. In either system, however, the victim's refusal to testify if a prosecution is attempted often is crucial to the decision to go forward.

If the facts gathered by the investigating officers are not conclusive, either the state prosecutors or federal district attorneys may refer the case to a "jury of inquiry," which can compel witnesses to testify under oath and can demand the production of evidence. This jury is referred to as a **grand jury** in most states because it has a larger number of members (20 or more in many jurisdictions) than the petit jury (6 to 12 members) that appears in a jury trial. If the grand jury develops enough evidence to indicate that a certain individual should be tried for the crime, it will vote out an indictment based on its oath. The **indictment,** like the information, is an accusation of criminal conduct against an individual.

Grand Jury: jury of inquiry

Indictment: grand jury accusation of criminal conduct

Arrest Warrant: order that person be arrested by competent authority

The indictment or information is forwarded to a judge or similar public official with the power to issue an **arrest warrant** (an order that a person be arrested by competent authority).

Pretrial Procedure

Once arrested, a person must be informed of the charge or charges against her or him and be allowed to plead guilty or not guilty. This is done at a court proceeding called an **arraignment.** After hearing the accused's plea, the court will hold a hearing to set bail, if such is to be allowed the defendant. **Bail** is the posting of property or bond with the court to ensure the accused's later appearance. If the accused fails to appear, the amount posted is forfeited to the court. If the accused pleads guilty at the arraignment, the appropriate court will pass sentence at a later time. If the accused pleads not guilty, he or she is scheduled to be tried as soon as possible in accordance with the constitutional guarantee of a speedy trial.

Arraignment: court proceeding to allow pleading to formal charge

Bail: posting of property or bond to ensure later appearance

If the defendant has been charged by an information and should he or she request it, the court is required to hold a preliminary hearing before trial. (Persons charged by grand jury indictment do not have the right to such a hearing.) During this **preliminary hearing,** the evidence against the accused will be presented by the prosecution. The court will then determine whether there is reasonable basis or **probable cause** to proceed with the trial. If the court decides that there is not, the accused will be freed and the charge(s) dropped. This does happen at times. If, for example, a necessary witness will not testify or the use of certain evidence is disallowed by the court, the case against the accused will be terminated. Usually, however, the court will find that there is probable cause to proceed with preparations for the trial. At times, as a result of the presentation of the evidentiary case against the defendant at the preliminary hearing, the prosecution or the defense, or both, will seek a **plea bargain.** A plea bargain is an agreement in which the defendant agrees to plead guilty to a reduced charge in exchange for the prosecutor's recommendation of a lighter sentence. Plea bargains are also used to lighten the workload of the prosecutors and the overcrowding of the courts by eliminating the trying of relatively minor cases.

Preliminary Hearing: court proceeding on basis for trial

Probable Cause: reasonable basis for charges

Plea Bargain: agreement to accept particular admission of criminal behavior and liability therefor

The Trial

If the court deems it proper and no plea bargain interrupts, the trial must take place without unreasonable delay. The **trial jury,** a group of persons selected according to law to impartially determine the factual questions of the case from the evidence allowed before them in court, is at the heart of our criminal system. Potential jurors are chosen from voter rolls in most jurisdictions. They are then carefully screened to eliminate any potentially biased persons. The right to a jury trial, if requested by the defendant, is guaranteed by the US Constitution. Certain defendants do not request a jury, especially those charged with such crimes as child abuse or the performance of especially gruesome acts.

Trial Jury: citizens appointed to determine factual questions from court-presented evidence

During the trial, the prosecutor will present evidence to prove the guilt of the accused "beyond a reasonable doubt," and the defense attorney will present evidence disputing that conclusion. Exactly what evidence it is proper to place before the trier of fact (usually a jury, but the judge if no jury is requested) is determined by the judge. If the material or testimony that either the prosecution or the defense desires to put into evidence might improperly bias the jury, it will not be allowed.

HYPOTHETICAL CASE

Charles DuBois was on trial for the armed robbery of a liquor store. His defense attorney called Bernard Strong to testify. Strong had been in the store when the crime was committed. When the police arrived, Strong overheard one of the police officers say, "It couldn't have been DuBois. I saw him in the park when this robbery was being committed."

If the prosecution objected to it, Strong's testimony would probably be thrown out by the court because it is **hearsay,** evidence stemming not from the personal knowledge of the witness but from what the witness heard another say. The jury would be ordered to disregard his testimony in reaching its conclusion.

Hearsay: testimony of what witness has heard another say

At the conclusion of the presentation of evidence by both sides, the judge will instruct the jury as to what it is to determine. The jury will then retire and try to reach a **verdict.** A verdict is a statement of whatever conclusions the jury has reached on the questions of fact (for example, "Is the defendant guilty of committing the crime?") submitted to it. If, after extensive deliberations, the jury cannot reach agreement on a verdict, it is labeled a **hung jury** and the case may be retired or perhaps even dropped.

Verdict: jury's conclusions

Hung Jury: jury unable to agree on verdict

If the jury returns a guilty verdict, the court will generally delay sentencing for a time so as to examine the criminal's past history and other circumstances. Some crimes require a mandatory sentence as dictated by the legislature or Congress.

Posttrial Procedure

On the other hand, a court may suspend the sentencing procedure and only place restrictions on the defendant's behavior for a certain period of time. If the defendant complies, there will be no official record of the conviction as sentence

Probation: conditional suspension of execution of sentence

Parole: conditional release of convict before full time served

was never passed down. A court may also pass sentence but suspend its execution, allowing the convicted party to go free on **probation.** The sentence will not be carried out if the person on probation leads an orderly life and complies with the terms set by the court.

Even if sentence is imposed and carried out by placing the convicted criminal in the county jail or the state penitentiary, the criminal may be given **parole,** a conditional release, when there is still a great deal of time left to be served. If the terms of the parole are violated, the criminal is returned to jail or the penitentiary to serve the rest of his or her term.

Should the convicted party feel that errors of law were made in the conduct of the trial or in the disallowing of certain defenses, an appeal may be taken to a higher court. Bail may be allowed pending the result of that appeal. If errors are found, the conviction may be thrown out. The prosecutor may then elect to retry the case or to let it drop, as shown in this example that parallels an actual case:

Conner was arrested for committing a felony. Shortly thereafter, his lawyer appeared at the police station but was not allowed to see him. Meanwhile, Conner was told that if he would confess, he could consult with his attorney. Conner thereupon confessed, and his confession was used to convict him. Upon appeal, the US Supreme Court ruled that before suspects in police custody are questioned, they must be informed of their rights, such as their rights to remain silent and to have counsel present if desired. Because these rights were denied Conner, both his confession and the conviction that resulted from its use were thrown out. (Nevertheless, the prosecutor later retried the case, using evidence other then the confession, and reconvicted Conner.)

What Constitutional Protections and Defenses Are Available to Those Suspected or Accused of Crimes?

We have learned that the essential elements of a crime are the physical act and the mental state. Unless these are proven to the trier of fact beyond a reasonable doubt, the accused cannot be convicted. Therefore, most defenses, such as overbroadness and entrapment, go to proving by competent evidence that either or both of these elements do not exist. The constitutional protections, on the other hand, are most often used to exclude improperly obtained evidence that could be used to prove the crime if presented at trial. So, to keep things in proper order, let's look at the constitutional protections first.

Miranda *Warning*

As indicated in the above situation involving Conner, any person taken into custody in a criminal case is protected by a number of rights. The *"Miranda* warning," stemming from the 1966 Supreme Court case of *Miranda* v. *Arizona,* is commonly read to all suspects of federal and state crimes. (Note that it does not apply to violators of municipal ordinances.) The warning, based primarily on the guarantees contained in various amendments to the US Constitution, details many of the protective rights. Any confession or other evidence developed by the authorities before a suspect has been properly informed of those rights cannot be used to convict the suspect. The warning has four parts:

1. That the person in custody has a right to remain silent (Fifth Amendment).
2. That any statement the person makes may be used as evidence against her or him.
3. That the person in custody has a right to an attorney's presence (Sixth Amendment).
4. That if he or she cannot afford an attorney, one will be appointed for him or her prior to questioning if so desired.

Other Significant Constitutional Protections

In addition, amendments to the US Consitution afford several other protections. As mentioned earlier, the Fifth Amendment prohibits double jeopardy. It also states that no defendant in a criminal case can be compelled to be a witness against himself or herself. Also, according to the Fourth Amendment, searches must be a result of probable cause. If not, the courts will not allow the use of whatever evidence they develop as a result of the search to convict the defendant. Among the other rights of defendants are the right to confront their accusers, the right to a speedy and public trial, and the right to be free from cruel and unusual punishment.

All of these constitutional protections, which often exclude evidence that would clearly show the guilt of the accused, are touted as safeguards against overzealous police efforts. Through these safeguards the legal system supposedly tries to live up to the idea that it should "free a thousand guilty lest one innocent be convicted." Critics of this approach say that present-day reality puts that quest in question. Innocents are still convicted. In addition, the thousand guilty who are freed by the exclusion of evidence showing their guilt all too often prey on countless more innocents after their release.

Moreover, the fruit of the truly successful criminal's labor often brings him or her substantial rewards that allow the hiring of the best defense attorneys. These attorneys ensure that their clients, who may be the most wicked and perverse persons in our society, receive the fullest protection of the law, whereas poorer defendants and certainly the victims do not. Rather than excluding improperly obtained but actual evidence of criminal behavior, an action that only hurts society, reformers today suggest that the defendant whose rights have been violated be allowed some form of action, such as a lawsuit, against the law enforcement officer and organization. This would leave the prosecutor with all the evidence she or he needs to have the best chance for a successful prosecution.

Defenses to the Showing of the Criminal Act

Even if legitimate and conclusive evidence is admitted against the defendant who committed the act in question, certain defenses are still available. One of these defenses stems from the attempts of prosecutors to make a law already on the books cover conduct it cannot legitimately reach. Consider this example:

> A criminal statute that prohibits the making and distribution of certain addictive drugs lists each of them by chemical formula. Sam Powers, the defendant, found a way to combine two of the cheapest "street drugs" on the list to make a third that was even more addictive. The combination drug had a formula different from those prohibited under the statute.

Overbroad: statute with too far-reaching application

If Powers were caught and tried for a violation of the statute, he could defend himself by pointing out that the drug he manufactured was not specifically prohibited. If he were nonetheless convicted by the trial court, the conviction would probably be thrown out on appeal as an **overbroad** or too far-reaching application of the statute.

Other defenses to a showing that the defendant committed the act in question include the defense that the statute was ambiguous in its definition of the act or that the statute makes a status, such as drug addiction, a crime. Note, however, that possession is not treated as a status and may therefore result in a conviction. The exercise of control over an item or even a vehicle, say one in which illegal drugs are found, is **possession** and enough of an act to satisfy the courts. Even refusing to act may be enough of an act to bring on criminal liability where the act is to fulfill a legally required duty. As mentioned previously, a lifeguard who refuses to attempt a rescue of a drowning person may be chargeable with manslaughter.

Possession: exercise of control over item

Defenses Relating to the Required Mental State

The second element of most crimes, the mental state, also provides grounds for many defenses. Note, that in a trial, the mental state of the defendant may be inferred by the trier of fact from the act itself. For example, a jury can conclude that the driver acted recklessly from a showing that she crossed and recrossed the interstate highway median at high speed prior to the collision. In such situations, the defense must present evidence that focuses directly on the defendant's actual mental state and not on what the act alone indicates it might have been.

Insanity Defense: inability to formulate criminal intent due to mental problem

The **insanity defense** is used in this way. When this defense is used, it must be shown that the defendant was suffering from a mental disease or defect that prevented the defendant from understanding the difference between right and wrong and therefore from formulating the evil intent that the criminal statute was meant to prohibit. A similar defense stems from the effect of an **irresistible impulse** (also known as the temporary mental defect), in which, because of a mental disease or defect, the defendant is temporarily unable to resist an impulse to commit a criminal act.

Irresistible Impulse: inability to resist desire to commit criminal act due to mental problem

Francis X. Tenguish, the fire chief of Flammable, Connecticut, returned home early from a stress clinic he had been attending for two weeks in rural Pennsylvania. The clinic had been prescribed as part of Chief Tenguish's treatment for job-related mental disorders. Unfortunately, the chief's unannounced return allowed him to catch his wife in bed with another man. Chief Tenguish immediately grabbed a 37 Magnum "extinguisher" from a bedside cabinet and shot his wife's lover twice in the lower abdomen. When the chief was charged and tried for criminal assault, his defense was that he had acted out of an irresistible impulse. The fact that he had just been undergoing treatment for a mental defect showed that his ability to choose right from wrong was seriously weakened and that it was easily destroyed by the impact of the event. The jury agreed and the chief was found not guilty. (This is based on an actual case. The wounded lover then sued the chief for damages in a civil lawsuit. See Chapter VI for an explanation of personal injury law.)

A defense that, like insanity, dispels the appearance of the criminal mental state is **entrapment.** If government agents have induced a person to commit a crime that she or he did not already contemplate, the accused has been entrapped and will be found not guilty. On the other hand, if the government agents provide only the opportunity for the crime to be committed, there is no defense. For example, individuals who sell goods they have stolen to an undercover cop acting as a fence have not been entrapped.

Entrapment: government agents improperly inducing person to commit crime

Mistake can be a defense when, because of honest error, the required criminal mental state is negated. Such a defense is provided if you take someone else's property because you honestly and reasonably believe it is your own.

Mistake: honest error that negates required criminal mental state

Phor O. Student purchased a gift for her friend, then took it to a gift wrapping service. She asked for a box of a particular size and for a particular style of wrapping paper. She then paid for the service and was told to return in 15 minutes to pick up her package. When she returned, a package just like the one she ordered was on the counter. Not seeing anyone around the counter area, she picked it up and left with it, not knowing that it contained someone else's very expensive purchase. Mistake would serve as a defense to charges of theft that might stem from the incident. (A mistake as to the existence or the reach of a criminal law is no defense, however. Ignorance of the law is still no excuse.)

Finally, accusations of criminal intent can be overcome if it can be shown that the defendant acted in **defense of self or others.** This defense is available if the defendant reasonably believed that there was danger of severe bodily harm or death from an unprovoked attack and used only enough force to repel that attack. Generally, retreat "to the wall," as it was once expressed, before defending oneself or others, is now required in only a few states and then only if faced with the use of deadly force and the retreat is not hazardous. When force is used in

Defense of Self or Others: use of appropriate force to repel attack

defense of others, some states require that those defended be members of the defender's family or household or someone else that the defender had a legal duty to protect. Other states allow the use of force in defense of others only if the party being defended actually (not just apparently) had a right to self-defense. In conclusion, note that only nondeadly force can be used in the defense of property alone.

APPLICATIONS OF WHAT YOU'VE LEARNED

Vocabulary Development

Fill in the blanks with the appropriate term.

Act	Felony	Mala in Se	Plea Bargain
Actus Reus	Grand Jury	Mala Prohibita	Possession
Arraignment	Hearsay	Mens Rea	Preliminary Hearing
Arrest	Hung Jury	Misdemeanor	Probable Cause
Arrest Warrant	Indictment	Mistake	Probation
Bail	Information	Motive	Recklessness
Breach of the Peace	Infractions	Negligence	Treason
Defense of Self	Insanity Defense	Overbroad	Trial Jury
or Others	Irresistible Impulse	Parole	Verdict
Entrapment	Knowingly		

1. The judge enters the judgment. A jury reaches its _____.

2. "I heard her say that he was present at the scene of the crime" is _____.

3. Acting in violation of the duty of due care may be negligence. Acting regardless of the high risk of harm to others is _____.

4. The conditional release of a convict before her or his full time is served is _____.

5. The conditional suspension of the carrying out of the sentence is _____.

6. The source of indictments is a _____.

7. A potential defense to criminal charges because government agents induced the commission of the offense is _____.

8. A _____ is a crime punishable by death or imprisonment for a year or longer.

9. A _____ is an honest error that negates the criminal intent usually required to convict someone of a crime.

10. At a preliminary hearing, the court will examine the evidence to see whether there is

_____

to go to trial.

Problems

1. Todd Chase Larue III, fresh out of the University of Virginia law school and destined to join the lucrative family law practice headed by Larues I and II, chuckled when he saw the motorcycle cop's lights flash in his mirrors. He didn't react at once. Instead he let his big engine push him a quarter of a mile more down the shore road. Finally, he pulled onto the shoulder. The motorcycle cop took off . . . her helmet. She was making out the ticket even then. Five minutes later, another citation for riding

without a helmet was in Todd's hands. Todd vowed that he would never pay any of them. They had no right to tell him he had to wear a helmet!

Does society have any interest to protect by requiring that we use helmets and other protective devices while traveling our roads, working in our factories, and so on? What has society invested in Larue III? What does society stand to lose beyond that investment if he is launched over the handlebars without a helmet on?

2. Marcia Benton watched the rain falling outside her hospital window, then, amused at herself about how vulnerable she was to suggestion, reached slowly for the glass of water by her bedside. Her hand trembled from the exertion. But she kept it moving, forcing it toward the glass by an act of will. A light sweat appeared on her forehead. Her body had withered away these last few years. The disease had so sapped her energies that just raising a hand took enormous concentration. Her children didn't understand her weariness, however. They remembered their mother from the days when she had protected them against all harm, comforted them with love, given them direction in life. She had told them of her current desire to die, but they had not taken her seriously. "You're kidding, Mom. You'll miss so much, grandchildren and all that," Bill had replied for all four of them. Even when the doctor had given them an estimate of the bill for keeping her on life support, they had remained resolute. She knew, though, that to keep her alive they would be paying the money they'd saved for their children's clothes, education, future . . . So when the other doctor had slipped into her room the day before and introduced himself, she was glad, even joyful. She had prayed that he would come, prayed that the hospital orderly would contact him as promised. The doctor would return this evening with his machine, set it up, and then she would activate it with a push button. When she did, it would gently administer a lethal dose of a drug that the doctor had assured her would be painless. Her children would ultimately realize that she had ended her life because she had to protect them . . . even from herself. Of course, the doctor would be in jeopardy. He was out on bail for rendering suicide assistance in another state. She grasped the water glass at last, but it fell from her hand and shattered on the floor. Marcia closed her eyes in dismay and sank back onto her pillows . . .

a. Should it be a criminal act to assist in suicides? If you believe that assisting suicides should be a crime, what should be the punishment for that crime (compare your answer with sentencing ranges for various crimes listed in Figure 7–1)?

b. Attempted suicide is a crime in some jurisdictions. What should be the punishment for it?

c. If an innocent bystander is accidentally injured in a suicide attempt (say because in such an attempt a car crashes into the bystander), should the person who made the attempt be punished for that injury?

3. Assume that you are the head prosecutor of a major metropolitan area. Two alleged rape cases on your desk are awaiting a decision on whether or not to go forward with trial. The first case involves a female victim who becomes hysterical whenever she is questioned about the incident. There is a high likelihood that the stress of a trial would cause her to suffer a severe breakdown. However, there is a great deal of evidence against the defendant, much of which suggests the use of extreme force: torn clothing, bruises and cuts on the alleged victim's body, and the recovery of a knife from the defendant similar to the one that the alleged victim described. The second case involves a defendant from a well-known and very wealthy entertainment family. The media coverage has been intense, and a decision not to prosecute would be regarded as favoritism. However, the only evidence in the case is the testimony of the alleged victim.

a. Which of the cases do you order to trial?

b. You have two assistant prosecutors who handle rape cases. One is an inexperienced woman. The other is a man with a superior conviction record over the six years he has been with your office. Which of these assistant prosecutors would you assign to the first case if it went to trial? Which would you assign to the second?

4. Assume that you are being arrested for a major felony. The police have handcuffed you and placed you in a patrol car for transport to headquarters. During the ride you have a few moments to think. As a person accused of a crime, what rights are you guaranteed under our federal Constitution? Given your present circumstances, what practical steps can you take to obtain the protection afforded by those rights?

ACTUAL CASE STUDY

United States v. John W. Hinckley, Jr.

525 F. Supp. 1342

Consider the case of U.S. v. Hinckley, wherein able and expensive attorneys utilized available constitutional protections and the insanity plea in the defense of their client

On March 30, 1981, as President Ronald Reagan left the Washington Hilton Hotel after giving a speech, he was wounded by one of a series of bullets allegedly fired by John Hinckley. Three other men were also wounded, including James Brady, the president's press secretary, who received a severely debilitating wound in the head. President Reagan underwent surgery shortly thereafter at a nearby hospital. Before the surgery he commented to his wife, "Honey, I forgot to duck," then eyed the surgeons and said jokingly, "Please tell me you're Republicans." He recovered and served two full terms.

John Hinckley was arrested at the scene with "smoking gun" in hand. Soon after his arraignment, he underwent two psychiatric examinations by order of the magistrate and then the chief judge involved in the case. Both examinations found him to be competent. On August 28, after being indicted by a federal grand jury, Hinckley pled not guilty to a battery of charges, including attempted assassination of the president.

His lawyers, however, were hard at work. First, they moved to suppress evidence garnered from Hinckley's interrogation by law enforcement officials soon after the shooting and before he had legal counsel at hand. The court held that although Hinckley had been informed of his *Miranda* rights three times prior to making his statements, his expression of a desire not to answer certain questions until he had consulted with his attorney was enough to invoke that right. The court therefore held that

interrogation should have been suspended until legal counsel was present and that Hinckley's answers to all questions relating to the investigation when he was without counsel would not be allowed as evidence. Second, Hinckley's lawyers moved to suppress evidence garnered from the diary and notes that he had mantained in his cell. In checking Hinckley's cell for contraband and indicators of a potential suicide attempt, his jailers had discovered allegedly incriminating material that he had written in the diary. Hinckley's lawyers argued that the substance of his writings had been improperly violated. The court held that the material garnered from those writings should be suppressed as the search and seizure rights of Hinckley's jailers went only to the two problem areas that they had been supposed to check. Finally, at trial, the defense was able to convince the jury, which debated almost 24 hours before returning a verdict, that John Hinckley was not guilty by reason of insanity. The defense introduced evidence of his psychiatric care immediately prior to the shootings and of his fixation on actress Jodie Foster. Hinckley apparently mused that Foster would have to notice him if he carried out an act such as the attempted assassination.

Hinckley was ordered confined at St. Elizabeth's Hospital, a mental institution in Washington, DC.

Questions

1. Hinckley was the son of very wealthy parents, and the law worked quite well in his defense. Do you think it would have worked as well in defense of an unemployed construction worker?

2. Should incriminating evidence be suppressed regardless of how it was obtained? Are there any alternatives to suppression?

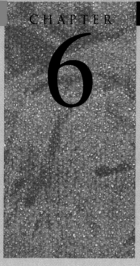

CHAPTER

6

How Are Injuries to Persons and Property Handled by Our Legal System?

CHAPTER OUTLINE AND OBJECTIVES

After studying this chapter, the student will be able to:

I. Define tort law and explain its relevance to other legal areas.
  a. Tort law's relationship to criminal and contract law
  b. Remedies available to correct tortious conduct

II. Distinguish among the kinds of conduct that will bring on tort liability.
  a. Intentional torts
  b. Negligence
  c. Strict liability
  d. Defenses to torts

III. Describe the procedure by which the courts resolve civil cases.
  a. Parties to the action
  b. Requiring the defendant to appear and answer
  c. Defining the issues to be resolved
  d. Pretrial preparations
  e. Trial procedure
  f. Appeal

IV. Observe how new torts are developed by reading *Nader* v. *General Motors*, which shows how the right of privacy was defined as a result of allegations of electronic eavesdropping, wiretapping, and worse against one of the nation's most powerful companies.

What Is a Tort?

A shopper backs his car into your new vehicle in the mall's lot.

A drunk punches you in the nose.

A newspaper improperly identifies you as the shoplifter picked up yesterday in a local store.

A truck overturns and spills gasoline that pollutes your land.

A competing business "bugs" your office with listening devices.

A doctor improperly diagnoses your problem as stomach flu when, in reality, you have appendicitis.

A lawyer improperly advises you, causing a $10,000 loss.

Do any of the above situations sound familiar? A wrong has been committed in each of them. In all of them the victim can use the courts to seek compensation. These personal injuries or wrongs for which the law will provide remedies are known as **torts,** and the person who commits a tort is known as a **tortfeasor.** It is the right of the injured party to sue the tortfeasor. If the injured party wins the lawsuit, the court will order the tortfeasor to pay that party an appropriate amount of money for the harm done. This compensation is known as a damage award or just as **damages.**

History has shown us that if the opportunity to right personal injuries in a court of law is not available, wronged individuals often seek revenge with their own hands. The resulting violence endangers, and may even destroy, the peace and stability that mark civilization.

Torts: personal injuries or wrongs with legal remedies

Tortfeasor: person who commits tort

Damages: monetary compensation

Tort Law's Relationship to Criminal and Contract Law

Note that tort law differs from other types of law in significant ways. Criminal law, for example, requires that the wrong be defined beforehand. Citizens then owe a duty to society not to commit criminal acts. When a crime is committed, however, it is society that has been injured because it is the peace of society that has been violated. Therefore, it is up to the prosecutor for the state or federal government to seek the fining and/or imprisonment of the violator on behalf of society. Tort law, on the other hand, is far more flexible than criminal law. It recognizes only a general duty of each citizen to refrain from harming another in negligent or intentional ways. The specific harmful act does not have to be identified beforehand and could occur in an ever-growing number of possible ways. If such harm occurs, it is then up to the injured person to seek damages and/or other suitable remedies in court. These available remedies are far less severe than the fine and/or imprisonment punishments meted out to violators of the criminal law. However, it should be realized that criminal acts often include conduct that constitutes a tort: Angered when a female fan at ringside repeatedly insulted his hairdo, famous wrestler Stan ("The Hummingbird") Solo hit her over the head with a folding chair. As a result, he was arrested and prosecuted for criminal assault. Afterward the fan sued him for the tort of battery and recovered $75,000 in damages.

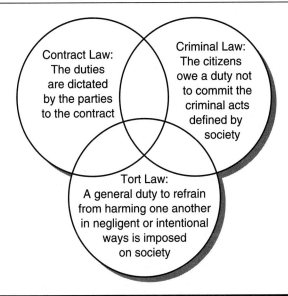

The Overlapping Duties of Criminal, Tort, and Contract Law   **Figure 6–1**

Contract Law: The duties are dictated by the parties to the contract

Criminal Law: The citizens owe a duty not to commit the criminal acts defined by society

Tort Law: A general duty to refrain from harming one another in negligent or intentional ways is imposed on society

Tort law also differs from contract law. As with criminal law, under contract law the enforceable duties are defined beforehand. However, the definition of those duties is written by the parties to the contract and not by society. In addition, the contractual parties owe the duties primarily to each other. It is up to the party injured under the contract to sue to collect damages when such a duty has been unfulfilled or violated. Regardless of the differences between the parties, however, contracts can also produce grounds for tort actions.

HYPOTHETICAL CASE

The Melbourne Marsupials, an Australian team of the World Intercontinental Football League (WIFL), needed a coach. Desperate, the Marsupials contracted with Danny Uprights, successful head coach of Pennsboro State University (PSU) of Missouri, for his services. Coach Uprights, however, had just signed a five-year contract with PSU and would have to break it to be able to coach the Marsupials. Should he do so, PSU could sue the Marsupials for the tort of intentional interference with contract.

Remedies Available to Correct Tortious Conduct

A person who initiates a tort suit is attempting to correct the supposed wrong done by asking for damages or an injunction, or both. An **injunction** is a court order directing that some action be either taken or halted. For example, if your neighbor is dumping toxic waste into a stream that flows onto your land, you might sue for a court order directing that the neighbor stop the dumping and clean up the toxic waste.

Although the availability of an injunction as a remedy is significant, it is the

Injunction: court order prohibiting an act that might injure or compelling an act to undo an injury

Litigants: those who engage in lawsuit

Actual Damages: monetary compensation for real harm done

promise or threat of a damage award that most often draws natural persons, associations, partnerships, corporations, and even the government (acting as a private individual) into court under the tort law. So, before discussing torts in detail, let's take a look at the various types and amounts of damages that may be available to **litigants** (those who engage in a lawsuit).

Actual damages (also referred to as compensatory damages) are the most important and most frequently sought damages. These damages are intended to compensate the victim for the real harm done. If property is damaged or destroyed, then the amount necessary to repair or replace it would be awarded. If a person is injured, damages would include payment for lost wages, medical bills, and the pain and suffering that the person endured.

Exemplary Damages: monetary compensation set to make example of defendant

In some cases the victim may be awarded even more than actual damages in order to punish or make an example of a defendant who acted maliciously or wantonly. These additional amounts, called **exemplary damages** (or "punitive" damages in some jurisdictions), are arbitrarily set by the jury and bear little, if any, direct relationship to the amount of actual injuries sustained by the victim. For example, imagine that, after waiting in line overnight, you are about to buy the last available tickets to a live concert of your favorite rock group. Suddenly, Anthony ("Little Mountain") Sanderson pushes you out of the way to get them for himself. You resist, and he punches you in the stomach. Then, while you are lying on the sidewalk, he buys the tickets, and leaves. Even if the punch did you no lasting harm, most courts would allow you to recover a small amount for it and thousands of dollars in exemplary damages from Sanderson to prevent the recurrence of such conduct. Unlike damages awarded for negligently caused harm, such exemplary damages are not dischargeable in bankruptcy.

Nominal Damages: token damages

Note that where there has been improper conduct but little in the way of actual loss, as in the preceding example, the law still awards a small amount of damages to the victim. Such awards are referred to as **nominal damages.** At times, these damages may be all that the victim receives as a result of her or his lawsuit. However, they do represent an acknowledgment by the law that the victim's rights have been violated.

Finally, do not forget that attorney's fees and expenses will not be awarded by the court in these cases. They are instead payable out of the pocket or recovery of the litigants. Many tort suits are brought on a percentage of recovery basis. Under such an arrangement, anywhere from 25 percent to 40 percent of the recovery may go to the attorney.

What Kinds of Conduct Will Bring on Tort Liability?

For a defendant in a tort case to be required to pay damages, it must be shown that he or she has harmed someone in one of three basic ways: (1) intentionally, (2) accidentally due to a failure to exercise reasonable care, or (3) by engaging in certain enterprises that bring on liability regardless of the degree of care taken.

Intentional Torts

The first of these three ways, that is, intentionally or purposefully bringing about harm to another's person or property, is the basis for the **intentional torts.** You've probably heard of some of the best known of these torts, such as assault, battery, and false imprisonment.

Placing an individual in reasonable fear of a harmful or offensive touching is an **assault.** Actually touching someone in a harmful or offensive way is a **battery.** Improper restraint or confinement of another without authority, justification, or consent is **false imprisonment.** Case examples of assault and battery will be discussed shortly in order to show how intentional tort law works. Other intentional torts and their specific impact on businesses will be discussed in Chapter 7.

It is extremely important to realize that the victim of an intentional tort is able to recover not only actual damages but exemplary damages as well. So the stakes can be extremely high.

To win an intentional tort case, several key points, called elements, must be proven to the jury. For the case of battery these elements include:

1. An act—this must be a result of the actor's will and not of a reflex or spasm. Thus, if a person hits me because he is in the throes of an epileptic seizure, I cannot recover for battery as he did not hit me willfully.
2. An intent—the defendant must have intended to bring about a harmful or offensive touching. Note that intentionally hitting someone with either a baseball bat or an unwanted (and therefore offensive) kiss can be the basis for a battery suit.
3. Actual contact—there must be actual contact, not just a swing (or pucker) and miss situation. Hitting a person's clothes while they are being worn or a person's purse while it is being carried is considered the same as hitting the person.
4. Causation—the defendant's action must be a substantial factor in the injuries suffered by the victim.
5. Damages—evidence of the harm caused by the defendant must be shown.

These elements differ a little for the closely related intentional tort of assault. Assault requires that the defendant intended to place the victim in reasonable apprehension of a harmful or offensive touching. No actual touching has to occur, it simply has to be reasonable to presume that you're about to suffer such a touching. However, there has to be an overt act by the defendant to bring on that presumption. Words alone are not enough.

To understand assault and battery better, consider this real-life example. You are in a high school English class whose teacher frequently hurls pieces of chalk at sleeping or inattentive students. Kelsay, who sits in front of you, is whispering with a new female student while the teacher is lecturing. As the teacher's voice drones on, you stare at the back of Kelsay's head thinking about last weekend's . . . Suddenly, the teacher fires a piece of chalk at Kelsay. Seeing it coming, Kelsay ducks violently, pinches a nerve in his neck, and loses consciousness. Unseen by you, the chalk pops you in the mouth and breaks off part of your

Intentional Torts: torts in which the tort feasor(s) purposefully inflicted harm

Assault: place in fear of harmful or offensive touching

Battery: touching someone in harmful or offensive way

False Imprisonment: improper restraint or confinement of someone

front tooth. Both you and Kelsay can bring suit for actual damages (his hospital-ization caused him to lose $80 by missing two days' work, he paid $4,500 in medical fees, and he requests $20,000 for pain and suffering) and exemplary damages (which will be arbitrarily set by the jury and may total $50,000 or more due to the nature of the incident). His suit will be based on assault as the force set in motion (the chalk) by the teacher did not actually hit him. Your suit will be for battery only as you were the victim of a harmful touching but had no notice or apprehension of a forthcoming harmful touching.

Defenses to Intentional Tort Cases.   As is obvious to any participant in or observer of a contact sport, not all injurious physical touching results in a successful lawsuit. That is because **consent,** a willing and knowledgeable assent to what would otherwise be tortious conduct, is a defense in intentional tort cases. The consent of the injured party may be implied or actual, and it must not be acquired by fraudulent means.

Consent: defense based on assent to tortious conduct

Self-defense and defense of property also provide limited protection against intentional tort suits. For information on these defenses, read the following scenario and consider the questions that follow.

HYPOTHETICAL CASE

> At 3 AM, JJ awakened when she heard a car engine idling roughly on the street. Knowing something was wrong, she slid out of bed and peered out of the window. A car was parked at the head of her driveway with its lights out and its trunk partly open. The side door of her new car, which was also parked in the driveway, was open, but its interior lights weren't on. A dark, shadowlike figure was sprawled on the seat of her car working at something under the dash. JJ called 911 and reported what was going on. As she hung up, she realized that the person was after her CD system, which was worth nearly $2,500 and uninsured. She grabbed her dad's old .45-caliber service pistol from the drawer in the night table and slipped out the side door. As she reached the driveway, the figure in the car got out, carrying her CD system. JJ was between him and his car. "Stop," she yelled, aiming the pistol at him. The man smiled at her and started walking to his car. As he walked past her, JJ chambered a round and yelled again: "Stop, I'll shoot and you better believe it!"

If JJ shoots the man in the knee, do you think he should be able to successfully sue her for doing so? The answer is that JJ will certainly be liable if she shoots him merely to prevent him from taking her property. The law holds that reasonable force may be used in defense of property. This does not include force that might cause substantial bodily harm or death. Presume that JJ doesn't shoot at first but that after putting her CD system in the trunk of his car, the man walks toward her with a tire iron in his hand, saying, "Now get out of the way so I can get the speakers." Would his subsequent lawsuit against her be successful if she kneecaps him at that time? The law holds that in self-defense a person must use only reasonable force to prevent a threatened battery. Such force may include inflicting substantial bodily harm or death on the aggressor, but only so long as a convenient or reasonable means of escape is not available. As JJ could have gotten out of the thief's way and not had to use deadly force, she would probably be held liable for assault and battery.

Negligence

The second way which a defendant may be held liable under tort law is to harm someone or something accidentally due to a failure to exercise reasonable care. This is termed **negligence.** If our property or person has been injured because of another's negligence, we may sue in court for the actual damages. Exemplary damages are not awarded to compensate for the harm caused by negligence.

Negligence: tort caused by lack of reasonable care

Elements of Negligence.   Of course, filing suit alleging that another negligently caused us harm is one thing; proving negligence is another. Proof of the tort of negligence typically requires producing evidence that shows each of the following elements:

1. An act or omission—unlike the intentional torts, which require an overt act, negligence may occur if the defendant simply fails to act when there is a special duty to do so. A bridgekeeper might be negligent if he or she failed to lower the traffic barriers before raising the bridge.
2. A duty of due care—this is defined by asking how a reasonable person would have acted under the circumstances. We all have the obligation to recognize and take reasonable precautions against harming others. In some instances society may inform us as to what it thinks is due care, for example, with highway speed limits, but even these indicators are not conclusive in all cases. It still comes back to an individual decision as to what is reasonable under the circumstances. It would not be a defense to negligence to claim that you were under the 65-mph speed limit when you were driving 63 mph on a road sheeted with ice and snow immediately before you crashed into the highway department's truck.
3. A breach of the duty of due care—the trier of fact (usually a jury, but a judge if a jury is not requested) will compare the defendant's behavior with its standard of how a reasonable person should have behaved under the circumstances. If the defendant's conduct, as shown by the evidence, falls below that standard, then there has been a breach of the duty of due care. In certain situations where there is not enough evidence to show the conduct of the defendant, such as airline crashes, the law will presume a breach of the duty of due care and will require the alleged tortfeasor (the airline) to show otherwise. The idea here is that the act (the crash) speaks for itself. Similarly, in assessing the potential liability of professionals they are charged with knowledge of the facts they "reasonably should have known," not just the facts they were actually aware of.
4. Causation—the law tries to be just by requiring that the negligence of the defendant be both the actual and the proximate cause of the harm done. By **actual cause** the law means that the harm would not have occurred but for the defendant's negligence. If the harm would have occurred regardless of that negligence, the defendant is not held responsible. By **proximate cause** the law

Actual Cause: indispensable factor producing harm

Proximate Cause: indispensable and immediate factor producing harm means that the harm caused must fall within the range of consequences (of the negligent act) for which the defendant is legally responsible. If the defendant's negligent act is not both the actual and proximate cause of the harm done, then the defendant is not liable.

HYPOTHETICAL CASE

"Spoke too Sooooon," a bicycle delivery service, was employed by several businesses in New York City due to the speed of its bikers. Delivery of important packages and messages was guaranteed within 30 minutes from the point of pickup in a 4-mile radius. After picking up a box marked "Danger, Explosive" from the Caustic Chemical Company on Fifth Avenue, Sue E. Side, Spoke's best deliveryperson, raced crosstown. Unfortunately, she was delayed by an accident on Broadway, so that she arrived at the destination with barely seconds to go. In her haste to beat the deadline, she negligently dropped the box, which exploded as it hit the ground. Sue was blown into some bushes and walked away with minor scratches. Glass shattered from nearby windows by the blast cut several individuals. Hiram Hackster, while driving his cab nearby, heard the noise and took his eyes off the road to see where the explosion came from and then crashed into the rear of a bakery truck, causing $8,500 in property damage. Spoke and Sue would be liable for the injuries to the individuals cut by the glass as their negligence was both the actual and proximate cause of the harm done. However, Hackster and the cab company would be liable for the harm done in the collision as Hackster's negligence in diverting his attention from his driving was the most proximate cause of that harm.

5. Damages—actual damages are awardable for negligence. So evidence of such damages—for example, lost wages, medical bills, and pain and suffering—is needed here.

Defenses to Negligence.   The defendant in a negligence case can offer a number of defenses. The most effective defense is **contributory negligence,** which disallows any recovery whatsoever for an injury if the injured party's own negligence contributed to that injury. In actual practice, contributory negligence has caused some very unfair results, but, even so, it was enforced in most states for many years. It is still the rule of law in several. For an example, consider the case of Sammi Shovel, licensed private investigator:

Contributory Negligence: defense disallowing recovery if injured party's negligence contributed to injury

HYPOTHETICAL CASE

Driving to a late night surveillance job, Sammi was tailed by undercover police detectives. One of the detectives had just clocked her driving 37 mph in a 35-mph zone when she was broadsided in an intersection by a huge garbage truck negligently driven through a red light. Her car was totally destroyed, and she suffered internal injuries and broken bones. After a short foot chase, the police detectives apprehended the truck driver, Stan ("Garbage Is My Life") Langston, and arrested him for driving while intoxicated. Langston suffered no personal injuries from the crash, and his truck had only a small dent in the right fender. Langston, who persisted in calling himself a "refuse manager" throughout his interrogation, proved to be the owner of the local trash collection service and had a long record of traffic convictions.

continued on page 71

concluded

Nevertheless, when Sammi brought suit for the injuries to her property and person, which totaled over $125,000, she could not recover. Under her state's contributory negligence rule, proof that she had been driving over the established speed limit immediately prior to the crash was enough to show negligence and to totally preclude her recovery.

Fortunately, most states have replaced contributory negligence with comparative negligence. **Comparative negligence** is a defense that does not deny all recovery when the injured party is somewhat negligent. Instead, it allows recovery according to the relative degree of fault of the parties to the accident. In Sammi Shovel's case, comparative negligence would require the trier of fact to assign each party a percentage of responsibility for the harm done. So if Langston were held to be 95 percent responsible, he would have to pay for 95 percent of the damages he had inflicted on Sammi and to bear 95 percent of his own damages. Sammi would be responsible for the remaining 5 percent of each.

Comparative Negligence: defense requiring recovery only according to degree of fault

A final defense worth mentioning is **assumption of risk.** If the injured party knew of the specific risk involved, yet voluntarily assumed it, recovery may be limited or even precluded. The operator of a portable TV camera on the sidelines of a football game would probably be held to have assumed the risk of the "Bubba factor," that is, the risk that a 245-pound linebacker would crash out of bounds into the operator.

Assumption of Risk: defense based on injured party's acceptance of risk

Strict Liability

Ultrahazardous Activities.   Under the doctrine of **strict liability,** regardless of how much care has been taken, if harm results from the defendant's conduct or activity, the defendant will be liable for it. This doctrine is applied when the defendant is involved in a hazardous activity, such as detonating explosives or

Strict Liability: actor liable regardless of safety precautions

---

A Comparison of the Elements of Proof for Two Intentional Torts and for the Tort of Negligence

Figure   6–2

Tort		
Negligence	**Assault**	**Battery**
Act or omission	Act	Act
Duty of due care	Intent to place in apprehension of a harmful or offensive touching	Intent to touch in a harmful or offensive way
Breach of the duty of due care	Reasonable apprehension	Actual touching
Actual cause	Causation	Causation
Proximate cause	Damages	Damages
Damages		

damming streams. Also, keeping wild animals, other than in a zoo or for public exhibition, exposes the owner to strict liability. So if your pet cobra, mongoose, or lion—or your pet penguin, for that matter—escapes from you and wreaks havoc, no matter how much money you invested in a restraint system, you're going to be liable for the harm it does.

Product Liability.   While we are discussing strict liability, it is a good idea for us to focus for a moment on a fast-growing area of the law that is in the process of embracing strict liability principles. That area is product liability. Until the last few years, if you were injured by a defective product, your only way to collect was by producing enough evidence to prove the negligence of the manufacturer. Attempting this often proved to a difficult, expensive, and unsuccessful proposition. This was due mainly to the complexity of the engineering involved in modern products and to the fact that the evidence was initially in the hands of the manufacturer.

Gradually the law has changed, so that today the injured party does not have to show how the product came to be defective due to the manufacturer's or seller's violation of the duty of due care. Instead, it is enough to show the following:

1. That the injury came from the use of the product in the manner intended.
2. That there was an unreasonably dangerous defect in the product.
3. That the defendant was engaged in the business of manufacturing or selling the product.
4. That the product had not been substantially altered by the time of the injury.

So a person injured while using his lawn mower to trim his hedge could not recover. However, the family members who were injured in a car crash caused when the car's air bags deployed upon hitting a dropout pothole in a bridge could bring suit and recover. (See also the table found in Problem 2 following the *Blevins* v. *Cushman* case in Chapter 17. It is useful in comparing the elements of negligence with those of strict product liability in tort.)

Defenses to Torts

"The king can do no wrong" was the binding adage of the English legal system for the simple reason that the courts were set up by and belonged to the monarch. The judges only had power because he granted it to them, and they certainly were not about to "bite the hand that fed them." After our Declaration of Independence on July 4, 1776, this freedom from responsibility changed slightly, but it was retained as what we know today as "governmental immunity." This protection from the consequences of tortious governmental acts has been weakened in recent years, but it still remains as a shield that most governmental bodies can hide behind, even though their citizens generally cannot. Spouses, parents, and charities also enjoyed the biased favor of the courts until recently. Today, however:

The federal government can be sued for its negligent conduct (but not for its intentional torts) or to hold it strictly liable. As an example consider this true story: to study the spread of infectious diseases, a US "intelligence" agency released a unique viral strain in the San Francisco Bay area. The agency then monitored how long the disease took to show up on the east and southern coasts. Lawsuits against the US government for losses due to the medical bills and lost wages of those who fell ill would be thrown out of court due to governmental immunity as the agency had acted intentionally.

At the state level, governmental immunity is still the rule.

Charitable immunity, due to the availability of insurance and the size of many charitable organizations, is generally a thing of the past. So a negligence suit against a hospital run by the Order of Merciful Medical Missionaries, a charitable group, which would have been thrown out of court in decades past, would be tried today.

Intrafamilial immunity, which once prevented all parent/child suits for tortious conduct, now applies only to negligence. A child can now sue his or her parents for intentional torts such as assault and battery.

Interspousal tort immunity still holds in several states for personal injuries, due to the worry that a husband and wife might conspire in a fraudulent scheme to collect money under a liability insurance policy. However, suits for property damage inflicted by one spouse on holdings of the other spouse are now prosecutable, whereas a few decades ago they too were not.

What Procedure Do the Courts Follow to Resolve Civil Cases?

Parties to the Action

Court actions that are brought because of a private injury or wrong, such as those arising under tort or contract law, are called civil cases. Such an action is usually begun when an injured party files a document called a **complaint** with the clerk of a court with original jurisdiction over the matter. The complaint states the injured party's version of the facts of the case and shows why the court has jurisdiction over it. The complaint then makes a request or "prayer" for relief in the form of damages and/or a court order directing the defendant to do or to stop doing something. The person who initiates a lawsuit in this fashion is called the **plaintiff.** The person complained against is known as the **defendant.** Note that the law also allows lawsuits against entities that are not flesh and blood persons. For example, corporations are considered artificial persons and can sue and be sued.

Complaint: injured party's document stating claim for relief

Plaintiff: person initiating complaint

Defendant: person complained against

Requiring the Defendant to Appear and Answer

Upon receiving the complaint, the clerk will see that a summons is issued and served upon the defendant along with a copy of the complaint. This "service of process" informs the defendant of the nature of the claim involved and the court that has jurisdiction over it. The **summons** also demands that the defendant respond to the complaint within a given time.

Summons: instrument giving notice of suit, court's jurisdiction, and required appearance

Service of Process:
presentation of summons
and complaint to a party
to the suit

Presenting the summons and complaint to the defendant, termed **service of process,** is vitally important. Otherwise, the defendant will not have proper notice of the lawsuit and cannot exercise the right to be heard. Once notice has been given, however, the defendant may react in a number of ways. First of all, the defendant may dispute whether the court is the proper one to judge the matter. For example, if the complaint is filed in a state circuit court, but the matter involves over $50,000 and the parties to the dispute are from different states, the defendant may request removal of the case to a federal court. Second, the defendant may suggest that the service of process was improper and, therefore, that the summons was not effective. If the defendant is correct about improper service, no response to the complaint is required.

Defining the Issues to Be Resolved

Answer: response to
complaint

Counterclaim: claim
defendant makes against
plaintiff in suit

Cross-Claim: claim
defendant makes against
another defendant in suit

Third-Party Complaint:
claim against party not
previously involved in suit

If both the court and the service are proper, however, the defendant must answer. The **answer** is the defendant's response to the complaint. In it the defendant either admits to or denies the claims of the plaintiff. The defendant may also make claims at this time. A claim that the defendant makes against the plaintiff based on the incident at hand is called a **counterclaim.** A claim that the defendant makes against another defendant in the same case is a **cross-claim.** Another procedural device, called a **third-party complaint,** reaches beyond the original parties and makes a party not previously involved a part of the suit. The good thing about the use of the complaint, the answer, and claims is that they tend to clarify and narrow the issues to be resolved at trial. For example, if you file a complaint against me based on my alleged negligent driving that ended in a collision with you, my answer may dispute the issue of negligence but will probably admit that I was involved in an accident with you on the date and under many of the circumstances you stated. In court, then, you won't have to prove that I was present or driving the car or even that there was a collision. You may focus instead on proving the heart of your case, the allegation of negligence. This makes for far more efficient use of the court system than would otherwise be possible. Formal written statements exchanged prior to trial, such as the complaint and the answer, are referred to as the **pleadings.**

Pleadings: formal written
statements exchanged prior
to trial

**Motion for Judgment on
the Pleadings:** request for
court rule on issue without
trial as no facts in
contention

It is very important to understand that at times a comparison of the various pleadings may reveal that there are no factual issues to be resolved in the case. When this occurs, a party may make a **motion for judgment on the pleadings.** This motion notes that since there is no factual issue, there is no reason to hold a full trial. Instead, the judge should just decide which laws to apply to the facts agreed to in the pleadings and enter judgment accordingly.

Pretrial Preparations

If a trial is to be held, our legal system wants all sides to have the best evidence available in their hands to present to the trier of fact. The system is also biased against surprises during trial, thinking it better that each side have the fullest possible ability to know the other side's case before it is presented. Such knowledge often leads the parties to settle out of court. Many jurisdictions enhance the possibility of such a settlement by requiring a **pretrial conference.** In such a conference, the judge and the attorneys for both sides try to get the parties to settle their problems without a formal trial.

Pretrial Conference: judge-supervised attempt to settle without trial

Should settlement efforts fail, either side is empowered to determine the evidence that the other side has to offer at trial. The process by which this is accomplished is appropriately termed *discovery.* Discovery involves a variety of ways in which one side can request information from the other side:

1. By interrogatories—a written list of questions that the other side must answer. Interrogatories are used to find out the names of the witnesses and their likely testimony or documents and physical evidence that are likely to be used as evidence,
2. By depositions—a procedure allowing witnesses or other parties to be placed under oath and made to respond to questions from opposing attorneys. A record of the answers given is made by court personnel and can be used against those testifying if their stories change,
3. By physical examinations conducted by qualified medical personnel. This allows the determination of injuries and conditions,
4. By requests for tangible evidence—to allow the opposition to examine evidence such as documents, photographs, weapons, defective products ... anything significant to the case.

If a party does not comply with proper requests for discovery, the court will compel it to do so and will penalize it if it still refuses. Of course, there are limits to discovery; for example, attorney-client conversations are "privileged" and therefore not subject to discovery. Properly used, however, discovery allows each side to intelligently prepare its case so as to make the best use of its opportunity in court.

Trial Procedure

If the case goes to trial and a jury is requested, the selection of that panel becomes the first order of business. (Remember that if a jury is not requested, the judge will sit as the trier of fact.) The members of the jury must be impartial and competent. Prospective jurors are therefore interrogated to ensure that they do not have a relationship to the parties or witnesses that would affect their judgment.

After the jury panel has been selected, the trial formally begins with the opening statements of the attorneys. These statements tell the jurors what the case is about and what each side will endeavor to prove. After the opening statements, the plaintiff's case is presented through her or his attorney. Documents, physical evidence, and the testimony of witnesses are introduced to convince the jury that the plaintiff's statement of the facts is correct. The evidence is not allowed to be considered by the jury if, among other things, it might unduly bias the jurors. Evidence is also rejected if it is not the best evidence for the purpose, if it is hearsay, or if it is solely the product of leading questions by the attorney. Objections to the admission of various types of evidence dot the average trial. The judge must make the proper legal ruling on each objection or face the possibility that the trial result will be overturned on appeal.

Direct Examination: questioning of witness by calling side

Cross-Examination: questioning of witness by opposition

The attorney who calls a witness conducts what is termed a **direct examination** of that witness. The opposition is then given an opportunity to challenge the testimony of the witness by cross-examining that person. Note that the **cross-examination** is confined to topics introduced in the direct examination. If the opposition wishes to introduce a new subject area, it must call the witness as its own. The calling side may conduct a re-direct to clarify matters developed by the cross-examination, and, finally, the opposition is given the chance for a re-cross.

After the plaintiff completes the presentation of evidence, the defense takes over. When the defense rests, the attorneys give their closing statements, which stress what they consider significant evidence and what they expect the jurors to conclude therefrom.

The judge then instructs the jury on the rules of law that it must use to reach proper findings of fact as to who, if anyone, is liable and as to damages. As mentioned in Chapter 5, these findings of fact are referred to as a verdict. After the judge finishes instructing the jury, it retires. If the jury is able to agree on a verdict, it returns to the courtroom and announces the verdict. In the event of a hung jury, the judge will end the current proceeding but allow the case to be brought again later.

If a verdict is returned by the jury, the judge will review it to be sure it has been correctly and fairly arrived at. If so, the judge will accept the verdict and enter judgment accordingly. Typically, the losing side will be required to pay a fee for the use of the court and the public officers involved in the trial. Generally, each party must pay his or her own attorney, regardless of whether the party won or lost. (See the special INSIGHT section on how attorneys are compensated.)

Appeal

Appeal: resort to higher court to correct error of law

After judgment has been entered, the losing side has a set period of time to file a notice of its intent to appeal. An **appeal** is a complaint made to a higher court of an error of law made during the conduct of a case. An appeal cannot be based on supposed errors in factual conclusions. For example, if a videotape made by a bank camera showed a defendant holding a submachine gun during a robbery, the defendant could appeal the judge's decision to allow the jury to see the tape. The appeal could be based on the claim that, as a matter of law, the tape would have such an impact on the jury that any and all other evidence could not overcome that impact. The appeal could not be based on the claim that the jury made an improper conclusion of fact once the tape was admitted into evidence.

Writ of Execution: court-directed seizure and sale of loser's property to satisfy judgment

If a judgment of liability and damages is allowed to stand by the appellate court or courts that review it, the loser has to pay the judgment. If payment is not made "voluntarily" within a set time, the court can order property of the loser seized and sold by the sheriff to satisfy the judgment. Such a court order is called a **writ of execution.** Any proceeds of the sale remaining after the judgment has been paid are returned to the loser. Rather than seize property, some individuals to whom a judgment is owed will ask the court to order the loser's wages or bank account paid into the court. Termed a **garnishment,** such an order is quite effective as it is directed to an established third party, say an employer or a bank, that is much more likely than the loser to comply rather than risk being held in contempt of court.

> **Garnishment:** proceeding to obtain money owed to defendant/judgment debtor

Regardless of the method utilized to satisfy the judgment, hopefully it will bring a successful and just conclusion to the elaborate and complex process known as the civil lawsuit.

APPLICATIONS OF WHAT YOU'VE LEARNED

Vocabulary Development

Fill in the blanks with the appropriate term.

Actual Cause
Actual Damages
Answer
Appeal
Assault
Assumption of Risk
Battery
Civil Case
Comparative
 Negligence
Complaint

Consent
Contributory
 Negligence
Counterclaim
Cross-Claim
Cross-Examination
Damages
Defendant
Direct Examination
Exemplary Damages

False Imprisonment
Garnishment
Injunction
Intentional Torts
Litigants
Motion for Judgment
 on the Pleadings
Negligence
Nominal Damages
Plaintiff

Pleadings
Pretrial Conference
Proximate Cause
Service of Process
Strict Liability
Summons
Third-Party Complaint
Tortfeasor
Torts
Writ of Execution

1. When Brenda Hone did not repay the loan of $500 he had made to her, Jan Stokes sued her in small claims court. He received a judgment in his favor of $500 plus $52 in interest and costs. Brenda did not pay the judgment. So, 30 days later, Jan asked the court to order her employer to pay part of the money due her as wages to satisfy the judgment. Such a court order is called a(n) _____.

2. Damages arbitrarily set to punish the defendant are termed _____.

3. The _____ initiates a lawsuit by filing a complaint.

4. The _____ must answer the complaint and may then counterclaim or cross-claim.

5. An injury from a negligent act could not have occurred but for a(n) _____.

6. A person who commits an assault, a battery, or a negligent act would be known as a(n) _____.

7. Token damages, which are generally awarded to acknowledge that a party was correct in suing but lacking in injury, are known as _____

8. To intentionally cause in someone a reasonable apprehension of a harmful or offensive touching is to commit a(n) _____.

9. To intentionally touch someone in a harmful or offensive way is a(n) _____.

10. A(n) _____ served on a prospective litigant gives notice of suit, of the court's claim of jurisdiction over the matter, and of a required appearance.

Problems

1. Take a minute to think about the relative positioning of contract, tort, and criminal law. It will help you keep things straight. For example, consider:

   a. Who sets the standards of behavior or duties expected of the parties under contract, tort, and criminal law?

   b. What sanctions are available to the court when those standards are violated—under contract law, under tort law, and under criminal law?

2. Woody Blankbrains' vacation was over. He had just lost his trip funds at the Hot Springs, Arkansas, racetrack on a 20-to-1 shot named Thunderchicken. The horse finished nearer the 20 than the 1. Angry, Woody went to a local bar to have a few drinks and "settle down." An hour later, he threw a beer bottle at a fellow gambler who called him a fool for betting on "the chicken," as Woody's steed was affectionately called around the track. The bottle mistakenly hit Darlene Dramshop in the face. Injured severely, Darlene called the police, but Woody was not prosecuted over the incident. However, upon hearing that Darlene had filed a lawsuit against him for over $40,000 in damages, Woody returned to his home in New Orleans. Since he was not served with process while in the state, the Arkansas courts could not hear the case (remember the federal courts require over $50,000 in contest before they'll serve as a forum for a diversity of citizenship case). As a consequence, Woody swore never to return to that state. A year later, Woody boarded a commercial jet in St. Louis, Missouri, for a nonstop flight to New Orleans. About halfway through, Woody's seatmate, an attractive woman, pointed out the window. "Look," she said "isn't that Little Rock, Arkansas, down there?" Woody looked out and replied, "Sure enough, little lady." As he did so the woman grabbed his hand and slapped a court summons and complaint from the Dramshop case in it.
   Questions:

   a. In your opinion, has Woody been properly served with process within the boundaries of the state and therefore brought under the jurisdiction of the courts of Arkansas? How far above and below the ground does the state of Arkansas extend? (Consider what would happen if someone had shot at a plane and hit someone high above the state or if someone had killed someone in a plane high above the state. Who would have jurisdiction then?)

   b. Presume that the Arkansas courts do have jurisdiction. When the case goes to trial what type of tort action will Darlene pursue? Negligence, assault, battery?

   c. Would any of the defenses we have mentioned work in Blankbrains' favor? Consent, assumption of the risk, contributory negligence, immunity?

3. Would you believe that Darlene recovered $38,000 from Woody in the lawsuit? Her attorney, who had been working under a contingency fee agreement, ended up with 40 percent or $15,200 for the trouble. In a surprise ending, a few months after the payoff, Woody bumped into Darlene in Hot Springs. They started dating and eventually married. Two years later, Darlene, in a fit of anger picked Woody's aunt's birthday gift to him, a large flower vase that she hated, off their mantle and tossed it at her husband. It hit a dodging Woody square in the head inflicting an injury that caused over $20,000 in lost wages and doctor's bills, as well as the loss of the $7.99 vase.

   Could Woody recover for any of these losses? If so, which?

4. Presume you are a judge on an appellate court. An attorney is appearing before you claiming that new evidence has been discovered that would reverse the result of a recent trial in a lower court and produce instead a holding in his client's favor. Which of the following factors do you consider important in determining whether or not to grant the new trial?

   A. The severity of the effect of the result of the loser.

   B. Whether it was a criminal or civil trial.

   C. How easy it was to find the new evidence.

   D. The workload of the lower court.

   E. The likelihood the new evidence would alter the original result.
   Suppose it was a murder trial and the attorney's client is on death row. The confession is from another inmate on death row who is known to be a publicity hog, yet the details of the confession are very accurate and the confessor

Nader v. General Motors

Court of Appeals of New York
255 N.E.2d 765

Like the law as a whole, the area of torts is constantly growing and being refined. The following opinion concerns the right of privacy and its development and definition in the latter half of this century. The case involved a David in the form of Ralph Nader and a Goliath named General Motors.

The well-known consumer advocate Ralph Nader came to national prominence in the mid-60s as consequence of a book he authored entitled *Unsafe at any Speed.* The book alleged serious safety problems with the Chevrolet Corvair, a General Motors (GM) product. A few years later Nader brought suit against GM, alleging various invasions of his privacy. Specifically, Nader alleged that GM (1) had had him accosted by women for the purpose of entrapping him into illicit relationships; (2) had conducted interviews with his acquaintances about him and had cast aspersions on his political, social, racial, and religious views, his integrity, his sexual proclivities, and his personal habits; (3) had kept him under surveillance in public places for an unreasonable length of time; (4) had made threatening, harassing, and obnoxious telephone calls to him; (5) had tapped his telephone and eavesdropped, by means of mechanical and electronic equipment, on his private conversations; and (6) had conducted a continuing and harassing investigation of him. In a landmark decision, the highest court in the New York State system, the Court of Appeals, addressed each of these allegations to determine if any of them constituted a basis for an invasion of privacy suit.

The classic article by Warren and Brandeis (The Right to Privacy, 4 *Harvard Law Review* 193) was premised to a large extent on principles originally developed in the field of copyright law. The authors thus based their thesis on a right granted by the common law to "each individual . . . of determining ordinarily to what extent his thoughts, sentiments, and emotions shall be communicated to others. Their principal concern appeared to be not with a broad "right to be let alone" but, rather, with the right to protect oneself from having one's private affairs known to others and to keep secret or intimate facts about oneself from the prying eyes or ears of others . . .

It should be emphasized that the mere gathering of information about a particular individual does not give rise to a cause of action under this theory. Privacy is invaded only if the information sought is of a confidential nature and the defendant's conduct was unreasonably intrusive. Just as a common law copyright is lost when material is published, so, too, there can be no invasion of privacy where the information sought is open to public view or has been voluntarily revealed to others . . . In order to sustain a cause of action for invasion of privacy, therefore, the plaintiff must show that the appellant's conduct was truly "intrusive" and that it was designed to elicit information which would not be available through normal inquiry or observation.

. . . We deem it desirable that we . . . indicate the extent to which the plaintiff is entitled to rely on the various allegations in support of his privacy claim.

. . . we cannot find any basis for a claim of invasion of privacy, . . . in the allegations that the appellant (GM), through its agents or employees, interviewed many persons who knew the plaintiff, asking questions about him and casting aspersions on his character. Although these inquiries may have uncovered information of a personal nature, it is difficult to see how they may be said to have invaded the plaintiff's privacy. Information about the plaintiff which was already known to others could hardly be regarded as private to the plaintiff . . . If, as alleged, the questions tended to disparage the plaintiff's character, his remedy would seem to be by way of an action for defamation, not for breach of his right to privacy.

Nor can we find any actionable invasion of privacy in the allegations that the appellant caused the plaintiff to be accosted by girls with illicit proposals or that it was responsible for the making of a large number of threatening and harassing telephone calls to the plaintiff's home at odd hours . . . where severe mental pain or anguish is inflicted through a deliberate and malicious campaign of harassment or intimidation, a remedy is available in the form of an action for the intentional infliction of emotional distress.

The one [allegation] that most clearly meets the requirements [for an invasion of privacy cause of action] is the charge that the appellant and its codefendants engaged in unauthorized wiretapping and eavesdropping by mechanical and electronic means. [Finally,] it is manifest that the mere observation of the plaintiff in a public place does not amount to an invasion of his privacy. But, under certain circumstances, surveillance may be so "overzealous" as to render it actionable. Whether or not the surveillance in the present case falls into this latter category will depend on the nature of the proof. A person does not automatically make public everything he does merely by being in a public place, and the mere fact that Nader was in a bank did not give anyone the right to try to discover the amount of money he was withdrawing. On the other hand, if the plaintiff acted in such a way as to reveal that fact to any casual observer, then, it may not be said that the appellant intruded into his private sphere.

Questions

1. After this appellate decision Nader was able to go forward in the court with original jurisdiction with suit based on invasion of privacy on only two of the six grounds he originally alleged. Which two?

2. Would it be an invasion of my privacy for you to listen in to calls I make on an unscrambled cellular phone? Assume that it is a phone whose transmissions are easily intercepted on any and all of the frequency scanners sold at Radio Shack and other electronic stores.

3. Would it be an invasion of your privacy if I shared with a newspaper reporter some of the tales you've told me about your love affairs?

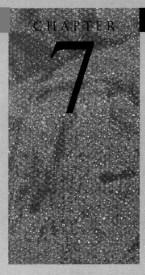

CHAPTER

7

What Crimes and Torts Most Affect Businesses?

CHAPTER OUTLINE AND OBJECTIVES

After studying this chapter, the student will be able to:

I. Identify the crimes that most affect businesses.
   a. Violent crimes
   b. Nonviolent crimes

II. Recognize the torts that most directly affect business.
   a. Wrongful interference with business contractual relationships
   b. Infringement of patents, trademarks, and copyrights
   c. Disparagement of reputation
   d. Injuries stemming from RICO-prohibited activities

III. Analyze the potential problems related to sexual harassment by reading the case of *Pease* v. *Alford Photo Industries, Inc.*

What Crimes Most Affect Businesses?

In this half of the chapter we discuss the criminal behavior that most often affects businesses. It is crucial for a businessperson to be able to recognize such behavior and its potential effects so as to take proper precautions. Criminal behavior can be classified as either violent or nonviolent.

Violent Crimes

You've probably seen the scenario on TV a dozen times—the armed bandit in front of the bank teller's cage or across the counter from the convenience store operator, but until the dark lethal holes of the twin muzzles of a sawed off shotgun or similar weapon have been pointed at your own chest, it's all make-believe. Nevertheless, this scenario is an example of robbery, the most frequently practiced crime of violence against businesses. It is defined below as well as several other crimes of violence.

Robbery. The taking of goods or money in the possession of another, from his person or in his immediate presence, by the use of force or fear is **robbery.** Notice that the items taken need only be in the possession of another and need not actually belong to that person. Also, in a number of jurisdictions the use of certain weapons, such as a handgun, in carrying out the crime of robbery, brings on a stiffer penalty. Generally, the additional penalty is a mandatory period of imprisonment beyond the usual term for robbery.

Robbery: taking goods or money from another by using force or fear

Burglary. The original common law definition of burglary, which was discussed in Chapters 2 and 5, has been altered in ways that make it applicable to business situations. "At night" or "nighttime" has been struck from the definition. "Dwelling house" has been replaced by "building" or "structure." So breaking into and entering a structure belonging to another to carry out a felony is now burglary in many states. The felony involved could also be grand larceny (discussed shortly) or even arson.

Arson. Arson, like burglary, was made a crime by the common law to protect the home, where, while sleeping, citizens were most vulnerable either to a fire raging out of control or to theft or other felonies. Today, as with burglary, the definition of arson has been broadened, so that it now means more than intentionally setting fire to a dwelling house. Currently, **arson** is defined as the willful and malicious burning of a structure. **Malice** in such a case implies a wrong, evil, or corrupt motive.

Arson: willful and malicious burning of a structure

Malice: wrong, evil, or corrupt motive

Extortion: using threats to get consent to take property

Extortion. A potentially violent crime that also takes its toll on businesses is extortion. **Extortion** is defined as using threats of injury to the victim's person, family, property, or reputation to get consent to take property. Popularly referred to as blackmail, extortion must be dealt with firmly and immediately. Otherwise, the more resources the extortionist receives, the more likely she or he is to increase demands or carry out threats.

Nonviolent Crimes

Violent crimes catch the spotlight far more frequently than nonviolent crimes. Yet the total losses in all bank robberies around the country over the last two years did not exceed $75 million according to FBI figures, whereas the losses in one scandalous savings and loan (Lincoln S&L in California) failure (bailed out by tax dollars) totaled over $2.5 billion. Obviously, nonviolent crimes account for losses far greater than those caused by violent crimes and thus pose a far greater threat to the vast majority of businesses.

Larceny. Take away the threat or use of violence from robbery, and the result is larceny. Defined as the unlawful taking and carrying away of another's goods or money, **larceny** is usually divided into two categories: grand and petit. Taking and carrying away more than a certain amount of another's goods or money, say $250 or more, is considered grand larceny and a felony. Doing the same to goods or money of less than that amount is petit larceny and just a misdemeanor. The dollar amount that is the dividing line between the two crimes is set by the various state legislatures. Note that what is commonly known as shoplifting is actually larceny.

Larceny: unlawful taking and carrying away of another's property

Embezzlement and White-Collar Crime. A crime very similar to larceny is **embezzlement.** The only difference between larceny and embezzlement is that in embezzlement the property taken is entrusted to the embezzler, who then wrongfully converts it to his or her personal use. Embezzlement poses a continual concern for businesses as most of those who commit it have no criminal record. Up until the time they act criminally, usually to support a lifestyle that has gotten out of hand, they are model employees, agents, executives, and the like. As noted above, embezzlement and similar criminal activities by well-respected agents and executives, called **white-collar crime,** account for losses far greater than those caused by crimes of violence.

Embezzlement: converting entrusted property to personal use

White-Collar Crime: crime committed by executives or agents of a business

Computer Crime. An accomplice of many white-collar criminals is the computer. A computer program often consists of thousands of lines of complex directions and logic. As a consequence, white-collar criminals are attracted by the ample opportunities it provides to hide and conduct embezzlement or larceny schemes. Also, computers and the data they contain are very vulnerable to unauthorized use or destruction. **Computer crime** is a developing area of the law that deals with these problems.

Computer Crime: unauthorized use or destruction of a computer or its data

HYPOTHETICAL CASE

As she neared the completion of her task, Bitsy Binari once again asked her boss, Sam Shadee, whether he would keep her on after she completed it. "Of course, of course," he replied. Nonetheless, as soon as she finished the program, Shadee fired her. Bitsy said nothing as she left. The next month, however, according to instructions she had programmed into the computer, it checked to see whether her Social

continued on page 86

concluded

Security number was still on the payroll. Seeing that it was not, the computer inverted the pay scale for the 12,000 employees of the business. Custodians received what Shadee normally did, and Shadee received the minimum wage. Then the computer completely erased the payroll program, the payroll database, and a variety of new project records before programmers discovered what was happening and pulled the plug. Shadee attempted to have Bitsy prosecuted for what she had done, but the evidence had been wiped out. In addition, the prosecutor pointed out that Bitsy's alleged "logic bomb" had only changed electronic impulses. There had been no taking of property. Without a taking of identifiable property, no crime had been committed under state law.

As the above example brings out, the law has a great deal of trouble with defining what is punishable as computer crime. Many of the computer crime statutes currently on the state lawbooks are very vulnerable to constitutional challenge. Valid federal laws, however, do make it a crime to access certain governmental computers without authorization.

Bribery.   Often crime flourishes because public officials find it more personally advantageous to look the other way. When something of value has been offered, given, received, or asked for (solicited) in return for influence on how an official carries out a public or legal duty, the crime of **bribery** has occurred. Whether or not the offer is accepted, a crime takes place when it is made. If, however, the offer is accepted, both parties are equally guilty.

Bribery: improperly influencing official action by offering, giving, receiving, or soliciting of value

Public officials often face bribery charges. In a notorious case that started in early fall of 1973, Vice President Spiro Agnew denied accusations that he had accepted bribes from contractors for aid in getting contracts with the state of Maryland. It was charged that he had received these bribes while an executive of Baltimore County, governor of Maryland, and vice president of the United States. At University Hall in Charlottesville, Virginia, the vice president elicited cheers from the assembled thousands when he said "I will never resign," and then concluded his speech with characteristic attacks on the media and liberal politicians. On October 10, 1973, however, he proved himself a liar and resigned his position of trust a "heartbeat from the presidency." Subsequently, Agnew pleaded nolo contendere (no contest) to a single charge of failure to pay his full income tax for 1967. The judge in the case declared his plea a full statement of guilt, sentenced him to probation (unsupervised) for three years, and fined him $10,000. However, other bodies did more than just slap his wrist for his wrongdoing. In 1974 the Maryland Court of Appeals disbarred him, an action that prevented him from practicing law in the state. Finally, in 1981, another Maryland court ordered the ex–vice president of the United States to pay the state $248,735. This was the amount of the bribes that Agnew had taken in his positions of public trust plus interest.

Bribery goes beyond payoffs to public officers. In most states it is also a criminal act, usually referred to as commercial bribery, to pay business employees to influence their actions for their employer. For example, the Joseph Schlitz Brewing Company was recently convicted of commercial bribery because it had its salespeople grossly overtip for service they received at bars to induce the buyers for those establishments to buy Schlitz products. In an attempt to curtail such activity, many employment contracts have a "nonacceptance of gift" clause. Overseas, American businesspeople are prohibited from bribing the officials of foreign nations in order to obtain or retain business. However, the federal statute involved, the Foreign Corrupt Practices Act, does allow what are called grease payments. Such payments are made as a matter of course overseas to get public officials to perform or expedite routine services, such as the issuance of a visa or a permit to do business.

Forgery and Bad Check Offenses.   Whenever someone with an intent to defraud falsely makes or alters a written document so as to create or change a legal effect of that document, a **forgery** has taken place. This crime takes in everything from altering the age on a driver's license to signing another's name on a deed or a check. Where checks are concerned, however, another crime, encountered even more frequently than forgery, is **issuing bad checks.** In committing this crime, a person writes a check on his or her account knowing that funds to cover the check are not available and that the check will probably not be paid by the financial institution on which it is written. If the financial institution does indeed fail to pay it, the person who wrote it is chargeable with issuing a bad check.

Forgery: fraudulently making or altering legal effect of document

Issuing Bad Checks: writing insufficient funds check

Racketeering.   Most crimes against businesses are isolated events, planned and carried out by one person or a small group. For at least the last 35 years, however, Congress and many state legislatures have also worried about the effects of organized crime on businesses. As a consequence, Congress passed the Racketeer Influenced and Corrupt Organizations Act (RICO) in 1970. This act prohibits using a pattern of racketeering activities, such as murder, kidnapping, arson, and mail and wire fraud, in the conduct of business. It also prohibits using a pattern of such activities or the income from them to acquire or maintain an interest in a business. In addition to providing for the criminal prosecution of violators, RICO also allows lawsuits for damages by the victims.

Monopolizing Conduct.   Although it is now popular to think of government with its regulations and paperwork as the main adversary of business, history shows that there is a far more important adversary, an adversary that puts far more companies out of business than any other. That adversary is competition. Seldom is government more than a thorn in the side of businesses. Competition, however, eliminates inefficient companies and keeps the economy healthy by keeping it populated mainly with companies that sell quality products for the lowest cost. As a consequence, in the past some businesspeople sought to eliminate competition. The common law responded by making conduct that tended to consolidate control over the production of a good or the provision of a service into one person's or one firm's hands illegal. Such control was referred to as **monopoly.** The initial victims of monopolizing conduct are those who seek to compete with the would-be monopoly. Ultimately, of course, the consumer has to bear the loss, for example, in the form of higher prices and diminished quality of the monopolized product.

Monopoly: control of area of commerce by one entity

As businesses grew in size, the ability of a single state's legal system to stop monopolies from forming decreased. So, near the turn of the 20th century, the US Congress passed the first of several statutes intended to stop the monopolizing conduct that it saw as threatening to dominate interstate commerce. The first act is

Table 7–1   **Comparative Sentencing Ranges for Selected Business and Other Crimes**

Arson	From 5 to 15 years
Bad checks	Up to 1 year
Bribery	
Of a public official	From 0 to 5 years
Commercial bribery	Up to 1 year
Burglary	From 5 to 15 years
Computer crime	
Damage under $1,000	From 0 to 5 years
Damage over $1,000	From 0 to 7 years
Forgery	From 0 to 7 years
Library theft	Up to 15 days
Murder (first degree)	Death or life without possibility of probation or parole (except by governor)
Rape (forcible)	From 10 to 30 years or life imprisonment
Robbery	From 10 to 30 years or life imprisonment
Unlawful receipt of a food stamp coupon	From 0 to 5 years

known today as the Sherman Antitrust Act. At the time of its passage, the primary way of consolidating control over businesses into a monopoly was through the use of a legal device called a trust. Thus, the word *antitrust* was applied to acts opposing such behavior. "Every contract, combination in the form of trust or otherwise, or conspiracy, in restraint of [interstate or international] trade or commerce" was declared illegal by the Sherman Act. The act also made it illegal for any person "to monopolize or attempt to monopolize" interstate or international trade or commerce. Other antitrust acts and amendments have followed over the years. They are discussed in Chapter 38.

Table 7–1 shows the various sentencing ranges for selected business and other crimes.

What Torts Most Directly Affect Businesses?

Without question, criminal behavior takes a severe toll on businesses. However, so does tortious conduct. Crimes are public wrongs for which the law provides a penalty. Torts are private injuries or wrongs for which the law provides a remedy. Several of the most serious and frequent torts that target business operations are discussed in the following sections. Again, it is extremely important for business-people to be able to identify them so as to take appropriate action when they pose a threat to business operations.

Wrongful Interference with Business Contractual Relationships

Every business is encouraged by our systems of law and economics to compete fairly with other businesses. Advertising a product's strong points or the true weak points of another's product is at the heart of capitalism. Luring customers from competitors with better prices and financing, if these are not set artificially low, drives our market mechanism. However, when a company breaches the level of fair competition by making false attacks on another company's reputation or products or by preying directly on another company's customers, an intentional tort has been committed.

Wrongful Interference with Contract Formation.

Valentino's Video store invested thousands of dollars in advertising for a two-for-one membership enrollment sale. Pirated Videos, a competing store, stationed an employee in front of Valentino's to tell its would-be customers that Pirated Videos had no membership fee. If these actions of Pirated Videos improperly took away whatever benefit Valentino's expensive advertising campaign might have brought it in new members and rentals, Valentino's could sue Pirated for the tort of wrongful interference with contract formation.

Note, however, that some third-party actions that might base a tort suit for wrongful interference with contract formation are privileged. This means that a successful suit cannot be brought. Over a decade ago, for example, the federal courts held that the First Amendment right to freedom of speech protected a National Organization for Women boycott of states that did not support the proposed Equal Rights Amendment to the US Constitution (*State of Missouri* v. *National Organization for Women, Inc.,* 620 F.2d 1301).

Inducing Breach of Contract. Causing one party to an already existing contract to breach that agreement may also give rise to an intentional tort lawsuit. Certainly, a person adversely affected by another's failure to perform her or his contractual obligations can bring suit against the nonperforming party for breach of contract. But if it can be shown that an outside party intentionally caused the breach, that third person can be sued for the intentional tort of inducing breach of contract.

Slippery Oil, Inc., of Dallas contracted to sell its outstanding shares of stock to a group of Japanese investors for $115 per share. Two weeks after the agreement was signed, the president of Slippery accidentally met the president of another American oil company, Continental Shelf Unlimited, Inc., at the Los Angeles airport. When Slippery's president told Shelf's president of the impending deal, Shelf's president offered $125 a share for the same stock. Slippery's president accepted the offer. When told that the deal with it was off, the Japanese investor group filed suit against Continental for inducing breach of contract and won. Since the suit was brought as an intentional tort rather than a contract action, the damages awarded included punitive damages and therefore ran into the billions of dollars. (For an actual case that closely parallels these facts, read *Texaco, Inc.* v. *Pennzoil Company,* 729 S.W.2d 768, in which Pennzoil won some $9 billion.)

Infringement of Patents, Trademarks, and Copyrights

In Section 8 of Article I, our Constitution gives Congress the power to "promote the Progress of Science and useful Arts, by securing for limited Times to Authors and Investors the exclusive Right to their respective Writings and Discoveries." Congress used this power to reward those who produce useful goods (often called intellectual property) with their minds instead of their backs. The **patent,** a nonrenewable legal monopoly over the right to make, use, or sell a device, was made available to the inventor of the device. The **copyright,** an exclusive right to the publishing, printing, copying, reprinting, and selling of the tangible expression of an author's or artist's creativity, was given to the copyright holder. A system for the registration and protection of the right to exclusive use of **trademarks**—the identifying symbols, words, or designs by which a business distinguishes its products to consumers—was also created by Congress in response to its constitutional charge. (Patents, copyrights, and trademarks will be covered in more detail in Chapter 30.)

When these rights of inventors, authors, artists, and businesses are violated, the tort of **infringement** of patent, copyright, or trademark has occurred.

Patent: legal monopoly over right to make, use, or sell a device

Copyright: exclusive right to author's or artist's work

Trademark: a distinguishing business symbol

Infringement: violation of patent, copyright, or trademark rights

Disparagement of Reputation

Defamation is the damaging of another's reputation by the making of false statements. It is divided into the intentional torts of slander and libel. **Slander** involves the communication of the false statements in a temporary form, such as orally. **Libel** involves the communication of the false statements in a more permanent form, such as in writing or in the visual medium of videotape.

To base a lawsuit, the false statements must be made or conveyed to a third party. If the person defamed is the only one to hear the false statement, no tort has occurred.

Our laws give journalists and their publishers (the members of our society with the greatest ability to spread false statements to others) special protection against certain lawsuits for defamation. Specifically, this protection is against libel or slander actions brought by public officials or public figures. In the eyes of the law, public officials and figures seek to gain the attention of the people by means of news carriers of all kinds, from supermarket tabloids to the most serious daily papers, and must therefore take the good with the bad. So the law allows public officials and figures to recover for defamation only if they can show actual malice by the journalist in putting together the alleged falsehoods in a story. Actual malice means that the reporter or publisher had to know the story was false or had to recklessly disregard the possibility that it was false. These are hard standards to overcome. As a consequence, nearly all such suits fail. It is significant to note that other nations require a higher standard of truth from their media than ours does and yet maintain a free press.

A person other than a public figure or a public official need only prove that the published statements were false and show damages in order to recover in court. In

Slander: legally harmful false statements in temporary form

Libel: legally harmful false statements in more permanent form

a step beyond that, some categories of statements have been identified by the law as so harmful that the plaintiff does not even have to prove damages. These categories include falsely accusing someone of having a communicable sexual disease, of committing a criminal offense, or of lacking the ability to perform the duties of an office, employment, or profession. Such statements are said to be **defamatory per se.**

Businesses confront the effects of defamation in two main areas. One of these areas involves the making of false statements about the reputation of the business itself or about the quality of its products. This is called **disparagement of reputation.** The other area involves defamation suits by former employees. Such suits stem from statements made in letters of reference written by businesses to prospective employers of former employees. The legal systems of most states recognize a need for candor in these letters and therefore require that actual malice by the former employer be shown before the former employee can recover. Regardless, because of the large number of suits and the high legal fees involved in defending against them, many businesses now refuse to provide useful references.

Defamatory per Se: false statement not requiring showing of damages for recovery

Disparagement of Reputation: legally harmful false statements about business or its products

Injuries Stemming from RICO-Prohibited Activities

As mentioned in the subsection on racketeering, in addition to allowing criminal prosecutions of violators, RICO allows civil suits. In such suits the victims can recover three times the actual damages (**treble damages**), court costs, and attorney's fees. RICO's provision for civil lawsuits, and especially for the recovery of attorney's fees, has led to some very creative applications of the statute by lawyers. This is especially true because the "pattern of racketeering activity" prohibited in the statute may be found in as few as two instances of related criminal activity within 10 years.

Treble Damages: three times actual damages

HYPOTHETICAL CASE

The prestigious John W. Booth School of Graduate Studies in Acting at the State University let the parents of several marginally qualified applicants know that their children would be admitted only if the parents contributed $15,000 each to the Booth School Foundation. The foundation regularly gave Christmas and summer fellowships to the deserving faculty and administrators of the graduate school. Over the course of five years, some $300,000 was raised in this manner. The parents of a student who dropped out after the first semester brought suit for a violation of RICO. The court held that they had been damaged to the extent of their contribution to the foundation. They were awarded $45,000 in treble damages (3 × $15,000) plus their attorney's fees of $17,000 and court costs.

All of the crimes and torts mentioned in this chapter can pose a threat to a business. Hopefully, knowing more about them can greatly reduce, if not eliminate, their potential for loss.

APPLICATIONS OF
WHAT YOU'VE LEARNED

Vocabulary Development

Fill in the blanks with the appropriate term.

Bribery	Embezzlement	Larceny	Slander
Computer Crime	Extortion	Libel	TrademarkTreble Damages
Copyright	Forgery	Monopoly	White-Collar Crime
Defamation per Se	Infringement	Patent	
Disparagement of Reputation	Issuing Bad Checks	Robbery	

1. Legally harmful false statements made in print: _____

2. Taking the property of another by means of force or threat of violence: _____

3. If a plaintiff received $100,000 in actual damages in a RICO-based civil case, she or he could receive $300,000 in _____ .

4. Falsely calling someone a murderer orally or in print is _____ .

5. An exclusive right to an author's or artist's creative work is termed a(n) _____ .

6. Violating an exclusive right to a patent is _____ .

7. Making payments to illegally influence the conduct of a public official is termed _____ .

Problems

1. After graduating from school, you take a position in the family business, a neighborhood supermarket. It has been in operation in the same location since the early 50s, and you represent the third generation to become involved with it. Unfortunately, your neighborhood has been changing:

Identify the following crimes.

Sam Sterling and two members of his street gang visit your store and threaten to frighten off your customers by hanging around near your entrance unless you pay $50 a month to them. The crime is _____ .

When you refuse, they begin their threatened campaign, but you are able to get the police to move them along with threats of prosecution under the loitering ordinance. They send gang members into your store to shoplift whatever they can. Your losses mount. Although certain jurisdictions have statutes that simply call their crime shoplifting, your jurisdiction still refers to it as the more general crime of _____ .

You hire security guards and install video camera surveillance and are able to put several of the gang members in jail temporarily. Then one night three men, whom you suspect as being gang members, hold up your store, using knives and guns. The crime is _____ .

One of the security guards was stabbed during the commission of the crime. Several of your employees quit shortly thereafter. When, after two months, no one has been arrested for the crime, you pay a visit to the prosecutor. She informs you that what happened to you was one of nine such crimes on that particular night and that it was a typical night in your neighborhood. Nonetheless, she promises renewed action on the case. Determinedly, you go back home and consider whether you can afford to continue doing business in such an environment. You decide to take a close look at your books. When you do, you discover that one of your long-term employees has been submitting bills from a nonexistent supplier. Trusting her, you have paid without a second thought. When confronted, she admits to having acquired the habit of visiting the horse track every day after work. Her crime is _____.

You discharge her without prosecuting. That evening a fire breaks out in your storage area. It burns more than 70 percent of the store. The fire marshal investigates and finds that an accelerant (gasoline) was used to help the fire along. The crime is _____. Subsequently, your insurance company refuses to pay for the damage and you close down the store.

2. Suppose you invented a beacon-type device that allows physically distressed individuals to identify their residences to emergency personnel summoned to help them. To give you time to profit from your stroke of genius, you might seek a 17-year government-awarded monopoly called a _____. If you give your product a unique name, such as Rescue Ray, you might protect the name by registering it as your _____. If you write ad copy to promote the sales of the Rescue Ray, you might secure a _____ for the ad to prevent others from using it.

3. In what was labeled an "Ad Parody—Not to Be Taken Seriously" in small letters next to the bottom margin of the page, a noted men's magazine printed a supposed interview with Jerry Falwell, televangelist, on his "first time." In the ads allegedly being parodied, the interviewees talked about the first time they used liquor. Some of the

questions and answers in the Falwell "ad" went in a different direction, however:

Interviewer: I see. You must tell me all about it (the "first time").

Falwell: I never really expected to make it with Mom, but then after she showed all the other guys in town such a good time, I figured, "What the hell!"

Interviewer: But your mom? Isn't that a bit odd?

Falwell; I don't think so. Looks don't mean that much to me in a woman. . . .

Interviewer: Did you ever try again?

Falwell: Sure . . . lots of times. But not in the outhouse. Between Mom and the . . . , the flies were too much to bear.

Jerry Falwell brought suit against the magazine for defamation and infliction of emotional distress. The US Supreme Court voted 8–0 in favor of the magazine. This prompted the magazine to return the ad with the following caption: "In the 200-year history of our Constitution, one of the most important decisions in support of the First Amendment was handed down because of this ad parody . . . We thought everyone who has heard the news, or is interested in press freedom, would like to see the parody that started it all."

From the chapter material, what basis do you think the Court used in reaching its decision. Can you recommend a different balance or compromise between press freedom and individual rights?

ACTUAL CASE STUDY

Stephanye Pease v. Alford Photo Industries, Inc.

667 F. Supp. 1188

Consider the following case related to sexual harassment. It represents a growing trend in the law and one that managers of both sexes are wise to be aware of.

Mrs. Pease had been working at Alford Photo Industries, Inc., for two weeks when she met Mr. Jimmy Alford, president of the company. According to Mrs. Pease, at the first meeting he discussed her prior employment and her work. At the second

meeting he inquired about her personal life. During a subsequent meeting he allegedly approached her from behind, put his hand on her shoulder, and rubbed her arm. The behavior was allegedly repeated during a later meeting. Mrs. Pease testified that she had felt terrible on both of these occasions and had pulled away and tried to focus the conversation on her work. A hugging incident occurred a few days later. Mrs. Pease stated that while carrying work material in a hallway, she had met Mr. Alford. He called her over, checked her work, handed t back to her, then slipped his hand under her lab coat and fondled her breast for less than a minute. She pulled back angrily. Later she left the plant with permission. When she returned to work the next day, she discussed the incident with Jimmy Alford's son, Steve, another executive of the company. Steve then alerted Jimmy's wife, Frieda, to the matter. Later Mrs. Pease repeated her story in Frieda Alford's office, and subsequently her employment was terminated.

Mr. Alford testified that he did put his hands on the shoulders of female employees. He said that he liked these employees. He noted that they reciprocated and that no one thought anything about it. Two of his female employees, Julie Campbell and June Gafford, had sat on his lap several years ago. He testified that he used his hands a lot in communicating with people and that he considered himself a warm, affectionate person. According to Mr. Alford, touching is a friendly thing, a way of saying "I like you." He indicated that what the world needed was a lot more touching and hugging.

Both sides stated that submission to such touchings had never been made an explicit condition of employment. Also, no one had been asked to go to bed with the employers or to leave the plant with them.

The district court held that Mrs. Pease had proven by a preponderance of the evidence that she had been a victim of sexual harassment and had been subject to a violation of her civil rights. As a consequence, she was entitled to back and future pay. The court also held that Mrs. Pease had proven that she had been the victim of several common law torts and that she would receive actual and punitive damages for those.

Questions

1. The proof here was by a preponderance of the evidence. What other standard of proof would be used if this were a criminal trial?

2. What common law torts were involved? What is the significance of the punitive damage award?

3. What specific conduct was involved in each of the torts?

4. Why do we have laws making sexual harassment an offense? Should those laws protect lesbians and gay men from harassment?

INSIGHT

How Do You Find the Law That Affects You

An Introduction to Legal Research

Right off the top, I must warn the reader that the techniques we're going to discuss are only an introduction to legal research. The "answers" produced are often only a starting point for further research by a trained professional. Even so, you'd be surprised at the difference in response from an attorney if she or he is approached by someone with some foreknowledge of the area of the law in question rather than by someone who is acting out of total ignorance. Accountability and service go way up, I promise you. Also, there are some matters wherein you just can't afford to hire an attorney to get the job done. Many of my students, having completed my basic business law course and being required to do some research, have used their knowledge to emerge victorious from minor legal skirmishes ranging from small claims court to the traffic division.

Also, realize that the techniques we're going to discuss will not do you any good if you're dealing with municipal ordinances or administrative law. Finding a municipal ordinance that applies to your situation in a typical municipal ordinance book requires a combination of good luck and a decent index. Frankly, in my experience neither is usually available, so you must hunt and peck through the table of contents. (Welcome to the world of local government.) On the other side of the coin are the administrative agencies. Their rules and regulations are typically organized to a level so detailed that the forest is not only lost for the trees but even the sawmill is overgrown.

What I can help you with is research into law directly created by the federal and state court systems, Congress, and the various state legislatures—in short, the law we discuss in the great majority of the chapters of this book.

Organization

The key to it all is realizing that there are two main places to look for the law that concerns you: codes and digests. A "code" is a compilation of statutory law at the individual state or federal level. It is generally arranged by the authorities of the jurisdiction involved according to the subject matter of its various statutes. An "annotated code" improves on a mere code by grouping around each statute quotes from various court decisions that help clarify, define, or apply the statute. A "digest" is best described as a topical encyclopedia of legal terms composed of similar explanatory quotes taken from relevant cases in a particular state or federal jurisdiction.

These quotes are selected by a publisher's editors, who are experts in the various subject areas of the law concerned. These editors read all of the decisions from the federal courts and from the state appellate courts in order to select the best passages.

So, for example, if you feel that your employer acted improperly by obtaining a credit report on your spouse while considering you for an important position, you could turn to the Fair Credit Reporting Act, indexed at Title 15 Section 1681 in the *United States Code Annotated* (USCA) volumes, to see whether such latitude is allowed. In addition to reading the pertinent section (Section 1681b— "Permissible purposes of consumer reports"), you might also discover a case in which a similar issue was considered. In fact, such a case does exist and the pertinent quote from the annotation reads:

> That intended purpose and actual use of credit report on spouse of employee being considered for security-sensitive position is to evaluate employee's trustworthiness for position, does not permit employer, under Fair Credit Reporting Act, to obtain credit report on spouse. *Zamora* v. *Valley Federal Savings and Loan Association of Grand Junction,* 811 F.2d 1368.

Or let us say that a person of considerable wealth who was engaged to marry your sister had promised to pay off the mortgage on your family's house in Memphis, Tennessee. Unfortunately, he had not done so by the time he unexpectedly died. He had, however, paid for a new privacy fence for the backyard and the pool it surrounded. Could his promise to pay off the mortgage be enforced against his estate? Using your basic knowledge of the law obtained from this text and other studies, you recognize the issue as one involving gifts. You turn to the *Tennessee Digest,* and under that topic you find a strikingly similar case involving Elvis Presley and the family of his fiancée, Ginger Alden, at the time of his death, August 16, 1977. Reading the case, given as *Alden* v. *Presley,* 637 S.W.2d 862, in the digest, will provide you with some beginning insight into the issues involved and will perhaps help you determine whether you should pay an attorney for a consultation on the matter.

How do you find that case or the *Zamora* case? The notations following the case names (811 F.2d 1368 or 637 S.W.2d 862) give all the directions you need. See the Insight section "How Are Case Decisions Reported?" to find out how those notations work. Finally, don't forget that, as I pointed out at the beginning, the ability to do a modest amount of legal research is only the first step in a potentially long journey. You should always refer to a competent legal professional, if this is cost effective, before taking action on any results of your own research. Nonetheless, knowledge, no matter how summary, generally cannot hurt. So I encourage you to attempt to learn all you can on your own regarding any legal matter in which you are involved. Ignorance is definitely not bliss where the law is concerned.

The Legal Environment of Business Contracts

CHAPTERS

What Is a Legally Enforceable Contract?

CHAPTER OUTLINE AND OBJECTIVES

After studying this chapter, the student will be able to:

I. Define contract.

II. Use the terminology of contract law.

   a. Express, implied, and quasi contracts

   b. Valid, voidable, and void contracts

   c. Executed and executory contracts

   d. Unilateral and bilateral contracts

III. Identify the six essential elements of a legally enforceable contract.

   a. The agreement

   b. Between competent parties

   c. Based on genuine assent

   d. Supported by consideration

   e. In the proper form

   f. For a legal purpose

IV. Analyze the case of *Brooke Shields* v. *Garry Gross*, which considered the right of a 16-year-old minor to disaffirm a contract, consented to by her mother, that allowed a photographer to take nude pictures of her six years earlier.

What Is a Contract?

Contract: agreement between parties creating an obligation

A **contract** is an agreement between two or more parties that creates an obligation. The freedom to make such agreements is so important to our economic system that the framers of the Constitution guaranteed it. In Article I, Section 10, just before the clause forbidding the states to "grant any Title of Nobility," the states are ordered not to "pass any . . . Law impairing the Obligation of Contracts." This restriction on state power has been echoed by numerous legal decisions through the two-plus centuries since the Constitution was adopted. Even so, the freedom of contract is not without legal bounds. For example, note that the prohibition against interfering with the obligation of contracts is not directed at the federal government but at the states.

In addition, realize that having the freedom to make contracts does not necessarily mean you can get our court system to enforce them. For example, the law will generally not waste its time enforcing social contracts.

HYPOTHETICAL CASE

Armed with flowers and candy, Ted Turntable stood waiting at the door of Jane's apartment. He'd done everything for this date, even canceled the meeting with Sherwood Adams on the Blackwood Apartments closing. Doing that had probably cost him the $15,000 commission. It's worth it for her . . . The rented limo was outside. Dinner reservations were for 6:30. Then the concert at 8. The tickets to the concert alone, center front, had cost him a small fortune. Then Jane opened the door and stood there—in an old robe, her hair in curlers, her face covered with some form of green paste. She stared at him for a moment, smirked slightly, then spoke. "Bill . . . , isn't it? I'm so sorry. I tried to call you about five minutes ago. I can't go out tonight. I need to have a makeover done for a party I'm going to tomorrow night. We'll try it again sometime." "Ted, the name's Ted," he blurted out as the door closed in his face. The next day Ted called his attorney and asked him to bring suit against Jane for the losses he had incurred because of the aborted date and for his investment in it. His attorney laughed but drew up the petition anyway, billed Ted at $250 an hour, and filed the complaint with the state circuit court. The judge read it and threw it out immediately after Jane's attorney filed a motion to dismiss. "The courts of this state," commented the judge, "could not possibly have the resources to save all the Teds of this world from the folly of their social lives."

There are many other situations in which courts will not enforce contracts. Certainly, if a person can't get such help from the legal system, the risk of loss in contracting goes way up. Thus, the ability to pick out which contracts can be enforced in court and which cannot is very important to us all. Chapters 8 through 13 are therefore devoted to equipping you with knowledge of the common law that applies to most contract issues. Afterward, in Chapters 14 through 17, we will study a body of statutes, called the Uniform Commercial Code or UCC, which was written to apply specifically to commercial sales contracts. The UCC alters the common law of contracts somewhat to make doing business easier and less risky.

Before we get to the UCC, however, you must acquire a firm grounding in the common law of contracts. To enable you to achieve this goal, we will first define some terms that are helpful in understanding contracts. Then we will introduce and study the six "essential elements" that must be present before a court will consider a contract enforceable.

What Terms Are Most Useful in Working with Contracts?

Express, Implied, and Quasi Contracts

Contracts can be categorized in many ways. One of the most important is to categorize them as to how explicitly their terms are stated. An **express contract,** to begin with the most likely, has its terms set down in a clear-cut fashion either orally or in writing. (Realize that from a technical legal standpoint, an oral contract is generally just as binding as a written one. However, it is usually much easier to prove the terms of a written contract. So it is the practical favorite.) On the other hand, the terms of an **implied contract** are not stated. Instead, they must be determined from the surrounding circumstances or a foregoing pattern of dealings.

Express Contract: contract with terms clearly defined either orally or in writing

Implied Contract: contract with terms implied from circumstances or previous dealings

HYPOTHETICAL CASE

JJ bought his roast beef sandwich there every lunch hour. Joe, the counterman, always had a joke or two that he would pass on while he rang up the transaction on the convenience store's register. Then JJ would buy a soda out of the machine, grab a section of the paper the store provided, and settle into one of the booths to read. JJ had only 20 minutes for lunch. So he made the most of them. One day he came in to find the store packed with Benton high school students. On their way to a semifinal game in the state basketball playoffs, their bus had stopped for them to buy lunch. Twelve of them were waiting in line at the register. Seeing his lunch time evaporating, JJ held up the sandwich where Joe could see it and laid the customary price on the back counter. Joe nodded, winked, and grabbed the money for the register. An implied contract between the two, based on their foregoing pattern of dealings, had just been made.

Unlike express and implied contracts, a **quasi contract** (also referred to as an implied-at-law contract) exists only by the direction of the court. It does not stem from the agreement of the parties to it. In reality, it is not even a contract, as courts cannot impose contractual obligations on someone who has not assumed them. Instead, it is best viewed as a remedy that the courts utilize to return value to someone who has enriched another person in the absence of an express or implied contract between them. Generally, the price in such a contract will be set at a "reasonable amount" by a jury as trier of fact, or by a judge if a jury is not present. Consider the following example.

Quasi Contract: contract created by a court to avoid unjust enrichment

Basil swerved and hit the brakes as soon as he saw the front tire of the kid's bike stick out from behind the parked car. The brakes locked. The 18-wheeler skidded sideways across the opposite lane and into a guardrail. The impact snapped Basil's head into the door glass. Basil felt the blood streaming down over his ear. He opened the door of the cab and staggered out. A man in a postal uniform ran up to him. "Is the kid . . . all right?" Basil stammered. "Sure. Good job. The kid's fine but you're not" came the man's reply, which seemed to fade off at the end. Basil realized he was losing consciousness. "Please don't sent me to a hospital . . . can't afford it." Basil slumped to the ground. An ambulance came and rushed him to St. John's, where quick treatment saved his life. When he awoke in a hospital bed, he tried to leave and refused to pay. Regardless of his refusal, a court would find that a quasi contract existed and would force payment of a reasonable value for the hospital's services. Otherwise, Basil would be unjustly enriched.

So, whenever the plaintiff has conferred a benefit on the defendant, the plaintiff had a reasonable expectation of compensation in so doing and the defendant will be unjustly enriched if he or she is not required to compensate the plaintiff, the courts will utilize the quasi-contract theory to set things right.

Valid, Voidable, and Void Contracts

Valid Contract: legally binding and enforceable contract

Voidable Contract: contract with legal effect cancelable by party

Avoid: cancel

Rescinded: cancellation of contract's effect plus restoration of parties to original positions

Another set of terms that are useful in describing contracts is *valid, voidable,* and *void.* A **valid contract** is one that is legally binding and enforceable. Most of the forthcoming chapters on contracts will be about how to form or recognize such a contract. In the event of a problem, any party to a valid contract can take it to court for enforcement.

A **voidable contract** is a contract whose legal effect can be cancelled by one or more of the parties to it. This power to cancel or **avoid** a contract is given by law to individuals whose ability to enter into binding agreements is in question. Contracts made by minors, for example, are voidable until some time after they enter their legal adulthood (usually at age 18 for contracts), at which point they can legally confirm their contractual obligations. When a minor uses his or her right to avoid, the contract is **rescinded.** This means not only that any current or future effect of the contract is cancelled but also that the minor is restored as much as possible to her or his previous position. (See Chapter 10 for a full explanation of a minor's contractual rights.)

Lola ("Wheels") Rattler took a last look at the car. The Model A Ford Coupe was a classic. She had restored it during her junior year in high school. She drove it every day until she went away to college. Coming home on summer vacation after her freshman year at Berkeley, she knew it was time to sell it. She placed an ad in the hometown paper. To no one's surprise, the "A" car sold immediately. Moments

continued on page 103

concluded

later the buyer returned with the cash to pick it up. He was young, not more than 17, Shawn somebody, and he had been saving his funds since he was 12. He handed over the cash, took the keys and title, and jumped into the car. He let the engine idle for a moment, then shifted into reverse, and, with a wave to Lola, backed out of the driveway directly into the path of an oncoming garbage truck. In the collision, the Model A was destroyed. Shawn survived without a scratch, then avoided his contract with Lola. She refused to return his money at first, but her father's attorney informed her that she had no choice. Lola was left with the pieces and with a lesson about the dangers of contracting with minors.

Finally, a **void contract** is one that has no legal effect whatsoever. Generally, the courts will not even recognize its existence. Gambling and bribery agreements are typical examples. A man recently sued in the Arkansas court system to recover a bribe he allegedly paid to one of the system's judges for a favorable verdict. The judge did not deliver, so he wanted his money back. The case was dismissed.

Void Contract: contract without legal effect

Executed and Executory Contracts

An **executed contract** is one that all parties have fully performed. On the other hand, a contract in which some performance, however slight, has yet to be rendered is termed an **executory contract**.

Executed Contract: contract fully performed by all parties

Executory Contract: contract with some performance yet to be rendered

HYPOTHETICAL CASE

Ed Cell contracted to sell his car to Stew D. Baker for $4,000. On May 1, Cell delivered the car to Baker and received his $4,000. However, as Cell still had to procure the legal title from his credit union, which was holding it due to a loan the union had made using the car for security, the contract was still deemed executory. It was not considered executed until the title form had been properly obtained, made out, and transferred to Baker.

When a dispute about a contract arises, the types of remedies available in a court of law depend on whether the contract is executed or executory. More about this in a later chapter.

Unilateral and Bilateral Contracts

A **bilateral contract** is one that places a mutuality of obligations on its parties to fulfill their promises. A **unilateral contract** is a contract in which one party is obligated to fulfill a contractual promise only if another party performs.

Bilateral Contract: contract with mutuality of obligations

Unilateral Contract: contract with one party obligated only if other performs

Are you bewildered by the above terms? Keep reading. They'll become clearer.

To really understand what we're discussing here and how the terms are applied, we have to define some more basic contractual terms. To begin with, someone who proposes a bargain or exchange to another party or parties is

Offer: proposal of bargain or exchange with another

Offeror: person making offer

Offeree: person to whom offer is made

Promisor: person making contractual vow

Promisee: person to whom contractual vow is made

Obligor: person who must perform contractual promise

Obligee: person to whom performance of contractual promise is owed

making an **offer.** The person making the offer is termed the **offeror.** The person to whom it is made is termed the **offeree.** For example, if I proposed to sell you my Macintosh computer for $2,200, I would be the offeror and you the offeree in relation to that offer. I made the offer to you. Assume that we haggle for a while. Finally, you counteroffer $2,000, and I agree. We thereby form a contract that calls for you to buy the computer for that amount. That contract involves two promises or declarations to which we may be bound: I promise to transfer ownership of the computer to you. You promise to pay me $2,000 (in cash, unless we agree otherwise) at the time I do so.

In relation to my promise to transfer ownership, I am the maker of that promise, or, at law, the **promisor.** You are the person to whom the promise is made, or the **promisee.** In relation to your promise to pay, you are the promisor and I am the promisee. Finally, our exchange of promises to each other creates obligations to fulfill those promises. I am the **obligor** who must fulfill my obligation to transfer ownership. Your are the person to whom I am obliged, or the **obligee.** In like manner, you are the obligor in relation to your promise to pay $2,000 in cash for the computer. I am the obligee of that obligation.

In short, we are mutually obligated, one to another, to fulfill our contract. When a contract includes such a mutuality of obligations, the law terms it a *bilateral contract.*

Unilateral contracts are most often found in reward situations. I offer to pay $25 to anyone in my college class who returns to me the notebook I left behind the last time the class met. Does the offer obligate any of my classmates to perform the act? Not at all. But if any of them does perform that act, I am obligated to pay that person the $25. Thus, the contract is unilateral. As such, it obliges me to perform only if another party performs according to my offer.

What Are the Six Essential Elements of a Legally Enforceable Contract?

Having defined some of the most important contractual terms and classifications, we must now take an introductory look at the key elements of a contract. (Bear in mind that these elements will all be fully explained in the chapters that follow.) There are six of these, and they are "essential" to successful contract formation. The six elements must be found to be present before a court will conclude that one or all of the parties to a contract are bound to carry out its terms. Specifically, the essential elements of a legally enforceable contract are (1) an agreement (2) that is between competent parties, (3) based on genuine assent, (4) supported by consideration, (5) in the proper form, and (6) for a legal purpose.

The Agreement

Composed of the offer and the acceptance, this cornerstone of contracts will be covered in Chapter 9.

Flowchart of Requirements for a Legally Enforceable Contract   **Figure 8–1**

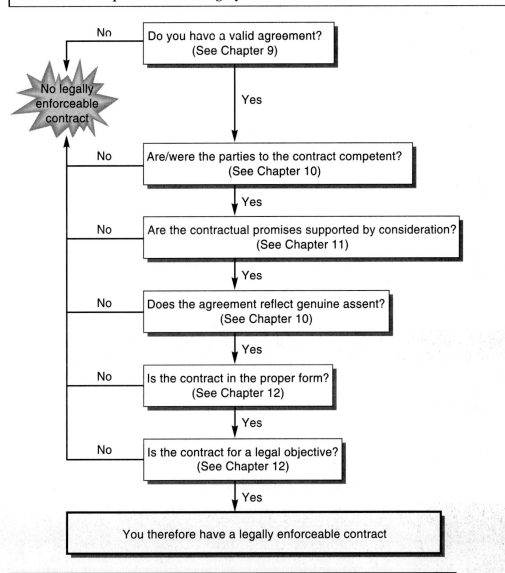

Between Competent Parties

In most instances, minors, the intoxicated, and the insane lack the capacity to contract. Chapter 10 details how the law handles contractual situations in which such people are involved.

Based on Genuine Assent

At times, individuals may enter into contracts as a result of circumstances that deny them the ability to say no. Duress, the undue influence of others, mistake, misrepresentation, and fraud may all compel less than genuine assent to a contract. Chapter 10 reveals when the lack of genuine assent will allow a party to back out of a contract.

Supported by Consideration

Generally, the law will not enforce against us a promise for which we receive nothing in return. What the promisor in a contract says he or she wants in return for giving a legally enforceable promise is referred to as consideration. Chapter 11 deals with this indispensable element of a legally binding contract.

In the Proper Form

Generally, oral contracts are legally valid, binding, and enforceable. In certain legal situations, however, a written statement of the contract terms signed by the person against whom enforcement is sought is necessary. Chapter 12 tells when to get your contract in writing.

For a Legal Purpose

As mentioned earlier in this chapter, the law will not enforce contracts for improper objectives such as bribery or gambling. Chapter 12 covers these eventualities.

After the in-depth discussion of the essential elements of contracts provided in Chapters 9 through 12, Chapter 13 discusses how contractual duties are ended. Then it discusses the remedies that are available in court if contractual duties are not properly accomplished. The end result of this six-chapter block on contracts should be to leave you with a clear idea of what contracts are enforceable and what results you can expect if you resort to a court for the enforcement of such contracts.

APPLICATIONS OF WHAT YOU'VE LEARNED

Vocabulary Development

Fill in the blanks with the appropriate term.

Avoid	Express Contract	Offeree	Rescinded
Bilateral Contract	Implied Contract	Offeror	Unilateral Contract
Contract	Obligee	Promisee	Valid Contract
Executed Contract	Obligor	Promisor	Voidable Contract
Executory Contract	Offer	Quasi Contract	Void Contract

1. John and Bill agree to the sale of John's Fiat to Bill for $2,000. In relation to his promise to transfer ownership of the car to Bill, John is both a(n) _____ and a(n) _____. In relation to John's promise, Bill is both a(n) _____ and a(n) _____.

2. Once John has delivered the car and Bill has paid, the contract will be deemed a(n) _____.

3. Because the terms were explicitly stated, the contract between Bill and John is termed a(n) _____.

4. If Bill turns out to be a minor, the contract is deemed a(n) _____. If Bill chooses to cancel or _____ it, the courts will see that the contract is _____.

Problems

1. Bart Sampson, a bachelor, lived at 353 East Nucleus Avenue in Reactor City, Florida. One day he drove home for lunch only to find a swarm of Acme Painters' workers painting his house a nice shade of white. For a moment this puzzled Bart, who then remembered that Bandy Simpson, his next-door neighbor, had mentioned that his (Bandy's) house was going to be painted. Bandy lived at 355 East Nucleus. Bart smiled and drove away. As he did, an Acme worker saw him. Later Acme discovered its mistake and sued Bart for payment for the work it had done. The worker is sure to testify that Bart drove by when his house was being painted. Should Acme win? Under what type of contract or contractual theory would Bart have to pay? Who would set the price?

2. Sandy walked to the window for the umpteenth time. Where was Ben? The prom started in 10 minutes, and her parents wanted to take pictures and be sociable for a while. She pushed back the curtain and started out into the street. Where was "Benjamin Bradley the Third," as he was fond of calling himself? The phone rang. Sandy started for it, but her dress and heels slowed her down. Her Mom picked up the phone, scowled, then handed it to Sandy. "SS . . . Sandy?" The voice was slurred. "Sandy??" "Yes, Ben," she answered. "SS . . . Sandy, sssome of my old buddies showed up and got me drunk. I'm afraid we're going to have to call it off. I'm sick." Sandy heard the phone clatter as Ben dropped it, heard him stumble away. Then a glass broke and a door slammed. Sandy laid the phone down and cried. The next day she filed a small claims action against Ben for breaking their contract. She sought $575 in damages— $450 for her prom dress, $75 for the shoes that were dyed to match the dress, $40 for her perm, $10 for her nails. Should she recover? Will she recover?

3. Clyde ("Da Bears") Longstreet of Springfield, Illinois, gave his friend Hank Billings $750 to place a bet on a certain Chicago team to beat the point spread in a playoff game. The Monday after that team did beat the point spread, Clyde asked Hank for his winnings. Hank replied that he had not placed the bet and was keeping the money. Clyde threatened to sue him for breach of contract. What kind of contract did the two men have? Will Clyde recover? If, so, will he recover the $750 or the amount he would have won had the bet been placed?

4. The key to separating the contracts that the law will help you enforce from all other contracts is to examine these contracts for the required six essential elements. These six elements must be found before a court will bind the parties to a contract. Specifically, a legally enforceable contract has to have an _____ made between competent _____, based on genuine _____, supported by _____ in the proper _____, and for a _____.

Brooke Shields v. Garry Gross

451 N.Y.S.2d 419

Consider the case of the mother who consented to pictures being taken of her ten-year-old daughter in the nude.

When Brooke Shields was 10 years old, her mother and professional manager, Teri Shields, signed broad consent forms giving photographer Gross the unrestricted right to "use, reuse, and/or publish or republish" various photographs he took of Brooke. The photos were taken pursuant to arrangements made by Playboy Press. Some of the photos were nude shots of the 10-year-old in a bathtub. In others she was clothed. Several of the photos were later published in *Photo,* a French magazine. At that time negotiations were begun to buy back the rights to the photos. When these negotiations broke down, a lawsuit seeking damages and a permanent injunction to prevent further use of the photos was brought under sections 50 and 51 of the New York Civil Rights Law. At this time Brooke was 16. The lower court, sitting without a jury, dismissed the complaint and denied the injunction except to order that the photos not be published in pornographic publications or in publications of a predominantly prurient appeal. The Appellate Division of the Supreme Court of New York State then took the case and decided it. (Note that the courts with original jurisdiction in New York are the supreme courts. Above them are the courts of the Appellate Division, and above those courts is the highest court in New York State, the Court of Appeals.) The decision of the Appellate Division was as follows:

In this state, as elsewhere, it has long been the general rule that an infant has the right to disaffirm a contract even when the contract has been entered into on behalf of the infant by a parent or guardian . . .

We do not perceive in the wording of [our] Civil Rights Law, sections 50 and 51, any clear manifestation of a legislative intent to limit the long-established rights of infants to disaffirm contracts approved by a parent with regard to actions brought under those sections. Section 50 provides: "A person, firm, or corporation that uses for advertising purposes, or for the purposes of trade, the name, portrait, or picture of any living person without having first obtained the written consent of such person, or if a minor of his or her parent or guardian, is guilty of a misdemeanor."

Section 51 makes a violation of section 50 actionable in a civil suit [such as this one].

. . . The manifest purpose of the requirement of parental consent in these sections was to protect someone who secured such consent from being prosecuted criminally, or subject to an action for damages or injunctive relief, with regard to activities embraced in the sections during the period the consent was effective. Nothing in the sections even purports to address the infant's right to disaffirm such consent, and we see nothing in the language of the sections nor the rights that they were designed to protect that would require an interpretation so inconsistent with the general common law principle and the clear meaning of the statutory pattern described above.

Accordingly, the judgment dismissing the complaint, and denying, except in one limited respect, plaintiff's right to a permanent injunction is modified and defendant is enjoined from using any pictures of plaintiff at issue here for purposes of advertising or trade.

Questions

1. Can the photos be used? Why or why not? What form of relief is used by the appellant court in this case?

2. Under the New York laws cited above, would a child have the right to disaffirm an agreement in which a parent contracts for the child to play a violent professional sport?

3. Is the result ethical?

CHAPTER

9

What Are the Requirements of a Valid Agreement?

CHAPTER OUTLINE AND OBJECTIVES

After studying this chapter, the student will be able to:

I. Distinguish a valid from an invalid offer.

   a. The test of contractual intent

   b. The test of definiteness

   c. The test of communication to the offeree

II. Identify the events that can terminate an offer before it can be accepted.

   a. Expiration of a reasonable time

   b. Revocation by the offeror and effect of an option

   c. Rejection and counteroffer

   d. Death or disability of a party

   f. Destruction of specific subject matter

   g. Subsequent illegality

III. Explain the importance of complete and unconditional acceptance of an offer.

   a. The mirror image concept

   b. Communication of acceptance

IV. Evaluate the importance of the type of contract used in a court enforcement action, using the case of *United Steel Workers of America* v. *U.S. Steel Corporation*.

In the last chapter, we discussed the six essential elements that are required for a contract to be legally enforceable. The first of these, the agreement, is the most crucial. In this chapter, we'll break down the agreement into its two elements, the offer and the acceptance, and test them for their legal validity.

How Do You Determine Whether an Offer is Valid?

Over the years, the law has devised several tests to tell whether an offer, defined in the last chapter as a proposal of a bargain or exchange with another, is valid. These tests pose three main questions: Did the party making the offer intend a contract to result? Was the offer definite enough to be accepted? Finally, was the offer properly communicated to the offeree?

The Test of Contractual Intent

Often our lips blurt out things before we can think to stop them. We'd prefer that most such statements not be repeated and that even fewer be held to in court. So when a pickpocket or a purse snatcher is running away with your valuables and you scream out, "Stop thief—I'll pay anyone who stops that person $5,000," the law regards the statement as having been made in the heat of excitement without enough thought to involve contractual intent. As a consequence, if someone chases and stops the thief and recovers your valuables, you will not be legally bound to pay the $5,000.

As discussed in the last chapter, the law does not find contractual intent in social invitations either. So, in the vast majority of states, individuals cannot sue or be sued over broken dates, missed birthday or dinner parties (RSVP or not), and so on.

Objective Standard: impartial observer's conclusions from express behavior

An offer made as a joke has also been held to lack contractual intent. The only problem here is that in most cases the law uses an **objective standard** to determine whether contractual intent is present. This means that, if a reasonable person observing the occurrence impartially would conclude from the conduct of the parties that the offer embodied contractual intent, a contract can be formed. In the case of some alleged jokes this can work a very harsh result, as in the following example, which is based on an actual case.

Buford Jones and his wife agreed that Yancy was a social climber. He had next to nothing, yet he was constantly badgering them about selling their family estate in Dorchester County to him. When they met him that night in the bar at the Elk's Head Inn, he started in on them again. Finally, they had had enough. While Yancy was in the rest room, Buford suggested to his wife that they play a cruel joke on the upstart. They would offer to sell him the estate for $250,000, just half of its market price. Not being able to pay would show Yancy up once and for all. So, when Yancy returned, Buford made the offer. Yancy thought for a moment, then thrust out his

continued on page 113

concluded

hand. "A deal for sure, Buf." They shook hands. Then Yancy suggested that they put the deal in writing. Buford did so. Before Yancy signed, he proofread the agreement and suggested changes due to typos and misspellings. Buford redrafted the document with the changes and signed. Yancy then also signed. A few minutes later, Yancy said good bye and left with his copy. He was barely out the door when he turned around, came back to the bar, and had Mrs. Jones sign the contract as well. A few weeks later, in accordance with the contract, Yancy produced the $250,000. The Joneses then discovered that their "ne'er-do-well" had just married a very wealthy woman. They refused to sell, claiming that the offer was a joke, although a cruel one. Yancy sued for title to the estate. The court concluded that a reasonable person using the objective standard would have believed from the conduct of the parties in drafting and redrafting the document, then having Mrs. Jones sign, that no joke was being played. It then ordered Mr. and Mrs. Jones to sign over the estate.

Judging from the above example, sometimes the better the deception, the more likely it is that the objective standard will bind the parties to the joke's legal punch line—a contract.

Another area in which contractual intent is not found is an **invitation to negotiate.** Such invitations may take many forms, but they are most commonly found in advertisements. Whenever most Americans see a good priced for sale in a store window, on a store's shelves, in a magazine or newspaper, or on television, they believe that the person who placed and priced it is legally obligated at law to sell it for that amount. In most cases this is not so. Generally speaking, an ad is construed by the law as merely a way of inviting someone to make an offer, or, in other words, to open negotiations. Haggling over the price of an item for sale, whether in the finest shop or with a street vendor, is a way of life in other countries.

Invitation to Negotiate: solicitation of offers

HYPOTHETICAL CASE

Andy Pottero of Plainview, Nebraska, visited Costa Rica on his first trip abroad. In a small native shop, Andy found a beautiful scarf for his wife. It was priced at only $0.50 in American money. He laid the purchase price down on the counter and was shocked by the shopkeeper's scornful look. Afterward, Andy asked a Costa Rican friend why the shopkeeper had reacted in this way. The friend informed him that by not haggling over the price, Andy had impliedly said to the shopkeeper that he was too wealthy to bother with such trivial matters, thus placing himself in a social status way above that of the shopkeeper. "Let it go," said the friend. "Most Americans display the very same insensitivity. That's why you are not as well liked as travelers of other nationalities."

Haggling over prices was the expected standard in this country as well until J. C. Penney supposedly made it a policy of his stores that they would sell at the same marked price to all comers. J. C. Penney's policy did not change the law, however, which was based on the premise that placing a price on a good is just an invitation to get the customer into the store to make an offer.

Before she married Tom Terra of Bloomingville, Indiana, Annie lived to surf. After the nuptials and the move back to Indiana, however, Annie found that the closest experience to surfing offered by the Midwest was slashing across some boat's wake on a pair of water skis. So she placed a "want ad" in the Bloomingville paper to sell her surfboard. Thinking there would be little appreciation of the board's quality, she priced it at $750, about half of the price it would bring in California. The day the ad appeared, her phone rang for a solid hour with people asking for her address so that they could come by and see it. Annie, realizing that the price she put in the paper was far too low, waited until a crowd had assembled and then sold the board to the highest bidder for $1,150. One man objected, saying that she should have sold it to the first person to arrive with $750 in cash. Annie replied that the price in the ad was just an invitation to negotiate. She insisted that she had as much right to talk people into paying more as they had to get her to lower her price.

Bait and Switch Scheme: sales device using low-priced and understocked goods as bait to bring in buyers, who are then switched to more profitable goods

To prevent sellers from taking advantage of ads that they consider invitations to negotiate only, statutes outlawing fraudulent advertising and **bait and switch schemes** exist. (In such a scheme a seller lures a buyer with an extremely low price on an understocked, underfeatured item, then "switches" the buyer to a far more expensive product. However, even if convicted of these crimes, a seller does not have to go through with the deal set out in the "invitation." In this situation, as in those mentioned earlier, contractual intent is a necessity.

The Test of Definiteness

Many times, what appears to be an offer will prove unenforceable in court because its terms are vague, ambiguous, confusing, or just incomplete. For example, if I offered to pay you "a little over minimum wage to guide a few of our tours to the tulip festival in a nearby town," the offer would be unenforceable due to a lack of definiteness. At a minimum, the court must be reasonably certain of four items in each enforceable contract: (1) the parties involved; (2) the cost in money or value paid for the good or service (referred to as the **price**); (3) the good or service involved in the contract (called the **subject matter**); and (4) the time for performance.

Price: contractual cost in money or value paid for a good or service

Subject Matter: good or service involved in the contract

Cost-plus Contract: development cost plus profit percentage paid by purchaser

Be aware, however, that courts will overlook the absence of these terms in certain instances. For example, many contracts requiring a great deal of research and development are made on a cost-plus basis. Under a **cost-plus contract,** the purchaser must pay the developer the amount of money it cost to create the product plus a certain percentage of that cost for a profit. Weapons systems are often developed for our government under cost-plus contracts.

"Yeeouch. Come 'ere you little . . ." Major General H. E. Airburst, US Army, was under attack by his son's remote-controlled miniature dune buggy. Traveling faster than a man could run, the device had just slammed into his foot. "Next Christmas, you get the violin," the general screeched at his son as he tried to stomp the shiny black toy into a state from which no alkaline battery could resurrect it. Suddenly, an idea followed the pathway that the pain had opened into his brain. The "Wheeled Remote Controlled Land Mine Project" was born. The next fiscal year the Army contracted with Childproof, Inc., a leading toy company, to develop the weapon. Because new materials would have to be built into the device to withstand battlefield conditions, the contract was made on a cost-plus basis. Three years later Congressman Hynd Syte, noted for his crusades against government waste, found that Childproof had just billed the government for $77 million under the contract. Syte raised such a furor over the project that the government refused to pay the money, saying that the contract was indefinite and unenforceable because it did not have a price term. Childproof sued the government. In court, the company was able to show that the $70 million in development costs had been reasonably and fairly arrived at. Those costs plus the agreed-to 10 percent profit of $7 million totaled $77 million. The court responded to Childproof's evidence by holding that there was an enforceable contract. It then ordered the government to pay immediately.

Other types of enforceable contracts that seem too indefinite include requirements and output contracts and reference to standard form contracts. A **requirements contract** obligates one party to buy all it needs of a particular kind of good from the other party for a set period. An **output contract** is similar. Under it the maker of a product must sell all of its output of that product during a set period to the other party to the contract. The amount of the subject matter cannot be determined from the contract in either instance. However, the court produces an enforceable contract by simply requiring both parties to act in good faith in making or requiring the product during the set period.

The **"reference to standard form" contract** appears even more indefinite than all of the above, yet remains enforceable. Such a contract typically refers the parties to a page in a recognized publication. The page contains a contract form with blanks to fill in the names of the parties, the price, the subject matter, the time of performance, and other terms. One of the parties numbers the blanks, then, on the contract beside the appropriate numbers, fills in the terms. The resulting contract looks like a sheet of paper with some unconnected but sequentially numbered facts on it. If, however, it is signed and otherwise valid, that sheet of paper and the terms it incorporates by reference are enforceable. With the widespread use of photocopying equipment, the rate of use of this type of contract has become very infrequent.

Requirements Contract: all of purchaser's needs for specific good bought from only one party for set period

Output Contract: all of party's production of specific good sold to one party

Reference to Standard Form Contract: signed list of items filling in blanks of predetermined prototype contract

The Test of Communication to the Offeree

HYPOTHETICAL CASE

Kim knew what Sharon would do, could only do, to return the deep forehand. A feeling of triumph swept through Kim's body. Years of training to get here, and now she had her archrival at match point for the championship. Sharon swung, aiming to lob the ball into Kim's backcourt. As the ball arced skyward, Kim smiled. It wasn't hit deep enough. It would allow Kim the perfect putaway, an overhead right at the net. The ball floated down. Kim heard the crowd draw in a collective breath. Sharon was running off the court to get out of the way. Now! Kim swung . . . and completely missed the shot she had hit dozens of times in a row in practice. The ball bounced off her head. Laughter skipped through the sun-drenched crowd. Overcome, Kim fell to her knees and pounded her fists into the clay. Finally, she rose and walked up to the judge. "I forfeit," she heard herself saying. Then she left. That evening she ran into Bobby, one of the touring pros in town for the pro-am tourney. "Bobby," Kim said, "I've thought about this since I left the court today. I'm quitting tennis. I'm going to sell my racket to Sharon for $75 and buy a bowling ball." Bobby laughed. "That racket is worth 10 times that. Come on now." Kim scowled at him. "Yep, I'm doing it," she insisted. "Maybe that racket will curse her the way it has me." Kim rose and left. A few hours later, Bobby saw Sharon and told her Kim's intentions. Sharon cashed a check for $75, then found Kim and pressed the money into her hand. "Bobby told me about your offer, and it's a deal," she said. "Go get me the racket." Kim refused, saying that she had changed her mind. Can Sharon enforce a contract of sale for the racket against Kim in court?

As you may have guessed, the answer to the above question is no. The courts have held that it takes communication of the offer to the offeree . . . by the offeror (or by some mechanism that the offeror sets in motion—for example, telling Bobby to tell Sharon if he saw her) to have a valid contract result. Such communication confirms the contractual intent of the offeror. Without it, there can be no resort to the courts for enforcement.

What Events Can Terminate an Offer Before It Can Be Accepted?

Of course, a valid offer standing alone doesn't make an agreement. It takes timely, appropriate action of at least one other party to produce a legally enforceable contract. Before that action occurs, a number of events can take place that will kill the offer before it can be accepted.

Expiration of a Reasonable Time

One of the most common of these events is the expiration of a reasonable time during which acceptance should have taken place. All too often, offers are made without the pinpointing of a specific time at which the ability of the offeree to accept ends. As it would be unfair to require that such offers remain open indefinitely, the courts will hold that only a "reasonable time" is available within which a binding acceptance can be communicated to the offeror. The length of this period varies with the subject matter of the contract. For an offer to sell 1,000 shares of IBM stock, a reasonable time might be measured in minutes; for an offer to buy a house or farm, it might be measured in weeks. The court will rely on its trier of fact—a jury, if one is sitting in the case—to tell it how long the period was. If this period had expired, no contract was formed by the attempted acceptance.

Revocation by the Offeror and Options

Whether or not the offeror set down a period within which the offeree could accept, he or she can still recall or take back the offer as long as this action, called a **revocation,** is taken prior to acceptance.

Revocation: offeror's recall of offer before acceptance

Henry walked quickly down the sidewalk toward the storefront. He recognized it as soon as he turned the corner. It was the same shop they'd been in a few hours earlier, one of the dozens lining the streets near the corner of Orchard and Delancey in New York City. He could still remember the way Diane had looked at the bracelet. A copy of some top designer's work, it sparkled with precious stones. The owner of the shop had made a great offer to them—$500. It was worth several times that, but she had said no. It was all the "mad money" they had, and if they didn't spend it, they could use it to fix up their apartment after the honeymoon. Just as they left the shop, the owner had said the offer was good all day, then winked at Henry. He had taken her back to their hotel room and then had made an excuse to go back out . . . He pushed the shop door open. The owner looked up, recognized him, and shook his head sadly. "I'm sorry, sir. I thought you'd come back. Your wife is so beautiful, but I have to cancel my offer. Just after you left, another person came in and wanted it. I told her you might be back. She'll pay $750. You can have it for that, but no less." Henry was crestfallen, but he knew the law. The shopkeeper could revoke his offer before acceptance if he wanted to even if he'd offered Henry a month to take him up on it. Henry shrugged and left the shop.

Henry could have made sure the offer would still be open by making an **option contract** with the shopkeeper. Such a contract binds the offeror to his or her promise to keep an offer open for a set period of time. For example, Henry could have paid the shopkeeper $10 for an option to buy the bracelet for $500 anytime that day. He would then have had a legally enforceable position if the shopkeeper promised it to another.

Option Contract: offeror bound to hold offer open set period of time

Rejection and Counteroffer

The actions of the offeree can also terminate an offer. If I offer to sell you my Fiat Spyder convertible for $2,000 and you reply that you'd never be caught dead in a foreign car, that expression of a lack of interest in my offer, called a **rejection** at

Rejection: expression of lack of interest in offer

law, terminates it. Afterward, if you suddenly remembered that an acquaintance of yours had told you she would pay $4,000 for my car, you could not come back and accept my offer. It was terminated at the time of the rejection. Any subsequent statement you made to me of being willing to buy it for $2,000 would be considered an offer by the court, not an acceptance of my offer. The same result would occur if instead of rejecting my offer, you said, "I wouldn't pay $2,000 for it, but I will pay $1,000 just to help you out." Your response to my offer, which alters the terms of that offer and which the court would label a **counteroffer,** terminates my offer, just as the rejection did.

Counteroffer: offeree's alternative terms given in response to offer

Death or Disability of a Party

The death of a offeror, whether or not communicated to the offeree, automatically terminates the offer. The same result occurs if the courts find the offeror to be insane or a habitual drunkard.

Destruction of Specific Subject Matter

Belinski offered to sell Chance the 2-carat or better cuttings from a 122-carat diamond just discovered in the Carpathian mines. While Chance considered the offer, the diamond was safely flown to New York for cutting. Unfortunately, when the cutter's tool smashed into the stone, it hit a previously undetected flaw. The diamond shattered into tiny pieces, the largest of which was one-third of a carat. That destruction of the specific subject matter of the offer terminated it.

Subsequent Illegality

Some offers are terminated when a lawmaking body renders their subject matter or performance illegal. For example, assume that Sherlock Holmes had a standing offer to pay Dr. Watson 5 quid for every fresh pack of opium he brought in for the famous detective's use. If Parliament later declared possession and use of opium illegal, performance would be made legally impossible by the new law. Consequently, the offer would be unenforceable.

Why Is Complete and Unconditional Acceptance of an Offer Important?

The Mirror Image Concept

Acceptance: indication of desire to be bound by terms of offer

Technically, an **acceptance** under contract law is a sign by which the offeree indicates that she or he will be bound by the terms of the offeror's offer. As you can gauge from the preceding section on rejection and counteroffer, an offer must be accepted without change. In other words, the acceptance must be a mirror

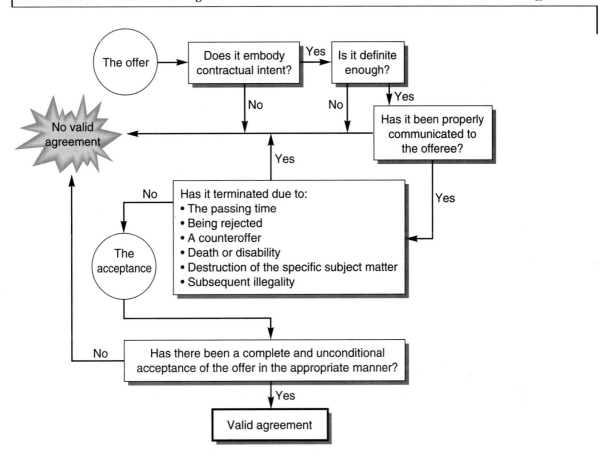

image of the offer. If not, what seemed to be an acceptance will be treated as a counteroffer and will terminate the original offer.

Communication of Acceptance

In unilateral contracts, problems with letting the offeror know the bargain is accepted do not generally occur. Action, not a return promise, is what is expected from the offeree. If I offer a reward for my missing dog, I expect someone to show up with the dog, not to call and promise to do so.

In bilateral contracts, however, a return promise is expected. This generally poses no problem if the contract negotiations are being conducted face-to-face or over the phone. If, instead, the parties are communicating by mail, telegram, fax, or a like medium, the rules become complex.

First of all, the offeror may require that a certain medium be used. If such is the case, remember that the offeror is master of the offer. So, "acceptance by mail required" means just that, and a communication of the acceptance by fax, phone, or otherwise will not bind the bargain.

If the offeror doesn't stipulate the medium, then the best idea is to send an acceptance in the same medium that was used to send the offer, mail if the offer was sent by mail and so on. If this rule is followed, the acceptance is effective when it is placed in the control of a representative of that medium—for example, when it is delivered to the post office with the proper address and postage. If a different medium is used, say the offer came by mail and the acceptance is faxed to the offeror, the acceptance is effective only when it reaches the offeror's office, home, or other location (usually whatever is indicated as a return address on the offer). The offeror doesn't actually have to open or read the acceptance for it to be binding. Note that unlike the acceptance, a revocation is effective only when the communication bearing that revocation arrives at the offeree's location.

Before closing out your study of this chapter, realize that all of the rules concerning the agreement (expressed in concise form in Figure 9-1) and the other essential elements of contracts are the result of centuries of common law experience. We in business today benefit greatly from that experience. In effect, the costly mistakes of our predecessors enable us to prevent our own. Ignorance of such law, therefore, is definitely not bliss.

APPLICATIONS OF WHAT YOU'VE LEARNED

Vocabulary Development

Fill in the blanks with the appropriate term.

Acceptance	Invitation to Negotiate	Price	Requirements Contract
Bait and Switch Scheme	Objective Standard	Reference to Standard	Revocation
Cost-Plus Contract	Option Contract	Form Contract	Subject Matter
Counteroffer	Output Contract	Rejection	

1. If you say to me, "I'll pay you $50 to keep that offer open for a month," you are attempting to make a(n) _____ with me.

2. If you agree to buy all the computer chips you need for the next month from me, we have made a(n) _____.

3. If you agree to buy all the computer chips I can make for the next month, we have made a(n) _____.

4. If you agree to repay the reasonable ammounts that I spend for developing a new chip and throw in an additional amount for a profit, typically a percentage of the reasonable amounts I spend, we have made a(n) _____.

5. If, coming into my store in response to my ads for a two-cycle push lawn mower at a very low price, you find that the lawn mower has been sold out but that my salespeople are ready to talk you into our new, air-conditioned, riding, garden plowing, and, oh yes, lawn cutting apparatus, you might

suspect that you are being manipulated in a(n) _____ .

Some terms from Chapter 8 may be required to answer the following questions.

6. If I advertise a 1-carat diamond ring on TV for $255 without mentioning any other terms, I am making a(n) _____ .

7. If you see the ad referred to in problem 6, drive immediately to my store, and slam down the $255 plus tax on my counter, you

are making a(n) _____ _____ to me for the ring.

8. If I take the money and ring up the sale on my cash register, my conduct implies a(n) _____ of your proposal.

9. If instead of taking your money as in Question 8, I explain that there was a mistake in the placement of the ad and that I will not contract for the sale at that price, my conduct amounts to a(n) _____ of your proposal.

Problems

1. Colossal Discounters advertised a compact disc player/changer for $75. When Anton Snider made it to the store on the morning the ad ran in the local newspaper, the player/changer stock was sold out. Anton slipped around and asked a friend of his on the sales staff how many of the item had been stocked. His friend replied, "One." Later that morning, Anton went to the courthouse and swore out a criminal complaint against Colossal for a

_____ .

If the prosecutor is successful in pursuing the charge and brings in a conviction, will Anton then be able to buy the player/changer for $75?

2. Madilyn Sanderson purchased her seat on the stock exchange right after she sold her real estate business to a large corporation. Since that time she had bought and sold with the best of them, and in the recent bull market she had made money hand over fist. So, two days ago, when she saw a chance to make financial history, she jumped at it. It happened when IBM announced that it had received a major order for its new computer line. Madilyn had just finished researching the computer line and knew that IBM could not produce all the chips for the new order internally. "Big Blue," as IBM was known, would have to buy those from external sources, and there were only two. Madilyn immediately placed

a "buy at market price" order for the stocks of the two companies with a Philadelphia broker who made a market in them. The broker responded that she would try to find some of the stock for sale and would get back to Madilyn. Now, 48 hours later, IBM had just announced that it was turning down the order for its new computer line because the purchaser was not able to pay enough up front. Madilyn tried to reach the broker to withdraw her offer but could not get her. Would Madilyn's buy offer still bind her? Why or why not?

3. Which of the following contract offers is (are) unilateral?
   a. I offer a reward for my missing camera.
   b. I offer to pay you to look for my missing camera.
   c. I offer a 50,000 prize to the first solar-powered plane to fly across the Atlantic.
   d. I offer to pay you $5,000 for your promise to perform at a concert I'm promoting.

4. Which of the offers in Problem 3 potentially involves a mutuality of obligations?

5. If my offer to you stipulated that you had to appear in person and verbally accept, would there be a contract if you sent me a videotape in which you stated that you accepted?

United Steel Workers of America v. U.S. Steel Corporation

492 Federal Supplement 1

Consider what a difference it makes as to how a contract is categorized by the courts—whether a contract was a unilateral or bilateral contract meant the difference between having a job and a home or not to the workers in a U.S. Steel plant

When the losses at its Mahoning Valley plants became intolerable, U.S. Steel Corporation laid plans to close them down. In response, the workers at the plants indicated a willingness to work hard at making them profitable and keeping them that way. U.S. Steel Corporation acknowledged these statements by the workers and communicated its willingness to keep the plants open if and so long as the workers made them profitable. When continuing losses

eventually forced the shutdown of the plants, the workers brought suit for breach of contract and damages.

In its decision the court held that the contract with the workers was unilateral. Therefore, the contract would not come into existence until the workers achieved and sustained profitability. Since the contract had not come into existence, it could not be breached.

Questions

1. Did U.S. Steel Corporation have to pay damages to the workers?

2. Would the decision have been different if the contract had been characterized as bilateral?

CHAPTER

10

Whom Will the Law Excuse from the Performance of Contractual Obligations?

CHAPTER OUTLINE AND OBJECTIVES

After studying this chapter, the student will be able to:

I. Identify parties who may be excused from their contracts because they lacked the contractual capacity to enter into them.

  a. Minors

  b. The insane

  c. The intoxicated or drugged

II. Identify the circumstances that can legally excuse individuals from their contracts because their assent was not genuine.

  a. Mistake

  b. Concealment

  c. Misrepresentation and fraud

  d. Undue influence and duress

  e. Unconscionability

III. Evaluate the importance of acting free of the above circumstances even in the most extraordinary situations by reading a hostage bargaining case, *United States* v. *Gorham and Wilkerson.*

It is a fact of life that individuals often hire attorneys to get them out of unfavorable contracts. Many times these individuals, looking for a loophole to slip out of, are disappointed because "the law loves a bargain." In other words, the law works to keep in effect contracts that have been fairly negotiated and entered into by able parties who had their eyes open at the time. If such contracts are now working a hardship on such parties, the law leaves them with only the option of blaming the person they see in the mirror each morning.

In certain limited situations, however, the law will allow a party out of an otherwise binding contract. These situations generally involve individuals who do not have the ability or the freedom to properly evaluate and control the contracts they enter into. The crucial ability to appreciate the consequences of entering into a contract is termed **contractual capacity.**

Contractual Capacity: ability to appreciate consequences of entering into a contract

Who Can Legally Be Excused from Their Contracts because They Lacked the Ability to Enter into Them?

Minors

Remember from previous discussions that, according to the law, a child under the age of seven can commit neither a crime nor a tort. This is because the law recognizes that such youngsters usually lack the ability to appreciate the consequences of crimes or torts and therefore does not hold them legally responsible for those consequences. Under contract law there is a similar rule relating to minors. In particular, contractual capacity is only recognized in individuals who are in their **majority,** or in other words, in those who are at or beyond the legal age to contract. This age varies from state to state but is generally set at 18. A person under this age is deemed a **minor** and therefore to lack such capacity to contract. The insane or mentally incompetent and, and in some cases, intoxicated persons are also deemed to lack such capacity under our laws.

Majority: legal age

Minor: person under legal age

Power to Avoid Their Contracts. The primary way in which the law protects minors from those who would take advantage of their lack of capacity to contract is to allow minors to avoid or **disaffirm** their contracts. Note that this power to avoid is given only to minors and not to the adults involved in contracts with them. The power was discussed somewhat in Chapter 8. In most states, even minors who lie about their age to cause adults to contract with them can avoid the contracts that result. If avoidance is allowed, the contracts will be rescinded and the minors put back on their original footing. Minors enjoy this status under the law to prevent them from being taken advantage of by adults. (Minors overseas are also shielded in this way, the age of capacity to contract being set at 20 in Japan and at 18 in continental Europe.) Note that, upon avoidance, minors are required to return any consideration still in their possession that they have received from the bargain. A businessperson who deliberately or inadvertently chooses to deal with a minor, even if the businessperson realizes the

Disaffirm: to repudiate intent to be bound by contract

error, must continue to follow the terms of the contract. This holds true even if doing this increases the businessperson's potential losses should avoidance occur.

Ratification.   Even after minors enter majority, they are given a reasonable amount of time to evaluate their contracts and to avoid them if they so desire. By the same token, minors may instead choose to ratify their contracts. **Ratification** is the display of a willingness to be bound by a contract's terms. Ratification can be inferred from certain actions. For example, either letting the reasonable period of time after turning 18 pass without avoiding the contract or making payments called for by the contract after turning 18 would be enough to prove ratification. Note, however, that a minor cannot effectively ratify a contract before entering majority.

Ratification: display of willingness to be bound by contract's terms

Unavoidable Contracts and Necessaries.   As you may have guessed, there are exceptions to the rule allowing minors to avoid their contracts. For example, some states bind minors to contracts in which they have misrepresented their age or to contracts that benefit their business interests. With this in mind, consider the following situation:

HYPOTHETICAL CASE

Both Ronald's and Sharlene's parents had known the marriage wouldn't last, but they had caved in and allowed the two minors to marry. Now, five months later, the two 17-year-olds were having big problems. Ronald, despondent over the pay he was earning at the car wash and without even mentioning the possibility to Sharlene, had just enlisted for a five-year stint in the Army. He would be in boot camp and advanced training for months. It was the last straw for Sharlene. She was packed and out of their tiny apartment just hours after he told her. Ronald was shocked when she left and even more shocked when she called and said that she would avoid their marriage contract if he went into the Army. Realizing that he had made a tremendous mistake, he called the Army recruiter to avoid his enlistment contract. Will either of these minors succeed in avoiding the contracts that bind them?

As you may have suspected, the answer is no in both instances. Minors cannot avoid valid enlistment or marriage contracts. In a somewhat similar vein, minors can be made to pay a reasonable value under executed contracts they make for items required to sustain life. Such items are termed *necessaries* by the law. In most states they include only food, clothing, and shelter (a few states added televisions and cars). If the law allowed minors to completely avoid contracts for necessaries, sellers would fear that after eating the food, wearing the clothing, and using the shelter, the minor would demand his or her money back. Sellers would therefore refuse to provide necessaries to anyone under 18.

Parental Liability.   Generally, parents are not liable for their minor child's contracts, but they may agree to assume such liability by serving as cosigners. However, the minor's right to avoid is not taken away by the parents' action.

Billie Buchard, barely 17 years old, watched as her dad cosigned the purchase contract and loan papers for her new speedboat. She had paid $2,000 down from her savings, and she could make the $147.60 monthly payments from her paycheck at McDonald's. The boat was perfect for her waterskiing and for entertaining her friends. As soon as her dad laid down the pen, Billie grabbed the keys on the salesman's desk and ran down to the dock. She warmed the 100-horsepower engine for a moment. By then her dad was at the dock shouting at her to wait. She laughed, waved at him, then gave the boat full throttle. Too late she thought of the stern line. As the boat shot forward, the thick rope played out for a fraction of a second, then stiffened and, with a tearing sound she would remember for years, ripped the back third of the boat off. Billie was thrown free and swam to shore as the boat, totally destroyed, sank to the bottom of the inlet. Her parents were so angry that they grounded her for six months. Out of spite, Billie then avoided her contract with the dealership. The dealership paid her back her $2,000 down payment and then billed her dad for it and the monthly payments. (Realize that if her parents had not cosigned, the dealership would have had to bear the whole loss, as Billie, upon avoiding, would have received her $2,000 back regardless.)

Finally, as discussed previously, minors can avoid most of the contracts that their parents have made for them. (See the *Brooke Shields* v. *Garry Gross* case at the end of Chapter 8.)

The Insane

In legal issues relating to capacity to contract, the insane are treated somewhat like minors. This holds especially true for individuals found by a court to be insane when they entered into a contract. If such individuals are found to be only temporarily insane, they are allowed to affirm or avoid their contracts whenever they become clearheaded (lucid) again. In the case of the permanently insane (as described below), their court-appointed representative may act to affirm or avoid. Regardless, the parties claiming this defense will be held liable to pay a reasonable value for necessaries. Note that mentally retarded individuals are presumed to have full capacity to contract unless the contrary is shown in court.

The treatment given the permanently insane under contract law is quite different. Realize that it takes a court proceeding to confer this status on a person. If the court does determine that a person is permanently insane, it will appoint a guardian for that person. The **guardian** is an individual who has been given the responsibility of taking care of the insane party. The guardian is also given the power to manage the **estate** of the insane party, meaning the real and personal property interests of that party, for the insane party's benefit.

Guardian: individual responsible for affairs of incapacitated party

Estate: property interests of person or entity

Once a person has been held to be permanently insane, that person's subsequent contracts, checks, notes, deeds, wills, and other legal actions are considered void. The court will intervene to rescind the contracts and otherwise preserve the interests of the insane party. It is even a crime in many states to knowingly take advantage of such a person. However, obligations for a reasonable value for necessaries provided to the insane can be enforced against the estate of an insane person.

Algernon L. Flowers, 84 years old and of substantial wealth, was declared permanently insane by the Greene County Court on July 24, 1992. Three months later, in response to her advances, he fell madly in love with Sally Benton, his nurse at the Last Daze Retirement Home. Nurse Benton, 41 years his junior, convinced Algernon that they should run away and be married. The following Saturday, Sally drove Algernon to a nearby state, where they were married. She then persuaded Algernon to sell his rings and expensive watch to finance their honeymoon. He did so. With the proceeds of the sales Algernon immediately rented the honeymoon suite in a nearby hotel and ordered champagne and caviar for their wedding feast. Algernon then gave Sally the remainder of the money he had with him, some $2,500. She was counting it when a deputy sheriff, alerted by a suspicious desk clerk at the hotel and by a missing person's report, knocked on the door of the suite. As a result of the deputy's investigation, Algernon was immediately returned to the retirement home. The legal effects of the "elopement" were longer lasting. Sally was charged under a state statute making it illegal for anyone to take advantage of an insane party. Sally's later claims to half ownership of all Algernon's property based on their marriage were rendered groundless when Algernon's guardian had the marriage contract canceled. The contracts for the sale of the rings and watch were rescinded. Finally, the hotel was paid out of Algernon's estate for the reasonable value of the shelter and food it had provided at his request.

The Intoxicated or Drugged

The law handles intoxicated or drugged individuals in a manner similar to its handling of the insane. Those individuals whom a court holds to have been temporarily incompetent due to alcohol or other drugs during the time they were making a contract will be allowed to avoid the contract. However, to be considered temporarily without capacity due to alcohol or other drugs, the persons claiming such incapacity must show that at the time they did so they did not even know they were entering into a contract. This is much harder to prove than the normal standard for lack of capacity, which is just being unable to understand the consequences of a contract.

A person considered by the law to be permanently without capacity to contract due to alcohol or drug use is termed a **habitual drunkard.** A habitual drunkard is a person who exhibits an involuntary tendency to become intoxicated as often as the temptation to do so is presented. The person may be more often sober than drunk. However, once the court has been shown that the person lacks the willpower needed to control his or her appetite for alcohol or drugs, it will relieve the person of his or her capacity to contract permanently.

Habitual Drunkard: person who becomes intoxicated whenever tempted

As with the permanently insane, a guardian will be appointed to handle the estate of the habitual drunkard. All contracts, checks, notes, will, deeds, and other legal actions taken by the incompetent will thereafter be considered void.

However, the doctrine of necessaries will apply to the habitual drunkard's contracts for food, clothing, or shelter.

HYPOTHETICAL CASE

Beth Lewis gingerly entered the hot bathwater. From the living room she could hear the sounds of the twins playing. The baby slept in his carrier beside the tub. Beth breathed deeply, exhaling slowly and softly. At last, she felt the tension start to melt away. George had gotten angry again this morning, especially when she had asked for some money to buy school clothes for their two oldest children. His drinking had gotten so much worse this last year. His booze was costing the better part of what was left after the bills were paid. Beth felt herself tense up again. She had to get the new clothes. George Jr., the oldest of the five Lewis children and a seventh grader, had come home practically in tears a week ago. His classmates had been teasing him about his old clothes. Beth knew that it would be months before the current styles appeared on the secondhand clothing racks she carefully shopped. The boy's grades were dropping too. He was so bright, but without a scholarship he'd never see college and neither would the other children. Beth was sure that George Sr., in a manner of speaking, would drink to that and would then get angry. She was worried about what his drunken fits of ill-temper would lead to. The children were frightened of him when he was drunk. They had all seen him hit her when he finally came home last Saturday night, and he'd threatened to do so again last night. Beth didn't want a divorce. When George was sober, he was wonderful. She had to stop his drinking, but how?

Of course, the reason for the above unfortunately stereotypical example is to suggest that the law might be able to help Beth and, in the long run, George Sr. If George Sr. were declared a habitual drunkard with Beth as his guardian, she would control the family's expenditures and George's access to cash. The liquor stores and the bars would soon realize that they could not expect payment for his checks as, at Beth's direction, the bank would not honor them. A good court-required alcohol abuse treatment program would also help. Times might be rough for a while, but no rougher than they would be if George continued on his present course. The jeopardy to the children's future alone should compel Beth to take the risk.

What Circumstances Can Legally Excuse Individuals from Their Contracts because Their Assent Was Not Genuine?

HYPOTHETICAL CASE

John Elza taught a high school business law class. One day, to explain a point about contract law, he offered to sell his 1982 convertible to anyone listening for $2,000. No one from the class spoke up, but another teacher, Sandra Pugh, who was walking past the classroom's open door, heard the offer. Sandra had ridden in the car and liked it. She poked her head in and said, "I'd pay $1,800." John replied, "$1,900."

continued on page 131

concluded

Sandra responded, "It's a deal." At that moment the bell rang. Most of the students left. Three hung around to ask questions. Before turning to the students, John asked Sandra whether she was serious. "Certainly," she responded. "I just can't pay you until the first of next month." John thought a minute, then said, "It'll cost you $1,925 if I have to wait that long." Sandra grimaced but agreed. John then turned to the students and answered their questions. After they left, John mentioned that the car's transmission was having problems that would take around $200 to fix. Sandra frowned. "Then I'll pay only $1,725." As if in agreement, John sat down and wrote out a contract. They photocopied it in the principal's office and signed both copies, each keeping one. That evening Sandra read the written contract for the first time and was angered to find that John had made the price $1,825. Would Sandra be bound by the written contract? Read further to find out.

At times, competent individuals may be forced, tricked, or otherwise improperly induced to enter into contracts. The desire of these individuals to be bound by such contracts may seem genuine. However, once they discover that they have been duped or once they are no longer threatened by whatever forced them into the bargain, they turn to the courts for release from the contractual obligations. The law does not always allow such individuals a way out. The freedom to contract we so prize includes a freedom to enter into bad bargains as well as good. In the following paragraphs we'll take a look at the most common problems in this area to see how the courts handle them. We begin with mistake, the excuse most commonly used by individuals who want out of their contracts.

Mistake

Mistakes can be made by one or all parties to a contract. A mistake made by only one party is called a **unilateral mistake.** If both or all parties err, it is termed a **mutual mistake.**

Unilateral Mistake. Unilateral mistakes can be of law or of fact. Where the mistake is in not knowing of a law or not knowing how a law is to be applied, the answer the courts give is simple. "Ignorance of the law is no excuse" expresses that answer best. The contract in question is then held to be valid and is enforced against the protesting party.

The most frequent unilateral mistake of fact is a failure to read the contract. In the above example Sandra Pugh committed such an error, and it could be costly to her. The law is impatient with individuals who do not act to protect themselves, especially by not doing something so simple and effortless as reading. Also, realize the complexity of the dispute involved if this written contract is placed in question before a court. Most of the business law class could be called on to testify that the real contract was for $1,900. Three students would indicate that the contract was for $1,925 with payment due on the first of the next month. Then the actual parties to the contract would offer two other versions, one for $1,725 and the other for $1,925.

Because of these and like problems, the law has devised several rules to simplify and lessen the burden of the court in such matters. The first rule is called

Unilateral Mistake:
contractual error made by only one party

Mutual Mistake:
contractual error made by both or all parties

Doctrine of Incorporation: writing that represents culmination of preceding oral bargaining

the **doctrine of incorporation.** This doctrine disregards oral bargains struck before a contract has been reduced to writing. It utilizes the commonsense argument that the parties will much more carefully deliberate over and choose the terms of a contract that they put in writing. They will pick whatever terms they want from any preceding oral attempts at the same bargain and incorporate those terms into the final written deal. So the doctrine of incorporation properly focuses exclusively on that writing.

Reinforcing the effect of the doctrine of incorporation is a second rule of like importance. This is called the **parol evidence rule.** It supports the doctrine of incorporation by disallowing oral (parol) testimony that contradicts, adds to, or modifies a written contract. The only exceptions to this rule are for situations in which evidence of fraud, incompleteness, ambiguity, or a similar problem is inherent in the contract.

Parol Evidence Rule: rule that disallows most of oral statements contradicting written contract

As you have probably guessed by now, these rules mean that bad news is in store for Sandra. Given the facts above, she will have to pay $1,825 for the car under what the law will hold to be a valid contract. Her unilateral mistake in failing to read the contract cost her $100. The only exceptions allowed by the courts in cases like Sandra's are for fine print appearing on what are essentially claim checks, such as those given out by parking garages, cleaning establishments, and so forth. The courts have consistently refused to enforce the fine print terms against the customers of such establishments. The courts feel that such customers only view the tickets as the means to reclaim their property, not even suspecting that they contain contract terms.

As a general rule, then, unilateral mistakes, whether of fact or law, do not release the mistaken parties from their contracts. The contracts remain valid, legally binding, and enforceable against those parties.

Mutual Mistake. Mutual mistakes can also be of either fact or law. As you can probably infer from the discussion on unilateral mistakes of law, mutual mistakes of law still result in a valid contract. Mutual mistakes of fact, however, are a different story.

HYPOTHETICAL CASE

Angelica owned an art gallery located in a very exclusive section of New York City. Her collection included two landscapes by a French painter named Slopée. One of the landscapes, entitled "Parisian Fields," was valued at over $50,000; the other, entitled, "same old field," at less than half that. Late one afternoon Gaston Dubarr the Third came into her office. He pounded his ivory-headed walking stick on the floor to get her attention, then announced, "I'll buy the Slopée landscape for $30,000." Angelica, presuming that he was bidding on the "same old field," since a Dubarr would never make such an insultingly low bid on "Parisian Fields," immediately accepted. She asked an attendant to place the painting in a suitable container while she collected Mr. Dubarr's check. Just as the shop closed, Mr. Dubarr left with his painting. That evening Angelica purchased three new sculptures for the shop with the funds from the Slopée sale. The next morning Mr. Dubarr's cane was banging on the shop door a half hour before opening time. Angelica let him in. With him came his chauffeur, who unceremoniously thrust the "same old field" at Angelica. Mr.

continued on page 133

concluded

Dubarr then insisted that he had bought "Parisian Fields" and demanded that painting. Angelica refused. Mr. Dubarr then demanded his money back. Angelica refused again. They next saw one another in court.

Angelica and Mr. Dubarr have made a mutual mistake of fact as to the identity of the subject matter of the contract. If their mutual mistake had been one relating to the appropriate value of a particular painting, such as "Parisian Fields," the court would rule the contract valid. In this situation, however, in which the parties were negotiating for altogether different items, the court will hold the contract not voidable but void. The court will then rescind the contract. As a consequence, Angelica will have to return the $30,000 to Dubarr, and he will have to return the "same old field" painting to her.

So if the mutual mistake concerns a difference in the valuation of an item properly identified to both parties, that difference is a matter of opinion and the contract is valid. If the mistake concerns the identity of the subject matter, that is, which item, the contract is void but will be rescinded by the court.

Concealment

As a general rule, a person negotiating a contract is not under a duty to voluntarily reveal everything known about the subject matter. The resulting contract is valid regardless. If the other parties want to know something, they are free to ask. The answer, if given, cannot knowingly be false. In addition, if the other parties should be able to discover a material fact about the subject matter with a reasonable investigation, the contract will be enforceable even by a party with knowledge of it who says nothing. **Material fact** as used here means a fact crucial to making or not making a contract. The court's logic here is simple. It does not want to spend its time getting people out of situations that they themselves could have prevented with reasonable diligence. A contracting party who wants to find out should ask. The other party will be held legally accountable if he or she then gives a knowingly false answer.

Material Fact: fact crucial to contracting

However, there are exceptions to this rule. In particular, courts recognize that certain relationships are rightly founded on trust. These are called **confidential relationships** (they are also called fiduciary relationships). For those in such a relationship who are contracting with each other, the law recognizes a legally enforceable duty that all material facts be revealed. So when contracts are formed, for example, between parents and children, doctors and patients, and attorneys and their clients, concealment of material facts, or, as it is legally phrased, "silence when it is one's duty to speak," can render the contracts voidable by the party from whom material information is withheld.

Confidential Relationships: personal associations built on trust

Misrepresentation and Fraud

Rather than concealing material facts, parties to contracts often misstate them. If this is done innocently, the resulting contract can be avoided by the improperly informed party. For example, if I am selling you my big-screen TV and tell you the three-year "parts and labor" warranty that still has 22 months to run will transfer to you when it will not, you can cancel the contract due to that misstatement. In other words, if I innocently misrepresented a material fact such as that, the courts will rescind the contract. We'll each get back what we put into the bargain.

However, if I intentionally lied about it, you might be able to show fraud. The courts would then allow you to cancel the contract, get your money back, and recover damages. **Fraud** occurs when someone makes an untrue or recklessly made statement of a material fact to induce another party to enter into a contract. The other party must enter the contract as a consequence of relying on the misstatement and be damaged as a result. To this rather lengthy list of elements that must be shown to prove fraud, some courts even add the requirement that the person who relies on the misstatement be unable to check on its accuracy by exercising due diligence. In short, fraud is rather difficult to prove. Making this even more difficult is the law's acceptance of the natural tendency of a seller to elaborate on the qualities of whatever is up for sale. Somewhat like the fisherman whose hands cannot get closer to each other than 2 feet when he or she is showing the length of the one that got away, the salesperson is expected to exaggerate somewhat. As long as the salesperson's statements are of opinions and not of facts, they are not considered fraudulent. For example, someone trying to sell parents a set of encyclopedias might state that having them available would raise their children's grades. This would not provide a basis for a fraud suit if little Jenny's grades plummet instead.

Fraud: improper deception in contracting

Undue Influence and Duress

We have just discussed mistake, concealment, innocent misrepresentation, and fraud, all of which deal with not knowing the correct facts to be used in deciding whether to enter a contract. Now we turn to undue influence and duress, which deal with forces that destroy the capability of persons to make a reasonable decision about contracting, whether or not they know the facts of the matter.

Both involve domination of one party by another. It is just the means by which this domination is effected that separate them. **Undue influence** is found where the dominating party to a confidential relationship (attorney to client, physician to patient, parent to young child, child to aging parent) has exerted irresistible pressure on the dominated party to enter a contract that benefits the former. Whether or not the dominating party lost his or her free will to contract under such circumstances is usually a question for the jury. If the jury concludes that such is the case, the contract is voidable by the dominated party.

Undue Influence: improper domination of contractual party

Legal **duress** is a wrongful threat that denies a person her or his free will to contract. The resulting contract is voidable by the party upon whom the duress was inflicted. Generally, a threat of bodily harm or death against the contracting party or his or her immediate family, a threat to burn down the contracting party's home, or a threat to bring a criminal action against the contracting party is considered legal duress. A threat of a civil suit or a threat that involves economic harm ("sign or you'll never do business in this town again") is not considered legal duress and thus does not render voidable the contract that results.

Duress: improper coercion to enter contract

Whom Will the Law Excuse from the Requirement to Fulfill Contractual Obligations?		Figure 10–1

Parties Excused Due to a Lack of Capacity	Parties Excused because They Contracted Without Giving their Genuine Assent Due to:
• Minors • The insane • The intoxicated	• Mistake • Concealment • Misrepresentation • Fraud • Undue influence • Duress • Unconscionability

Unconscionability

All of the problems with genuineness of assent that we've discussed so far are individual ones. They focus on the contracting party's lack of ability to properly evaluate and freely enter a contract due to factors peculiar to that person or the contractual setting. However, our courts have also had to deal with cases in which fully informed, capable individuals out of necessity entered contracts that gave lopsided advantages to the other parties. Typically, such contracts met all of the traditional tests for a valid, legally enforceable, contract. To somehow grant relief from such oppressive bargains, the courts had to formulate a new doctrine. That doctrine was unconscionability.

An **unconscionable contract** is one entered into as a result of the greatly unequal bargaining power of one party, who makes a take it or leave it offer to the other party without any viable market alternative. If the resulting contract is grossly unfair to the weaker party, the offending section of the contract is void.

Unconscionable Contract: grossly unfair bargain

APPLICATIONS OF WHAT YOU'VE LEARNED

Vocabulary Development

Fill in the blanks with the appropriate term.

Confidential Relationships	Duress	Majority	Ratification
Contractual Capacity	Estate	Material Fact	Unconscionable Contract
Disaffirm	Fraud	Minor	Undue Influence
Doctrine of Incorporation	Guardian	Mutual Mistake	Unilateral Mistake
	Habitual Drunkard	Parol Evidence Rule	

1. "This car is the best bargain I've had on my car lot since I opened it." "Of course, I can do your surgery. I have the steadiest hand in the entire country when it comes to working on a person's brain." "I'm sure I can win this case. I always put the best interests of my clients ahead of my own, just like all other attorneys."

   These exaggerations would probably not be a basis for a _____ suit.

2. How many miles a car has been driven is usually a(n) _____
   _____ in the bargaining for the sale of a car.

3. "Sign the contract, or I'll report your tax dodge to the IRS for prosecution" is a good example of _____ .

4. A person under the age of capacity is termed a(n) _____ .

5. "Every party I go to with her she gets intoxicated. I'm afraid to let her drive home. She just can't turn down a drink." These words might describe a(n) _____ .

6. If a court declares the person described in Question 5 incompetent, it will appoint a(n) _____ to manage the _____ of that person.

7. Making four monthly payments on a financing contract for a car after turning 18 is good evidence that a(n) _____ of the contract by the minor obligor has occurred.

Problems

1. Brenda Sanders, 17 years old, bought the dune buggy from a dealership in Santa Monica, California. She drove it home, parked it in the driveway, got out and found her father waiting for her. "Take it back right now. The bank called and said you'd cleaned out our joint account of all your college money for a down payment. Go get your money and your future back from those car salesmen." Brenda frowned, then shrugged her shoulders and without comment fired up the engine. She drove around the house's circular drive and came to a stop at the street. To the left was the beach; to the right was the dealership. Brenda turned right and smashed head-on into a new limousine. Luckily, no one was injured. The property damage totaled over $7,000. When Brenda filed for coverage under the family car insurance policy, which covered new purchases without requiring notification up to 10 days, the insurance company refused to pay, saying that the car dealership's policy should cover the damages because Brenda had avoided the contract. Do you agree? Why or why not?

2. Can a minor ever avoid his or her contracts after attaining majority? Why or why not? Can a minor ever ratify her or his contracts before attaining majority? Why or why not? Should minors be able to use their minority status to take unfair advantage of parties that would sell to them (for example, should minors be able to buy tickets from airlines, use the tickets, and then avoid the contract to get their money back)? Why or why not?

3. A court-determined habitual drunkard goes into a bar and runs up a $357 tab. He then buys two bottles from the liquor store affiliated with the bar. He writes a check to pay for the amount he owes and leaves. What is the status of the contracts the drunkard made in the bar and liquor store? Who can stop payment on the check? Is it ethical to treat such businesses as the bar and liquor store in this manner?

4. Now drop back over a century for a classic true case. Two ships, each bearing the name *Peerless,* were scheduled to leave Bombay, India, for England. One was to leave it in October, the other in December. A buyer accepted an offer to sell bales of cotton on the ship he believed was sailing in October. The seller was instead referring to bales of cotton on the ship sailing in December. How did the court resolve the breach of contract suit that the buyer filed when the cotton did not arrive on time?

5. Bill and his wife, now divorced, were separated when he signed an agreement dividing up the marital property. Today he greatly regrets entering into the agreement and claims that he did so only because of his wife's threat to bring criminal child abuse charges against him. Can he get out of the agreement if this is shown to be true? Could be get out of it if he maintained that he entered into it because of his wife's threat to sue him for damages for battering her?

ACTUAL CASE STUDY

United States v. Gorham and Wilkerson

523 F.2d 1088

Consider the "appeal of the miffed escapees" based on the idea that "if you can't trust the commissioner of corrections who can you trust?"

For some time prior to October 11, 1972, while appellants Gorham and Wilkerson, a/k/a Robert Jones (hereinafter Jones), were confined as inmates at the District of Columbia jail, they conspired to escape from that facility and in furtherance of the plan, obtained a loaded .38-caliber pistol. In the early morning hours of October 11, 1972, Jones feigned sickness, and when two correction officers entered his cell to assist him, Gorham assaulted them with the pistol and took them as hostages. Gorham and Jones proceeded to take control of the entire cellblock and to release other prisoners to assist them in obtaining additional hostages. These hostages eventually included Kenneth L. Hardy, District of Columbia Corrections Director. In furtherance of their demand that they be released, appellants made numerous threats of violence against their hostages, used some of them as shields, and with the inmates who had joined them employed other stratagems in pursuit of their freedom. All of their efforts were thwarted, and the jail authorities eventually reacquired control of the cellblock and the entire jail complex.

In the aftermath of this episode Gorham and Jones were transferred to the maximum security

"penthouse" area of the jail. While they were confined there, appellants obtained several hacksaw blades, sawed through two iron bars in a window, and on October 25, 1972, effected their escape by means of a "makeshift Jacob's ladder, fashioned from bedsheets in the classical manner" (quoted from trial brief).

In this appeal, appellants contend that the trial judge's failure to recognize as binding an agreement made during the riot was reversible error. This agreement, in which the government agreed not to punish the prisoners for their actions, made the subsequent confinement of Gorham and Jones in the maximum security cells improper. The agreement was extracted from D.C. Corrections Director Kenneth Hardy while he was a hostage.

In ultimately deciding this case, the Court of Appeals stated, "We find no merit to these contentions and no error in the trial and affirm all convictions on all (22) counts."

Questions

1. On what basis do you think the courts refused to regard as valid the agreement not to punish the prisoners?

2. Considering the possibility of future hostage situations, is disregarding the agreement a wise policy decision? Do you think "policy" entered into the judge's decision to ignore the agreement?

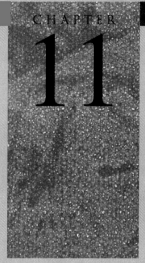

CHAPTER

11

When Is Consideration Present?

CHAPTER OUTLINE AND OBJECTIVES

After studying this chapter, the student will be able to:

I. Provide the legal definition of consideration and explain its importance.
   a. Legal effect of a promise without consideration
   b. Adequacy of consideration

II. Distinguish what the law holds to be legally binding consideration from nonbinding consideration.
   a. Legally binding consideration
   b. Nonbinding consideration

III. Identify the exceptions that the law allows to its rule requiring consideration and explain why these exceptions are allowed.
   a. When a debt is barred from collection by the Statute of Limitations or a bankruptcy proceeding
   b. When the court uses promissory estoppel
   c. When the promises are made for the support of charitable institutions or other nonprofit organizations.

IV. Analyze the case of *United States* v. *McBride et al.* to see how a court used the concept of consideration to determine whether a deal between the US government and a group of extortionists was valid.

At the very heart of the freedom to contract is the ability to "name your price." In other words, you have a right to indicate what you must receive in return for being bound to your offer. For example, let us assume that we are bargaining over the sale of my grand piano to you when you finally state, "All right, I'll buy that piano for $2,500." Now you'd expect to be bound to your offer only if I promised to transfer ownership of that piano to you in return for that amount of money. That promise to you is, in effect, what you demanded in return for making your offer into a promise that is binding against you. In general, then, the supplying of what would-be promisors require in return for being bound to their offer is one of the main things the law looks for in a contract suit. This chapter focuses on how the law makes sure this essential element of an enforceable contract, labeled consideration, is present.

What Is the Legal Definition of Consideration?

Consideration: whatever is demanded to bind promisor to promise

To express it in more concise legal terms, **consideration** is what the offeror demands and, in most situations, must receive in return for making his or her offer into a promise that is legally binding against him or her.

Legal Effect of a Promise without Consideration

Gift: donation

If someone offers to do something for you without naming the consideration that she or he wants in return, the offer can be no more than a stated intent to make a gift. A **gift** is a transfer of property by one party, acting voluntarily and without consideration, to another party. Under our legal system, a statement of intent to give standing alone is unenforceable in a court of law. "I'll give you my piano" is far different from "I'll give you my piano if you'll pay me $2,500 for it." The former is interpreted as a stated intent to make a gift and needs much more to be legally binding. The latter, of course, is a contractual offer.

In almost all gift situations, the stated intent to donate must be accompanied by a delivery and acceptance of the subject matter of the gift to be of any legal significance. As a consequence, getting the promisor of a donation to complete the intended gift typically remains only a moral issue between the would-be **donor** (giver) and the **donee** (intended recipient of the gift). This is not the case in several other Western legal systems, particularly those of Western Europe, in which a promise to make a gift can be legally enforceable against its maker.

Donor: giver of gift

Donee: recipient of gift

In our legal system, however, rather than making all such promises enforceable, we let the presence or absence of consideration guide us in picking which of them we'll let our courts enforce.

Adequacy of Consideration

As long as the would-be promisor is capable of making a genuine offer, the law gives each of us the latitude to determine what amount of consideration is adequate for the good or service we're offering. If I want to sell my Picasso to you for $10,000 cash even though its market value is over $100,000, the law leaves that decision to me. Perhaps I need the money right away, or perhaps my decision is based on tax considerations; the reason doesn't matter as long as I am a capable adult making a legally enforceable offer.

Madison Barnes was in his last year of law school when his mother was approached by Horace Hillbarn. "He just walked right up and asked me to sign away my rights in that old warehouse your dad owned before he died," Mrs. Barnes told Madison over the phone. "He said he'd been in it over 10 years now and that if I didn't sign, even though he can't find the deed to the property he claims your dad gave him, he'd take me to court for it. You're about to become a lawyer, son. Can you come out and defend me if he does?" Madison thought a moment, then replied. "Sorry, Mom, I can't do that till I'm licensed by passing the bar exam, and that'll be months yet. Otherwise, the only way I could argue the case would be if it were my own property. Then I could appear on my own behalf. Anyone can argue their own case under our system. It's called appearing "pro se." Of course, here in school they say that the lawyer who argues his own case has a fool for a client." Both Barneses laughed. Finally, Mrs. Barnes said, "All right, Madison, how about this? Would you like to buy my rights for $1? You may end up owning a warehouse." Madison replied quickly, "Good idea, Mom. I'll buy it for that. At least Horace won't get the property without a fight, and legal fees can be expensive. The only thing is, I've got to actually give you the $1. The courts won't care how much I bought your rights for, but the other attorney will check to be sure that we went through with the transaction." Madison then sent Mrs. Barnes a check for $1 which she cashed and spent. He used the canceled check and a written contract of sale he'd drawn and had Mrs. Barnes sign as evidence of his rights in the warehouse. Later that year, after graduation from law school and while studying for the bar, Madison argued and won the lawsuit for himself. He later sold the warehouse for $45,000 and gave an undisclosed amount of the sale price to his mother.

What Does the Law Hold to Be Legally Binding Consideration?

The law is full of surprises. Some of these surprises come in what the law does and does not hold to be legally binding consideration.

Legally Binding Consideration

Promises.   Generally, a promise is held to be legally binding consideration. When a person offers to sell you a big-screen television for $2,000, he or she doesn't expect that you'll have the cash with you. Instead, the offeror will want you to accept the offer by giving him or her a promise to pay that amount at some time in the future. That promise is consideration, and it will legally bind the offeror to a promise to transfer ownership of the television to you.

Exchange of Value. Another form of valid consideration is found in things of value that are immediately given to the promisor to bind her or him to his promise. **Money** is the thing of value most frequently used in this way. It is a medium of exchange that a government has selected or created for just this purpose. Typically, what we refer to as "cash" has little, if any, functional use except to serve as a standard for determining relative value. Without money, we must barter good for good for the things we need or desire. Without money, statements like, "I'll give you two chickens and that stack of cherrywood over by the barn for that rocking chair you just made" would be the rule, not the exception. Of course, goods and services are legal consideration in their own right. When they are exchanged for other goods and services without the use of money, the exchange is called a **barter.**

Money: governmentally endorsed medium of commercial exchange

Barter: direct exchange of items in commerce without use of money

Forbearance

> Marsha Hollander glared across her desktop at the soles of Will Stuart's size 10s. His desk fronted on hers. Now, head thrown back, staring at the ceiling of the newsroom, Will was smoking another of his cigars. The smoke rose 2 feet above his head, where it formed a spiraling cloud of toxic elements that reached out to engulf her. As in the past, Marsha felt her sinuses tightening; she knew that the first of a freight train of body-convulsing sneezes was on its way. He had ignored her past complaints, and shooting him was eliminated by the number of witnesses, so now it was time for plan B. Marsha grabbed her nose, then made Will Stuart an offer she prayed he couldn't refuse. "Look, Will, you know what those cigars do to me. I know you've got every right to smoke them, but they're killing me. Would you take $500 not to smoke in here for a year?" With a smile, Will nodded and stuck out his hand.

Forbearance: refraining from exercising right

If Will does not smoke for a year, would he be able to hold Marsha to her promise in a court of law? The answer is certainly. Refraining from doing something you have a legitimate right to do is termed **forbearance.** Either a promise to forbear or the actual forbearance is sufficient consideration to bind those who demand that forbearance in return for their promise. A promise not to follow through on your intention to sue someone where you have a reasonable right to do so is also consideration. So if I promise to pay for the harm done to your car plus $250 if you won't sue me for my negligence in an accident, your forbearance would bind me to my promise.

Nonbinding Consideration

Past Consideration. Sometimes, however, promises that appear to be valid consideration are not.

Grateful to his friend, Helen, who had taken him in one bitterly cold evening years ago, John Stroll, a formerly homeless person, wrote out the following promissory note: "For goods provided and services rendered, I promise to pay to the order of Helen Santos $15,000." The note was dated and signed. When John presented it to her before leaving, she frowned and said, "No, John, I can't." He smiled. "Remember, Helen, how you said we all need our dignity. This will help preserve mine." She thought a moment, then took the note. "Goodbye . . . you were the son I never had." John hugged her, grabbed his suitcase, and walked out the door.

A nice story, a gracious lady, and a gentlemanly exit, but Helen could not collect on the promise John put in writing. Why? Because all that Helen did for John is termed **past consideration.** Such consideration is not legally binding as it was given without expectation of or demand for a binding promise in return. Even when placed in the form of a promissory note, a promise without legally binding consideration is unenforceable in a court of law.

Past Consideration: something previously given without demand for anything in return

Promise to Perform a Preexisting Obligation. Another circumstance in which what appears to be consideration is not occurs when the return promise requires the performance of a task that the promisor is already obligated to do.

Such a return promise is not taken as legal consideration.

For example, suppose you promise to pay:

A member of the city fire department $50 a month to check your building every night before she goes off duty.

An on duty cop $7.50 each time he shows up at your store at closing to protect you as you transfer your cash to the bank.

Windblown, Inc., $950 for each sail it provides instead of the $750 price it agreed to under its two-year contract with your sailboat manufacturing company.

Are these promises legally binding against you? The answer is no. This is because in each instance the consideration you received for your promise is merely a **promise to perform a preexisting duty.** In other words, it is a promise to do something that the promisor is already legally obligated to do, either by a previous contract with you or by a duty owed to the public. In the first two instances, the public servants involved are already obligated to perform the duties mentioned, so their promises cannot be valid consideration. The promises you made in return are therefore not legally binding on you. In the last instance, the result is the same, but it stems from the private contractual obligation to you that Windblown, Inc. had previously assumed.

Promise to Perform a Preexisting Duty: stated intent to accomplish an established legal responsibility

What Exceptions Does the Law Allow to Its Rule Requiring Consideration for Every Binding Promise?

At times, the law will abandon the general rule that consideration is required for a promise to be legally binding.

When a Debt Is Barred by the Statute of Limitations or a Bankruptcy Proceeding

Statute of Limitations: legal time limit for bringing civil or criminal action

If I borrowed money from you 12 years ago and have not yet repaid it, your right to enforce that debt against me today in a court of law would be barred by the **statute of limitations** in our state. Such statutes limit the time a person has to bring suit. The limits vary, depending on the nature of the possible action. For oral contracts, the limits range from a minimum of 2 years in a few states to a maximum of 10 years in one state; most states set the limits between 3 and 5 years. For written contracts, the limits range between 3 and 15 years.

However, even after the statute limits have been passed, if I reaffirm the debt, no consideration is necessary to bind me to my new promise. The same rule applies to debts I owed you before I filed bankruptcy but which, because of the legal effect of that process, now cannot be collected through the courts. For example, if I meet you at our 15th high school reunion and, feeling guilty or embarrassed or missing your friendship or for no recognizable reason, promise that I will pay back the money you loaned me on graduation day, that promise will be effective against me without consideration. In most states the promise is enforceable even if made orally. If the promise is to reaffirm a debt barred by bankruptcy, however, the current federal Bankruptcy Act requires a formal statement at a hearing. (Read more about the fascinating, tricky, and sometimes even rewarding world of bankruptcy in Chapters 23 and 24.)

When the Court Uses Promissory Estoppel

Equity: basic fairness

Promissory Estoppel: equitable remedy stopping promisor for claiming lack of consideration for promise upon which promisee has relied

At times a rigid adherence to the letter of the law can produce injustice. As a consequence, the law allows courts to counteract this effect by taking certain actions in the name of **equity** (basic fairness). One such action that the courts can take is the use of the doctrine of promissory estoppel. When brought into use (or "invoked," to be more accurate) by the courts, **promissory estoppel** prevents promisors from stating that they did not receive consideration for their promises. Now, if you think for a moment, you'll realize that, under the doctrine of consideration, if the courts stop people from stating that they didn't get what they demanded in return for being bound to their promises, then those promises can be enforced against them.

To get a court to invoke promissory estoppel, the person who requests it has to show first of all that a promise was made that could reasonably be expected to induce action on the promisee's part. Then, if the promisee acts in response to that promise and if an injustice can be avoided only by the court's enforcement of the promise, it will invoke promissory estoppel. All of these requirements filter out a

Exceptions to the Requirement of Consideration for a Legally Binding Promise

Table 11–1

A promise to renew a debt barred by the statute of limitations or a bankruptcy proceeding.

Instances in which a court estops a promisor from claiming a lack of consideration for his or her promise.

Situations in which a promise is made for the support of a charitable institution or another nonprofit organizations.

lot of situations in which the doctrine cannot be used, mainly because centuries of experience have provided other remedies. Promissory estoppel therefore remains only a last resort used by the legal system to correct injustices that have slipped through the cracks of established contract law.

HYPOTHETICAL CASE

Diamond Gym, a regionally famous East Coast entertainer whose real name was James Barrett, had been offered a six-month run as a single act at the Lagoon Lounge in Atlantic City. The owner of the Lagoon, Arty Slaw, had said he would pay three times what Barrett was making. So Barrett had given notice that this evening would be the last show of his current engagement. He fished in his pocket for Slaw's card, found it, and called him. The phone rang for only a fraction of a second. "Yeah," Slaw's voice thundered. "Arty," Jim responded, "I just ended my current contract, and I'm ready to appear at the Lagoon. Didn't you mention that I could start next week." There was a pause at the other end. Then Slaw said, "Look, kid, I hired a new act just yesterday. Shoulda called you but didn't. Them's the breaks. Keep in touch." Without waiting for a reply, Slaw slammed down the receiver. Diamond Gym stared at his phone for a while. It was true that there wasn't a contract, but Slaw must have known that Barrett would end his current contract so that he could go to work at the Lagoon. The other clubs where Barrett normally performed were booked months ahead. Despondent, he picked up the phone to call his lawyer.

Should Diamond Gym elect to sue Arty Slaw, his attorney will probably request that the court use the doctrine of promissory estoppel. If the court agrees, it will not let Slaw raise lack of consideration as a defense. As a consequence, Slaw will be bound to his promise of employment and will have to pay damages to Barrett for breaking it.

When the Promises Are Made for the Support of Charitable Institutions or Other Nonprofit Organizations

Universities, hospitals, public broadcasting, churches, charities ranging from the Red Cross to Save the Seals, and many other beneficial organizations depend on their donors for their very existence. Their annual budgets and the special projects they undertake are based on reliable sources of funds. Therefore, as a matter of public policy enforced by the application of promissory estoppel, courts have held that pledges of contributions to such organizations are binding on the parties who make those promises.

APPLICATIONS OF WHAT YOU'VE LEARNED

Vocabulary Development

Fill in the blanks with the appropriate term.

Barter	Equity	Past Consideration	Promissory Estoppel
Consideration	Forbearance	Promise to Perform a	Statute of Limitations
Donee	Gift	Preexisting Duty	
Donor	Money		

1. Bart said to Brett, "I'll trade you this fine stallion of mine for that quarterhorse colt of yours." This is an example of a proposed __barter__ contract.

2. To bind Brett to his promise in Question 1, Bart has named the __consideration__ he must receive.

3. If Bart had instead said, "Because you took care of my ranch while I was in jail, even without my asking you to, this stallion is yours," the delivery of the stallion by Bart and its acceptance by Brett would have completed a(n) __gift__.

4. Brett's taking care of the ranch would be _____ _____

for Bart's promise to transfer ownership of the stallion to him.

5. Assume that Brett relied on Bart's promise to give him the stallion and spent a lot of resources in anticipation of owning it and that Bart then changed his mind and decided to keep the stallion. Out of a sense of basic fairness or _____, a court might listen to a request by Brett to force Bart to transfer ownership of the stallion to him.

6. The court might even use the doctrine of _____ _____

to disallow any attempted showing by Bart that he didn't get any consideration to bind him to his promise.

Problems

1. Terry Firm owned a minerals and precious gems shop. He often sold his merchandise at weekend flea markets. At such a market Crystal Beam, a seven-year-old, bought a "pretty rock" from Terry for $5. Crystal paid for the stone with her own money. Later a licensed gemologist valued her purchase at over $24,000. Hearing of this, Terry then sued to undo the sales contract because he had not received adequate consideration for the purchase and because Crystal was a minor. Will Terry succeed? (This account is based on an actual incident.)

2. Football coach of the LeBrea High School Reptiles, Brutus ("Who Needs Helmets") Concussionus offered to pay the math teacher of one of his linemen $20 per hour to tutor the lineman each day during a free school period. The money was to be

paid in December out of the Reptile's Nest Booster Fund. The teacher accepted the offer. By the end of the season, the teacher was owed some $1,700. However, the fund's board of directors refused to pay. The teacher brought suit, but the court upheld the board's refusal because of a problem with the consideration that the teacher gave to bind the Reptile's boosters to the contract. What was that problem?

3. Bono Chumpson loaned his son's baseball coach $750 to keep the bank from foreclosing on the coach's house. The coach never repaid the loan. When Bono finally brought suit in small claims court over four years later, the judge threw out the case as the statute of limitations had run out. One day in the Mall, Bono asked the coach in front of

witnesses why he had not repaid the loan. The coach was embarrassed and promised to do so. Can Bono enforce this new promise? Why or why not?

4. Al Lumus of Brooklyn, New York, was contacted by a representative of Hosanna High during its "buy a piece of heaven" fund drive. Hosanna was a grade and high school set up by the famous televangelist Helen Razor. It was supported by charitable contributions from around the United States and Latin America. Caught up in the spirit of the moment, Al, a 1978 Hosanna graduate, pledged

over $72,000 to help fund a new media center at the school. A few weeks later Al noticed an article in New York–based *SSSHHHH! Magazine* relating that Hosanna was making films opposing family planning of any and all types and sending the films to developing countries. As Al believed fervently that the overpopulated developing countries needed family planning, he thereafter refused to send in the amount of his pledge. Can Hosanna High legally compel him to pay it the money he promised? Why or why not?

ACTUAL CASE STUDY

United States v. John McBride, Michael Allen Worth, Theodore Duane McKinney, and Jill Renee Bird

571 Federal Supplement 596

On September 28, 1982, the president and the three vice presidents of Gulf Oil Corporations received a letter announcing that the "Gulf Chemical Cedar Bayou Plant and one other Gulf facility have been sabotaged." The letter also stated that "in excess of 10 explosive charges have been placed within the Cedar Bayou Plant. These charges are both radio actuated and time actuated. The radio charges may be detonated from any point within a twenty (20) mile radius of this facility. The time-actuated charges will self-detonate starting 120 hours after 10:00 AM on the morning you receive this letter; the time charges will continue to detonate up to seven days after this time . . . The purchase price to Gulf for the locations and deactivation sequences for the bombs at Cedar Bayou and one other plant to be discussed is $15 million, a fraction of Cedar Bayou's value and annual producing income."

Investigating FBI agents arrested Michael Worth and Theodore McKinney in Phoenix, Arizona, in the course of arranging by telephone to have them pick up the $15 million. Agents later traced the plot to John McBride and Jill Bird and arrested them in Durango, Colorado. Shortly after McBride's arrest, he stated to an FBI agent that he would give the government everything it needed in exchange for the government's agreement to certain terms, including the release and nonprosecution of Bird.

Assistant US Attorney Patrick T. Murphy, under pressure to accept McBride's offer from a variety of sources, including the FBI, bargained with McBride

concerning these terms. In considering his decision, Murphy contacted an assistant US attorney in Houston, Texas, because both Colorado and Texas had jurisdiction over the matter. Murphy later testified that he accepted the deal after suitable consultation, during which he received approval to go ahead. McBride thereupon revealed that all of the bombs had already been found and dismantled.

Regardless, Bird was released by order of the Colorado US Attorney's Office in accordance with the agreement but then indicted by the US Attorney's Office in Texas. She made a motion to dismiss the indictment based on the government's agreement.

The testimony of Assistant US Attorney Langoria, who was the party in the Texas office contacted by Murphy before he decided to make the agreement, is extremely significant in the court's decision. That testimony, as summarized by the court, is as follows:

He [Langoria] said that he viewed McBride's offer as coercive, that it seemed to him they were being extorted, and he indicated to Murphy that he believed the agreement was voidable. On the other hand, he testified that he did not express dissatisfaction with approval of the agreement but, on behalf of the United States Attorney in Houston [who later secured the indictment of Bird], agreed that the agreement was a good deal. He testified that the government was getting something in exchange for something: that the something they were getting was the peace of mind that they would have in knowing that there were no more bombing devices in the refinery, and that the government entered the agreement in good faith. He testified that the government's reputation is only as good as its word, but also that good faith meant that the government would keep its promise, all other things being equal . . . Langoria concluded his testimony by stating that the government should honor its agreement, assuming it was valid and the government was going to get what it bargained for.

Questions

1. Would you rule to uphold the agreement in this case? Why or why not?

2. How do you think the court ruled?

3. Can you trust the government?

4. If you reach an agreement with the federal government to avoid prosecution under a federal criminal statute for, let's say, kidnapping, do you think you could still be prosecuted by a state government for the same crime?

CHAPTER

12

How Do Statutes Affect the Form and Enforceability of Contracts?

CHAPTER OUTLINE AND OBJECTIVES

After studying this chapter, the student will be able to:

I. Explain the law's position on oral contracts.
   a. The general rule
   b. Practical matters of enforcement

II. Identify which contracts must be in writing to be enforceable.
   a. The Statute of Frauds
   b. Rules of evidence that reinforce the effect of the Statute of Frauds
   c. Contracts that require a writing

III. Identify contracts that are unenforceable by the courts due to their improper objectives.
   a. Contracts partially or wholly unenforceable due to illegal objectives
   b. Contracts partially or wholly unenforceable due to being against public policy

IV. Analyze *In the Matter of Baby M*, a case that dealt with the ethical and contractual issues surrounding the use of surrogate mothers.

Are Oral Contracts Valid and Enforceable in a Court of Law?

The answer to this question lies in the historical ties of our legal system to English law. Through those ties we can trace the origin of our contract law back five or more centuries to a time when few people could read or write. As you can infer, the people of that day made mostly oral contracts. The law confirmed the existence of those contracts through the testimony of witnesses under oath. Although there were many problems with having to rely on oral testimony, the courts had no choice if they were to serve the needs of the people.

The General Rule

The general rule in force then remains in force today: Oral contracts are legally valid, binding, and enforceable in a court of law.

Practical Matters of Enforcement

Of course, such a rule presents all kinds of practical problems. Chief among those problems is finding witnesses who heard and accurately remember all of the terms agreed to. Perjury runs a close second on this list of problems. However, the alternative of not enforcing any oral contracts would present a problem of a far greater magnitude. At the extreme, it is possible for a contract case to be conducted without witnesses other than the parties to the contract. Such a case would boil down to having just those parties testify in court as to what was involved. It would then be up to the trier of fact to determine whom to believe about what was agreed to. The court would then enforce the contract resulting from this process.

Which Contracts Must Be in Writing to Be Enforceable?

The Statute of Frauds

History. As the years went by, the number of people who could read and write increased. At the same time, the courts became more and more uncomfortable with the enforcement of all oral contracts due to the uncertainty of their terms and the possibilities for injustice that they presented. In the middle of the 17th century, England was swept by allegations of widespread lying under oath concerning the existence and terms of some very important contracts. Parliament reacted in 1677 by passing the Act for the Prevention of Fraud and Perjuries. This act, which is today in use in one form or another in each of our states, has become known as the Statute of Frauds.

Liz Fisher shook her head and began to cry. They were going to take it all from her. Today three pushy real estate developers were going to testify against her in court. Their stories parroted one another. They would each lie by saying that she had promised to take their combined offer of $1.5 million for her 40-acre estate. Oh, they had talked with her about a $7.5 million deal. And it was true that they had even given her a check for $50,000. She had deposited the check and was spending it because she needed the money. But they had given it to her in return for her promise not to sell the estate to anyone else for three months. She hadn't agreed to sell it to them. Now one of the developers even said that right after their negotiations he had made a memo of the deal that he would show the court. It may be hopeless. Liz thought, but if I have to fight, then fight I will. She went into her bedroom to change clothes for court.

Form and Interpretation. In its current form, the **Statute of Frauds** requires that in certain contract situations a written contract be produced in court. This "writing" must be signed by the party against whom enforcement of the contract is sought. For Liz in the above situation, this is good news, as agreements to sell land come under the Statute of Frauds. Therefore, if she denies that there was a contract for the sale of her estate, the developers will have to produce a writing. Such a writing must, at a minimum, identify the subject matter of the contract (the estate), specify the consideration (the price), and be signed by the party against whom enforcement is sought (Liz). The signatures of the developers are not necessary as they are bringing suit for the contract's enforcement and must therefore submit to those terms. Note, though, that if Liz admits to the contract in court under oath, the contract will be enforceable without a writing.

Statute of Frauds: law requiring written contract for enforcement

We will discuss the various situations that require a writing in just a moment. However, now is a good time to emphasize that getting a contract in writing is a good idea anytime, not just when this is required by the Statute of Frauds. The old saying "Strong fences good neighbors make" has its place in contract law. A writing is a strong guarantee that a court will enforce what it contains. Therefore, both parties are more likely to stay with the terms of a written agreement than with those of an oral agreement.

Rules of Evidence That Reinforce the Effect of the Statute of Frauds

The Parol Evidence Rule. Also realize that the strength of a writing used as evidence in court is reinforced by court procedure in the form of the parol evidence and best evidence rules. As discussed in Chapter 10, the parol evidence rule will not allow oral (parol) testimony in court that would change or add to the terms of a written contract. This is because a written contract takes more time and deliberation to prepare and is therefore more likely to be in a final form agreeable to all before it is signed. Also, the alternative, oral negotiations, may give the appearance of contract formation to innocent witnesses and yet be only a part of the progress toward a final agreement. To illustrate:

HYPOTHETICAL CASE

Professor Lee Galese used his car, a Fiat convertible, as the subject matter for his examples of how contracts work. He would lecture, then make an offer to sell the car to a class member. "I'll sell you my 1982 Fiat convertible for $2,000" became a joke among many students. During one lecture, however, a student named Johnson surprised Galese by making a serious counteroffer of $1,700. Just as the period ended, Galese agreed to the deal in front of the whole class. The classroom emptied quickly. As the last three students filtered out, they overheard Galese's and Johnson's oral contract fall apart when Johnson said he could not pay Galese until the first of the month. Galese then said that he would take $1,750, the additional $50 being his payment for waiting until the first. Johnson agreed. The three students then left. As the classroom door closed behind them, Galese remembered that his alternator light had been coming on as he drove in that morning. "I just remembered," Galese said, downcast, "the car probably needs a new alternator. It will cost $100." Johnson thought a moment, then replied, "Tell you what, I'll pay you $1,625 for it as is. That's the $1,750 less the $100 for the part and $25 for my labor in installing it." "Fine," said Galese. "Let's put it in writing." Galese wrote out the contract, then they photocopied it, and each signed the other's copy. The first of the month came around and Galese refused to take $1,625 for the car, saying he had a classroom with some witnesses who would say that the deal was for $1,700 and others who would say that the price was $1,750. Which contract would the courts enforce?

In this and similar situations in which a party denies the validity of a written contract, the law avoids a complex trial by enforcing the parol evidence rule. If it did not, the courts would face innocent, sincere witnesses (such as the various class members in the above situation testifying to the existence of contract terms totally different from those of the real bargain). So, in the case of *Johnson* v. *Galese,* Galese would have the written contract enforced against him for $1,625 as long as Johnson held on to his copy for evidence. Note that if the writing leaves important terms out or is ambiguous, then parol or other less reliable evidence will be allowed to clarify the intent of the parties.

Best Evidence Rule: allows only primary evidence before court

The Best Evidence Rule.   As mentioned, the **best evidence rule** also reinforces the strength of a writing as the determinative evidence of a contract. It does so by allowing only primary evidence, for example the original of a contract, to be placed before the court. Such secondary evidence as copies of the contract will be allowed only if the original contract has been lost or destroyed.

The combined effect of the parol and best evidence rules is to make an original of a written contract vastly superior to any other documentation of that agreement in the eyes of the court.

Contracts That Require a Writing

In most states the Statute of Frauds specifies five or six situations in which a writing is required. The situations most frequently included are the following:

For the Sale of Real Estate.   Land and things permanently attached to land are referred to as **real estate.** When a contract is made for the transfer or sale of an interest in such property, it must be in writing to be enforceable. A detailed discussion of real estate or real property interests is included in Chapter 30.

Real Estate: land and things permanently attached thereto

Note that there are a number of important exceptions to the general rule requiring a writing in this area. First of all, in most states, if you make a contract for the rental of real property for a period of less than a year, the contract does not have to be in writing to be enforceable. Second, even if the contract for the sale of land is oral, should the seller convey the title, he or she can collect the purchase price. This is because the whole idea of the Statute of Frauds was to protect the seller against untruthful allegations that she or he made an oral contract for the sale of land. The buyer was not taken into consideration.

For Contracts That Cannot Be Completed within One Year

HYPOTHETICAL CASE

Abe Backus stared at the mailbox. It was one minute before midnight, April 15. The carrier from the main post office took out his key and slid it into the box's lock. Abe waited till the last second, then slipped the tax return through the slot. The carrier grinned, unlocked the box, picked out the mail including Abe's return, then looked up, "Not letting them have your money till the last minute, eh?" Abe nodded. The federal mismanagement, the congressional perks and scandals—of course they weren't getting his money till the last moment, and not at all if he could work it. Unfortunately, the tax rules were becoming too complex and time-consuming to keep up with. So, just a few hours previously, Abe had made two contracts with a tax preparation service, Loopholers, Inc. One contract was to do his taxes for this calendar year, and the other covered the calendar year after this. Did either of these contracts have to be in writing?

The rule is reasonably simple. When the performance required under a contract cannot be accomplished within a year from the date on which the contract was made, the contract has to be in writing. This rule was put into the Statute of Frauds because over the course of a year's time people often forget the detailed terms of an oral contract. The result in the eyes of the law is litigation and loss of resources that can be avoided. In applying the one-year rule, however, problems arise in determining which contracts truly cannot be finished within a year. In the example with Abe, the answers are relatively straightforward. Loopholers, Inc., can do his taxes for the current calendar year within that time, whether or not it does. Therefore, the contract for the current calendar year does not have to be in writing. However, the contract to do the taxes for the next calendar year obviously cannot be fulfilled until that year is over. That is a year and three quarters from now. Therefore, a writing is required.

Now assume that you contract to buy 50,000 standard washers from my factory. Using our sole assembly line, we are currently able to produce only 24,000 per year by running three continuous shifts. Comparing those figures, you might think that a writing would be required. But as it is possible for us to purchase any shortfall on the open market, the contract can be done in a year. Therefore, no writing is required under the one-year rule. (But see the next section on contracts for the sale of goods valued at more than $500.)

Employment contracts are often made with an indefinite term in mind as such contracts may go on for the lifetime of the employer or the employee. However, because that lifetime may end before the year is up, no writing is required under the one-year rule. Similarly, unilateral contracts whose demanded action can be performed within a year although the promise that brought it on takes longer than a year to perform do not have to be in writing. For example, if someone offered to pay $1,500 at the rate of $100 a month for 15 months for the return of a champion Irish setter that escaped, the promise would not have to be in writing to be enforceable by the party returning the dog.

For Contracts for the Sale of Goods with a Purchase Price of $500 or More.
In the washers purchase mentioned above, the contract may have to be in writing if the amount of the purchase equals or exceeds $500. There are a number of exceptions to this rule. One exception is for goods specially manufactured for the buyer, such as an expensive tailored suit, that cannot be resold for their value elsewhere. Another exception is made for that part of a goods shipment that has been paid for or the delivery of which has been accepted.

For Promises to Stand Good for the Debt of Another Made to the Other Person's Creditor

HYPOTHETICAL CASE

Abraham Klaus stared at the door handle as the knocks began again. They were louder this time, more insistent. "Whoever it is must know I'm here," thought Abe. His hand shook as he opened the door. Two men in coveralls stood on his porch. One of the men spoke, "Mr. Klaus?" Abe nodded. The man went on. "Mr. Klaus, we're from Garton's Appliance Store. I'm sorry, sir, but we're here to repossess your refrigerator due to the delinquent payments. If you make any move to stop us, we'll leave and return with a police officer who will insure there's no breach of the peace while we do our jobs." Abe moved slowly aside, head down, and motioned the men in. "Stop right there," a voice boomed from behind the two. "Garton's men, right?" The voice continued, "You don't even put your name on the side of the truck." Abe looked up just as his neighbor, Bill, and two other men reached his porch. "Abe here's retired and spent every dime to help his wife fight her cancer. But he owes you, right?" Both of the men in coveralls nodded, but Abe noticed that they had begun backing off the porch. One of them fumbled in his pocket and produced a bill for $252.50, Abe's balance due. Bill looked at it, then shoved three 20s at the Garton's men. "That'll bring him up to date. If he has trouble paying in the future, have your office get ahold of me and I'll take care of it. Got it?" The men nodded, grabbed the $60, and trotted toward their truck. As they clambered into the cab, one yelled back at Bill, "We'll remember that. When the old coot doesn't pay, we'll send the law to come knocking on your door. You got that!" The truck roared off. Abe

continued on page 157

concluded

> turned to Bill and said, "I'll pay you back somehow, Bill. It's just that the hospital and funeral bills are chewing me up right now. They'll probably be dogging you with a court suit next month." Abe shook his head. Bill smiled. "Forget it, Abe. I remember how good you and Ruth treated my kids. Besides, those boys don't know much about the law."

Bill is correct. At law, the promise that he just made to Abe's creditors has to be in writing to be enforceable against him. The general rule under the Statute of Frauds is that whenever a person promises a creditor to pay a debtor's debt if the debtor cannot, the promise must be in writing to be enforceable. Note, however, that if the promise is made to the debtor instead of the obligee creditor, it does not have to be in writing. So, if Bill had promised Abe instead of Garton's Appliance Store, the promise could have been enforced without a writing. Also, the Statute of Frauds requires a writing only if the promise is to pay if the debtor cannot. Therefore, if a person promises to be directly liable as a codebtor, regardless of whether or not the other person can pay, no writing is required.

For Promises to Stand Good for the Debts of a Deceased's Estate.

When a person dies, someone is selected to manage and distribute that person's property according to the laws. Whenever this manager makes a promise to pay the debts of the deceased person out of the manager's personal funds, the promise must be in writing to be enforceable. In the eyes of the law, this situation closely parallels the one we just discussed, in which someone promises a creditor to stand good for the debts of a certain debtor.

For Promises Made in Consideration of Marriage

HYPOTHETICAL CASE

> Brenda Koch looked across the table at her brother Brent, who was four years her junior. "It doesn't matter, Brent," she whispered. "Besides, Mom knows enough to take care of herself." Brent shook his head and spoke out loud, "She's in love. He's some young stud that she has the hots for, but after they're married, when she dies he might sell the ranch, the business . . . everything . . . everything Dad built, then take half of the money and disappear." As he spoke the last few words, Brent glanced up from his coffee. Brenda was looking over his shoulder, eyes wide. Brent didn't turn around. He knew that his stepfather-to-be had come quietly down the stairs into the kitchen and overheard all he'd said. "But you'd never do that, would you, Stephen?" Brent continued. Stephen Kline slapped Brent a little too hard on the shoulder and replied quietly, "Of course not, Brent, all that belongs to you two. I just love your mother, nothing more. That's good enough for me. You've got my word on that. You two can keep all the property." After a confirming hearty slap on Brent's shoulder, Stephen left. Brent waited, then spoke, "I think we need to get that in writing, Brenda. Don't you?" Brenda shrugged and dialed her attorney.

As you might suspect, Stephen's verbal promise is not enough under the Statute of Frauds. However, it is true that the basic marriage contract, to meet and exchange vows, is fine in an oral form. To be enforceable, any additional promises given as consideration for marriage beyond those vows must be placed

Figure 12-1   **When Is a Writing Required under a Typical Statute of Frauds?**

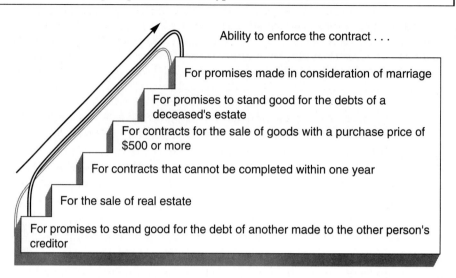

Ability to enforce the contract . . .

For promises made in consideration of marriage

For promises to stand good for the debts of a deceased's estate

For contracts for the sale of goods with a purchase price of $500 or more

For contracts that cannot be completed within one year

For the sale of real estate

For promises to stand good for the debt of another made to the other person's creditor

---

Prenuptial Agreement: promises given in consideration of marriage other than the traditional vows

in a writing before the marriage. Such a writing is known as a **prenuptial** (also premarital or antenuptial) **agreement.**

A summary of the situations requiring a writing under a typical Statute of Frauds appears in Figure 12–1.

What Contracts Are Unenforceable by The Courts due to Their Improper Objectives?

Contracts otherwise enforceable may fail because of their improper objectives. Such objectives include those that are illegal and those that are against public policy.

Contracts Partially or Wholly Unenforceable due to Illegal Objectives

HYPOTHETICAL CASE

"The winner is number 3913. Who's got the winning ticket?" The voice reverberated throughout the gymnasium. Sanford Davis looked around. A man was running toward the stage from the other side of the floor. It was Brandon Johnson, the son of Michael Johnson, owner of Johnson's Exotic Car Shop. The '67 Mustang was his. Odd, thought Sanford, out of over 2,000 purchasers of the $25 tickets, the son of the man who had donated the car for the lottery had won it. Of course, buying new uniforms for the high school's Marching Terrapin band was a great cause. Still . . . Impulsively, Sanford pushed forward through the crowd. Near the stage he found the band director carrying a box with the receipts in it. "I want my money back," said Sanford, "or I'll prosecute you for holding an illegal lottery." The band

continued on page 159

concluded

director replied that it had been an honest drawing and that he wouldn't refund Sanford's $25. Sanford nodded and without another word turned and pushed his way out of the gym. The next morning, after a lengthy session with Sanford, the local prosecutor brought felony gambling charges against the organizers of the lottery.

Gambling Contracts.   **Gambling** is paying something of value to win a prize in a game of pure chance. Most gambling contracts, including the ones in the preceding example, are illegal. A positive motive behind drawings like the one in that example does not give them a legal status. However, most prosecutors will shy away from bringing charges against those holding such games unless a complaint is filed. If a complaint is filed, however, the charge and the result are very serious. Most gambling contracts are considered void by the courts. Therefore, the individual who ends up with the money keeps it, regardless of the bargain he or she struck to obtain it.

> **Gambling:** game involving prize, chance, and consideration

Many states have legalized state-run lotteries in order to generate revenue. The $8–10 billion total per year that these games of chance bring to the states that have set them up is used for schools, roads, and general state needs. In some states, not-for-profit civic groups can also run games of chance, such as bingo. However, these exceptions do not make other lotteries legal or make the contracts underlying illegal games of chance enforceable in a court of law. Note, too, that many people associate investing in the stock market or on commodity exchanges with gambling. However, this is not gambling in the legal sense. Certainly, a lot of money is won and lost in such investing, but, because that investing incorporates the elements of skill, experience, and knowledge along with chance, it is not held to constitute "gambling" under the law.

Bribery Contracts.   As mentioned previously, in a recent Arkansas case, a citizen of that state sued one of its judges for the return of bribery money he had paid the judge. Normally, as you know, contracts involving the improper buying of influence over public officials are void. In the Arkansas case, however, the person who paid the bribe maintained that he was not **in pari delicto** (of equal guilt) with the judge. If this claim is proven to the satisfaction of the court, the court often steps in to protect, usually by the return of consideration, the innocent or more nearly innocent party to an illegal contract. In the Arkansas case, of course, the courts refused to do so. Therefore, allegedly, the judge was left with the money from the bribe and certainly with a damaged reputation.

> **In Pari Delicto:** of equal guilt

Usurious Contracts.   Many states set a maximum on the interest rate chargeable for the loan of money. Charging an interest rate in excess of this legal limit is **usury.** In most states, usury limits are currently set at around 10–15 percent. (Note that we are talking about the lending of money, not the sale of goods on credit. For such sales, the interest rate can exceed 30 percent in some jurisdictions.) Some states hold that a contract charging more than the set limit is void. Therefore, the lender cannot collect the amount due through the courts and the borrower cannot get back excess interest paid. Other states just enforce the

> **Usury:** charging an interest rate above the legal limit

contract for the maximum interest chargeable and refund any excess amount to the borrower.

Other Illegal Objectives.   Contracts for prostitution, the sale of illegal drugs, or other objectives that involve the commission of a crime are treated as void by our legal system.

Contracts Partially or Wholly Unenforceable due to Being against Public Policy

Barth ("Rug") Baldwon stared at his image in the large mirror of the clinic. "Hair," he cried. He grabbed a small mirror off the sink and checked the back of his head. "More hair!" he shouted. The replacement surgery had been successful. Dr. Claudia Von Klippen, the noted ex–East German hair specialist, watched her patient for a moment, then walked out of the room. Dr. Klippen's administrative assistant met the specialist in the hallway. "He's ready for the bill," said Dr. Klippen with a smile. The assistant nodded and winked. Dr. Klippen's practice, opened upon her arrival from Berlin barely three months ago, was doing well. There was some question about the validity of Dr. Klippen's license, which was not recognized by the New York State Licensing Board for Physicians, but it hadn't stopped the customers or the cash flow . . . at least not yet. The assistant made a mental note to find out what effect lack of a license would have on the contracts the good doctor made.

Where Unlicensed Parties Are Involved.   Dr. Klippen and her assistant have quite a bit to worry about. If a license is required for the protection of the public, such as a license for a physician, contracts made without the license are treated as void. Therefore, if Barth Baldwon refused to pay, Dr. Klippen could not use the courts to recover the money due. However, if a license is required just to generate money for a community, such as a license for a typical business, the contracts will still be enforceable.

Contracts Made on Sunday.   Despite the constitutional requirement of the separation of church and state, many courts continue to uphold the use of state statutes or local ordinances to give workers a "day of rest" on Sunday. In the states that utilize this approach, the treatment of contracts made on this day of rest varies widely. For example, some states allow contracts made on Sunday to be ratified or confirmed on a weekday. Other states hold that such contracts are illegal and therefore altogether void. Some states even delegate the choice of prohibiting or allowing such contracts to local governments. In the jurisdictions that retain them, laws that regulate the making or performing of contractual obligations on Sunday, called **blue laws,** are still a factor to be considered in determining the enforceability of contracts.

Blue Laws: limitations on contracting on Sunday

Contracts Curtailing the Freedom to Marry. Society places great emphasis on the family and home. A part of this emphasis concerns the preservation of the freedom to marry. Except for laws reinforcing **monogamy** (being allowed only one spouse), most limitations on that freedom are against public policy. This is especially true for contracts that restrict or prohibit marriage and contracts that foster divorce. If Jane takes $5,000 in return for agreeing never to marry, or not to marry for the next three years, or not to marry a particular individual, she may do so anyway, as such contracts are void. Similarly, if Jane is paid $5,000 in return for promising to divorce her husband, she may keep the money and her husband if she so desires, as that contract is also void. However, property settlement agreements between divorcing spouses are not void.

Monogamy: being allowed only one spouse

Other Contracts against Public Policy. In addition to looking with disfavor on the contracts mentioned above, the law looks with disfavor on contracts that interfere with the administration of justice and public service (such as contracts that place restraints on trade and commerce and contracts that improperly limit liability for a party's actions).

APPLICATIONS OF WHAT YOU'VE LEARNED

Vocabulary Development

Fill in the blanks with the appropriate terms.

Best Evidence Rule
Blue Laws
Gambling
In Pari Delicto
Monogamy

Parol Evidence Rule
Prenuptial Agreement
Real Estate
Statute of Frauds
Usury

1. Yi-Ling put $1 into the jar, then walked out on the first tee. The $5,000 hole-in-one prize had last been awarded when the pro tour came through several years ago. One of the tour leaders had put in $121 before hitting the cup. The flag was only 220 yards away, but on a dogleg turn. Yi-Ling teed up her ball, made three or four practice swings, then smacked a drive that banked near the hole and rolled in. When she went into the office to claim her prize, the manager refused to pay, even with the witnesses. Yi-Ling brought suit, but the lawyer for the golf course said that the game involved prize, chance, and consideration and therefore was _____ and illegal. The court should therefore declare the contract void and not force the golf course to pay. The judge listened for a moment, then said, "Sure there's a prize, $5,000, and sure there's consideration, the $1 Ms. Yi-Ling chipped in, but that hole in one wasn't chance, that was skill. Pay her, gentlemen."

2. Fisk looked down at the contract. He had signed it, sure, but these weren't the terms that they'd agreed to. Why did he ever let Henson put it in writing? Why didn't he read it as a precaution before signing. Now Fisk's attorney advised him that because of the _____, Fisk couldn't even testify to the real terms. Fisk put his head in his hands and sighed in resignation.

3. Hester held a garage sale. Thelma, her friend, advised her not to open on Sunday because the _____ made contracting on that day illegal.

4. When Saundra and her bookie, Angela, were caught

by the police, Angela was holding a $1,000 bet of Saundra's. Angela refused to return the money, and Saundra sued for it, claiming that she was not _____ _____ _____ with a bookie. Therefore, Saundra argued, the court should not throw the case out but instead order her money returned.

Problems

1. What other approaches could the law take today to preserve the enforceability of oral contracts rather than having them reduced to writing? Evaluate the strengths and weaknesses of each.

2. Laurel Davis put her house up for sale after her divorce from David became final. She offered it as "for sale by owner" by putting an ad in the local newspaper, placing a large sign in her front yard, and even sending out a notice over the computer network at the plant where she worked as a drafting engineer. After several months, Holly Seeler, a fellow worker at the plant, contacted her through the electronic mail. She asked to see the house. The day after Laurel took her through the house, Laurel found an offer from Holly to buy it on the computer bulletin board. Laurel counteroffered and Holly agreed. Afterward, Laurel and Holly left the contract for sale in the computer database. Therefore, when a dispute arose about the terms, the only contract they could produce was a printout from a source that either of them could have tampered with. The printout, of course, did not contain the signature of either Laurel or Holly. Would it satisfy the Statute of Frauds? Should it be considered best evidence?

3. Which of the following contracts have to be in writing?
   a. A contract giving the phone company permission to run underground lines across your real property.
   b. A contract for the purchase of $450 in model train equipment that usually takes over a year to make by hand.
   c. A promise to your friend to pay his debts if he cannot.

4. Which of the following contracts would the court enforce?
   a. A contract under which you owe $2,500 to a dentist who performed root canal surgery on you without the appropriate state license.
   b. A contract with a customer of your retail business that you made before you secured a city license to do business.
   c. A contract with a professional engineer to draw up the structural plans for your new office building. The engineer is licensed in several neighboring states but not in the state where the building is to be erected.

ACTUAL CASE STUDY

In the Matter of Baby M (a pseudonym for an actual person)

Supreme Court of New Jersey
537 A.2d 1227

When William Stern learned that his wife would be in considerable danger of blindness and paraplegia if she had children, he was deeply concerned. All the other members of his family had been destroyed by the Holocaust. As the only survivor, he very much wanted to continue the bloodline. Consequently, Mr. Stern, Mrs. Mary Beth Whitehead, and Mrs. Whitehead's husband at the time entered into a surrogacy contract. The contract provided that Mrs. Whitehead (since divorced and remarried) would be artificially inseminated with Mr. Stern's sperm. She would then carry the child to term, deliver it to the

Sterns, and thereafter do whatever was necessary to terminate her maternal rights so that Mrs. Stern could adopt the child. For these services, Mr. Stern would pay Mrs. Whitehead $10,000 after the child was delivered to him.

Not wanting anyone at the hospital to be aware of the surrogacy situation, Mr. and Mrs. Whitehead posed as the parents of the newborn baby, which was named Sara Elizabeth Whitehead on the birth certificate, with Mr. Whitehead listed as the father. The Sterns visited the hospital unobtrusively to see the child.

Almost from the moment of birth, however, Mrs. Whitehead concluded that she could not part with the child. She broke into tears when the Sterns told her what they were going to rename the child. She also commented on how much the baby looked like her other daughter.

Ultimately, Mrs. Whitehead refused to turn over the baby to Mr. Stern. Mr. Stern filed suit for custody, but the Whiteheads fled to Florida with baby M. The Whiteheads, fearing the loss of the child, lived in roughly 20 different hotels over the next three months. Finally, the police located the baby and forcibly took her into custody. The trial court then heard the Sterns' complaint, which, in addition to seeking possession and custody of the child, sought enforcement of the surrogacy contract. The contract, among other things, required that Mrs. Whitehead's parental rights be terminated and that Mrs. Stern be allowed to adopt the child.

The Superior Court (trial court) upheld the validity of the surrogacy contract and granted the Sterns' request for its enforcement. The case was appealed to the New Jersey Supreme Court, which ruled as follows:

We invalidate the surrogacy contract because it conflicts with the law and public policy of this State. While we recognize the depth of the yearning of infertile couples to have their own children, we find the payment of money to a "surrogate" mother illegal, perhaps criminal, and potentially degrading to women. Although in this case we grant custody to the natural father, the evidence having clearly proved such custody to be in the best interests of the infant, we void both the termination of the surrogate mother's parental rights and the adoption of the child by the wife/stepparent. We thus restore the "surrogate" as the mother of the child. We remand the issue to the trial court . . . We find no offense to our present laws where a woman voluntarily and without payment agrees to act as a "surrogate" mother, provided that she is not subject to a binding agreement to surrender her child. Moreover, our holding today does not preclude the Legislature from altering the current statutory scheme within constitutional limits, so as to permit surrogacy contracts. Under current law (prohibiting the sale of babies), however, the surrogacy agreement before us is illegal and invalid. [Mrs. Whitehead was allowed visitation rights with the child.]

Questions

1. Do you feel that the court's decision reflected the "wisdom of Solomon" that we discussed earlier?

2. Should surrogacy contracts be allowed? What problems do you foresee if they are?

3. Can you distinguish surrogacy contracts from contracts to aid in the suicide efforts of a terminally ill patient? What are the similarities between these two types of contracts?

How Are Contractual Obligations Discharged, and What Can Be Done if They Are Not?

CHAPTER OUTLINE AND OBJECTIVES

After studying this chapter, the student will be able to:

I. Identify to whom and by whom contractual duties must be rendered.

   a. The parties to the contract

   b. Third-party beneficiaries of the contract

   c. Assignees of contractual duties

   d. Delegatees of contractual duties

   e. Those with joint and/or several liability

II. Explain how contractual obligations are discharged.

   a. Performance levels necessary to discharge contractual obligations

   b. Nonperformance means of discharging contractual obligations

III. Identify the remedies available for the breach of contractual duties.

   a. Damages

   b. Rescission and other equitable remedies

IV. Evaluate the meaning of an incidental beneficiary in *Neal* v. *Republic Airlines, Inc.*, the case of the missing body.

To Whom and by Whom Must Contractual Performance Be Rendered?

The Parties to the Contract

In most contractual situations, the rights and duties created by the agreement fall on the parties to it. In fact, the law requires that for every right there be a corresponding duty. Persons who are not parties to a contract, however, do not have to perform its duties. By the same token, such persons generally cannot expect to receive benefits from the contract. In the main, contractual performance is to be rendered by and for the benefit of the parties who negotiated and concluded the agreement.

However, there are exceptions to this rule. At times the parties to a contract may intend that benefits flow to persons besides themselves. Such a person is known as a third-party beneficiary. Life insurance contracts made between the insured and her or his insurance company are a good example. Such agreements call for a payment to a third party outside the contract in the event of the insured's death.

In addition to creating rights in others during contracting, parties to a contract may later transfer their rights and duties to others who were not original parties. Such a transfer of rights is termed an **assignment.** A transfer of contractual duties is termed a **delegation.**

Third-Party Beneficiary: noncontracting recipient of contract rights per intent of parties

Assignment: transfer of contract rights to third parties

Delegation: transfer of contractual duties

Third-Party Beneficiaries of the Contract

Before we discuss assignment, we need to take a closer look at third-party beneficiaries. This designation is important because true third-party beneficiaries can sue to enforce the contract that benefits them. Realize that contracts often benefit many parties. For example, a contract to buy a new car might benefit the dealership, the dealership's employees, its creditors and suppliers, and its owners. The same contract might benefit the purchaser; the purchaser's children, spouse, and other relatives; and the purchaser's lending institution, insurance company, and garage. Obviously, however, the courts could not open themselves up to suits by all of these potential beneficiaries should the contract not be properly performed.

As a consequence, the courts allow only true third-party beneficiaries to sue. Others, labeled **incidental beneficiaries,** are considered only the unintended recipients of a contract's direct or indirect benefits. Incidental beneficiaries therefore cannot bring suit to enforce the contract.

Among third-party beneficiaries are creditor beneficiaries and donee beneficiaries.

Incidental Beneficiaries: unintended recipients of contract's benefits

The thunderous wave of cheers cascaded down the aisles and crashed over him as he came out on stage. His blood surged into his fingers. The first notes from his guitar slashed back at the audience. The roar increased momentarily, then died away as the crowd of over 60,000 packed into the St. Louis Wonderdome settled in to enjoy the concert. Three hours and five encores later he was back in his hotel room. Ben Jackson, his agent, had just told him that the box office gross was over $1.5 million. It was more than enough to bail out the overdue bank loans on his estate and the new theater he'd opened in Branson, Missouri. Now that drugs were behind him, he hoped, it would be a new world. Just to be sure, though, his contract with the concert promoters stipulated that the money due him was to be paid directly to his creditors as third-party beneficiaries. Whatever was left after that, he would party on, without drugs, please, please without drugs.

A **creditor beneficiary** is a third party to a contract to whom payment of some obligation is expressly directed by a contractual party who has incurred that obligation. In the above example, the entertainer's creditors were creditor beneficiaries. As such, they could sue to enforce the contract between the entertainer and the promoters. By law, such a suit on behalf of a creditor beneficiary can be directed against either of the parties to the contract.

Creditor Beneficiary: third party to whom fulfillment of obligation is directed under contract by contracting party

A **donee beneficiary** is a third party who receives her or his rights under a contract as a gift from a party or parties to that contract. Most life insurance contracts are made in favor of a donee beneficiary. By naming a person as the recipient of the face value of a life insurance policy, the insured is making a gift, not responding to the demands of an obligee. Unlike the situation with a creditor beneficiary, a donee beneficiary can sue only the promisor of the benefit, not the promisee. So as a third-party beneficiary under a life insurance policy, one can sue only the insurance company for failing to abide by the policy's provisions, not the person who took out the policy.

Donee Beneficiary: third party to whom rights under contract are given by contracting party

Assignees of Contractual Duties

After an agreement has been concluded, one of the contracting parties may want to transfer to someone else the right to receive a performance due under it. If I construct an apartment building, for example, as part of the deal I might transfer to the bank that made the construction loan the right to receive the rent from the tenants for a certain span of time. I might also contract to transfer to a private repair firm the duty of keeping the building in good shape. As noted above, the transfer of a person's rights under a contract to another party is known as an assignment. The party who assigns the contractual rights is known as the **assignor.** The party to whom they are assigned is known as the **assignee.** (See Figure 13–1.)

Assignor: transferor of contractual rights

Assignee: transferee of contractual rights

Figure 13–1   Assignment

Generally, a landlord has:

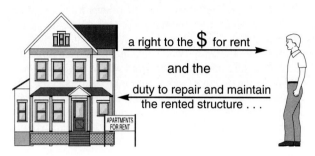

a right to the **$** for rent

and the

duty to repair and maintain
the rented structure . . .

However, the landlord may assign the right to the rent money
and delegate the repair and maintenance duty. For example:

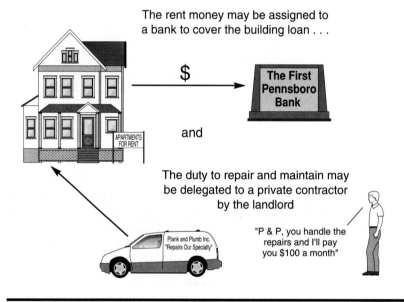

The rent money may be assigned to
a bank to cover the building loan . . .

$ **The First Pennsboro Bank**

and

The duty to repair and maintain may
be delegated to a private contractor
by the landlord

"P & P, you handle the
repairs and I'll pay
you $100 a month"

Plank and Plumb Inc.
"Repairs Our Specialty"

Novation: release of one
contractual party and
substitution of another

In general, contractual parties can assign their rights and delegate their duties as they see fit. In fact, the transfer of an entire contract to a third party by a contracting party carries with it a full assignment of rights and a full delegation of duties. Of course, contracting parties can secure a complete release from their contractual duties if the other parties allow it. When a contracting party secures such a release by substituting someone else to perform his or her contractual obligations, the maneuver is termed a **novation.**

When Halfman Construction Company (Hafa) discovered that it had run out of low-cost fill material for construction of the concrete foundation at the new stadium, its executives were able to secure a novation from the other contracting parties by finding another company, Gem Construction Company (Gem), to perform the same work for the agreed-upon price. Unfortunately, Gem's fill material was substandard and the concrete foundation was too weak. Gem was sued and recovered against as a consequence. When Gem later brought suit against Hafa for some of the money it paid out as damages (*Gem* v. *Hafa*), the court held that the release Hafa had obtained as part of the novation prevented any such recovery.

Note that if no release is obtained, even with a legally allowable assignment of rights and delegation of duties, the original party remains liable on the contract. In the preceding example, if Hafa had not secured the release, even if it were blameless for Gem's failure to perform the contract, it would have remained liable to the original obligee for damages for not fulfilling its obligations under the contract.

By law, some contract rights cannot be assigned. For example, an assignment of contractually required personal services that greatly increases the obligation of the person providing those services is not allowed. In other words, if you contract for the services of a certified public accountant to do your company taxes, you cannot assign that accountant's services to my much larger company instead of using them yourself. Also, restrictions on the assignment of contractual rights may be put in the contract itself.

"Just sign at the bottom on the blank line, sir." The rental car clerk smiled at Eddie Bonet. The car keys dangled from her left hand. Eddie read the wording above the blank signature line. "This says I've read the terms on the back of the agreement and agree to the incorporation of those terms into our agreement." The clerk smiled and shrugged, "That's right, sir. Nobody reads them though." Eddie thought a moment. "Well, let me take a few minutes anyway," he said as he flipped the contract over. The back contained a full page of small print. The first few terms were general statements that had little impact on the rental contract. "Whoa, what's this?" Eddie blurted. "I can't let anyone drive it who's under 21, and every time I leave the vehicle the doors are to be locked and the windows up." The clerk nodded, "Standard terms, sir. Also, you can't assign your contract rights to the possession and use of this car to anyone else." Eddie thought a moment, then said, "So if I violate any of these terms, even for the best of reasons, and something goes wrong, I'm automatically liable for breach of contract." Again the clerk nodded, "That's right, sir. Take it or leave it." Eddie looked out the window at the car, shrugged his shoulders, and signed.

So, in this true-to-life example, Eddie could not assign his right to the car to anyone else due to the contract terms themselves. Note that an assignment, unlike a contract, does not require consideration to be enforceable. Also, assignments need be in writing only if the original contract was required by law to be in writing.

Finally, it is important to provide notice of the assignment to the person who must render the assigned performance. If notice is not given and the obligor performs for the assignor, the assignee cannot demand that a similar performance be rendered for her or him. For example, presume that I assigned to you the right to receive a $100,000 payment owed me by a debtor under a contract. If the debtor, acting without notice of the assignment, paid me and I disappeared, you would have to get the money from me, if you could find me. However, if you gave the debtor notice of the assignment and the debtor still paid me, you could legally take the debtor to court for the $100,000 payment, regardless of whether or not the debtor could find me to recover the mistaken payment.

Delegatees of Contractual Duties

Delegation of duties under contracts requiring personal services is also limited.

HYPOTHETICAL CASE

Angie heard her husband, Dave, from across the yard. "Do we know? You bet. It's a boy. You ought to see the ultrasound!" Angie didn't hear the rest, but Dave and their neighbor, Bill Bradford, burst out laughing a moment later. A smile flashed across her face, then faded. Angie was worried about her doctor. On the first pregnancy and through most of this one, she'd been with Susan Medford, MD. Now, barely two months before her due date, they'd received a letter stating that Dr. Medford had gone into partnership with the two male doctors Angie had met during her last office visit. Angie liked Dr. Belton, who was short and rather pudgy. But Dr. Davis, who was tall and pale, gave her the creeps. As Dave walked toward her, she could hold back no longer. "Dave, I just don't want Dr. Davis to touch me. If he's on call the night I deliver, I won't let him handle it. But when I called the hospital to tell them this, they said that if I didn't use Dr. Davis, I'd just have to wait my turn for an emergency room doctor. It isn't fair. Can Dr. Medford do this? Our contract was with her."

The legal answer to Angie's question is a simple no. Without Angie's permission, Dr. Medford cannot delegate such a personal contractual responsibility to either of the other two doctors. Only a standardized performance, such as one performed by unskilled labor, can be delegated.

Those with Joint and/or Several Liability

Where two or more parties sign a contract as obligors, the very wording of the contract is crucial in determining which of them may be required to perform or who may be responsible if performance is not properly rendered. If all three doctors promised in the same contract to deliver Angie's baby as a cooperative effort, they would be **jointly liable** for whatever occurred. This would mean that

Jointly Liable: status of co-obligors under contract

if Angie had a problem with the birth procedure, she would have to sue all three together to recover. If the doctors instead each promised to do the same thing individually, they would be **severally liable.** In order to recover, Angie would have to sue only one of the doctors for the full amount due. Finally, for some obligations, such as the payment of income taxes by a husband and wife, the obligors are **jointly and severally liable.** This status allows the obligee of the performance to bring suit against any one, a few, or all of the obligors should the obligation not be properly fulfilled.

Severally Liable: status of person individually obligated by contract

Jointly and Severally Liable: status of person responsible individually or as co-obligor under contract

How Are Contractual Obligations Discharged?

In a legal sense, **discharge** means to free from a legal obligation. When talking about effective discharge under contract law, it is crucial to realize that the vast majority of contractual obligations are discharged simply by performing them. Of course, where performance is complete and satisfactory, little law is made. So don't be fooled by the small amount of space devoted to such performance. Our society could not survive without willful and full compliance with the vast majority of its contracts. In this section we'll discuss the various levels of performance, and then we'll focus on other means for discharging contractual obligations.

Discharge: free from legal obligation

Performance Levels

Ideally, every contract would be concluded by **complete performance,** that is, performance in which all of the parties fulfilled every promise as expected. Given the complexity of many contracts, it should come as no surprise that reality often falls short of this standard. As a consequence, in most cases the law allows substantial performance to discharge the contractual obligations owed by the parties. **Substantial performance** results from a good faith effort that meets contractual expectations except for minor details. The difference between complete performance and substantial performance is that reimbursement for the minor shortcomings of substantial performance can be obtained at law.

Complete Performance: effort fulfilling every promise

Substantial Performance: effort fulfilling contract except for minor details

Even so, at times individuals do not want to be satisfied with any performance short of that which meets their full personal expectations. These individuals will insert such words as "performance to my satisfaction" or "satisfactory to [a named individual]" into the contract requirements. The courts do not always enforce such **satisfactory performance** terms, however. If there is an objective standard that the courts can rely on to determine whether performance is satisfactory, they will do so. If none exists, the courts will hold the obligor to the requirement that he or she must satisfy the obligee's personal tastes in order to render a proper performance.

Satisfactory Performance: effort intended to fulfill obligee's expectations

If the contract is silent as to certain terms relating to performance, the law will place its own into effect. For example, if the time of performance is not mentioned, the law will read "in a reasonable time." If a lawsuit develops, the court will ask the trier of fact to determine what that time should have been. When "time is of the essence" is used in a contract to bind a person to a set performance date, the courts will look at the circumstances closely to find out whether time truly was of the essence before allowing any consequential recovery. For example, if I have arranged for a $7,500 shipment of a variety of ice-cream flavors to be delivered on the day before the grand opening of my ice-cream shop, I would be able to justify a "time is of the essence" requirement in a contract I make with you for the installation of my freezer.

If the method of payment is not stipulated, US coin or currency is required. A check may be used as a substitute only if this is agreed to by the obligee. Finally, performance may hinge on the satisfaction of a condition concurrent, a condition precedent, or a condition subsequent.

Condition Concurrent: requirement that both parties perform contractual obligations nearly simultaneously

A **condition concurrent** requires both parties to perform their contractual obligations at the same time. Payment on delivery is the most common condition concurrent term. Even when this condition is not explicitly mentioned, it is often implied by the courts.

Condition Precedent: specific event required before obligation arises

A **condition precedent** is a contractual term specifying an event that must occur before an obligation to perform is placed on one or all of the parties to a contract. An example is, "If you'll mow the yard before 5 PM, I'll pay you $15."

Condition Subsequent: specific event whose occurrence extinguishes obligation

A **condition subsequent** is a contractual term specifying an event that will extinguish an obligation to perform if it occurs. Let me paraphrase offers we've all heard for an example: "Keep the 10 compact disks of oldies remastered off Edison's original recordings for up to 30 days. If you're not satisfied, return them before that time expires and pay nothing." If you contract for the disks, fulfilling the condition subsequent by returning them before the 30 days expire will terminate your obligation.

Nonperformance Means of Discharging Contractual Obligations

A number of ways can lead to the discharge of contractual obligations without performance. The release involved in a novation and the action of a condition subsequent, both already mentioned, can accomplish this end. In addition:

Mutual Rescission: setting of contractual parties on original footing concurrent with discharge of obligations

Mutual Rescission.   **Mutual rescission** can also discharge contractual obligations without performance. Typically, it involves an agreement whereby the parties to a contract can obtain a discharge from the contractual obligations by returning whatever they've received under the contract (or equivalent value). If the original contract was required to be in writing, the agreement calling for mutual rescission must also be in writing.

Tender of Performance: ready, willing, and able offer to perform per contract

Tender of Performance.   Having a tender of performance turned down will also discharge most contractual obligations. (A **tender of performance** is a ready, willing, and able offer to perform in accordance with the terms of the contract.)

James Ford was in charge of booking a band for the 50th reunion of the Miller High School Class of 1945. Turning through the listings of available bands, he came across the Bennie Goodman Band and mistakenly presumed that it was the famous swing era band of nearly the same name. He therefore called in and contracted for a two-hour show. When the band arrived on the fateful night, James realized that he had mistakenly booked a rap group composed of female impersonators. He then refused the band's tender of performance and thus discharged its obligation to perform under the contract. However, Bennie and the band would still be able to claim their paycheck.

Note that a tender of payment of a debt is an exception to this rule. If such a tender is refused, the refusal does not discharge the duty to pay. Out of fairness, however, any interest and charges for nonpayment stop running at the time such a tender is made.

Impossibility of Performance

To Sandra Stuart it felt like opening a time capsule. The old garage had stood behind her grandfather's house for years and years. He had never mentioned anything about it to her. Now, through his will, whatever was in there was hers. She turned the key that the attorney had given her in the old but well-oiled padlock. It clicked open. She removed it from the hasp, grabbed the door, and tugged. The light of day stabbed into the dark interior, disclosing something white . . . a car. Not just any car. Sandra remembered the movie *American Graffiti*. It was a very rare '55 T-bird, portholes and all, and Sandra noticed that the odometer read 7,700 miles. All in all, the car looked just as it did when it was driven from the showroom so long ago. Three weeks later, Sandra had sold it for $27,000 to a Ford dealer in Chicago. Then tragedy struck. A grass fire started by derelicts in a nearby vacant lot burned across her grandfather's yard, left unmown since his death, and destroyed the garage and the car. The car dealer and Sandra were discharged from their contract because of the obvious and irreversible impossibility of delivering the car.

Destruction of specific subject matter.   The destruction of the '55 T-bird is a good example of the first of several forms that impossibility of performance can take, that is, the destruction of subject matter specifically referred to in the contract. The destruction of such subject matter will terminate the contract. If the contract is not specific, the promisor must bear the extra expense of locating like subject matter and providing it to the obligee instead.

Incapacity of the performing party.   Death, disability in relation to a necessary skill, or incompetence as a result of insanity or substance abuse will terminate certain contractual obligations that require a special talent. For example, whether a star guitarist dies, breaks an arm, or is declared incompetent due to drug use, she or, upon her death, her estate is no longer bound to meet the demands of a personal appearance tour. However, her estate would be liable to pay off a bill for a new guitar that she had purchased just before her death, as making the payment is a simple effort not requiring special talent.

Commercial frustration.   In exceptional cases the law will excuse a party from performing a contractual obligation when such performance requires an extraordinary and wasteful commitment of resources. For example, fulfilling a contract to supply gasoline during an oil embargo might require buying crude petroleum at triple its preembargo price. Enforcing such a contract would serve no practical public policy end. Therefore, the obligor might be discharged from his or her obligation. Before releasing the obligor, courts usually look for the occurrence of an unexpected event whose risk was not allocated between the parties by either the contract or custom. If such an event makes performance commercially impracticable, the doctrine of commercial frustration will be utilized; if not, the obligation remains. Several decades ago the Suez Canal was closed due to international hostilities. Its closure greatly increased costs for ships leaving the United States for Iran, India, and other destinations in the Middle and Far East due to the necessitated long detour around Africa's Cape of Good Hope. A US federal court refused to use the doctrine of commercial frustration to allow shippers to recover additional costs under contracts for such journeys made before the canal's closing, saying that the increased costs were not great enough (approximately $45,000 added to a contracted price of $305,000).

Effect of Law.   A variety of laws may also affect the legal necessity for an obligor to perform. For example, the law occasionally changes so as to ban the performance of certain contractual obligations. Such changes discharge the contractual obligations in question. So, if you have a contract to distribute a fine Scotch whiskey distilled in Great Britain throughout the United States just as another prohibition act goes into effect, you are no longer legally required to follow through on your promise. The same holds true for drugs that the Food and Drug Administration takes off the market and for other products subject to governmental regulation.

Statutes of limitations may also affect performance. Such a statute sets the time limits within which a lawsuit must be brought. There is such a statute in each of the states. For action on a written contract, the case must generally be brought within 6 to 10 years, depending on the state. If it is not, the right to use the courts to resolve contract disputes over a lack of or improper performance is lost.

The federal bankruptcy statute produces the same effect for obligors under the control of its procedure. One result of a "successful" bankruptcy filing is that obligees are barred from using the courts to secure performance of the obligations due them. The bankruptcy statute is covered in Chapter 24.

Note that both the bankruptcy statute and the statute of limitations do not actually discharge performance obligations. They merely bar the obligee from using the courts for enforcement of those obligations.

The means of discharging contracts are summarized in Figure 13–2.

Means of Discharging Contracts   **Figure 13–2**

- Performance
- Mutual rescission
- Tender of perfomance
- Impossibility
- Effect of law

What Remedies Are Available for Breach of Contractual Duties?

When there is a **breach of contract** (an unexcused failure to perform according to the terms of the agreement), the injured party has a right to a legal remedy. As you might suspect from common sense, improper performance by one party also discharges the other party from having to perform further. It also enables the injured party to seek a legal remedy to the problem.

Breach of Contract: unexcused failure to perform according to agreement

Potential remedies include damages, rescission, and specific performance. We'll get to those in a moment. Before we do, realize that there are times when an obligor under a contract expressly states or clearly implies that he or she is not going to perform at all. When such a statement is made even before performance has begun, it is termed a **repudiation.** In response to a repudiation, the obligee can either bring suit immediately or wait to see whether the person who has repudiated will change his or her mind before the actual date that performance was to begin. The latter is the wisest course as it is usually a far more practical way to get the performance desired under the contract rather than by relying on a court-imposed substitute. If suit is brought, however, the repudiation is treated as an **anticipatory breach** because it precedes the beginning of performance.

Repudiation: clear indication of intent of nonperformance

Anticipatory Breach: preperformance expression of intent not to comply with contract terms

Damages

You have already been introduced to compensatory damages, the type of damages most often sought in a contract law suit. As you may recall from Chapter 6, those damages are meant to provide the injured party with the amount of her or his actual loss (they are therefore often called actual damages). Compensatory damages can be arrived at by calculating (1) how much a like performance would cost from a source other than the obligee, or (2) the incremental cost of making a substandard performance whole, or (3) the lost profit on a sale. The trier of fact, usually the jury, fixes such damages to equal the financial loss borne by the injured party.

Consequential damages are also recoverable. These are damages reasonably foreseeable as being caused by the breach. Do not forget, however, that lawyer's fees, perhaps up to 40 percent or more of the damage award, almost always come

Consequential Damages: indirect, foreseeable damages to injured party

out of that award. This is one reason why in most circumstances bringing a hasty lawsuit rather than waiting for proper performance is not a good idea.

Punitive or exemplary damages are not available in the vast majority of contract suits. Some statutes do allow them in consumer contract cases in which there has been exceptionally improper behavior by a party. Nominal damages are also awarded at times under contract law to acknowledge that someone who suffered only minimal harm had a cause of action. In addition, courts may award **incidental damages** to cover costs expended by an innocent party to stem the loss.

Incidental Damages: compensation for innocent party's costs of stemming loss

Finally, realize that, like most of us, courts do not like uncertainty. As a consequence, the law will not speculate as to the amount of a loss just to see a recovery of some sort by the injured party. If a monetary figure for harm done cannot be determined with reasonable certainty, the court will not allow damages to be awarded. So if you're opening that brand new ice-cream store we spoke of earlier, you cannot recover lost profits when the refrigeration company doesn't put in the freezer in time for the opening. In the eyes of the court, the amount of the lost profits would not be reasonably ascertainable because you don't have any history of income for the store.

The way around this dilemma is to stipulate an amount for liquidated damages in the contract. **Liquidated damages** are a realistic approximation of the damages that a court should award in the event of a breach of the contract. They must be arrived at in good faith by the parties to the contract. If the liquidated damages are excessive given the nature of the breach, the court will not award them because such damages would be punitive.

Liquidated Damages: contractually noted approximation of harm from breach

Mitigation of Damages.   Finally, realize that a party injured by a breach of contract has a duty to act to minimize the harm done, in other words, to **mitigate** the damages. So, given time, the Bennie Goodman group must try to find another booking when its tender of performance is turned down. The ice-cream store without a working freezer, thanks to the refrigeration company's contractual breach, must try to find another location to store the ice-cream delivery rather than just stand by and see it melt. Even if the efforts fail, the injured parties must try to mitigate. If they fail to do so, they may lose part or all of their right to recover. Assume that if the effort were made, Bennie Goodman could have still gotten a suitable booking for later that night. If this were shown in court, the amount that would have been paid or that was paid for that booking would be deducted from the damages due under the Miller High School reunion contract.

Mitigate: act to reduce harm from contract breach

Rescission and Other Equitable Remedies

Another remedy for breach of contract is rescission. The injured party who has performed may simply sue to recover what she or he has put into the contract. If the contract is for the sale of goods, damages may be sought in addition to the recovery of the items sold.

Of course, there are times when damages and rescission simply are not adequate remedies. For example, assume that you have entered into a contract for the purchase of 7 acres on the best corner in town. You have already lined up your financing and prospective tenants for a new shopping center when the seller breaches. Would you be satisfied with available damages, rescission, or even another 7-acre tract? Of course not. Land is unique, as are certain other items, such as paintings, ancient relics, and collector's items. You may therefore request as a remedy that the court order the other party to fulfill the contract. This remedy is called **specific performance.** Note that the court will not order specific performance of contracts calling for nonstandardized personal services because this would come too close to a violation of the Thirteenth Amendment's prohibition of involuntary servitude (slavery).

Specific Performance: court-ordered fulfillment of contract terms

HYPOTHETICAL CASE

"What do you mean he isn't coming," Burl Wilson screamed into the phone. "We've sold over 3,000 advance tickets at $25 plus a pop. The show's been scheduled for months." Burl's eyes bugged. "You squirrelly little . . . " Benton Ellis clapped his hand over Burl's mouth and grabbed the receiver. "Look, Mr. Charles, if Rod doesn't appear here, we'll go to court and sue for damages. We've got our time in this, it cost a bundle to print the tickets, and we'll have to refund every one of the advance sales." Benton stopped and listened. "You will. Well, that'll help some. We'll consider it. I know the courts wouldn't give us our lost profits yet because there are still 11,000 tickets to sell for the concert, so your covering our expenses will help. Still, he's supposed to appear here, not in the Twin Cities." Benton listened a moment longer, then said "I'll call you back on this" and hung up the phone. He turned and put his hands on Burl's shoulders. "Look, Burl, our little promotion just dies unless we can find some way to get Rod to change his mind. The courts can't order him to perform here, and Rod's management promised to pick up our expenses. Still, it's nowhere near what we could make if he showed up and sang. Tell you what: Let's call our lawyer and see if we've got any other options."

Although it is true that, due to the Thirteenth Amendment, a court would not order Rod to appear, Burl and Benton's lawyer may advise them that other remedial court action is possible. The most effective remedy in this situation might be an injunction. An **injunction** is a court order prohibiting or requiring someone to do something. Rod could be prohibited from appearing at any other location on the date that he was to be onstage for Burl and Benton. If Rod disobeyed, he could be held in contempt of court and fined or imprisoned, or both. The fine would go to the court and thus would not help the promoters financially. However, the threat of such a consequence might force Rod's management to reach a satisfactory compromise with Burl and Benton.

Injunction: court order prohibiting or requiring someone to do something

The contractual remedies we have discussed above are satisfactory as a last resort. But it is important to realize that they do not take the place, from either an individual or a societal perspective, of satisfactory performance under the contract. The reliance that can be placed on such performance in most contractual situations is what fuels our culture's growth and independence.

APPLICATIONS OF WHAT YOU'VE LEARNED

Vocabulary Development

Fill in the blanks with the appropriate term.

Anticipatory Breach	Condition Subsequent	Injunction	Repudiation
Assignee	Consequential Damages	Jointly and	Satisfactory Performance
Assignment	Creditor Beneficiary	Severally Liable	Severally Liable
Assignor	Delegation	Jointly Liable	Specific Performance
Breach of Contract	Discharge	Liquidated Damages	Substantial Performance
Complete Performance	Donee Beneficiary	Mitigate	Tender of Performance
Condition Concurrent	Incidental Beneficiaries	Mutual Rescission	Third-Party Beneficiary
Condition Precedent	Incidental Damages	Novation	

1. A(n) _____ involves the release of one party from contractual duties and the substitution of another party.
2. To be _____ is to be individually fully responsible for certain contractual obligations.
3. If a carpenter builds your gazebo to your contractual specifications with just a few minor deviations, the carpenter has rendered a(n) _____.
4. If a court responds to your complaint by ordering the electrician to complete his contract with you by installing wiring in the gazebo, the remedy used by the court is termed _____.
5. When you also try to get the court to order the painter to fulfill her contractual obligations, the court notes that the contract requires completion of the carpentry and the wiring before any latex goes on the structure. This requirement is termed a(n) _____ to the painter's obligation.
6. When the roofers hear about your court actions against the electrician and the painter, they ask to be let out of their contract. As you have spent a lot of money pursuing those lawsuits, you agree. Each party to the roofing contract will return the other party to that party's previous position. This is an example of a(n) _____.
7. A ready, willing, and able offer to perform contractual obligations is termed a(n) _____.

Problems

1. When Bob Hayes's wife died, her insurance company refused to pay Bob, as beneficiary, the amount of her insurance policy due to the suspicious nature of her death. Bob was in debt to a number of creditors, including the local bank, at the time of his wife's death and had planned to use the insurance proceeds to pay them. When the insurance company refused to pay him, he decided to just let the matter drop and take bankruptcy to clear his debts. In relation to the insurance contract, what type of beneficiaries are Bob's creditors? Can they sue to enforce the policy?
2. In Problem 1, assume that Bob threatens the insurance company with a lawsuit. What type of beneficiary is he? Can he sue to enforce the contract with the insurance company?
3. Good news for Bob's creditors: The insurance company decides to pay off to avoid being sued. Bob then assigns the right to receive the policy amount to the creditors and in writing informs the insurance company of his assignment. The insurance company erroneously pays Bob, who then buys a ticket for Brazil and disappears with the payoff amount. The creditors then sue the insurance

company for the money due them as a result of the assignment. The insurance company replies that the creditors must find Bob and get their money from him. Who is correct? Why?

4. Bernice contracts with XXXX-Terminate to rid her property of various insects. She owns some stock in the company and likes to think she will get a part of her money back as a dividend payout. Bernice is upset, however, when XXXX-Terminate, so as to fulfill its obligations of a big government contract, delegates its contractual duty to another established exterminator. She maintains that only XXXX-Terminate can perform the contract. XXXX-Terminate replies that any unskilled laborer can accomplish the job and that it can therefore delegate the job as it sees fit. Who is correct?

5. The Bombay or Bust Shipping Company contracted to transport several thousand tons of concrete yard ornaments to India by the beginning of the new year. Unfortunately, a major conflict in the Near East caused the Suez Canal to close and shipping costs to quadruple. Bombay or Bust wants to be released from its contract. You are the company's attorney. On what theory would you base your argument?

6. Our Grass Is Greener Company, a lawn care firm, contracts to mow the 2-acre yard of Mrs. Bailey's estate for $200 a month during the current year. Later Mrs. Bailey's grandson offers to do the same job for $50 a month. Mrs. Bailey tells Our Grass Is Greener that she is canceling the contract. The company responds by noting the $2,000 liquidated damage clause in the contract. What would be the effect of this clause in court?

7. Assume that in a lawsuit based on the scenario of Problem 6 it is shown that Our Grass Is Greener could have taken another job to replace Mrs. Bailey's that would have paid $150 per month at the estate next door to hers. How does this affect any potential recovery by the company?

ACTUAL CASE STUDY

Neal v. Republic Airlines, Inc.

605 Federal Supplement 1145

Consider the case of the missing deceased and how the court used contract law to solve it.

When Mrs. Neal died in Chicago on November 23, arrangements were immediately made between Inman Nationwide Shipping and Republic Airlines to ship her remains to her birthplace in Sulligent, Alabama.

Republic Airlines took charge of her remains on November 24 for its Flight 480 to Alabama. Through some error, however, they were instead flown on other flights from Chicago to Memphis to Atlanta to Greenville, Mississippi, and then back to Memphis again. They did not arrive at the proper destination until the afternoon of the 25th, which significantly "interfered with the timely and proper burial of their mother by plaintiffs" (to quote the complaint).

The Neals thereupon brought suit against Republic Airlines for breach of contract and for other causes of action based on the breach. Should the Neals be allowed to recover in this action? Why or why not?

INSIGHT

How Do You Choose an Attorney?

Most of us choose an attorney only when forced to do so by immediate events. As a consequence, such choices are often haphazardly made, and all too often they doom the client to a less than optimal conclusion of the matter at hand. For example, say that you've been involved in a car accident or a contract dispute and need an attorney. A friend mentions the satisfactory result that a particular attorney achieved in the settlement of an estate, the inference being that the attorney who does well in one kind of case can handle all kinds. Under the pressures of time and uncertainty, you throw your problem at that attorney and hope for the best. This scenario illustrates two errors. The first, and more obvious, is the use of a poor method in selecting an attorney at such a crucial time. The second, and perhaps more important, is the failure to prevent a situation in which the selection of an attorney is forced under pressure.

One way to avoid both errors is to establish an ongoing professional relationship with an attorney in general practice before events force such a hasty choice. As continuity is especially important in such a relationship, you should choose an attorney who is likely to be available throughout your productive years (the actual mechanics of making such a choice will be described in a moment). Like your relationship with your dentist (and at times at least as painful as that relationship), your attorney–client relationship should be based on periodic evaluations by your attorney of the legal needs that you may encounter. These evaluations will result in your attorney's recommendations of steps that you can take to preclude such needs or at least to reduce their effects. In addition, whenever a legal need arises that is beyond your attorney's normal practice range, he or she may be used as a good source of recommendations to enable you to find an attorney who is well versed in the required legal specialty.

Of course, you still need to know how to choose your long-term attorney or, if you are among the vast majority of Americans who don't have one, how to choose your attorney for use in an immediate legal dispute. Available attorneys are listed in most yellow pages. Along with that listing you will often find ads that identify the areas in which they most frequently practice. These yellow page ads are sometimes a full page in size, and they may even contain a picture of the attorney. Some attorneys or law firms also advertise on television or billboards to secure business. In addition, most local bar associations provide referrals over the phone. However, those referrals are often just read in turn from a precomposed list, so the referral you receive may be merely a random function of the calls that the bar association receives. Instead of using these relatively haphazard methods of obtaining possible choices of legal representatives, you might consult a nationwide directory of attorneys and law firms published annually by Martindale-Hubbell. This directory is found in most public libraries. It gives areas of concentration, and it lists clients. Therefore, at the very least, you can evaluate all of the available attorneys on the basis of the major clients they service.

Regardless of how the names of attorneys are acquired, it is very important to investigate more than one. Many attorneys will give you a free half-hour's consultation on your problem. Take advantage of it. Present your case to a few of them. Ask them about their compensation schedules, workload, areas of specialty, staffing, and so on. Be especially aware of the ease with which you can contact them. While it is true that many attorneys have to be in court and therefore cannot be reached immediately, their secretaries should know where they are and they should be reliable in returning your call. Finally, pay careful attention to their preliminary conclusions and to their professionalism, their appearance, their offer of support, and the apparent extent of their enthusiasm for your cause. Take notes. Don't contract immediately. Take some time to consider all factors before you form the relationship that will likely make you either a winner or a loser in a court of law.

The Legal Environment of Business: Sales

CHAPTERS

What Is the Uniform Commercial Code, and How Does It Apply to the Sale of Goods?

CHAPTER OUTLINE AND OBJECTIVES

After studying this chapter, the student will be able to:

I. Explain the origin and the current significance of the Uniform Commercial Code (UCC).
   a. Origin of the UCC
   b. Current significance of the UCC

II. Describe the relationship between the law of sales and law of contracts.

III. Identify the crucial terms we need to know to better understand the application of the law of sales.
   a. Goods
   b. Sale and contract to sell
   c. Merchant
   d. Good faith

IV. Analyze the million dollar difference a definition can make in the case of *Liberty Financial Management Corp.* v. *Beneficial Data Processing Corp.*

What Is the Origin of the Uniform Commercial Code (UCC), and What Is Its Current Significance?

If you're doing business with individuals in another state, it is important to know just how likely you are to receive what you bargained for. If the risk is great due to political or economic instability or to the possibility of underhanded dealings, you will increase your bargaining demands to compensate for that risk. Doing so reduces the amount of your economic activity and therefore impairs the well-being of all concerned. To correct this situation, a drive to standardize the commercial laws of the various states has been underway in these "United" States since the late 19th century.

Since its founding in 1892, the National Conference of Commissioners on Uniform State Laws (National Conference) has turned out nearly 200 uniform acts. These "acts" lack the force of law until they have been adopted by the states that care to put them into operation. Each uniform act is put together by including the best part(s) of the existing laws on a particular subject in the various states. The resulting act is then referred to the state governments for their consideration and possible adoption.

Legal Realism: philosophy calling for selection of desirable actual practices as laws

This approach reflects the application of a school of jurisprudence (remember from Chapter 1 that *jurisprudence* is synonymous with *legal philosophy*) called **legal realism.** This school holds that the law should reflect the most desirable real-life practices in use in a particular area. Judging from the economic success of our nation, brought about in part by the adoption of the National Conference's uniform and predictable laws in most states, this idea seems to have worked.

Origin of the Uniform Commercial Code

In the early 1940s the National Conference took on its most ambitious assignment: the creation of a uniform code of laws covering most commercial areas. It enlisted the help of the American Law Institute, whose membership comprised hundreds of the country's leading judges, lawyers, and law professors. A decade later the first edition of the **Uniform Commercial Code** (UCC) appeared. It has since been adopted in whole or in substantial part by nearly all the states, and significant portions have been updated as the need arose.

Uniform Commercial Code: statute (in force in all but one state) governing certain areas of trade

Current Significance of the UCC

In the remainder of this book we will lean heavily on the UCC as our source for the most likely form of the law in the legal areas it covers. As the UCC is statutory, it supersedes conflicting common law holdings in these areas. Figure 14–1 shows what areas the various articles of the UCC cover and where in our text those areas are discussed.

Just reading the subject matter of the articles in Figure 14–1 gives you some idea of how much about the details of business law you can learn from the UCC. The UCC is a law that facilitates the operations of businesses. It was drafted to

Summary of The Uniform Commercial Code   **Figure 14–1**

Uniform Commercial Code Articles and Coverage	Topic Area	Covered in Chapter(s)
Article 1: General Provisions—here are definitions and general guidelines on how to apply the act.		
Article 2: Sales—here are the laws that cover transactions in goods as well as the laws on contracting, performance, and remedies.	Sales of Goods	14–17
Article 2A: Leases—here are the laws that cover the leasing of goods.	Property Law	30–31
Article 3: Commercial Paper—these laws cover the use of checks, notes, drafts, and similar instruments.	Commercial Paper	18–21
Article 4 and 4A: Bank Deposits, Collections, and Transfers.	Financial Institutions	21
Article 5: Letters of Credit—these laws cover conditional commitments by banks to honor instruments drawn on them.	Commercial Paper	18
Article 6: Bulk Transfers—these laws govern the sale of major parts of the transferor's materials, supplies, and merchandise.	Sales of Goods	15
Article 7: Documents of Title—these laws control the use of instruments that signify ownership of goods.	Sale of Goods	16
Article 8: Investment Securities—these laws help govern the issuance of stocks and other securities.	Security Regulation	39
Article 9: Secured Transactions—these laws govern the interests lenders and sellers may have in the property of others.	Creditors and Debtors	22–24

keep businesspeople out of court, not to lay roadblocks requiring detours that lead to litigation.

The learning process begins with the area of sales law. As you can tell from Figure 14–1, Article 2 of the UCC pertains to sales. This is probably the most important area covered by the UCC.

What Is the Relationship between the Law of Sales and the Law of Contracts?

The answer to this question stems from the fact that the law of contracts is meant to apply to any and all contracts made within our society, whereas the law of sales is tailored to businesses.

Contract law may cover agreements relating to transfers of merchandise, land, buildings, services, and other things tangible and intangible. The law of sales deals only with transfers of rights in and to "goods"—a term referring to a relatively narrow class of items that we will define in a moment.

Also, the UCC's law of sales often requires knowledge beyond that demanded of the layperson by the law of contracts. You will quickly see that Article 2 both recognizes and demands the possession of more knowledge by a certain class of businessperson. (Note, however, that this article also provides standards for nonbusinesspersons involved in sales.) In return for its demands, it gives such businesspersons the ability to cut corners in ways not possible under contract law.

So, really, after having given you a great deal of backgrounding, we are just now embarking on the study of true business law. We begin, as noted, with Article 2 of the UCC. The knowledge it imparts is specialized, challenging, and, like all knowledge, will either give you an advantage in your dealings or come back to haunt you if you fail to acquire it.

What Crucial Terms Do We Need to Know to Better Understand the Application of the Law of Sales?

Goods

Goods: movable items identified to a sales contract

As mentioned above, Article 2 of the UCC, which contains the law of sales, governs the transfer of rights in and to goods. **Goods** are defined as things that are movable at the time they are identified as the subject matter of the sales agreement. This definition is given in section 105 of Article 2 (which is expressed as "2–105" in the common notation used to identify UCC sections). It is a good idea to turn to the UCC Appendix of this book right now to get a feeling for how the UCC actually expresses the definition. Note that section 2–105 specifically excludes money and investment securities (covered in Article 8 of the UCC) from the definition. Excluded by implication from the definition are things not traditionally considered "movable" in the eyes of the law, in particular real property.

Real Property: land and buildings and items permanently attached to them

Real property is defined as land and buildings and items permanently attached to land and buildings. Note that the transfer of ownership rights in real property is covered by areas of the law that have been established for longer than the UCC. (Real property will be discussed in detail in Chapter 30.) Put another way, Article 2 generally focuses on things other than real property. This brings us

Personal Property: all things not classified as real property

to the subject of personal property. **Personal property** is best defined as encompassing all things that are not real property—clothes, cars, books, and so on. The law of sales found in Article 2 is correctly regarded as applying to the transfer of ownership of most tangible, movable personal property. (Some personal property is intangible—contract rights, for example. See Chapter 30 for a fuller explanation.)

Of course, none of these terms from property law mesh exactly with the UCC. This is because the UCC is based on current business experience, which is constantly changing. The time-tested but relatively inflexible rules of property law, on the other hand, reflect centuries of development. They embody the conflict between the historical school and the legal realism school of jurisprudence.

Sale and Contract to Sell

Sale: passing of title to goods from seller to buyer for price

Another vital term is *sale*. In UCC 2–106(1), a **sale** is defined as the passing of title to goods from a seller to a buyer for a price. Two terms in this definition—

price and title—require explanation. The **price,** as you might suspect from contract law, is defined as the consideration required to be transferred in exchange for the goods. This price can be in money, other goods, or services.

Price: consideration given for goods

The other term, *title,* requires an explanation grounded in the area of property law. Simply put, property as we know it comprises many rights. For example, you may have the property rights of possession and use of this textbook, but some other party may really "own" it. In other words, that party may have the formal ultimate legal right to the textbook's ownership. This is the property right that the law refers to as **title.**

Title: formal legal right of ownership

HYPOTHETICAL CASE

Horton rented his specially constructed buses to rock groups on tour. Such a group would have possession and unrestricted use of a bus during the tour and then would have to return it. One group, Wild Irish Rose, liked its bus so much that a month after its tour ended, it made an offer to purchase the wheeled home. Horton finally accepted a price of $250,000 and transferred title to the group. However, Wild Irish Rose would have to wait until the bus was returned by the group currently using it before they would be able to have possession and use it.

The point of all this is that the seller may not have possession and use of goods at the time their sale takes place. In addition, the law of sales in Article 2 is applicable even if the goods are not in existence or identified to the contract at the time of the contracting. The law refers to such goods as **future goods.** An agreement involving future goods is known as a **contract to sell.** Note that even though Article 2 governs the transaction, according to UCC 2–105(2) no interest in goods can pass until they are both in existence and identified to the contract. As a consequence, the distinctions between goods and future goods and sale and contract to sell become important when questions of performance or risk of loss are raised by the parties to the contract. More about that later.

Future Goods: subject matter not in existence or identified to contract at time of contracting

Contract to Sell: agreement involving future goods

Finally, it is important to realize what a "sale" under Article 2 is not. It is not a gift, a providing of services (e.g., automobile repair or restaurant tablewaiting), a transfer of only possession for money (e.g., a rental or lease—see Chapters 30–32), or a process whereby a creditor is given rights in goods to secure payment of the obligation (e.g., a security interest—a very important tool for sellers and creditors—see Chapter 22).

Merchant

The more you understand about the definitions of goods and sale, the clearer the pervasive coverage of Article 2 will be. Given that and the fact that most of you studying this material either have a career in business or are planning one, another term of considerable importance is **merchant.** This is especially true because under the law of sales a person classified as such is held to a higher standard than the layperson. The definition is more drawn out than most, so read it carefully.

Merchant: person dealing in goods involved in transaction or possessing expertise in or hiring expertise for the transaction

Merchant means a person who deals in goods of the kind or otherwise by his occupation holds himself out as having knowledge or skill peculiar to the practices or goods involved in the transaction or to whom such knowledge or skill may be attributed by his employment of an agent or broker or other intermediary who by this occupation holds himself out as having such knowledge or skill.

This definition may be complicated but it also is very important. (Sometimes it seems that the same person who writes assembly instructions for children's toys was hired by the Uniform Law Conference to formulate the UCC definitions.) So let me paraphrase and, hopefully, clarify it. People who regularly buy and sell the goods in question are considered merchants by the UCC. Also considered merchants are two other types of people: (1) those who make a living by selling their expertise in the goods involved in the transaction and (2) those who hire individuals with that expertise.

Good Faith

Good Faith: honesty in fact

We've just noted that under the UCC merchants are held to higher requirements than laypeople. Now let's see what that means in terms of good faith, the one unalterable standard that affects the interpretation of every UCC contract. **Good faith** is defined as honesty in fact by UCC 1–201(19). For merchants, however, it carries a further meaning (or requirement) added by UCC 2–103(1)(b). That UCC section demands of merchants not only honest behavior but also the observance of reasonable commercial standards of fair dealing in the trade.

HYPOTHETICAL CASE

Barney Stallings stood in the kitchen and stared out the screen door at the dark clouds on the southwest horizon. Just after he had cut and baled the hay on his north 40 acres, Barney had contracted with a regional stockyard. The stockyard people agreed to buy the hay at $2.40 a bale and had promised to pick it up from the field within seven days of the contracting. Of course, every farmer knew that the contract was void if it rained on the hay before they could get to it. This was due to the possibility of spontaneous combustion and spoilage when wet hay was put in storage. The stockyard people knew that too, and Barney suspected that they'd been watching the weather forecasts just as he had. The price of hay had fallen by a quarter a bale right after the contract was made, so maybe they had decided to play it cute by letting it rain on his bales and then buying cheaper from someone else. They still had two days to pick up the hay before the week was up, so they could wait if they wanted to, couldn't they? Suddenly the rain began. Barney groaned. Then he turned away from the screen door and placed a call to an attorney he knew in town.

Barney's attorney should have some good news for him. Even though the stockyard people may have been within the bounds of good faith in waiting to pick up the bales until near the end of the seven days, as merchants they are held to a higher standard. If they indeed postponed picking up the hay so as to get a better deal elsewhere, they are in violation of the UCC's requirement of reasonable fair dealing in the trade. In short, they should have picked up the hay because of the possibility of rain. Under these circumstances Barney should be able to recover damages from the stockyard.

Vocabulary Development

Fill in the blanks with the appropriate term.

Contract to Sell **Legal Realism** **Price** **Title**
Future Goods **Merchant** **Real Property** **Uniform Commercial**
Good Faith **Personal Property** **Sale** **Code**
Goods

1. The formal legal designation of ownership of goods is _____.
2. An apartment building is classified as _____.
3. A wristwatch is classified as _____. If the same wristwatch were the subject matter of a sales contract, it would be classified as _____.
4. Jonathan wanted to buy a horse for his wife. He knew little about evaluating horses, so he hired Jack P. Allance, a horse trader and ex–cattle drive boss, to pick one out. In relation to this transaction, Jonathan is considered a(n) _____.
5. The consideration paid for goods in a transaction is termed the _____.
6. If I contract to buy the first 500 television sets you manufacture next month, the sets are _____ The contract is a(n) _____.

Problems

1. Which article of the UCC covers each of the following transactions?
   a. You sign a contract to purchase your new car, a Fordolet Thunderchicken.
   b. You sign a note to finance the purchase of the car.
   c. You write a check for the down payment on the car.
   d. The car dealership deposits your check in its bank, which then collects the funds to pay the check from your bank.
   e. The dealership makes so much money on your purchase that it decides to sell more stock to finance its expansion.
   f. The dealership contracts with Fordolet to buy 100 Thunderchickens.
   g. The bank receives rights from the dealership to take control over the Thunderchickens in the dealership's stock if the dealership's debts are not paid off properly.
2. Consider each of the following disputes, and determine whether it would be resolved by contract law or by the law of sales in Article 2 of the UCC.

   a. John Holland will not turn over the title to 7 acres as required by a contract for sale of the land.
   b. Jean Holland, John's wife, sues her employer for overtime that she says her employment contract allows.
   c. Joe Holland, John's brother, sues John concerning the delivery terms in a contract by which Joe bought 100 bags of concrete from John.
   d. Jerri Holland, John's aunt, sues the department store from which she bought a $250 bottle of Confusion perfume, on the grounds that it did not throw her intended mate into a state of ecstasy as advertised.
   e. Jim Tunnel, the Holland family lawyer, brings suit against each member of the Holland family mentioned above for nonpayment of attorney's fees.
   f. The Fordolet corporation sends the Thunderchickens mentioned in problem 1 to the dealership by rail and sends the dealership separately a document showing that it has title to the cars in the shipment.

g. A few months later the dealership, unable to find enough customers to buy its remaining Thunderchickens, has to sell off its assets, equipment, and inventory.

3. Amy Irving holds a garage sale each weekend. Would she be considered a merchant under the UCC?

ACTUAL CASE STUDY

Liberty Financial Management Corp. v. Beneficial Data Processing Corp.

670 S.W.2D 40

Finally, consider how the characterization of a contract as a sale of goods (or not) made a million dollar difference to two feuding companies.

Liberty Financial Management Corporation (Liberty) contracted with Beneficial Data Processing Corporation (Beneficial) for on-line computer data services for Liberty's many accounts. Dial, a company with which Liberty had grown disenchanted, had previously provided it with similar services. In order to provide the services to Liberty, Beneficial had to transfer to its own system thousands of accounts and records from data tapes that it obtained from Dial. In the transfer, Beneficial allegedly negligently lost some 5,000 account records and duplicated 20,000 others. The loss to Liberty was enormous, and it brought suit.

In the contract between Liberty and Beneficial was a clause limiting the liability of Beneficial for negligence to out-of-pocket expenses but not lost business. Citing public policy considerations embedded in the UCC, the trial court threw out the limited liability clause and awarded Liberty nearly $2 million, mainly for lost business.

Beneficial appealed on the grounds that since it was providing a service, not selling goods, the law of contracts applied, not the UCC, and the limitation on liability should be enforced.

Questions

1. What good or service is being transferred?
2. Does the transaction fall under the UCC or not?
3. Who ultimately wins as a consequence of your decision in Question 2?

CHAPTER

15

What Are the Requirements of a Valid Sales Contract?

CHAPTER OUTLINE AND OBJECTIVES

After studying this chapter, the student will be able to:

I. Identify the proper form for sales contracts.

   a. Approach of the UCC

   b. Impact of the Statute of Frauds

   c. Exceptions to the Statute of Frauds

   d. Requirements of the writing under the UCC

II. Explain how the UCC changes the law of contracts to fit sales situations.

   a. Offers under the UCC

   b. Acceptances under the UCC

   c. Performance under the UCC

III. Describe the special rules that apply to situations involving bulk transfers and auction sales.

   a. Bulk transfers

   b. Auction sales

IV. Apply knowledge of the requirements for sales contracts to *Sedmak* v. *Charlie's Chevrolet, Inc.*, the case of the elusive Corvette Pace Car.

What is the Proper Form for Sales Contracts?

Approach of the UCC

Frankly, the standards used under the UCC to determine whether a contract has come into existence are quite relaxed. Any conduct showing that the parties have reached an agreement will bind them unless the Statute of Frauds requires a written contract. (More about that in a moment.) In other words, the basic thrust of the UCC is to support as legally binding any oral contract, any written contract, and any contract that can be implied from the actions of the parties. Thus, under the UCC many elements of a contract can be omitted without dooming it. To keep the basic contractual intent intact, the UCC rules will at various times fill in price, subject matter, date of execution, and other items whose omission would easily make a contract unenforceable under the common law of contracts. Preserving bargains is the watchword of the sales portion of the UCC. It will go to seemingly extraordinary limits to do this. Compared with the more ordinary contracts we discussed in Part II, it is much easier to get into and much harder to get out of sales contracts. Do not forget that.

Impact of the Statute of Frauds

As far as the Statute of Frauds is concerned, UCC 2–201(1) states formally what we have already discussed in Chapter 12:

> (1) Except as otherwise provided in this section a contract for the sale of goods for the price of $500 or more is not enforceable by way of action or defense unless there is some writing sufficient to indicate that a contract for sale has been made between the parties and signed by the party against whom enforcement is sought or by his authorized agent or broker. A writing is not insufficient because it omits or incorrectly states a term agreed upon but the contract is not enforceable under this paragraph beyond the quantity of goods shown in such writing.

HYPOTHETICAL CASE

Jennifer Robinson owned the Fender-Bender Repair Shop, which specialized in fixing and selling top-of-the-line guitars. When one of her best-selling manufacturers came out with a new line, Jennifer immediately ordered by phone 20 of each of the manufacturer's four new models from her wholesaler. During the phone conversation, the wholesaler's salesclerk advised her that the bill would be over $52,000. Seven weeks passed, and her customers asked time and again when she would be getting in the new line. Finally, a competing store obtained the guitars and Jennifer began losing sales. She contacted the manufacturer and was told that she could buy such a large order direct from it at a considerable saving. She then placed an order with the manufacturer. The very next day the guitar shipment arrived from her wholesaler. She refused it. When the wholesaler sued, Jennifer claimed that there was no writing to clarify what was agreed on and to prevent fraud. Since the wholesaler could not satisfy the requirements of the Statute of Frauds, the court dismissed the case.

As noted earlier, $500 is the limit for oral contracts. Section 2–201 makes that plain. The last part of the section also states clearly that mistakes or omissions of terms do not signify the death of a contract. We'll discuss shortly what the UCC does in that event. However, we must now take a look at the exceptions to the Statute of Frauds that call for a writing that are provided by the UCC. Section 2–201(1) alludes to them at the start. (See Figure 15-1 for a listing of these exceptions.)

Exceptions to the Statute of Frauds

Three of these exceptions are applicable to everyone. A final exception applies only to merchants and is a part of the specialized knowledge that merchants need in order to come out ahead in the game of buying low and selling high.

However, the first three exceptions get top billing. They deal with (1) court admissions, (2) specially manufactured goods, and (3) the effect of payment, receipt, and acceptance.

Court Admissions.   If the person against whom enforcement is sought admits in court pleadings, testimony, or otherwise that a contract for sale was made, the Statute of Frauds barrier is lifted. Note, however, that the contract is good only for quantities up to the amount admitted to by the party making the pleading, giving the testimony, and so on. In the case of the Fender-Bender Repair Shop, for example, if, in answering the wholesaler's complaint, Jennifer's side admitted that the contract existed, the UCC's requirements would have been satisfied.

Specially Manufactured Goods

Yi-Ling stared at the black cookie, broke it in her hands, and pulled out the slip of paper concealed inside. "You will not leave the restaurant alive," it read. She shook her head and tore it into tiny pieces. It would have been far better if she had never heard of "misfortune cookies." Kuo Ming, who had come up with this idea, had intended to use such cookies as a joke for his new restaurant. He had ordered thousands, over $4,200 worth, from Yi-Ling's Chinese Bakery. Then the bank had cut off his financing. Yi-Ling opened another cookie. Its slip said, "You will meet three tall, dark, and handsome IRS agents." Then another: "You don't look a day over 70." Now Kuo was refusing to pay for the cookies. Yi-Ling had not made him sign a written contract, although a number of people could testify to their oral discussions. No one in his or her right mind would buy the cookies. Without a written contract, Yi-Ling felt, there was no way she could win a lawsuit. Is she correct?

As you might suspect, the answer to the above question is no. Yi-Ling could win a lawsuit even without a writing signed by Kuo Ming, the party against whom enforcement is sought. The UCC makes an exception to its requirement of a writing in the case of specially manufactured goods. As long as those goods are not suitable for resale to others in the ordinary course of business and the seller

Figure 15–1   **Exceptions to the Statute of Frauds Requirements for a Writing**

- Admissions to the contract have been made in court.
- The goods have been specially manufactured.
- The goods have been accepted.
- Written confirmation of an oral agreement between merchants meets with no objection from its recipient.

has made a "substantial beginning of their manufacture or commitments for their procurement," the contract is enforceable without a writing.

Accepted Goods.   A final exception to the requirement for a writing is made for goods that have been either paid for and accepted or received and accepted. **Acceptance** occurs when the buyer, after a reasonable opportunity to inspect the goods, signifies to the seller that the goods are fine, performs an act inconsistent with the seller's continued ownership, or simply fails to reject the goods.

Acceptance: occurrence showing buyer's intent to exercise ownership of goods

Transactions between Merchants.   As mentioned, the three previous exceptions apply to all parties. A special exception, however, deals specifically with transactions between merchants. (Remember the definition: Merchants deal regularly in the goods involved, hold out their expertise in the goods for hire, or hire someone with such expertise.)

Assume that, as often happens, two merchants come to an oral agreement that is then confirmed in writing by one or the other of them. Unless the recipient of the written confirmation objects to the terms stated in it within 10 days, the written confirmation allows enforcement of the oral contract. In the hypothetical situations described above, Jennifer Robinson's wholesaler and Yi-Ling would have saved a great deal if they had sent such a confirmation and it was not objected to within 10 days after receipt.

Requirements of the Writing under the UCC

As mentioned, the UCC's bottom-line requirements for a writing to satisfy the Statute of Frauds are minimal. A writing that will do the job need only contain some reference to a contract for the sale of goods, specify the quantity, and be signed by the person against whom enforcement will be sought. Realize, however, that the ability of a party to get past the hurdle of the statute does not necessarily mean that the party will win the case. Without a writing or the use of one of the exceptions, however, the case will not be heard.

How Does the UCC Change the Law of Contracts to Fit Sales Situations?

As mentioned, the thrust of the UCC is to streamline the process by which binding contracts can be made. This has been attempted by simplifying the law of contracts, especially in the areas of offers, acceptances, and performance. For some, this simplification is seen as benefiting all concerned because it encourages more contracting, more exchanges of goods, more business activity. To these supporters of the UCC, more business activity means progress and a better standard of living for all concerned. To others, of course, it means more resources converted or destroyed, more pollution, more uncontrolled growth. Regardless of which side of this never-ending argument you happen to favor, one thing can be agreed on: The UCC rules have curtailed the diversion of a great deal of funds into litigation. Here's how:

Offers under the UCC

A lot of things can go wrong when an offer is made. Terms crucial to the bargain may be omitted. Other terms may still be under discussion when the bargain is made or, if agreed to, may conflict with preexisting terms. In addition, these potential problems may be affected by the fact that the parties are merchants or parties that deal with one another regularly. As such, they may have ongoing understandings from their previous dealings or they may be subject to rules that others in the trade adhere to. The UCC is equipped to handle all of these situations.

Absent Terms.   One of the most important terms that can be omitted from a contract is the one that sets the price. Under the law of contracts no contract results if the price is not specified. Under the UCC, however, an **open price term** does not eliminate the reality of a contract (UCC 2–305). The court holds that a contract exists whenever that is the intent of the parties, regardless of whether or not they've agreed on a price. They are then given time to agree to that term. If they cannot agree, the court will set the price at a reasonable amount determined as of the time of delivery.

Open Price Term: omission from sales contract of specification of consideration due for goods

HYPOTHETICAL CASE

Wayne C. Barnum knew a good thing. The 74 merry-go-round horses were extravagantly designed and painted. They were exactly what he needed to get his new amusement park off the ground. Smiling, Wayne approached Jim Bailey, the craftsman who made them, with an offer. Bailey counteroffered. Barnum said, "Look, we've got a deal here. I need to get my employees on the job setting up the whirl. So let me get busy on that. We'll agree to the price later." Bailey agreed. A court enforcing the UCC would give them time to work out a price. If they could not, the court would have the trier of fact determine what a reasonable price for the horses was at the time Barnum's employees took delivery of them.

Where the exact quantity of the subject matter purchased is omitted in favor of such statements as "all of the item we need" or "all of the item we can produce," the UCC will enforce the contract. We have already discussed such requirements and output contracts. The law of contracts did not support them until the UCC's standards of good faith and performing to reasonable expectations proved workable in these areas. Place of delivery and terms of payment may also be inferred by the courts through these standards.

Course of Dealings: understandings between parties from previous transactions

Trade Usage: pattern of dealing established in commercial aea in which parties are dealing

The UCC's course of dealings and trade usage rules are additional sources of aid to courts trying to keep alive a sales contract with missing terms. **Course of dealings** refers to the understandings that the parties to the contract have developed in their previous transactions. **Trade usage** is a pattern of dealing established in the area of commerce in question that the parties to the contract can be expected to adhere to. Finally, the course of dealings of the parties to the contract, what they did and did not do, may also be referred to for guidance. All of these sources can be drawn on to fill in terms absent from the contract. However, when the actual terms of the contract conflict with or rule out the use of either course of dealings or trade usage, the contract's terms prevail.

HYPOTHETICAL CASE

The Baldknobber's Noose, a tourist-oriented store in Branson, Missouri, sold concrete lawn furnishings. Normally, the Noose placed an order for 25 concrete miniature outhouses from its supplier in midseason and the supplier accepted the order and delivered the outhouses to the Noose's front door. This time, however, due to being extremely busy transporting a large order to a national park in the Southwest, the supplier did not deliver them. Orville Waxworm, owner of the Noose, called the supplier when the outhouses were not delivered. When told that he would have to bear the cost of having a truck line transport them, Oliver did so under protest and then sued the supplier.

As you might suspect from our discussion, the court handling the "Noose" suit would hold that the course of dealings between the two merchants indicates that the supplier was to deliver the outhouses and was responsible for the costs of so doing.

Firm Offers. For offers, as for other areas, merchants must adhere to a higher standard than that required of nonmerchants. In particular, no consideration is required to hold a merchant to a promise to keep an offer for the sale of goods open for a certain time. This is true as long as the offer is made in writing, is signed by the merchant, and is not to be effective for more than three months. Such an offer is referred to as a **firm offer** under the law of sales (UCC 2–205). Under the law of contracts, we knew it as an option. Other than under the law of sales, such an option has to be supported by consideration to be legally enforceable. Put differently, the offeror has to be paid something of value to keep the offer open. Otherwise, the offeror can withdraw the offer at any time even before the promised period had run.

Firm Offer: written offer signed by merchant

HYPOTHETICAL CASE

Jeremy Bean placed a newspaper ad to sell his old bike for $50. His first call came from Mike Terratola, who offered Jeremy $40. Jeremy counteroffered with $45. Mike said he'd have to come over and take a look at the bike before he'd go any higher. Jeremy replied that he'd keep the $45 offer open till the following morning. By the time Mike showed up, Jeremy had received calls from several other parties who were on their way over to see the bike. Jeremy therefore withdrew his offer of $45.

Even though a sale of goods was in question, Jeremy was able to do this because he was not a merchant and had not made a firm offer. Had Jeremy been a merchant and had he put the offer to sell at $45 anytime before the next morning in writing and signed it, the offer would be binding against him.

Acceptances under the UCC

The UCC has made three important changes with regard to acceptances. The first change involves the mode of acceptance, the second involves additional terms in the acceptance, and the third involves the more specialized case of prompt shipment.

Mode of Acceptance. Under the law of contracts, if the offeror requires a particular mode of acceptance, such as phone, letter, telegram, or fax, that mode must be followed to produce a contract. Also under the law of contracts, if no particular mode is required, the acceptance is effective if it is sent in the same mode as that used by the offeror to make the offer. For example, a contract results at the moment that, in response to a mailed offer, the offeree drops her or his acceptance in the mail. If a different mode is used, for example, if a fax is sent in response to a mailed offer, the acceptance is effective only when the offeror receives it. Got all those rules? There are more, but . . .

The UCC simplifies all that. UCC 2–206 states that "unless unambiguously indicated by the language or circumstances," the offeree is allowed to accept in any reasonable manner or by an reasonable medium. Such an acceptance is effective when sent. End of discussion.

Additional Terms in the Acceptance. In the same vein as its rules relating to mode of acceptance, the law of contracts dooms any would-be acceptance that contains additional terms. Successful acceptances are required to be absolute and unconditional. Again not so under the UCC.

According to UCC 2–207, which deals with additional terms in the acceptance, a sales contract is formed even if the "definite and seasonal expression of acceptance . . . sent within a reasonable time" includes some different terms. These additional or altered terms are treated as proposals that will be added to the contract if and when nonmerchant parties agree to them. Merchant parties, however, have to be more alert. Why? Because for merchants, if the new terms are not **material** (essential), they will become part of the contract unless the recipient gives some notification of objection to them within a reasonable time or unless the offeror expressly limited acceptance to the terms of the offer. If the terms are material, they cannot become a part of the contract without the actual assent of the offeror.

Material: essential

HYPOTHETICAL CASE

Murphy Anderson ran Chips 'n' Dips, an electronic goods store. Late one fall she mailed the following order to her wholesaler: "Send me 250 computer chips set to run at 50 megahertz at the price shown in your fall catalog. If you don't have that
continued on page 202

concluded

chip at that price, just forget it." The wholesaler faxed back an acceptance of her offer that read as follows, "Will ship 250 chips at Fall Catalog price but set at a slower megahertz unless we hear from you within 10 days. We will ship by UPS second-day air COD with insurance." Murphy did not communicate further with the wholesaler, who then sent the order some 15 days later. When Murphy refused to pay upon delivery, the wholesaler sued for enforcement of the contract and the shipment costs. The wholesaler argued that the additional terms it had proposed in its acceptance had not been rejected within a reasonable time and that Murphy was a merchant, so those terms therefore became part of the contract. The court held for Murphy, stating that she had restricted acceptance to the goods requested in her original offer and that the subject matter in question, namely the type of chip, was a material term. Therefore, UCC 2–207 prevented a contract from coming into existence. Without a contract, the additional terms of the acceptance relating to shipment had no bearing.

Prompt Shipment.　The latitude that the UCC rules allow sellers when buyers demand prompt shipment also has a significant impact on acceptances. If Murphy Anderson had said "I need these chips yesterday" or had used other words to indicate the necessity of prompt shipment, the wholesaler could have accepted by simply shipping immediately. Doing so brings problems, however. Hopefully, the shipped goods will be **conforming goods,** that is, goods specifically fulfilling the seller's obligations under the contract with the buyer. If, however, the goods deviate from the buyer's specifications or are defective in some way, they are labeled **nonconforming goods.** The shipment of nonconforming goods may act both as an acceptance binding the seller to the contract and as a breach of that contract. This will be true unless the seller notifies the buyer that such goods are being offered merely as an accommodation. An accommodation is an arrangement or favor to the buyer, done perhaps because the seller who could not fill the order as given wanted to stay on the buyer's good side. It is not treated as consideration that would bind the buyer to the contract. If the buyer accepts the accommodation of substitute goods, then a contract would result only for the purchase of those goods. So if the wholesaler promptly shipped Murphy Anderson the nonconforming goods without giving notice that the goods were merely an accommodation, the wholesaler would be bound to the contract. If, however, the wholesaler sent notice that the substitute goods were an accommodation, then the wholesaler could not be sued for breach because no contract would be held to exist for the goods originally ordered. If Murphy refused the substitute goods, then no contract would have resulted for either set of goods.

Conforming Goods: subject matter fulfilling contract specifications

Nonconforming Goods: subject matter deviating from contract specifications

Performance under the UCC

Once the contract has been solidified, the UCC is very plain as to what it expects of the parties. UCC 2–601 states that "if the goods or the tender of delivery fail in any respect to conform to the contract, the buyer may (a) reject the whole; or (b) accept the whole; or (c) accept any commercial unit or units and reject the rest." In short, a **perfect tender** is expected. Should it not be forthcoming, the buyer may use any of the remedies listed above.

Perfect Tender: offer to perform conforming completely to contract obligations

Perfect Tender Requirement.   We'll discuss the remedies in detail in Chapter 17. The important point here, however, is the absolute nature of the requirement on the seller of the goods. Note, though, that when a contract requires performance to the satisfaction of the buyer, that performance is judged from the perspective of what the buyer's reasonable expectations should be, not what they actually are.

HYPOTHETICAL CASE

Grandma Jones was a "whittler" in the language of the Ozark Mountains of Missouri. Well known regionally, she turned out statuettes of hillbilly figures. After viewing some of her work, representatives of a large New York City department store contracted with her for several carvings "suitable for our customers." When the whittled figures were delivered, the department store sued because they were not of sufficient detail to meet the standards of its customers. The carvings closely resembled those that Grandma Jones made for her regional trade. The court held that they were acceptable goods under the sales contract as they should have matched the reasonable expectations of the buyer.

Tender of Delivery.   Another hedge on the perfect tender requirement is the seller's opportunity to cure. **Cure** under the UCC means the ability to replace a defective tender with one that is proper under the contract.

Cure: right to replace defective tender with proper one

UCC 2–508 allows the seller to cure in only two circumstances. If there is still time to perform properly under the contract or if the seller had reasonable grounds to believe that the tender of nonconforming goods (with or without a money allowance for the shortcomings of the tender) would be accepted, the seller can give notice and try again. In the latter situation, even if the time to perform has expired, the UCC will allow the seller "a further reasonable time to substitute a conforming tender."

Tender of Payment.   Unless otherwise agreed, the tender of conforming goods is contingent on the concurrent requirement for a proper tender of payment. Such payment can be by any means or mode normally used in business unless the seller demands payment in legal tender (money). If the seller makes this demand, she or he must give the buyer a reasonable time to obtain it. If the seller accepts payment by check, it is conditional on the payment of that instrument by the bank (UCC 2–511).

That about does it for the UCC changes in the standard way of handling things under the law of contracts. However, before concluding our discussion, we need to look at the auction and the bulk transfer, two sales situations that are given special treatment by the UCC.

What Special Rules Apply to Situations Involving Bulk Transfers and Auction Sales?

Both bulk transfers and auction sales involve the sale of goods. However, due to their unique problems, special rules are applied to them.

Bulk Transfers

Bulk Transfer:
extraordinary trading away
of major part of
commercial enterprise's
assets

Under the UCC a **bulk transfer** is a trading away of a major part of a commerical enterprise's inventory, supplies, and/or equipment in a transaction that does not occur during the ordinary course of doing business.

The problems come when a business tries to undercut the rightful claim of its creditors by such a transfer. The creditors expect the debts owed them by the business to be satisfied at least in part by the value of its inventory, supplies, and equipment. Merchants who saw the end nearing for their business all too often sold off such assets. They then used the proceeds from the sale in ways (such as payments to investors in the business) that left unpaid creditors with nothing to execute their claims against. Bulk transfers were therefore made the subject of a special UCC article, Article 6.

This article puts a special burden on the transferee of the goods involved in a bulk transfer. Certain very specific requirements must be met. If not, creditors of the transferor can demand the return of all the goods involved without having to compensate the transferee. The requirements are as follows:

1. The transferee must get a list from the transferor of the latter's creditors, their addresses, and the amounts due each of them.
2. The transferee and transferor must make out a schedule of the property subject to the transfer so that the items can be identified.
3. The transferee must have the list and the schedule available for inspection for up to six months after the transfer.
4. The transferee must give the creditors notice of the transfer at least 10 days before paying for the goods or taking possession of them, depending on which occurs first.

Creditors who have failed to act to stop the transfer after the transferee has observed these requirements have lost any right to do so that they might have had.

Auction Sales

Auction: authorized public
sale of property to highest
bidder

**Auction Sale with
Reserve:** auctioneer's
withdrawal of goods before
completion permitted

**Auction Sale without
Reserve:** auctioneer's
withdrawal of goods before
completion not permitted

An **auction** is defined as a public sale of property to the highest bidder by someone authorized to conduct the sale (the auctioneer). UCC 2–328 covers this type of sale. It mentions two types of auctions. In the first, an **auction sale with reserve,** the auctioneer is able to withdraw an item at any time before she or he announces the completion of its sale. In the second, an **auction sale without reserve,** the auctioneer cannot withdraw an item after he or she asks for bids on it.

Note that the description of the items up for sale and the request for bids all fall under the heading of an invitation to negotiate from contract law. The bids are considered offers. As such, they may be withdrawn by the bidder at any time before a contract has been concluded by the auctioneer. The auctioneer usually indicates this conclusion or acceptance by banging down the gavel and saying "Sold." The bidder (offeror) can withdraw the offer at any time before this indication has been given. Such a retraction, however, does not revive any previous bid.

If the gavel is falling just as a new bid is made, the auctioneer may go ahead with the auction using the new bid or just sell the item under the bid on which the gavel is falling.

Some auctions are rigged by the sellers. They do this by planting individuals (often called shills) in the crowd who bid against the innocent, unsuspecting bidders to produce higher prices for the goods on sale. This practice is forbidden by the UCC except in a forced sale, such as a sale of foreclosed property by the sheriff. In a normal sale, however, if a shill is utilized, the buyer can avoid the sale or buy the good at the last good faith offer made prior to the completion of the sale. This penalty often produces a significantly lower price for the buyer at the seller's expense.

APPLICATIONS OF WHAT YOU'VE LEARNED

Vocabulary Development

Fill in the blanks with the appropriate term.

Acceptance	**Auction Sale**	**Course of Dealings**	**Open Price Term**
Auction	**with Reserve**	**Material**	**Perfect Tender**
Auction Sale	**Bulk Transfer**	**Nonconforming Goods**	**Trade Usage**
without Reserve	**Conforming Goods**		

[Some of the answers may be drawn from the preceding chapter.]

1. Hanson's business was on the ropes. Before his creditors knew what was going on, he sold his inventory and delivery fleet to a competing store for a fraction of its value. He then took the proceeds of the sale and paid himself a high salary. The sale of the goods was a(n) _____.

2. An offer to produce goods that conform exactly to the sales contract is a(n) _____.

3. Omitting the amount of consideration payable for the goods sold is to leave a(n) _____.

4. When goods are not in existence at the time of contracting, they are labeled _____.

5. The pattern of doing business that the parties to the sales contract have established in their previous transactions is termed a(n) _____.

6. Land and buildings are termed _____ property.

7. A watch is labeled _____ property.

8. A(n) _____ term to the contract is essential to its enforceability.

Problems

1. Assume Sports Wholesalers sent a written confirmation that Putting Green received on May 15. Putting Green, a golf pro shop, rejected the confirmation's terms on May 30. Would Putting Green be bound to the confirmation's terms? Why or why not?

2. On May 12, Putting Green orally ordered $1,500

worth of golf gloves from Sports Wholesalers. The gloves came on May 18. Six weeks of the season passed before Putting Green tried to negate the contract by refusing to pay. Putting Green claimed that since there was no writing, it was not obligated. Do you agree? Why or why not?

3. Colling's Hardware Store ordered 500 pounds of 12

and 16 penny nails from its usual supplier. When Colling's checked on the price by phone over a week before it placed the order, the nails were wholesaling for 18 cents a pound. However, no price was mentioned when the order was placed. When the nails were delivered, a bill for $100 (20 cents a pound) came with them. Colling's refused to pay, saying no contract existed because a price term had not been agreed to. When the case was litigated before the small claims court, the nails were selling at 15 cents a pound. The court found in favor of the supplier, holding that under the UCC a contract did exist between the two merchants. What price will the court require Colling's to pay for the nails?

4. When Phil's Floral Shoppe ran out of poinsettias for the holidays, it placed an order for prompt shipment of five dozen more with its wholesaler. The wholesaler shipped five dozen Irishsettias, a similar potted plant, with notice that they were an accommodation. Phil's kept the Irishsettias and sold several. After the season, however, Phil's sued the wholesaler for a breach of contract for the poinsettias. Will it succeed?

5. Glory Daze, a religious broadcasting station with its own satellite transponder, bought the equipment and tape library of a competing station. The deal, a tremendous bargain, was closed quickly. Two months later Glory Daze received notice that creditors of the competing station were demanding the return of its assets. Under what law could they take this action? Would Glory Daze have to return the assets even if it could not get back the money it paid for them?

ACTUAL CASE STUDY

Sedmak v. Charlie's Chevrolet, Inc.

622 S.W.2d 694

In July 1977, Dr. Sedmak read in *Vette Vues,* a Corvette fancier's magazine, that the Pace Car, a special edition of the Corvette, would soon be manufactured. He was a collector of Corvettes and wanted one of the 6,000 that were to be placed on sale. In January 1978, Mrs. Sedmak gave Charlie's Chevrolet a $500 check as a deposit on a Pace Car and specified the options that the Sedmaks desired. She was then informed that the purchase price of the car would be around $15,000. In April 1978, the Sedmaks were notified that the Pace Car, equipped as specified, had arrived but because of the increased demand for the car, it would be put up for bids. The Sedmaks did not submit a bid; instead, they filed a suit for specific performance.

The trial court found that the parties had entered into an oral contract. If that contract could be excepted from the application of the Statute of Frauds, the court would order specific performance as requested. Charlie's would then have to sell the car to the Sedmaks at a reasonable price, which, given the options added, would be around $15,000.

Questions

1. Should the oral contract be excepted from the application of the Statute of Frauds?

2. Assuming that the contract should be so excepted, which one or more of the acceptable grounds would you use to justify the exception?

When Does Ownership of the Goods Transfer in a Sales Contract?

CHAPTER OUTLINE AND OBJECTIVES

After studying this chapter, the student will be able to:

I. Explain the importance of title within the overall concept of ownership.
   a. Valid and void title
   b. Voidable title
   c. Title to entrusted goods

II. List the rules that determine when the attributes of goods ownership, that is, title, risk of loss, and insurable interest, are obtained during a sales transaction.
   a. Insurable interest
   b. Title and risk of loss
   c. Exceptional situations

III. Recognize special situations that affect the application of these rules.
   a. Sale on approval
   b. Sale or return

IV. Apply the rules of risk of loss to *Prewitt* v. *Numismatic Funding Corp.*, a case involving $60,000 in lost coins.

What Is Meant by Ownership of Goods?

When we began our study of sales back in Chapter 14, we defined title as the ultimate legal right to ownership of property. The concept of ownership, however, takes in far more rights than just title. Possession, use, the right to sell or mortgage, and a number of other rights are all bundled together to form our concept of ownership of a good. It is possible for each of these rights to be in the hands of a different person. For example, I may have possession of my son's car but allow my wife to drive it to various locations while I ride as a passenger. My son is the legal titleholder, true, but he has allowed the bank the right to take the car away from him if he fails to make payments on his car loan. In a sense all three of us and the bank have property rights in the car, but the predominant right is title.

Valid and Void Title

Valid Title: legally enforceable claim of ownership

Void Title: nonexistent claim of ownership

Whenever goods are purchased, the presumption is that the seller had **valid** (legally enforceable) **title** to them. This is not always the case, however. The seller may have been offering stolen goods for sale, in which case, the title that passed to the buyer is termed a **void** (or nonexistent) **title.** In short, the buyer receives nothing but possession and use. The true owner maintains valid title to the goods and may come in and claim them at any time. This is true no matter how innocent the purchase may have been or how many innocent purchasers and sellers may have transferred the goods previously. The innocent purchaser of stolen goods is left with only the alternative of suing the seller, who, all too often, has disappeared with the money.

Voidable Title

Voidable Title: claim of ownership terminable by party to sales contract

Instead of receiving void title by purchase of stolen goods, a buyer may buy problems by purchasing voidable title. **Voidable title,** like a voidable contract, may be terminated at the option of one of the parties. Until that occurs, however, the title is considered valid. Such a faulty title can originate in a situation in which goods are obtained from minors or others incapacitated in contracting. It can also be obtained through duress, undue influence, or fraud. The difference in effect between void and voidable title is that an innocent purchaser of a good whose seller has voidable title receives valid title.

HYPOTHETICAL CASE

Stanley Spoke decided to have a garage sale to raise money for his motorcycle group's annual road ride to a bikers' get-together in the Midwest. Herb Ignatius, a Boy Scout leader who happened by during the sale, bought a color television set for the Flaming Bison troop's den room and four handheld scanner radios for the upcoming all-troop hike to the headwaters of the Santa Ana River in lower California. Later the police visited Herb. They informed him that the radios had been stolen from an electronics store in downtown LA and that the color TV set had been

continue on page 211

concluded

purchased by Spoke from a widow for $5 after members of the club threatened to beat her cat. Since Herb was an innocent purchaser, although he would have to return the stolen merchandise as his title to it was void, he and the scouts did have valid title to the color TV. Herb and the troop, however, voted to return it to the widow.

Title to Entrusted Goods

HYPOTHETICAL CASE

Helene Heartburn, noted star of the long-running TV soap opera "Destiny's Fate," took her new watch in for repairs. The watch was nearly pure gold with diamond-studded settings. Unknown to Helene, the jeweler, Mitch Wastrel, had run up some very serious gambling debts. To cover these debts, Mitch put her watch up for sale, then gave her a cheap replica. Winna Winsome, an innocent purchaser, bought the real watch for $27,500. A few months later, Helene was showing the replica to another jeweler, who exclaimed that it was a fake. Helene then realized what had happened. In the meantime, however, Mitch Wastrel had gone out of business and disappeared. Helene then determined from his business records that Winna had purchased her watch. Can she recover her valuable timepiece from Winna?

Especially since the Great Depression, when confidence in the market system was greatly shaken, a major emphasis of the law has been to give consumers assurances about what they buy. The UCC follows suit in section 2–403(2) when it states: "Any entrusting of possession of goods to a merchant who deals in goods of that kind gives him power to transfer all rights of the entruster to a buyer in the ordinary course of business." A later subsection states that this holds true regardless of "any condition expressed between the parties" to the entrusting. In short, whenever you turn over your possessions to a merchant, you are giving that merchant the power to transfer good title to any innocent purchaser of those possessions in the ordinary course of business. Therefore, the merchant's reputation and many other factors should play a role in your decision as to whom to entrust with your valuables. The more important the possession, the more care you should take. As you may suspect, Helene's only recourse is against Mitch. Under the UCC, Winna has acquired good title by virtue of her good faith purchase in the ordinary course of business. The watch cannot be retaken from her by legal action.

What Rules Determine When Title, Risk of Loss, and Insurable Interest in Goods are Obtained During a Sales Transaction?

All too often, even when the requirements for forming a valid contract for a sale have been complied with, something goes wrong. Goods are lost, stolen, damaged, or destroyed before, during, or after transit. Whenever something of that nature occurs, it becomes necessary to determine whether the buyer or the seller must suffer the loss. This risk of loss is often determined by simply finding out who has title as, generally, the loss then falls on that titleholder. However, there are exceptions to this rule which we will discuss in the latter portions of the chapter.

Insurable Interest

Insurable Interest: indemnifiable property right in goods

Knowing the hazards involved, a wise party to a sales contract may take out insurance to cover a potential loss of the goods. As a consequence, it becomes important to determine who has an insurable interest in them. An **insurable interest** is a property right in goods whose potential loss can be indemnified (protected against).

Identified: specified as subject matter of sales contract

The seller has such an interest until title passes to the buyer. The buyer obtains an insurable interest as soon as the contract has been made and the goods have been identified to it. **Identified** to the contract means that specific goods are selected by some party as the subject matter of the deal. They may be tagged, marked with the name of the buyer, placed in a certain part of the warehouse or shipping area, wrapped together, gathered off the shelves into the buyer's cart, and so on. How the goods are identified is generally immaterial. Fungible goods are the only exception. Salt, grain, sugar, oil, and gas are examples of such goods.

Fungible Goods: subject matter of which one unit is the equivalent of any other unit

In essence, **fungible goods** are those goods one unit of which is acknowledged by trade usage to be identical with any other unit. Therefore, identification of a certain amount of fungible goods occurs whenever the bulk from which it will come is indicated. The exact amount of salt or whatever other fungible good does not have to be segregated for that fungible good to be identified to the contract.

The point, however, is that both the buyer and the seller may have an insurable interest in the goods at the same time during the sales transaction. Typically this overlap occurs between the time when the goods are identified to the contract and the time when they are received and accepted by the buyer. During this time, both parties would recover if the goods were to be damaged or lost.

Title and Risk of Loss

Aside from the period of overlap, title remains the most important determinant of which party (or which party's insurance company) must bear a loss when it occurs. Unless the parties specifically agree otherwise, as soon as the goods are identified, title typically passes to the buyer when the seller delivers those goods in accordance with the contract terms.

Shipment Term: requires turning over of goods to carrier for delivery to buyer

There are two categories of delivery terms in sales contracts. The first is the **shipment term.** This category calls for the seller to turn the goods over to a carrier for delivery to the buyer. Once this has been done, the seller has no further responsibility for seeing that the goods reach their destination. In a sales contract with a shipment term, title and the risk of loss pass to the buyer upon the seller's delivery of the goods to the carrier.

Destination Term: requires delivery of goods by seller to buyer

The second category is referred to as a **destination term.** Such a term requires the seller to be responsible for the delivery of the goods to their destination. Title and the risk of loss then pass to the buyer when the seller makes a **tender of delivery** (an offer to turn over the goods to the buyer) at that location.

The business world uses a shorthand to specify which type of term is controlling in a particular sales contract. If you read "Free On Board (FOB) place of shipment" in the contract, this indicates that the costs of shipment to the destination are being paid for by the buyer. "FOB place of destination" indicates that the costs of shipment to the destination are being borne by the seller. Risk of loss and title then pass as described above. Note that a term with similar effect relating to sea transportation is Free Alongside Ship (FAS) either at the seller's or buyer's dock or port, again with title and risk of loss passing accordingly. If no terms of shipment are specified, the contract is assumed to be a shipment contract.

Tender of Delivery: offer to turn over goods to buyer

HYPOTHETICAL CASE

While Missouri Valley tennis champion in the 60 and older category, Joe Crowson purchased 12 cases of tennis balls from Double Fault, a mail-order discount house for tennis supplies in San Andreas, California. As the contract did not cover shipping, Double Fault arranged for the pickup and delivery of the cases by a local trucking firm. When the balls were destroyed in a wreck of the trucking firm's only vehicle, Joe had to bear the loss as Double Fault's risk ended with the satisfaction of the contract, which was implied to be a shipment contract by the UCC. However, should it still be solvent, Joe might recover from the trucking firm.

Other terms that affect delivery include Cash On Delivery (COD) and Cost, Insurance, and Freight (CIF). COD requires the shipper to collect the cost of the goods (and often of shipping as well) before turning them over to the buyer. CIF (or sometimes just CF if insurance is not included) requires the carrier to collect the cost of the goods, the insurance, and the shipping in one lump sum.

Exceptional Situations

"Buyer Pick Up" Sales Contracts. When the buyer agrees to pick up the goods rather than have them delivered, special rules apply. The title passes at the time of contracting. If the seller is a merchant, however, the risk of loss passes when the buyer actually receives the goods. If the seller is not a merchant, the risk of loss is passed to the buyer when the seller makes the goods available for pickup by the buyer.

HYPOTHETICAL CASE

Stacy Portman had just moved into her first apartment since graduating school, and it was bare. But it wouldn't be long. Smiling, Stacy made a left turn into McClernon's Furniture. It was having its big annual red-tag sale . . . Half an hour later she drove out of the McClernon's lot, the proud owner of a new living room set. Rather than pay the shipping charges, Stacy had told McClernon's that before the day was out,

continued on page 214

concluded

she would return with her pickup to get the furniture. McClernon's had promised that it would be on the loading dock waiting for her. On her way to get the pickup, Stacy bought a bedroom suite at a yard sale from a teacher who was moving to another city. When the teacher said that she could take the suite with her immediately, she replied that she would be back within the next two hours to pick it up. Unfortunately, before Stacy could return to McClernon's or the yard sale, a sudden rain-, wind-, and hailstorm hit without any warning and destroyed both sets of furniture. Who must bear the loss in each instance, and why?*

Documents of Title.   Another exception to the general rules for passage of title involves the use of ship's bills, bills of lading, warehouse receipts, and other **documents of title.** These instruments evidence the power of the person who possesses them to control the instruments themselves and the goods they cover. In certain sales situations, the purchaser is given a document of title instead of immediate possession. When presented to the appropriate warehouse or carrier, the document of title will allow the purchaser to receive the goods. Unless the parties agree otherwise, when a document of title is used in a sales transaction, both the title and the risk of loss are transferred to the buyer upon the delivery of that document.

Documents of Title: instruments evidencing possessor's control over them and goods they cover

HYPOTHETICAL CASE

José purchased 100 video cameras from their manufacturer in Yokohama, Japan. As José wanted the goods delivered to the United States, the manufacturer placed them aboard a merchant ship headed for San Diego, California. The ship's master inventoried them as they came on board. When the ship left port, the manufacturer was issued a ship's bill, a document of title to the video cameras. When the manufacturer received payment for the goods, it signed the ship's bill over to José and sent it to him by Express Mail. When the goods arrived in San Diego, José was able to pick them up by presenting the document of title. He had become the titleholder and responsible for any loss of the video cameras at the time the document arrived.

Agreements.   As has been mentioned in passing, if the parties to the contract specifically agree on the time when title and risk of loss are to be passed, that agreed-to time takes precedence over the UCC rules concerning the matter. This is not the case only when the parties agree that the seller is to retain title even after shipment or delivery to the buyer. In section 2–401 the UCC identifies this arrangement as the retention of a security interest by the seller. A **security interest** is a property right that allows its holder legal recourse against specific property (in this case the goods) if a debt or obligation is not paid off. (Chapter 22 will cover security interests in depth.) When such a situation occurs, title passes as though there were no agreement of the parties.

Security Interest: right of legal recourse against specified property if obligation not fulfilled

---

*McClernon's must bear the loss for the living room set. Since the store is considered a merchant under the UCC, even though Stacy owned the set as of the time of contracting, the risk of loss stayed with the store because she had not *received the goods.* In the case of the bedroom suite, however, the seller is not a merchant but a teacher. Therefore, both title and the risk of loss passed to Stacy, the former at contracting, the latter when the goods were tendered by the teacher saying take them with you, in other words by making an offer to turn them over to her. Stacy must therefore bear the loss of the bedroom suite.

When the Buyer Says No.   UCC 2–401(4) covers a ticklish area:

> A rejection or other refusal by the buyer to receive or retain the goods, whether or not justified, or a justified revocation of acceptance revests title to the goods in the seller. Such revesting occurs by operation of law and is not a "sale."

"Justification" in the meaning of 2–401(4) is usually found in defective or nonconforming goods. Of course, revesting title in the seller still leaves the risk of loss undetermined. UCC 2–510 controls that issue. If the rejection occurs because the goods are nonconforming, the risk of loss remains with the seller until cure or acceptance. If a defect is discovered after acceptance and the acceptance is consequently revoked by the buyer, the risk of loss depends on the insurance coverage of the buyer. According to 2–510, the buyer must cover the loss up to the amount of her or his insurance, if any, and the remainder of the loss falls on the seller.

So much for the buyer's justifiable actions. If, instead, the buyer breaches the sales contract after the goods are identified to the contract, the risk of loss beyond the seller's insurance coverage may be shifted to the buyer for a commercially reasonable time. Let that sink in. Once again, the risk of loss shifts after identification, not after shipment, delivery, or acceptance. Also, if the seller has no insurance coverage, the buyer has the full risk of loss during the period. This makes breaching a sales contract potentially even more damaging should a loss of the goods occur.

What Special Situations Affect the Application of These Rules?

The desire to capture customers often causes suppliers of goods to offer special deals. These deals often pose particular problems for the application of the rules we have just discussed. The two most often encountered deals involve terms calling for sale on approval or for sale with the right of return.

Sale on Approval

HYPOTHETICAL CASE

Angela Coy listened enraptured as the announcer spelled out the terms of the transaction: ". . . and if you do not want to keep the Wonder Carpet Coater, simply return it before the 30-day trial period is up for a full refund . . . just call 1-800-289-7226—that's 1-800-BUY-SCAM—and never have to vacuum your carpet again." Angela punched the 1-800 number into her portable phone without hesitation. A few days later the device came, complete with supplies. Angela immediately ran the Carpet Coater over her rugs. Afterward the pile of the carpet glistened with the newly applied stain- and dirt-repellent coating. Sure enough, as guaranteed, the carpet did not have to be vacuumed. In fact, the carpet pile had turned as hard and slippery as sheet ice. Then days after purchasing the Carpet Coater, Angela decided to return it. She informed 1-800-BUY-SCAM of her decision. Unfortunately, as she was driving downtown to ship her purchase back, her car was sideswiped by a large truck and overturned. The Carpet Coater was destroyed. Who had the risk of loss of the Carpet Coater at the time of the accident?

Sale on Approval: deal allowing buyer/user to return even conforming goods

A **sale on approval** is a transaction in which the buyer is allowed to return the goods within a reasonable period even if they conform to the contract. A sale on approval is distinguished from a sale or return, which we will discuss in a moment, by the fact that the goods involved are intended primarily for the buyer's use instead of for resale.

In a sale on approval, the title and risk of loss stay with the seller until the buyer accepts the goods. This acceptance may be found in the oral or written statements of the buyer. It may also be indicated by showing extreme carelessness in handling the goods or by keeping them beyond a reasonable time. Acceptance is not found in the trial use of the goods in an expected way. So in Angela's case, her working on her carpet would not show acceptance. Therefore, the risk of loss was still on the seller when the Carpet Coater was destroyed. Also note that as title had not passed to Angela, none of her creditors (should any exist) could satisfy the amounts due them from the value of the Carpet Coater.

Sale or Return

Sale or Return: deal allowing buyer/reseller to return even conforming goods

In a **sale or return,** goods sold primarily for resale may be returned even though they conform to the contract. Title and risk of loss pass to the buyer upon acceptance. Therefore, the buyer's creditors can reach the goods and if the goods are destroyed, for instance, the buyer must still pay for them. The buyer must take reasonable care of the goods in case they are to be returned. Finally, the return is at the buyer's expense and risk.

APPLICATIONS OF WHAT YOU'VE LEARNED

Vocabulary Development

Fill in the blanks with the appropriate term.

Destination Term	**Insurable Interest**	**Security Interest**	**Valid Title**
Documents of Title	**Sale on Approval**	**Shipment Term**	**Voidable Title**
Fungible Goods	**Sale or Return**	**Tender of Delivery**	**Void Title**
Identified			

[Some of the answers may be drawn from the preceding chapter.]

1. Bills of lading, airbills, and warehouse receipts are examples of _____.

2. A legally enforceable claim of ownership to goods is referred to as _____.

3. A(n) _____ involves the contractual right to return conforming goods that were purchased for resale.

4. A written offer signed by a merchant is termed a(n) _____.

5. Waldo bought a new car by borrowing money from his credit union. In return for the loan he agreed to make payments of principal and interest to the credit union. He also created in the credit union the right to repossess and sell the car if he failed to keep up with the payments of principal and interest. This right is referred to as a(n) _____

6. A contract provision calling for the seller to transfer the goods to a shipper for delivery to the buyer is known as a(n) _____.

7. Salt, grain, sugar, and other items with identical units when taken as subject matter to a sales contract are termed _____.

Problems

1. Marshall Mishappe innocently bought a wristwatch from Deals in Digitals, a watch repair and sales shop. The watch he bought had been mistakenly placed on sale after Annie Analog brought it in for repair. What kind of title did Marshall have to the watch? What claim does Annie Analog have, and against whom?

2. Marshall Mishappe innocently bought a stolen bicycle for $375 from Deals on Two Wheels, a cycle repair and sales shop. What type of title did he acquire to the bike? What legal action was open to him after the original owner reclaimed her property? In what court would he be likely to file his action?

3. Marshall Mishappe and his wife, Missy, ran a religious bookstore called HyMMMs. A church in the Mishappe's community ordered 100 hymnals from them. The hymnals were taken out of the Mishappes' warehouse and stamped with the name of the church. Before they could be shipped, however, the church replaced its old pastor. The new pastor called the Mishappes, informed them that the ordered hymnals were blasphemous, and tried to cancel the order. The hymnals were destroyed that very evening, when the Mishappes' store was hit by a bolt of lightening and burned to the ground. The Mishappes did not have insurance. Who bears the cost of the loss of the hymnals?

4. The Mishappes had displayed several racks of greeting cards for sale that were transferred to them under a contract with a sale or return feature. When their store burned, the cards were destroyed. Who bore the risk of their loss?

ACTUAL CASE STUDY

Prewitt v. Numismatic Funding Corp.

745 F.2d 1175

On February 10, 1982, Numismatic Funding Corporation mailed Frederick Prewitt, a commodities broker in St. Louis, Missouri, gold and silver coins valued at more than $60,000. The corporation sold rare and collector coins by mail throughout the United States. It had dealt with Prewitt on two previous occasions. The terms were stated in literature enclosed with the coins: "Everything is available to you on a 14-day approval basis." The invoice stated that title did not pass until the buyer paid the account in full and that the buyer had 14 days from the date of receipt in which to settle the account. The literature gave no directions on how to return unwanted coins.

In the words of the court, "Upon receiving the coins, Prewitt instructed his wife to return them via certified mail for the maximum amount of insurance available—$400 for each package (2 packages). She mailed the coins on February 23, 1982, but Numismatic never received them. Thereafter, Prewitt brought this action seeking a declaration of his nonliability for the loss in mailing."

Questions

1. Who must bear the $60,000-plus loss for the coins, Prewitt or Numismatic? Why?

2. Numismatic's sales technique was to ask each buyer by phone to agree to consider a number of coins for purchase. Upon the prospective buyer's agreement, Numismatic would then send the coins out on the terms cited above. Prewitt informed the court that he had complained to Numismatic that it often sent out more coins than had been agreed to (unsolicited merchandise). Given your answer to Question 1, would you recommend that Numismatic change its tactics. If so, how?

What Product Liability and Breach of Contract Remedies Are Available in a Sales Transaction?

CHAPTER OUTLINE AND OBJECTIVES

In the three preceding chapters we have dealt with the law covering that special area vital to our way of life called sales. We have seen how a relatively new body of law, the UCC's Article 2, was molded to provide clear, uniform, and current standards by which sales contracts and performances under them were to be judged. According to most, this effort was successful. However, beyond the sales contract itself lie other areas extremely important to such a transaction. Among these areas are the characteristics of the goods themselves and the remedies available for problems that arise under the contracts for their sale.

The impact of the characteristics of the goods is covered in this chapter's discussion of warranties and product liability. Following that, in the latter part of the chapter, the discussion turns to remedies for breach of sales contracts. These remedies are divided into those belonging to the buyer and those belonging to the seller. First, however, here's a hard look at warranties.

What Is the Significance of Warranties in Sales Transactions?

Warranty: guarantee

A **warranty** is nothing more or less than a guarantee. It is used to describe the product and the product's quality and performance. Within the context of a sale of goods, this means that a warranty is an assurance that is either expressly made by the seller (orally or in writing) or that will be implied against the seller by a court of law.

Express Warranties

Express Warranty: seller's oral or written assurance or its equivalent about good

To be legally exact an **express warranty** is an oral or written term or its equivalent in the sales agreement in which the seller makes some statement of assurance about the good being sold. According to UCC section 2–313, an express warranty can be created by a sample, a model, a description, or an "affirmation of fact or promise made by the seller to the buyer," any of which then becomes part of the "basis for the bargain."

HYPOTHETICAL CASE

> Jo Lee demonstrated a working model of his Life-light to a large department store chain. The customer would use enclosed Velcro strips to affix the Life-light to a visible outside portion of a house or apartment. Then, when the customer dialed 911, in an emergency situation, the light would come on and be a beacon to emergency vehicles. The department store chain bought 5,000 Life-lights. When these arrived, it was found that they lacked the computer chip necessary to turn on the light when 911 was dialed. Based on the model, which did contain such a chip, the department store chain brought a successful suit for breach of an express warranty.

Puffing: exaggerated statement of opinion by salesperson

Be sure to realize that the UCC distinguishes between an express warranty and puffing. **Puffing** is an exaggerated statement of opinion by a salesperson. Such statements as "This is the finest, most reliable car I've ever tried to sell off my lot" are easily recognizable as puffing by most people. Statements of this kind do not become the basis for the bargain and thus cannot be considered a warranty.

Magnuson-Moss Warranty Act

Of importance in the area of express warranties is the Magnuson-Moss Warranty Act. This act was passed by the federal government in 1975 to see that consumers were better informed about the warranties on the products they bought. The application of the act is strictly limited. In effect, it applies only to voluntarily issued written warranties on consumer products costing more than $15. These **consumer products** to which the act applies are defined as items of tangible personal property used for personal, family, or household purposes.

Whenever a written warranty is given on goods that fall under the act, three requirements must be observed. First, the warranty has to be available before the consumer's "buy" decision. Second, the warranty has to be expressed in easily understood language—no "legalese." Finally, the warranty must state whether it is a **full warranty** (the seller's promise to cover the costs of the labor and materials necessary to fix the product) or a limited warranty.

Given all of these requirements, it is easy to see the value of such a warranty. It is also easy to imagine the burden a warranty of this kind puts on those that give it.

If a manufacturer or seller of a consumer product does not choose to give a full warranty, it may nonetheless offer a written warranty meeting some of the requirements of a full warranty. Such a restricted written guarantee is termed a **limited warranty.** The ways to cut back on a full warranty are numerous. Perhaps the warranty extends to parts and not labor, or vice versa. Other limits include covering only the first purchaser within a fixed period, giving only a partial credit or refund for damaged goods depending on how far into the warranty period it is, and placing on the owner the burden of transporting a heavy good to the seller or the place of repair. Regardless, the point is that any written warranty on consumer goods costing over $15 without all the attributes required of a full warranty is treated as a limited warranty. Given the maker-planned obsolescence of many of the consumer products in our marketplace, we all need to take the time to understand warranties and to make them an integral part of any purchase.

Consumer Products: tangible personal property used for personal, family, or household purposes

Full Warranty: seller's promise to cover labor and material cost necessary to fix product

Limited Warranty: restricted written guarantee

HYPOTHETICAL CASE

Tiny's Ice Cream Parlor ordered a new freezer. The freezer came with a warranty; however, it limited the warrantor's responsibility, if a problem developed, to replacing the defective parts. Labor and other costs of repair were the responsibility of the owner. When, barely a month after it came, the freezer broke down and $17,000 worth of ice cream melted, Tiny's owner, Tim, sued the warrantor for the costs of both the labor and parts necessary to repair it. Tim insisted that those costs should be covered under the "full warranty" required by the Magnuson-Moss Act. Is he correct?*

*No. Magnuson-Moss applies only to consumer products. This warranty is on business equipment and covers only what is stated by the issuer.

Implied Warranties

Implied Warranty:
guarantee imposed by law

Implied warranties, the second basic type of warranties, are guarantees imposed by law. Since, first and foremost, they are seldom found in writing or mentioned orally, they contrast sharply with the express warranties contained in the statements, samples, or product descriptions given during negotiations between buyers and sellers. Implied warranties are agents of the law that act to bring about higher standards of conduct in business transactions. There are three such warranties: the implied warranties of merchantability, fitness for a particular purpose, and title.

Warranty of Merchantability:
guarantee of goods' fitness for their ordinary intended use

Merchantability. From the standpoint of the purchaser, the most important implied warranty is that of merchantability. This warranty is read by the law into every sale by a merchant (manufacturer, wholesaler, or retailer) of goods of the type sold in the transaction. Nonmerchant sellers are not bound by it. At its heart, the **warranty of merchantability** is a guarantee that the goods sold are fit for their ordinary intended use. The UCC, in section 2–314, sets the following standards for merchantable goods:

> They must at least be (a) able to pass without objection as goods of the contract description in the trade area involved, (b) fit for the ordinary purpose for which such goods are used, (c) uniform in quality and quantity within each unit, (d) adequately "contained, packaged, and labeled as the agreement may require," (e) in conformance with facts or promises made on the container or labels, and (f) in the case of fungible goods, of reasonable average quality within the description of the goods given.

Given the detail of these requirements, you can easily see why the warranty of merchantability is a favorite of buyers. You can also see that this warranty clearly applies to food and drink as well as other goods.

HYPOTHETICAL CASE

John sank back in his car seat. It was late. The lights of the Burger-Banger franchise had blinked out just as he pulled out of its drive-through. He raised the hamburger to his lips. "Ahhhh," he said to his friend Lissa, "here goes the first bite of the day." Soon after he began chewing, a shriek erupted from his lips. A large piece of bone had come between his good teeth and a new partial filling his dentist had put in place earlier that day. Most of the filled tooth was crushed. John found the bone, showed it to Lissa, and headed into the Burger-Banger. The bone was large enough to violate the warranty of merchantability pertaining to adulterated food. As a consequence, when the dentist told John the next day that the remnant of the tooth would hold a cap, the Burger-Banger had to pay for the procedure plus the pain and suffering and other damages that John incurred.

A stumbling block to many suits based on the implied warranty of merchantability is showing that the goods were nonmerchantable when they were sold. Often the defect complained of does not surface until the product has been in use for an extended period. It therefore becomes difficult to prove that the problem was not caused by ordinary wear and tear. This is especially true in suits alleging defects in motor vehicle tires, shock absorbers, and muffler and steering systems.

Fitness for a Particular Purpose

When Claude first came up with the idea of glassing in their porch to produce the hot, humid environment necessary for growing night crawlers, Gladice had tried to stop him. Finally, she gave up and called an air-conditioning firm. She told the firm's representative that the system had to be able to keep the house at around 70 degrees on the hottest days, even with the extra heat from the "worm room." The firm had installed the system it thought best, but since being put in operation three weeks ago, the system had been unable to produce a temperature lower than 80 degrees during the heat of the day. Gladice asked the firm to check the system. However, it was running perfectly. Gladice then thought of the public broadcasting show on consumer law that she had watched last night. Several warranties had been mentioned. One of them was an express warranty. Unfortunately, the air-conditioning firm had made no express representations as to how cool the house could be after the system was installed. The warranty of merchantability didn't apply either because there was no defect in the equipment. Gladice had to admit it was running fine—continually, but fine. So what was left? Gladice shook her head in dismay. Maybe an answer would come to her.

An answer to Gladice's dilemma may be found in UCC 2–315, which provides for the **warranty of fitness for a particular purpose.** This warranty applies to any seller, not just a merchant, who knows or should know the buyer's intended use for the goods and upon whose skill or judgment the buyer is relying to obtain suitable goods. (Note that it is the seller's duty to ask the buyer questions that define the buyer's intended use.) The warranty of fitness for a particular purpose fills a void, as Gladice's case has illustrated, where no express warranties are extended and there are no defects in the goods to bring in the warranty of merchantability.

Warranty of Fitness for a Particular Purpose: guarantee of goods' suitability for buyer's intended use

Title.   A **warranty of good title** is another implied warranty that is effective against any seller, not just a merchant. This warranty, expressed in UCC 2–312, is given by the seller. It guarantees that the title transferred to the buyer is good and that the transfer is rightful. It also provides that the goods will be delivered free from any claims of other parties about which the seller has knowledge.

Warranty of Good Title: guarantee of validity of ownership right and transfer

Figure 17–1   **The Implied Warranties**

- Title
- Fitness for Particular Purpose
- Merchantability

Bertram sold Angela a freezer he had recently purchased on credit from Sears. Sears had a claim for the unpaid credit balance that it could bring against the freezer no matter who owned it. When Bertram stopped making payments on the freezer, Sears did exactly that. Angela could and would have to sue Bertram for breach of the implied warranty of good title to cover her loss.

Is It Possible to Eliminate Such Warranties, and If So, How?

The answer to the first question is, of course, yes. The UCC sanctions three main ways to bring about this result:

First, by using the words "as is," "with all faults," or similar language in the contract. Such phrasing cancels all implied warranties except title.

Second, by allowing the buyer to examine the goods. Whether the buyer does so or not, any implied warranty that would have covered a defect discoverable by such a reasonable inspection is thereby terminated.

Third, by using specific disclaimers for the implied warranties of merchantability and fitness for a particular purpose. If such disclaimers are in writing, they must be conspicuous, typically in large and very bold type. In addition, a disclaimer of the implied warranty of merchantability must mention it by name. For example, "THE SELLER OF THIS TEXTBOOK HEREBY EXCLUDES THE WARRANTIES OF MERCHANTABILITY AND FITNESS FOR A PARTICULAR PURPOSE."

In the area of consumer goods, however, the Magnuson-Moss Warranty Act curtails the seller's ability to eliminate warranties by the above means. Thereunder, if either a full or limited express written warranty is given or if a service contract for the goods is sold within 90 days of their sale, the implied warranties of merchantability and fitness for a particular purpose cannot be disclaimed during the effective period of the warranty. Finally, any clause attempting to eliminate or limit consequential (indirect but foreseeable at the time of contracting) damages must be conspicuously noted on the warranty.

How Can a Person Recover for Breach of Warranty or a Like Injury?

Lawsuit for Breach of the Warranty

The primary remedy available when a warranty is breached is the threat of or actual initiation of a lawsuit against the violating party. However, to be eligible to recover in such ways for a breach of warranty under the UCC, the injured party must satisfy two requirements: notice and privity.

Requirements for Recovery

Notice. UCC 2–607 provides that a buyer must give the seller notice of any breach within a reasonable time after the breach has been or should have been discovered. If this is not done, the buyer is barred from any remedy.

As you may suspect, this failure to give notice within a reasonable time also adversely affects the buyer's chances of recovering for breach of the sales contract itself, not just for breach of warranty. We will discuss the remedies for breach of the sales contract in the next section.

Privity. If you reflect a moment, you will realize how much the availability of warranties depends on the interaction between the parties to the sales contract. This mutual relationship between buyer and seller based on the establishment of a bargain between them was known as **privity.** Prior to the UCC, warranties were regarded as being extended only to the actual buyer by the seller because only those two were "privy" to the deal. Typically, the seller did not look beyond the buyer to other potential users of the product nor did the buyer bargain for warranties for such later users. However, it ultimately became obvious to society that confining warranties to those in strict privity to the contract left without a remedy others who might be injured by a defective product. Therefore, the suggested provisions of the UCC abolished the requirement of privity and gave the states three replacement options to choose from in the process of enacting the code (a state could also draft its own option, of course, and a few of the 50 states did so). These options are summarized as follows:

Privity: relationship between buyer and seller based on bargain between them

Option A: Extends express or implied warranties to any natural person who is a member of the buyer's family or household or a guest of the buyer if it is reasonable to expect that such person will consume, use, or be affected by the goods. Limits recovery to personal injuries.

Option B: The same as A but drops the requirement that the natural person be a member of the buyer's family or household or a guest of the buyer.

Option C: Drops the requirement of a natural person and the restriction of recovery to personal injuries.

Most states have adopted A, the most restrictive option. Fewer than 10 states have adopted B. A mere handful have adopted C, the most liberal option. Check in your state's commercial code at section 2–318 to see which of the three options covers your fate. Note that a very few states (under five) have retained the original privity requirements.

Once a person is considered authorized to sue under the UCC for breach of warranty, the question of who can be sued comes up. The problem is that all too often the retailer who sold the defective product turns out to have insufficient assets against which to recover. Fortunately, the trend of cases has been to allow suits against the manufacturer of the defective product. This is because it is often the manufacturer's massive advertising campaigns that have developed the demand for the product in the first place.

Product Liability

It is important to remember that, although this chapter emphasizes remedies based on warranty or the sales contract itself, there is an important alternative. That alternative is a product liability action under tort law rather than contract law. This alternative was covered in detail in Chapter 6. It focuses on the safety of the product rather than on the conduct of the parties. Potential plaintiffs for product liability actions are not limited to the options described above. Individuals without any relationship to the original sales transaction may seek damages for injuries brought about by a defect in a product under consideration. Despite this broad applicability of product liability tort law, however, warranty law retains great significance within the area of sales.

What Remedies Are Available for Breach of the Sales Contract itself?

Adequate Assurance of Performance

Adequate Assurance of Performance: action satisfactorily indicating intent to fulfill contract

One of the most important remedies actually works to forestall a possible breach of the contract. It is termed an adequate assurance of performance. Often during the contractual period the actions of one of the parties can be interpreted as showing an intent to breach the contract. UCC 2–609 provides a means of clarifying this intent short of having the other party stop performance and go into a breach mode. Under this section the worried party may suspend performance and demand an **adequate assurance of performance** (action satisfactorily indicating intent to fulfill the contract) from the other party. The demand must be in writing, and the party making it must wait for the assurance for a reasonable time (but not over 30 days). If it does not come, the party demanding the assurance may safely treat the contract as repudiated. Under the UCC a repudiation allows the injured party to suspend his or her own performance and either wait for performance by the repudiating party or choose from the remedies for breach of contract discussed below.

| The Legal Remedies Available for Breach of the Sales Contract | Figure 17–2 |

Remedies Available to the Seller	Remedies Available to the Buyer
■ To *cancel the contract*. Upon the breach by the buyer, the seller stops all efforts to comply with the terms of the agreement. The seller may also select any of the following remedies if appropriate. (UCC 2–106) ■ To *withhold or stop delivery of the goods*, if appropriate. (UCC 2–703 and 705) ■ To *resell undelivered goods and sue for damages*. This remedy applies whether or not the goods are in finished condition. The seller is not required to invest additional resources in bringing the goods into compliance with the order. The unfinished material may be sold as scrap and suit brought for the difference between the price of the scrap and the contract price. Note that good commercial judgment to minimize loss must be used in this procedure. Any good faith purchaser of the goods at such a sale takes them free and clear of the buyer's rights. (UCC 2–706) ■ To *retain the goods and sue for damages*. The seller may then sue for either the lost profit (which includes incidental damages of stopping delivery; transporting, caring for, and attempting to resell the goods; etc.) or the shortfall between the contract price and the market price when the breach occurred. [UCC 2–703(e)] ■ To *sue for the price*. If the goods have been accepted, the seller may initiate an action to recover the sales price. (UCC 2–709)	■ To *cancel the contract and sue for money paid*. In addition, the buyer may select from any of the following remedies that are appropriate. ■ To *sue for damages*. When the seller fails to deliver the goods, the buyer may bring suit for the amount of the difference between the contract price and the market price at the time of the breach. Incidental and consequential damages may also be recovered in such an action (UCC 2–710 and 2–711) ■ To *cover*. The buyer "covers" the sale by purchasing similar goods in the marketplace within a reasonable time. Suit for damages for any increase in cost may then be brought as described above. [UCC 2–711 (a)] ■ To *retain improper goods already delivered and seek an adjustment*. If no adjustment is forthcoming, suit may be brought for damages measured as the difference between the value of the goods delivered and the value of the goods contracted for. (UCC 2–714) ■ To *sue for specific performance*. This remedy is allowed under UCC 2–716 where the goods are unique and money damages will not suffice.

When there is a breach of contract, which we defined in Chapter 13 as an unexcused failure to perform according to the terms of the agreement, the injured party has the right to a legal remedy. This same right extends to those injured by a repudiation leading to an anticipatory breach of the contract. As Figure 17–2 shows, under the UCC the potential remedies from which such a party may choose are rather extensive for both the buyer and the seller.

These remedies, broad and thorough as they may seem, are worth nothing without the resolve to right the wrong done. The UCC recognizes this fact by providing a statute of limitations of four years on breach of contract actions under Article II. Beyond that time frame there appears little reason for allowing the threat of a potential lawsuit to hang over the heads of the litigants.

APPLICATIONS OF
WHAT YOU'VE LEARNED

Vocabulary Development

Fill in the blanks with the appropriate term.

**Adequate Assurance
of Performance**
Consumer Products
Express Warranty

Full Warranty
Implied Warranty
Limited Warranty
Privity

Puffing
Warranty
**Warranty of Fitness for
a Particular Purpose**

Warranty of Good Title
**Warranty of
Merchantability**

[Some of the answers may be drawn from preceding chapters.]

1. Flashy Dan "The Used Car Man" looked you straight in the eye and said, "You don't want these drag slicks on this car if you buy it? No problem. I'll put some recaps on. They'll be better than new tires. Frankly, I don't see why they bother making new tires with such bargains as recaps on the market." When Flashy Dan said that, he was probably _____ in relation to the capabilities of the recapped tires.

2. The implied warranty that covers adulterated foods is the _____.

3. A written warranty that covers the cost of the labor and parts necessary to repair a defective product is a(n) _____.

4. You ask a hardware store employee for a nontoxic paint to cover and seal the interior walls of your concrete swimming pool. When she sells one to you, you receive an implied warranty with the paint. It is the _____.

5. Bills of lading, ship's lading, and airbills are examples of _____.

6. The mutual relationship between the buyer and seller in a sales contract is referred to as _____.

Problems

1. Hiram Stone knew he needed to have his car painted. So when a car repair shop in town advertised its "Watch Out for the Early Bird" special, he drove to the shop immediately. Under this special, the shop would paint any car for $250 in the five paint colors that it had overstocked. After looking at five cars in the shop's parking lot, each painted in one of the colors, Hiram selected the "sun-burn red." When the shop was done painting his car, however, the color looked more like "blush pink" than the red he had picked. After considerable argument, the shop admitted that it had thinned the red with some white to make it go further. Hiram felt that the shop had breached its warranty to him and refused to pay. What type of warranty is Hiram referring to?

2. Is the following a full or limited warranty under Magnuson-Moss. Why?

   "This warranty covers any defect or malfunction of the RB–71 unit. Repairs will be made free of charge for labor or materials within a reasonable time after notice of the problem is given, if such notice is provided within ONE YEAR AFTER DATE OF PURCHASE. This warranty applies to anyone who is a member of the purchaser's household. If repairs cannot return the unit to a serviceable condition within one month after notice, a new unit will be provided free of charge."

3. If it is to be eliminated, what implied warranty must be mentioned by name in a written disclaimer?

4. L. A. Botomy prided himself on the condition of his yard and shrubbery. One summer day, just hours before the city's annual "best lawn" contest was to begin, L. A.'s hedge trimmers fell apart. Knowing that he had to act decisively or lose the contest that he had won all of the past five years, L. A. picked up his lawn mower and proceeded to trim his shrubs with it. (Believe it or not, this problem is based on an actual case!) As he was about to finish, a stout part of the bush he was working on snapped and

was flung back, hitting L. A. in the face. L. A. brought suit for a breach of the warranty of merchantability and on product liability grounds. Review both areas and make the best case for Mr. Botomy that you can. Do you think he recovered?

5. Henpecked Farms, Inc., sold 3 tons of chicken parts to the Mystery Meat Hot Dog Packers Company.

The chicken parts were to be delivered in three 1-ton shipments. What prebreach remedy would you recommend to Henpecked Farms if Mystery Meat's check for the first shipment bounced?

6. If Mystery Meat was thereafter deemed to be in breach of contract, what remedy or remedies would you recommend to Henpecked?

ACTUAL CASE STUDY

551 S.W.2d 602 **Blevins v. Cushman Motors**

Maxwell and Blevins teed off on 13, then hopped into their golf cart and motored out to Maxwell's ball. Maxwell fired his second shot, then drove the cart toward Blevins' ball. As the cart approached the ball at approximately 5 mph, it entered a shady area of the course, on which a light dew lay. At that point the cart went into a skid for 10 to 15 feet—it was "like being on ice"—and then tipped over. Maxwell was thrown free. However, Blevins, who failed in his attempt to jump from the cart, was pinned under it when it came to rest.

Blevins brought this suit on product liability grounds based on strict liability in tort, not negligence. He sued for personal injuries. In addition, his wife brought suit for loss of consortium (the fellowship of husband and wife in companionship and sexual relations). Both of them received very substantial rewards in the trial court that were upheld before the Missouri Court of Appeals. The case was then appealed to the Missouri Supreme Court.

Among other unsuccessful contentions, Cushman argued that although Missouri courts had used strict liability in tort to decide cases involving a defect in manufacturing, the courts of the state should not use this theory to decide cases involving a defect in design. Instead, the negligence theory should be used in such cases to determine whether the maker of the product was liable. The Missouri Supreme Court replied:

In *Kenner* [a precedential case in Missouri on this issue], this court established that an action sounding in strict liability in tort may lie to recover for injuries caused by a product which is unreasonably dangerous as manufactured. It is only logical that in this case we permit an action in strict

tort liability to obtain for the recovery of injuries caused by a product which is unreasonably dangerous as designed because, "There is no rational distinction between design and manufacture in this context, since a product may be equally defective and dangerous if its design subjects protected persons to unreasonable risks as if its manufacture does so" [quote from California appellate court].

Questions

1. According to what the court said, was strict liability in tort to be used to determine this case?
2. Consider the following:

The Elements of Negligence	The Elements of a "Strict Tort" Product Liability Action
Act or omission	Injury from intended use
Duty of due care	Injury from intended use
Breach of the duty of due care	Unreasonably dangerous defect
Actual cause	Manufacturer is the defendant
Proximate cause	Manufacturer is the defendant
Damages	No alteration before injury

a. Which would you rather try to recover under, negligence or a "strict tort" product liability action?
b. What actual proof requirements would be added in this case if the court chose negligence as the standard instead of strict liability in tort?

INSIGHT

How Do You Compensate an Attorney?

Most people are hesitant about asking an attorney the most important question: "How much is all this going to cost me?" Admittedly, prior to approximately two decades ago, the state bar associations prescribed minimum fee schedules and threatened to disbar anyone who broke the fixed price. So at that time trying to do comparative shopping for legal services usually didn't pay off. The prescribed schedules disappeared after a successful antitrust suit against a state bar association, so that today the prices of legal services vary significantly. Even with price competition among lawyers, however, there are still certain fee benchmarks that can serve as a basis for comparison.

To begin with, some attorneys occasionally do work "pro bono" (without fee). These cases are taken either by order of a court or simply as a function of the attorney's conscience. I would not count on having an attorney do your work for free. Attorneys use two methods in billing the vast majority of cases. One method is to charge an *hourly rate* for their services and for the services of their staff and their legal assistants. Such rates fluctuate from under $50 per hour to the more than $400 per hour that the federal government reputedly paid attorneys who handled the savings and loan cases. The other method is to bill on a *contingency fee* basis. In essence, under this method the attorney gets a percentage of the take. Usually, this is as follows:

25% of the recovery	If the action is settled without trial
33% of the recovery	If the action is won at trial
40% or higher	If the action must be won on appeal

If these fees seem high, remember that the attorney is gambling her or his time against the probability of your recovery in the cause of action and will receive nothing if you do not recover.

Exceptions

Some law firms call themselves "legal clinics" and offer standard services for flat fees. For example, they might charge $750 for an uncontested divorce, $150 for a name change, and so on. The flat fee is increased as the complexity of the case increases.

Another exception arises whenever an action is created by statutes that authorize the billing of attorney's fees and costs to the loser. Remember that in most cases you must pay your attorney out of your recovery or out of your own pocket, depending on the situation. However, in statutory actions, such as actions taken under the Fair Credit Reporting Act, the court can award a recovery and the collection of the plaintiff's attorney's fees from the defendant.

Finally, individual clients may carve out their own exceptions by bargaining with the attorney. When I was in law school, a close relative slipped on a jar of broken mustard and injured her knee while shopping. I recommended to her that she not contact an attorney immediately but instead deal with the store's insurer until she received its settlement offer. She did so. The amount offered was $2,000. I then selected an attorney for her from the data in Martindale-Hubbell (see the Insight section "How Do You Choose an Attorney?"). He was the head of the local bar association. We concluded an arrangement under which he would receive a slightly higher contingency fee percentage than what he normally charged on whatever he won for my relative over the $2,000. The case resulted in a mistrial. Before the second trial began, my relative succumbed to the pressure and took the $2,000 settlement offer. Her attorney, who had compiled a file 2 inches thick on the case, received nothing for his months of work. Nonetheless, as he parted from my relative, he shook her hand, said he understood, and sincerely wished her well. In the years since, I have not seen a better example of what an attorney should be. So do not hesitate to bargain for the best deal. Bargaining does work, and it may save you thousands of dollars.

The Legal Environment of Business: Commercial Paper

CHAPTERS

18

What Is Commercial Paper, and What Purpose Does It Serve?

CHAPTER OUTLINE AND OBJECTIVES

After studying this chapter, the student will be able to:

I. Define commercial paper and explain why it is used.

II. Identify the types of commercial paper and their uses.

   a. Checks

   b. Drafts

   c. Trade acceptances

   d. Promissory notes

   e. Certificates of deposit

   f. Letters of credit

III. Explain the risks involved in the use of commercial paper.

IV. Analyze the case of *Means* v. *Clardy* to find out whether it's possible to pay a promissory note in cabinets.

What Is Commercial Paper, and Why Have It?

Commercial Paper:
written promise or order to pay a sum of money.

Article 3 of the UCC provides the laws that govern the area of **commercial paper,** which is defined as a written promise or order to pay a sum of money. The definition is generic because checks, promissory notes, and a number of financial instruments you may never have heard of all have to be covered by it. You'll learn a lot more about it as we discuss them all in detail. However, the best way to understand why we have "commercial paper" in our society is to go back a few years to the era of the Great Depression.

HYPOTHETICAL CASE

Hutton L. ("Nub") Turnback stood in the cold of an early winter day and watched the crowd file in and out of the building. The word that the Farmers and Merchants Bank was about to go bankrupt had spread like wildfire among those who still had money. Fearful that they would lose all they had, anxious depositors had lined up before 6 that morning to withdraw their cash. Nub had no such worries. Instead, he had come on the scene at about 11 AM, when the line was at its peak. As time went on, about 25 other out-of-work men and women had joined him. Nub checked the City Hall clock. It was past 11:30 PM on this Tuesday, the 28th of November, 1932. Most of the people watching with Nub were surely as hungry as he was. Most had families who were also hungry. They stood silently, immobilized by what was happening and by the steady gaze of two mounted police officers. In desperate consideration they eyed those who were walking out of the bank with cash stuffed in their pockets. The story was always the same. Relief at having retrieved their money was written on each ex-depositor's face as he or she came out through the bank's doors. Then they paused. The expression on their faces changed. They sensed the destitute mass of raggedly clothed people watching them, knew that the cash they were carrying meant food, warmth, and shelter to the watchers. They each then turned and walked resolutely to the bank across the square from the Farmers and Merchants. They deposited their funds in that bank, and left it carrying a new checkbook. They preferred to trust their funds to the machinations of yet another banker rather than risk the desperation of the people on the street.

Bill of Exchange:
historically, paper ordering transfer of precious metal from one party to another

The above is a true story. It illustrates the classic purpose of commercial paper, such as checks, drafts, and notes over the last several centuries. That purpose is to relieve individuals of the need to carry large sums of gold, silver, or cash by providing them with a safe means of payment in commercial and other exchanges. In fact, the forerunner of the check was called a **bill of exchange.** It was simply a piece of paper on which the owner of precious metals wrote an order requiring that a certain amount of those metals be transferred to the person named in the order. The order was addressed to an individual or a company who made it their business to hold such metals in safekeeping away from robbers and other threats. The individual or company holding the precious metals carried out the order after validating the signature of their owner.

Even though the current system is more sophisticated, a check still fulfills the same function. By this instrument we order a certain financial institution in which we have deposited our money to "pay to the order of" a particular individual or company to whom we want to transfer cash. The point here is that, although today there's a lot of law and electronic encoding surrounding the use of such instruments as checks, those instruments are still understandable from a commonsense viewpoint. Why? Because their basic use or purpose hasn't changed. So don't be overcome by the terminology. It has to be precise due to the great importance of commercial exchange. Recognize it as a "necessary" for your professional knowledge. Once mastered, it helps a great deal in understanding what's going on. We'll have a go at the terminology in the next section, on types of commercial paper.

What Are the Types of Commercial Paper and Their Uses?

The two basic types of commercial paper are drafts and notes. We'll define each of these types and explain their function in detail shortly, then move on to some less frequently used types. First, however, it's probably best to start our discussion with an instrument that almost everyone is familiar with, a type of draft called the check.

Checks

A **check** is the most important type of draft. It is defined as an unconditional written directive to a bank to pay deposited funds on demand to the order of an individual named on the instrument or to the **bearer** (a person in possession of a valid instrument that does not specifically identify its owner). Here are some important points to note about this definition:

Check: unconditional written directive to bank to pay deposited funds on demand to order of individual named on instrument or to bearer

Bearer: person in possession of valid instrument that does not specifically identify its owner

1. A check must be drawn on an institution chartered as a bank by either the federal or state government. A savings and loan or credit union does not qualify. (The instruments drawn on such institutions fall into the broader classification of drafts, which we will discuss in a moment.)
2. "On demand" means that the check is to be paid whenever it is physically presented to the bank for payment by the person authorized to do so. Other terms, such as "at sight" or "on presentment," imply the same thing.
3. The instrument must be unconditional. Such conditions as "Pay to the order of Ajax Construction as soon as it finishes the construction of my home" make the instruments that bears them ineligible to be a check.
4. The instrument must be in writing. The following subsection, "Form of the Check," explains how this requirement applies.

The legal terminology associated with a check is relatively simple. The person who issues the order to pay found in a check (or in any other draft) is termed the

A Check Drawn (Issued) by Lois Kent Ordering a Payment to Be Made Out of the Funds She Has Deposited with The First National Bank in a Checking Account

Figure 18–1

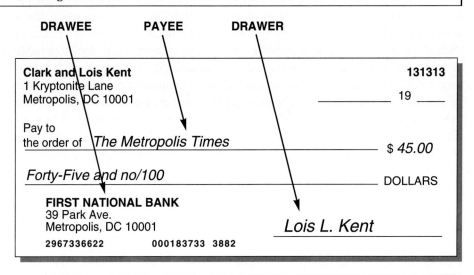

Drawer: issuer of check or draft

Drawee: person ordered to pay in check or draft

Payee: person named to receive funds

drawer. The drawer in the check shown in Figure 18–1 is Lois L. Kent. The bank that is directed in the check to pay to the order of someone is termed the **drawee.** The drawee ordered by Lois to pay the $45 is the First National Bank of Metropolis. For that order to be effective, Lois must have sufficient funds in the drawee bank. The person named to receive the funds or the power to order them paid to someone else is labeled the **payee.** Again referring to the above example, the *Metropolis Times,* one of the two newspapers serving the city of Metropolis, is named as the payee.

More than one individual may be named as payee on the same instrument. The UCC specifically allows **joint payees.** In this arrangement the payees' names are separated by the word *and.* "Pay to the Order of Joan and Ted Stanley" is an example of joint payees. Both parties so named must consent before the instrument can be exchanged for value. In other words, both Joan and Ted have to **indorse** (sign the reverse of the instrument) before the instrument can be cashed.

Joint Payees: persons named on instrument, each with equal right in funds to be paid

Indorse: to sign reverse side of instrument

Alternative Payees: persons named on instrument, each with full right to all funds to be paid

The UCC also allows **alternative payees,** wherein the payees' names are separated by the word *or.* "Pay to the Order of Joan or Ted Stanley" is an example. In the case of alternative payees, the instrument can be cashed if only one of the two payees consents. Typically, consent is shown by the payee's indorsement.

Assuming you have a checking account in a bank, are you the debtor or the creditor of the bank in relation to that account?

I hope you said creditor because that's correct. Don't forget you have given the bank your money for safekeeping. They are your debtor. Think about how your creditors treat you when you are dealing with your bank concerning your checking account.

Form of the Check. Today most bank depositors are used to writing checks on uniform, neatly printed, electronically encoded forms provided by banks at their depositors' expense. The uniformity and encoding facilitate the speedy processing of these instruments by financial institutions. However, they were not used when the checking system began and they are not required today. By law, any written instrument that fulfills the definitional requirements of a check is acceptable as such.

Chad Keck turned to Bill Glass, his buddy, for a favor. "Bill, I wrote my last printed check for the groceries back at that convenience store, but I still need some cash. Could you lend me $50?" Bill thought a minute, then replied, "Sure thing. But instead of an IOU, just write me out a check for that amount on this sheet of paper. I'll cash it when I get back to town." Chad frowned. "You can't do that. It's not a check unless it's on the form." Bill smiled. "Tell you what, Chad, make it out for $100. If I can't cash it, you don't owe me a thing. If I can, the $100 is mine." Chad agreed. Figure 18–2 shows how the instrument read. Bill presented the instrument at the People's Bank of Pennsboro the next day. The teller he showed it to called a supervisor, who, in turn, called the bank's lawyer. After studying the instrument for a short time and comparing Chad Keck's signature on it with the signature that the bank had on file, the lawyer told the teller to pay the check.

Note that we'll discuss several special types of checks, such as cashier's and certified checks, toward the end of Chapter 21. Right now, however, we will concentrate on the basic types of commercial paper. That brings us to the draft.

Drafts

A **draft** is similar to a check in many ways. It is defined as an unconditional written order to a person to pay money, usually to a third party. Notice that the order is given to "a person." This means either a natural person or an "artificial person" such as a corporation (in the case of a check, a banking corporation). Also, the payment is not necessarily due on demand. It may be due after a certain

Draft: unconditional written order to person to pay money, usually to third party

A Legally Effective Check Written without a Printed Form   **Figure 18–2**

August 8th, 19**

To the People's Bank of Pennsboro, Pennsboro, Missouri. Please pay to the order of Bill Glass on demand $100.00 from my checking account.

Chad Keck

Figure 18–3

Time Draft Drawn by Joey Kleeman to Pay B. A. Hill from Money Owed Him by Collyer Hardware, an Instrument on Which Jim Collyer Has Accepted Primary Liability and Which He Must Pay When It Is Due

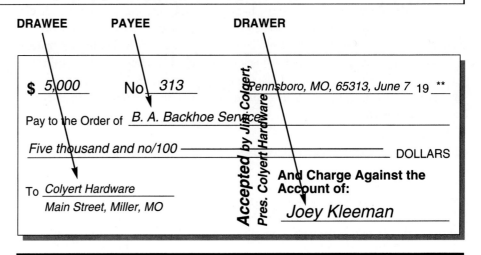

Time Draft: draft due after certain period

Sight Draft: draft due on sight

Postdated Check: draft bearing issue date set in future

Antedated Check: check issued bearing past date

period, such as a number of days or months, in which case it is a **time draft.** On the other hand, it may indeed be payable on demand, which would make it a **sight draft.** It is also possible to combine the two. A draft that reads in part "due and payable 90 days after sight" is an example of such a combination. Finally, note that a **postdated** check (an instrument issued bearing a future date) is treated as a time draft. It will become a demand instrument on the date entered on its face. An **antedated check** (a check issued bearing a past date) is treated as a check in all respects. UCC 3–114 requires that the date on any dated instrument be presumed to be correct.

Figure 18–3 shows a time draft. It was written because Joey Kleeman, the drawer, had completed a construction job for Collyer Hardware, the drawee, as a part of Collyer's expansion plan. Collyer owed Joey $6,500 as a consequence. When B. A. Hill asked Joey for the $5,000 Joey owed him for backhoe work in Joey's new subdivision, Joey convinced him to take the draft instead. B. A. then

Acceptance: undertaking of liability to pay instrument according to its terms

Dishonored: instrument not accepted by party meant to undertake liability thereon

presented the instrument to Jim Collyer for **acceptance** (an assurance that he would be liable on the draft and would pay it according to its terms). If you look at Figure 18–3, you will see that Collyer has correctly indicated this by writing "accepted" and his signature across the instrument. If Collyer refused to agree to pay the draft, it would be considered **dishonored.** Banks must make the same type of decision daily on millions of checks.

Trade Acceptances

Trade Acceptance: draft drawn by seller on payoff due from buyer

Like the check, the **trade acceptance** is a type of draft. It can be extremely helpful in certain business situations. It is written by the seller of goods on the money owed to him by the buyer of those goods. If the buyer accepts the liability on the instrument, the seller has a valuable piece of commercial paper that can in turn be sold. Here's an example of how it works in real life:

Susan Bentley's clothing store, Unmatronly, was in trouble. Antoinette ("Toni") Zelos, salesperson for Femuline, the store's main supplier of women's business suits, knew it. The new freeway was going nearby. During the construction, Unmatronly's business had dropped off by 40 percent. Still, Toni thought, the freeway will be done in two months and then Unmatronly will be doing twice its original level of sales. The only question was how to provide a stock for Unmatronly in the meantime. Toni had been selling to Susan's store on "open account." In other words, Toni's company would provide whatever stock Susan ordered on terms requiring that it be paid for in 30 days. Unfortunately, the winter shipment, whose invoice price was $7,000 hadn't been paid for yet. In fact, it had been over 90 days since that batch of suits had been shipped to Unmatronly. As a consequence, Toni's company had just informed her that it would not provide Susan's new order for $4,000 of additional merchandise on the same terms. Suddenly, Toni recalled her old business law teacher talking about how a trade acceptance was used. It might work. She called the company's legal adviser and her boss, received permission, and drew one up. It is shown in Figure 18–4.

When the new shipment of goods arrived, Susan would inspect them, then sign the trade acceptance. The good part of it was that this instrument (for the $11,000 balance that would then be due on the account) could be **discounted** (sold at less than its face amount) to a financial institution. Even if it brought only $10,000 from the financial institution, that money would at least be available for Femuline to use. When the instrument came due, the financial institution would make money as it would collect the full $11,000. Susan would stay in business, and Toni would keep a customer and get a commission on the sale.

Discounted: instrument sold at less than face amount

From this example, you can see how handy the trade acceptance can be. Of course, the same is true for the other kind of draft, the check, and for the basic draft itself. They were born of necessity to solve various problems. They remain with us because they continue to do so. The second basic type of commercial paper, the promissory note, has a similar role.

Promissory Notes

Gomeranna Pyle and her mother, Anna Pyle, walked into the dealership. Her car to be, a brand-new Ford Patriot, was waiting on the showroom floor. Their salesperson, Manbart Simpson, motioned for them to come into the "settlement room." There they were given various documents to sign, including the contract of sale. Finally, Manbart said, "Now we just need a check for the $3,000 down, and then you both need to sign this note. Ford Credit will send you," he nodded to Gomeranna, "a payment book in about a week." Gomeranna wrote out the check. She and her mother then read the promissory note, shown in Figure 18–5, and signed it. Manbart smiled, dug in his pockets for a moment for the keys, then stood up and ceremoniously presented them to Gomeranna. "The temporary tags are on her. Happy driving."

Figure 18–4

A Trade Acceptance Drawn by the Seller, Antoinette Zelos, Acting as an Agent, of Femuline, in Favor of That Company as Payee. This Trade Acceptance is Drawn on Unmatronly but Will Have to be Accepted by an Appropriate Representative of That Shop (Susan Bently by Her Signature on the Line for the Drawee, Unmatronly, Inc.) before It Is Payable According to Its Terms

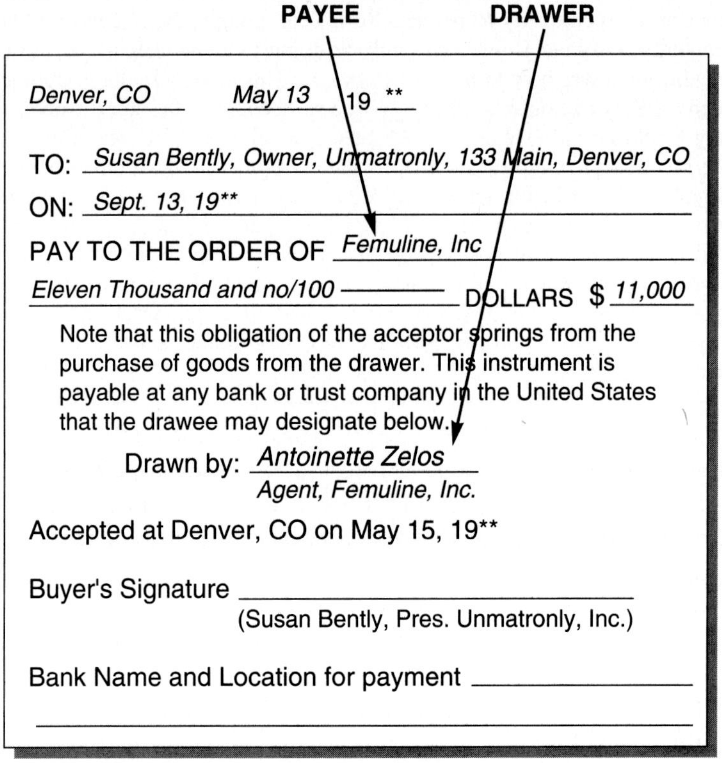

PAYEE   DRAWER

Denver, CO   May 13   19 **

TO: _Susan Bently, Owner, Unmatronly, 133 Main, Denver, CO_

ON: _Sept. 13, 19**_

PAY TO THE ORDER OF _Femuline, Inc_

Eleven Thousand and no/100 —————— DOLLARS $ _11,000_

Note that this obligation of the acceptor springs from the purchase of goods from the drawer. This instrument is payable at any bank or trust company in the United States that the drawee may designate below.

Drawn by: _Antoinette Zelos_
          Agent, Femuline, Inc.

Accepted at Denver, CO on May 15, 19**

Buyer's Signature _____
          (Susan Bently, Pres. Unmatronly, Inc.)

Bank Name and Location for payment _____
_____

Figure 18–5

Promissory Note Evidencing Obligation Undertaken by the Pyles to Repay $12,000 in Installments over Five Years

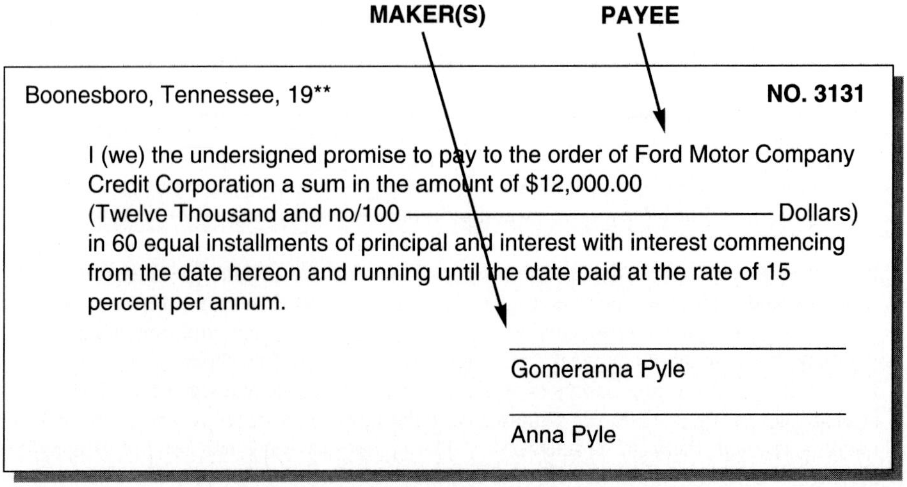

MAKER(S)   PAYEE

Boonesboro, Tennessee, 19**   NO. 3131

I (we) the undersigned promise to pay to the order of Ford Motor Company Credit Corporation a sum in the amount of $12,000.00 (Twelve Thousand and no/100 ————————————— Dollars) in 60 equal installments of principal and interest with interest commencing from the date hereon and running until the date paid at the rate of 15 percent per annum.

_____
Gomeranna Pyle

_____
Anna Pyle

Promissory Note Payable on Demand of Lincoln Savings and Loan or Anyone to Whom Lincoln Properly Transfers Right to Collect. Bernard Bilgewater the III is the Maker of the Note and Obligated to Pay It Plus Interest When It Is Presented

Figure 18–6

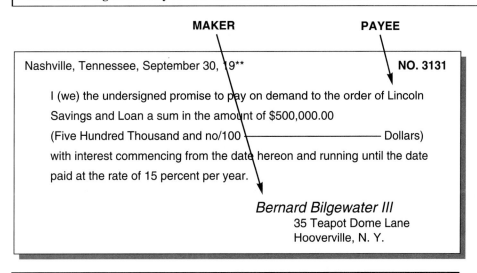

A **promissory note** is a written promise by one party to pay money to the order of another party. It is often used, as in the above example, as evidence of a debt. Unlike an IOU, which merely acknowledges the existence of a debt, a promissory note is legally enforceable because it contains a promise to pay.

The promisor on a promissory note is termed the **maker** (two or more promisors are referred to as **comakers**); the person named to receive the money is termed the payee. In the above example, Ford Credit was the payee of the promissory note and Gomeranna and her mother, Anna Pyle, were its comakers.

There are various types of promissory notes. A **demand note,** an example of which is shown in Figure 18–6, is a note that becomes due and payable whenever the payee or a subsequent owner presents it for payment. Both the face amount of the note (called the **principal**) and any interest are payable at that time A **time note,** unlike a demand note, is payable at a set future date that is noted on the face of the instrument. The note is said to "mature" or become due on that date. An **installment note** (refer to the instrument that Ford Credit used in the example involving Gomeranna) requires a series of payments of principal and interest until the debt has been paid off.

Promissory Note: written promise by one party to pay money to order of another party

Maker: promisor on note

Comakers: two or more promisors on same note

Demand Note: note due and payable when owner presents it for payment

Principal: face amount of note

Time Note: note payable at set date in future

Installment Note: note payable in series of payments of principal and interest

Certificates of Deposit

A **certificate of deposit,** or CD, as it is often called, is a written acknowledgment by a bank of the receipt of money coupled with a promise to pay it back, usually with interest, on the due date. Such certificates are issued rather frequently

Certificate of Deposit: written acknowledgment by bank of receipt of money coupled with promise to pay it back, usually with interest, on due date

because they give the bank some security as to how long it gets to keep (and make money with) the depositor's money. Also, the depositor is pleased as he or she receives a higher interest rate on a CD than, for example, on a savings account.

Letters of Credit

Letter of Credit:
instrument containing promise by person to honor and pay drafts drawn in compliance with its terms

A **letter of credit** is a promise by a person (typically a financial institution such as a bank) that it will honor and pay drafts drawn in compliance with the terms of the letter of credit. This instrument is often used to assure payment for foreign purchases when the buyer and the buyer's credit standing are unknown to the seller. Say that you have just taken a job with Harvey's Stereo Warehouse, a small electronics retailer in the Midwest. Harvey's makes most of its profits on the sale of the Sony MX–11 compact disc player and and its installation in automobiles. You have been at Harvey's less than three weeks when Greatest Buy Electronics, a national chain with a store less than a mile from Harvey's, starts offering the MX–11 and its installation at a price less than your cost. After a day or so of panic, you tell your boss that the only hope is to buy direct from Sony. Eliminating the reseller will bring your costs down to where you have a chance at competing with Greatest Buy. Your boss says that Sony will never sell to Harvey's because Sony doesn't know Harvey's from the Grand Old Opry. You tell him that you're sure Pennsboro National Bank, with which Harvey's keeps its accounts, will write a letter of credit to the bank of Yokohama that will give Sony the reassurance it needs to sell 250 MX–11s to Harvey's. Your boss asks you to give it a try. A few days later, after some negotiations, the President of Pennsboro National Bank writes the letter of credit shown in Figure 18–7.

You then notify Sony of your order and the letter of credit being held at the Bank of Yokohama. Sony's places the goods you ordered on a ship bound for the United States. The shipmaster inventories the goods and issues a ship's bill of lading for them. The Sony representative takes the ship's bill to the Bank of Yokohama, where it is compared with the letter of credit requirements. If satisfied that these requirements have been met, the Bank of Yokohama issues a draft for the amount of the purchase. The draft is drawn on Pennsboro National Bank and payable through the Bank of Yokohama. Sony's representative may then cash the draft or deposit it in Sony's accounts, from which it will make its way back to the bank of Yokohama. That bank will pay the draft, then demand the amount paid plus a service fee from Pennsboro. When payment is received, typically electronically, from Pennsboro, the ship's bill is sent to that bank. Pennsboro then requires that Harvey's pay it the amount it has expended plus a service fee. When Harvey's pays, it receives the ship's bill showing ownership of the goods. As Harvey's representative, you can then go down to the local warehouse to which the goods were shipped, present the ship's bill, and receive the goods. With them, hopefully, will come a promotion and a raise. If not, it's time to update the résumé.

The point here is that in a global economy, the use of such instruments as letters of credit is crucial to businesspersons who hope to compete today and in the future.

**Letter of Credit Allowing Bank of Yokohama to Issue Draft on
Pennsboro National Bank Payable to Sony Corporation,
If Sony Ships Ordered Goods to Pennsboro Client**

Figure 18–7

Letter of Credit
PENNSBORO NATIONAL BANK
PENNSBORO, MO 65713
July 27, 19**

TO: BANK OF YOKOHAMA, Yokohama, Japan

Good Day

   Upon recepit of suitable bill of lading showing the transshipment of
250 Sony Model MX-11 Compact Disc Players to Harvey's Stereo
Warehouse, Springfield, MO, you are authorized to draw on the
Pennsboro National Bank a sum of up to $50,000 in favor of Sony, Inc.
in payment for said goods. This letter will expire 90 days from above date.
No partial shipments are to be allowed or compensated.

Hutton L. (Nub) Turnback II, President

What Risks Are Involved in the Use of Commercial Paper?

Properly used, checks, drafts, and other forms of commercial paper greatly reduce the possibility of such dangers as theft of cash. As already discussed, that idea of reducing such dangers probably brought on the use of what we now know as commercial paper. But every solution gives rise to new problems. Crimes involving lost and stolen instruments, forgery, embezzlement, insufficient funds checks, and the like have marked society's increasing turn toward substitutes for hard cash. In response, the laws governing the use of commercial paper have been altered to reduce the risk of such problems to a manageable level. The bulk of the next few chapters will be devoted to familiarizing you with how to use these laws to protect yourself from the most common problems of this kind.

APPLICATIONS OF WHAT YOU'VE LEARNED

Vocabulary Development

Fill in the blanks with the appropriate term.

Acceptance	Comakers	Drawer	Postdated
Alternative Payees	Commercial Paper	Indorse	Principal
Antedated Check	Demand Note	Installment Note	Promissory Note
Bearer	Discounted	Joint Payees	Sight Draft
Bill of Exchange	Dishonored	Letter of Credit	Time Draft
Certificate of Deposit	Draft	Maker	Time Note
Check	Drawee	Payee	Trade Acceptance

1. _____ occurs when an individual agrees to pay a draft according to its terms by writing a word or words to this effect across the instrument and signing below that.

2. A check that the bank refuses to pay has been _____.

3. The person in possession of an instrument made out to cash can be labeled a(n) _____ of that instrument.

4. A check, issued today but bearing an earlier date, is labeled a(n) _____ check.

5. The face amount of a note, not including interest, is called the _____.

6. A note containing a promise to pay the amount due in a series of payments over a number of periods is a(n) _____.

7. To sign the reverse of a piece of commercial paper is to _____.

8. The person to whom a note is payable is labeled the _____.

9. The issuer of a check is termed a(n) _____.

10. The bank upon which a check is drawn is labeled the _____.

Problems

1. Will commercial paper become obsolete? Consider the alternative forms of rendering payment and transferring resources in your answer.

2. Flora and Deplora Adams, twin sisters, were arguing over the best place to establish a checking account. Flora wanted to place the account with her credit union, which paid interest even on such accounts. Deplora wanted to place the account in Pennsboro Bank because she received a lot of out-of-state checks and these would clear (be paid by the issuer's financial institution and thereby produce usable funds) almost a week sooner at the bank than at the credit union. After several days of dispute, Deplora pointed out that there was no such thing as a checking account in a credit union. Was she correct? Why or why not?

3. Tim Schulyer sold the Going-Going-Gone Company a load of ash timber for use in making baseball bats. As a result, the company owed him $7,500 on the purchase price. Before receiving the payment due, Tim found a used tractor that he wished to purchase. Its price was $5,000. Tim needed it immediately and did not want to borrow from the local bank for its purchase. What type of commercial paper could he use to order Going-Going-Gone to pay the seller of the tractor the $5,000 due? Is the commercial paper likely to be a demand instrument or a time instrument?

4. Sure-Fire Wood Stove Company delivered five of its airtight models to Taylor's Stove and Hardware Store over six months ago. The store has still not paid on its account. Several Sure-Fire executives have recommended suing Taylor's for the $3,500 balance due. The salesperson in charge of the Taylor's account has pointed out that the store was a good customer in the past and that the winter just concluded was mild and the costs of fuels competing with wood were therefore low. What type of commercial paper would you recommend that Sure-Fire require Taylor's to sign in lieu of bringing a lawsuit against it? What could then be done with that paper to provide working funds for Sure-Fire?

5. Abraham Manufacturing Company sells Omar's, a chain of clothing stores for oversize men, 100 suits. In the trade acceptance based on this transaction, which firm was the drawer? Which firm was the drawee? Which firm was the acceptor? Which firm was the payee?

6. What risks are associated with the use of means other than commercial paper for transferring resources? How could these risks best be avoided? Consider credit cards, voiceprint money ordering, electronic fund management, and so on.

Means v. Clardy

735 S.W.2d 6

Gary Means and his coappellant, Fred Barry, brought this case before the Western District of the Missouri Court of Appeals. They were seeking to collect on a promissory note in the amount of $31,000 purportedly signed by a Nancy Clardy as partial payment for a cabinetmaking business that she allegedly purchased. Two weeks after the note was made, it was to be paid by $5,000 in cash. Then the remainder of the principal and interest was "to be paid in cabinets figured at the prevailing builder's price for Jefferson City" and in a final lump-sum payment. When the note was not paid, Means and Barry brought suit for the nearly $22,000 still due. During the trial, Nancy Clardy testified that she did not sign either the note or a bill of sale buying the business. She alleged that her son, Bruce, had done so and had drawn $5,000 from a "remodeling" fund to make the initial payment on the note. Bruce took the Fifth Amendment (protection against self-incrimination) when asked about this at the trial. However, a witness to the signing of the promissory note and the bill of sale testified that

Bruce Clardy placed the signatures of Bruce and Nancy Clardy on the note.

Questions (After composing your own answers, compare them with the footnotes below.)

1. Is the jury most likely to hold that Bruce Clardy forged his mother's signature?[1]

2. If the note is payable in money, the Uniform Commercial Code will apply. The UCC requires that a forger be liable on the signature she or he forged. If the note is not payable in money, Gary Means and Fred Barry will be treated only as assignees of the contract rights to collect on it. In addition, although Bruce Clardy may face criminal charges for forgery, neither Bruce Clardy nor Nancy Clardy will be personally liable on the note. Is the note payable in money????[2]

3. Why do we give a decided advantage to takers of an instrument that falls under the coverage of the UCC?[3]

---

[1] As a jury in a civil case such as this decides on the "preponderance of the evidence," they will almost assuredly conclude Bruce forged the signature. This will have no bearing on a later criminal prosecution for such an act (should it occur).

[2] Not in the eyes of the Uniform Commercial Code. Although the instrument is made out for a total value of $31,000, the payments are mainly in the form of a commodity, i.e., cabinets. The value of the cabinets depends on too many variables to be considered money and therefore the instrument does not fall under the rules of the UCC.

[3] Because we as a society benefit greatly from the flexibility that commercial paper's use gives to our economic system. Therefore, we want to enhance its use by decreasing all inappropriate risks associated with it.

19

What Protection Does the UCC Provide for Those Who Deal with Commercial Paper?

CHAPTER OUTLINE AND OBJECTIVES

After studying this chapter, the student will be able to:

I. Explain how being a holder in due course reduces the risks of using commercial paper.
   a. Purpose of the holder in due course status
   b. Requirements of a holder in due course

II. Identify the powers of mere holders or assignees in relation to an instrument.
   a. Mere holders
   b. Assignees

III. Determine which instruments are negotiable by whether or not they meet the definitional requirements.
   a. A writing
   b. Signed by the maker or drawer
   c. Unconditional
   d. For a sum certain in money
   e. Payable on demand or at a specific time
   f. Payable to order or to bearer

IV. Understand the importance of negotiability in the case of *Centerre Bank of Branson* v. *Campbell*.

What is a Holder in Due Course, and What Does That Status Have to Do with Reducing the Risks of Using Commercial Paper?

At the end of the last chapter, we discussed briefly some of the problems associated with the use of commercial paper. These problems, which include worthless instruments, embezzlement, forgery, and many others, can never be eliminated, but they can be brought under control by a variety of means. Good management is at the top of the list of those means. Among the wise courses of action that indicate good management in this regard are selecting personnel after suitable background checks, incorporating internal audit procedures in day-to-day business operations, and carefully screening customers from whom checks, drafts, promissory notes, and other instruments are taken. Finally, the application of foresight and good negotiating skills to agreements from which negotiable instruments may issue can also help a great deal. (In this connection, it is interesting to note that the UCC does not define the word *default*. That definition is left to the contracting parties. For example, late payments, the obligor's bankruptcy, or the obligor's insolvency are among the definitions that could be included in the agreement on which the issuance of commercial paper is based.)

Other means of protection are also available. In fact, it is the primary aim of this chapter and the next few chapters to provide information on how to utilize for protective purposes the holder in due course status made available by the UCC's Article 3.

Purpose of the Holder in Due Course Status

Holder: person possessing instrument issued or indorsed to her or him or made payable to bearer

The holder in due course status allows a qualified **holder** (a person possessing an instrument issued or indorsed to her or him or made payable to bearer) to overcome legal defenses that often prevent someone from collecting on a piece of commercial paper.

What are these defenses? The ones most commonly used are breach of contract and failure of consideration, both of which should be familiar to you from our discussion of contract law.

HYPOTHETICAL CASE

Commerce Bank bought two promissory notes from their payees at a discount. One note was issued by Babbling Brook, Inc. (the maker), to Fearless Chemical Company (the payee) in part payment for a shipment of cleaning chemicals. The face amount of this note was $2,000; Commerce bought it for $1,750. The other note was issued by Aggressive Agriculture, Inc. (the maker), to Kikkstart of Japan (the payee) for two garden tractors. Its face amount was $5,250; Commerce acquired it for $4,500. When the notes became due, Babbling Brook refused to pay because the chemicals

continued on page 251

conclude
did not do the job warranted (this is a failure of consideration defense). Aggressive Agriculture also refused to pay, stating that it had never received the tractors as promised by Kikkstart (a breach of contract defense). Commerce Bank could legally overcome both of these defenses and collect on the notes if it has the status of holder in due course. If Commerce is an assignee or a mere holder of the notes, the defenses will be upheld by the court and collection will not be possible against the makers.

Definition of a Holder in Due Course

A holder qualifies as a **holder in due course** (HDC) by giving value for the piece of commercial paper in good faith without any notice of defect or dishonor. Let's take a close look at what is meant by the various elements in this definition.

Holder in Due Course: holder who gives value in good faith without notice of defect or dishonor

Value.   Under Article 3 of the UCC, value is defined as akin to "consideration" in contract law. However, there are some significant differences. For example, value must actually have been given to qualify under Article 3 rather than merely promised as under contract law (remember that under contract law a promise is taken as consideration to support another promise). Also under Article 3, value is considered given if an instrument is issued as payment of a foregoing debt (this would be considered past consideration under contract law and, therefore, would not bind a promisor to a promise).

HYPOTHETICAL CASE

Xuan Li's restaurant, Little Saigon, was behind by 180 days in paying on the balance in the open account provided to it by its major supplier, Oriental Foods, Inc. Finally, before Oriental Foods would fill another order for Li, it required him to sign a promissory note in the amount of the overdue balance. By law, this substitution of the note for the antecedent (preexisting) debt, would be taken as value given by the payee, Oriental Foods, Inc.

The adequacy of the value given, as in the analysis of the adequacy of consideration, is immaterial. Whether $1 or $50,000 is given for an instrument with a $50,000 face value does not matter in determining whether value has been given. However, if the instrument is transferred as a gift, the donee is not credited with giving value.

Finally, realize that, by law, value is not given when an instrument is acquired in a sale brought about through legal process or as part of a bulk transfer.

Good Faith.   To qualify as a holder in due course in relation to an instrument, a person must take the instrument in good faith. **Good faith** is most closely defined as subjective honesty. Although the adequacy of the consideration given for an instrument is immaterial in determining whether value has been given, adequacy is very relevant to the question of whether the acquirer of an instrument has acted in good faith. Giving $1 for a $50,000 instrument may be taken as a clear indication that in the buyer's opinion something is wrong with the transaction. Therefore, it may be concluded that the buyer did not act in good faith.

Good Faith: subjective honesty

Figure 19–1   **Requirements of the Holder in Due Course Status**

- Give value
- In good faith
- Without notice of defect or dishonor

Without Notice of Defect or Dishonor. Notification of a defect in an instrument or the past dishonor of an instrument that would prevent a holder becoming a holder in due course may be acquired in a number of ways. Such notification may be by actual knowledge given by someone or something directly to the would-be holder in due course. Being told by a credible witness that a promissory note was issued because of an illegal gambling debt, for example, would disqualify the recipient of the information from being a holder in due course of that instrument.

Notification may also be found in knowledge that is imputed to the would-be holder in due course. Imputed knowledge may be inferred when such a person is aware of a circumstance from which he or she should have concluded that there was a defect or dishonor. Acquiring an instrument already past its due date is one example of this. Consequently, you need to know that a time instrument becomes overdue the day after the maturity date specified on its face. Also, by law (UCC 3–304), a check is overdue 30 days after it has been issued. This does not mean that it cannot be cashed even years after the 30-day period. It does mean, however, that anyone who takes the check after those 30 days have elapsed cannot be a holder in due course. Demand drafts and notes are typically held to be overdue about 60 days after their issue date.

There are other signs from which notice of potential defect or dishonor can be inferred. Discovery of these signs requires more than a cursory glance at the face of the instrument. For instance, a person should inspect an instrument to see whether there has been an obvious alteration, such as crossing out one figure and entering another for it. Individuals sometimes even initial such changes as though that would reduce their effect. It does not. Other important inquiries that should be made include the following: Does the amount deliberately written out in longhand agree with the amount shown in numbers? Is the instrument incomplete? Does the instrument have missing or incomplete indorsements? Is there evidence on the face or reverse that the instrument has been presented for payment and dishonored? Such defects will prevent a would-be holder in due course from acquiring that less risky status in relation to the instrument.

Finally, there is always the danger of some type of public notice, say a bankruptcy filing by the issuer of the instrument, that would eliminate the possibility of this status.

What Powers Do Mere Holders or Assignees Have in Relation to an Instrument?

Mere Holders

The failure of a person to qualify for the status of holder in due course does not mean that the instrument involved cannot be collected. A mere holder of the instrument has the power to transfer ownership of that paper, to demand payment on it, and to exercise any and all rights that the person who transferred the instrument to the holder could have exercised.

This last power of a holder, to have and exercise the rights of her or his transferor, led to the creation of the status of a holder through a holder in due course in the UCC's Article 3. A **holder through a holder in due course** (HHDC) is a holder who cannot become a holder in due course (HDC) on his or her own but who acquires an HDC's rights by acquiring the instrument after an HDC has held it.

Holder through a Holder in Due Course: holder who acquires HDC's rights

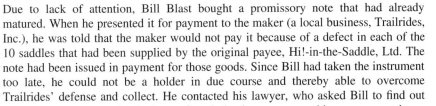

HYPOTHETICAL CASE

Due to lack of attention, Bill Blast bought a promissory note that had already matured. When he presented it for payment to the maker (a local business, Trailrides, Inc.), he was told that the maker would not pay it because of a defect in each of the 10 saddles that had been supplied by the original payee, Hi!-in-the-Saddle, Ltd. The note had been issued in payment for those goods. Since Bill had taken the instrument too late, he could not be a holder in due course and thereby able to overcome Trailrides' defense and collect. He contacted his lawyer, who asked Bill to find out whether the person who had transferred the instrument to him, an equestrienne named Stacy Shipman, had been an HDC. Bill learned that she had been. He therefore acquired her rights, and as a holder through a holder in due course he could recover the amount due on the instrument despite the maker's defense of failure of consideration.

Note, however, that a previous mere holder of an instrument cannot improve her or his status by reacquiring it. For example, if Hi!-in-the-Saddle knew or should have known of the saddles' defects, it could not be a holder in due course of the instrument but only a mere holder. The UCC would not allow it to improve its position by reacquiring the instrument from Stacy Shipman, an HDC. Hi!-in-the-Saddle would still be restricted to the powers of a mere holder. Therefore, it could not improperly use the law associated with the HDC status to overcome the defense of failure of consideration stemming from defects in the saddles it supplied.

Assignees

Thus far we have focused our attention solely on the requirements of persons who try to acquire the powers of holders and, more important, the powers of HDCs. If such persons, no matter how qualified, take a defective instrument, they are treated as only assignees of that instrument. They retain this status until the defects have been corrected, if this is possible, at which time they can become a holder, an HDC, or an HHDC. Unfortunately, some defects cannot be corrected. It therefore becomes important for businesspersons to examine an instrument to determine which are defective and which are not. In the terms of the UCC, before acquiring an instrument, a potential investor or buyer should determine that it is negotiable and that it has been properly negotiated. Otherwise, the investor or buyer will end up being treated as only an assignee of the instrument and will thereby lose out on the protection that the UCC can afford the wise acquirer.

How Do You Determine Which Instruments Are Negotiable?

Negotiable Instrument: unconditional written promise or order payable to order or bearer signed by maker or drawer for sum certain in money due on demand or at specific time

In the remainder of this chapter, we will devote our attention to determining in detail what a negotiable instrument is. Chapter 20 will then cover how an instrument should be transferred so as to have been properly negotiated. A **negotiable instrument** is (1) a writing (2) signed by its maker or drawer (3) that is unconditionally payable (4) in a sum certain in money (5) on demand or at a specific time (6) to order or to bearer.

Most of the elements of the definition have been discussed in a surface way in the preceding sections and chapter. Now, however, we need to focus in depth on the case law and the UCC sections pertinent to each of these elements.

A Writing

This requirement is very flexible. The writing may be done in pen, pencil (although this invites alteration), or even blood as long as it is legible. The surface on which the writing is executed must be capable of being circulated (so writing an instrument on a 10-ton rock is out), but that's about the only constraint. Of course, the use of anything out of the ordinary invites detailed examination and delay, so the most practical choice is to execute your instruments in the same way as others do.

The fact that an instrument is in writing means that the parol evidence rule governs the admissibility of oral evidence to contradict the terms of the instrument. Therefore, evidence of fraud, incompleteness, inconsistency, and the like is required before testimony on the terms of the instrument will be allowed in court. There are also rules for interpreting problems that tend to recur frequently in the making out of such an instrument. When there is a conflict of terms, for example, the written term takes precedence over the typewritten term or over any printed form term. In other words, flexibility is emphasized. On the other hand, if there is a conflict between the written amount and the amount expressed in numbers, the former wins out due to the deliberation required to state it.

Signed by the Maker or Drawer

This second requirement is relatively straightforward. The actual or authorized signature of the issuer is required for the instrument to be negotiable. Unlike situations that require the interpretation of the writing, in which the parol evidence rule may potentially block testimony, oral evidence is admissible to identify the signer of an instrument. In any region of the country, after all, there are typically several people bearing the most common names. So we allow the appropriate person to testify as to which of the ten John Smiths possible actually was the maker of the note or draft.

Further, if another person signs for the issuer (for example, all corporations must employ this method to utilize commercial paper), the person signing must be authorized to do so or be bound personally to pay the instrument. A failure to indicate that a person is signing in such a capacity, even if so authorized, obligates the signer personally as well as the issuer.

The Reverend Billie Samuel was president of the Bible College of the Ozarks, a small accredited four-year school located in Pennsboro, Missouri. Each Friday, she signed the payroll checks and other pieces of commercial paper for the school. She was authorized to do so by the school's governing body. She signed only her own name and did not indicate that she was signing in her capacity as president of the institution. Recently, due to the publicized infidelities of several TV evangelists, the donations to the school had dropped overnight. As a result, the payroll checks and several other outstanding instruments were dishonored. If the college cannot pay these instruments, their employees and other obligees may take Reverend Samuel's home, car, bank account balances, and so on, by bringing suit against her for the money due.

Two final points: First of all, any form of signature is permissible as long as it indicates an intent to issue the instrument. So any instrument signed with the proverbial *X* is sufficient (witnesses to such a signing are usually a good idea but not required technically). Second, the signature may appear anywhere on the face of the instrument, not necessarily at the end. Obliquely across the face and embedded in the body are both acceptable options. For example, the instrument in Figure 19–2, written by the obligor, Thomas Hart Benton, was considered complete with signature.

Handwritten Promissory Note Containing Valid Signature of Thomas Hart Benton

Figure 19–2

8/8/**

I, Thomas Hart Benton, promise to pay to the order of Fouro Student $500.00 on demand.

Unconditionally Payable

This requirement maintains that the promise or order to pay contained in the commercial paper must not be conditional on any outside event. The requirement is based on the role of commercial paper in our economic system. To enhance the transferability of such instruments as checks and notes, we want to avoid a situation in which every potential purchaser of an instrument must somehow take time to determine whether a condition has been fulfilled. Allowing instruments bearing such statements as "Pay to the order of Wilmouth Builders, Inc., if it has completed construction on our house" to be negotiable would so inhibit the transfer of commercial paper that its use would practically disappear. Requiring that something be done or that a specific event occur before an instrument can be collected on reduces the instrument to the status of a simple contract whose rights, at best, can merely be assigned.

A Sum Certain in Money

Sum Certain: amount clearly ascertainable from face of instrument

The requirement of a **sum certain** means that the amount must be clearly ascertainable from the face of the instrument. To qualify the instrument in question as negotiable, this must be capable of being done at two distinct times. First of all, when the would-be holder considers buying the instrument, he or she should be able to calculate from the information on its face the exact minimum amount payable on it. Second, at maturity, the holder must be able to calculate from the face the exact amount due.

It does not disqualify an instrument if it is payable in installments or with a particular interest added on because even if this is the case, the amounts mentioned above can still be calculated. Even if an instrument promises the recovery of reasonable attorney's fees and court costs in case of default, the courts have held that it is still negotiable.

Money: medium of exchange officially adopted by any government as part of its currency

A second requirement is hidden in the requirement of a sum certain, namely the requirement that the instrument be payable in money. **Money** is defined as the medium of exchange that any government has officially adopted as part of its currency. So if an otherwise negotiable instrument states that it is "payable in 10,000 German marks," we have no problem with it.

In addition, if an otherwise negotiable instrument bears such wording as "payable in 10,000 German marks or my 1986 Ford Pickup at the holder's option," it too would still be negotiable as long as the holder (obligee/owner) of the instrument can choose to be paid in *money*. Whether or not she or he does so is immaterial; the instrument is negotiable.

On Demand or at a Specific Time

To satisfy this requirement, the time the instrument is payable must be determined in one of two ways. We are more familiar with "on demand" because this is the only way legally allowable for checks. At law, *on demand* is synonymous with *at presentment* or *at sight*. All of these terms reflect the acceptable condition that the holder has the option of choosing the time when she or he is to receive payment. Equally acceptable is specifying the time when the instrument matures. Such expressions as "due and payable on or before March 3, 19**," "due and payable 60 days from sight," or "due and payable 60 days from March 3, 19**" (that is, a particular date, such as the date of issue), are all acceptable. The point is that the holder must be able to determine from the face of the instrument the latest possible time it can be paid without default.

Acceleration Clause: clause allowing obligee to declare full amount due and payable upon occurrence of particular event

Even if the instrument is subject to an **acceleration clause** (a clause allowing the obligee to declare the full amount due and payable upon the occurrence of a particular event, such as the failure to make a payment), as long as a specific date is otherwise named, the instrument is still negotiable.

Note that making an instrument due and payable upon the death of a person, although such is sure to occur, is not acceptable because the date is not specific enough. Finally, even though an instrument's due date may be extended, at the holder's option, it is negotiable. However, this would not be the case if, instead, the obligor could extend the time of payment indefinitely.

Payable to Order or to Bearer

This last requirement is the most straightforward. An order instrument must be "payable to the order of the named payee(s)," "payable to the named payee's order," or some equivalent wording. A bearer instrument must be written "pay to bearer," "pay to cash," "pay to the order of the bearer," "pay to the order of the named payee(s) or bearer," or something very similar. Finally, if an instrument is made out to an obviously fictitious person, such as Superman, it is treated as a bearer instrument.

A negotiable instrument, then, is one that satisfies all of the above requirements. The negotiability of an instrument is something that is basically determined or determinable when the instrument is first issued. Just because an instrument is negotiable, however, does not necessarily mean that a holder who acquires it in good faith and gives value without notice of defect or dishonor can be a holder in due course. The instrument must also have been properly negotiated as it made its way to that holder for him or her to attain the valuable status of an HDC. As mentioned above, we will discuss negotiation itself in the next chapter.

APPLICATIONS OF WHAT YOU'VE LEARNED

Vocabulary Development

Fill in the blanks with the appropriate term.

Acceleration Clause
Good Faith
Holder
Holder in Due Course

Holder through a Holder in Due Course
Money
Negotiable Instrument
Sum Certain

[Some of the answers may be drawn from the preceding chapter.]

1. An individual who cannot of himself or herself be a holder in due course but acquires the same rights as those of a holder in due course by taking an instrument from a holder in due course is labeled a(n) _____.

2. Subjective honesty is known at law as _____.

3. To qualify as a holder in due course of an instrument, a mere holder has to take the instrument in good faith without notice of defect or dishonor and give value for it. The instrument itself has to be _____ and properly negotiated to the would-be HDC.

4. A(n) _____ allows the obligee of an instrument to declare it fully due and payable if certain conditions occur.

5. A check issued on May 12, 19**, but bearing the date May 31, 19**, is a(n) _____ check.

6. A check issued on May 12, 19**, but bearing the date May 3, 19**, is a(n) _____ check.

7. The _____ of a check must be a bank.

Problems

1. On Christmas eve, Christina Cringle was racing to catch her plane for home. As she reached the boarding area, she realized that she needed to phone a friend and ask him to pick her up on arrival. Desperate to place the call, she had to trade for $1.25 in coin a $50 check her parents had given her during her October vacation. Why would Ebeneezer Grennich, the person who paid $1.25 for the check, not be a holder in due course?

2. Would Grennich be able to collect on the instrument anyway? Why or why not?

3. Horatio Bornlower, principal of the East London Home for Wayward Boys, signed so many documents that he had his signature duplicated onto a rubber stamp and used it instead. One day, when about to write out the home's payroll checks, he hit upon the idea of using the signature stamp to sign these checks as well. Can he do so and still produce a negotiable instrument?

4. Assuming that all other requirements for negotiability have been satisfied, would an instrument bearing the following wordings be negotiable?

   a. "Payable upon completion of the construction contract for our home."

   b. "Payable to Ajax Construction Company as required in the construction contract for our home."

   c. "This debt is secured by a mortgage."

   d. "Payable out of account number 313 only."

5. A promissory note issued by Chet Brinkley to payee David Huntley included this statement: "The obligor of this instrument reserves the right to extend the due date indefinitely." All the other requirements of negotiability were satisfied. Was the instrument negotiable? Would your answer be the same if the statement read, "The obligor reserves the right to extend the due date by one six-month period"?

6. Is the instrument in Figure 19–3 negotiable?

Figure 19–3

IOU given by Carlton Marlboro in exchange for $500 payment to Him from Benjamin Longstreet III

To Benjamin Longstreet III
August 9, 19**

I. O. U. $500.00

Carlton Marlboro

ACTUAL CASE STUDY

Centerre Bank Of Branson v. Campbell

744 S.W.2d 490

Now decide whether or not the instrument in the following case is negotiable.

The Campbells signed a note obligating them to pay $11,250 that contained the following term: "Interest will be payable semiannually. Interest may vary with bank rates charged to Strand Investment Company." The note was sold to Centerre Bank. Upon default Centerre sued to collect. The Campbells refused to pay, claiming that there had been a failure of consideration when Strand Investment Company failed to establish the limited partnership promised in return for issuance of the note. The trial court entered judgment in favor of the bank, saying that it

was a "holder in due course of the note sued upon." As such, it could overcome the Campbells' defense of failure of consideration and recover.

Questions

1. Assume that you are the judge and that you are about to write the deciding opinion for the appellate court. Would you consider the bank a holder, an HDC, an HHDC, or what? What is the basis for your classification?

2. Should Centerre Bank be allowed to recover from the Campbells as a consequence of that classification?

CHAPTER

20

How Is Commercial Paper Negotiated and What Defenses May Stop Holders from Collecting?

CHAPTER OUTLINE AND OBJECTIVES

After studying this chapter, the student will be able to:

I. Negotiate commercial paper using the proper indorsements.
   a. Bearer paper/blank indorsement
   b. Order paper/special indorsement

II. Explain the effects of other types of indorsements.
   a. Sources of an indorser's potential liability
   b. Qualified indorsement
   c. Restrictive indorsement

III. Recognize the defenses to collection and evaluate their effectiveness.
   a. Real (Universal) defenses
   b. Personal (Limited) defenses
   c. Consumer transaction defenses

IV. Identify the various commercial paper warranties and their effect.

V. Solve the case of *Blue Cross Health Services* v. *Sauer*, in which checks totaling over $22,000 were sent to the wrong person.

How Is Commercial Paper Negotiated?

Negotiation: transfer that results in transferee being one of three types of holder

To begin with, remember that commercial paper must be both negotiable and properly negotiated to have the potential for making a transferee a holder in due course. In fact, **negotiation** is defined as a transfer that results in the transferee being at least any one of the three types of holders we've defined (holder, HDC, or HHDC). If either of these elements (negotiability or negotiation) is missing, a transfer of the commercial paper is regarded as merely an assignment and therefore the transferee cannot be a holder in due course. As has been discussed in brief and as you will gather from the discussion on defenses in this chapter, the HDC status can be extremely important. In fact, it can mean the difference between collecting and not collecting on an instrument.

As a consequence, the final part of the preceding chapter focused on being able to determine whether or not an instrument is negotiable. Now this is the key question: Presuming that you have negotiable paper, how do you properly negotiate it? The key issue in answering this question is whether you have bearer or order paper, as bearer paper is negotiated in one way and order paper in another. Let's consider bearer paper first.

Bearer Paper

Bearer Paper: instrument payable to cash or equivalent and without any indorsements or on which last indorsement is blank indorsement

Blank Indorsement: signature of transferor

What is it? **Bearer paper** is commercial paper that is found in only one of two forms: (1) issued payable to cash, bearer, or the equivalent and without any indorsements; or (2) issued payable to cash or to the order of someone, but the last indorsement is a blank indorsement. A **blank indorsement** does not designate a person who is to receive the payoff on the instrument. It is merely a signature.

How do you negotiate bearer paper? Proper negotiation of bearer paper is accomplished by a mere transfer of possession. No indorsement is necessary.

Order Paper

Order Paper: instrument issued to specific party and not as yet indorsed or with special indorsement at end of its indorsement chain

Special Indorsement: transferor signs instrument, writes indorsee's name, and directs that instrument be paid to endorsee

What is it? **Order paper** is commercial paper that, like bearer paper, is found in only one of two forms: (1) it has been issued to a specific party and has not yet been indorsed or (2) whether issued to cash or to a specific person, it has a special indorsement at the end of its indorsement chain. A **special indorsement** names the indorsee and directs that the instrument be paid to the indorsee. In such an indorsement, the expression "pay to the order of" or "pay to" is followed by the name of the recipient. (Note that, for brevity's sake, on the reverse of an instrument "pay to" is legally treated as the equivalent of "pay to the order of.")

How do you negotiate order paper? Proper negotiation of order paper must be by indorsement of the holder accompanied by a transfer of possession to another party. A transfer without the proper indorsement is classified as an assignment.

Consider the accompanying examples closely.

• An Instrument created as negotiable, order paper

Carryl Taylor bought a shipment of vitamins for his business from his supplier, Wayne Washam. He made out a check to Wayne, naming him as payee, and handed it to him. At that point the check was considered order paper and would require Wayne's signature and transfer of possession for a proper negotiation.

Carryl Taylor	**No. 1313**
Rt. 2	
Pennsboro, MO 65707	*December 10* 19 **
Pay to the Order of *Wayne Washam*	$ *237.50*
Two hundred and thirty-seven and 50/100 ——	DOLLARS
People's Bank of Pennsboro	*Carryl Taylor*

• Indorsed in blank, thereby becoming bearer paper

Wayne used the check to pay off a debt to Buff Chassie. To do so, Wayne indorsed the instrument in blank and transfered possession to Buff.

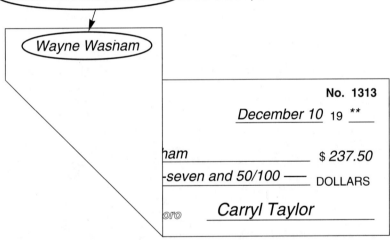

• Left unchanged as negotiable bearer paper

Chassie bought some fuel for his furnace. The bill came to $250. Chassie negotiated Taylor's check over to Shore Oil, Inc. simply by handing it to their cashier (transferring possion – as it was bearer paper) and paid the additional $12.50 in cash.

• Given a special indorsement to become negotiable order paper

Shore Oil Company's President, Paula Sweetcrude, then signed the check over to Shore's supplier, Cielnoir, Inc. with a special indorsement and a transfer of possession. **Note that the transfer of possession was all that was required for a proper negotiation in this instance** but Sweetcrude wisely created order paper by her special indorsement. She did this so that Clienoir's indorsement would serve as some evidence of the transaction.

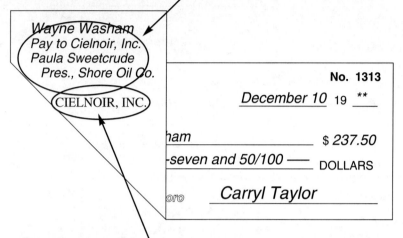

• Deposited in bank for collection

When Cielnoir deposited the check in its bank, it indorsed the instrument (this time with a stamp) in blank. When the bank tried to collect, Carryl Taylor refused to pay the instrument because the vitamins he had bought with it proved to be spoiled once the containers were opened. Because the instrument was negotiable and properly negotiated to it and because it gave value in good faith without notice of defect or dishonor, Cielnoir was an HDC and could recover the amount of the check from Taylor regardless of his defense of failure of consideration. Carryl would have to sue Wayne Washam to recover for his (Carryl's) loss.

What Other Kinds of Indorsements Are There, and What Are Their Effects?

As shown above, the proper method of future negotiation of a piece of commercial paper may be determined by the use of either a blank or a special indorsement. However, two additional types of indorsements, the qualified indorsement and the restrictive indorsement, may also affect the use of commercial paper. The qualified indorsement helps determine the degree of the transferor's exposure to liability based on his or her use of the instrument. The restrictive indorsement curtails the rights of the indorsee, but it does no more than that. We'll take a look in depth at each of these indorsement types right after a brief discussion of liability on commercial paper.

| | Parties Who Are Primarily and Secondarily Liable Based on Signature | Figure 20–1 |

	Notes	Drafts
Primary	Maker	No one until acceptance of primary liability by drawee
Secondary	Indorsers unless qualified (see the section on "Effect of the Qualified Indorsement")	Drawer and indorsers (unless indorsers are qualified)

Sources of an Indorser's Potential Liability

Whenever a check, note, or other form of commercial paper is circulated, there are two different types of potential liability that may attach to parties through whose hands the instrument passes. The first type of liability stems from warranties that the courts may imply against parties to any transfer of such an instrument. These warranties will be discussed in the last section of this chapter.

The second type of potential liability comes from signatures. As a general rule, only a person whose signature appears on the instrument is exposed to this type of potential liability. There are a few exceptions to this rule. One exception makes a forger or someone who signs another's signature without authorization liable on that signature as if it were his or her own. A second exception makes the person whose signature is forged or given without authority liable if she or he **ratifies** (approves or confirms) the act. Typically, other than as a result of these exceptions, a person must sign the instrument in his or her own name in order to be liable on that signature.

Ratifies: approves or confirms

Signature-based liability on commercial paper is either primary or secondary. **Primary liability** is defined as the unconditional responsibility to pay an instrument whenever it is due. The maker of a promissory note or a certificate of deposit is primarily liable thereon; although no one is primarily liable on a draft when it is issued, the drawee becomes so upon acceptance.

Primary Liability: unconditional responsibility to pay instrument whenever it is due

Secondary liability is the legal responsibility to pay an instrument whenever the party primarily liable does not. It is owed to the current holder and all subsequent indorsers. Secondary liability attaches only when the instrument has been properly presented for payment to the party primarily liable, when that party has refused payment, and when notice of the refusal or dishonor has been given to the parties who are potentially secondarily liable. The drawers of drafts are secondarily liable thereon. Indorsers of all forms of commercial paper can be secondarily liable unless they use a qualified indorsement.

Secondary Liability: legal responsibility to pay instrument whenever party primarily liable does not

Effect of the Qualified Indorsement on Such Potential Liability

A **qualified indorsement** is one that uses "without recourse" or a similar phrase in conjunction with an indorsement. Qualifying an indorsement in this manner

Qualified Indorsement: "without recourse" or similar phrase used above transferor's indorsement

Figure 20–2 **Blank, Qualified Indorsement That Eliminates Signature-Based Liability to Subsequent Holders and Indorsers**

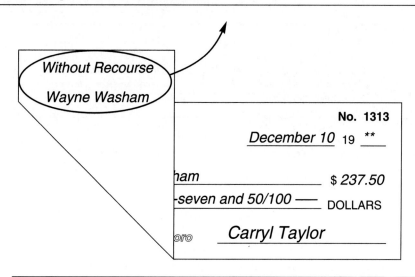

eliminates signature-based liability (but not liability based on the warrantee). Figure 20–2 shows an example of the use of "without recourse" as used by Wayne Washam to cancel his potential signature-based liability on the instrument.

Restrictive Indorsements and the Rights of the Indorsee

Restrictive Indorsement: rights of transferee curtailed or restricted by statement above transferor's signature

A **restrictive indorsement** is one that curtails or restricts the rights of the transferee. Examples include such expressions as "for deposit only," "for collection only," "pay to [indorsee's name] only," and the wording in Figure 20–3, which would be considered a special, restrictive indorsement.

There are two important things to remember about restrictive indorsements. One, already mentioned, is that the indorsement restricts only the rights of the immediate transferor and does not prevent further negotiation. So a check indorsed "for collection only, Bill Blaase" could be treated as though it had only a blank indorsement by future holders except for the party who took it from Bill Blaase and for some reason did not act to collect on it. An immediate transferee who does not follow the restriction imposed by the indorsement may be liable for the tort of conversion.

The second important thing to remember about restrictive indorsements is that putting them on a conditional basis may not affect the negotiability of the instrument. Recall, however, that a condition imposed at the time of issuance ("pay to the order of Cielnoir, Inc., only upon delivery of T–32 pump as per order" on the face of the instrument) would defeat the instrument's negotiability. But such conditions can be imposed on the reverse to accompany indorsements.

Special, Restrictive Indorsement Imposing a Condition on Cielnoir, Inc., That Must Be Satisfied before Shore Oil Company Is Secondarily Liable on Instrument **Figure 20–3**

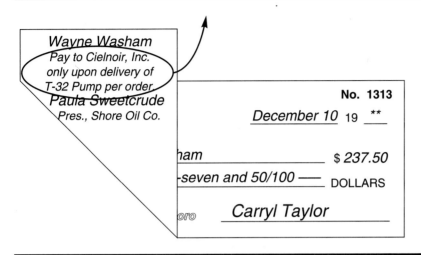

A Few Miscellaneous Points about Indorsements. If wording on the reverse of an instrument reads like an assignment, the UCC insists that it is instead to be treated as an indorsement. Thus, if the reverse reads "I hereby assign all my rights under this instrument to Timothy Leery" and is signed by the holder, Bill Blaase, then transferred, the effect is that of a negotiation (UCC 3–202).

Another quirk in the law comes from the pressure of necessity. In particular, the law allows a **depository bank** (the first bank to which an instrument is transferred for collection) to act as an agent of its customer (the depositor) by supplying his or her indorsement if it is missing from the instrument. This facilitates collection by eliminating the delay of holding the instrument until the proper signature has been obtained.

Depository Bank: first bank to which instrument is first transferred for collection

Finally, if a situation arises in which the indorsee's name is misspelled, UCC 3–203 allows that party to indorse with the correct spelling or the previous incorrect spelling, or both. However, a transferee giving value for the instrument may, again by the dictate of UCC 3–203, require the transferor to sign both ways.

If a Person Who Has Acquired the Rights of a Holder in Due Course Tries to Collect on the Instrument and Is Refused, Which of the Defenses Raised By the Obligor Can Be Overcome and Which Cannot?

Hopefully, having worked your way through the material on HDCs, negotiability, and negotiation, you can now grasp the crucial point of commercial paper law. We've alluded to it before. Basically, the point is that a person who becomes a holder in due course and takes a negotiable instrument that has been properly negotiated has greatly reduced the risk of being unable to collect on the commercial paper involved. This risk reduction comes because a person with an HDC's rights can overcome many of the defenses traditionally raised against someone trying to collect on a check, draft, note, or any other instrument in question. Now, to build on this key point, let's look at the range of possible defenses and see which of them fall into the category of defenses that are good against all holders. Then we'll examine defenses in the second category, which consists of defenses that can be overcome by the rights of an HDC.

In other words, a valid defense from the first category will prevent holders, HDCs, HHDCs, and, of course, mere assignees from collecting on a check, draft, or other piece of commercial paper for which they may have paid good money. This category is labeled the **real** (also called universal) **defenses.**

The second category of defenses consists of defenses that are good only against mere holders and assignees but can be overcome by HDCs and HHDCs. This category is labeled the **personal** (also called limited) **defenses.**

Real Defenses: defenses that can be successfully raised against all kinds of holders

Personal Defenses: defenses that are good against mere holders and assignees but can be overcome by HDCs and HHDCs

Real Defenses

The key to most of the real defenses is that a void transaction is or was involved in the issuance of the instrument.

Illegality.   An example of illegality as a defense is a situation in which an instrument has been issued in conjunction with an illegal gambling debt. Since the transaction underlying the issuance is void, the real defense of illegality can be raised in court and will prevent collection by any and all holders of the check or promissory note that resulted. Instruments resulting from bribery or extortion also fall into this subcategory.

Forgery or Unauthorized Signature.   Again, the underlying transaction is void. Consequently, the defense of forged or unauthorized signature of the maker or drawer is valid against all holders. The only exceptions to this rule are situations in which the negligence of the drawer or issuer have contributed to the forgery or unauthorized signature.

HYPOTHETICAL CASE

> Bruce negligently left his checkbook in the child's seat of his shopping cart at the supermarket. It disappeared but was returned shortly by store personnel. They reported finding it near the magazine rack at which Bruce had been standing. Bruce, thinking that he had merely dropped the checkbook, did not examine the numbered checks and thus did not notice that the last five had been ripped out. Consequently, when checks in the amount of several hundreds of dollars were passed over his forged signature, the court had to choose between placing the loss on Bruce and placing it on the innocent holders of the instruments. Because Bruce's negligence was evident, he had to sustain the loss.

Discharge as a Result of Bankruptcy Proceedings.   Chapter 24 contains a lengthy discussion of bankruptcy and its effects. Right now it is enough to say that the determinations of a bankruptcy proceeding can result in a real defense against the collection of any of the bankrupt's outstanding instruments.

Material Alteration.   Among the many examples of material alteration are adding figures to the amount or deleting figures from it, no matter how small their significance; unauthorized completion; and changing the date or dates involved. If made with a fraudulent intent, such changes produce a real defense against collection of the instrument. The extent of the defense differs. It is a defense to the full amount due when a mere holder seeks to collect. A person with the rights of an HDC, however, can enforce the instrument for its original amount or even for an amount fraudulently inserted on an incomplete instrument (due to the issuer's negligence in leaving part of the instrument blank).

Fraud in the Execution

HYPOTHETICAL CASE

Billy Boots, a sudden smash country-and-western star, walked down the stairs after an evening performance at the *Star on Stage* review in Branson, Missouri. Several fans pushed toward him. Billy signed their playbills without glancing at them. One, a blank piece of stiff, white 67-pound paper, was immediately pulled back by the person who had offered it, a tall raven-haired woman of about 30. Billy caught her eye for a brief moment, and she self-consciously smiled at him, then disappeared into the darkness. Two months later Billy received a call from his business manager. Commercial Bank of Branson had just called for payment of a $100,000 promissory note it was holding. Commercial had bought the note from a "Suzanne Williams," one of its depositors. It had paid $95,000 for the note and wanted the $100,000, as the note had just become due. When Billy examined the instrument, he remembered the raven-haired woman, who had evidently printed the note around his signature on the blank piece of paper. In the meantime Suzanne Williams had disappeared. Will the bank as a holder in due course be able to overcome Billy's defense of fraud?

The answer is no (1) if Billy did not act negligently or carelessly in succumbing to the fraud, and (2) if Billy did not know he was creating an instrument or was totally deceived as to the instrument's essential terms. **Fraud in the execution,** in which the party does not even realize that she or he is issuing a piece of commercial paper, is a real defense. If that defense were successfully established in court, the bank could not collect from Billy. Given the above circumstances, such would probably be the case. The bank would then have to recover against Suzanne Williams, the secondarily liable party, or just bear the loss. (Be sure to compare fraud in the execution with fraud in the inducement—which will be discussed shortly.)

Fraud in the Execution: real defense stemming from fact that defrauded party does not realize she or he is issuing a piece of commercial paper

Infancy.   As you may suspect, minority as it relates to the capacity to contract produces a real defense to commercial paper issued in the contractual context. Otherwise, if, for example, a minor issued a check to pay for an expensive car, she could avoid the contract but would be required to pay the check. This would defeat the law's purpose.

Insanity and Habitual Drunkenness.   As you probably recall, whenever the law recognizes either insanity or habitual drunkenness in an individual, it appoints a guardian for that individual. This renders void all contracts made by the protected party. Thus on behalf of the protected party's estate, the guardian can enter a real defense against any commercial paper that the protected party issues.

Extreme Duress.   If commercial paper has been issued by a person under **extreme duress,** its issuer can raise a successful real defense to its collection. In most states extreme duress is defined as a threat against the issuer or his or her immediate family. The threat must be of death, severe bodily harm, or the destruction of the issuer's home, and it must cause the issuer to act in a way that she or he would not have acted otherwise. (Be sure you understand the difference between extreme duress and ordinary duress. Ordinary duress is discussed later in this chapter.)

Extreme Duress: real defense against collection arising from threat of force or violence against person, family, or home of party

Statute of Limitations.   Many states impose a statute of limitations on the collection of commercial paper. If this period (typically one year to three years) has run, it will produce a real defense.

Personal Defenses

The defenses in this category are good only against mere holders and assignees. HDCs and HHDCs will be able to collect regardless of the personal defenses being raised against them.

Breach of Contract or Failure of Consideration.   In situations in which commercial paper has been issued to bind a transaction, a personal or limited defense is available when the contract has not been properly executed or the consideration is faulty or lacking.

HYPOTHETICAL CASE

Stan Crucial owned a restaurant in St. Louis. Deciding to go into catering, he bought a new delivery van from Sally's Service Vehicles. He issued a check for $3,000 as a down payment for the van and signed a promissory note for the $27,000 balance. Unfortunately, the delivery of the van was delayed several weeks past the promised date. Consequently, Stan lost considerable business for which he had already signed contracts. When the van was finally delivered, its faulty heating and cooling systems caused food spoilage. Stan tried to use the breach of contract (late delivery) and failure of consideration (faulty good) as offsets to the amounts due on the commercial paper he had issued in the transaction. Unfortunately, Stan had to pay the check as Sally's had transferred it to an HDC, which could overcome the defenses. When Sally's tried to collect on the note, however, Stan could offset his damages from the amount due Sally's. This was because of the knowledge of the van's defects attributable to Sally's as the seller. Sally's, therefore, could not be a holder in due course on the instrument, and as a mere holder it could not overcome Stan's personal defenses of breach of contract and failure of consideration.

Fraud in the Inducement and Similar Defenses

When a person is deceived or defrauded into issuing commercial paper, a personal defense of **fraud in the inducement** results. In fraud in the inducement, unlike fraud in the execution, the issuer knows that she or he is making out an instrument.

Other circumstances leading to a voidable contract also produce personal defenses to commercial paper issued in the voidable transaction. Misrepresentation, undue influence, temporary insanity, and temporary intoxication all produce this effect in most jurisdictions. **Ordinary duress,** which is typically found in economic threats or legitimate threats of criminal prosecution, also results in a voidable contract and a personal defense.

Fraud in the Inducement: personal defense in which defrauded party knows he or she is issuing an instrument but is deceived or defrauded into doing so

Ordinary Duress: personal defense found in economic threats or legitimate threats of criminal prosecution

Consumer Transaction Defenses

Finally note that nearly 20 years ago, in response to a multitude of consumer complaints, the Federal Trade Commission (FTC) issued a rule that greatly affected the collection of commercial paper issued in a consumer transaction. In effect, the FTC decreed that in a transaction in which commercial paper is issued in payment, all claims and defenses available to a consumer are effective even against a person with the rights of a holder in due course in relation to that paper. In other words, where consumer credit instruments (drafts and notes) are concerned, HDCs and HHDCs are treated in exactly the same way as mere holders are treated and are subject to whatever defenses mere holders are subject. See *Blue Cross Health Services* v. *Sauer,* the case at the end of the chapter for a real-life example of the difference this makes.

What Warranties Flow from the Use of Commercial Paper, and What Is Their Effect?

Earlier in the chapter we noted that there were two bases for liability on a piece of commercial paper. We have just looked extensively at the first of these two: liability based on signature. Now we need to examine the second: warrantee-based liability.

Just as it does in sales situations, the law implies certain warranties against the transferor of commercial paper. If the transfer is made by indorsement and delivery, the warranties flow to the immediate transferee and all later holders who take the instrument in good faith. If the transfer is made by delivery alone, the signature of the transferor does not appear on the paper and the warranties therefore flow only to the immediate transferee.

The warranties are as follows:

1. *Good title.* In effect, the transferor is held to warrant that she or he has good title or is authorized to act on behalf of the person who has good title to the instrument.

2. *Genuine or authorized signatures.* By this warranty the transferor is impliedly held to acknowledge that all foregoing signatures on the instrument are genuine. In the event of a forgery or an unauthorized signature on the instrument, no matter how distant from the transferor in the indorsement chain, the transferor is therefore held liable and may have to take the loss unless a transferor further up the chain can be saddled with accountability.

3. *No material alteration.* Given this warranty, you can understand the reluctance of a potential holder to take an instrument made out in pencil. With such an instrument, the possibility of undetectable alterations would pose too great a risk.

4. *No defense against the transferor by any party to the instrument.* This warranty is softened somewhat for qualified indorsers. They are held only to a warranty that they have no actual knowledge of any such defenses.

5. *No knowledge of any insolvency proceedings against the issuer or acceptor of the instrument.*

As you can tell, the coverage of the warranties is quite broad. Taken together with signature-based liability, they reduce significantly the potential for loss on commercial paper. That diminished potential for loss combined with the convenience of commercial paper has produced the flood of checks, drafts, notes, and other instruments in use in our capitalist system.

APPLICATIONS OF WHAT YOU'VE LEARNED

Vocabulary Development

Fill in the blanks with the appropriate term.

Bearer Paper
Blank Indorsement
Depository Bank
Extreme Duress
Fraud in the Execution

Fraud in the
  Inducement
Negotiated
Order Paper
Ordinary Duress

Personal Defenses
Primary Liability
Qualified Indorsement
Ratifies

Real Defenses
Restrictive Indorsement
Secondary Liability
Special Indorsement

[Some of the answers may be drawn from preceding chapters.]

1. The first bank into which a check is placed for collection is referred to as the _____.

2. While he's on vacation, Randy Realestate's secretary issues a check for a down payment on a piece of property he's been trying to buy for five years. When he returns, she informs him of what she has done. He agrees to pay the check or _____ it.

3. If a piece of commercial paper has been properly transferred so as to make the transferee a holder of some kind, the paper has been _____.

4. If a piece of commercial paper has not been properly transferred, it has merely been _____.

5. After Angelica threatened to vandalize his car, Bill gave her a check for $500. Bill's defense against collection of this instrument is

_____.

6. The maker of a note and the acceptor of a draft have

_____ on the respective instruments.

7. The drawer of a check has _____ on the instrument.

Problems

1. For the following examples, name the type of indorsement and then state what would be required to further negotiate the instrument.

2. For each of the following situations, determine whether or not the specified person with the rights of a holder in due course would be able to recover on the instrument in question. In each instance, be sure to specify the type of defense that the obligor would raise.

   a. Patsi Johnson wrote a $350 check in payment for a sophisticated electric-powered Jeep that she bought for her granddaughter. The Jeep's battery exploded, ruining the vehicle. Could a bank that qualifies as an HDC recover on the check?

   b. M. T. Pockets went through bankruptcy. After the process had been completed, the 1st National Bank of Pennsboro (an HDC) requested payment from him on a note that he had signed prior to his bankruptcy filing. Could the bank recover on the note?

a.

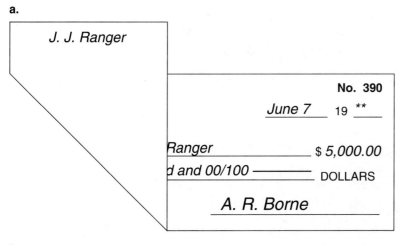

b.

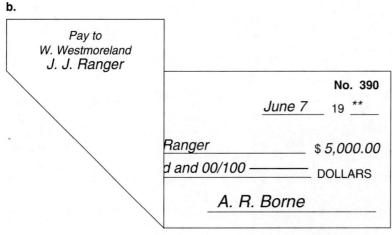

c.

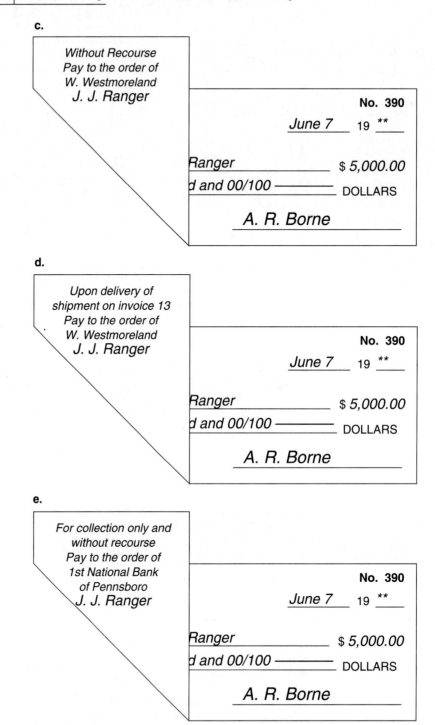

Without Recourse
Pay to the order of
W. Westmoreland
J. J. Ranger

No. 390

June 7   19 **

Ranger $ *5,000.00*
d and 00/100 ———— DOLLARS

A. R. Borne

d.

Upon delivery of
shipment on invoice 13
Pay to the order of
W. Westmoreland
J. J. Ranger

No. 390

June 7   19 **

Ranger $ *5,000.00*
d and 00/100 ———— DOLLARS

A. R. Borne

e.

For collection only and
without recourse
Pay to the order of
1st National Bank
of Pennsboro
J. J. Ranger

No. 390

June 7   19 **

Ranger $ *5,000.00*
d and 00/100 ———— DOLLARS

A. R. Borne

c. Charles Smith stoped payment on a check on which his name had been forged as a drawer. Could a bank that qualifies as an HDC recover on the check?

d. Lee Infant, while 16 years of age, wrote a check to pay for some records he purchased with money he had been saving for college. His parents had him avoid the transaction. Could a bank that qualifies as an HDC recover on the check?

e. Dee Seived wrote a $15,000 check to buy stock in a fraudulent scheme to purchase the Brooklyn Bridge and remove it to England for use as a tourist attraction. Could a bank that qualifies as an HDC recover on the check?

3. What is the advantage to the transferee of having bearer paper indorsed by the transferor?

ACTUAL CASE STUDY

Blue Cross Health Services v. Sauer

800 S.W.2d 72

Now decide what to do about the more than $22,000 in checks that Blue Cross sent to the wrong person.

Because of a clerical error, 33 checks totaling over $22,000 had been sent to William Sauer of Chesterfield, Missouri, instead of William Sauer of Milwaukee, Wisconsin. The Missouri man had been in the hospital at about the same time as the Wisconsin man's son. Both Sauers had been insured by Blue Cross, and the numerous checks had been sent sporadically over a seven-month span. When Blue Cross brought suit to reclaim the money paid erroneously to Sauer of Missouri, he claimed that he was a holder in due course of the instruments and therefore that he could collect on them regardless of any defense of failure of consideration or breach of contract that Blue Cross might raise. In examining this claim, the court determined that each check sent to Sauer of Missouri had been accompanied by an "explanation of benefits" form and that his father, who had been paying his Blue Cross premiums, had stopped paying them before Sauer of Missouri's most recent hospitalization.

Questions

1. Applying the definition of an HDC to Sauer of Missouri's circumstances, determine whether or not he must repay the money. What are your conclusions?

2. Ethically, should Sauer of Missouri be forced to repay the more than $22,000 in checks that were sent to him by mistake if it is shown that in cashing and spending the checks he acted in good faith and without knowledge of the mistake being made?

How Is Commercial Paper Discharged and What Part Do Financial Institutions Play in the Use of Commercial Paper?

CHAPTER OUTLINE AND OBJECTIVES

After studying this chapter, the student will be able to:

I.   Explain how commercial paper is discharged.
  a. By payment or satisfaction
  b. By cancellation or renunciation
  c. By impairment of recourse or collateral
  d. By reacquisition of an instrument by a prior party
  e. By other means

II. Discuss how our financial institutions enhance the use of commercial paper.
  a. By creating new methods of resource transfer
  b. By making specialty instruments available
  c. By day-to-day management of the commercial paper system

III. Identify potential changes in Articles 3 and 4 of the Uniform Commercial Code.

IV. Determine whether attorneys and judges ever use the wrong laws by deciding *Rotert* v. *Faulkner*, a case that ties together the concepts of negotiability and discharge.

How Is Commercial Paper Discharged?

Discharge: termination of legal obligation

In 3–601 the UCC provides a laundry list of potential means of **discharge** (termination of a legal obligation) of liability on an instrument. Realize that even after an individual's obligation on a check, draft, or other piece of commercial paper has ended, the paper can remain due and payable. When this occurs, the discharge is effective only if notice of it is given to subsequent HDCs. A qualified indorsement is an example of this. The expression "without recourse" gives notice to all later owners of the instrument that the qualified party is not liable on her or his signature. With that in mind, let's run down the most significant items on the UCC's list of potential ways to be discharged from responsibility on commercial paper.

By Payment or Satisfaction

It goes practically without saying that for the overwhelming majority of pieces of commercial paper, discharge comes from full, complete payment. It is a tribute to the adequacy of the laws governing the use and flow of such instruments that, relatively speaking, so few cases are adjudicated by our legal system.

Accord and Satisfaction: discharge from previous contractual obligation by fulfillment of terms to new contract

In dealing with discharge by payment, some cases involve the use of an accord and satisfaction. Basically, an **accord and satisfaction** involves the discharge of a party from a previous contractual obligation (satisfaction) by his or her fulfillment of the terms of a new contract (the accord). Here's an example:

HYPOTHETICAL CASE

Jason Tarleton, a contractor, lost $6,000 in penalties because he was late in completing the Barstone Causeway Project. Jason blamed his tardiness on the tardiness of one of his suppliers, Reliable Rebar, Inc. When he threatened suit, Reliable Rebar sent him the following check:

By indorsement, payee accepts this check in full satisfaction of all claims against Reliable Rebar, Inc.

No. 1313

September 30 19 **

Tarleton $ *2,500.00*

d and 00/100 DOLLARS

Hy Grade

as Pres., Rel. Rebar

Jason took the check, then lined out the wording on the reverse and substituted his own, which read:

continued on page 279

concluded

> ~~By indorsement, payee accepts this check in full satisfaction of all claims against Reliable Rebar, Inc.~~
>
> _____
>
> This check is accepted as part payment on full amount due under the claim for which this is offered as a settlement
>
> *JASON TARLETON*

A court eventually held that regardless of Jason's reasons for cashing the check as expressed in his indorsement, the drawer had offered an accord by sending the check to him. In cashing the check, therefore, Jason had brought about a satisfaction of the foregoing contractual dispute over Reliable Rebar's tardiness.

Note that some parties try to imply an accord and satisfaction by writing such comments as "payment in full" on the face of a check that is only one of many installment payments. Unless there have been foregoing negotiations supporting an accord in which one payment cancels the whole obligation, the notation on the check has no effect.

Effect of Tender of Payment. Unlike the tender of a ready, willing, and able offer to perform under a contract, a tender of payment will not discharge a due instrument. However, it will discharge the tendering party from liability for subsequent interest, attorney's fees, and other costs associated with collection. If the instrument is not mature, a tender of payment has none of these effects unless the terms include the acceptability of payment "on or before" the due date.

By Cancellation or Renunciation

Any holder of an instrument may, with or without consideration, cancel any party's obligation. This is done on the face or reverse of the instrument by striking out the party's signature or using any other means that conveys to a prospective holder that the party is no longer obligated on the instrument.

Cancellation can also be accomplished by simply destroying or mutilating the instrument.

Renunciation:
abandonment of right
without transfer

Renunciation, which is the abandonment of a right without transferring it to another, can be accomplished by the delivery of a signed writing to that effect to the party so discharged. It can also be accomplished by the surrender of the instrument to the party to be discharged (UCC 3–605).

By Impairment of Recourse or Collateral

This takes a bit of explaining. Once you grasp what's going on, however, the rule makes a great deal of common sense. Assume that Dannee Frail needed an education loan of $7,000 to pursue his studies and that he borrowed the money he needed from his friend, William Winton. Dannee then issued in Winton's favor a promissory note in that amount plus interest. To give further assurance that the loan would be repaid, Dannee also promised William Winton and anyone who took the note from him, the right, upon default, to sell Dannee's car and use the proceeds to satisfy whatever might still remain to be paid. Winton then sold the note to Theodore K. Runamukus; who sold it to Georgio Bushini. Bushini, as holder, bipartisanly released Dannee from his promise to let Winton sell his car to pay for any default on the note and canceled Winton's signature and secondary liability by lining through Winton's indorsement. The face (top) and the reverse of Dannee Frail's promissory note issued to William Finton as they appeared when Bushini tried to collect the balance due looked like this:

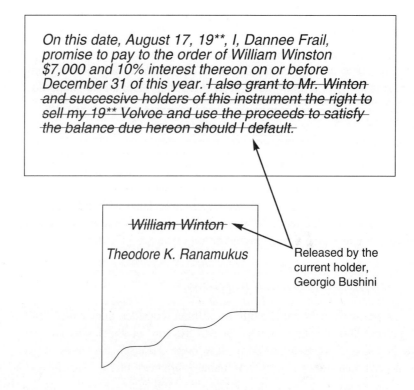

However, when Bushini tried to collect on the note, he found that Frail could not pay. Bushini then gave proper notice of default to Runamuckus so as to make him secondarily liable. Runamuckus was quick to point out that Bushini had impaired Runamuckus's chances of recourse against Winton by canceling Winton's obligation and Runamuckus's chances of recourse against the collateral (the Volvo) by releasing Frail from his promise to sell it to cover an amount due on default. As a consequence, according to UCC 3–606, Runamuckus had been discharged. Bushini immediately called his lawyer, who reluctantly agreed with Runamuckus.

The point is that it would be unfair to allow a current holder to cancel rights of a previous holder of an instrument and then expect that holder to pay off the instrument without them. The UCC rule prevents this inequity.

By Reacquisition of an Instrument by a Prior Party

Remember the rule that no one can improve his or her status by reacquisition? We ran into that rule in discussing holders who could not be a holder in due course on their own but tried to get the rights of an HDC by selling to one and then buying the instrument back. This rule follows the same principle. For example, forget about the release of parties and collateral by Bushini. Instead, just presume that Winton reacquired the instrument from Bushini. The instrument from the illustration below presumes that Bushini only considered releasing Winton from secondary liability and Frail's collateral but did not follow through because of the potential problems with collection. Instead, Bushini resold the instrument to Winton.

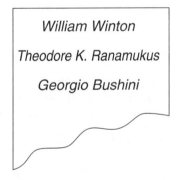

William Winton

Theodore K. Ranamukus

Georgio Bushini

To be consistent with the HDC application, we cannot allow Winton upon default to pursue Runamuckus and Bushini for secondary liability. If he were able to do so, he would have improved his status by reacquisition. Therefore, Runamuckus and Bushini are discharged.

By Other Means

The UCC also lists a number of other means by which parties can be discharged from their liability on an instrument:

Certification of a check. We'll discuss this in the next section.
Fraudulent and material alteration. We've already discussed this under defenses.

Unexcused delay in presentment or notice of dishonor. We've also discussed these possibilities.

Acceptance varying a draft. When the potential acceptor negotiates with the holder to vary the terms of the draft itself as a condition for acceptance, the drawer and indorsers are discharged unless they agree to still be held accountable to the new terms.

By any of the means discussed above, then, the obligation of the paper itself or that of any of the parties to the paper can be discharged. However, it is important to bear in mind that the vast majority of instruments are discharged simply by being paid according to their terms. Considering the volume of instruments of all types that the commercial paper system must handle, it is an extremely reliable and well-functioning facilitator of our commercial and personal endeavors.

How Do Our Financial Institutions Enhance the Use of Commercial Paper?

Our banks, savings and loans, credit unions, and other financial institutions all play a crucial part in making the commercial paper system work. In addition, the federal government administers a very efficient transmittal and clearance procedure for the instruments that are the heart of that system. Methodology that has been in use for well over a decade can even make checks and similar instruments obsolete.

By Creating New Methods of Resource Transfer

Electronic Fund Transfers: electronic/ computer-based substitute for hardcopy commercial paper

The major innovation in this regard is the use of **electronic fund transfers** (EFTs). EFTs employ a powerful combination of electronics and computer technology as a substitute for the instruments, such as checks and drafts, that we have relied on for so long. Without any action by the depositor, paychecks are automatically deposited in employee accounts and drafted on to pay recurrent bills automatically; automatic bank tellers "work" around the clock, allowing the customer to make most bank transactions without contacting any human employee of the institution; retail purchases are charged off directly against the account balance; and on and on. The only paper trail for what occurs is found in a computer printout or a computer-printed form notifying the party at interest of what has occurred.

Of course, this system invites unchecked error, fraudulent schemes, and theft. Since the system is of great advantage to financial institutions as well as a convenience to its users, the financial institutions are burdened with the greater potential for loss in exceptional circumstances. For example, when an EFT card is lost or stolen and used without authority, the card's owner can limit her or his liability to $50 if the issuer is given notice within two business days. (The liability limit of the card's owner becomes $500 if notice is given between 2 and 60 days, and after 60 days his or her liability is unlimited.)

Although computers have an aura of infallibility, computer errors occur all too frequently. For example, consider the case of an 85-year-old woman, Jewell M. Miller, who was recently indirectly declared dead by her bank. The bank's computer refused to deposit in her account her EFTs from the Veterans and Social Security administrations. Those agencies, "thinking" she was indeed dead, immediately stopped sending her the monthly checks on which she depended for her livelihood. Mrs. Miller checked her pulse and then reported the error to her financial institution. Nevertheless, it was a full three months before her income was reinstated. According to the Electronic Fund Transfer Act of 1978, the law that governs EFT transactions (and provides the rules for lost and stolen EFT cards), a consumer has 60 days to report such an error (discovered through a careful review of the bank statement and receipts) to the responsible institution. Upon notification, the institution has 10 business days to investigate. If it takes longer to complete the investigation (up to 45 days are allowed), it must at least recredit the customer's account with the amount in dispute after the 10 days. In Mrs. Miller's case this recrediting had to be done as the dispute took far longer than 10 days to resolve.

By Making Specialty Instruments Available

Financial institutions facilitate the satisfaction of consumer needs by making several special kinds of instruments available for use. Traveler's checks, cashier's checks, and certified checks are the most noteworthy in this regard.

Traveler's Checks.   These checks are issued by various types of financial institutions in addition to banks (although the use of the word *checks* implies that only banks are involved). The checks are purchased for the security they provide and for the ease with which they can be cashed even when the person who cashes them is far from her or his home area. These attributes stem from the way in which they are placed in circulation. A financial institution is both drawer and drawee of a **traveler's check.** However, when traveler's checks are purchased, the buyer signs each of them in the presence of the issuer. Thereafter, each traveler's check can be cashed only if its possessor is identified to the payee and countersigns in the payee's presence. Thus, the risk for the person who takes the traveler's check in payment for merchandise or cash is greatly reduced by simply requiring a picture ID and comparing signatures. The risk for the person carrying the checks is also greatly reduced as his or her signature, given in the payee's presence, is required to negotiate them. Moreover, many issuers of traveler's checks pride themselves on their promptness in replacing lost or stolen checks.

Traveler's Check: commercial paper instrument of which financial institution is both drawer and drawee and which requires user's signature before issuer and payee

Cashier's Checks.   With a **cashier's check,** as with a traveler's check, a financial institution (in the case of a cashier's check the institution must be a bank) is both the drawer and the drawee. A cashier's check can be issued payable to its purchaser or to any party its purchaser specifies. Since the bank has drawn the check on itself, the check is a good as the creditworthiness of the bank itself. This greatly enhances the likelihood that the instrument will be taken by a third party in lieu of cash. Also, the payee or holder knows that, by law, payment

Cashier's Check: commercial paper instrument of which financial institution is both drawer and drawee

cannot be stopped on such a check, because by issuing it, the bank has already accepted primary liability.

Murkey Hubbell agreed to buy a new telescope for $1,300 from a 1-800 discounter in New York State. The discounter required payment by credit card or cashier's check. Murkey went to a local bank and purchased a cashier's check for $1,305 (the bank charged nondepositors a $5 service fee). She mailed the check by Priority Mail. The discounter shipped her telescope upon receipt of the cashier's check, so that she received her new purchase barely a week after her original phone call. When she opened the package, however, she discovered that the telescope's mirror was scarred. She immediately contacted the discounter, who referred her to the manufacturer. The manufacturer stated that the discounter was not an authorized retailer for its products and refused to talk to her. Murkey then tried to get the bank to stop payment on the cashier's check. The bank refused to do so, stating that, by law, it had already accepted the primary liability to pay the instrument. (Note that some 1–800 discount retailers will accept a personal check but will not ship the goods until the check clears.)

Certified Check:
depositor-issued instrument on which financial institution has accepted primary liability

Certified Checks.   A **certified check** is the check of a depositor in a bank on which that institution has indicated, by writing "accepted" or "certified" accompanied by the date and the signature of a bank official, its warranty that sufficient funds are available for payment. According to the UCC, this certification is the equivalent of actual acceptance. Upon certifying such an instrument, most banks immediately subtract from the depositor's account the funds for payment of the instrument.

By certification the bank acquires primary liability to pay the instrument. However, the identities of the secondarily liable parties on such an instrument depend on who requested the certification. If the drawer of the check requested the certification, then that drawer and all indorsers are secondarily liable. However, if a holder had the instrument certified, the drawer and the intervening indorsers are discharged. Here's an example:

Boyer bought $7,500 of sports equipment from Javier, for which he paid by check. Javier used the check to pay a debt to White. White then signed it over to Euchre as a down payment on a business. While Euchre was discussing the matter with White, he received a call from his employer informing him that he was being transferred to the West Coast immediately. To obtain access to funds at this new location, Euchre took the check to Boyer's bank to have the bank certify it. When the bank did so, Boyer, Javier, and White were all discharged from secondary liability on the instrument. This is only fair as their secondary liability was only contingent on the bank's refusal to accept the check. It was accepted, so the potential liability ended at that point.

By Day-to-Day Management of the Commercial Paper System

At the heart of the commercial paper system are the financial institutions that, through their relations with their customers, keep the system intact and efficient. These relations are most frequently defined in contract form, in particular in the form of a depository contract. It is important to note at the outset that this contract is solely between the financial institution and its depositor/customer. Rights under the contract are not assigned by a depositor or a payee by the issuance of an instrument. So, for example, if a bank refuses to pay a check even if there are funds available, the payee/holder cannot bring suit to force it to do so. Any suit for payment of the amount due must instead be directed at the parties secondarily liable on the instrument or against the issuer based on the underlying contract, if there is one. The depositor can sue the bank for its failure to pay as a breach of the depository contract, but, once again, the holders of the instrument cannot.

Since the depository contract is pivotal to the functioning of the commercial paper system, we need to take a closer look at the relationship it creates.

Primarily, it establishes the financial institution as the caretaker of the depositor's funds. The financial institution is to preserve them, keep them safe, and place them at the disposal of the depositor on that person's demand. The financial institution also serves as the **agent** (a person authorized by another to act in her or his stead) of the depositor in collecting negotiable instruments payable to the depositor. Any type of use of the money that the **depository bank** (the bank into which the instrument is deposited for collection) gives the depositor before the instrument has actually been paid by the bank on which it is drawn is only temporary, however. As a consequence, the depository bank can, under the depository contract, revoke the use of the money if the instrument is dishonored.

Agent: person authorized by another to act in her or his stead

Depository Bank: bank into which instrument is deposited for collection

Turning the situation around, the depositor's bank is under a contractual duty to honor all checks drawn on the depositor's account when there are sufficient funds in it. If there are not sufficient funds in the account to cover a check, the bank may pay it nonetheless and bill the depositor for an administrative charge in addition to the amount of the **overdraft** (the amount of the check in excess of the deposited funds). If a bank decides not to pay the overdraft, it may nonetheless levy an administrative charge for reviewing the situation. Many institutions negotiate a line of credit that can be automatically drawn against in the case of a depositor's overdraft. Whether by using a line of credit or by simply paying an overdraft, the bank converts its position from that of the depositor's debtor to that of the depositor's creditor.

Overdraft: amount of check in excess of deposited funds

Should a **payor bank** (the bank by which an item is payable as drawn or accepted) wrongfully dishonor a check, for example, when there are adequate funds in the depositor's account to pay it, the bank is liable for the proximate (direct) damages to the depositor that follow. These damages may include (to quote UCC 4–402) "damages for an arrest or prosecution of the customer or other consequential damages. Whether any consequential damages are proximately caused by the wrongful dishonor is a question of fact to be determined in each case."

Payor Bank: bank by which item is payable

Bart Black and J. Silverheels had a long-standing dispute over the ownership of a horse named Scout. Finally, Black agreed to pay Silverheels $500 to settle things. To do so, he drew a check in that amount on his account at the National Bank of Pennsboro. Unfortunately, even though there were sufficient funds in the account, the bank refused to honor the check. As a consequence, Silverheels brought bad check and grand theft charges (for taking Scout) against Black. Black later sued the bank and received payment for the harm caused him by the dishonor. His recovery included actual damages (the expenses of finding another horse to replace Scout) and consequential damages (his lawyer's fees and other costs).

Midnight Deadline: midnight of banking day following day instrument in question has been received

Such mistakes, given the number of instruments presented for payment each day, are infrequent. An unavoidable factor complicating this process is the requirement that the decision to pay or not to pay each instrument must be reached by the payor institution's **midnight deadline.** This refers to midnight of the banking day following the day on which the instrument in question has been received.

Although the risks of banks are increased by some rules, such as those relating to the midnight deadline and the availability of proximate damages, other rules affect the bank–depositor relationship in a manner protective of banks.

Stale Check: check presented for payment over six months after issue date

Stale Check Rule.

A **stale check** is a check presented for payment over six months after the date of issue indicated on its face. The rule is that a bank is not liable for failing to pay such a check. In addition, a bank is not liable if it in good faith honors such an instrument. These rules are especially important due to the time limits imposed on stop-payment orders.

Stop-Payment Order: directive to drawee not to transfer funds in accordance with issued draft

Stop-Payment Orders.

A **stop-payment order** is a directive to the drawee institution not to transfer funds in accordance with the terms of a previously issued draft. The drawee institution is given a reasonable time to execute the order. Thereafter, however, if it pays the instrument, it is liable to the depositor. UCC 4–403 states that an oral stop-payment order is effective for 14 calendar days only unless it is confirmed in writing during that period. A written stop-payment order is effective for 6 months unless it is renewed in writing for another term. Beyond that time, if the bank, given the notice of the stop-payment order, pays the check (or if it doesn't), it could be exposed to potential liability were it not for the stale check rule.

Death or Incompetence of a Customer.

Similarly, a drawee financial institution is not liable (UCC 4–405) if it pays a check before it has received notice of the death or incompetence of a depositor. Even with knowledge, it may continue to certify or pay checks for 10 days after it has received notice.

Forgeries and Unauthorized Signatures.

UCC 4–406 places squarely on the shoulders of the depositor the duty to examine promptly and with reasonable care his or her account statement. This statement and accompanying items must be made available to the depositor in a reasonable manner. The depositor must then report unauthorized signatures and other problems promptly to the bank. A depositor who fails to do so cannot hold the bank liable for any loss sustained because the bank paid on a forgery, an unauthorized signature, or a material alteration.

What is "prompt" is undefined except in the case of a string of forgeries, of which the first one or so is included in a statement. In that circumstance, the forgery must be reported in 14 days or the customer will have to bear the loss for all like items up to the time the bank actually has notice of what has been happening. The UCC also sets an absolute limit of one year for notification of a forged or altered check and a three-year limit for notification of a forged indorsement.

The Impostor and Fictitious Payee Rules.   In addition to avoiding liability by means of the above rules, the financial institution can avoid liability if it can be shown that the depositor's negligence contributed to a loss resulting from an unauthorized signature or a material alteration. For example, negligently leaving your checkbook in a golf cart from which it was stolen would preclude you from forcing the bank to recredit your account for any forged check from the checkbook that it paid on. Therefore, you would most likely take the loss for what occurred unless you could find and recover from the forger. This rule not only protects financial institutions but rightfully places responsibility for such problems on the party most able to prevent them, that is, the party whose negligence gave rise to the problems.

The idea of placing responsibility on the party most able to prevent the problem is also reflected in the **impostor rule.** If one party is duped into issuing an instrument to a person whom the issuer has misidentified, the loss from the resulting forgery falls on the careless issuer.

Impostor Rule: legal guideline placing loss on issuer duped into making instrument by one person posing as another

Vaughn Richthoften's barnstorming air show business had just gone bankrupt, and he desperately needed money to start over. Finally, he hit on a plan. Knowing that Charles Snootz, one of the 12 wealthiest persons in the world, supported almost all of the children's charities, Richthoften called Snootz and posed as the local campaign chairperson for the Jerry Lewis Telethon. As such, he obtained Snootz's promise to donate $100,000 to the latest effort. Richthoften later drove up to the Snootz estate and collected the check personally. He then forged the telethon's indorsement and cashed the instrument. Snootz's accountant discovered the deception a few days after the bank statement came. Richthoften could not be located. Snootz sued to get the bank to recredit his account as it had paid on a forgery and the rule is that the loss falls on the person who takes from the forger. Unfortunately for Snootz, his negligence in failing to unmask the impostor by requiring proper identification and the like caused the court to shift responsibility from the bank to him. As a consequence, Snootz had to bear the loss and the bank did not have to recredit the account.

Fictitious Payee Rule:
legal guideline placing loss on issuer duped by trusted employee into making instrument in favor of improper payee

The **fictitious payee rule,** a rule, similar to the impostor rule works a like result in a slightly different circumstance. The rule is used when an employee tricks her or his employer by providing the name of a payee to whom the employer is to issue an instrument in payment of a supposed obligation that is in reality nonexistant. The employee then takes the instrument, indorses it with the payee's signature, and cashes it for his or her own benefit. In such an event, the rule is invoked to force the employer to bear the loss because the loss is held to result from the employer's negligence in placing the employee in the position of trust that allowed execution of the scheme.

The protection that the above rules afford is generally well deserved by our financial institutions, especially if they are to fulfill all that our commercial paper system demands and those who benefit from it expect.

Potential Changes in Articles 3 and 4 of the Uniform Commercial Code

In 1990, a major revision of UCC Articles 3 and 4 was offered to the individual states. (Remember that since the UCC is a state law, changes in the UCC must be adopted–and often amended in the process–by each state legislature in order to be effective.) As of this writing, almost half a decade later, only the following 20 states have adopted part or all of the proposed revision: Arkansas, California, Connecticut, Florida, Hawaii, Illinois, Kansas, Louisiana, Minnesota, Mississippi, Missouri, Montana, Nebraska, New Mexico, North Dakota, Oklahoma, Pennsylvania, Utah, Virginia, and Wyoming.

If the proposed changes have been put into effect in your state, they may include the following significant alterations:

1. The definition of bank has been expanded to include "savings bank, savings and loan association, credit union, or trust company." [UCC 4–105]
2. The title of Article 3 has been changed from "Commercial Paper" to "Negotiable Instruments," and the forms that negotiable instruments may take have been simplified to "promise" and "order" instruments, which are then labeled notes and drafts, respectively. [UCC 3–104 (e)]
3. The outer limit on the "reasonable period" allowed a depositor to inspect her or his bank statement for unauthorized signatures or alterations has been extended from 14 days to 30 days. [UCC 4–406(d)(2)]
4. A promise or order is no longer made conditional "because payment is limited to a particular fund or source." [UCC 3–106](b)(ii)]
5. Banks can pay postdated checks before the indicated date without incurring liability unless they have been properly notified not to by the customer. [UCC 4–401(c)]
6. The time allowed from the date of issue before a check becomes overdue has been increased from 30 days to 90 days [UCC 3–304(a)(2)]

Vocabulary Development

Fill in the blanks with the appropriate term.

Accord and	Depository Bank	Impostor Rule	Renunciation
Satisfaction	Discharge	Midnight Deadline	Stale Check
Agent	Electronic	Overdraft	Stop-Payment Order
Cashier's Check	Fund Transfers	Payor Bank	Traveler's Check
Certified Check	Fictitious Payee Rule		

[Some of the answers may be drawn from preceding chapters.]

1. Electronic tellers and direct deposits are examples of _____.

2. A(n) _____ must be signed by the user in front of the issuer and the payee.

3. A(n) _____ , which is an instrument over six months old, does not have to be paid by its drawee bank.

4. A(n) _____ has a bank for its drawer and drawee, and a stop-payment order is ineffective against it.

5. A bank accepts primary liability on a(n)

_____ issued by its depositor, then allows the instrument to be returned to circulation.

6. An agreement to discharge a party from a preexisting debt upon payment of a late charge of 10 percent on the debt plus principal and interest is a(n) _____.

7. The amount of a check that is in excess of the checking account balance is known as a(n)

_____.

8. An oral _____ is good for two weeks, but if placed in writing, it is good for six months.

Problems

1. Ben Cartwrong thought he could get out of making the remaining 34 monthly installments (totaling over $14,000) on his new car by writing "accepted as payment in full" on the top of the reverse side of the current check he was sending in as payment. He had not communicated with the creditor at all.

   a. If the payee/creditor signs under the indorsement, does Ben still owe the remainder of the payments?

   b. What circumstances can you envision that would make such an indorsement binding against the creditor?

   c. What legal terminology would be used to describe such an arrangement if it were effective?

2. Having unexpectedly received a large estate settlement, Anton went around to his creditors to pay them off. He owed one of them, Silas, $5,000 on a promissory note that was to mature in a week.

When he talked to Silas, however, she refused to take the payoff. Anton set the money aside to pay her in a week, but instead spent it on a new car for his daughter. As a consequence, he did not have the cash to pay Silas when the note came due. When he finally went to pay Silas several months later, Anton refused to pay more than the principal plus the interest that was due up to the time he tendered payment. Is Anton correct in maintaining that he has to pay only this reduced amount?

3. Ajax made out a check to Bold, but before delivering it to that payee, Ajax took the check to the bank and had it certified. Once Bold had the check, she negotiated it by special indorsement to Chear. Chear then negotiated it, again by special indorsement, to Duzz. If the check is not paid upon presentment, which parties are secondarily liable on it? If, instead of being obtained by Ajax, certification had been obtained by Duzz, who would be secondarily liable?

ACTUAL CASE STUDY

Rotert v. Faulkner

464 S.W.2d 463

Now work your way through this case. It might prove to you that you know more about certain aspects of commercial paper law than some judges and attorneys.

Charles and Alice Faulkner signed a $25,000 note as makers. The note was made out to Elmer Miller and Ronald Rotert as co-owners of the instrument. It was payable in monthly installments of principal and interest. However, the interest and principal came due only upon the death of Elmer Miller. The note was delivered to Miller upon issue. Nine months later Miller wrote the following on the note:

July 12, 1978
Paid in Full
for Services Rendered
Elmer E. Miller

In fact, the Faulkners paid nothing to Miller during his lifetime and they did nothing to Rotert before or after Miller's death. Because of the Faulkner's failure to pay upon Miller's death, Rotert brought suit. The lower court treated the instrument as negotiable and consequently applied UCC 3–116 to it. That section reads:

An instrument payable to the order of two or more persons . . . if not in the alternative is payable to all of them and may be negotiated, discharged, or enforced only by all of them.

As the instrument was not payable in the alternative (i.e., "pay to the order of Elmer Miller or Ronald Rotert"), it has not been discharged under the UCC. Therefore, the lower court awarded Rotert a judgment against the Faulkners for the full $25,000 with interest from the date of Miller's death as well as attorney's fees, costs, and expenses of over $3,500.

The Faulkners appealed to the Missouri Appellate Court. In their appellate brief they admitted liability for the half of the amount of the note not discharged and for the attorney's fees, costs, and expenses.

Questions

1. Why was the lower court incorrect in treating the note as a negotiable instrument?

2. If the note was not negotiated to Miller, how was it transferred legally?

3. What body of law should be applied to resolve the situation, if the negotiable instrument law embodied in Article 3 of the UCC is not to be used? How much should the Faulkners pay ultimately?

The Legal Environment of Business: Secured Transactions, Debtor–Creditor Rights, and Bankruptcy

CHAPTERS

Why Should a Creditor Take Security for a Debt, and How Is This Done under the UCC?

CHAPTER OUTLINE AND OBJECTIVES

After studying this chapter, the student will be able to:

I. Recognize why it is so hard to collect on debts.

II. Understand how having security for a debt increases the chances of collection upon default.

III. Explain how a creditor obtains the protection of a security interest.

    a. Attachment

    b. Perfection

IV. Discuss the strength of the protection afforded by holding a security interest.

    a. Time period of effectiveness

    b. After-acquired property may be covered

    c. Automatic perfection in the proceeds of the sale of collateral

    d. Out-of-state coverage

    e. Uniform default procedure

V. Determine, by reading *In re Midas Coin Co.*, whether any better collateral for a loan than money can be found.

Why Is It So Hard to Collect on Debts?

It was *Hamlet*'s Polonius who warned us, "Neither a borrower nor a lender be." In a society that, arguably, has continued to flourish in the face of immense economic problems because of the credit device, we may be inclined to dispute the validity of that warning. However, the warning is very apropos, or "on point" as the legally inclined might say, whenever there has been a default on a loan made against the general credit of the debtor. For the person failing to pay, that event (default) brings on the potential of lawsuits, personal embarrassment and expense, and the curtailment or elimination of a positive credit standing.

For the creditor, matters are even worse, if possible. Upon default, the creditor's interest must be pursued in an environment of increasing animosity. Gentle reminders of an overdue payment give way to threats, veiled and otherwise, as to the debtor's loss of credit standing. The use of collection agencies and the filing of lawsuits against the debtor may soon follow. If the default has been anything but an oversight on the debtor's part, the creditor will ultimately have to utilize some, if not all, of these alternatives. Usually, the creditor will find that there are other lenders in the same position relative to the defaulted debtor. So the game comes to involve not only finding any resources of the debtor that can be used to satisfy the outstanding balance but beating others in so doing. If the creditor is a natural individual (usually individuals—friends and relatives—are turned to last by debtors on the verge of default), she or he is usually up against institutions that know far more about winning the collection game. If the creditor is an institution, a bank, a credit union, or some other financial entity, it is usually up against other institutions with the same expertise. In addition, such institutions are very closely monitored by their governmental auditors. Such monitoring is mainly a reaction to the "deregulation" trend of a decade ago, whereby a lack of governmental oversight ultimately cost the taxpayers almost as much as the entire conflict in Vietnam. Uncollectible loans hurt these institutions and inhibit their ability to make money by future lending.

The strictly legal alternatives, lawsuits and bankruptcy, are very costly. Bankruptcy kills almost all chances that the debtor will work his, her, or its way out of the situation. In addition, as we will discuss, the bankruptcy procedure takes the better part of a year and usually returns under 15 cents on each dollar owed. A lawsuit also takes a long time. After other collection methods have failed, a lawsuit might be filed. Given scheduling problems, postponements, and other delays, the case might be heard four to six months after default. Even after a judgment has been entered against the debtor, most jurisdictions allow the debtor four additional weeks to come in and pay what is due under that court directive. Only if the debtor fails to do this can court procedures (which still take time and money) be initiated to collect the amount due against the debtor's liquid (cash or readily convertible to cash) and static assets. The creditor may then find that those assets are already **encumbered** (subject to a legal claim other than that of the debtor). If such is the case, the creditor gets only what is left after the encumbrance has been satisfied, and please don't forget the legal fees and costs that must be paid as well.

In short, 99.9 times out of 100, it is a no-win situation if a creditor has no option other than to try to collect against just the debtor's assets in general.

Encumbered: subject to legal claim of another other than debtor

How Does Having Security for a Debt Increase the Chances of Collection upon Default?

Of course, there are remedies for this problem. However, they require varying amounts of knowledge, expertise, time, and expense. One remedy is the pledge. A **pledge** involves the transfer of possession of personal property to the creditor, who has the right to sell it upon default to pay off the debt. Such an arrangement is the basis for pawnshop operations everywhere. The problem with the pledge is that the debtor does not have possession of the **collateral** (the property subject to the creditor's claims) during the term of the obligation. This inhibits the use of the pledge, as the use of the collateral often figures significantly in the debtor's ability to pay off the debt.

Pledge: transfer of possession to creditor with right to sell upon default

Collateral: property subject to creditor's claims

As a consequence, another procedure has evolved that allows a creditor sufficient assurance that a loan will be repaid even if the debtor retains the collateral. This assurance, legally referred to as **security,** is obtained by having the debtor give the creditor a property right in the debtor's collateral. That property right, given to the creditor by the debtor in return for the loan, allows the creditor to sell the collateral on default and to satisfy (pay off) the loan therefrom. The property right we are describing is known as a **security interest.** Be sure you understand that this right is created in the creditor by the debtor. It is not something the creditor gets automatically by just loaning the debtor money. A **secured loan,** therefore, is one in which the creditor has a security interest in specific property that can be utilized in the event of default. An **unsecured loan,** the situation described in the first section of this chapter, allows the creditor no such option. As described therein, the creditor must instead proceed against the general asset position of the debtor.

Security: assurance that loan will be repaid

Security Interest: property right, given to creditor by debtor, allowing sale of collateral to satisfy loan

Secured Loan: indebtedness in which security interest of creditor in specific property can be utilized in event of default

Unsecured Loan: indebtedness with no assurance of repayment other than debtor's general credit

Because of the importance of security interests to lenders and, through the results of lenders' efforts, to the economy as a whole, the state governments have set up UCC procedures that streamline and coordinate the use of security interests taken in personal property. (Similar procedures for recording encumbrances are followed in relation to land and other real property in the county recorder's offices throughout the nation.) These procedures are intended to offer creditors some protection with regard to one very important drawback of using security interests, namely that a debtor could use the same property as collateral for more than one loan. When this occurs, the first properly established loan has top priority. All the proceeds from the sale of the collateral are used to satisfy that debt. Whatever is left after that trickles down to those who established their security interests later.

HYPOTHETICAL CASE

When Wayne Myers needed $1,500 to start his own cable TV show, he borrowed the money from his uncle. In return, Wayne gave his uncle a security interest in his car, a slightly road-weary Pacer. Later Wayne needed more money, in this case $5,000, to fund a movie production. He borrowed it from his friend Dana Garth and gave her a security interest in the same Pacer. When the movie grossed only $500, Wayne defaulted on the loans. His uncle ultimately took possession of the Pacer and had it

continued on page 296

> concluded
>
> sold. The car brought $1,600, of which $1,435 was taken by Wayne's uncle to satisfy his remaining security interest and $165 went to Dana Garth. To recover the $4,865 still owed her, Dana would have to go wherever in the world Wayne's property was located and start a court proceeding against it as a general creditor.

As a consequence of such difficulties, the UCC sets up an orderly procedure to be followed in establishing a security interest in personal property. It also provides for the maintenance of a registry of such security interests at a location designated by the state. (Typically, states require that security interests be filed with the secretary of state or with the county clerk of the debtor's county, or with both.) So when a lender is considering giving money to a person in exchange for a promise to repay that is secured by particular collateral, the lender need only check the registry to see whether this is a wise thing to do. If someone else has already taken out a security interest in the collateral, this will most likely be on record and as a result the would-be lender will probably say no.

As a creditor or a potential creditor, you will therefore find it quite important to learn how to reduce risks by properly establishing an enforceable security interest.

How Does a Creditor Obtain the Protection of a Security Interest?

As mentioned above, we will deal with security interests in land and buildings (real property) in Chapter 30. Right now, however, we will concentrate on items other than land and buildings; such items are the most frequently used subject matter of security interests. To do this, we must look closely at Article 9 of the Uniform Commercial Code. Article 9 was created to bring understandable uniformity to the wide and confusing variety of pre-UCC means for obtaining security interests in items other than land and buildings. The statutory format and procedure required by Article 9 are the subjects of this section.

Attachment

Security Agreement: written agreement creating security interest

Attachment: creditor's acquisition of right to take collateral to satisfy debt

The most important requirement for the creation of a legally effective superior security interest under Article 9 is that the agreement by which the collateral's owner creates the security interest in the creditor must be in writing. The agreement we are referring to is termed a **security agreement** by the UCC. It must clearly identify the collateral, and it must be signed by the debtor.

With few exceptions, the security agreement is indispensable to the procedure for creating the desired security interest. It is at the heart of the first of the two important stages in this procedure. This first stage is referred to as **attachment.** It begins when the creditor (who may be a lender of money or a seller of the collateral) acquires a legally enforceable right to take the collateral and sell it to satisfy the debt.

There are three requirements for attachment. First, the debtor must have property rights in the collateral. Typically, these rights stem from ownership of the collateral, although the right to possess the collateral may be sufficient in certain instances. Second, the creditor must transfer to the debtor something of **value** (typically this refers to money from a lender, but it may also refer to the buying power in the form of credit to purchase the collateral that the seller extends). Value is technically defined in UCC 1–201(44) as contractual consideration, a past indebtedness, or a credit extension. Third, the creditor must receive a security interest in the collateral from the debtor (as evidenced by a security agreement) or the creditor must take possession of the collateral (as in the pledge).

Value: contractual consideration, past indebtedness, or a credit extension

Once these requirements have been satisfied, the secured party acquires the right to **attach** (seize) and sell the collateral. The proceeds from the sale are then applied to the satisfaction of the debt involved. A problem here is that there can be more than one party whose debt has attached or may attach to the collateral in question. Therefore, the proceeds from the sale may have to be shared with others. There is, however, a way for a secured party to obtain the full use of the proceeds to satisfy his or her debt. That way is through the "perfection" of the secured party's interest in the collateral, as explained in the following section.

Attach: seize

Perfection

After attachment, the next stage in the Article 9 procedure allows a secured party to obtain a set priority in the collateral. This stage is called **perfection.** If a secured creditor is the first in priority, that creditor will be able to satisfy her or his entire debt from the collateral or from the proceeds of its sale before anyone of lesser priority can claim a penny. (Of course, this holds true only if the collateral is valuable enough.) The priority thus established cannot be disturbed by subsequent attempts to satisfy judgments by attaching and selling the collateral.

Perfection: securing of a set priority in collateral

There are a number of ways to perfect a security interest in collateral. The one used depends mainly on the circumstances of the underlying transaction. The first and simplest way is by possession. Remember that the last requirement for attachment is the security agreement or the pledgee's retention of possession of the collateral? Well, possession also works the same result for perfection. If the creditor holds onto the collateral, perfection has been achieved as of the moment of possession. It's that simple.

The second way to perfect applies only to consumer goods. **Goods** are items that are tangible and movable at the time the security interest attaches. **Consumer goods** are goods that are purchased primarily for personal, family, or household purposes. A lender or seller that provides the value to purchase specific consumer goods acquires a perfected security interest in those goods at the time of attachment. This is called a **purchase money security interest.** It is available only in consumer goods. Allowing perfection through attachment greatly curtails the time, expense, and inconvenience associated with obtaining perfection in other ways. Perfection through attachment enhances the flow of consumer goods at a

Goods: items that are tangible and movable when security interest attaches to them

Consumer Goods: items purchased for personal, family, or household purposes

Purchase Money Security Interest: creditor's right, perfected on attachment, in consumer goods

lower cost and protects the creditor against the claims of most others. Some additional risk over the other ways of perfection is involved, however. This risk will be discussed shortly.

HYPOTHETICAL CASE

Sonny Salvatore bought a new home. After a week, he decided that it was time to cut his 4-acre lawn for the first time. After mowing with his old push mower for a little over two hours, he decided that it would be wise to mechanize. He and his new wife, Cherilyn, drove to a nearby mall and, after several hours of shopping, picked out the Blade Babe, a riding lawn mower. Unfortunately, the mower carried a price tag of over $2,000. Just as the couple were about to break into "I Ain't Got You, Babe," a new song that they had written on the spot, a salesperson informed them that Sark's, the store that sold the mower, would be glad to finance their purchase with only 25 percent down. Salvatore slapped down the $500. Stark's produced a security agreement that described the mower in detail and gave the store the right to repossess and sell it upon default to help pay for any outstanding debt. Sonny and Cherilyn signed the agreement and took the mower home. Later a court judgment was entered against the couple. To satisfy the judgment, the sheriff tried to attach the mower and sell it. However, Sark's was quick to notify the court that its security interest had a superior priority because that interest had not only attached but been perfected (when the security agreement was signed). As a consequence, the court could not utilize the lawn mower or proceeds from its sale to satisfy the judgment. The court then used some of the couple's other property instead.

The third way of achieving perfection is by filing a brief documentation of the security interest's existence with the appropriate governmental office. This documentation is referred to as a **financing statement.** It must contain three items: (1) the debtor and secured party's names and addresses, (2) a description of the collateral, and (3) the signature of the debtor. The financing statement's place of filing varies with the state and the type of collateral, as described below.

Financing Statement: documentation of security interest filed with government

Collateral can be tangible or intangible. As mentioned earlier, items that are tangible and movable items when the security interest attaches are referred to as goods. In addition to the class of consumer goods, which we have already defined, this general category of collateral is broken down into three other classes:

Equipment: goods used primarily in ongoing business

1. **Equipment**—goods used primarily in an ongoing business. A forklift in a warehouse or a dentist's chair would fall into this class.
2. **Inventory**—goods bought for sale or lease.
3. **Farm products**—livestock, crops, and supplies used or produced in farming operations that are in the possession of the debtor-farmer.

Inventory: goods bought for sale or lease

Farm Products: livestock, crops, and supplies used or produced in farming operations that are in debtor-farmer's possession

Intangible collateral includes amounts owed on account to the debtor, negotiable instruments, and documents of title. All of these are frequently used as collateral for a secured loan. It is interesting to note that under the UCC money itself, as a medium of exchange, is not considered a good and therefore cannot be used as collateral.

The filing of the financing statement is typically done at the local county courthouse for farm products and, if desired, for consumer goods. A financing statement identifying inventory or equipment as collateral is usually filed with the state's secretary of state. However, regardless of where the documentation is to be filed under the law, if it is done properly, it will provide constructive notice to whoever else considers taking the same items as collateral. A prudent lender will always check for such a filing before completing a loan.

A prudent secured party will almost always file a financing statement for perfection also. There are filing charges, of course, and in high-volume sales of consumer items a significant amount of additional work is involved. As a consequence, some retailers just rely on the purchase money security interest rule that attachment is perfection. When we discussed this option, however, we mentioned that it entails additional risk. That risk stems from the fact that whereas a filing is constructive notice to all comers that a security interest has been perfected in the collateral, using attachment as perfection does not provide such wide notice. In fact, what is called the neighborhood exception haunts retailers in this area. Let's go back to Sonny and the Blade Babe to explain it.

HYPOTHETICAL CASE

Sonny Salvatore was awakened at around 7 AM by a knocking. He staggered downstairs, still half-asleep, and opened his front door. A large woman with a huge pair of sunglasses pushed up into her hair stood with her hands on her hips in front of him. "The garage sale here, buddy?" she asked. Sonny shook his head, "Not until 8:30, lady." He started to shut the door, but she took a step forward. "Look, mister, I want to buy that Blade Babe in the worst way." Sonny paused. He needed the money for some hospital bills, but he hadn't planned on selling the mower. He still owed Sark's $1,200 on it. He'd parked it by the garage after mowing yesterday. Still ... Sonny shrugged, "I'd sell it for $1,500," he said. "$1,200," the woman replied as she pulled her sunglasses down onto her nose. "$1,350," Sonny counteroffered," but I've got to warn you that Sark's has a security interest in it and I still owe them $1,200." The woman scowled. "That's not good. Not a penny over $1,200." Finally, Sonny agreed to the $1,200. A few months later Sonny and Cherilyn hit on hard times and couldn't make any more payments on the lawn mower. When Sark's came to repossess it, Sonny admitted selling it. He was able to provide Sark's with the name and address of the purchaser. A few days later Sonny received a call from Sark's lawyer. The lawyer asked him whether he had told the purchaser about the loan on the lawn mower. Sonny said that he had. The lawyer then told Sonny that when someone sells a consumer good on which documentation of the security interest has not been filed, an innocent purchaser usually gets the title free and clear. If that were the case, Sark's could not take the lawn mower back and sell it. Since Sonny had given notice of the security interest to the purchaser, Sark's would be able to take the lawn mower back and sell it to satisfy the amount due from Sonny. However, the lawyer cautioned, the purchaser would be able to sue Sonny for the amount she paid him.

In other words, if retailers opt for the purchase money security interest exception to the rules, that is, if they depend on acceptance being recognized as perfection in consumer transactions, they run the risk of losing their security interest to aninnocent, good faith purchaser. Filing as perfection would eliminate this risk, but it's more expensive and time-consuming.

How Strong Is the Protection Afforded by Holding a Security Interest?

Lien: claim on property for payment of debt

To begin with, realize that upon default Article 9 affords creditors substantial protection by providing for self-help repossession of the collateral and priority in the proceeds of its sale. In addition, under the Article 9 procedure the **lien** (claim on property for payment of a debt) itself is both flexible and tenacious in addressing problems short of default.

Time Period of Effectiveness

The term of the lien, for example, can be as long as five years, and it can be renewed for another five if renewal is filed for in the last six months of the first five-year term. This is proving more and more important as the increasing price of items, such as automobiles, coupled with high interest rates forces creditors to allow buyers longer to repay. When I purchased my first automobile, the maximum time allowed for repayment of such loans was 24 months and most car loans were made for 12–18 months. Today the maximum financing period is 60 months (coincidentally, the Article 9 limit on unrefiled liens).

After-Acquired Coverage

After-Acquired Property Clause: security agreement term making subsequently acquired items collateral

UCC 9–204 allows the security agreement to cover future advances made to the debtor. In addition, property acquired after the agreement to replace collateral identified in the agreement may be made subject to the lien set up by the agreement. Such an **after-acquired property clause** is found in many security agreements. It is especially useful when the collateral is inventory that may be sold and replaced frequently. Note that buyers who in the ordinary course of business purchase inventory subject to a security interest take their purchase free and clear of that interest unless they had actual knowledge that the sale violated the terms of an inventory loan.

Automatic Perfection in the Proceeds of the Sale of Collateral

Unless reinvested in replacement goods in accordance with an after-acquired clause, the proceeds from a debtor's sale of the collateral may disappear. With the proceeds go any hedge based on Article 9 that the lienholder may have against the risk of default. As a consequence, the UCC provides for the secured creditor to have automatic perfection in the proceeds from the sale of such collateral for 10 days. After that time, unless there is reinvestment under an after-acquired property clause, the creditor loses the priority position in relation to the debtor's assets. In the example with Sonny Salvatore, if Sark's had known of the sale of the lawn mower in time, it could have executed its security interest against the $1,200 in proceeds to pay off the remainder of the debt. Note that the 10-day period of perfection in the proceeds can be extended if the debtor agrees to the extension.

Out-of-State Coverage

An obvious ploy of a desperate debtor would be to remove the collateral from the state in which the security interest is effective. Then, in a new state, she or he could use the property as collateral for a new loan. To deal with such situations, the UCC provides for the old creditor's perfection in the collateral in the new state by filing in that state within four months. If the previously secured creditor has not filed for protection in the new state by that time, that creditor's priority in the collateral is lost.

HYPOTHETICAL CASE

Charles Berry pulled the last strap tight over the U-Haul trailer load of his goods, then jumped behind the wheel of his station wagon. Maybe Alabama would bring better things for him. It couldn't be worse there than here in Michigan. General Motors had shut down the plant 18 months ago. His unemployment had run out several weeks ago. He was exhausted from job hunting and avoiding creditors. It was time to head back home. Fourteen hours later he was in Birmingham safe and sound. Four weeks later he'd found a minimum wage job and was looking for something better. In the meantime, he needed money for enrollment in a technical college. Desperate, he went to Templars, a local loan office that promised almost universal acceptance but charged extremely high rates. When it requested collateral for the loan, Charles offered the refrigerator and freezer he had brought down from Michigan. He knew that the appliances were still subject to the purchase money security interests he had given Sears back in Detroit. However, it was school and a future or nothing. So, with barely any hesitation, he signed the necessary papers and took the money. Templars filed a financing statement as required to perfect its security interest. A few weeks later Sears filed against Charles's appliances in Alabama and thereby perfected its Michigan security interest in the southern state. Due to a lack of payments, Sears then repossessed the appliances and kept them in satisfaction of the amount due on them. Templars was left without collateral for its loan as a consequence.

Uniform Default Procedure

Another advantage of Article 9's reworking of the old laws on secured transactions is uniformity among jurisdictions with regard to claim priorities and default procedure as follows:

Priorities.   When two or more parties claim an interest in the same collateral, the UCC provides a means of listing them in the order of their priority. Perfected

Figure 22–1   **Creditor Protection Under Article 9 of the UCC**

- Extended time protection
- After-acquired property can be made subject to lien
- Automatic perfection in proceeds if sold
- Out-of-state protection
- Uniform default procedure

claims are at the top of the list. They have priority over attached and unsecured claims. If two parties have perfected claims in the same collateral, the first to perfect wins out. Remember that a "winner" here is permitted to satisfy the entire amount due from the proceeds before others further down the priority list get anything. If there are not enough proceeds to satisfy the entire debt of any party with a secured interest, that party becomes an unsecured creditor with a claim against the general credit of the debtor for the balance due. Finally, among those whose security interests have merely attached, the first in time wins out.

Procedure upon Default.   A self-help repossession (in the event that the security interest is not evidenced by a pledge) is the first step usually considered upon default. As long as this can be accomplished without a disturbance of the peace, it is the creditor's best hope of getting back the value it has invested. If a disturbance of the peace may result from an attempt at repossession, the person making the attempt must seek an alternative method.

If the collateral is repossessed, the creditor may either keep it in full satisfaction of the claim or sell it. If the creditor decides to keep it, the debtor and any other secured creditor must be notified. If any of these parties object within 21 days, the collateral must be sold and the proceeds used to satisfy the secured party's claims. Any money left over must be given to the other secured party or parties or to the debtor. If the sale doesn't produce enough money to pay off the debt(s), the debtor is liable for the remainder. As you might expect, the law requires that any sale be conducted in a commercially reasonable manner. This typically calls for advertising and conducting the sale in a manner calculated to bring top dollar from appropriate prospective buyers. Finally, if the collateral consists of consumer goods, this procedure is altered somewhat. In that case, if more than 60 percent of the cash price has been paid, the secured party is not allowed the option of keeping the goods. They must be resold, and the debtor must be told of the sale and have the right to buy the goods at the sale.

Once the debt has been satisfied, by whatever means, the secured interest holder who perfected by filing a financing statement must file a termination statement with the same governmental office at which the financing statement was filed. This **termination statement** gives notice that the property used as collateral is no longer encumbered. The debtor can then apply for other loans and offer the property as security.

Termination Statement: public filing of notice that property used as collateral is no longer encumbered

Vocabulary Development

Fill in the blanks with the appropriate term.

After-Acquired Property Clause	Encumbered	Lien	Security
Attach	Equipment	Perfection	Security Agreement
Attachment	Farm Products	Pledge	Security Interest
Collateral	Financing Statement	Purchase Money Security	Termination Statement
Consumer goods	Goods	Interest	Unsecured Loan
	Inventory	Secured Loan	Value

[Some of the answers may be drawn from preceding chapters.]

1. The transfer of possession of collateral to a creditor is called a(n) _____. It is the basis for pawnshop operations.

2. _____ can be found in consideration that would bind a simple contract or a preexisting obligation.

3. Goods used in the operation of a business are known as _____.

4. Goods for lease or purchase are labeled _____.

5. Both the tangible, movable items referred to in questions 3 and 4 above can be taken as _____ for the security interest of a creditor.

6. A(n) _____ is a document that is filed in a governmental office to give notice of the existence of a security interest.

7. At the direction of a court, a sheriff or a similar official may _____ or seize items.

8. Property subject to a legal claim of someone other than its owner is said to be _____.

9. _____ are purchased for personal, family, or household use.

Problems

1. Why does Article 9 of the UCC exist? Is there an obligation to assist creditors in lowering the risks of lending? Does the average person profit from such efforts?

2. Who "owns" a property right such as a security interest before it has been transferred to a creditor? Why does the law require that a security agreement be in writing and signed by the debtor?

3. Burney loaned Sampson $4,000 to buy a car. Sampson issued a promissory note in favor of Burney for that amount. Also, when he registered the new car, Sampson had Burney's name entered on the title as lienholder. Later Sampson took out a loan from the First National Bank of Pennsboro. After a few months, he defaulted on both the bank loan and the promissory note. The bank filed suit and obtained a judgment against Sampson that it sought to execute against the car. Burney maintained that he had a security interest in the car that took precedence over the Bank's claim. Who do you think won?

4. Matt Lawnder bought a washing machine and a dryer from the Pennsboro Department Store. The store financed the transaction and perfected its security interest by filing shortly after the sale was closed. Two years later, still owing a substantial amount on the appliances, Lawnder sold his house and moved to another state, taking the washing machine and dryer with him. Three months after his move, Lawnder lost the job he had acquired in the new location. He then sold the appliances to a local dealer for $400 and deposited the money in his bank account. Two weeks later the Pennsboro Department Store discovered what had happened. The proceeds from the sale are still in Lawnder's account. Can the store recover the $358.75 still owed on the appliances from the account?

ACTUAL CASE STUDY

In re Midas Coin Co.

264 Federal Supplement 193

Finally, consider the following case and then use it to remind yourself that at times the statutory law goes a bit berserk and needs a judge to straighten it out.

In order to take out a loan, the Midas Coin Company offered some of its rare US coins to St. John's Community Bank as security. The bank took possession of the coins and thought that it therefore had a perfected security interest in them. When problems arose concerning Midas's ability to meet its obligations, it was contended that as the UCC does not allow money to be taken as collateral, Midas did not have the priority of a perfected secured party in them. Therefore, other creditors could share in the proceeds from the sale of the coins.

Questions

1. Should St. John's Community Bank be allowed a secured position in the coins? What argument would you make to support the position that it does not? That it does?

2. Who will win if it does not? Will the bank lose out entirely if it does not have the highest priority security interest?

CHAPTER

23

What Protections for Creditors and Debtors Are Found Outside the UCC?

CHAPTER OUTLINE AND OBJECTIVES

After studying this chapter, the student will be able to:

I. Identify how our laws protect certain types of lienholders.

   a. Involuntary liens in real property

   b. Involuntary liens in personal property

   b. Guarantors and sureties

II. Recognize what protections debtors are afforded under our laws.

   a. Consumer debtor protection

   b. Bankruptcy

III. Analyze the interpretation of the consumer credit protection laws in *Carroll* v. *Exxon Co.*, which pits a single employed woman with hardly any credit history against a corporate giant.

How Are Certain Types of Lienholders Protected by Our Laws?

In Chapter 22 we dealt with liens established through the cooperation of the debtor. The law refers to such liens as "voluntary" encumbrances. Usually, the debtor "volunteers" to subject her or his property to a lien in return for value of some sort or money. As you probably suspect, there are also "involuntary" liens, to which we must now turn our attention. These liens do not require the property owner's assent. Instead, they arise by operation of the law.

Involuntary Liens in Real Property

Tax Lien: encumbrance against property subject to taxation for unpaid levy

Tax Liens. The primary example of these involuntary encumbrances is the **tax lien.** If certain property taxes remain unpaid for an extended time, they become a lien against the property taxed. Ultimately, the governmental entity owed the taxes can cause the property to be sold to satisfy the amount due. Liens for nonpayment of governmental services can also be placed against the property.

HYPOTHETICAL CASE

When the grass on his lot in downtown Pennsboro grew too high, the city asked disc jockey Robert ("Howling Bob") Logan to mow it. Insulted, even though the vegetation stood over 3 feet above the 1-foot limit set by city ordinance, Howling Bob took to the airwaves to protest. His loyal listeners picketed Pennsboro City Hall carrying signs that read, "Hell, no, we won't mow." After repeated warnings, the city sent its own personnel to mow Howling Bob's lot. Afterward, as called for by city ordinance, the city attorney filed a lien against the property for the cost of the mowing, some $14. Howling Bob again refused to cooperate. Finally, the city asked the court to sell the lot to pay for the mowing. The court complied. The lot sold for $1,725, from which the $14 plus the city's legal costs and the court costs were deducted. Ultimately, a little over $1,400 was returned to Howling Bob, who, due to the publicity the case attracted, had just been offered—and had accepted—a new job with a major station in Chicago.

Mechanic's Lien: encumbrance against real property for unpaid bills for labor and supplies used in improvements thereon

Mechanic's Liens. Workers and suppliers of material used in building or improving real property have at their disposal a similar involuntary lien. This encumbrance, called a **mechanic's lien,** ensures the proper payment of those who add value to buildings or land through their labor or other resources. Plumbers, carpenters, electricians, landscapers, lumberyards, hardware stores, and you-name-it are all empowered by law to file a lien against property improved by their efforts or materials. The lien must be filed within a certain time after the work has been completed. Usually, the limit is no longer than 60 or 90 days. Once filed, however, the lien typically takes priority over all other encumbrances.

Martina and Nat met in graduate school and married soon after they met. After graduation, they dreamed of and designed their own house. A few years of saving later, they bought some land and found J. Elza Fudgling, a contractor they believed could build their dream house. Fudgling had been building custom homes in the area for years and liked their plans. His bid came in at $350,000. Martina and Nat quickly secured a line of credit for the project through the Pennsboro National Bank by giving the bank a security interest in the house. Eight weeks later J. Elza presented them with the keys to the house. Nat checked the line of credit, found that only $335,000 had been used, and then gave J. Elza a bonus check of $5,000. A troubled look flickered over J. Elza's face as he took the check, but he quickly recovered, smiled, and thanked Martina and Nat for their business. A week later, as Nat went out to get the paper, he was shocked to see a parade of pickups in his driveway. Representatives of every firm that had put labor or materials into construction of the house, including the lumber company, the plumbers, the carpenters, the electricians, and even the installer of the automatic sprinkling system, came at him. None of the firms had been paid. J. Elza had guaranteed all of them their money by 5 PM the previous day and hadn't come through. "What do you mean?" said Nat. "I asked for and got releases from all of you." A lanky man wearing a carpenter's apron spoke for the assemblage, "Not from us you didn't. We've been checking, and ol' J. Elza may have outfoxed us all. He probably worked up his own copies of our release forms that he's handled over the years and made out the ones he gave you himself. There are three other high-dollar homes around town he's pulled the same thing on. Over one-and-a-half million dollars. Rumor is his wife was suing him for divorce, so he cashed it all in and headed south. Reckon you'll be owing us and your mortgage company now." Nat shook his head in dismay, turned, and reentered his house. As he slammed the door behind him, one of the men yelled, "See you in court." Nat watched through the window as the pickups, to a vehicle, pulled out of the drive, and, sure enough, headed toward the courthouse. A few days later Nat and Martina worked up a total of the full amount due. The mechanic's liens that had been filed against the house totaled over $250,000. Although those claims took priority over the $340,000 that Nat and Martina had drawn against the line of credit, the latter amount would still have to be paid back after the "mechanics" were paid. Nat looked up from the list, "Martina," he asked, "didn't your dad say he could recommend a good bankruptcy attorney for us?"

Involuntary Liens in Personal Property

The Artisan's Lien.   In case you hadn't noticed, a car mechanic in modern terms would not be able to avail herself or himself of a mechanic's lien. This contradiction becomes understandable if you realize that Webster's primary definition of the word *mechanic* reads "of or involving skill or manual labor." So painters, carpenters, and the like can all enjoy the protection of mechanic's liens due to the application of their skill and labor to real property. Car mechanics have to use the **artisan's lien.** This possessory lien is given to someone who has improved or added value to the personal property of another. Two points must be made here. First, a "possessory lien" is effective only while the lienholder maintains possession of the property that has received the benefit of the artisan's

Artisan's Lien: possessory security interest against personal property for unpaid improvements thereon

Artisan: person skilled in trade or craft requiring manual dexterity

efforts (legally, an **artisan** is a person skilled in a trade or craft requiring manual dexterity). Second, as the lien is intended to ensure the payment due for the services performed, it places the lienholding artisan in a very powerful position that is not under a court's immediate supervision. That position can lead to abuse.

HYPOTHETICAL CASE

Herman Petite decided to have his convertible painted at The Reubens Auto Salon, an upscale car detailing shop near Beverly Hills, California. The "colour" he selected was "flaming fall," a muted reddish orange. The color was based, according to the "artistes" at The Reubens, on "the glorious daunting colours of a sugar maple in the autumnal pause." Regretfully, when Herman returned to pick up the car, he found that the color resembled a coat of rust inhibitor. Herman refused to pay the bill, and the Auto Salon, in turn, refused to relinquish possession of the car. The Salon's salesperson noted that if the bill remained unpaid for over a month, the Salon would enforce its artisan's lien by having the car sold and taking the bill amount plus storage charges of $40 per day out of the proceeds. Unfortunately, Herman needed the car to drive to work. So, after a few phone calls, Herman found a friend who could come down to the Auto Salon. When the friend arrived, he told her what was going on and had her witness his payment of the bill under protest. (After hearing his complaints, the Auto Salon would take only cash.) The president of the Salon took the money, then relinquished possession of the car and, thereby, the Salon's artisan's lien. Herman realized then that to get his money back he would have to bring suit in court under contract law.

From the above account, it can be seen that physical labor and skill invested in the property of another may bring on an artisan's lien. It should be noted, however, that in most states this does not mean that accountants or lawyers or doctors have such a lien on the materials of their clients or patients.

The Hotelkeeper's Lien. Another possessory lien established without the property owner's consent is the **hotelkeeper's lien** (also referred to as the innkeeper's lien). This lien allows the provider of lodging to take the property a guest brought into the establishment, except for the property in the guest's immediate possession, as security for payment of that guest's bill.

Hotelkeeper's Lien: possessory security interest in guest's property for unpaid lodging

The Warehouseman's Lien. A similar possessory lien allows a warehouse to hold stored property as security for payment of the storage charges. This is termed a **warehouseman's lien.** The warehouse must be careful to list all property stored by a customer on a receipt provided to that person. Otherwise, its security interest in the unlisted, yet stored, property may not be recognized.

Warehouseman's Lien: possessory security interest in stored items for unpaid storage costs

The Attic, a storage warehouse in Boca Raton, Florida, repeatedly stored unused store fixtures (tables, racks, display counters, etc.) for Idling Shoppers, a chain of walk-in or drive-thru convenience stores. Because of the frequency of the chain's storage and retrieval trips to the warehouse, the Attic stopped issuing warehouse receipts to it. Late last year, Idling Shoppers went into bankruptcy owing over $7,000 in storage bills to the Attic. When the Attic tried to claim Idling Shoppers' nearly $20,000 worth of stored property as security for the storage bills, the bankruptcy court would not allow it because of the lack of receipts. The Attic therefore became an unsecured creditor, and when the bankruptcy proceeding was concluded, it received only $948.52 instead of the full $7,000 it would probably have received if its debt had been property secured.

Carrier's Lien.   A **carrier's lien** is, as you may suspect, also involuntary and possessory. It is given to a person engaged in transporting cargo for hire. The specific cargo transported is the lien's collateral. Like the warehouseman, the carrier must be careful to properly list all property received in the **bill of lading** (the receipt provided to the person contracting for the shipment).

Carrier's Lien: possessory security interest in cargo for unpaid shipping charges

Bill of Lading: receipt for goods provided to person contracting for their shipment

Guarantors and Sureties

Although the law offers a great deal of protection through Article 3 of the UCC and the liens we have just discussed, that protection comes with complexities, delays, costs, and uncertainties that may inhibit lenders. Consequently, the most practical protection for a creditor is often found by adding another person to the list of those responsible for paying off a loan. Both for the debtor who has yet to establish a credit standing worthy of the sought-after loan and for the prospective lender, this arrangement often provides the final measure of assurance necessary. The individuals who assume the responsibility for payment do so under varying conditions.

A person who agrees to be primarily liable for the payment of a debt (or the performance of an obligation) of another is known as a **surety.** A person who agrees to be secondarily liable for the payment of a debt (or the performance of an obligation) is known as a **guarantor.**

The difference between the positions of surety and guarantor is often quite significant. A surety makes the same promise as the principal debtor and is usually a party to the original instrument creating the debt or other obligation. An example, shown in Figure 23–1, is a promissory note signed by a father as surety for a loan made to enable his son to start a small business. The point to be made here is a vital one. From the way the obligation is assumed, the surety is liable for the loan from the beginning. Such is not the case with a guarantor, who becomes liable only upon the default of the principal debtor.

In particular, the guarantor does not make the same promise as that made by the principal debtor whom the guarantor is sponsoring. Instead, the guarantor

Surety: person who agrees to be primarily liable for debt or obligation of another

Guarantor: person who agrees to be secondarily liable for debt or obligation of another

Figure 23–1 **A Note Signed by Tyrone Lancaster II as Surety for the Loan of $5,000 to His Son, Tyrone Lancaster III**

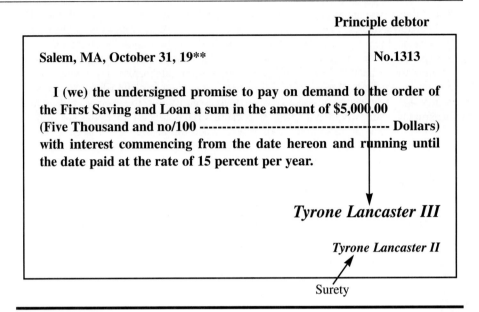

promises to stand good for the debt only upon the default of the principal debtor and upon the provision of suitable notice. It is a separate undertaking altogether, and typically it must be supported by separate consideration. Also recall that under the Statute of Frauds a promise to a creditor to stand good for the debts of another must be in writing to be effective.

Whether the additional party is a guarantor or a surety, however, the additional assurance provided by that party's credit standing is often all that a sensible lender requires.

What Protections Are Afforded Debtors Under Our Laws?

To balance out the various forms of assistance given to creditors, our legal system offers debtors—especially consumer debtors—certain protections. In addition, it offers all debtors the shelter and potential rehabilitation of our Bankruptcy Act.

Consumer Debtor Protection

Defenses Preserved against HDCs. A primary means of protecting consumer debtors, already mentioned, is the preservation of defenses against the enforcement of commercial paper by all types of holders. (See Chapter 20 for more about this important area.) With the exception of the bankruptcy provisions, the most significant of the remaining federal laws for debtor protection are found in the Consumer Credit Protection Act (CCPA). The act covers most aspects of

Example of Retailer's Advertisement that Mentions a Credit Term and Therefore Must Include the Other Credit Terms

Figure 23–2

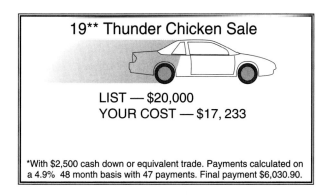

19** Thunder Chicken Sale

LIST — $20,000
YOUR COST — $17,233

*With $2,500 cash down or equivalent trade. Payments calculated on a 4.9% 48 month basis with 47 payments. Final payment $6,030.90.

the consumer–lender relationship. (See Title 15 of the US Code beginning with section 1601 for the full text of this act.)

Requiring Information Allowing Loan Comparison. A portion of the CCPA commonly known as the Truth in Lending Act (TILA) requires that prospective borrowers for personal, family, household, or agricultural purposes (and prospective purchasers of goods and services on credit) be provided with a written disclosure of comparative information about the loan. The most important items in that disclosure are:

The **finance charge**—the actual cost of the loan expressed in dollars and cents. This cost is computed by summing the interest plus add-on charges such as loan initiation fees.

> **Finance Charge:** actual cost of loan expressed in dollars and cents

The **annual percentage rate**—the interest rate of the loan expressed as a yearly figure. An interest rate of 1⅔ percent per month, for example, would have to be expressed as a 20 percent APR.

> **Annual Percentage Rate:** interest rate for loan expressed as yearly figure

Note that TILA only provides that the consumer be informed of the interest rates. It does not set limits on those rates. The states set interest limits in what are termed **usury laws.** These limits vary considerably from state to state. Also, many of the loans made with real estate as security are not covered by TILA.

> **Usury Laws:** state statutes that set limits on interest rates

Finally, TILA requires a certain format in advertising credit terms. If an interest rate is mentioned, it must be in APR terms. If one credit term is stated (e.g., "no money down"), the other credit terms must also be stated. (See Figure 23-2 for our example.)

Ensuring Equal Opportunity for Credit. The Equal Credit Opportunity Act, another act of significance to debtors, attempts to provide consumers with fair access to loans and other extensions of credit. All lenders who regularly extend credit must comply with the act. Such lenders include not only banks, finance companies, credit unions, and the like but also retailers and credit card companies. Individuals who apply for credit may not be asked to disclose the following information about themselves:

Religion, sex, race, or national origin.

Marital status (unless applying for a joint account or in the states of California, Arizona, Nevada, New Mexico, Washington, Idaho, Texas, Louisiana, and Wisconsin, all of which have laws giving one spouse certain property rights in property held in common with the other spouse) *or whether widowed or divorced.*

Plans for raising children.

Receipt of alimony, separate maintenance, or child support (if that income is not relied on).

In addition, would-be creditors are prohibited from considering these factors:

Age (unless applicant is a minor or over 62 and the information will result in favorable consideration).

Public Assistance, except in the same manner as other income.

Applicants for credit have a right to know the results of their application within 30 days. If rejected, they have a right to be advised of the reasons for that rejection within 60 days.

Violators of the Equal Credit Opportunity Act can be sued by the applicant(s) harmed for the applicant's losses, attorney's fees, and court costs. Punitive damages are also available.

Correcting Billing Errors. Billing disputes that concern consumers are covered under the Fair Credit Billing Act. Under this act a creditor must mail bills at least 14 days before they are due. A consumer who discovers an error has 60 days from the mailing date to notify the creditor. That notification must contain the identity of the consumer, the account number, and a description and explanation of the error. An acknowledgment of the consumer's notification is required within 30 days. The creditor then has 90 days to investigate. If an error is discovered, it must be corrected. If the account is believed to be correct, an explanation must be sent to the consumer.

A less well-known addition to this act allows the holder of a credit card to withhold payment for defective items or unsatisfactory service valued at over $50 and purchased with the card within the cardholder's state or within 100 miles of the cardholder's mailing address. If the cardholder withholds payment and the party at fault fails to correct the problem, the cardholder may use that failure to defend a suit by the credit card issuer for the amount due. Cardholders cannot be given a poor credit evaluation because of such actions.

Protecting Against Improper Bill Collection Practices. To prevent abusive techniques from being used to collect debts, Congress passed the Fair Debt Collection Practices Act. The act regulates the activities of those who are in the business of collecting debts for others. In particular, a debt collector:

Must not attempt to locate a debtor by informing others that the debtor owes money. The use of postcards to collect debts is also forbidden due to the public nature of the message they carry.

Must communicate solely with the debtor's attorney if one is known to be representing the debtor.

Must not communicate with the debtor at the debtor's place of employment (if the employer prohibits such communication) or at unreasonable hours. The typical proper hours are 8 AM to 9 PM unless information to the contrary is provided to the collector.

Must not communicate, in connection with collection of a debt (not locating a debtor), with anyone other than the debtor, the debtor's attorney, the creditor's attorney, or a credit reporting agency.

Must, upon the debtor's written notification of the debtor's refusal to pay the debt or the debtor's desire that the collector cease communication, cease contacting the debtor except to notify the debtor of a specific action.

Must not use harassing or abusive means to collect the debt. For example, threats of violent action, profanity, criminal activity, and frequent telephone contacts are ruled out.

Must not use a form of communication that would cause the debtor to mistake it for legal process.

Violators of the Fair Debt Collection Practices Act can be sued for actual and punitive damages, court costs, and attorney's fees.

Assisting in the Reporting of Accurate Credit Ratings. In a society like ours in which credit is often regarded as the vehicle to prosperity, our ability to utilize that vehicle is often dependent on the evaluation of our ability to repay debts that has made by certain credit bureaus. This evaluation is termed a **credit rating.** To enable us to be as certain as possible that such ratings are fair and accurate, Congress passed the Fair Credit Reporting Act. If consumers are disallowed credit, insurance, or employment because of a bad credit report, the act requires that they be told of this and that they be given the name and address of the credit bureau from which the credit report was obtained. If they do this within 30 days, the act allows them to see without charge the files that the credit bureau maintains on them. Such files contain reports from many sources and are reviewed by credit bureaus to determine the credit ratings of their subjects. Upon reading the contents of such a file (including the sources of the information but excluding any medical information contained therein), a consumer can point out alleged errors to the credit bureau. The bureau must then investigate. If the investigation proves that the consumer was correct, the improper information must be deleted or changed. If the bureau decides that the information objected to was accurate and retains it in the file, the consumer can still file his or her version of the story with the bureau. The consumer's version must be maintained in the file with the other version.

Credit Rating: evaluation of subject's ability to repay debts

Bankruptcy

The bankruptcy provisions of the federal laws assist greatly in the maintenance of fairness in the credit dealings of consumers (see also Chapter 36 for laws dealing with credit card use by consumers). Without these laws, the balance of power in such dealings would easily tip toward the lenders. However, consumers are not the only debtors who at times need protection from the consequences of an overwhelming debt load. The availability of the protection afforded by the federal bankruptcy laws has been and will be of prime importance to all classes of debtors. The various aspects of that protection and the procedure necessary to avail oneself of them will be discussed in Chapter 24.

APPLICATIONS OF WHAT YOU'VE LEARNED

Vocabulary Development

Fill in the blanks with the appropriate term.

Annual Percentage Rate	**Carrier's Lien**	**Guarantor**	**Surety**
Artisan	**Credit Rating**	**Hotelkeeper's Lien**	**Tax Lien**
Artisan's Lien	**Finance Charge**	**Mechanic's Lien**	**Warehouseman's Lien**
Bill of Lading			

[Some of the answers may be drawn from preceding chapters.]

1. A credit bureau evaluates your ability to repay debts and gives you a(n) _____.

2. A mother who agrees to pay off a car loan if her son cannot is a(n) _____ in relation to the loan.

3. The involuntary security interest afforded by the law to the unpaid plumber who installed the bathrooms at the Bates Motel is termed a(n) _____.

4. The involuntary possessory security interest afforded by the law to the person who repaired Mr. Bond's Lotus sports car is termed a(n) _____.

6. A mother who agrees to be primarily liable on a car loan made to her son is a(n) _____ in relation to the loan.

Problems

1. Which of the following involuntary liens are not possessory?

   a. Mechanic's
   b. Hotelkeeper's
   c. Warehouseman's
   d. Tax
   e. Artisan's
   f. Carrier's

2. Which of the types of liens in Problem 1 would each of the following have if it were unpaid for providing its goods or services?

   a. Bro' Lex's Watch Repair Shoppe

b. Lawrence County Assessor's office

c. Minnie Pixel's Television Repair Shop

d. Hardis Nailz House Carpenter Company

e. Kent Uke Ohm Electrician

f. Bill Lading's Commercial Storage Company

3. Flashy Dan, the Amusing Appliance Man, placed the following ad:

BLACK HOLE

As used by the Astronauts
on the Mars Mission!
0 %   F i n a n c i n g   (A P R)

What law is Dan overlooking? What must he do to comply with that law?

4. The Pennsboro National Bank of Pennsboro, Missouri, used the following application form for its individual line of credit:

What is improper about the form? What recourse does an applicant have for dealing with the violations of law inherent in the form?

PNB Loan Form 27-93-(individual line of credit)

Please supply the following information:

Name _____   Sex M F   Date of application _____

Address _____   Years at this address _____

Employer _____   Years at this job _____

Salary _____   Spouse's name _____

Spouse's employer _____   Spouse's salary _____

If single, have you been divorced? _____   Widowed? _____

Number of children _____   Planning for more? _____

Have you currently involved in a lawsuit that may result in a judgment against you? (If yes, please explain.) _____

_____

If you are currently receiving income other than your salary and want us to consider it, please list the amount and its source _____

Amount of line of credit requested: $ _____

Thank you. We will inform you of our decision in 45 days.

ACTUAL CASE STUDY

Carroll v. Exxon Co.

434 Federal Supplement 557

Now consider the effectiveness of the consumer credit protection laws in the case of:

When Exxon denied Kathleen Carroll a credit card, she requested that it furnish her with the specific reasons for its action. In its subsequent correspondence with Carroll, a single employed woman, Exxon failed to state the name and address of the credit bureau on which it had relied in denying the credit application. Carroll brought suit. In the court proceeding, it was shown that her credit bureau files contained little, if any, information. AsAs a consequence, it was held that Exxon did not have sufficient information available for a determination of her worthiness as a credit risk.

Questions

1. What consumer credit protection laws did Exxon violate? How?*

2. What could Exxon have done to fulfill the requirements of these laws?

---

*Answer: Exxon failed to provide the name and address of the credit bureau or agency from which it received information on Carroll. This is a violation of the Fair Credit Reporting Act. Exxon also failed to state a specific reason for the denial of credit, which is a violation of the Equal Credit Opportunity Act. Actual damages, punitive damages, and attorney's fees and costs could therefore be assessed against Exxon.

Who May Take Bankruptcy, How Is It Done, and What Are the Effects of So Doing?

CHAPTER OUTLINE AND OBJECTIVES

After studying this chapter, the student will be able to:

I. Explain what bankruptcy is and why bankruptcy is provided as an alternative to remaining in debt.

II. Identify what type of protection the Bankruptcy Code makes available to debtors.
    a. Eligibility and administration
    b. Types of protection available

III. Discuss the procedure followed in Chapter 7 liquidation
    a. The filing of the petition
    b. The order of relief
    c. The automatic stay and appointment of the bankruptcy trustee
    d. Informational filings by the debtor
    e. The creditors' meeting
    f. The collection and liquidation of the debtor's assets
    g. Payout of bankruptcy proceeds
    h. Discharge of the debtor's obligations
    i. Revocation of discharge and debt reaffirmance

IV. Debate, on the basis of *Pennsylvania Dept. of Public Welfare* v. *Davenport*, whether the Bankruptcy Code should be available for use by convicted criminals to avoid paying fines or restitution.

What Is Bankruptcy, and Why Do We Provide It as an Alternative to Remaining in Debt?

Discharged: released

Bankruptcy: court-supervised procedure established by federal law through which qualified debtors can seek relief from obligations

Our society has a history of harsh treatment of debtors. At one time it maintained prisons to punish persons unable to pay off their obligations. Our Constitution, however, took a more enlightened approach. The authors of the Constitution offered an alternative to imprisoning such individuals or, perhaps just as debilitating, leaving them to suffer under overwhelming debt loads for years. In Article I, Section 8, Congress is given the power to "establish . . . uniform Laws on the subject of Bankruptcies throughout the United States." In other words, Congress was authorized to provide a procedure whereby citizens overburdened with debt could be **discharged** (released) from their obligations.

However, Congress has not seen fit to utilize this power frequently. The first federal bankruptcy act was not passed until 1800. Our current bankruptcy statute, the Bankruptcy Reform Act of 1978, was the first substantial modification of the bankruptcy laws since 1898. The changes it brought about were controversial at best. In fact, this latest bankruptcy act was perhaps too generous in its terms. The rate of bankruptcies doubled almost overnight. The act also left open so many obvious loopholes and created so many administrative problems that most observers were amazed at the seeming lack of competence shown by Congress in drafting it. Ultimately, the act was successfully challenged on constitutional grounds and had to be substantially amended, first in 1984 and again in 1986. Most attorneys refer to its current form as the Bankruptcy Code.

Realize that the word *bankrupt* is not used in the Bankruptcy Code. Instead, the word *debtor* is used. This omission was intentional perhaps to avoid applying the stigma of the term it replaced to those who seek the protection of the code.

The word **bankruptcy,** however, has acquired a legal meaning. It refers to the procedure by which debtors' eligible assets are utilized to discharge them from some, if not all, of their obligations. Note that the discharge of debts through bankruptcy is available to a debtor only once every 6 years and that the debtor's credit record typically reflects the discharge for 10 years. However, neither government bodies nor private employers can discriminate against someone who has gone through bankruptcy (for example, by firing). Nevertheless, seeking protection under the Bankruptcy Code provisions is an option that should be considered only as a last resort.

What Type of Protection Is Made Available to Debtors by the Bankruptcy Code?

The Statutes of the United States contain the provisions of the Bankruptcy Code in Title 11. This title is subdivided into several chapters that contain the eligibility requirements, procedures, and protections authorized by Congress. Note that each chapter, with the exception of Chapter 12, has been given an odd number. So if you look up the statute to find more detailed information, do not spend time trying to discover what has been done with Chapters 2, 4, 6, 8, 10, and 14. They simply do not exist.

Eligibility and Administration

The chapters that you will find fall into two general groupings. Chapters 1, 3, 5, and 15 contain procedures and information relevant to whomever might become subject to the Bankruptcy Code. Chapter 1 gives the eligibility guidelines. Chapter 3 creates and empowers the various official positions associated with the bankruptcy process. Chapter 5 contains the principles to be used in determining which of the debtor's properties are legally accessible to satisfy the creditors' claims. Finally, Chapter 15 sets up the position of **bankruptcy trustee** and specifies its duties and powers. The bankruptcy trustee is the individual selected to administer the debtor's estate in bankruptcy. (An **estate** is a person's rights and interests in property of all types.) The trustee's job is to maximize the assets of the debtor's estate so as to provide more for the creditors upon **liquidation** (sale for cash) of those assets.

Bankruptcy Trustee: individual selected to administer debtor's estate in bankruptcy

Estate: rights and interests of person in property of all types

Liquidation: sale for cash of other forms of assets

Types of Protection Available

Each of the remaining chapters in the Bankruptcy Code—7, 9, 11, 12, and 13—sets up a different type of bankruptcy protection:

Chapter 7—"Discharge of Debts by Liquidation and Payout"—provides for the form of bankruptcy that most people are familiar with. It calls for the discharge of the debtor's eligible obligations after a payout to creditors. This payout comes from the proceeds of the liquidation of the debtor's statutorily unprotected assets. We'll discuss this form of bankruptcy in depth shortly.

Chapter 9—"Adjustment of Debts for Cities"—gives municipalities facing a funding crisis the latitude to restructure their obligations.

Chapter 11—"Reorganization to Avoid Liquidation for Active Businesses"—

Forms of Bankruptcy Protection Available for Debtors under the Federal Bankruptcy Statutes

Figure 24–1

Chapter 7	All of the debtor's assets (with certain exemptions) are sold. The cash proceeds are distributed to the creditors according to a statutory priority order. Then, except for certain nondischargeable items, all debts, paid and unpaid, are discharged and thereafter cannot be collected by the debtor's creditors.
Chapter 9	Provides a means for reorganizing the debts of financially stressed municipalities.
Chapter 11	Emphasizes the preservation of the debtor as an ongoing entity. Therefore, the court reorganizes the debt and equity structure of the entity, often discharging some of its obligations in order to preserve it.
Chapter 12	Reorganizes family farms under court supervision with the objective of preserving each farm as an ongoing entity.
Chapter 13	Provides a procedure enabling natural persons as debtors to discharge their debts without liquidating their assets, usually following a three-year plan of regular payments to creditors.

This chapter is meant to afford ongoing businesses a last alternative before full bankruptcy under Chapter 7. Compliance with the Chapter 11 procedure may allow a business that would otherwise be terminated due to inability to meet its obligations to restructure them, remain in possession of its most important assets, and continue doing business in some form. Participation in a Chapter 11 proceeding may be initiated voluntarily by the business, or it may be forced to follow Chapter 11's requirements by its creditors.

The point is that keeping a business in operation, employing individuals and filling a social need, is typically far more beneficial to society than selling off its assets piecemeal. Often, however, this result cannot be achieved without losses to obligees of the business. For most creditors these losses are generally far smaller than those sustained if the business is liquidated. (As mentioned previously, a rule of thumb in a full Chapter 7 "straight bankruptcy" is that each unsecured creditor will get back only about 15 cents on the dollar. Chapter 11 reorganization usually promises to pay back far more than that.)

Under Chapter 11's procedure, a reorganization plan is filed with the court by the debtor or, if a trustee has been appointed for the debtor's estate, by any interested party. The plan must designate classes of claims—for example, secured debts, unsecured debts, business accounts payable, workers' claims, and pension plan claims—and it must indicate which class or classes will have their claims impaired (reduced) by it and which will not. It is forwarded to the various classes of creditors to approve or reject.

Even if not all classes approve the plan, if the court feels that the plan is fair and equitable, it may put the plan into operation. This is called the "cramdown" provision of Chapter 11, the idea being that the plan may be imposed on some creditors even over their objections. Chapter 11 plans can even result in modification or avoidance of collective bargaining agreements between workers and the debtor firm. However, such action by a bankruptcy court is the exception today.

HYPOTHETICAL CASE

Due to financial problems incurred during a retailing downturn, Herb's Department Store was in serious trouble. Although it owned its main building in downtown Springton, Herb's had entered into very expensive leaseholds in two upscale malls in the suburbs. The lease payments and a lack of turnover in its inventory left it teetering on the brink of bankruptcy. In desperation, Herb's board of directors was able to locate a prospective buyer out of state. The buyer, Slashed Enterprises, had considerable resources and ran a chain of discount department stores in the Chicago area. Unfortunately, when the news of the impending sale was announced, the malls threatened to sue Herb's to block the transaction. The malls pointed to a provision in their agreement with Herb's prohibiting the marketing of low-quality and/or discounted merchandise on their premises. When Herb's attorneys admitted that the malls' suit would probably be successful, Herb's filed for a Chapter 11 reorganization. Ultimately, the bankruptcy court accepted a plan put together by Herb's attorneys that postponed some payments for Herb's inventory and eliminated other payments. The court also voided the provisions in Herb's leases with the malls that allowed the malls to sue to block the sale of Herb's but required that the buyers maintain Herb's reputation as an upscale store. As a consequence, the sale went through and Herb's is again flourishing.

Chapter 12—"Discharge of Debts without Liquidation for Family Farm Owners"—which was added to the Bankruptcy Code in 1986, adheres to the procedure for relief provided in Chapter 13, on which it was modeled. Chapter 12 is meant to provide assistance for the family farmer who finds the debt limits of Chapter 13 too low and the expense of Chapter 11 filings too high.

Chapter 13—"Discharge of Debts without Liquidation for Individual Debtors" (natural persons only)—is commonly called the "wage earner's plan." It is available only to those with regular income. In addition, the person who voluntarily files a Chapter 13 action must have less than $100,000 in unsecured debt and less than $350,000 in secured debt. (Chapter 12 requires that the family farmer's debts not exceed $1,500,000).

The Chapter 13 procedure requires the debtor to propose a plan that includes the signing over of future income to a trustee who is to pay creditors. Under a Chapter 13 plan, both unsecured and secured debts can be reduced in amount or the time allowed for making payments can be extended. In most instances, however, the plan cannot run for more than three years, although in some situations its duration can be extended to five years. The plan is reviewed by the court to make sure it provides the creditors with advantages over what they might expect in a Chapter 7 liquidation.

If the plan is approved by the court, at the end of the three- or five-year period of payments, practically all debts have been discharged, with the debtor retaining title to and possession of all her or his property. (Alimony and child support are not dischargeable by this method.) Before Congress moved to close the loopholes in its latest round of amendments, there was an abundance of instances in which debtors used their prefiling credit standing to load up on luxury goods just before taking Chapter 13 bankruptcy—fur coats, jewelry, expensive cars, and the like— would all be acquired by the debtor simultaneously with large cash advances. Timing was important so that the credit load for one item would not show up on a credit report requested by the seller of another item. In this way, individuals were earning tens and even hundreds of thousands of dollars simply through their ability to read and follow Chapter 13's procedure. After a wait of six to eight years, Congress acted to stop this practice by making debts nondischargeable if they were acquired from the purchase of $500 or more of luxury items within 40 days of a bankruptcy filing or from cash advances totaling over $1,000 taken out within 20 days of a filing.

What Procedure Is Followed in a Chapter 7 Liquidation?

The most common form of bankruptcy protection is also the harshest. It is available under Chapter 7 of the Bankruptcy Code. Under this chapter's procedure the discharge of debts follows a liquidation of the debtor's property. This quid pro quo produces a more dramatic change in the debtor's financial environment than any other bankruptcy alternative. Of course it wouldn't be the law we were discussing if there weren't exceptions. Not all of the filer's debts are eligible for discharge. Not all of the filer's property must be liquidated. To determine which debts and property belong in which category and to produce the fairest result in a situation with no real winners, a strict procedure is followed. (See Figure 24-3 for our overview of this procedure.)

The Filing of the Petition

Bankruptcy Debtor: any natural individual or business eligible under law for bankruptcy

Voluntary Bankruptcy: unforced filing of bankruptcy petition by debtor

Involuntary Bankruptcy: petition filing by debtor's creditors subjecting debtor to bankruptcy procedure

Insolvent: debtor unable to meet debts when they come due

The procedure commences with the filing of a bankruptcy petition. If the petition is filed by the **bankruptcy debtor** (any natural individual or business except those considered special cases, such as banks, savings and loans, building and loans, railroads, and insurance companies), what results is considered a **voluntary bankruptcy.** If the petition is filed by a debtor's creditors, what results is considered an **involuntary bankruptcy.**

Although subject to the same basic liquidation procedure, these two types of Chapter 7 bankruptcies are fundamentally different. In a voluntary filing, the petitioner does not even have to be **insolvent.** In other words, the debtor may be able to meet his or her debts when they come due, yet be eligible to file for *voluntary bankruptcy*. A contested *involuntary bankruptcy*, on the other hand, must include a showing of the debtor's insolvency to be successful. Insolvency under the Bankruptcy Code is not a test based on a balance sheet assessment that a debtor has more liabilities than assets. It is a status afforded someone who cannot meet his or her debts when they become due. If the bankruptcy court dismisses the involuntary petition for lack of such a showing, the debtor can be awarded costs, lawyer's fees, and damages (even punitive damages in certain cases).

A husband and wife can join in a voluntary proceeding, whereas an involuntary proceeding is individualized. Also, neither a charity nor a farmer can be forced into involuntary bankruptcy (nor can the types of businesses listed above as special cases). The farmer or the charity can, of course, take voluntary bankruptcy without objection.

To force an eligible party into involuntary bankruptcy, only one signer of the petition is required if the debtor has fewer than 12 creditors and the signer is owed $5,000 or more. If there are more than 12 creditors, at least 3 of them with unsecured debts totaling over $5,000 must sign the petition.

HYPOTHETICAL CASE

Due to medical problems, Victoria Baker fell behind in payments to her creditors. After several months, two creditors ignored her assurances that she would pay them back upon being restored to her job after recovery. The two creditors, Ava Rice and G. Reed, filed an involuntary proceeding against Baker showing that the total amount owed them exceeded $5,000. Baker contested the filing by saying that she had over 12 creditors (the petition showed only 8), so that at least 3 of them had to sign the petition. Baker insisted that her attorney argue that her phone bill of $37.50, the $50 she owed her mother, her Ward's credit card balance ($5.75), and the $12.50 she owed the paperboy brought the number of her creditors up to 12. The attorney reluctantly did so. The court examined the statute, found that no minimum amount was necessary to be a listed creditor, and therefore dismissed the petition and awarded Baker enough in damages to pay off all her debts.

The Order of Relief

Once an involuntary petition has been filed, the court will enter an **order of relief** (a declaration that the debtor is in a state of bankruptcy liquidation) if it determines that the petition will not be contested. If the debtor exercises her or his right to contest the petition, the court must hold a trial. The purpose of the trial is to determine whether the debtor is insolvent or whether the debtor's property is in the custodial care of another. Only if the court so determines will it issue the order of relief. Note that the very filing of a voluntary petition acts as an order of relief in that circumstance.

Order of Relief: declaration that debtor is in state of bankruptcy liquidation

The Automatic Stay and Appointment of the Bankruptcy Trustee

The order of relief has two important effects. First, by law it triggers an automatic **stay** (suspension or halt) to judicial and administrative proceedings against the debtor. It also stops the enforcement of any judgment or the creation or enforcement (by self-help or otherwise) of liens against the debtor. Any violation of the stay can result in the violator being fined or imprisoned for contempt of court. Note that the stay does not freeze the collection of alimony and child support or a criminal prosecution. Finally, realize that the stay, enforced by the watchful eye of the court, prevents creditors from receiving or achieving an unfair advantage over one another.

Stay: court-ordered suspension or halt

The second effect of the order of relief is to bring about the appointment of the bankruptcy trustee by the court. As mentioned, the bankruptcy trustee administers the debtor's estate. This involves discovering, assembling, and protecting the rights and interests of the filer, then liquidating them and using the proceeds to pay claims against the estate.

Informational Filings by the Debtor

Whether the debtor voluntarily files for bankruptcy or is involuntarily petitioned into bankruptcy, that party must provide certain information under oath:

A list of the debtor's creditors and the amount owed to each (an unlisted debt generally will not be discharged).

A list of all the debtor's property, whether or not it is exempt from the claims of the creditors. (For the federal list of property allowed to be claimed as exempted from the liquidation procedure, see Figure 24–2. Note that the Bankruptcy Code gives states the power to disallow their citizens' use of this federal list. Instead, states can compose their own list and either require that debtors use it or give debtors the choice between the federal list and the state list.)

A list of the debtor's current income and expenditures and a statement disclosing and explaining the debtor's financial affairs.

Figure 24–2

Exemptions Allowed under the Current Bankruptcy Act and Its Amendments

---

The Federal List of Exempt Property

Note: Only state exemptions are allowed in over half of our states. However, some states have more generous exemptions than those shown here.

1. A value of $7,500 in the debtor's residence (called the *homestead exemption*) and, in a macabre touch, the debtor's burial plot. (The state of Texas sets aside its homestead exemption by acreage—1 acre of urban or 200 acres of rural property—regardless of value—as long as the residence is there.)
2. Household and personal items valued at less than $200 up to a total of $4,000. (For several years Congress did not have a cap—the $4,000 total restriction—on this category. So debtors were breaking down all manner of items, even cars, into small parts, each worth less than $200, and thereby escaping their creditors' claims.)
3. Up to $500 in jewelry, $750 in professional books and tools of the debtor's trade, and $1,200 of value in a car.
4. Alimony, child support, Social Security, public assistance, pension, and veterans and disability payments.
5. Damages due in a personal injury suit, life insurance payments from a policy on someone on whom the debtor was dependent, and award pools for victims of violent crimes.

The Creditors' Meeting

Once the creditors have been identified, a meeting is scheduled for them. At that meeting, the debtor is required to answer their questions in person and under oath. If the creditors so desire, they can elect a trustee to replace the court-appointed trustee already in place. They can also elect a creditors' committee to consult and advise the trustee.

The Collection and Liquidation of the Debtor's Assets

Whenever a Chapter 7 proceeding is begun, an estate in bankruptcy is formed out of the debtor's property. This estate includes the property rights and interests of the debtor at the time of filing plus those to which the debtor becomes entitled during the next 180 days. In other words, insurance policy proceeds, gifts, inheritances, property awards and settlements from lawsuits (including divorces), and other property in which the debtor acquires rights and interests during this extra 180-day period will also be used to satisfy creditors' claims. Thus, the end of this period acts as a cutoff point for the bankruptcy process. After the 180 days have run, the estate can typically be settled as no other property will become available that the trustee can liquidate for the creditors' benefit. Property acquired after the 180-day limit will remain the debtor's.

During these 180 days a number of other events can occur:

Creditors, especially those not listed by the debtor in the informational filings or those who allege a different amount owed, can file a proof of claim (a document showing the debtor's obligation to them). The court will automatically allow such proofs of claim unless someone affected by the bankruptcy (trustee, debtor, or creditor) objects, in which case the court will review the matter to be certain that the alleged debt is enforceable against the debtor. Obviously, a creditor that does not correctly establish itself during the 180-day period will not be eligible for a portion of the payout when the estate is settled.

Secured creditors in general may petition the court to be allowed to execute their security interest before the 180-day period has run. Such a petition is usually granted if the property is perishable or will decline greatly in value during that period. If the sale does not satisfy the full amount of the claim, the secured party is treated as an unsecured creditor for the balance due. If there is an excess of proceeds, the excess amount must be used to help the creditor pay off reasonable fees and costs brought on by the debtor's default. Anything still remaining is to be paid out to the unsecured creditors. (Note that a consumer debtor must file a statement of intent regarding the secured collateral in her or his estate. This statement of intent, which must be filed before the creditors' meeting, details whether the debtor wants to surrender the collateral or keep it in the estate. The trustee is obligated to comply with the debtor's wishes within 45 days. If the collateral is to be turned over to the consumer debtor's creditors, they must determine whether to keep it in full satisfaction of the debt or to sell it for the proceeds, which are then utilized as in a non–consumer debt situation.)

The trustee in bankruptcy can accept or reject any of the debtor's executory contracts. In addition, the trustee collects the debtor's property and reduces it to money. This collection process may involve undoing some questionable transfers of property made by the debtor prior to filing for bankruptcy. In particular, the trustee is allowed to recover money or other property transferred by the debtor to a favored creditor on one of two grounds. The first type involves a transfer made by an insolvent debtor within 90 days of the filing of the petition. This **preferential transfer** must give the payee creditor more than that person would have received in a Chapter 7 proceeding. If the transfer is to a **bankruptcy insider** (a person with a close relationship to the debtor, such as a relative or partner), the 90-day period is extended to a full year before filing. The second type of transaction that the trustee can avoid consists of transactions made with the intent to defraud, hinder, or delay creditors. These are called **fraudulent transfers.** The trustee can undo fraudulent transfers occurring up to one year prior to the filing.

Preferential Transfer: payment giving creditor more than creditor would have received in Chapter 7 proceeding

Bankruptcy Insider: person with close relationship to debtor, such as relative or partner

Fraudulent Transfer: transaction made with intent to defraud, hinder, or delay creditor

Payout of Bankruptcy Proceeds

The Bankruptcy Code establishes a prioritized order in which the unsecured creditors are to be paid from the proceeds of the estate. (Remember that secured creditors have priority over all other creditors in the proceeds from the sale of their collateral.)

This payout of proceeds to the unsecured creditors is done in order of classes. All member of the class with the top priority must be fully paid before one cent is paid to anyone in the class with second priority. This procedure is followed through the eight classes until the money runs out. If a class cannot be fully paid, its members receive a pro rata share of the funds available. The priorities are as follows:

1. Court costs and attorneys' and trustee's fees (typically labeled administrative costs).
2. Claims against the debtor involuntarily petitioned into bankruptcy for expenses incurred between the filing of the petition and either the appointment of a trustee or the issuance of an order of relief.
3. Claims against the debtor for wages, commissions, and salaries earned within 90 days of filing. There is a $2,000 cap per claimant on this. The amount over $2,000 may be pursued as an unsecured claim (the last priority of claim).
4. Claims stemming from unpaid amounts to employee benefit plans for the last 180 days prior to filing. Again, there is a $2,000 cap per employee.
5. Claims against debtors operating fish and grain storage facilities brought by fishers and grain producers—$2,000 cap per claimant.
6. Claims by consumers who have deposited funds to purchase or rent consumer goods or services that were not provided—$900 cap, with amount in excess of $900 eligible for treatment as an unsecured debt.
7. Unpaid income and property tax claims due various governmental bodies.
8. Claims of general creditors.

Any money left after these claims have been satisfied is turned over to the debtor.

Discharge of the Debtor's Obligations

After the procedures detailed above have been properly followed, the bankruptcy court will order a discharge of most of the debtor's obligations. Some debts are not dischargeable by the court, however. These include:

Alimony and child support.
Back taxes accruing over the three-year period prior to the filing for bankruptcy.
Student loans owed to the government that were acquired over the last five years.
(However, a debtor can rid himself of this burden by proving that paying the loans would impose an undue hardship.)
Judgments or consent orders resulting from driving while intoxicated.
Judgments against the debtor resulting from willful or malicious conduct injurious to the person or property of another, such as assault, battery, defamation, or other intentional tortious conduct. Negligence awards, however, can be discharged through bankruptcy.
Claims against the debtor resulting from larceny, fraud, or embezzlement.

Note that in certain instances the court will not order a discharge of even eligible debts. These instances include situations in which the debtor has fraudu-

Steps in a Chapter 7 Bankruptcy   **Figure 24–3**

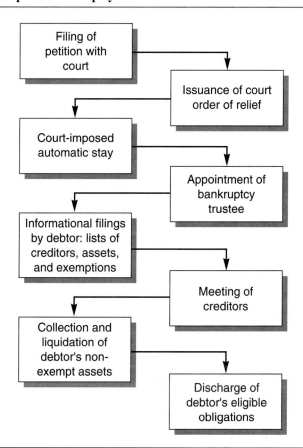

lently made a false oath, presented a false claim, used various means to withhold information on financial condition or business transactions, or attempted during the year before filing to keep property out of the creditors' grasp by fraudulent means. In addition, a debtor who fails to obey a lawful court order or who has received a bankruptcy discharge within the last six years will not receive a discharge. Finally, and most surprisingly, although most businesses can file and go through a Chapter 7 liquidation, corporations and partnerships cannot have their debts discharged as a result of so doing. They must instead go through a Chapter 11 reorganization or liquidate under state law. According to the Bankruptcy Code, only natural individuals can be discharged under Chapter 7.

Revocation of Discharge and Debt Reaffirmation

If the bankruptcy court should find at any time within one year of the discharge that the debtor acted fraudulently or in a dishonest fashion during the bankruptcy proceeding, the court may revoke the discharge. This leaves the creditors free to exact their claims against the debtor.

Reaffirmation Agreement: formal notification to bankruptcy court of debtor's intent to pay off debt after it has been discharged

Also, it is often the debtor's wish to pay off a discharged debt owed to a family member, a friend, or a vital supplier of the business. This can be done legally through a **reaffirmation agreement**. However, the agreement must be made before the discharge and notice of it must be filed with the court. It may be rescinded by the debtor at any time up to 60 days after it has been filed or before discharge, whichever comes later.

Through the extended, formalized procedure of bankruptcy that we have just detailed, thousands of Americans yearly seek the relief from debt necessary to allow them to become fully productive citizens once again.

APPLICATIONS OF WHAT YOU'VE LEARNED

Vocabulary Development

Fill in the blanks with the appropriate term.

Bankruptcy	**Discharged**	**Involuntary Bankruptcy**	**Preferential Transfer**
Bankruptcy Debtor	**Estate**	**Liquidation**	**Reaffirmation Agreement**
Bankruptcy Insider	**Fraudulent Transfer**	**Order of Relief**	**Stay**
Bankruptcy Trustee	**Insolvent**		

[Some of the answers may be drawn from preceding chapters.]

1. Paying off one favored creditor fully when the other bankruptcy creditors receive only 15 cents on the dollar owed is labeled a(n) _____.

2. Upon the filing of a voluntary petition, a(n) _____ is issued that would stop or _____ other proceedings against the debtor.

3. A person unable to pay her or his debts when due is _____.

4. The sale for cash of the assets in the bankruptcy estate is called _____.

5. A transaction by the debtor made in the one-year period prior to filing that was intended to hide assets from the bankruptcy creditors is labeled a(n) _____.

6. The rights and interests of an entity in property of all types is termed a(n) _____.

Problems

1. Considering the effects of taking bankruptcy upon a debtor's credit standing, do you feel that the bankruptcy law is achieving its objectives? Why or why not?

2. Under what ethical systems is the cramdown provision of Chapter 11 supportable? Do you agree with such actions? Two Texas brothers, oil barons R. E. and I. N. Quest, were recently forced into involuntary bankruptcy. Problems 3, 4, 5, and 6 were taken

from their filings of exempt property. Look through the problems, and inform them of just what the court will allow.

3. Both brothers live in a penthouse atop structures they own. R. E.'s penthouse is atop a $62 million office building. I.N.'s penthouse is atop a $71 million shopping complex. Each claims the 1 acre of urban property due him under Texas law. That acre encompasses both structures. Will both be allowed their multimillion-dollar exemptions?

4. R. E. separated his rare china collection into 1,217 individual pieces, each worth less than $200, and claimed them under the personal property exemption. Will this method enable him to save the collection from liquidation? Could it have enabled him to do so in the past?

5. One month before being forced into bankruptcy, I. N. retired from his position as president of the brothers' company. He then began drawing an amount equal to his old salary ($4 million per year) as his pension. He claimed that the pension was exempt from his creditors' claims.

6. I. N. divorced his wife a month before the filing. As part of the property settlement, he signed over all his properties to his ex-wife. In turn, his ex-wife agreed to pay him alimony in the amount of $4 million per year. I. N. now claims that the $4 million is exempt from his creditors' claims.

The Quests were insolvent for a year before they were forced into bankruptcy. During that period, they made the following transfers, which are now the subject of the trustee's attention as possible fraudulent or preferential transfers. Which property will the bankruptcy court order returned to the estate? Explain, if appropriate, which type of transfer it is.

7. R. E., a widower, gave his $13 million yacht to his son Charles a month before the filing.

8. I.N. paid off in full a note held by his friend and business partner, Charles Smith, 92 days before the filing. I.N.'s creditors can expect to receive only 11 cents on the dollar as a result of the current bankruptcy proceeding.

The Quests want the court to order the following debts discharged. Will they be?

9. An award of $2.5 million to Rodney Henry, a driver paralyzed in an automobile accident due to R. E.'s negligence.

10. A consent decree in which R. E. agreed to pay $1.2 million to the family of Bernard Tower, a driver killed in an automobile accident due to R. E.'s negligence. R. E. was issued a citation for driving while intoxicated.

11. Taxes amounting to $127 million owed to the federal and state governments since 1987.

12. Child support of $125,000 a year that R. E. agreed to pay as a result of a paternity suit brought against him four years ago.

Pennsylvania Dept. of Public Welfare v. Davenport

110 S. Ct. 2126

Now consider just how forgiving of debts society should be:

Ed and Deb Davenport pleaded guilty to welfare fraud and were sentenced to a year on probation. One condition of their probation was that they make payments of restitution for the welfare funds they had fraudulently kept from others. A few months after being sentenced, the Davenports filed for bankruptcy under Chapter 13. They listed the restitution payments as a debt from which they sought relief.

Questions

1. From an ethical perspective, should the relief be granted? What ethical system would support your answer?

2. The case was ultimately appealed to the US Supreme Court, which ruled on it in 1990. What do you think the Court held?*

3. What is your overall opinion of Chapter 13 plans?

---

*Answer: The court held that the requirement for restitution was a dischargeable debt in bankruptcy.

How Do You Become An Attorney?

If you are considering entry into the legal profession, you must begin your preparation as soon as possible. Graduation from an accredited law school is now an almost universal prerequisite to sitting for the bar exam. In turn, most law schools require a college degree for admission, and colleges, of course, look primarily for achievement in high school in selecting their students.

Preparatory Course Selection

But aside from just making good grades and retaining as much as you can from your educational experience, you can enhance your future chances in the law by wise course selection. In particular, courses at any level emphasizing communication skills, English, logic, and even Latin are recommended. Additionally, should specific law, constitutional, or business classes be offered at your educational institution, take them.

Law School Admission

As far as law school itself is concerned, competition to get in is especially tough. With the glut of people applying for admission, every law school can afford to be choosy about whom it lets in. Most law schools base their initial screening on a combination of the applicant's college grade point average and his or her score on the Law School Aptitude Test (LSAT). An exceptional score on the latter, which is a standardized test given to measure ability to study law, can often overcome a mediocre grade point average. Prelaw clubs in colleges around the country give courses to prepare persons for the LSAT. Also, workbooks and interactive computer programs are available to help persons study for it on their own.

Law School

Once admitted to a law school, every law student is required to take basic courses on such subjects as contracts, torts, property, and criminal law. These courses often run for a full year, with just one final exam on which the entire course grade is based. Elective hours are used to tailor one's skills to a particular specialty within the legal profession. Such areas as taxation, securities regulation, labor law, family law, and intellectual property law require preparation beyond the general background required of all law students. In addition, summer clerking jobs with law firms and members of the judiciary are helpful in providing the student with practical knowledge and in clarifying the student's long-term ambitions in the legal field.

The Bar Exam

After graduation from law school comes the final hurdle, the bar exam. That exam generally comes in two parts. There is a multistate part on legal principles that the given jurisdiction holds in common with most other jurisdictions and a part on legal decisions peculiar to the state for whose bar association the applicant is seeking to qualify. Retakes of parts not passed in previous sittings are generally allowed. After passing the bar exam, if the applicant is shown to be of good character, he or she is admitted to the bar and begins a career as a legal professional.

The Legal Environment of Business: Forms of Business Organizations

CHAPTER

25
What Are Your Choices in Selecting a Legal Form for Your Business, and How Do You Organize the Simplest of These Forms—The Sole Proprietorship?

CHAPTER OUTLINE AND OBJECTIVES

After studying this chapter, the student will be able to:

I. Identify the forms of organization that should be considered in starting a business.
   a. Sole proprietorship
   b. General partnership
   c. Limited partnership
   d. Corporation
   e. S corporation
   f. Limited liability corporation and others

II. Explain how to organize a business as a sole proprietorship.

III. Discuss the relative nature of the powers of business "ownership" after studying, in the case of *Pilsbury* v. *Honeywell, Inc.*, what happened when a corporate "owner" tried to stop some of the killing in the Vietnam War.

When You're Ready to Start a Business, What Forms of Organization Should You Consider?

It is the dream of almost every businessperson to become her or his own boss by establishing a business. The three chapters of this unit are specifically dedicated to helping you make that choice either now or at some future time. We'll begin by going over the most commonly used alternatives very concisely. Then we'll look in detail at the sole proprietorship (near the end of this chapter), partnership (Chapter 26), and corporate (Chapter 27) forms. A good rule of thumb is that the more complex the procedure you use to organize your business (and therefore the more professional legal help you require), the greater the benefits you can derive from it.

That said, we need to start our discussion with the sole proprietorship, the form of business that is simplest to organize and also the form of business that is most frequently used in the United States.

Sole Proprietorship

Sole Proprietorship:
business with one owner
who has full personal
liability for it

A **sole proprietorship** is a business owned by one person. That owner alone is personally liable for the obligations of the business. Partnerships have two or more persons as owners. Corporations provide a shield that protects their owner or owners from personal liability. But the sole proprietor stands alone. Typically, the business rises and falls on his or her contacts, contracts, expertise, business savvy, energy, or other resources. If it falls, the obligations it has incurred are enforceable not only against its assets but against the home, car, furniture, and other possessions of its sole proprietor.

Why be a sole proprietor then? Why expose so much to the control of the marketplace, especially when the corporate form is available, usually for under $500 in legal and filing fees? Mainly because the sole proprietorship is such an easy form to assume. Make your lemonade, set up a table on the street, and you are a sole proprietor. Aside from having a product, a price, and a prospective customer, the preparation involved is practically nil. The government may come along later and enforce such minor requirements as a tax number or a business license. However, you will not be shot or typically even fined for starting without these. "Just do it," seems the best way to express both the philosophy and the foresight required to get started in this form.

The sole proprietorship is also far more flexible and responsive to change than the other business forms—if the owner is properly involved in it. If not, the business is at peril. That's a major weakness of the sole proprietorship as well as its potential strength. Its very existence is the responsibility of one individual, the owner. If the owner loses interest, desire, financial or physical health, the business typically perishes. For this reason, it is difficult to hire long-term professional businesspeople into a sole proprietorship. In addition, both the initial capitalization of the sole proprietorship and its financial ability to respond to change and opportunity are limited to the resources that the owner can bring to bear from personal savings or indebtedness.

General Partnership

If to make a venture a success a businessperson needs more capital and greater skills than he or she alone can provide, the use of the partnership form might be advisable.

The basic partnership is known as the **general partnership.** It is statutorily defined as "an association of two or more persons to carry on as co-owners a business for profit." The use of the term *co-owners* here implies that, like the sole proprietor, each of the partners is individually liable for the obligations of the firm. As you may suspect, a partnership involves more legal considerations than does a sole proprietorship. In fact, this area of the law is governed by the Uniform Partnership Act (UPA). The UPA is a product of the Conference of Commissioners on Uniform State Laws. First offered to the states for adoption as law back in 1914, it has been enacted by every state but Louisiana.

Although involving more legal considerations than a sole proprietorship, the basic partnership form is relatively easy to assume. The UPA is oriented toward providing rules for situations that arise from use of the form rather than toward creating legally prescribed steps that must be followed to get into it. Note that should one of the partners die or withdraw, the partnership's legal existence comes to an end. However, its business may be continued if this is allowed by the partnership agreement—more about this in Chapter 26.

General Partnership: business with co-owners, each with full personal liability for it

Limited Partnership

The use of the general partnership form brings on the co-owner's unlimited personal liability for the obligations of the business. This can produce very unsatisfactory results.

HYPOTHETICAL CASE

Dick Lobe and Lea Pold met in college, where they were both journalism majors. After graduation they kept in touch. Lobe became a successful TV news anchor. Pold became the editor of a biweekly regional literary magazine. When Lobe inherited $750,000 from an uncle, he mentioned the inheritance to Pold. She then suggested that they enter into a partnership and open a small publishing firm. Lobe agreed and put the $750,000 into the business. Pold agreed to do most of the managing in return for 50 percent of the profits. Lobe assisted by reading some manuscripts but mostly involved himself in his work and in writing his own novel, which he expected to have the partnership publish. When he finished the book, he presented it to Pold, expecting her to put it in print. She refused to do so, saying that she had just paid a large advance to a well-known defense attorney for his autobiography and that there wasn't any money left to do anything else. Several months passed. One day Pold called a meeting with Lobe. At the meeting, she quickly announced that due to personal problems the attorney had not submitted a publishable manuscript. She went on to say that the partnership was out of funds and that she was dissolving it. After she left, Lobe checked the partnership books. Only then did he realize that due to contracts Pold had made, there were outstanding obligations of over $1,300,000. Lobe could find no record of any scheduled income. When the creditors sued for

continued on page 342

> concluded
>
> their money, Pold was discovered to be judgment proof (no recoverable assets). Lobe, however, was forced into bankruptcy and stripped not only of what few assets remained in the partnership but of most of his personal possessions, including his home, his summer house, his cars, and much more.

Limited Partnership: business at least one co-owner of which is its manager and fully liable personally

Limited Liability: investor's exposure to loss no greater than amount put in to business

Because of experiences paralleling Lobe's, a statutory alternative to the general partnership form has been created. It is called the **limited partnership**. Such a partnership is composed of one or more general partners with full personal liability and one or more limited partners whose liability for partnership obligations extends only to the amount of their investment in the business. This is termed limited liability. To retain their **limited liability,** limited partners must not participate in the general management of the business. If Lobe had been a limited partner, he would have been liable only for the $750,000 that he put into the business. The creditors would not have been able to reach his personal wealth.

As mentioned, the limited partnership is a statutory creation. The statute that created it, the Revised Uniform Limited Partnership Act (RULPA), set down a formation procedure that must be strictly complied with in order for the limited partnership status to be conferred. Nonetheless, because of the advantages of the limited partnership, many businesses employ this form.

Corporation

Corporation: legal entity created as artificial person through statutory authority

Stock: shares of ownership in a corporation

The ultimate in limited liability protection of investors is offered by the corporation, the form of business that almost all large firms choose. The **corporation** is defined as a legal entity that has been created as an artificial person through statutory authority. It can be owned by one or more persons (natural or artificial). Therefore, it can sue or be sued without its investors acquiring personal liability. Also, it continues in existence beyond the withdrawal or death of its owners. This is due to the free transferability of their ownership rights and equity in the form of certificates or shares of ownership called **stock.**

Shareholders: owners of corporation

The protection of limited liability coupled with the possibility of perpetual existence made the corporation the foremost device for attracting capital investment ever created. Of course, the sheer size of some corporations renders them unresponsive to the best interests of their owners and to the immediate challenges of the marketplace. Also the enormous earnings accumulated by corporations have made them the target of public criticism and, perhaps more important, of almost every public entity with taxing authority. Today, unlike the owner of a sole proprietorship or a partnership interest, the owner of a corporation is subject to double taxation. Because the corporation is considered a separate artificial person, it is taxed on its earnings. Then, when some or all of its after-tax earnings are paid out to the owners of the corporation, that is, the **shareholders,** the earnings are taxed a second time. This occurs because the stockholders are required to declare the earnings payouts as income on their personal tax returns.

Even so, if dollars were votes, the corporate form would be elected the world's most popular mode of business ownership for investors.

S Corporation

A significant stepping-stone between the partnership and the full corporate form is provided in the Internal Revenue Code. It is the **S corporation.** Organized in the same manner as a normal corporation, the S corporation differs from a normal corporation only in the fact that profits and losses are taxed directly to the stockholders. In that way, double taxation is avoided. To become an S corporation, a corporation merely has to file for the status with the Internal Revenue Service and to meet the following criteria:

S Corporation: corporation whose profits and losses are taxed directly to its owners

1. Have no more than 35 shareholders (partnerships and corporations are not allowed as shareholders).
2. Have the agreement of all stockholders to become an S corporation.
3. Have only one class or kind of stock shares.
4. Divide its profits and losses among its shareholders according to their proportionate holding of stock.

As with a normal corporation, limited liability, survivability, and free transferability of shares are features of the S corporation (as long as the 35-shareholder limit is not exceeded). Also, the passing through of losses is important to investors who can use them to cancel out income from other sources, thereby reducing the investors' overall tax burden. Losses cannot be passed through to the owners of a regular corporation.

When the time comes for the corporation to draw in more investors for growth purposes, the S corporation status can be dropped with another filing. Since its creation as an alternative form of business a little over a decade ago, the S corporate form has become increasingly popular with wise owners.

Other Forms Worthy of Mention

Limited Liability Corporation.   This form of corporation has swept across the country since a favorable Internal Revenue Service ruling on it in 1988. Currently, more than 20 states have passed a prototype statute making the **limited liability corporation** (LLC) form available to potential users. The LLC combines the advantages of the limited partnership and the S corporation form while eliminating the restrictions normally placed on each. In particular, the LLC, unlike the S corporation, is neither restricted in the number of its shareholders nor is it restricted to only one class of stock. At the same time, every member of an LLC is free to participate in management without losing the limited liability protection so important to a limited partner or a corporate shareholder. In addition, no general partner who is fully personally liable is required under the LLC statutes of the various states that have adopted this form. With all of these advantages and several others that we have not covered, the LLC still retains the ability to pass through losses as well as profits to the member owners. In short, the LLC seems almost too good to be true, and, in fact, after proposed congressional hearings are held, the tax loophole that began this business form may well be closed and the LLC eliminated.

Limited Liability Corporation: form of business organization combining advantages of limited partnership and S corporation but without their restrictions

Business Trust:
commercial enterprise with
trustees managing property
to provide return to
beneficiaries

Beneficiaries: individuals
receiving benefit of
another's action

Business Trust.   The **business trust,** which is still in use, was once a popular business form in some northeastern states that barred corporations from dealing in real property. It involves having selected trustees manage property (signed over to the trust by its owners) so as to provide income or other forms of return to certain individuals (labeled **beneficiaries** at law). It is formed by an instrument that generally must be crafted by attorneys to properly describe the trust property, the trustees' powers, and the rights and interests of the beneficiaries and the trust's creditors.

At one time, the business trust was not subject to either double taxation or other forms of governmental regulation. In addition, its participants were free from personal liability. Now, however, the business trust is taxed as a corporation and the trustees and any beneficiaries of the trust who have managerial power have personal liability for trust obligations. Accordingly, the popularity of the business trust has declined markedly.

Franchise: business
surrounding licensing of
trademark, trade name, or
copyright for use in selling
goods or services

Franchisee: recipient of
franchise

Franchisor: seller of
franchise

Franchise.   Another form of business that has recently become somewhat inhibited by regulation is the **franchise.** It is defined as a business arrangement surrounding the licensing of a trademark, trade name, or copyright for use in selling goods or services. A detailed and well-tested system of doing business often comes with the licensing. The capital for the business comes from the recipient of the franchise, called the **franchisee.** The franchisee can be a sole proprietor, a partnership, a corporation, or some other form of business, whatever is acceptable to the seller of the franchise (the **franchisor**). In return for her or his investment, the franchisee typically receives, in addition to the license and the business system, the benefit of national or regional goodwill from collective advertising and the cost-cutting power of collective purchasing. The franchisor receives the franchise fee, a percentage of the sales, and other reimbursements.

The successful franchises are practically legendary, ranging from Ray Kroc's McDonald's to a multitude of other names that crowd the highly trafficked thoroughfares of America and the world. The unsuccessful franchises, however, are equally numerous, if not more so. This has caused state and federal regulators to focus on how franchises are distributed. In 1979 the Federal Trade Commission required that prospective franchisors disclose material facts about their enterprise. A failure to properly reveal all information pertinent to a prospective franchisee's choice or a misstatement in the information disclosed may leave a franchisor wide open to suit. These informational requirements have been augmented by various state laws aimed at preventing franchisors from terminating franchises without good cause. Taken as a whole, the legal attention given to franchising has made it a field for the cautious and those with the resources to ensure compliance.

All of the forms of business discussed above have advantages and drawbacks (see Figure 25–1 for a summary of these). To help you when it is your turn to choose, we will take a look at the establishment of a sole proprietorship in the next section. Then, in the chapters that follow, we will do the same thing for the partnership and corporate forms.

General Attributes of Most Used Forms of Business

Figure 25–1

	Sole Proprietorship	Partnership	Corporation
Capitalization potential	Typically limited to proprietor's resources	Typically limited to partners' resources	Relatively unlimited
Owner's liability limited to investment?	No; proprietor's personal resources may be used to satisfy liabilities of business	No; partners' personal assets may be used to satisfy liabilities of business	Yes
Formal entry requirements	Negligible	Need partners' agreement; lawyer's services recommended.	Relatively complex; lawyer's services usually necessary
Potential lifetime of business	Limited by duration of proprietor's involvement	Ends upon death, disability, or withdrawal of any partner	Can be perpetual
Potential for attracting and retaining professional management	Poor due to limited lifetime and growth potential	Poor due to inherent instability of partnership	Excellent due to extent of life of business and possibilities for growth
Ability to respond to changing business environment	Excellent in short term due to lack of institutionalization; poor strategically due to lack of capitalization potential	Moderately able both tactically and strategically	Relatively slower to respond to tactical changes; excellent for long-term structural changes due to capitalization potential
Is business taxed as a separate entity?	No; earnings taken as personal income by sole proprietor	No; profits taken as personal income by partners	Yes; corporation taxed on earnings; owners taxed on dividends paid to them out of those earnings

How Do You Organize a Business as a Sole Proprietorship?

As indicated in the foregoing brief discussion of the sole proprietorship, the answer to this question is practically, "Open the doors." In most municipalities a business license is required. Even so, unless the business comes under some regulation because of its product or service, for example liquor, food, or toxic chemicals, obtaining a business involves the mere formality of paying a fee.

Michael Mansfield opened his gaming store and playroom in April. Some six months later a city inspector walked in and checked to see if the business was licensed. Finding no license displayed, he ordered Michael to procure one at his earliest opportunity. Michael did so at once. No fine or late charge was imposed. The license cost $10. The inspector returned the next week, saw the license, and thanked Michael for taking care of it so promptly.

Of course, if Michael had refused to obtain a license (a source of revenue for the city), he would have ultimately been closed down by the municipality involved.

Another requirement for businesses is a tax number. This number is provided free of charge by the federal government upon request. It or a similar number issued by an individual state is often used as identification to see that eligible businesses do not have to pay sales tax on their purchases of inventory. It also serves to identify businesses to the Internal Revenue Service so as to assure their payment of taxes and various other levies.

Beyond these minor requirements, the average sole proprietor need worry only about having, as mentioned above, the product, the price, and the prospective customer.

APPLICATIONS OF WHAT YOU'VE LEARNED

Vocabulary Development

Fill in the blanks with the appropriate term.

Beneficiaries **Franchisee** **Limited Liability** **Shareholders**
Business Trust **Franchisor** **Corporation** **Sole Proprietorship**
Corporation **General Partnership** **Limited Partnership** **Stock**
Franchise **Limited Liability** **S Corporation**

1. Shares of ownership in a corporation are evidenced by _____ certificates.

2. The seller of a franchise is known as the _____.

3. Individuals receiving the benefit of a business trust are labeled _____.

4. The form of business with one owner who has full personal liability for the business is known as a(n) _____.

5. The form of business with more than one owner, each of whom has full personal liability for the business, is known as a(n) _____.

6. The form of business with multiple owners, at least one of whom has full personal liability for the business, is known as a(n) _____.

Problems

1. You are a business consultant. A young engineering school graduate walks into your office one day. He has a patent on a new type of automobile braking system. He informs you that he knows a wealthy doctor who wants to invest in the development of the product. However, the doctor does not want to risk the possibility of liability from lawsuits if the product fails to perform and injures someone. The engineer does not want to use the corporate form because he feels that it might cause him to lose control of the business. What form of business do you recommend to him? Why?

2. Barney Phifendrum has worked for a large auto muffler shop for six years. Now he wants to go into business for himself, selling and installing mufflers at discount prices. He has saved barely enough money to buy an initial stock of different sizes of mufflers and to lease a suitable garage for six months. What form of business is Mr. Phifendrum most likely to establish? Why?

3. A year has passed, and Mr. Phifendrum's shop is a huge success. He has developed his own methods for advertising, pricing, and installing mufflers. The ads feature "Sy Lentz," the fictional spokesperson and owner of the shop that bears his name (Sy Lentz's Discount Mufflers). Mr. Phifendrum plans to establish a second shop on the other side of the city. However, he is worried about being able to attract a good manager for that shop and about the potential liability from improper installations. He does not like the corporate form because of the double taxation. What business form should he choose? Why?

4. Mr. Phifendrum's second shop is also successful. He has recently been approached by a number of people for help in setting up shops like his in nearby cities. What form of business would you recommend that Mr. Phifendrum consider at this stage of development of his business? Why?

5. Most of us have business ideas that we have promised ourselves to market-test someday. Think about yours, or reflect until you have such an idea. Then ask yourself, "Given my current situation in life, would I want to use the sole proprietorship form to develop a business around my idea?" What are the pros and cons of a sole proprietorship for you? Are you likely to use that business form?

ACTUAL CASE STUDY

Pilsbury v. Honeywell, Inc.

191 N.W.2d 406

Consider a case that points out the limits on the powers of ownership.

During the Vietnam conflict, Honeywell, Inc., made fragmentation bombs for use against enemy personnel. The bombs, nicknamed "shredders" by some veterans, were highly effective. Pilsbury, an antiwar protester, bought one share of Honeywell stock in order to communicate with other Honeywell shareholders. He wanted to persuade them to use their power of ownership to cause the company to cease production of the shredders and other munitions. As an "owner" of the company, he therefore requested a list of shareholders and records of its dealings with the Pentagon from its management. When his request was refused, he petitioned the court to order the documents released to him.

Questions

1. If Honeywell were a sole proprietorship and Pilsbury were its owner, would there be any question as to his ability to obtain the information he wanted? If it were a partnership and Pilsbury were a general partner, would there be any question?

2. The court refused Pilsbury's request. What reasons for its refusal can you think of?

3. Would the court be justified in refusing a similar

request from a member of a competing corporation's management who bought a share to obtain inside information about Honeywell? Would the court be justified in refusing a stockholder who believed that corporate management was defrauding the shareholders by not reporting all of the income from its munitions sales to the Pentagon and needed the records to confirm that belief?

4. Is Pilsbury a true "owner" of a business?

CHAPTER

26

When Should You Form a Partnership, and How Do You Do So?

CHAPTER OUTLINE AND OBJECTIVES

After studying this chapter, the student will be able to:

I. Identify the advantages and disadvantages of the general partnership form.

II. Explain how a partnership is created.

  a. By court acknowledgment

  b. By statute

  c. By agreement

III. Describe how the operation of a partnership is conducted.

  a. Management

  b. Profits, losses, and property rights

  c. Liability for business operations

  d. Fiduciary duties

IV. Discuss how partnerships are ended.

  a. Dissolution

  b. Notice of dissolution

  c. Winding up

III. Identify the advantages and disadvantages of the limited partnership.

IV. Judge, from the case of *Gridley* v. *Johnson*, whether or not one doctor in a clinic may be held liable as a partner when another doctor in the same clinic is sued for malpractice for operating on a woman he did not know was pregnant.

What Are the Advantages and Disadvantages of the General Partnership Form?

In comparing the different forms of business in the last chapter, we mentioned most of the advantages and disadvantages of the general partnership form. However, it seems a good idea to quickly restate them. In particular, the advantages include ease of entry, flexibility, greater capital formation potential and managerial resource availability than are obtainable with the sole proprietorship, lack of direct governmental oversight, and lack of double taxation. The most notable disadvantages are full personal liability for the partners, termination of the partnership upon the withdrawal or death of any partner, and the practical problem of keeping the partners acting as partners.

All too often, the greatest enemy of a partnership is the lack of a satisfactory balance in the effort or sacrifice required of each partner. As a result, resentments among the partners build up. Before long, it occurs to some of the partners that to work for the partnership is to reward "partners" who they feel are not carrying their share of the burden. The ultimate result is that the "partnership" perishes. (Consequently, a "word" to the wise would be: Never—repeat, never—go into a general partnership with anyone with whom you want to keep a long-lasting personal relationship.)

Lawyers are typically well aware of the perils of the partnership form. Therefore, when clients ask a lawyer to write a partnership agreement for them, the lawyer tries to build terms into that document that anticipate conflicts and, while the prospective partners are still working together, set out a means for resolving them. Unfortunately, doing these things requires asking the potential partners how they would resolve these conflicts. The clients, who have come into the attorney's office caught up in the euphoria of what they think the partnership could achieve, have the ice-cold water of experience poured on them. The lawyer, through her or his well-motivated questions, reminds them about all that could go wrong with the partnership. Before long, the euphoria changes to dread, the result often being that no partnership is formed. Thereby, lawyers earn time and again their reputation as "deal killers" and are paid for so doing. To avoid both horns of this dilemma and in the spirit of forewarning you about the challenges of the general partnership form, the next sections delve deeply into the legalities of creating, running, and terminating a general partnership.

How Is a General Partnership Created?

As mentioned, one of the advantages of the partnership form is ease of entry. This is borne out in real life by an examination of the two principal ways of forming partnerships. The first, as you might suspect, is by express agreement of the persons involved. Note that the "persons" referred to here may include various types of business organizations, especially corporations. We will discuss this way to form a partnership in detail at the end of this section.

By Court Acknowledgment

The second way a partnership is formed results from a court determination that a partnership exists because of how certain parties do business with one another. If a person maintains in court that a partnership exists, the court will examine the business dealings of the alleged partners for the existence of some **prima facie evidence** (proof goodand sufficient on its face upon which a factual presumption can be based) of the partnership. The most common prima facie evidence is the sharing of profits. If the court discovers that practice, it will hold that a partnership exists unless satisfactory evidence to the contrary is presented. (For example, profits may be paid out to a creditor or other obligee without making the recipient a partner.)

Prima Facie Evidence: proof good and sufficient on its face upon which a factual presumption can be based

HYPOTHETICAL CASE

McCord, Hunt, and Liddy formed a partnership to do household plumbing repairs. They leased office space in a well-known city landmark. To pay for their rent, they agreed to share 25 percent of their profits with their landlord, Creep, Inc. When the partnership failed to meet its obligations, several of its creditors hired the law firm of Cox, Sirica, and Jaworski to try to recover the amounts due. The law firm produced evidence showing that the plumbers did indeed share their profits with Creep. One of the plumbers, John McCord, even alleged that Creep was a partner. This was enough prima facie evidence to cause the court to presume that a partnership existed and therefore that Creep could be held liable for the partnership's obligations. Creep then came forward with documents and tapes of the lease negotiations showing that the payout of profits was strictly for rent. This was enough evidence to cause the court to overturn its presumption that Creep was a member of the partnership. It then held that Creep was not liable for the partnership's debts.

Other profit payouts, such as payouts to employees for wages, to creditors for debt repayment, to retirees as part of a pension plan, or to sellers as the price of goods sold, are not enough to make the payees partners either. Remember, though, that if prima facie evidence of partnership is found, it is then up to the party denying that a partnership exists to disprove the court's contrary presumption. The court will not look for evidence on its own. Once the prima facie evidence causes the court to erect its presumption, it must be shown that there was no partnership.

By Statute

Typically, statutes do not interfere to any great extent with the formation of a general partnership. (The Statute of Frauds does require, however, that the express contract on which the partnership is based be in writing if it cannot be carried out in less than a year.) However, the Uniform Partnership Act, which we discussed briefly in the last chapter, does provide terms that the courts are to use in handling partnership issues. These terms are to be used only if the partners did not reach agreement on their own terms. For example, section 18 of the UPA reads in part:

The rights and duties of the partners in relation to the partnership shall be determined, subject to any agreement between them, by the following rules:

(a) Each partner shall . . . contribute towards the losses, whether of capital or otherwise, sustained by the partnership according to his share in the profits.

*****

(e) All partners have equal rights in the management and conduct of the partnership business.

*****

(h) Any difference arising as to ordinary matters connected with the partnership business may be decided by a majority of the partners; but no act in contravention of any agreement between the partners may be done rightfully without the consent of all the partners.

Articles of Partnership: partnership agreement

These are only a few of the UPA rules that will apply unless the parties to the partnership agreement (referred to as the **articles of partnership**) stipulate otherwise. So in a state that has adopted the UPA, if you don't want every partner to "have equal rights in the management . . . of the partnership business" [16(e) above] or if you don't want to have "ordinary business matters . . . decided by a majority of the partners" [16(h) above], then you would have to put your desired way of doing these things into the articles of partnership.

In contrast to this approach, the UPA, in section 16, does provide for having certain individuals bear the responsibility for partnership obligations. In that section the UPA mandates the enforcement of partnership responsibilities against someone who improperly indicated by words or conduct that a partnership existed or who held herself or himself out as a member of an existing partnership. If an outside party was deceived enough to form a reasonable belief in these misrepresentations, the person who made them is held responsible for any subsequent liability just as though he or she were a partner. This is termed a **partnership by estoppel**. However, no real partnership is created thereby. Partners by estoppel don't get a share of the profits or assets. They simply lose the ability to deny at law their involvement in the partnership so as to avoid paying for its liabilities.

Partnership by Estoppel: person stopped from denying existence of partnership so as to avoid liability

HYPOTHETICAL CASE

A group of investors wanted to open a country music theater in Branson, Missouri. They pooled their money and formed a partnership. To attract customers, they paid famous country singer Ronny Money for the use of his name. A few months before the season was to begin, however, it became obvious that Ronny Money Country Music Jubilee would not be able to open its doors without a sizable loan. Knowing that Ronny was well regarded in the community and had an excellent credit rating, the partners asked him to accompany them to the bank from which they wanted to acquire the loan. Ronny, who would receive a substantial percentage of the jubilee's take when he appeared at the jubilee in person, agreed to do so. He even pretended to be a partner and represented himself as such to the bank. Because the bank knew Ronny's credit rating, it made the loan to the partnership. Due to other difficulties, the country music theater never opened. When the bank sought funds to cover its unpaid loan, it was able to proceed against Ronny as a fully liable partner. Although in actuality he was not, the court held that he was a partner by estoppel. He was therefore estopped or prohibited from denying that he was a partner for the purpose of avoiding responsibility for repaying the loan.

By Agreement

Although court acknowledgment focuses partnerships responsibility on some, a partnership is most often created by express agreement of the parties. As mentioned, that agreement can be oral (unless an oral agreement conflicts with the Statute of Frauds requirement of a writing for agreements that cannot be performed in a year or unless the partnership is to be engaged in the acquisition and sale of real estate).

The flexibility of the partnership form is shown by the various types of partners that may use it. For example, **general partners** participate in the management of the partnership and are fully liable personally for the partnership's obligations. **Silent partners** are properly and publicly acknowledged as partners but do not participate actively in the management of the partnership. **Secret partners**, on the other hand, are partners but are not known as such publicly. **Nominal partners** are not actually partners but hold themselves out as such or allow themselves to be held out as such. (As you have probably deduced, Ronny Money was a nominal partner.) Finally, **dormant partners** are neither acknowledged publicly as partners nor do they actively participate in the management of the partnership.

Regardless of the intentions of those that would establish a partnership (as mentioned, they may be corporations, individuals, or, in many states, other partnerships), the partnership form has proven to be flexible enough to serve any would-be partner's needs and imagination. The articles of partnership shown in Figure 26–1 present most of the items normally considered important in forming a partnership.

General Partners: partners participating in partnership management with full personal liability for partnership obligations

Silent Partners: publicly known partners not actively involved in management of partnership

Secret Partners: partners not known as such by public

Nominal Partners: nonpartners held out as partners

Dormant Partners: partners neither acknowledged publicly nor actively involved in management

How Is the Operation of a Partnership Conducted?

The rules determining how the operation of a partnership is conducted may be spelled out in the partnership agreement, if one exists. However, if partnership is not based on an express agreement or if it is based on an express agreement that is not thorough enough, some or all of the rules of its operation are contained in the UPA. So, we will use the UPA rules in the discussion that follows. Remember that the partners are free to select their own rules for the partnership agreement, which typically then supersede the UPA rules.

Management

Under the UPA, the day-to-day operations of a partnership business can be conducted by any of the partners. Each partner has equal rights in the management of the ordinary course of business no matter how small that partner's percentage of ownership may be. Any difference of direction among the partners over routine matters is to be resolved by a majority vote of the partners. Should that method fail, then any previous pattern of conducting business is retained, if appropriate. If no previous pattern exists or the failure to resolve the issue impairs the business routine and its profitability, the partnership must be dissolved.

Figure 26–1

**The General Partnership Agreement Forming
Leaks Anonymous**

**Date, identity of
partners, and
purpose of
partnership**

**Name, location,
and records
availability**

**Duration and
termination
procedure**

Capitalization

**Funding of
reserve**

**Division of profits
and losses,
payout
schedule**

**Account
location,
withdrawal
procedure**

**Duties and
limitations**

**Nonroutine
decision-making
procedure**

Signatures

By agreement made this 30th day of September, 19**, we, John McCord, Glenda Liddy, and Eduardo Hunt, the undersigned all of Leavenworth, Kansas, hereby join in general partnership to conduct a plumbing installation and repair business and mutually agree to the following terms:

1. That the partnership shall be called "Leaks Anonymous" and have its principal place of business at 715 South Oaklawn, Leavenworth, Kansas, at which address books containing the full and accurate records of partnership transactions shall be kept and be accessible to any partner at any reasonable time.

2. That the partnership shall continue in operation for an indefinite time until terminated by 90 days' notice provided by one or more of the partners and indicating his, her, or their desire to withdraw. Upon such notice an accounting shall be conducted and a division of the partnership assets made unless a partner wishes to acquire the whole business by paying a price determined by an arbitrator whose selection shall be agreed to by all three partners. Said price shall include goodwill, and the paying of same shall entitle the payor to continue the partnership business under the same name.

3. That each partner shall contribute to the partnership: $5,000 for initial working capital and the inventory and equipment (including trucks—which shall be marked with the partnership name, address, and logo) of their current individual plumbing businesses.

4. That in return for the capital contribution in article 3, each partner shall receive an undivided one-third interest in the partnership and its properties.

5. That a fund of $25,000 be set up and retained from the profits of the partnership business as a reserve fund. It being agreed that this fund shall be constituted of not less than 15 percent of the monthly profits until said amount has been accumulated.

6. That the profits of the business shall be divided equally between the partners, that the losses shall be attributed according to the subsequent agreement, and that a determination of said profits and losses shall be made and profit shares paid to each partner on a monthly basis.

7. That the partnership account shall be kept in the First National Bank of Pennsboro and that all withdrawals from same shall be by check bearing the signature of at least one of the partners.

8. That each partner shall devote his or her full efforts to the partnership business and shall not engage in another business without the other partners' permission.

9. That no partner shall cause to issue any commercial paper or shall enter into any agreements representing the partnership outside the normal conduct of the plumbing business without notice to the remaining partners and the consent of at least one other partner and further that all managerial and personnel decisions not covered by another section of this agreement shall be made with the assent of at least two of the partners.

IN AGREEMENT HERETO, WE ARE

John McCord   *Glenda Liddy*   *Eduardo Hunt*
(Signatures)

Lance and G. Daland Webb formed a partnership and took over their father's prosperous real estate brokerage when he retired. Unfortunately, conflicts soon developed between the two partners over employee tasks and office locations. One of them employed a programmer to integrate the use of computers into the office, them employed a programmer to integrate the use of computers into the office routine. The other saw the hiring as a budget problem and fired the programmer. Lance developed an advertising campaign. Daland canceled it. Before long, the well-meaning decisions of the two partners started to affect profits. Finally, because of their inability to agree on such ordinary business matters, the partnership had to be dissolved.

Extraordinary managerial decisions typically require the assent of all the partners. For example, using partnership property as collateral, bringing in a new partner, and selling the partnership's real property require unanimous consent of the partners. (Compare how the partners in Leaks Anonymous handled this area—see article 9 of Figure 26–1.)

Note that under the UPA partners can assign their partnership interests, such as profits, to nonpartners. If this is done, however, the assignees who receive such interests are not thereby given the right to take part in the management of the partnership business.

Profits, Losses, and Property Rights

Each partner is entitled to an equal share in the profits and losses of the partnership unless agreement to the contrary has been reached. As mentioned, however, it is often to the tax advantage of partners that have extensive outside income to take a larger share of the partnership's losses than is taken by those that do not have such income. Such an allocation can easily be provided for in the partnership agreement. (Note that, under the UPA, partners may call for an accounting of the partnership business to determine profits, losses, and other matters whenever this "is just and reasonable" [UPA section 22(d)].)

In addition to a share of profits and losses, the UPA gives each partner a co-ownership in partnership property. This **tenancy in partnership**, set up in section 24 of the UPA, provides that each partner has an equal right with the other partners to possess specific partnership property for partnership purposes. This right, unlike the partner's interest in the profits of the partnership, cannot be assigned. Likewise, specific partnership property cannot be used for personal purposes by any partner without the consent of the other partners. Consequently, a partner's creditors cannot attach or execute their rights against specific partnership property, whether or not the property is in that partner's possession. In addition, should a partner die, the deceased partner's rights in specific partnership property passes to the surviving partners. The surviving spouse, heirs, or next of kin cannot subject specific partnership property to their claims.

Tenancy in Partnership: form of partner's ownership interest in partnership property

Liability for Business Operations

All of these provisions of the tenancy in partnership act to provide the best possible opportunity for preserving the partnership's business in the face of individual misfortune. However, the partnership is liable for torts that a partner or an employee commits while engaged in the partnership's business. The liability is both joint and several for the partners for everything chargeable to the partnership in this manner. This means that each partner can be sued (or perhaps released from liability) separately without affecting the case against the other partners. It also means that several or all of the partners can be sued at once. If sued separately and recovered against in full, a partner is entitled to seek contributions from the other partners (or, if necessary, secure such contributions by court action).

If a partner commits a crime to further the partnership's interests, that partner is separately liable for the offense.

A contract action, unlike ones based on tortious or criminal conduct, must be brought against the partners jointly. The judgment received or the release given applies to all of the partners.

Fiduciary Duty above All

Fiduciary Duty: legal requirement that certain parties put a particular interest ahead of their own

Finally, in conducting the partnership's business, each partner owes a **fiduciary duty** to the partnership. This means that the partner must put the partnership's interest above her or his own. The partner must act in good faith throughout. Using partnership funds or other property for personal gain violates the partner's fiduciary duty, as does competing against the partnership. Consequently, the courts will hold the partner accountable to the partnership for any individual gain that he or she receives while on partnership business.

How Are Partnerships Ended?

Dissolution of Partnership: change whereby partner ceases association with partnership's business

In general, a partnership's legal existence may have to be terminated (brought to a legal end) because of intentional actions of the partners, because of the automatic operation of the law, or because a court has decreed that the partnership should end. Any one of these possibilities, which will be discussed in detail shortly, may result in a **dissolution of partnership.** The UPA defines such a dissolution as a change whereby any partner ceases to be associated with the carrying on of the partnership's business. However, the dissolution of a partnership does not necessarily mean that the partnership's business must end. Often the partnership agreement provides a way by which the remaining partners can buy out the interest of the departing partner. Article 2 of the partnership agreement shown in Figure 26–1 provides a mechanism that would allow the partnership business to continue under its established name after the departure of one or more partners.

However, if no such mechanism has been set up in the partnership agreement or if no one uses an available mechanism, the partnership business, like the relationship among the partners established by the partnership agreement, will have to be wound up and terminated. Winding up can be accomplished either according to a procedure set up in the partnership agreement or, lacking that, according to UPA rules. The **winding up** of a partnership requires the concluding of all business (no new contracts can be entered into except as necessary to fulfill existing obligations) and the selling of the partnership property. After the cash accumulated in this way has been used to satisfy the partnership's debts, any remaining funds are distributed to the partners. The partnership then ceases to function and the effect of the partnership agreement is terminated.

Winding Up: process by which partnership concludes all business, partnership property is sold, and proceeds distributed

Dissolution

Now that you have the general picture, let's examine the various ways in which dissolution can be initiated.

By the Intentional Acts of a Partner.   Many partnership agreements set down the term for the partnership. Once that period has run or a specified event has occurred (such as a fall in gross earnings falling below a certain amount or the expulsion of a partner or a unanimous partners' vote for dissolution), the partnership is dissolved. Some partnership agreements hinge dissolution on the accomplishment of a partnership's purpose (construct a bridge, provide food service at home football games for the coming season, etc.). If nothing is set down in the partnership agreement on the term of the partnership, then the partnership is considered to be "at will." Any partner can dissolve a **partnership at will** at any time without incurring any liability for doing so.

Partnership at Will: partnership dissolvable by any partner at any time without any liability for so doing

By Action of Law.   Certain events dissolve partnerships automatically. These events are set down in various laws. For example, the law prescribes that the death of a partner ends the partnership. The bankruptcy of a partner or the bankruptcy of the partnership works the same result. The loss of a professional status or license could bring on the dissolution of a partnership by making it inoperable.

Fresh out of school, Burma, Gore, Lurem, and Skewerem formed a partnership to practice dentistry. For several years they were quite successful. Then Lurem was charged with using too little anesthesia in her procedures. Eventually she lost her license to practice in the state. Since she could no longer take part in the partnership's activities, the partnership was automatically dissolved as a matter of law.

By Court Decree.   Although not automatic, other legal grounds can be used to dissolve a partnership by court **decree** (judgment). When circumstances render the partnership inoperable, yet do not bring on its automatic dissolution under the law or the partnership agreement, a court can be petitioned with the facts of the matter. The court is asked to judge whether or not the partnership can or should be continued. If not, the court will order it dissolved. Typical bases for such petitions are:

Decree: equity judgment

Disputes among the partners that cannot be reconciled.
A significant willful breach of the partnership agreement.
The inability to carry on the partnership's business except at a loss.
The incapacity of a partner to carry out the partnership agreement.

Regardless of what brings it about, dissolution affects not only the partners but those who deal with the partnership. In the dentistry partnership, knowing that Dr. Lurem would no longer be available might have made a significant difference to many of the partnership's patients. The consequent reduction in partnership income might have also made a significant difference to the partnership's creditors.

Notice of Dissolution

Because dissolution of a partnership affects the third parties that deal with it, the law has special provisions relating to the notice of dissolution due such parties. Creditors must receive direct personal notice of the dissolution. Others, until they receive implied or express notice of the dissolution, are protected if they continue to deal with the partnership in the same manner in which they had dealt with it previously.

Winding Up

As mentioned, the dissolution of a partnership does not necessarily mark the termination of the partnership's business. However, should that become necessary, an orderly procedure must be followed. The procedure begins with the sale of the partnership's assets. The funds raised are then used to pay off the partnership's liabilities. Whatever remains is distributed to the partners in accordance with the percentage of the profits each normally receives. It is important to remember three things about this procedure. First, until the partnership has been fully wound up, the partners still owe a fiduciary duty to one another. Second, once the procedure has begun, the partners are authorized to act only in ways that contribute to the winding-up process. Third, in paying off the partnership's creditors, nonpartner creditors receive their due before partner–creditors receive theirs.

Obviously, destroying an ongoing profitable business seldom does anyone any good in the long term. The employees lose their livelihood. The economy loses a viable participant. Even the partners who receive a payout from the process would probably get a better return on their money if the business continues to function. Nonetheless, if the business has to be wound up, following a fair and orderly procedure in the winding-up stages is the best insurance against expensive subsequent lawsuits.

What Are the Advantages and Disadvantages of the Limited Partnership Form?

A creation of statute, the limited partnership form is roughly similar to the general partnership form. It differs from the general partnership form in that it offers limited liability as an option for all but one of the partners involved in the business. It also differs in that, in return for the limited liability attribute, the law establishing the limited partnership form requires compliance with relatively strict governmental rules, denial of managerial input from limited partners, and the filing, in the appropriate governmental office, of a **certificate of limited partner ship** for notice to third parties dealing with the business.

The limited partnership form is ideal for putting two types of parties together as partners. The first type is the party who has the business idea and/or expertise and wants to retain control of the business but is without the capital needed to get it going. The second type is the party or parties who have the capital but do not want to be involved in running the business or to be exposed to full personal liability. The Revised Uniform Limited Partnership Act (RULPA), mentioned in the last chapter, sets down the requirements that enable these parties to be joined in a business form beneficial to both types.

However, the partners must always act in strict compliance with the statute. If the limited partners act as managers, they will be held fully liable personally as general partners. If the organizational requirements are not met, the business will be held to be a general partnership. If the certificate of limited partnership is not properly filed to give notice to parties who will be dealing with the limited partnership, the limited liability protection will be lost.

Regardless of these worries, the advantages of the limited partnership, often bring about its use, especially in more sophisticated investment situations.

> **Certificate of Limited Partnership:** notice of limited liability status to third parties dealing with business provided by filing with appropriate government office

APPLICATIONS OF WHAT YOU'VE LEARNED

Vocabulary Development

Fill in the blanks with the appropriate term.

Articles of Partnership	Dissolution of Partnership	Nominal Partner	Secret Partner
Certificate of Limited Partnership	Dormant Partner	Partnership at Will	Silent Partner
Decree	Fiduciary Duty	Partnership by Estoppel	Tenancy in Partnership
	General Partner	Prima Facie Evidence	Winding Up

1. The court formed its factual presumption from _____.

2. An individual member of a partnership who has full personal liability and participates in managerial decisions in relation to the partnership is known as a(n) _____.

3. An individual member of a partnership who has full personal liability but is unknown to the public and does not participate in managerial decision making is known as a(n) _____.

4. An individual member of a partnership who has full personal liability and is publicly known but does not participate in the management of the partnership is known as a(n) _____.

5. An individual who is not a member of a partnership but holds himself out as such or allows another to do so is known as a(n) _____.

6. An individual member of a partnership who has full personal liability and participates in managerial decisions while remaining unknown to the public is known as a(n) _____.

Problems

1. Explain the rationale behind each of the following observations
   a. "Do not go into partnership with your in-laws."
   b. "Lawyers are deal killers."

2. Houk wanted to involve everyone in her message delivery business. She therefore set up a compensation system under which her employees received a percentage share of the profits as their pay. Later she extended this system to retirees from her business. Unfortunately, the business acquired an overload of debts during a recession. Its creditors then maintained that the employees, retirees, and Houk were partners so as to hold them all personally liable. Will the court find prima facie evidence of partnership here? Are the employees, retirees, and Houk partners? Why or why not?

3. In an effort to save her business, Houk applied to an investment capital syndicate for a debt consolidation loan. As an adviser during her interview with the syndicate, she took along Marisa Mantle, a wealthy, well-known friend, whom she introduced jokingly as "my partner in crime." The syndicate members made the loan because they assumed that Marisa was a partner. Marisa did not receive any profits (or losses) from the business. When Houk's business collapsed after the loan was spent, the syndicate sued Houk and Mantle as partners. What theory might be used to cause Mantle to be liable as a partner for the debts of the business? Will that theory work? Why or why not?

4. Again desperate to save her business, Houk took in a partner, Hubert Spoke. Spoke, an ex-employee of a competing firm, had inherited his Aunt Chaney's fortune. Spoke's money bailed the business out. Later he and Houk had a number of disputes over how the business should be run. One of the disputes concerned Spoke's authority to make contracts for the business. Another involved Spoke's suggestion that a third partner be brought into the business. Houk and Spoke have no express partnership agreement, but the UPA is in force in their state. How would their disputes be resolved in court?

5. Which of the following occurrences would force a legal end to the partnership?
   a. The state medical malpractice board removes the license of one of the two physicians in Trauma Treaters, a professional partnership.
   b. One of three partners dies.
   c. The partnership declares bankruptcy.
   d. All of the above would end the partnership . . .

6. Remember the business idea that you promised yourself to market-test with a view to using the sole proprietorship form (Problem 5 of last chapter)? This time, ask yourself, "Given my current situation in life, would I want to use the partnership or limited partnership form to develop a business around my idea?" What are the pros and cons of these forms for you? Are you likely to use either of them?

Gridley v. Johnson

476 S.W.2d 475

Test your ability to judge whether or not a partnership exists in the following medical malpractice case.

Mr. and Mrs. Larry E. Gridley sued three doctors and a hospital for damages caused Mrs. Gridley by the alleged failure of the defendants to give her a pregnancy test before having her undergo a gall bladder operation and a dilation and curettage ("D & C"). Dr. Doane was one of the three doctors named as defendants. The plaintiffs were attempting to hold him liable for the alleged wrongful acts of Dr. Johnson by alleging that the two were partners in the operation of the Grandview Clinic, where Mrs. Gridley was seen. A letterhead and billheads submitted as evidence showed the name and address of the clinic at the center top and the doctors' names at the sides. Dr. Doane testified (Dr. Johnson was ill at the time of the trial) that the two doctors saw and charged their own patients. However, if one of the doctors were absent, the other would see the absent doctor's patient and receive the amount charged. The two doctors did not share each other's fees, but they did share the expenses of the clinic and its equipment.

Questions

1. Is Dr. Doane a partner of Dr. Johnson? Why or why not?
2. Should a partnership by estoppel be held to exist here? Why or why not?
3. What do you think the court held in this case?

When Should You Form a Corporation, and How Do You Do So?

CHAPTER OUTLINE AND OBJECTIVES

After studying this chapter, the student will be able to:

I. Discuss the considerations involved in choosing the corporate form for a business.

II. Explain the steps that are taken in forming a corporation.

   a. Promotion

   b. Stock subscriptions

   c. Articles of incorporation

   d. Issuance of the charter

   e. Sale of stock

   f. Organizational meeting

   g. Commencement of business

III. Identify the important legal considerations in the day-to-day management of a corporation.

   a. The business judgment rule

   b. Powers of the corporations and its officers

   c. Shareholder rights and responsibilities

IV. Analyze the case of *K.C. Roofing Center* v. *On Top Roofing* to appreciate the extent of the limited liability protection.

When Is the Corporate Form Optimal for a Business?

Finally, our discussion turns to the corporation, the form of business that large concerns choose almost exclusively. As mentioned in Chapter 25, although sole proprietorships and partnerships are far more numerous than corporations, in amount of capitalization the corporate form wins the popularity contest hands down.

Why is this? Primarily because of the combination of attributes associated with the corporate form. It offers limited liability coupled with a practically unlimited ability to attract capital and professional management. It not only protects investors against full personal liability but gives them an ownership interest that, typically, is freely transferable. It offers professional managers access to the resources necessary to carry out their plans. In addition, its survival—unlike that of a sole proprietorship or a partnership—is unaffected by the death or withdrawal of its owners.

For those who began the business as a sole proprietorship or a partnership however, the shifting into the full corporate form may eventually mean a loss of control. If the change breeds success, however, the increased scale of doing business and, hopefully, the increased profits of the business may provide suitable consolation.

With these considerations in mind, let's take a look at the typical steps followed in forming a corporation.

What Steps Are Taken to Form a Corporation?

Public Corporation: organization set up by government to accomplish governmental purpose

Private Corporation: organization set up by private individuals to achieve private ends

For-Profit Corporation: organization formed to produce investment return for its owners

Not-for-Profit Corporation: organization formed to achieve educational, charitable, or other ends without investment return

To begin with, we need to clear up a problem with terminology involving the specific type of corporation we are discussing. Because of the free transferability of most corporate stock among the public of private investors, people often refer to corporate stock as being "publicly held" and to the business form we are discussing as being a "public corporation." It is not. A **public corporation** is an organization set up by a local or state government or the federal government to accomplish a governmental purpose. Instead we are discussing what is legally referred to as a **private corporation,** that is, an entity set up, funded, and run by private individuals to achieve private ends.

A private corporation may be organized on either a for-profit or a not-for-profit basis. A **for-profit corporation** is set up to yield its owners a return on their investment. A **not-for-profit corporation** is created to achieve educational, charitable, or other ends without any return to its investors. As you may suspect, we'll focus on the for-profit form. By the time you're into setting up not-for-profit corporations, you'll have enough expertise to do so (or, more likely, more than adequate amounts of money to buy that expertise—and then some).

Finally, before we get into discussing how to promote a corporation to prospective investors, a few other labels that might confuse you need to be clarified. Private corporations are often labeled "domestic" or "foreign," depending on their state (not country) of origin. As the states write the laws that control the creation and empowerment of corporations, a corporation doing business in the state under whose laws it was organized as a legal entity is known as a **domestic corporation.** In all of the other states where it does business, except the state of organization, the corporation is a **foreign corporation.** (A corporation from outside the United States is referred to as an **alien corporation.**) Private corporations may also be referred to as closely held or **close corporations.** These labels indicate that the stock-based control of the corporation is held by a single individual or a tight-knit group of individuals. The stock is not traded publicly, and some states even allow the imposition of restrictions on the transferability of the owners' shares.

Also, a number of the labels explained above may apply to the same corporation. For example, you may own a private, for-profit, domestic, close corporation that has elected (and qualified) to be taxed as an S corporation. Finally, some states have created a specialized corporate form called a professional corporation. This form is available only to professionals who were previously statutorily prevented from incorporating, such as doctors, lawyers, public accountants, osteopaths, chiropractors, architects, optometrists, and veterinarians. The professional corporate form provides tax benefits to those who utilize it. However, it does not limit or insulate the professional from malpractice liability.

Domestic Corporation: corporation doing business in state where chartered

Foreign Corporation: corporation doing business in state where not chartered

Alien Corporation: corporation chartered in another nation

Close Corporations: corporation owned by one person or small group

Promotion

Hopefully, what we must do when we attempt to form a private, for-profit, corporation is already somewhat clear in your mind. The first step in this "long journey" is promotion. **Promotion** is the advocacy of the business idea and the corporate form for it to potential investors. The people who do this sales job are, as you might expect, labeled **promoters.** Some promoters are individuals bent on organizing the corporation and then participating in its day-to-day existence as officers, managers, and/or employees. Other promoters may merely be interested in selling the to-be-issued stock on a commission basis.

Even at this early stage, however, all promoters have a fiduciary duty to the corporation they intend to form and to its future stockholders. The promoters must put the interests of the corporation-to-be ahead of their own. They must act as its loyal servants. They must honestly and fully account for any contractual obligations they incur on behalf of the future corporation. If the corporation is not formed or if, once formed, it fails to fulfill these contracts, the promoters may be held personally liable.

Promotion: advocacy of business idea and corporate form for it

Promoters: advocates of business idea and corporate form for it

HYPOTHETICAL CASE

Because of the repeated success of the Johnson Family Racing Team in regional "street" stock car races, the Johnsons finally decided to move into a higher level of competition. As this new level, "modified" stock car races, required much more funding, the Johnsons also decided to finance the move by forming a corporation tentatively named The Checkered Flag Company. They planned to sell shares in the

continued on page 368

concluded

corporation to fans and other investors. While promoting the unformed corporation, the two oldest Johnson brothers, Brad and Charley, entered into contracts for equipment, space in a garage, and indorsements on its behalf. In each instance they worked hard to secure the best deals for the corporation-to-be. To do so, however, they had to cosign the contracts personally as well as on behalf of the corporation. As Brad, the older of the two promoters, said to Charley, his younger sibling, "If we don't get enough investors to put this corporation together, you and I are going to be in a real financial bind due to all these contracts we've signed."

Brad was right to worry. Moreover, as mentioned, even when Checkered Flag is formed, it will not be bound by any of the contracts that the two promoters made in its behalf until it performs some act indicating its acceptance of those contracts. For example, moving the corporation's tools and equipment into the garage or making a lease payment on it would show such acceptance and render the corporation liable. However, just having the corporation assume liability does not release the promoters from responsibility under the same contracts.

Stock Subscriptions

Despite the potential liability from contracts, the focus of the promoter must be on getting potential investors to commit themselves to buying the stock of the corporation-to-be. That stock will become available only after the formation of the corporation. The formation of the corporation in turn will occur only if enough investment capital has been committed to it. See the problem here? Which is to come first?

Subscription Agreement: written contract to buy stock when issued

The resulting impasse is usually solved by large measures of trust and, especially in the case of large stock offerings, by **subscription agreements.** Such an agreement is a written contract by which a potential investor agrees to buy a certain amount of stock if and when stock is issued. The resulting commitments, if sufficient in number, give those bent on organizing the corporation a foundation on which to proceed with the next step, incorporation.

Articles of Incorporation

Articles of Incorporation: application for corporate status

Incorporators: individuals signing articles of incorporation

The process of incorporation begins with the filing of a written application for corporate status with whichever state the corporation's organizers have chosen (it does not have to be the state in which the corporation is or will be located). This application is called the **articles of incorporation** because of the requirement that the state be provided with various items (or "articles") of information pertinent to the corporation-to-be. The individuals signing the articles of incorporation are known as **incorporators.** The Model Business Corporation Act, offered as a prototype incorporation act to the states by the American Bar Association, requires that each application contain the articles of information shown in Figure 27–1.

The laws of the state of incorporation control how a corporation is run. These laws vary significantly from state to state. Some states allow a great deal of latitude to corporate management; others require shareholder approval for nearly

**Articles of Information Required in an
Application for Corporate Status**

Figure 27–1

**The State of Missouri
Office of the Secretary of State
Articles of Incorporation
(As Required By Revised Statutes of Missouri Section 351.055)**

1. **The Name of the Corporation shall be:** The Checkered Flag Company
2. **The Address, including street and number, if any, of its initial registered office in this state, and the name of its initial registered agent at such address:** Omar Bradley Johnson, Agent, at 213 First Street North West, Miller, MO 65707.
3. **The number, class, and right of the holders of authorized shares:** 100,000 common shares each with full ownership rights and voting authority.
4. **A current shareholder's right to purchase shares in a new stock issue:** Each current shareholder shall have the right to purchase a pro rata share equal to her or his ownership percentage of each subsequent issue at the public offering price of that issue.
5. **The name and place of residence of each incorporator:**

   Omar Bradley Johnson   Miller, MO 65707
   Charles Edgar Johnson   Miller, MO 65707

6. **The number of corporate directors and the names and addresses of those chosen to fill those positions until the stockholders can elect their replacements:**

   Three (3) directors shall constitute the initial Board of Directors of The Checkered Flag Company. They are

   Omar Bradley Johnson, 213 First Street North West, Miller, MO 65707
   Charles Edgar Johnson, 1717 East Delmar, Miller, MO 65707
   Jacqueline Alexis Johnson, 213 First Street North West, Miller, MO 65707

7. **The number of years the business is to continue:** The business is to enjoy perpetual existence.
8. **The purpose(s) for which the business is formed:** The Checkered Flag Company is to involve itself in racing competitions with the hope of profiting thereby.

---

all major decisions. Most of our larger corporations have been formed under the laws of the state of Delaware, which provide management with a great deal of latitude. Businesses wanting to incorporate in Delaware need only follow that state's relatively simple regulations and employ a **registered agent** (a person to represent the corporation in receiving binding service of process) in the state. So a business with headquarters in New York City, for example, can still be "a Delaware corporation" if it so chooses.

Registered Agent: person designated to legally represent corporation in state

Also note from the articles of incorporation displayed in Figure 27–1 that the name of the business must include the word or the abbreviation of *company, corporation,* or *incorporated.* Finally, the duration selected can include any term up to and including the "perpetual" indicated for The Checkered Flag Company in article 7.

Issuance of the Charter

Once the articles of incorporation have been submitted, the appropriate state office will review them. This is usually the office of the secretary of state for whatever state the incorporators have chosen (the state of Missouri was chosen by

the incorporators of The Checkered Flag Company). If all of the legal requirements are met and all of the fees are paid, the state will issue a certificate of
incorporation, called a charter, to the applicants. Through the powers vested in the
state, the **charter** officially creates a separate legal entity, (i.e., an artificial person
according to the law) called a corporation.

Charter: certificate of
incorporation

Sale of Stock

Once the corporation has been officially chartered, it can commence doing
business. Its obvious first step is to acquire the necessary capital by selling stock
to those who have subscribed to the initial offering and to others as necessary.

Organizational Meeting

The stockholders are then summoned to an organizational meeting run by the
initial directors named in the articles of incorporation. (Note that some states have
adopted the Revised Model Business Corporation Act, which dictates that the
incorporators shall run the initial meeting.)

The first order of business at this meeting is typically the election of permanent **directors.** These stockholder representatives are charged with the overall
responsibility for management of the corporation. Although most directors are
shareholders, this is not a requirement for their selection. Many large corporations
have both **inside directors** (individuals who are employees, officers, or major
stockholders) and **outside directors** (individuals without a significant financial
interest in the corporation). Collectively, the directors are referred to as the **board
of directors.**

After their election the directors proceed to formulate and adopt the corporate
bylaws. These are the rules by which the internal organization and management
of the corporation proceeds.

Bylaws typically include provisions that:

Set the time and place for future meetings of the stockholders and the board of
directors.
Determine the number required for a quorum for such meetings.
Stipulate how vacancies on the board of directors shall be filled.
Identify the corporate officer positions and the qualifications required of those
who fill them.
Prescribe the duties of the corporate officers.

Like the promoters and the incorporators, the members of the board of
directors owe a fiduciary duty to the corporation and its investors. The formula-
tion of the bylaws and consideration of the contracts made by the promoters for
ratification should reflect the proper execution of this duty, as should the selection
of officers by the board.

Directors: stockholder
representatives with overall
responsibility for corporate
management

Inside Directors: directors
who are employees,
officers, or major
stockholders

Outside Directors:
directors without significant
financial interest in the
corporation

Board of Directors:
managing panel of directors

Bylaws: rules for
organization and
management of the
corporation

Commencement of Business

Once the company president, the company treasurer, and other necessary corporate officers and employees have been selected, the company can commence
doing business. As long as the proper legal steps have been taken in its formation,

The Steps in Forming a Corporation

Figure 27–2

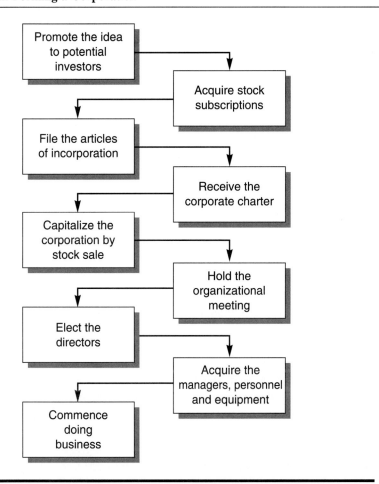

the company is now a separate legal corporate entity called a **de jure corporation.** Neither private citizens nor the state can challenge its status.

If an error has been made in the process of incorporation, yet the effort to incorporate was made in good faith, the corporation is said to be a **de facto corporation.** Such a corporation is afforded the same status as a de jure corporation as far as a challenge by private citizens is concerned. Only the state can challenge its position so as to correct the errors of incorporation.

Why would a private citizen or the state want to challenge the corporate status of a company? There could be many reasons for so doing, but the primary reason is to impose personal liability on the owners (i.e., the shareholders) of the company. This is called **piercing the corporate veil.** Although frequently sought, piercing the corporate veil has been achieved only in aggravated cases. However, if a corporation has been organized as a shield behind which its owners carry out improper or illegal acts, the courts will disregard the corporate status to make the wrongdoers pay.

By working through all of the steps mentioned in this section and diagrammed in Figure 27–2 a corporation can be formed and readied to do business. However,

De Jure Corporation: properly formed corporate legal entity

De Facto Corporation: corporate entity improperly formed due to good faith error

Piercing the Corporate Veil: court action imposing personal liability on owners

as the next section details, the legal considerations do not end when the business finally begins.

What Legal Considerations Are Important in the Day-to-Day Management of a Corporation?

As you may have inferred from the discussion about directors, in a typical corporation the directors are not the day-to-day managers. However, they are charged by law with the ultimate managerial responsibility. The directors fulfill this responsibility by appointing (hiring) what they feel is the necessary number of corporate officers. These officers may include a president, numerous vice presidents, a treasurer (with responsibility for financial plans and budgets), a secretary of the board, a comptroller (an official in charge of day-to-day expenditures), and a general counsel (attorney). In large corporations all of these positions are needed, and each of them is filled by a different person. In some close corporations, however, if allowed by state law, only one person may fill all of them. In other words, the same person may be the sole director, the sole corporate officer, and the sole shareholder.

The Business Judgment Rule

When it comes to the decisions made by managers and other officers of corporations, our court system typically adopts a hands-off approach. This is because the courts recognize the general overall competence of such people in making the resource allocation decisions for which they were hired. The courts adhere to this approach even when these decisions may place the good of the corporation ahead of the good of the community in which it is located.

In response to the passage of federal legislation creating a free trade zone between the United States, Mexico, and Canada, the management of the Zenith Corporation elected to move its Springfield, Missouri, manufacturing facility to Mexico. Although the move meant an end to the last domestic manufacture of certain electronic goods and the loss of over a thousand jobs, which would have a severely depressing effect on the economy of the Springfield region, the decision could not be successfully challenged in a court of law.

Rather than install costly preventive devices on its smokestacks, Sintax, Inc., chose to vent thousands of pounds of toxic wastes into the air breathed in by its neighbors in the Pennsboro, Missouri, community. The venting was allowable under the environmental control regulations of both the federal government and the state government.

In reviewing decisions such as the ones made by Zenith's or Sintax's officers, the courts use the **business judgment rule.** The rule's effect is to immunize management from liability resulting from business decisions made within the power and authority granted corporate officers in the corporate charter and state statutes. The decisions must be made in good faith and with due care for corporate interests. Moreover, in situations in which the managers personally benefit from their decisions made on behalf of the corporation, the law requires that at a minimum they fully disclose all crucial information, including their own involvement. Similarly, if a business opportunity develops that the corporation might take advantage of, the officer who knows of it and might take the opportunity herself or himself must disclose it to the corporation. If the corporation then rejects it, the officer may take it, but only then. All of this stems from the duty of loyalty to the corporation. If the officer violates the tenets of that duty, he or she is exposed to the full scrutiny of the court without the benefit of the business judgment rule.

Business Judgment Rule: insulates management from liability stemming from bona fide business decisions

Powers of the Corporation and Its Officers

As the business judgment rule protects only the officers whose decisions are within the legitimate powers of the corporation concerned, we need to pause and discuss the most significant of those powers. The primary rule defining corporate power comes from the law's recognition of the corporation's status as a separate legal entity, an artificial person. Therefore, unless the articles of incorporation or the state laws under which the corporation is formed set limits, the corporation has the same powers as a natural individual to do anything necessary to carry out its business and related matters. These powers typically include:

The power to acquire, hold, and dispose of property.
The power to act in the corporate name to bring suit against (and be sued by) others.
The power to contract.
The power to borrow and offer corporate property as security for loans.
The power to participate in other business organizations and to acquire, hold, and dispose of rights in them.
The power to employ agents with appropriate compensation and pension plans so as to fulfill the purposes of the corporation.
The power to contribute to the public good.
The power to conduct inter- and intrastate business by means of the powers explicitly noted above and any other legitimate implied powers that further the business interests of the corporation.

Any action taken by the corporation that goes beyond the powers granted by the express and implied delegations specified above or by statute is labeled **ultra vires.** In most states a corporation may use the fact that a corporate officer's act was ultra vires to protect itself from the enforcement of an executory contract against it. In fact, at one time all ultra vires corporate transactions were void. However, modern law does not hold a party contracting with a corporation to the responsibility of inquiring into what the corporation she or he is dealing with can or cannot do. If you are unaware of limitations placed on the actions of a

Ultra Vires: action exceeding bona fide corporate powers

corporation, then you are not bound by those limitations nor can you use them against the corporation. Similarly, the fact that a corporate act is ultra vires does not mean that it is illegal and void.

As part of the "full service" facility at its downtown branch, the Greater Pennsboro Savings and Loan operated a small convenience store, a laundromat, and a liquor store in its mall-like lobby. Chase LaRue, one of the town's leading citizens, ran up a large bill in the liquor store, then refused to pay it. When Greater Pennsboro brought suit for the balance due, Chase defended by contending that running a liquor store was an ultra vires act for a savings and loan. Therefore, the contract was void or, in the alternative, illegal and thereby void. The court disagreed, stating that as Chase had enjoyed the benefit of the contract without complaint, he could not now raise the ultra vires defense. The court also noted that even if the selling of liquor was ultra vires, this did not mean that the sales contract was illegal and thereby void. Many ultra vires acts are legal. Chase was ordered to pay Greater Pennsboro the full amount due.

Corporate Growth and Financing. As the corporation widens its business operations, encounters new obstacles, and, hopefully, overcomes them, its potential profit and exposure to liability expand accordingly. Although growth should not be considered synonymous with success, it parallels success in many cases. New markets beckon to the company with the currently superior product or service. Often the expansion necessary to take advantage of such markets cannot be financed through the internal generation of capital from profits. Therefore, the corporation may decide to seek more funds by turning once again to potential investors. Generally, it can do this in two main ways:

It can attract more capital by selling stock of various kinds to individuals who want to become part owners of the business or to increase the amount of their existing ownership. This is termed **equity financing** as it increases the investment of the owners in the business.

It can attract more capital by borrowing money from individuals and issuing them **bonds** (a certificate or some other evidence of debt requiring that the issuer/borrower repay the amount borrowed, the **principal,** plus interest according to a fixed schedule) in return. This is termed **debt financing** for obvious reasons.

Equity Financing: capitalization by increasing owner investment

Bonds: evidence of debt and required form of repayment

Principal: amount borrowed

Debt Financing: capitalizing by debt issue

Whichever method is chosen to generate capital, stock or bonds, the transaction comes under the scrutiny of the federal government and the state governments (see Chapter 39). There are advantages and disadvantages to either method. For example, bonds have a number of tax advantages, but if they are not paid as required, the corporation might face bankruptcy. Stock has no such demanding payout schedule. However, the issuance of more stock dilutes the ownership of the corporation, that is, it creates more owners to split the payout of earnings whenever these occur. Also, selling too much stock to newcomers might jeopardize the control of the original owners.

Because of these and other considerations, a large variety of types of stocks and bonds have been used in the past. The basic type of stock, and the type generally issued at the start of corporate existence, is called **common stock.** This type of stock gives its owner the right to vote (according to the number of shares held) in corporate elections. The owner of common stock also gets a proportionate share in the distribution of corporate profits, called **dividends,** whenever these are authorized for issue by the board of directors. Should the corporation be terminated, the owner of common stock also receives a proportionate share of the payout, if any. Other rights that accrue to common shareholders (and generally to shareholders of all types) include the right to transfer their shares, the right to receive information (financial and other reports) about the company, and the right to inspect corporate books and records.

Contrasting with common stock is a type of stock whose dividend amount is usually set ($1 per share, for example) and whose owners get paid in full before common shareholders are paid any dividends. This type is referred to as **preferred stock.** Unlike common stock, preferred shareholders do not have voting rights in corporate matters. This causes some investors to shy away from this type of stock. However, if the corporation desires, the basic position of a preferred shareholder can be enhanced by making preferred stock cumulative and/or participating. **Cumulative preferred stock** requires that all unpaid preferred stock dividends be paid, even from previous fiscal years, before the common shareholders receive anything. **Participating preferred stock** means that preferred stockholders are entitled to receive a pro rata share of the monies for common stock dividends left over after the preferred dividends have been paid.

Like stock, corporate bonds come in a variety of types. A debenture bond, or just a **debenture,** as it is commonly known, is a bond that has been issued without any security. It is to be paid back through the general credit of the issuing corporation without recourse against any specific corporate property. A **convertible bond** is exchangeable for a set amount of stock at the option of the bond's creditor.

Shareholder Rights and Responsibilities

In most states, the choice between these various forms of financing and several others not mentioned is left up to the voting stockholders of the corporation. In a widely held corporation, many of these owners cannot be present to cast their vote on the timing and amount of the dividend, the type of financing, or even the directors who will oversee the corporation. Consequently, the law allows voting by proxy. A **proxy** is an authorization by which a shareholder allows someone else to cast his or her vote. Significant disputes over corporate control or similar issues often manifest themselves as "proxy fights" to see which side can get the most votes of those shareholders who cannot be present. To enhance the possibility of treating corporate issues democratically, state incorporation statutes provide the option of **cumulative voting** in the all-important election of directors. Each share is given a number of votes equal to the number of directors to be elected. So if a person owns 1,000 shares and five directors are to be elected, the person can cast 5,000 votes among a general field of candidates for the positions. The five

Common Stock: basic corporate ownership interest with right to vote and share profits

Dividends: distribution of corporate profits

Preferred Stock: corporate ownership interest with priority in receipt of dividends but without voting rights

Cumulative Preferred Stock: preferred stock on which all missed dividends must be paid before common shareholders receive dividends

Participating Preferred Stock: preferred stock entitled to its dividend plus pro rata portion of common dividend

Debenture: bond issued without security interest

Convertible Bond: bond exchangeable for stock at option of bond's creditor

Proxy: authorization by shareholder for another to vote in his or her stead

Cumulative Voting: method of increasing likelihood of minority representation on corporate boards candidates with the most votes are elected. This method enhances the possibility that a minority view will be represented on the board. It contrasts sharply with the usual method, voting for each director's position individually, strictly between two or so candidates for that specific position. Under this latter method, someone controlling only 51 percent of the common stock could elect all five directors.

In addition to being given cumulative voting to protect their rights, shareholders are given the power to bring what are called derivative court actions to safeguard their own and corporate interests. This is typically done if the officers and directors have either acted improperly or have failed to pursue a claim of the corporation against a third party. Such an action is allowed only if a demand for such action is first made on the officers and directors.

Investors in corporations are protected by these shareholder rights, other devices and mechanisms, and by government oversight. Of course, none of these means or measures can replace individual vigilance. However, despite scandals of the greatest magnitude, colossal failures, and the unforgettable specter of the Great Depression, the corporate form today remains the foremost legal building block of our country's economic well-being.

APPLICATIONS OF WHAT YOU'VE LEARNED

Vocabulary Development

Fill in the blanks with the appropriate term.

Alien Corporation	**Cumulative Voting**	**Incorporators**	**Principal**
Articles of Incorporation	**Debenture**	**Inside Directors**	**Private Corporation**
Board of Directors	**Debt Financing**	**Not-for-Profit**	**Promoters**
Bonds	**De Facto Corporation**	**Corporation**	**Promotion**
Business Judgment Rule	**De Jure Corporation**	**Outside Directors**	**Proxy**
Bylaws	**Dividends**	**Participating Preferred**	**Public Corporation**
Charter	**Directors**	**Stock**	**Registered Agent**
Close Corporation	**Domestic Corporation**	**Piercing the Corporate**	**Subscription Agreements**
Common Stock	**Equity Financing**	**Veil**	**Ultra Vires**
Convertible Bond	**Foreign Corporation**	**Preferred Stock**	
Cumulative Preferred Stock			

1. A legal entity organized by the government to fulfill a governmental function is termed a(n) _____.

2. A separate legal entity organized for charitable purposes without the promise of a return to its investors is a(n) _____.

3. A corporation doing business in the state in which it was chartered it a(n) _____.

4. A corporation improperly organized due to a good faith error is a(n) _____.

5. A corporation owned by one or very few individuals is known as a(n) _____.

6. Capitalization of a company through the issuance of bonds and similar instruments is called _____.

7. Capitalization of a company through the issuance of stocks and other means of increasing the ownership investment is called

   _____.

8. A type of stock with a priority claim on dividends yet without voting rights is referred to as

   _____.

9. A type of stock like that defined in Question 8 but

with the additional attribute that all of its missed dividends must be paid before any dividends are paid on common stock is termed

   _____.

10. A debt instrument issued by a corporation that can be exchanged for a certain number of shares of the corporation's stock is termed a(n)

   _____.

Problems

1. Again, go back to that business idea that you promised yourself to market-test with a view to using the sole proprietorship form and the partnership form (Problem 5 of Chapter 25 and Problem 6 of Chapter 26). This time, ask yourself, "Given my current situation in life, would I want to use the corporate form to develop a business around my idea?" What are the pros and cons of this form for you? Are you likely to use this form? If so, then explain how you would promote, incorporate, and start doing a profitable business with it. Be demanding on yourself. The more clearly you define the steps now, the more likely you are to accomplish them later.

2. Following up on Problem 1, consider these questions: Do you have to incorporate in the state where your corporate headquarters are located? Do you have to incorporate in every state in which you do business? If you choose to incorporate in a state other than one in which you have a corporate office, how do you legally establish a presence in that state so that you can be chartered there?

3. Presume that your corporation has been properly formed and has been in operation for over a year.

Your reputation is spreading. Business opportunities in your line of operation are popping up every day. However, your considerable profits are still not enough to finance what you regard as a need to expand. What type of financing for the expansion would you try to use if you did not want to dilute your control (you currently own 51 percent of the common stock) or be forced to make payments back to your new investors unless you had the profits from which to make them?

4. As your company grows more and more successful, some criticism develops over the corporate projects that you are funding. As a result, a block of dissident shareholders set out to secure a position of the corporation's five-member board of directors. You have retained your 51 percent block of common stock. Without cumulative voting, how many directors can the dissidents hope to elect at the next shareholders' meeting? With cumulative voting, how many of the 20,000 outstanding shares of the corporation's common stock must they control before they are assured of electing at least one director?

K.C. Roofing Center v. On Top Roofing

807 S.W.2d 545

Examine how the limited liability aspect of the corporation may be manipulated.

Creditors brought suit to pierce the corporate veil of On Top Roofing, Inc., and affix full personal liability on its owners. The evidence submitted at trial included the following information:

That On Top Roofing, Inc., was actually incorporated in 1977 as Russell Nugent Roofing, Inc., but changed its name to On Top Roofing, Inc., in 1985.

That Russell and Carol Nugent were the sole shareholders, officers, and directors of the corporation.

That On Top ceased doing business in 1987 when RNR, Inc., was incorporated with Russell and Carol Nugent as the sole shareholders, officers, and directors.

That RNR went out of business in 1988 and RLN Construction, Inc. was incorporated in its stead with Russell and Carol Nugent again the sole shareholders, officers, and directors.

That RLN Construction went out of business in 1989 and Mr. Nugent then formed Russell Nugent, Inc.

That all of the companies were located at the same address, 614 Main in Grandview, Missouri, which was owned by the Nugents and used the same business telephone number.

That although three directors were required, only Carol and Russell Nugent had been directors for several years.

That Mr. Nugent's corporations did not produce records of any annual meetings in 1988 or 1989.

That in 1987 K.C. Roofing Center (the plaintiff) advanced about $45,000 in roofing supplies to On Top, which went unpaid, and fostered this suit.

That according to Mr. Nugent's testimony, he stopped buying materials from suppliers when they refused to advance any more material on credit.

Finally, that Carol and Russell Nugent received rent for 614 Main in amounts varying with the success of the corporations they owned and in 1986 included a $99,290 payment in addition to their $100,000 in salaries for that term.

Questions

1. Why should the court pierce the corporate veil and hold the Nugents personally liable to the creditors of their various corporations?

2. What reasons could be used to argue against piercing the corporate veil even in this case?

INSIGHT

How Are Case Decisions Reported?

In the Insight section on doing your own legal research, it was noted that both annotations and digests contain excerpts from cases. If users of these reference tools want to read the case from which a particular excerpt was drawn, they must be able to utilize a shorthand method of referral called "citations." A case citation typically includes the name of the case and the page, volume, and abbreviated name of the particular set of books, referred to as "reporters," in which the opinion of the court deciding the case can be found. These case citations, for example "*Alden* v. *Presley,* 637 S.W.2d 862," pass on all the information needed to locate the full report of a case in a reasonably equipped law library.

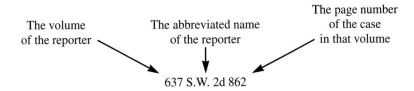

Each reporter typically covers a specific court or courts. The US Supreme Court, for example, has a number of reporters that carry only its decisions. One of these reporters, *U.S. Reports,* is labeled the "official" court reporter and is published by the Government Printing Office. The others, including the *Supreme Court Reporter,* published privately by West Publishing, are unofficial. Should a conflict arise between the official and unofficial versions of the same opinion, the official version is, by law, the correct one. Note that some reporters are into a second or later series. Thus you see a "2d" following the reporter abbreviation (S.W., for *South Western Reporter*) in the *Alden* v. *Presley* citation. This indicates that volume 637 of the *South Western Reporter*'s second series contains this case. Some of the most frequently encountered reporters, their abbreviations, and their coverage are shown in the following table.

Reporter	Abbreviation	Coverage
Atlantic Reporter	A. or A.2d	Appellate cases from the state court systems of Connecticut, Delaware, Maine, Maryland, New Hampshire, New Jersey, Pennsylvania, Rhode Island, and Vermont.
Federal Reporter	F. or F.2d	Cases of the US courts of appeals
Federal Supplement	F. Supp.	Cases of the US district courts and the US Court of International Trade
North Eastern Reporter	N.E. or N.E.2d	Appellate cases from the state court systems of Illinois, Indiana, Massachusetts, New York, and Ohio
North Western Reporter	N.W. or N.W.2d	Appellate cases from the state court systems of North and South Dakota, Iowa, Michigan, Minnesota, Nebraska, and Wisconsin
Pacific Reporter	P. or P.2d	Appellate cases from the state court systems of Arizona, California, Colorado, Idaho, Kansas, Montana, Nevada, New Mexico, Oklahoma, Oregon, Utah, and Washington
South Eastern Reporter	S.E. or S.E.2d	Appellate cases from the state court systems of Georgia, North and South Carolina, Virginia, and West Virginia
South Western Reporter	S.W. or S.W.2d	Appellate cases from the state court systems of Arkansas, Kentucky, Missouri, Tennessee, and Texas
Southern Reporter	So. or So.2d	Appellate cases from the state court systems of Alabama, Florida, Louisiana, and Mississippi
Supreme Court Reporter	S. Ct.	Cases of the Supreme Court of the United States
U.S. Reports	U.S.	Cases of the Supreme Court of the United States

Agency and Employment

CHAPTER

28

What Is an Agency, and How Is One Created, Run, and Terminated?

CHAPTER OUTLINE AND OBJECTIVES

After studying this chapter, the student will be able to:

I. Explain the distinctive function of the agency relationship.

   a. Agency distinguished from similar relationships

   b. The extent of an agent's authority

III. Describe the duties of the principal and the agent.

   a The principal's duties

   b. The agent's duties

IV. Discuss the situations in which principals and agents are liable to third parties.

   a. Principals

   b. Agents

V. Explain how agencies are terminated.

   a. By actions of the parties to the agencies

   b. By the law

   c. Notice of termination

VI. Answer the question "Is a husband an automatic agent for his wife when it comes to contracts with third parties?" by analyzing the case of *Missouri Farmers Association, Inc.* v. *Willie May Busse.*

What Is An Agency?

Agency: relationship whereby one party can bind another party by words or actions.

Principal: person authorizing another to act in her or his stead.

Agent: person authorized to act for another

Scope of Authority: range of power granted agent

Often in our lives we face the necessity of being in more than one place at one time, to be out making a sale while clearing up the paperwork from the last sale back in the office, to be on vacation while keeping up with bills and business, or, as is necessary for a member of the armed forces, to be on a combat mission while managing his personal affairs in his country of origin. As is the case for many other kinds of practical problems, dilemmas of this kind have bred a legal solution, in this case a relationship called agency.

When two parties establish a relationship whereby one may legally bind the other by words or actions, an **agency** has been created. The person authorizing another to act in her or his stead is labeled the **principal.** The person so authorized is termed the **agent.** As long as the agent acts within the power granted her or him by the principal (called the agent's **scope of authority**), the principal is bound by any deals that the agent negotiates with third parties.

 HYPOTHETICAL CASE

The Rasslin Reptiles, Cobrette and Vipera, could not find suitable matches for women with their talents. Wrestling promoters across the country would not return their calls. Finally, they hired a professional manager, Angela Drone, and gave her full authority to contract on their behalf as their agent. The manager then booked the Reptiles into a sequence of matches up and down the West Coast. In addition, she handled their finances, travel arrangements, and public relations through contracts she made on their behalf. The Reptiles were bound to those contracts, as the manager was their agent.

Agency Distinguished from Similar Relationships

To better grasp the meaning and practical functioning of agency, we must place it properly in regard to similar relationships, such as those existing between an employer and an employee or between an individual and the independent contractor hired for a project.

The principal–agent relationship is distinguished from a typical employer–employee relationship on the basis of the extent and type of control exercised. In the first place, whereas an agent can enter into contracts on behalf of her or his principal, the typical employee cannot. Second, although an employer (also labeled a "master" at law) can direct the on-the-job physical actions of the employee (also labeled a "servant" at law), the principal does not have the equivalent power over her or his agent. Should the principal contract for this power as well, the agent becomes an employee in the eyes of the law. Should this occur, the principal, like any other employer, is held liable for the harm caused by the agent in the physical conduct of the agency duties. In the alternative, should an employee be granted the power to contract on the employer's behalf, that employee becomes an agent of the employer and can render the employer liable for the agreements that he or she makes on the employer's behalf.

An independent contractor, on the other hand, contracts only to provide a result. The independent contractor, therefore, neither acts to bind another to legal agreements nor acts under the control of another and thus renders that other liable for damages caused by the independent contractor's actions. (See Chapter 29 for full discussion of the employer–employee relationship and the legal status of the independent contractor.)

The Extent of an Agent's Authority

As described in the material that follows, an agent may be empowered by a principal's express grants of authority or by implication from the nature of the agency. In addition, the circumstances in which individuals are clothed may indicate that they have an agent's authority and thus may cause those responsible to be bound to contractual obligations that result.

Power of Attorney: written authorization of agency

General Power of Attorney: authorization to do anything legally necessary to conduct principal's affairs

Limited Power of Attorney: authorization to carry out specific transactions or to act as agent for specific period of time

Express Authority. Express grants can either be made orally or be placed in writing. The important thing is that the terms are spelled out for both parties. A written agency authorization is called a **power of attorney.** That power may be either general or limited. A **general power of attorney** allows the agent to do anything legally necessary to conduct the principal's affairs. A **limited power of attorney** allows the agent to carry out only specific transactions or to act as agent for only a set period of time.

HYPOTHETICAL CASE

When their agent booked the Rasslin Reptiles into a six-month string of matches in Europe, Cobrette gave her brother, Herb, a general power of attorney to handle her interests while she was gone. Vipera, on the other hand, did not want to trust anyone with so much power. Consequently, she gave her lawyer only a limited power of attorney that restricted him to paying all of her monthly bills and to contracting for the necessary maintenance work on her properties while she was gone.

Implied Authority. Whether placed in writing or merely stated orally, an express grant of authority to an agent carries with it implied authority to do whatever is reasonably necessary to carry it out. For example, if while Vipera was away on the European tour, her car needed to be driven occasionally to keep it in proper condition, her lawyer had the implied authority to buy gas for it.

Apparent Authority

HYPOTHETICAL CASE

Snyder was a volunteer firefighter. She also ran a used car lot near the fire station in Pennsboro, Missouri. When a fire call came in early one afternoon, Snyder asked Angie Clark, a 16-year-old high school student who had stopped by to chat, to sit in

continued on page 386

concluded

the office of the used car lot and manage things until the emergency was over. Angie agreed. When Snyder returned from the fire, she found that Angie had accepted delivery on two used cars from a wholesaler. The wholesaler regularly toured the new car dealerships, bought trade-ins, and took the trade-ins to remote used car dealers. Snyder usually bought a couple each trip, but as sales had been slow, she had not planned to this time. Is she bound to the contract?

Apparent Authority: power of person seemingly authorized to act for another but in actuality not so authorized

If one person "clothes" another person with the appearance of an agent, the courts will often hold that the person so clothed had **apparent authority** to enter into contracts on the clothier's behalf. Such was the case for Angie, whom Snyder placed in a position of responsibility in relation to the used car lot. Because Snyder's actions created the appearance of agency in Angie, Snyder would be bound to the contract for the two cars. Those actions would cause a court to prohibit Snyder from denying the existence of the agency. In other words, apparent authority creates an **agency by estoppel.** As mentioned, the fact that Angie is a minor makes no difference where the principal is an adult. It should be noted here that the representations or conduct of an alleged agent cannot be the sole basis for the creation of such an agency. There must also be the reasonable appearance of authority originating from the alleged principal.

Agency by Estoppel: legal fiction created by court forbidding alleged principal to deny existence of agency

Generally, then, if a person acts without the express, implied, or even apparent authority of another, the alleged principal is not and cannot be bound. However, should the unauthorized act be **ratified** (expressly approved or impliedly approved by accepting the benefits of the unauthorized act), the ratifying party can be bound as a principal.

Ratified: expressly or impliedly approved by accepting benefits of unauthorized act

Note that if a minor becomes a principal in an agency relationship, that minor retains the power to avoid any contracts entered into in his or her behalf. In addition, the minor can avoid the agency contract itself. However, a person without contractual capacity, such as a minor, can be an agent. Therefore, the adult who makes a contract through an agent who is in her or his minority cannot avoid the contract on that ground.

What Are the Duties of the Agent and the Principal?

Once an agency has been established, the parties to the agency (depicted in Figure 28–1) owe distinct duties to each other.

Duties of the Principal to the Agent

To Compensate the Agent (if so agreed). This duty can be the most important of all. In particular, the principal must pay for the agent's services if this is required under the agency contract. If such payment is not required, the arrangement is referred to as a **gratuitous agency.**

Gratuitous Agency: principal not obligated to pay for agent's services

The Legal Duties That Form the Basis for the Principal–Agent Relationship

Figure 28–1

To the principal, the agent owes:	To the agent, the principal owes:
Obedience	Compensation as agreed
Loyalty	Reimbursement as agreed
The exercise of reasonable care and skill	Indemnification of contract and tort liability incurred by the agent without fault
The segregation of funds belonging to the agency	
A proper accounting upon reasonable demand	

To Reimburse the Agent. Again, if the agency contract requires, either expressly or impliedly, that the agent expend her or his own funds to carry it out, the principal is obligated to reimburse the agent for those expenses.

To Pay for the Agent's Liabilities to Third Parties. If, in properly carrying out agency duties, the agent incurs contractual or tort liability through no fault of his or her own, the principal has an implied duty to make good the agent's loss.

To Adhere in Good Faith to the Agency Contract. The principal must comply with the agency's terms openly and honestly. Also, the principal must not block or inhibit the agent's ability to carry out her or his duties.

All of these duties save the requirement of good faith are subject to revision or elimination by means of the agency contract.

HYPOTHETICAL CASE

The Nosmadas owned a shoe store. Wanting to retire, they listed the property with a realtor, Tex Porter. The agency contract with Porter stipulated that he would bear the expenses of advertising and showing the building as well as the responsibility for maintaining insurance to cover any liability he might incur in performing the agency. The contract also required that the Nosmadas pay him a 10 percent commission on the sales price of $50,000 if he produced a ready, willing, and able buyer. Two months after the Nosmadas made the listing contract with Porter, he produced such a buyer. Before the deal could be closed, however, the Nosmadas learned that the pension fund of Mrs. Nosmada's employer had been looted by the previous management to fight a takeover bid. As a result, they could not retire and they therefore refused to go forward with the sale. Nonetheless, they owed Tex a $5,000 commission for fulfilling his part of the agency contract.

The Agent's Duties to the Principal

Obedience. An agent is responsible for obeying the lawful directions of the principal. Any damages that result from his or her failure to do so are recoverable from the agent.

Kaila Moore managed the weekend early morning shift at the Rat Race Convenience Store in Pennsboro, Missouri. Because the Rat Race was open 24 hours a day and did a large cash volume, the owners required that all managers do a cash drop into a floor safe every time the cash on hand exceeded $200. Because Kaila found the procedure annoying, however, she ignored it. She only deposited her excess cash just before her replacement showed up. At 7:30 AM on the Saturday on which deer season began, while Kaila was on duty, the Rat Race was held up. Receipts showed that the robbers made off with over $1,700 that Kaila had left in the cash drawer in defiance of her principal/employer's instructions. She was therefore held personally liable for $1,500 of the loss.

Loyalty.   Just as the principal owes the duty of good faith to the agent, the agent is held to the duty to act loyally toward the principal. If the agent's personal interests are affected by a transaction for the principal, the agent must inform the principal that this is the case. The agency's business must not be conducted with intimates or businesses of the agent without the principal's prior approval. Such approval is also required before the agent can represent other parties in an agency transaction. Without the required approval, the transaction is voidable by the principal.

Reasonable Care and Skill.   When carrying out the principal's directions, the agent must exercise reasonable care and skill. Failure to do so renders the agent liable.

Bronowski owned a car brokerage on a corner of an intersection of two busy streets. He convinced Jonathan Brown that Brown's van would sell in just a few days if it were left at that location. Brown turned the van over to Bronowski on a Tuesday. By Thursday Bronowski had sold the vehicle. When Brown came to get his money, Bronowski informed him that the buyer's check had bounced and that the buyer had disappeared with the van. Brown asked Bronowski whether he had run a credit check or obtained any information from the buyer other than what was printed on the buyer's check. Bronowski replied that he had not as the buyer had shown up at closing. Brown sued and recovered the value of the van from Bronowski due to Bronowski's failure to exercise the degree of care that a prudent person would have exercised under the circumstances.

Segregation of Funds and Accounting.   The agent is charged with keeping agency funds and other property separate from her or his personal resources. In addition, the agent must be prepared to account for all agency funds and other property that are under his or her control. If for some reason the agent commingles personal and agency property in a way that makes it impossible to distinguish personal property from agency property or to separate personal property from agency property, the principal can claim all of the property.

Farmer Joan Jones made the Pennsboro Seed Company her agent to sell the barley crop of her north 40 acres. The company had barley of its own stored in a silo at company headquarters. When Jones appeared with her truckloads, the company mistakenly had her put her barley in the silo in which theirs was stored. Since neither Jones nor the company had any way of determining their respective shares of the barley in the silo, all of the barley in the silo was later awarded to Jones.

When Are Principals and Agents Liable to Third Parties?

The potential for liability of the principal and the agent to each other springs from the duties listed above. However, either of the parties to an agency can also become liable to third parties.

Principals

Certainly, a principal is bound by any contracts with third parties as long as those contracts have been negotiated by the agent acting within the boundaries of the authority that has been granted to the agent. As mentioned, the principal can also be held liable to third parties whenever he or she ratifies the actions of the agent even if those actions were not initially within the scope of the agency. In addition, any tortious conduct committed by the agent when acting within the guidelines set for the agency renders the principal (and the agent) liable. Finally, the principal is usually held to be without liability for criminal acts committed in carrying out an agency unless the specific criminal acts were approved by the principal or were later ratified by that individual.

Agents

Generally, an agent is not liable on contracts that she or he negotiates for the principal under the terms of the agency. However, there are exceptions to this rule.

For example, should the agent exceed the boundaries of the authority granted by the agency, the agent is liable under the contract that results. The principal, as indicated, is not liable in such a situation unless he or she has clothed the agent in apparent authority or unless she or he ratifies the contract.

An agent can also incur liability when she or he acts for an **undisclosed principal,** that is, under an agency contract that forbids the agent to reveal that he or she is acting for a principal, much less that principal's identity. In such a case, the third party may hold either, but not both, the agent or the principal liable for

Undisclosed Principal: party authorizing agent's actions whose identity cannot be revealed according to agency's terms

losses. (Note that if the principal's existence, but not her or his identity, can be revealed, that party is referred to as a partially disclosed principal.) Finally, should the principal be shown not to exist or not to have capacity to contract, the agent will be held liable.

The law firm of Williams and Manchester contracted to act as agents for a large amusement park chain that wanted to buy land near Branson, Missouri. Afraid that knowledge of its plans would drive land prices sky-high, the chain required that Williams and Manchester not disclose their principals. After thousands of dollars of land purchase contracts had been negotiated in the name of Williams and Manchester, the amusement park chain went bankrupt. The third-party sellers of the land could hold the firm liable under the purchase contracts.

How Are Agencies Terminated?

By Actions of the Parties to the Agencies

Agencies are so dependent on the relationship between the parties that the law generally allows both agent and principal the power to terminate the agency at any time even before the terms of the contract might cause it to expire. Except for cases in which the agency is terminable at will, however, the power of the parties to terminate their relationship does not mean that either has the legal right to so do. The exercise of the power to terminate in the face of legitimate contractual requirements to remain in the agency will cause the courts to hold those who exercise that power responsible for the harm that results from their action. In other words, even though the courts cannot force us to remain in agency contracts we do not wish to be in, they can make us to pay damages for the liability that results from our refusal.

Agency Coupled with an Interest: agent given interest in property in which she or he is dealing

Note that in one situation even the power to terminate the agency relationship is denied. This is the situation in which the agent is given an interest in the property in which she or he is dealing. That interest must be above and beyond the payment for the agent's services. The parties thereby create an **agency coupled with an interest,** which is irrevocable by the principal.

Ben Blackdeer was a professional bass fisher. Bass Pro Manufacturing of Springfield, Missouri, offered him the prototype of its new design of bass boats for two-thirds of the planned market price. In order to finance his purchase, Ben took out a bank loan of $12,000. The bank refused to accept the untested product as

continued on page 391

concluded

security for the loan, so Ben put up his $25,000 arrowhead collection instead. In addition, he made the bank his agent to sell the collection in case he defaulted on the loan. Because of the bank's security interest in the subject matter of the agency, Ben could not terminate it except by repaying the $12,000.

The agency can also be terminated by success, in other words, by the achievement of the purpose for which it was created. Finally, the agency can be terminated by mutual agreement of the parties.

By the Law

As you might expect, the death or permanent incapacity (for example, through insanity) of either the principal or the agent usually works an automatic termination of the agency. If an agent makes a contract with a third party on behalf of a principal who has, without the agent's knowledge, become incapacitated or deceased, the agent may be liable to the third party. This is because an agent is held to an implied warranty of having the principal's authorization to act. However, the third party cannot recover against the principal's estate.

Bankruptcy terminates many agencies. If the principal is the subject of the bankruptcy proceeding, the agency is canceled. If the agent is the subject, the agency may continue at the wish of the parties involved unless the agent cannot perform because of the need to commit personal funds to the endeavor. For example, a real estate agent who is the subject of a bankruptcy proceeding might lack access to the resources necessary to advertise and sell the principal's property.

Finally, if carrying out the agency becomes impossible, the agency relationship is terminated. The destruction of the subject matter or a change of law rendering essential agency actions illegal discharges the agency due to impossibility.

Notice of Termination Is Required

Except where the agency is discharged as a matter of law, the principal has the duty to give notice of its termination. This notice must be given to parties with whom the agent has had prior dealings for the principal. If the principal fails to give adequate notice, he or she is liable on contracts negotiated by the former agent with such parties.

Vocabulary Development

Fill in the blanks with the appropriate term.

Agency	**Agent**	**Gratuitous Agency**	**Principal**
Agency by Estoppel	**Apparent Authority**	**Limited Power of**	**Ratified**
Agency Coupled with	**General Power of**	**Attorney**	**Scope of Authority**
an Interest	**Attorney**	**Power of Attorney**	**Undisclosed Principal**

1. An agency that neither party has the power to terminate is the _____.

2. When the court stops a person from denying that an agency exists, a(n) _____ is in effect.

3. A written agency agreement is referred to as a(n) _____.

4. The range of power given an agent is called her or his _____.

5. An agency in which the agent does not receive any compensation is labeled a(n) _____.

Problems

1. Which of the following statements are true?
A minor can be an agent.
A minor can be a principal.
An employee can be made an agent of her or his employer.
A power of attorney must be in writing.

2. Wyn Drow sold used farm equipment as an agent for Agri-Vate Corporation. The terms of his agency agreement allowed him to keep half of whatever amount over cost he was able to obtain from the sale of the equipment. Wyn kept his money receipts from the agency in his personal bank account along with the money receipts from his other businesses. When a fire burned his records, he could not determine how much of the money in the account he owed Agri-Vate. Agri-Vate brought suit. How much of that money could the court award Agri-Vate to satisfy its claim?

3. Chung ("Stretch") Minh delivered custom-made limousines to various points around the country for the Elegant Transportation Company of Pennsboro, Missouri. He also served as the company's agent in selling such vehicles to those who inquired about them during his trips. Unbeknownst to Elegant, Chung took several friends along on these trips. His friends would enjoy use of the limos' built-in TVs, VCRs, sound systems, liquor cabinets, and other luxury appointments. They would also pose as famous personalities. During Chung's last trip, his friends got out of hand and caused him to negligently run off the road, through a fence, and into the African game preserve of the famous Animal Land of Ohio. The downed fence allowed the escape of several exotic animals, some of which were never recovered. In addition, in an argument that followed the accident, Chung assaulted the preserve's owner. Is Elegant liable for the damages to the preserve or to the person of its owner?

4. The limo was barely damaged. When Chung called in to report the accident, he was ordered to return to Pennsboro and was told that not only was he no longer an agent of Elegant but that he would be terminated as an employee as soon as he got back. Acting out of spite, Chung then drove the limo to the home of an individual who had asked him about buying one several weeks earlier. There he negotiated the sale of the limo to that individual for about one-third of its regular price. Is Elegant bound by the sales contract? Does Elegant have any recourse against Chung?

Missouri Farmers Association, Inc. v. Willie May Busse

767 S.W.2d 109

Consider whether one spouse has the authority to bind the other spouse to contracts without the knowledge of that other spouse.

Tom and Willie May were farmers. Raising cattle was part of their business. On March 18, 1978, Tom executed a credit agreement with the Missouri Farmers Association, Inc. (MFA). That agreement obligated Tom to pay the balance due, court costs, attorney's fees, and finance charges if the account became delinquent. When Tom died, an outstanding balance of $17,000 was owed to the account. Although Willie May did not dispute that supplies were received from MFA and that $17,000 was due on the account, she asserted that she was not liable personally for the amount due. She stated that

although her part in the cattle business included ordering and picking up cattle feed and grain from the MFA, she did not know of the credit agreement and did not remember being present when Tom signed it.

Questions

1. Do you think that one spouse should be an implied agent able to bind the other spouse to contracts? Why or why not?

2. Do you think the law holds that, without any other proof, the marital relationship alone creates such an agency?

3. What argument other than the existence of an implied agency could you make for binding Willie May to the credit agreement?

How Is the Employment Relationship Created, Managed, and Terminated?

CHAPTER OUTLINE AND OBJECTIVES

After studying this chapter, the student will be able to:

I. Explain what employment is and why it is important to distinguish employment from similar relationships.

II. Identify the basic duties imposed by law on the employer and the employee.
  a. Duties of the employer
  b. Duties of the employee

III. Explain how an employment contract is terminated.

IV. Describe how the employment relationship is regulated by government.
  a. The National Labor Relations Act
  b. The Fair Labor Standards Act
  c. The Occupational Safety and Health Act
  d. The Equal Employment Opportunity Commission
  e. Workers' Compensation laws
  f. Social Security programs for workers
  g. The Americans with Disabilities Act and the Family and Medical Leave Act

V. Discuss the issue of sexual preference and employability after reading the case of *John Doe* v. *William Webster, Director, Central Intelligence Agency.*

What Is Employment, and Why Is It Important to Distinguish It from Similar Relationships?

The second of these two questions needs to be answered first, at least in broad terms. Why distinguish employment from similar relationships? If for no other reason, to motivate us to study the employment relationship. Simply put, without that relationship most of the productive work in our society would not get done. The alternatives to that relationship, such as slavery, the feudal system, and the communistic production credo ("From each according to his ability, to each according to his need") have been cast aside. Basically, if we want to be properly fed, clothed, and housed, employment is important to us. However, a second reason is probably more relevant to the subject matter of this book, namely that the employment relationship is blanketed with more statutory and administrative regulations than any other. We'll discuss a lot of those regulations later. For now, however, it is sufficient to say that a businessperson who fails to distinguish employees from agents or independent contractors and to treat those who are employees accordingly will quickly be ensnared in violations, regulators, and legal fees.

Employment: relationship in which one party pays another to do work under the control and direction of the first party

Employee: payee of employer and party working under employer's control and direction

Employer: payor of workers and party providing workers with control and direction

Independent Contractor: party performing job for another but not subject to the other's direction and control

Actually, **employment** is simply defined as a relationship in which one party (the **employer**) pays another party (the **employee**) to do work under the control and direction of the first party. The detailed terms of this relationship are found in the employment contract that binds the parties, which can be oral or written. The terms of the contract can be either expressly set down or implied by the court from the course of dealings. Like any other contract, it must contain all the essential elements of a contract in order to be enforceable.

The employment relationship is distinguished from an agency by the fact that whereas the agent is authorized to contract on behalf of her or his principal, the employee under the basic employment contract is not so authorized. An **independent contractor,** like an employee, is someone who agrees to do a job for another, but unlike an employee, an independent contractor will perform in his or her own way and is not subject to the direction and control of the person with whom he contracted to do the job. Generally, only the final result need be satisfactory to that person for whom the independent contractor is working. Of course, that is not the case with the employer–employee relationship, in which the employer controls the details of the employee's performance.

HYPOTHETICAL CASE

The Larger Area of Pennsboro Stock Exchange (LAPSE) needed a new manager. Consequently, it decided to pay an independent contractor, ExecuTrak, $5,000 to locate five candidates with the special skills necessary to do the job. When Execu-Trak submitted its list, the LAPSE made its former manager its agent to interview the candidates and ultimately negotiate an employment contract with the one who its former manager considered best qualified. The former manager did so, and thereby provided the LAPSE with a new manager who was also a new employee.

The degree of the employer's control over and, as a consequence, responsibility for what happens to the employee, the product, and the consumer is the rationale for the close regulatory scrutiny that employers are given. Before we examine the regulatory web that envelops the employment relationship, we need to go over the basic duties that the common law identifies as being owed to each other by the parties to the employment contract.

What Basic Duties Are Imposed by Law on the Employer and the Employee?

Before detailed regulation of the work environment began several decades ago, the common law had created legal standards that it enforced against the participants in the employment relationship. Those standards are still valid today. They are usually stated in terms of the duties that the participants owe to each other and are in addition to the duties expressed in an oral or written employment contract. Most of them parallel the duties pertinent to agency law.

Duties of the Employer

Compensation.   As you may suspect, the employer's primary duty to the employee is to compensate the employee, principally by wages or salary, for the work done by that employee. Such compensation can include **fringe benefits.** These are forms of payment not directly related to work performance such as pensions, vacation time, and free insurance.

Fringe Benefits: forms of payment not directly related to job performance

Many employment contracts are **terminable at will** unless they specify a fixed term. Such at will relationships can be ended without notice by either party at any time without producing a litigable cause of action. However, if a fixed period of employment has been contracted for and compensation has not been provided according to its terms, the employee is justified in quitting. In fact, as long as the employee shows herself ready, willing, and able to perform during the fixed period, the compensation is due whether or not any work was performed.

Terminable at Will: contract that either party may legitimately end at any time without notice

HYPOTHETICAL CASE

The Miracle Motor Company of Lockewood, Colorado, hired three full-time employees for a period of one year. The three were to do the dealer prep work on the new car models that the company sales staff sold during this period. Unfortunately, due to a strike at the manufacturing plant, no new models were available for sale during most of the year. Nevertheless, the three showed up for work each day, ready, willing, and able to perform. Miracle Motor Company therefore had to pay them for the entire period.

Reasonable Range of Duties and Treatment.   A second duty owed by the employer to the employee is to properly set out a reasonable range of tasks for the employee and to treat the employee properly in the performance of those tasks.

The employee cannot be required to perform acts outside the scope of the job as defined in the employment contract. Such extracontractual requests would provide the employee with adequate legal grounds to justify termination of the employment relationship. However, quitting a job merely because the treatment is harsher than expected or the tasks are more difficult than expected is not legally defensible.

In addition, the employer is not permitted to subject the employee to unreasonably harsh treatment, such as assaults or batteries. For example, should the employer inflict a beating on the employee, the employee can quit without any fear of liability for breach of contract.

HYPOTHETICAL CASE

To make money for school, O'Neil agreed to work through the summer as a detail person at a local car wash. She would dry each car with a chamois, then clean the ashtrays and floors of the vehicle. Late one afternoon, she inadvertently spilled a half-full container of milk that had been left open on the dash of a brand-new luxury car. Her boss saw her do so and yelled at her, calling her a "clumsy fool." He then helped her clean up the mess. Unfortunately, they could not get out all of the milk. When the milk that had soaked deep into the pile curdled and started to smell, the owner brought the car back and demanded new carpeting. The cost to the car wash came to over $1,100. When O'Neal's boss got the bill, he walked up to her, pulled her by the hair, and threatened her. O'Neal then quit and sued him for assault and battery.

Note that insulting O'Neal by calling her a "clumsy fool" did not give her a legal basis for quitting. Only the later assault and battery provided her with a legal basis for quitting without fear of legal recourse for breach of the employment contract.

Proper Work Environment. Because of the employee's lack of control over the details of how the work is done, the law maintains that, as a minimum, she or he is entitled to a safe work environment. Unsafe working conditions provide the employee with another justification for ending the employment relationship without liability for breach of contract. The employee's recourses against the employer for injuries sustained in an unsafe work environment are covered later in this chapter.

Duties of the Employee

As with the duties of the employer, many of the employee's duties, such as obedience, loyalty, and reasonable care and skill, find their basis in agency law. However, the first duty of the employee discussed below, providing production in return for compensation, is at the heart of the exchange inherent in all employment relationships but is not found in all agencies.

Production.   The primary duty of any employee is to produce a satisfactory work product. Work that is below standard in either quality or quantity can result in justifiable discharge of the employee.

Obedience.   Implicit in the employment relationship is the employee's agreement to submit to the detailed control and direction of the employer. As noted earlier, it is this detailed oversight that distinguishes the employment relationship from that involving the independent contractor or agent. Unlike them, the employee must obey the lawful orders and rules of the employer that fall within the scope of employment. Failing to do so provides grounds for dismissal.

HYPOTHETICAL CASE

A government safety inspector ordered Dark-Oak Enterprises, a woodworking firm, to provide all of its employees with safety glasses. The firm did so and issued a rule that all employees were to wear the glasses while within 5 feet of a woodworking machine. Johnson found the glasses annoying, especially in the heat of summer. She therefore refused to wear them. After several warnings, Dark-Oat properly terminated her employment.

Loyalty.   In return for the compensation paid, the employer buys not only obedience but an expectation of loyalty. Loyalty does not extend beyond the job, however. So although it is certainly justifiable for an employer to expect that its employee will not reveal confidential information or otherwise do harm to its business, the employer cannot demand that the employee use its products in his or her private life.

Reasonable Care and Skill.   Unless hired to take part in a training program, the employee impliedly warrants that she or he has the skills needed to perform the job properly and with the proper care. If experience shows that this is not the case, the employer is justified in discharging the employee.

One of the main reasons for the employer to discharge an improperly qualified employee is the potential liability if such an employee injures someone or something while acting within the scope of employment. In such a situation, the employer can be held vicariously liable for the harm done. **Vicarious liability** is a legal doctrine that imposes responsibility on the party for the actionable conduct of another party based on an existing relationship between the two parties. In the areas of employer–employee or principal–agent relationships, the rule of law placing vicarious liability on the employer or principal is known as **respondeat superior** (let the master answer). This rule allows an injured party to hold the servant and the master jointly liable for the harm done by the former. As you probably suspect, the justification for the rule lies in the high degree of control that the employer exercises over the employee. As long as the employee is acting within the scope of employment, the detailed training and directives given by the employer make the employer accountable for the employee's harmful actions. However, holding a "deep pocket" such as the employer liable does not release the employee from responsibility.

Vicarious Liability: doctrine imposing legal responsibility on one person for the actionable conduct of another

Respondeat Superior: let master answer

Figure 29–1　　　**Duties of the Employee and the Employer**

Employee's Duties	Employer's Duties
To produce a satisfactory work product	To compensate the employee
To obey lawful orders and rules of the employer that are within the scope of the employment	To be reasonable in defining jobs
	To treat employees properly
To be loyal to the employer's best interests	To provide a proper work environment
To perform with reasonable care and skill	

In contrast to the willingness of the courts to affix civil liability on the employer for the employee's tortious acts, criminal acts generally remain the sole responsibility of the employee. Unless the employer has specifically authorized the crime, the criminal intent of the master simply cannot be inferred from the servant's acts. There are exceptions to this rule, the most glaring being the criminal responsibility placed on the employers of those who, even against their employers' directions, sell impure foods or alcoholic beverages to minors or to persons too inebriated to drive.

How Is an Employment Contract Terminated?

The general rule regarding termination of the employment relationship is that unless termination is inhibited by an employment contract or a collective bargaining agreement, the relationship can be ended at any time by any party to it for practically any reason. This is the "at will" termination that we mentioned earlier. Such terminations do not ordinarily give rise to any litigable causes of action (again, unless there is a contract or an agreement setting standards for dismissal).

There are exceptions to this rule. Some (but few) states require that firings be made as a result of good faith evaluations of the various factors involved in employment. Other states protect employees who are fired for refusing to violate the law or for failing to waive their rights under certain laws, such as workers' compensation. Most states, though, still cling to the at will perspective. Finally, the federal government has legislated exceptions in favor of "whistle-blowers," persons who alerted the authorities to improprieties in the conduct of their employer (even when the federal government was that employer).

Agreements Not to Compete: employment contract terms constraining former employees from entering into competition with former employers

Note that employers who must impart secret information on product formulas or vital processes often have **agreements not to compete** in their employment contracts. Such agreements limit the ability of a worker to enter into competition with his or her former employer for a reasonable period after termination of the employment relationship. If written too broadly, agreements of this kind fly in the face of federal laws intended to spur competition. The courts will either void such an agreement or "blue-pencil" (reduce) it to reasonable proportions.

Angela Pilet worked for Crowson's Fried Chicken in Columbia, Missouri, for three years. Shortly after she left its employment, she started her own fried chicken restaurant, using the recipes and the cooking and serving processes that she had learned at Crowson's. Crowson's promptly filed suit asking the court to enforce the agreement not to compete in Angela's employment contract with it. The contract term read, "I will not compete with Crowson's for a period of three years after leaving its employ or within a 10-mile radius of any of its stores." The court agreed to uphold the agreement, but only after blue-penciling it down to one year and 1 mile from the Crowson's outlet in which Angela had worked.

How Is the Employment Relationship Regulated by Government?

The government often seeks to intervene in the employment relationship, typically to balance out the degree of control vested in the employer. Such intervention comes mainly from the federal government in the form of statutorily authorized regulation.

The National Labor Relations Act (also referred to as the Wagner Act)

Government measures prior to the passage of the National Labor Relations Act (NLRA) in 1935 had legitimized negotiations over conditions and terms of employment between representatives of a work force and its employer (called **collective bargaining**), but the NLRA went further by creating a system of governmental oversight that sought to assure fairness and order in the process. It set up procedures for selecting a bargaining representative as well as for conducting collective bargaining. In addition, the NLRA made illegal certain activities on the part of a union or an employer. The prohibited activities were referred to as **unfair labor practices.** They included the refusal to participate in collective bargaining, firings or other discriminatory actions in retaliation for union activity, the inhibition of employees' right of organization, and improper interference with or control over the creation or running of a union.

Collective Bargaining: negotiations between representatives of work force and its employer

Unfair Labor Practices: employee or employer behavior outlawed by NLRA

Finally, the NLRA created an administrative body to oversee its application. This body, called the National Labor Relations Board (NLRB), investigates and makes determinations on complaints of NLRA violations, especially as to unfair labor practices.

After World War II, in a much more positive economic environment than that of the depression-burdened 1930s, Congress passed, over President Truman's veto, amendments to the NLRA in the form of the Taft-Hartley Act of 1947. Taft-Hartley attempted to achieve a better balance in the provisions of the NLRA by stipulating a number of unfair labor practices that

Strike: refusal to work for employer in order to win contract demands

Boycott: refusal to do business in order to obtain concessions

Secondary Boycott: entity pressuring third parties to agree to cease doing business with firm with which entity is involved in dispute

restricted unions as well as employers. It prohibited union coercion of individual employees, made it illegal for unions to refuse to bargain collectively with an employer, required unions to give notice of their intent to **strike** (refuse to work for an employer in order to win contract demands), allowed employers more freedom of speech to comment on unionization, and prohibited secondary boycotts. (A **boycott** is a refusal to do business with a particular person or firm in order to obtain concessions. A **secondary boycott** involves causing third parties to agree to cease doing business with a firm with which a union is involved in a dispute.)

HYPOTHETICAL CASE

> The Retail Clerks and Busboys Union of Pennsboro, Missouri, had organized the workers in that community's largest chain of grocery stores. Other stores remained without unions but paid union scale wages. In response, the Retail Clerks placed billboard ads at a number of locations near the nonunionized stores urging the general public to boycott those stores. One of the nonunionized stores, Smithson's, filled a complaint with the NLRB against what it termed the secondary boycott urged by the ads. The complaint, however, was disallowed as no agreement was involved.

Right-to-Work Laws: state laws prohibiting collective bargaining agreements from requiring union memberships as condition of employment

The Taft-Hartley Act also contained provisions allowing the president of the United States to request through the US attorney general that a federal district court order an 80-day "cooling-off" period in the event of a strike severely endangering the nation's well-being. During the 80 days, the strikers must return to work and may be required to vote on the latest contract offer during the 61st–75th days. Finally, the Taft-Hartley Act allowed the individual states to pass laws prohibiting collective bargaining agreements from requiring union membership as a condition of employment. Such laws, called **right-to-work laws,** are in place in about 40 percent of the states.

In 1959 another set of significant amendments was made to the federal labor laws. These provisions were intended to help clean up corruption within the unions. Titled as the Labor-Management Reporting and Disclosure Act (also referred to as the Landrum-Griffin Act), the law contains a statement of rights for union members, including the right of voting in union elections, the right of access to union financial statements, and the right to voice their concerns at union meetings.

The Fair Labor Standards Act

Another piece of legislation that directly affects the employment relationship also originated in the 1930s. The Fair Labor Standards Act (FLSA), passed in 1938, sets the basic parameters of hours and wages for any person who works in or produces goods for interstate commerce. Many state laws echo the FLSA standards and make them applicable to persons not covered under the FLSA. Under the provisions of the FLSA, no covered worker can be employed for more than 40 hours a week without being paid time and a half for overtime. In addition, the law sets a floor under hourly wages, called the **minimum wage,** and prohibits the employment of individuals who are 13 or younger.

The exemptions from the FLSA standards are numerous. Among those who lack the protection of the act's provisions are managers; scientists; local, state, and federal employees; employees of retail and service businesses with gross annual sales of less than $250,000; outside salespeople; and those for whose exemption special permission has been wrested from the US Department of Labor. In the same vein, exemptions are granted to certain occupations for minors. For example, minors 13 and under can be employed to deliver newspapers, act, and work on farms as long as the work is not hazardous. Between the ages of 14 and 16, minors can also be employed as office workers and gas station attendants but not in factories or around machines or in hazardous work areas.

The Occupational Safety and Health Act

In 1970 Congress created the Occupational Safety and Health Administration (OSHA). OSHA's purpose is to establish and enforce federal health and safety standards in the workplace. Employees have the right to request an OSHA inspection if they suspect a violation of an OSHA rule or regulation. If the inspection reveals such a violation, the employer is cited and required to appear at a hearing to defend against being penalized. OSHA inspectors conducting an investigation are required to have search warrants if they do not receive the employer's voluntary assent to inspection.

Willy Hastings worked in the paint shop of a small manufacturer in Tabletop, Kansas. His co-worker, Tom Allen, had been painting the manufacturer's products for years. After work Willy and Tom would occasionally meet for a few beers at a local pub. Willy would watch as Tom hacked up clots of the orange rust inhibitor they used in most of their jobs. The "paint shack," as their boss called it, was not ventilated, and even while Willy and Tom wore masks, the hovering vapors penetrated into their air passages and lungs. One day, Tom did not show up for work. When Willy inquired, he was told that Tom had collapsed at the bowling alley the previous evening and was in the hospital. Two months later Tom died of a rare lung disease. Willy then called OSHA and, requesting anonymity, reported the lack of ventilation in the paint shack. OSHA investigated and cited the employer. Eventually, a ventilator was installed. However, the employer came to suspect Willy as the reporting party. Although never questioning him about the matter or discussing it with him directly, the employer served Willy with implicit notice that his future with the company might be limited. Willy quit the next year to return to school. [Based on an actual incident.]

The Equal Employment Opportunity Commission and Discrimination

Every time factors other than the ability to perform the task at hand affect who is hired, promoted, or discharged in the workplace, we all pay a higher price for our goods and services because they have not been produced by the most efficient employees. In addition, when the best worker is turned away because of improper discrimination based on such factors as sex, race, and color, we are lowered in an ethical sense. The apathetic acceptance of such activities by a citizenry and its leaders debases a nation. In recognition of these facts, Congress passed the Civil Rights Act of 1964. That act established the Equal Employment Opportunity Commission (EEOC) and authorized it to utilize litigation and conciliation to fight against **discrimination in employment.** Title VII of the Civil Rights Act makes such discrimination illegal and defines it as hiring, promoting, or discharging on the basis of race, color, sex, religion, or national origin. Amendments to the Civil Rights Act gave the EEOC power to compel employers (with over 15 employees whose business has an impact on interstate commerce), unions, employment agencies, and other entities to eliminate improper direct discrimination on these bases. In addition, the EEOC can act against the more subtle discrimination inherent in supposedly neutral rules that have an improper impact (requiring security guards to be at least 6 feet tall and to weigh at least 200 pounds, for example, a requirement likely to produce an all-male force).

> **Discrimination in Employment:** hiring, promoting, or discharging on basis of race, color, sex, religion, or national origin

The EEOC also enforces the Equal Pay Act of 1963, which precludes the use of sex as a basis for paying one worker less than another who is performing similar work. The opportunity for all aspects of compensation, from overtime to pensions, must be equal for men and women doing jobs that are performed under similar working conditions and require the same levels of effort, skill, and responsibility.

Another act enforced by the EEOC is the Age Discrimination in Employment Act. This federal law, passed in 1967, makes it illegal for private employers to discriminate against persons because they are 40 or over. In addition to prohibiting age discrimination in hiring, firing, promotion, or pay, the act prohibits advertising for job applicants in terms that suggest a preference for youth or for persons in a particular age bracket. Even advertising a desire for a "recent graduate" is improper.

Other statutes in the area of discrimination include:

The Rehabilitation Act—requires the hiring and promotion of handicapped individuals by employers who do more than $2,500 worth of government business in a year.

The Pregnancy Discrimination Act—requires that an employer treat pregnancy, giving birth, and the recovery from delivery in the same manner in which other physical problems producing an inability to work are treated.

Federal Regulation 29—requires the elimination of harassing sexual advances, requests for sexual favors, and other verbal or physical abuse of a sexual nature. When such sexual harassment comes from a supervisor, the employer is strictly liable for the improper conduct. When it comes from co-workers, the employer is liable only if the supervisor knows or should have known of the conduct and have not taken effective action to eliminate it.

Bona Fide Occupational Qualifications. It is important to note that exceptions are made in some of the discriminatory categories mentioned above. These exceptions typically fall under what are termed *bona fide occupational* *qualifications* (BFOQs), which are occupational qualifications that allow types of discrimination that are reasonably necessary to the conduct of a specific business. Here, what is "reasonable" is the issue. Is it reasonable to have only Baptists as faculty members at a Baptist college? Is it reasonable to have only men as guards in an all-male maximum security prison? Is it reasonable to have only men as frontline combatants in war? The answers vary dramatically from person to person, interest group to interest group, government entity to government entity, political party to political party, time to time, and at law.

Affirmative Action Plans.   One of the most controversial current areas in discrimination law involves **affirmative action plans.** Such plans are "voluntarily" created by employers according to EEOC guidelines. They set down methods and time frames for actions to eliminate the adverse impact of an employer's past discriminatory practices on certain such subgroups as women and racial minorities. Percentages are used as general guidelines to determine whether or not an adverse impact exists. Individuals in the adversely impacted subgroups may then be hired or promoted ahead of similarly or better-qualified employees to achieve a satisfactory balance. Such actions lead to charges of **reverse discrimination** (government-endorsed favorable hiring, promoting, or discharging based on the prohibited categories of sex, race, etc.) and the use of **quotas** (the setting aside of a certain number of positions to be filled exclusively by the adversely impacted subgroup.)

Affirmative Action Plans: plans to eliminate adverse impact of employer's past discriminatory practices on certain subgroups

Reverse Discrimination: government-endorsed favorable hiring, promoting, or discharging based on otherwise prohibited categorization of workers by sex, race, color, etc.

Quotas: reserving certain number of positions for members of adversely affected subgroup

Workers' Compensation Laws

Long before OSHA, the common law offered workers some hope of protection from unsafe working conditions. If injured because of such a condition, an employee could bring a negligence suit against the employer. If victorious, the employee would not only secure compensation for his own injury but would also serve notice on the employer that failure to correct the condition responsible for the injury could result in additional successful suits. Regretfully, the state of the law at the time was such that even if the employer's negligent violation of the duty to provide reasonably safe working conditions could be shown, recovery by the employee was often prevented by certain defenses. These defenses included contributory negligence, assumption of the risk, and the acts of fellow workers.

Contributory negligence of the injured employee, say in not observing safety rules set down by the employer, precluded any recovery even in situations in which the negligence of the employer far outweighed that of the employee. Recovery was also precluded by assumption of the risk, evidenced by the employee remaining on the job after having been shown the dangerous condition that later caused the injury—for example, the open pit or the unsheathed saw blade. Finally, the fellow servant defense meant that if the employer could show that another employee caused the harm, the injured employee could recover only from that employee, not from the employer.

In the 19th century these defenses were commonly available in part because our society wanted to protect its growing businesses. Therefore, the legal system enforced rules that caused individual employees and their families to bear the consequences of disabling on-the-job injuries. Around the turn of the century, as the capitalization of our industrial base became more secure, these defenses slowly eroded. Employee negligence suits became more frequent, and the dollar awards of such suits increased. As an alternative to possibly ruinous recoveries, employers then supported the passage of workers' compensation statutes at the state level. These statutes required employers to buy insurance that would pay injured employees appropriate benefits regardless of fault. Such assurance of benefits was given to employees as a substitute for bringing a negligence suit against the employer. The benefits awardable by the statutes generally encompassed only medical expenses and a certain percentage of the injured employee's lost wages. This eliminated the potential recovery for the pain and suffering derived from the injury. It also proved a good bargain for employers as, by rule of thumb, the recovery for pain and suffering in a court of law is 5 to 10 times the medical expenses.

Vocational Rehabilitation: training to allow new employability

If the employee cannot continue in her or his former occupation because of the injury, the system provides for **vocational rehabilitation** (training to assume another type of job). This takes the place of a recovery for lost future earnings under negligence law.

HYPOTHETICAL CASE

Sherman Henry, the sole breadwinner for his family of six, worked as a master carpenter for an Arkansas construction company. While constructing the roof on a new house, one of Sherman's fellow employees, newly hired and without proper training, placed a thin sheet of plywood over a chimney hole. Sherman stepped on the sheet, broke through, and plummeted three stories. In the fall, he broke his pelvis and several bones in his arm. The workers' compensation system paid for his medical treatment, reimbursed him for several months of lost wages, and assisted in his vocational rehabilitation at a nearby university. The total amount that the system expended on Mr. Henry was $17,000. (Based on an actual incident.)

Eligibility. Most of the injuries that fall under the workers' compensation systems occur while the employee is on the job and are related to the work. In the phrasing of the typical state workers' compensation statute, the injury must "arise out of and in the course of the covered employment."

Potential for Lawsuit regardless of Workers' Compensation System. In certain exceptional instances, the employee is not bound by the workers' compensation laws and can pursue suit against the employer. For example, if the employer does not subscribe to the workers' compensation insurance program although required to do so, the employee may bring suit. In that event, the employer is forbidden to use the defenses mentioned above (fellow servant, assumption of risk, contributory negligence).

The employee may also bring suit if the employer has intentionally acted to harm the employee or has permitted conditions it knows will bring injury to the employee.

Karen Silkwood's father, as administrator of her estate, brought suit against Kerr-McGee because his daughter had been contaminated by plutonium at that company's Cimarron nuclear fuel plant, where she worked. The jury found for Karen's estate and awarded $10 million in punitive damages for the company's tortious conduct.

Finally, suit is still allowed where the employee or the injury is not required to be covered by workers' compensation. In such cases, however, the employer may use the previously mentioned defenses.

Social Security Programs for Workers

The Social Security Act provides programs that supplement some of the others mentioned above. These programs provide relief for qualified individuals who lose their jobs, become disabled, or retire. An in-depth discussion of these aspects of governmental regulation of the employment environment is contained in Chapter 34.

The Americans with Disabilities Act and the Family and Medical Leave Act

The statutory requirements imposed by the recently enacted Americans with Disabilities Act (ADA) also affect what an employer must do for her or his disabled employees. Under the ADA an employer must provide "reasonable accommodations" for a qualified worker who happens to have a substantial physical or mental impairment. What accommodations are reasonable varies with the nature and cost of the impairment and the work requirements. The impairments can be the result of diseases or accidents. The accommodations can include visual aids, hearing aids, alterations in ventilation, lighting (in one case a teacher was allergic to fluorescent light and a classroom therefore had to be rewired for incandescent bulbs), and other elements of the work environment.

The Family and Medical Leave Act (FAMLA) also imposes new requirements on employers. Specifically, employees in covered businesses (those with 50 or more employees) must be allowed to take up to 12 weeks of leave without pay if a child is born or adopted or if the employee or member of the employee's immediate family member develops a serious medical condition. In addition, the employer must maintain health insurance on the employee during the leave and reinstate the employee in the same job or an equivalent job upon return.

APPLICATIONS OF
WHAT YOU'VE LEARNED

Vocabulary Development

Fill in the blanks with the appropriate term.

Affirmative Action Plans	Employee	Quotas	Terminable at Will
Agreements Not to Compete	Employer	Respondeat Superior	Unfair Labor Practice
	Employment	Reverse Discrimination	Vicarious Liability
Boycott	Fringe Benefits	Right-to-Work	Vocational
Collective Bargaining	Independent Contractor	Secondary Boycott	Rehabilitation
Discrimination in Employment	Minimum Wage	Strike	

1. The _____ is the lowest legal hourly wage.

2. A(n) _____ is a work stoppage intended to coerce employers into yielding on disputed issues.

3. The doctrine of _____ allows an employer to be held as the respondeat superior of her or his employees.

4. _____ provides training in new occupations for the disabled.

5. Pension plans, vacation time, and profit sharing are all _____ of certain jobs.

6. _____ laws make it illegal to require that an employee be a union member.

7. A(n) _____ involves a refusal to do business with someone.

Problems

1. In terms of control over his or her work, distinguish an employee from an agent and an independent contractor.

2. The Pennsboro Baptist Church employed Hiram Goodrest, a retired carpenter, to drive a bus for the church school. One evening, while driving the school's basketball team to an away game, Hiram negligently rammed the rear of a car, thus injuring several elderly women. If the women bring suit, whom do you think they will probably name as defendants? What legal doctrine allows this? Would they be able to sue the same parties if Hiram Goodrest were an independent contractor hired to drive for this one trip only?

3. Mike Mass owned and operated a nationwide job hunt service for nuclear engineers. To help him in his work, he hired Sharon Newtron. Mike taught her the entire business. He introduced her to many of his clients and to the entities with which he found them jobs. After five years Sharon quit to found her own job search business for all employees in the nuclear industry, including the engineers. Mike brought suit to enforce the agreement not to compete portion of Sharon's employment contract with him. The agreement specified that for three years after leaving his employ Sharon could not open a competing business or contact any of the clientele or employers she had become acquainted with while in his employ. Sharon responded that, because the nationwide nuclear industry consisted of only a small number of employing entities, enforcing the agreement would exclude her from the market. What do you think the court should do ?

4. Every day at the morning coffee break, the office secretaries gather in the lounge. Steve, the only male secretary, is often chided by female secretaries and occasionally propositioned by them. He has reported the problem to his boss, Victoria Adams, but nothing has been done to correct matters. Can he sue and recover against his employer for sexual harassment?

5. Caprice Whimsey worked as a chemist in a secure area leased by a defense contractor from Grand Bluffs Air Force Base in Kentucky. While working

late one evening, she was raped, badly beaten, and left for dead by Jeremiah Stanton, a custodial employee who had a record of sexual assaults. Her employer had neglected to check its staff for

criminal records. Will she be covered by workers' compensation or instead be allowed to sue her employer for negligence? Why?

ACTUAL CASE STUDY

John Doe v. William H. Webster, Director, Central Intelligence Agency

769 F. Supp. 1

Consider the case of a covert CIA operative who was fired when he told the agency about his homosexuality.

"John Doe" was hired by the Central Intelligence Agency (CIA) in 1973. By 1977, thanks to consistent evaluations of his performance as excellent or outstanding, he was promoted to a position as a covert electronics technician. In early 1982 Doe voluntarily informed a CIA security officer that he was a homosexual. The CIA then placed him on administrative leave and conducted an investigation of the ramifications of his homosexuality. During a polygraph examination, he admitted that he had engaged in homosexual conduct but denied ever having had homosexual relations with any foreign national or ever having discussed classified information with a sex partner. After the evaluations were concluded, Doe was asked to resign. He refused and was then, in May 1982, dismissed by order of the director of the CIA. At that time, he was informed that the agency would give him a positive job recommendation during his job search but that if he applied for a job requiring a security

clearance, it would inform the prospective employer of its conclusion, namely that his homosexuality posed a threat to national security.

Doe maintained that he was denied due process because his dismissal resulted from a blanket CIA policy baring homosexuals who engaged in homosexual activity from CIA employment. Doe maintains that without the individualized appraisal guaranteed by due process through notice and a hearing, he cannot present evidence showing his trustworthiness and employability.

Questions

1. Do homosexuals pose a greater risk to the intelligence services than heterosexuals? (If you have access to a law library, read *High Tech Gays* v. *Defense Industrial Security Clearance Office,* 895 F.2d 563 at p. 568 for a detailed consideration of this issue.)

2. If homosexuals do pose a greater risk, should that justify a blanket policy against their employment by the intelligence services?

3. Should Doe receive the due process he requests?

The Legal Environment of Business: Property, Bailments, and Leaseholds

CHAPTERS

CHAPTER

30

How Is Property Legally Acquired, Held, and Transferred?

CHAPTER OUTLINE AND OBJECTIVES

After studying this chapter, the student will be able to:

I. Define property.

II. Identify the rights and interests that comprise property.

    a. Title

    b. Possession

    c. Use

    d. Alienation

III. Distinguish between the two types of property, real and personal.

IV. Discuss how property is acquired.

    a. Intellectual property

    b. Other personal property

    c. Real property

V. Select the appropriate legal form for holding the ownership of property.

    a. Individual ownership

    b. Joint ownership

VI. Discuss, using the case of *Doe* v. *Keane* as a basis, the issue of a surrogate mother's property rights in the unborn child she carried.

Behold, my brothers, the spring has come . . . Every seed is awakened, and so has all animal life. It is through this mysterious power that we too have our being, and we therefore yield to our neighbors, even our animal neighbors, the same right as ourselves, to inhabit this land. Yet, hear me, people, we have now to deal with another race . . . They claim this mother of ours, the earth, for their own and fence their neighbors away; they deface her with their buildings and their refuse.

Sitting Bull, Sioux warrior and chief, 1877, reacting to US government order that the Sioux leave their treaty-guaranteed hunting grounds, where gold had been discovered

What Is Property?

Rent: pay for right to use or occupy

Property: rights and interests in things

This seemingly simple question has a complex answer. Many of us think of property as things—things we can own or **rent** (pay consideration for the right to use or occupy) or otherwise obtain some right or interest in. In the law, however, a more proper and accurate definition is emphasized. There, **property** is best defined as the rights and interests we recognize that each of us can have in things. Property is not the things themselves. In fact, under our capitalist system, many people can have rights and interests ("property") in the same thing at the same time. For example, you might have the right of ownership of this book by virtue of having purchased it from its previous owner, a campus bookstore. However, you might rent the book to a friend for a semester so that she won't have to buy her own. She might, in turn, let another student have the possession of it to check his notes. All of these individuals have distinct property claims (ownership, possession, and use) on the book. To put it directly, all have property in the same thing. So, it is crucial that you recognize at the outset that "technically" at least, any particular thing is not property. Property is only the rights and interests in things that a particular society allows its citizens. Societies other than ours did not and do not always place the same value on property as we do.

As long as the sun shines and the waters flow, this land will be here to give life to men and animals. We cannot sell the lives of men and animals; therefore we cannot sell this land. It was put here for us by the Great Spirit, and we cannot sell it because it does not belong to us.

A Blackfoot chief rejecting an offer of money by US delegates in return for the tribal lands of the Blackfoot.

What Are the Rights and Interests That We Recognize as Property?

Title: legally endorsed claim of ultimate ownership

The most important of the rights and interests that the law labels property is title. **Title** in property law means a legally endorsed claim to the ultimate ownership of

**The Rights and Interests That We May
Have in Things**

Figure 30–1

- Title
- Possession
- Use
- Destruction, consumption, and alienation

---

something. **Ownership,** in turn, refers to a variety of rights allowing the use and enjoyment of things. These rights, as indicated by the discussion in the preceding section, may be split among many individuals, but the claim of title is their origin and the point to which they return.

Ownership: rights allowing use and enjoyment of things

Possession is another property right. Most of us have heard that it is nine-tenths of the law. Although this greatly overstates the case, **possession** does mean immediate control or power to the exclusion of all others over something. Given what can be done to something in a person's possession, other rights and interests may prove irrelevant.

Possession: immediate control or power over something

Use is a third right of importance. In the case law of property, **use** is defined as the enjoyment of things by their employment. Don't be misled by the word **enjoyment** in the definition. At law, enjoyment means the exercise of a right, not the taking of pleasure, the sense in which the word is commonly used.

Use: enjoyment of things by their employment

Enjoyment: exercise of right

Finally, there are the rights that allow the owner of property to destroy, consume, and **alienate** (transfer title by sale, gift, will, etc.) some or all of it.

Alienate: transfer title to property

HYPOTHETICAL CASE

Eileen bought the old *Pennsboro Press* building from the last editor of the newspaper. Her purchase included all of the property located in the building. Back issues of the *Press* were part of that property. Although Pennsboro's mayor and other Pennsboro citizens asked her to have the issues microfilmed at their expense so as to help preserve the city's history, she declined to do so and burned the issues.

What Are the Different Kinds of Property?

Property is divided into two classifications, real and personal. **Real property** is defined as rights and interests in land, buildings, and fixtures. Note that land is viewed as extending downward to the very center of the earth and upward into the atmosphere above it.

Real Property: rights and interests in land, buildings, and fixtures

Fixtures are tangible, movable things that become permanently attached to land or buildings, such as an oven built into an apartment wall or a trailer permanently moored to a piece of land. Generally, once a tangible, movable thing has become permanently attached to real property, its ownership vests in the owner of that property. This is true regardless of who owned the thing before it

Fixtures: tangible, movable things permanently attached to land or buildings

Trade Fixtures: things permanently attached to real property by someone using that property for business purposes

Premises: real property subject to current legal action

Personal Property: all property save land, buildings, and fixtures

Intangible Property: something that is evidence of value

was attached. **Trade fixtures** are an exception to this rule. Such items are attached to another's realty by a renter to facilitate a business the renter is carrying on in the property. Pizza ovens bolted to a storefront wall or walk-in-freezers in a grocery store or an ice-cream parlor are examples. The ownership of trade fixtures remains with the party renting the **premises** (real property subject to the legal action at hand) and may be taken with her or him after the rental period is complete.

Personal property is basically everything that is not real property. It can be tangible (say a shoe or a pen) or intangible. **Intangible property** is generally some evidence of value, such as a stock certificate, a promissory note, a patent, a copyright, or a trademark. The last three of these items are the main evidences of the intellectual property we defined in Chapter 7.

How Do You Acquire Property?

Intellectual Property

How property is acquired varies with its type. In particular, acquiring intellectual property, unlike acquiring the other categories of personal property, depends largely on compliance with government regulation. As a consequence, we'll first take a look at how patents, copyrights, and trademarks come to be owned by someone. Then we'll deal with the traditional methods of acquiring all categories of personal property. Finally, we'll examine how real property is acquired.

Patent: governmental grant of exclusive rights to use, make, and sell qualified invention for set period of time

Design Patent: governmental grant of exclusive rights in unique configuration or appearance of surface or components of object

Utility Patent: governmental grant of exclusive rights to novel, nonobvious, useful invention

Novel: previously unknown idea typically representing "burst of genius"

Obvious: plainly evident to person with average skill in particular field involved

Useful: possessing utility to society

Patents.   Article I, Section 8, of the US Constitution empowers our government to grant a qualified applicant the exclusive rights to use, make, and sell her or his invention for a set period. Such a grant is called a **patent.** It is the equivalent of a legal monopoly. However, it requires that the inventor make public the substance of the invention so that others may use the ideas it contains as a basis for further developments. The two most important types of patents are the design patent and the utility patent.

A **design patent** protects the unique configuration or appearance of an object's surface or components. To qualify for such protection, the configuration or appearance must be ornamental, original, and not obvious. The term of a design patent's protection is 14 years. Note that some items that qualify for a design patent can also be copyrighted (see below). For example, an automobile manufacturer might try to protect the unique shape of a particular model by acquiring a design patent for it.

The most common type of patent, however, is the **utility patent.** Its 17-year run of exclusive rights is granted for a novel and useful invention that is not obvious. By **novel,** the law impliedly requires a previously unknown idea typically representing a "burst of genius." An idea is **obvious,** and therefore not patentable, if it is plainly evident to a person with average skill in the field involved. **Useful** implies that the invention has a utility of some kind that will reward society for granting patent rights to the applicant.

The subject matter of the invention can be a machine (such as an intermittent windshield wiper), a process (such as xerography), a composition of matter (various prescription drugs), or other articles of manufacture.

If a person **infringes** another's patent (exercises any of the rights granted without authority to do so), the holder of those rights may sue for an injunction stopping the infringement. The holder may also sue for damages, which are usually set in the amount of what would have been a reasonable **royalty** (compensation for the use of property) for the patent rights in question.

Infringement: exercise of right without authority to do so

Royalty: compensation for use of property

HYPOTHETICAL CASE

Arnold Cruise invented a device that "scrubbed" or cleaned over 99.9 percent of the pollutants in the smoke from coal fires for a fraction of the costs of the scrubbers currently in use. On the advice of people he approached to invest in the development of his device, Arnold contacted a patent attorney. The attorney immediately had a computer search conducted through the US government Patent and Trademark Office's database to see whether similar devices had already been patented. Two "hits" came back. The attorney then ordered descriptions of the patented devices. She and Arnold studied the descriptions and determined that they were not that close to Arnold's idea. Next the attorney had a draftsman draw up detailed plans of Arnold's invention. Then she and Arnold sat down and wrote up the "claims" they would make for his invention. These claims or distinguishing points had to be sufficient to cause the patent office to agree that Arnold's invention differed significantly from those previously registered. The patent application was then submitted to the patent office. In the meantime, Arnold made a prototype of the invention and marked it "patent pending." Many investors promised their financial support if the patent did indeed issue. Unfortunately, the patent office turned down the application. Arnold, nonetheless, got together a small amount of capital and began making the devices. Soon the holder of one of the other patents brought suit against him and received an injunction requiring Arnold to cease production. The patent holder was also awarded some $97,000 in damages for lost royalties.

Copyrights. Article I, Section 8, also empowered the federal government (Congress in particular) to "promote the Progress of . . . useful Arts, by securing for limited Times to Authors . . . the exclusive Right to Their . . . writings." The original copyright statute, passed in 1790, granted exclusive protection for such writings for 14 years with a provision for renewal for another 14. Under the current statute, which became effective in 1978, authors of books, composers of music, and originators of similar artistic productions have their works protected for the life of the creator plus 50 years. The **copyright** thus awarded places the exclusive rights to copy, publish, and sell published or unpublished works in the hands of their creator. The works that can now be copyrighted include everything from the traditional books to sound recordings, motion pictures, and videos.

Copyright: exclusive right to copy, publish, and sell published or unpublished works

Should a copyright be infringed, the holder may sue for injunctive relief, damages, and lost profits. Also, the injured holder may ask that the unauthorized copies be destroyed.

Given the widely disseminated copying means now available, such as the photocopier, the VCR, and the cassette deck, one of the main sources of friction in copyright law has to do with permissible copying. How many magazines, newspapers, books, compact discs, and movie tapes have not been sold due to would-be purchasers' access to copying equipment? What has been the long-term effect of such access on the publishing, movie, television, recording, and related industries?

Fair Use Doctrine: rule defining circumstances for lawful unauthorized reproduction of copyrighted material

Regardless, under the **fair use doctrine** the copyright law provides for the unauthorized reproduction of copyrighted material if this is done reasonably so as not to injure the rights of the copyright holder. Accordingly, teachers, reporters, researchers, and commentators can copy items for use in their work. Libraries and like facilities can make unauthorized single copies of copyrighted articles for noncommercial purposes.

Trademarks.   The maker or seller of particular goods often identifies them with a distinctive name or symbol known as a **trademark.** From Coca-Cola to the MGM lion, such marks identify to consumers the level of quality, reliability, and many other attributes of products. For many, the Campbell soup label is protection against the possibility of botulism that haunts the user of the generic brand. (Nonetheless, the holder of the trademark can license its use to others.) Also, under a relatively new federal statute, businesses can even preregister a mark for up to three years before its use if they file the proper application, certify they intend to use the mark, and pay a fee every six months.

Trademark: distinctive name or symbol

Unlike the regulation of patents and copyrights, the regulation of trademarks is not given to the federal government by the Constitution. Instead, there are both state statutes (to handle marks used intrastate) and a federal statute, the Trademark Act of 1946 or Lanham Act (to cover marks used in interstate commerce). The state statutes vary widely. However, the federal statute grants protection to registered marks for 20 years, with the possibility of renewal for additional 20-year periods until the mark has been abandoned.

Marks can also be lost if they lose their distinctive nature. In the 1980s Xerox Corporation became worried because its distinctive name was being genericized. "I'm going to xerox something on the _____ photocopier" (name your own brand here) was being heard all too often. Xerox therefore launched a multimillion-dollar ad campaign to remind consumers that the company name stood for a particular entity and a particular level of service and quality.

Other Personal Property

A wide variety of ways exist to acquire all types of personal property. Asked how you acquire personal property, one person jokingly suggested, "You steal it." Surprisingly, in a sense she was correct. You can acquire possession that way. However, possession is all you will have. Title will remain forever in the true owner, to whom you, and all future possessors, innocent or not, have a legal duty to return the stolen item. Of course, what we are looking for here is how you acquire legitimately full ownership of personal property.

The best place to start is where most law school courses on property start—with wild animals. Back when our forebears were hunter-gatherers, a lot depended on whose property the deer or other felled game was. Once a society was stable enough for such questions to be answered by courts instead of what Will and Ariel Durant in their series of books on civilization referred to as the law of natural society, "which knows no rights except cunning and strength," the answer came through loud and clear:

HYPOTHETICAL CASE

> Barney of Oxfordshire and Fred of Bree, shooting from opposite sides of the deer, each lodged an arrow in it at the same time. The deer bolted. Both men gave chase. The deer collapsed and died after running about 100 yards. Barney was first to it and claimed it. When Fred arrived, he showed that his arrow had produced the mortal wound. To whom should the deer be awarded?

The answer, said the courts, is that the deer belongs to Barney, the first person to reduce it to her or his possession. Barney's family eats well. Fred's ends up hunting lots of edible roots in the forest.

Recovery of Lost, Mislaid, and Abandoned Property.   A similar rule applies to **abandoned property** (property in which the owner has given up all intention of maintaining rights or interests). In such cases the first party to establish dominion and control over whatever has been abandoned owns it.

Lost property is a different story. Such property has been parted with involuntarily due to the negligence or inadvertence of the true owner. When lost property is found, the finder is allowed to retain it until the true owner is found. Lost property must be distinguished from mislaid property. **Mislaid property** was consciously laid aside by the owner, who intended to retrieve it later, but now it cannot be found. When mislaid property is found, the finder must surrender it to the person most likely to contact the true owner during the true owner's search for the property. Whether property is considered lost or mislaid depends on what can be inferred from where it was discovered. For example, a $50 bill found on the floor of a barbershop would probably be treated as lost property and retained by the finder (until the true owner appeared). The same bill found on a counter near the coatrack of the barbershop would be considered mislaid and legally should be rendered to the barber to enhance the chances of its being returned to the true owner.

Both the finder and the ultimate holder of mislaid property have a duty to try to return the property to its rightful owner. Many states have statutes that allow individuals with lost or mislaid property to acquire ownership by making a sincere effort to locate the true owner over a period of time (usually by advertising the situation in a publication of general circulation for a certain number of times over a period of one year). In many jurisdictions, converting lost property to

Abandoned Property: things in which owner has given up all intention of maintaining rights or interests

Lost Property: things owner has involuntarily parted with

Mislaid Property: things owner consciously laid aside but now cannot find

the finder's own use without attempting to find its true owner is considered larceny. In addition, failure to take reasonable care of found property can result in liability for the finder or holder.

Professor Abraham folded up his notes and then watched the students file out of his 9 AM Law I class. The last one, a Bill Turner from nearby Springfield, turned toward him. "Here, Dr. Abraham, this was left in the row down from mine. It's not from our class." Turner headed Abraham a large backpack. Abraham thanked him, then put the backpack on a chair near the door and left a message on the board about it. The backpack disappeared. Due to his failure to take reasonable care (for example, by storing it in his office rather than leaving it where anyone could make off with it), Professor Abraham could be liable if the backpack were taken by someone other than its true owner.

Escheat: right of state to property without existing claimants

Lost or abandoned property without any rightful claimants eventually, usually after several years, reverts to being the property of the state. The right of the state to property without existing claimants is referred to as **escheat** by the common law. (Today, many states have put into law the Uniform Disposition of Unclaimed Property Act to cover this and similar issues.) It was rumored that W. C. Fields, a famous comedian of the 1930s, opened accounts under fictitious names in banks throughout the country, then never returned to collect the money he deposited. In most states, after a 20-year period the unclaimed funds would have escheated to the state in which each of the banks was located.

Gifts. Although it may not happen as often as you'd like, personal property may also be acquired by having it given to you. What could be more simple, right? Well, as you may by now suspect, simplicity in the law is like fairness in the Tax Code—it hasn't happened yet. First of all, the law has determined that you need three elements to have a transfer of ownership. Those three are the intent to give, the delivery of the gift, and the acceptance.

Donor: person or other entity giving gift

Donee: recipient of gift

Inter Vivos: between the living

Causa Mortis: in anticipation of death

The intent of the **donor** (the person or other entity giving the gift) is controlling. If the intent is to make a gift at the present time, then for the gift to be complete it need only be shown that the item involved was delivered to and accepted by the **donee** (the recipient of the gift). Such an absolute, nonconditional gift is labeled **inter vivos** (between the living).

A gift given in anticipation of death, on the other hand, is labeled **causa mortis.** In other words, if a living person, in contemplation of her or his death from a known cause, gives someone a gift, the gift is regarded as conditional. Therefore, should the donor not die as anticipated, either within the projected time frame or of the supposed cause, the gift is legally ineffective. The ownership of the subject matter of the intended gift is then returned to the would-be donor or the donor's estate. The same result (that is, the return of the gift to the donor) is reached if the donee dies before the donor or if the donor takes the gift back before dying of any cause.

HYPOTHETICAL CASE

Sensing his death from cancer to be near, Jim Jones gave Antoine Carver, his longtime friend, a check for the $210,000 in his checking account. Jones then took an overdose of sleeping pills and died. Since Jones did not die of the anticipated cause, the court ordered that the $210,000 be returned, as the gift was causa mortis, that is, conditional on Jones's near immediate death from cancer. As Jones died without a will, the court would split up the money along with the rest of Jones's assets among Jones's surviving relatives.

Legal questions regarding gifts also arise as to delivery. Since people often publicly state their intent to make a gift but do not follow through, the courts must see evidence of delivery to have a completed gift. Transfer of dominion and control over the subject matter of the gift is typically good enough. Even if the physical delivery of the property is not made, for example, transferring the means of access or control to the donee (e.g., the key to the safe-deposit box containing the jewelry) is enough. Such a symbolic act is known as **constructive delivery.**

Constructive Delivery: symbolic transmittal of subject matter

Finally, to be complete a gift requires the donee's acceptance. Such acceptance is generally presumed or, if questioned, can be inferred from an act of the donee indicating that he or she intends to treat the subject matter as his or her own.

HYPOTHETICAL CASE

When she found out that her friend Taipei had voted a split ticket in a recent election, Hillary bought her a mule and a young elephant. She then had them delivered to Taipei's house along with a card indicating the nature of the gift. Taipei, although amused and flattered by Hillary's attention, wanted to refuse the gift. Indecisively, she waited so long to act that the reasonable time during which she could have repudiated passed. As a result, the animals became hers by law.

The area of gifts poses a few other problems for the law. For example, the common law held that gifts given to minors really belonged to the parents. As a consequence, many states have passed Uniform Gifts to Minors acts that prescribe procedures for making sure that such gifts are used in the minor's best interest or will be kept for the minor until she or he reaches adulthood. Another problem is the gift of an engagement ring. In many states the courts hold that if the engagement is broken, the ring is to be returned to the donor. The courts of some states hold just the opposite if it was the donor who broke the engagement. In several states, the position of the courts on this problem seems to change every few years, leaving it a question to which the law cannot give a conclusive answer.

Purchase: transmittal of property from one person to another by voluntary agreement based on valuable consideration

Purchase.   **Purchase** is the most frequently utilized means of acquiring personal property. Purchase is defined as the transmittal of property from one person to another by voluntary agreement based on valuable consideration. Chapters 8–17 on contracts provide in-depth coverage of this method of acquiring personal property.

By Descent or by Will.   Personal property is also acquired through the distribution of the assets of a deceased. Such a distribution is done either according to the wishes of the deceased as expressed in a will or according to the provisions of state statutes should no will be involved, or both. For the details on how this occurs, see Chapter 41.

Accession: acquisition of property by natural increase of property already owned

Accession and Confusion.   Two other means of acquiring personal property are worthy of mention. Both are rather specialized. **Accession** involves the acquisition of property by the natural increase of property already owned (for example, when a cow produces a calf, the calf belongs to the cow's owner) or by the affixing of things to property already owned (for example, a carburetor placed on a car's engine during repairs becomes the property of the car's owner).

Confusion: blending of indistinguishable goods of two or more owners so that share of each cannot be identified

   Confusion is the blending together of indistinguishable goods of two or more owners so that the share of each owner cannot be identified. When such a situation arises, the most innocent party usually receives the ownership of the intermixed whole.

Bailment: acquisition of possession of personal property of another subject to agreement to return it or to deliver it to third party

Bailments.   A **bailment** is the legal relationship created by the acquisition of possession of the personal property of another, subject to an agreement to return it or to deliver it to a third party. Although short of full ownership, this transfer of a personal property right is also worthy of mention here (and full coverage in the next chapter) due to the frequency with which it occurs. From property rentals to "loaning" someone your textbook so that she or he can use it to study for the next exam, bailments involve the transfer of an important part of personal property, the right of possession.

Deed: formal written instrument utilized to transfer title to real property

Warranty Deed: document conveying title and binding assurances

Grantor: transferor of property

Grantee: transferee of property

Quitclaim Deed: document passing whatever claim or interest grantor may have in real property

Real Property.   Like personal property, the ownership of real property can be acquired by gift or by purchase. Should either of these methods be involved, the result is evidenced by a **deed,** a formal written instrument utilized to transfer title to real property. There are two basic types of deeds. The first and most frequently used is a **warranty deed.** Such a deed not only conveys title from the **grantor** (transferor of property) but also contains several warranties for the benefit of the **grantee** (transferee of property). These warranties include legally enforceable assurances that the grantor has title and the right to transfer it, that the grantee will not be disturbed in her or his ownership by someone with a superior claim, and that the property is free from all encumbrances (liens) at the time of transfer. Such assurances are usually very important to a new owner of real property.

   The other type of deed, in contrast to the warranty deed, has none of these protective assurances. Instead, a **quitclaim deed** merely passes whatever claim or interest the grantor may have or might receive in the real property. So if the grantor has only a disputed or partial claim, that's all the grantee gets. No warranties are made in the deed.

By Descent or Will. Like personal property, real property may also be acquired through the distribution of the assets of a deceased. Such distribution is done either according to the wishes of the deceased as expressed in a will or according to the provisions of state statutes, should there be no will, or both. See Chapter 41.

By Adverse Possession. In all of our 50 states ownership of real property can be acquired by occupying it for an extended period. Such occupancy must be open, continuous, exclusive of others, notorious (generally known), and under some rightful claim. The period required varies from 5 to 30 years, depending on the state. Note that land belonging to the government cannot be adversely possessed. Also, the possession has to be without the owner's permission. In some states the adverse claimant's payment of taxes on the land shortens the period necessary for adverse possession. Finally, adverse possession can apply to small portions of land. For example, presume that after a neighbor builds his fence 1 foot onto your land, you protest but take no further action. After the statutory period has run, the neighbor owns the land enclosed by the fence.

HYPOTHETICAL CASE

After her husband, Hutton Larue, died and left her several pieces of real property, Jewell Larue, then 75 years old, pulled into herself. As a consequence, she neither realized nor cared when Benton Hill moved onto one of the pieces, claiming that her husband had sold it to him before he died. A little over 10 years afterward, Benton Hill sued in court for an acknowledgment that he had adversely possessed the land and thus obtained a title to it. The court agreed and awarded the land to him.

Eminent Domain. At times, ideally for the good of the whole, private land has to be taken for public use. The right of governments and other public bodies at the federal, state, and local level to do so is referred to as **eminent domain.** Hospitals, schools, parks, and highways for public use are all made possible through the use of this right. The owners of the public land must receive "just compensation" according to the Fifth Amendment to the US Constitution. The amount of this compensation can be determined by a court if necessary. However, as has often been pointed out, no amount of money can make up the loss to the elderly widow who is forced out of her home that she shared with her lifemate and in which she raised her family and stored the memories of a lifetime.

Eminent Domain: governmental right to take private property for public use

HYPOTHETICAL CASE

Mrs. McWilliams, an 85-year-old widow living near campus, refused the University of Springfield's final "fair value" offer for her home. The university's population was expanding, and the land was said to be needed for a parking lot. Upon her refusal, the university went to court for a final determination of the amount that Mrs. McWilliams would have to accept for her property.

Leaseholds, Easements, and Profits. Rights and interests short of full ownership are also acquirable in real property. For example, a **leasehold** gives the recipient the right to the exclusive possession of the premises involved for a certain term. Leaseholds are discussed in detail in Chapter 32. An **easement** gives someone the right to use the land of another for a variety of purposes. Utility companies often need to obtain easements from property owners in order to run their lines. Also, owners of an adjacent parcel of land may have an easement across another property to allow them access to theirs. A **profit** is the right to take from the soil of the land of another, for example, to mine for minerals, extract timber, or drill for oil.

Leasehold: right to exclusive possession of premises for a certain term

Easement: right to use land of another

Profit: right to take from soil of land of another

HYPOTHETICAL CASE

> Wildcatters, Inc., bought the right to drill for oil on Tricia Horton's land. However, in order to reach the spot on which they intended to place their oil rig, Wildcatters had to and did purchase an easement from Grant, who owned the adjacent property. Wildcatters did not have to purchase a similar right from Horton because the profit they had already obtained from her implied the right of access across her land. When Grant subsequently leased his land to Buford, Buford still had to allow Wildcatters its access.

Other Interests in Real Property. Creditors often acquire interests in the property of their debtors. A **mortgage,** for example, is a device that transfers the right to have the subject real property sold to satisfy an unpaid debt. Such a right or lien is given by the debtor (**mortgagor**), who thereby transfers one of the ownership rights that he or she has in the property, to the creditor (**mortgagee**), who lends value to the debtor in return for such secured repayment. Mechanic's and tax liens, discussed in Chapter 23, allow roughly the same rights as the mortgage, but generally without the debtor's direct assent. Finally, individuals can have certain privileges in using the real property of others. For example, a deliveryperson or a business customer may be allowed access to real property, depending on the circumstances. (See the discussion on trespassers, licensees, and business invitees in Chapter 32.)

Mortgage: right to have subject real property sold to satisfy unpaid debt

Mortgagor: transferor of mortgage

Mortgagee: transferee of mortgage

What Are the Legal Forms for Holding the Ownership of Property?

Individual Ownership

Persons who own property may do so individually or with others. In the former situation, where there is only one owner, that owner is said to hold the property in **severalty.** This is the simplest and most common form of ownership. When there are two or more owners, property can be held in a variety of ways. These are

Severalty: ownership of property by one individual

**By What Means Can an Individual Acquire
Ownership of Real and/or Personal Property?**   **Figure 30–2**

- By intellectual creativity
- By establishing dominion and control over abandoned property
- By gift
- By purchase
- By receiving it from a decedent's estate
- By accession
- By confusion
- By deed
- By adverse possession

---

discussed below and include tenancy in common, joint tenancy, and tenancy by the entirety. (Note that, back in Chapters 25–27, we have already discussed the combined ownership of property by individuals grouped as business entities. Also note that we will discuss various tenancies relating to the sole right of possession of property in Chapter 32.)

Joint Ownership

All three of the above-mentioned tenancies involve different rights that various co-owners enjoy in the subject property. A **tenant in common,** for example, is a co-owner of the undivided property in question who can transfer her or his ownership interest without the permission of the other co-owners. Like the other cotenants, a tenant in common is entitled to possess the entire premises. The creditors of a tenant in common can use her or his interest to satisfy their legal claims. Also, a tenant in common can call for **partition** (division of the property or of the value received for it) if desired. Finally, the shares of tenants in common do not have to be equal to one another.

> **Tenant in Common:** coholder of transferable ownership right to share of undivided property in question

> **Partition:** division of subject property or of value received for it

Like a tenant in common, a **joint tenant** is defined by and enjoys a different set of rights in relation to the subject property. Specifically, a joint tenant is legally considered to own all of the subject property. As all joint tenants are considered to have equal rights in the subject property, this means that each of the two, three, or more owners is considered by the law to own all of a single thing. Life in general teaches us that such an obvious divergence from reality is indicative of a need for either therapy or a good lawyer. In this case the divergence is what is known as a legal fiction and as such is accepted as an irrefutable tenet of belief by the entire legal profession, and so you must accept it as well. In addition to owning all of the subject property, each of the joint tenants also has the **right of survivorship.** This means that when a joint tenant dies, the entire ownership remains with the surviving tenants and is not subject to the claims of the deceased's family or estate. If a joint tenant transfers his or her ownership rights, the transferee becomes a tenant in common with the other joint tenants. Finally, partition is allowed and the creditors of one joint tenant may

> **Joint Tenant:** coholder of transferable ownership right to entire undivided property in question

> **Right of Survivorship:** upon death, ownership of subject property remains solely with surviving cotenant(s) of deceased

reach the property held by all of the other joint tenants to satisfy outstanding debts.

Tenants by the Entirety:
husband and wife coholders of nontransferable ownership right to entire subject property

Tenants by the entirety must be husband and wife. The old common law treated spouses as one person, so such tenants each own all of the property in the same manner as joint tenants. Thus, each spouse has the right of survivorship in relation to the subject property. However, the separate action of one spouse, such as falling into debt, cannot work a detriment on what is owned by both as tenants by the entirety. In other words, neither creditors solely of the husband nor creditors solely of the wife can reach property that both hold as tenants by the entirety. Both husband and wife must have signed any debt instrument in order to allow the creditor of the debt to take the collateral held in tenancy by the entireties upon default. (Note that, unlike the situation in states accepting the common law approach that each spouse owns whatever he or she earns unless both spouses agree to share, in nine of our states each spouse is automatically considered to have an undivided one-half interest in whatever the other spouse earns. In those states the creditors of one spouse can reach the property of the other spouse, at least partially, without the other spouse's signature. See the materials on "community property" in Chapter 41 for a further discussion of this approach to marital property.) Should the couple divorce, however, they are no longer considered tenants by the entirety but instead become tenants in common and the creditors can descend on them and their holdings.

APPLICATIONS OF WHAT YOU'VE LEARNED

Vocabulary Development

Fill in the blanks with the appropriate term.

Abandoned Property	**Escheats**	**Mortgagee**	**Real Property**
Accession	**Fair Use Doctrine**	**Mortgagor**	**Rent**
Alienate	**Fixtures**	**Novel**	**Right of Survivorship**
Bailment	**Grantee**	**Obvious**	**Royalty**
Causa Mortis	**Grantor**	**Ownership**	**Severalty**
Confusion	**Infringement**	**Partition**	**Tenant in Common**
Constructive Delivery	**Intangible Property**	**Personal Property**	**Tenants by the Entirety**
Deed	**Inter Vivos**	**Possession**	**Title**
Design Patent	**Joint Tenant**	**Premises**	**Trade Fixtures**
Donee	**Leasehold**	**Profit**	**Use**
Donor	**Lost Property**	**Property**	**Useful**
Easement	**Mislaid Property**	**Purchase**	**Utility Patent**
Eminent Domain	**Mortgage**	**Quitclaim Deed**	**Warranty Deed**
Enjoyment			

1. A creditor who receives the right to have property taken as security sold to satisfy a debt is known as a(n) _____.

2. A coholder of a transferable ownership right to a share of the subject property is a(n) _____.

3. The division of the subject property of an ownership tenancy or the division of the value received for it is termed _____.

4. Rights and interests in things are known at law as _____.

5. Use is the _____ of things by their employment.

6. Rights and interests in land, buildings, and fixtures are known collectively as _____.

7. The unauthorized exercise of a right is known as _____.

8. Compensation paid for the use of intellectual property is known as a(n) _____.

9. A(n) _____ gift is one given in anticipation of death.

Problems

1. Given the quickly diminishing resources of our planet and the skyrocketing population, is it wise of us to adhere to a concept of property that regards everything as capable of being under the exclusive ownership and control of one person or a few persons?

2. Are people really nothing more than property? Ask yourself what rights and interests other people have in you. Who has the equivalent of title, possession, use, and alienation in you and under what circumstances? When does your body itself become property? (*Hint:* Consider blood and tissue donations, parental rights over children, life-support systems and their cost, etc.)

3. Bartholomew Wentworth III of Sandcranial, California, buys two high-quality cooking stove and oven combinations. One he builds into the wall of the townhouse he is renting; the other he bolts to the floor and wall of his restaurant, which is located in space rented from the Sandcranial Mall. Who now owns each stove and oven combination? What legal terms and doctrines are applicable to this question?

4. State at least three situations in which possession of property can ultimately produce ownership.

5. Which would you rather live in, a community property state or a common law state? Why? Which do you feel is the fairer approach to the treatment of marital assets, the community property approach or the common law approach?

ACTUAL CASE STUDY

Doe v. Keane

658 F. Supp. 216

Now reflect on whether or not we should allow a surrogate mother property rights in the fetus she is carrying?

Jane Doe (a pseudonym for the plaintiff mother in this case) contacted a Michigan attorney in early 1985 to inquire about becoming a surrogate mother.

After several months of deliberation she agreed to a parenting contract that promised her $10,000 if she carried an artificially inseminated child to term and $1,000 if she miscarried in the fifth, sixth, or seventh month of pregnancy. Jane was then subjected to the efforts of four doctors who each tried separately to artificially inseminate her. Perhaps because of one of these efforts, she had to be treated at Lansing General Hospital for a swollen uterus. Ultimately, she became pregnant. However, the child was born prematurely and died immediately afterward. Plaintiff then called the defendant and demanded the $10,000. After negotiation she accepted $7,000 in return for signing a document releasing Keane and the four doctors from all potential claims.

Plaintiff now brings suit for malpractice and negligence against Keane and the attendant doctors. She also alleges a violation of the Thirteenth Amendment prohibition of slavery.

Questions

1. Even though Jane signed a release, can you think of reasons why it might be just to allow her to bring the suit for malpractice and negligence?

2. The Thirteenth Amendment reads:

Section 1. Neither slavery nor involuntary servitude, except as punishment for crime whereof the party shall have been duly convicted, shall exist within the United States, or any place subject to their jurisdiction.

Section 2. Congress shall have power to enforce this article by appropriate legislation.

   a. What actually constitutes slavery?

   b. Does Jane Doe have a point in alleging that the parenting contract was slavery?

3. Is the aspect of our society's current concept of property that allows a person to buy a human being from another person consistent with your moral views?

CHAPTER

31

What Are Bailments, and How Are They Originated, Managed, and Terminated?

CHAPTER OUTLINE AND OBJECTIVES

After studying this chapter, the student will be able to:

I. Recognize a bailment.

II. Identify the principal types of bailments.

   a. Bailments requiring ordinary care

   b. Bailments requiring extraordinary care

   c. Bailments imposed by law

III. Explain the rights and duties of the parties to bailments.

IV. Determine what was adequate care in *Inter-Ocean (Free Zone)* v. *Manaure Lines, Inc.*, the case of the 600 missing color TV sets.

What Is a Bailment?

Bailors: individuals who bail goods

Bailees: individuals to whom goods are bailed

Lease: agreement for transfer of exclusive possession of real property or possession, use, and enjoyment of personal property

Mutuum: loan for consumption of subject matter

In Chapter 30 we defined a *bailment* as the legal relationship created by the acquisition of possession and control of the personal property of another subject to an agreement to return it (or, in certain types of bailments, to deliver it to a third party). That definition makes the subject area seem relatively complex and the likelihood of any further use of the term remote. However, this surface impression is incorrect. Bailments actually occur with great frequency in our society. We just use less accurate terminology to describe them in real life. For example, if you need to use my textbook, you do not ask me if I'll bail it to you. Instead, you want me to "loan" or "give" it to you for a few days so that you can study for the exam. If you need the use of a trailer to move your furniture and other belongings to a new apartment, you do not look under **bailors** (individuals who bail goods) in the yellow pages. Instead, you look under "rental centers" or "trailer rentals." Similarly, if you need someone to transport a package for you to a friend in a faraway city, you do not look under **bailees** (individuals to whom goods are bailed). Instead you look under "delivery services" or, perhaps, "common carriers." If you need money and pawn your compact disc player to get a quick loan or if you find someone else's lost money—*all* of these situations and many more involve bailments but just aren't called such in everyday life.

Bailments must be distinguished from somewhat similar transactions. A sale, for example, unlike a bailment, involves not only the transfer of possession to another party but also the transfer of title to that party. The same is true of a gift. The person who receives these property rights is not under any duty to return the goods or to deliver them to a third party.

A **lease** is an agreement under which exclusive possession of real property or possession, use, and enjoyment of personal property are temporarily transferred. A bailment is a term describing a transfer of only personal property subject to an agreement such as a lease. A leasing of space alone, such as a locker in a bus station, part of a large shipping container, or a parking space downtown, is not a bailment either. This is mainly because the immediate control of the goods remains with the person who contracts for the space.

Finally, a bailment is not a mutuum, or vice versa. I know you'll sleep well just knowing that. Actually, we all involve ourselves in mutua fairly frequently, as a **mutuum** is a loan for consumption. For example, if you lend me a gallon of gas for my lawn mower to save me the time I'd use going to the gas station, you don't expect to get that very gallon of gas back, yet in both our minds the transaction is still a loan. The gas will be consumed as I mow, but I still owe it to you. Even if the item consumed is to be replaced by an identical good and that good is to be returned to you as soon as possible, the transaction is still not a bailment.

Finn needed some white paint to finish a job. As it was a holiday, no stores were open. Wanting to get done, he asked Sawyer whether Sawyer had any that he would lend. Sawyer rummaged through his garage, eventually finding 2 gallons. According to the terms of the mutuum, Finn was to replace them as soon as the stores opened the next day.

So, to generalize from all of this, realize that a few key things distinguish a bailment:

Possession and control are the rights transferred, albeit only temporarily.
Only personal property is involved.
The goods bailed have to be returned or delivered to a third party.

What Are the Principal Types of Bailments?

Now that you have a summary idea of what's inside the extensive area that the law refers to as bailments, we need to start a more detailed examination. The best way to do so is to set up some categories within which we can file the many examples of bailments that will be encountered. The three we'll use are:

1. Bailments requiring ordinary care by the bailee.
2. Bailments requiring extraordinary care by the bailee.
3. Bailments imposed by law.

The first two are voluntarily entered into by the parties, while the third is thrust upon individuals by a combination of circumstance and legalities.

Bailments Requiring Ordinary Care

Ordinary care means reasonable care under the circumstances. This standard would be violated if the bailor's negligent or even more substandard care resulted in harm to the bailed goods.

Ordinary Care: reasonable care under the circumstances

Living Room Chariots, Inc., sold a special type of reclining, vibrating, deep-cushioned chair with a built-in alarm clock, heater, and universal remote control for the "fermented couch potato." Winstone Bobblesock bought the last of this year's models off the showroom floor. Unfortunately, in trying to move the chair to the loading dock, the staff at Chariots gouged a forklift tine through its back. Chariots' negligence violated the requirement of ordinary care in such a bailment.

Gratuitous Bailments: bailments for sole benefit of one or other of parties

Mutual Benefit Bailments: bailments under which both bailor and bailee receive payment of some kind

Pawn: bailor transfers personal property to bailee as security for loan

Bailments requiring ordinary care can be broken down into bailments for the sole benefit of one or the other of the parties (called **gratuitous bailments**) and mutual benefit bailments. The intent of **mutual benefit bailments** is that both the bailor and the bailee will receive payment of some kind. A common example of a mutual benefit bailment is a **pawn** (also referred to as a pledge). In a pawn arrangement, the bailor transfers his or her personal property to the bailee as security for a loan.

Gratuitous bailments involve a flow of use or value in one direction only. For example, if I let you borrow my riding lawn mower to finish a part of your yard where the grass has grown exceptionally high, that is a bailment for the sole benefit of the bailee—you. I do not expect payment for my neighborly favor. The next time we go on vacation, however, look for me to show up on your porch with all of my wife's ferns and a note with the following directions: "They need watering every day, and I was hoping you wouldn't mind if I left them with you. Don't forget to talk to them—Marge keeps them up on all the neighborhood gossip. Thanks, Flanders." This arrangement is a gratuitous bailment for the sole benefit of the bailor. Under modern bailment law, ordinary care is required in all situations involving mutual benefit and gratuitous bailments.

Note that in a few states the old common law rules still apply. Under these rules, the bailee in a bailment for the sole benefit of that bail*ee* must exercise *great care,* which is care that a person of superior foresight and prudence would exercise (in other words, you'd better be extra careful with my riding lawn mower). Such a bailee will be responsible if harm occurs as a result of even slight negligence on her or his part.

Gross Negligence: intentional reckless disregard of duty with knowledge of harmful consequences

Conversely, in a bailment for the sole benefit of the bail*or*, the bailee must exercise only *slight care,* so my wife's ferns could be in trouble. The bailee is liable only for **gross negligence** (intentional reckless disregard of duty with knowledge of the harmful consequences). Remember, however, that in most states ordinary care is required rather than the extremes just mentioned.

Bailments Requiring Extraordinary Care

Extraordinary Care: standard of responsibility holding bailee liable for damage to bailed property unless attributable to war or unforeseeable acts of God

Hotelkeeper: person who operates establishment renting overnight accommodations to public

In certain bailment arrangements, bailees must take extraordinary care of the property entrusted to them. **Extraordinary care** implies a standard of responsibility that holds the bailee liable for any loss or damage unless it is solely attributable to unforeseeable war, time circumstances or the acts of God. In short, the bailee becomes a near insurer of the goods. Such strict liability arises in business settings only. The foremost examples of bailees who must take extraordinary care are hotelkeepers and common carriers.

A **hotelkeeper** (also occasionally labeled innkeeper by the law) operates an establishment that provides overnight accommodations to the public. The common law imposed on hotelkeepers a duty to accept all guests. Further, these offerors of accommodations for profit became insurers of the property that their guests turned over to them for safekeeping.

Arraonson stored his jewelry samples in the safe of the Knightlite Inn, where he had taken a room. One night a fire started in the hotel kitchen. During the chaos that followed, two masked individuals overpowered the guards, held up the hotel, and made off with the jewelry. The Knightlite Inn would be liable to Arraonson for the loss of the bailed items.

This unenviable level of responsibility for bailed goods is also placed on businesses that hold themselves out to the general public to transport goods for a fee. Such businesses are referred to as **common carriers.** They, like hotelkeepers, must take extraordinary care of items bailed to them. Common carriers must be distinguished from **private carriers,** such as Sears or Ward's, companies that transport in their own vehicles their own goods or goods they have sold or leased, and **contract carriers**, companies that transport goods only for those with whom they care to do business. Of the three types of carriers, only private carriers are not regulated by the federal Interstate Commerce Commission and only common carriers must exercise extraordinary care.

A bailment of goods to a common carrier for shipment is known as a **consignment.** When the common carrier receives goods for shipment, it issues a document called a **bill of lading.** The bill of lading states the terms of the shipping contract for the consigned goods. It also contains a description of those goods and details who has the right to demand the goods by presentation of the bill of lading upon the arrival of the goods at their destination. Some bills of lading are *negotiable.* Like commercial paper, they (and thereby the right to receive the shipped goods) can be made to the order of a named person or to a bearer. Other bills of lading are *nonnegotiable,* which means that the consignee of the goods involved must deliver them to the person named on the bill of lading.

Common Carriers: transporters holding themselves out to general public to carry goods for fee

Private Carriers: transporters carrying their own goods in their own vehicles

Contract Carriers: transporters hiring themselves out to carry goods only for those with whom they care to do business

Consignment: bailment of goods to common carrier for shipment

Bill of Lading: document stating terms of shipping contract for consigned goods

Interactive Instruction Incorporated (III) sold the Pennsboro public schools 15 of III's compact disc–based learning systems. III shipped the systems from San Francisco by common carrier, but by mistake III's employees sent only 13 systems. The agent of the common carrier issued the bill of lading without checking to see how many systems were actually turned over to the common carrier. As a result, when only 13 systems arrived in Pennsboro, the city's school system held the common carrier liable for the "loss" of the other 2.

Bailments Imposed by Law

What do the following individuals have in common?

Willa finds another student's textbook.
James buys a stolen compact disc player.

Harry keeps the $175 in a wallet he found even though the owner of the wallet is clearly identified by documents contained in it.

Sandra borrows Angela's car to drive back and forth to work but on occasion uses it to go shopping in a nearby city.

John refuses to return Carlos's jack after changing a tire.

The answer is that even without a controlling agreement these individuals are all treated as bailees by the law. The law thrusts bailment-based duties on a variety of individuals, ranging from a finder of lost property to a person who commits the tort of conversion by converting another's property to his or her own use. The situations in which this happens can be divided into involuntary bailments and tortious bailments.

Involuntary Bailments.   A situation in which personal property inadvertently ends up in the hands of a stranger is referred to by the law as an **involuntary bailment.** The misdelivery of a package and the taking of lost property into the possession of its finder are both examples of involuntary bailments. The person who thereby holds the property must then exercise a level of care similar to that required of a bailee in a bailment for the sole benefit of the bailor (ordinary care in most states, as noted earlier).

Involuntary Bailment: personal property inadvertently transferred into the hands of a stranger

Tortious Bailments.   When personal property wrongfully comes into another's hands, a **tortious bailment** is created by law. Tortious bailees are the equivalents of insurers for any damage that occurs to property in their possession. The last four situations mentioned above are typical examples of such bailments; James, Harry, Sandra, and John are all bailees who owe extraordinary care to the true owner of the property in question as they are all wrongful recipients of another's personal property.

Tortious Bailment: personal property wrongfully transferred into another's hands

What Are the Rights and Duties of the Parties to Bailments?

Generally, the rights of one party to a bailment are the mirror images of the duties owed by the other party to that bailment. For example, in the case of a bailment requiring ordinary care, it is the duty of the bailee to treat the bailed property with that level of care and the right of the bailor to expect such treatment.

In addition to a matching of rights and duties with regard to the level of care owed to the bailed goods in the various situations mentioned in the preceding section, other rights and duties are also matched. In a voluntary mutually beneficial bailment, for example, it is the duty of the bailor to deliver goods that are safe to use and, again, the right of the bailee to expect such. However, when the voluntary bailment is not mutually beneficial, the rules change. In a bailment for the bailee's sole benefit, the bailor is liable only for injuries to the bailee caused by defects in the bailed property of which the bailor had actual knowledge. In a bailment for the bailor's sole benefit, the bailee has the right to be reimbursed for reasonable expenditures for the care of the bailed property.

| Types of Bailments | Figure 31–1 |

Those voluntarily entered into
Where ordinary care of the bailed property
  is required of
    The gratuitous bailee
    The mutual benefit bailee
Where extraordinary care of the bailed property
  is required of (among others)
    Hotelkeepers
    Common carriers

Those imposed by law
Upon
  Involuntary bailees
  Tortious bailees

HYPOTHETICAL CASE

For safekeeping, Ben Range left his classic Ferrari Sportster with his son, Feral, while Ben went on a long cruise. Every few days Feral took the Sportster for a short drive to keep it roadworthy. The car developed a hole in the manifold, and the exhaust system had to be replaced in order to legally drive the vehicle. The cost was over $1,600. When Ben returned, he had a duty to reimburse Feral for his expenditures for the gas and oil necessary to drive the vehicle and for the repair of the exhaust system.

In a bailment for the sole benefit of the bailee, the expenses associated with the use of the property must be borne by the bailee. However, the bailor must pay for expenditures not attributable to daily use.

HYPOTHETICAL CASE

After the cruise was over, Ben loaned the Ferrari to his daughter, Medusa, for a trip to the East Coast. On her trip, the car's transmission locked up. The mechanic who replaced it (for $3,472.78) said that long-term wear and tear had caused the problem. Therefore, although Medusa was responsible for the gas, oil, and tires expenditures on her trip, Ben would have to pay or reimburse the $3,472.78.

In any voluntary bailment, the bailee has the right to use the subject property according to the terms of the bailment agreement. If the bailee uses the subject property in ways that violate those terms, however, the bailee becomes a tortious bailee, is liable for the tort of conversion, and is responsible for any damage to the subject property.

Vocabulary Development

Fill in the blanks with the appropriate term.

Bailees	Contract Carrier	Involuntary Bailment	Ordinary Care
Bailors	Extraordinary Care	Lease	Pawn
Bill of Lading	Gratuitous Bailment	Mutual Benefit	Private Carrier
Common Carrier	Gross Negligence	Bailment	Tortious Bailment
Consignment	Hotelkeepers	Mutuum	

1. Another word for _____ is pledge.

2. A finder becomes a party to a(n) _____.

3. A(n) _____ transports her or his own goods in her or his own trucks.

4. A(n) _____ holds himself or herself out to the general public to transport goods.

5. A thief has a(n) _____

6. A bailment for the sole benefit of the bailor or bailee is a(n) _____.

Problems

1. Which of the following is not a bailment?
   a. Your neighbor loans you a cup of sugar.
   b. Your mother has you hold her purse while she tries on some clothing.
   c. You lease a yacht for a round-the-world cruise.
   d. You find $20 on a football field after the game.

2. Paula borrows John Henry's gasoline-powered chain saw to cut firewood for the fireplace of her lake cabin. John Henry lets her use the chain saw for free. However, he has just finished cutting with it and the chain is loose. When Paula fires it up, the chain slips off and slashes her arm. Three stitches and a tetanus shot are needed. The total expense is over $250. Who is ultimately responsible for the bill?

3. Due to John Henry's generosity in letting her borrow the chain saw, Paula decides not to pursue the issue. Instead, she waits a day, then borrows a pickup from her neighbor, Beau Lombard. She drives into the nearby national forest, where she has a permit to cut pine trees. While she is cutting, two things happen. First, she forgets to replace the oil cooling the blade and engine of the chain saw. As a result, the chain saw overheats, ruining its motor. Second, a strong wind blows a tree trunk over the cab of Beau's pickup, doing severe damage. Who is liable for the harm in each situation?

4. Paula still needs to bring in the firewood she has cut. To do so, she borrows an all-terrain vehicle (ATV) from another friend, explicitly for that job. This time her mission is a success. After unloading the firewood, however, she uses the ATV on a night fishing trip near the waterfall on the other side of the lake. Regretfully, during the night the ATV is stolen even though Paula has hidden it and removed its key. The ATV is never recovered. Who is responsible for the loss?

ACTUAL CASE STUDY

Inter-Ocean (Free Zone) v. Manaure Lines, Inc.

615 F. Supp. 710

Even the FBI was baffled in the case of the missing color TVs, but someone had to pay.

A full container load of color TV sets (600 in number) and 11 cartons of audiotapes was delivered into the possession and control of Strachan Shipping Company, Inc., the Manaure Lines' stevedore at the Port of Miami. The delivery was receipted by a Strachan employee. The trucker delivered the container, then parked it at spot E–32 in Strachan's area and left. When Strachan employees came to retrieve it, it was missing. Strachan's container depot at the Port of Miami was fenced on three sides. The fourth side was open to Biscayne Bay for loading operations. According to the testimony of Strachan's manager of stevedore operations, the depots of all other stevedores at the Port of Miami were completely surrounded by fencing. In addition, the gate to Strachan's depot was always left open and unguarded during the day. Two months prior to this loss, another cargo container disappeared from the same Strachan depot. Strachan maintains in its defense that if its clerks or other employees observed the theft, they could have called the security personnel at the main gate to the Port of Miami, who could have easily apprehended the thieves. Passes were required to enter or leave the port through that gate.

Questions

1. Should Strachan be liable for the loss of the goods? Why or why not? What steps should be taken to prevent similar incidents?

2. What party, other than individuals wanting to ship goods with Strachan, Strachan itself, and the shipping lines with which Strachan works, would be financially interested in the security of the depot?

How Are Leaseholds Created, Managed, and Terminated?

CHAPTER OUTLINE AND OBJECTIVES

After studying this chapter, the student will be able to:

I. Define the term lease.

II. Identify the types of leaseholds that can be created by a lease of real property.
   a. The periodic tenancy
   b. The tenancy for years
   c. The tenancy at will
   d. The tenancy at sufferance

III. Explain the rights and duties of the landlord and the tenant.
   a. The landlord's rights and duties
   b. The tenant's right and duties

IV. Describe how a leasehold is terminated.

V. Review, through the case of *Draper and Kramer, Inc.* v. *Baskin-Robbins, Inc.*, the validity of a lease term that gives a mall store exclusive rights to "hand packed ice cream, ice cream cones, or soda fountain items."

What Is a Lease?

To begin with, you have to realize that as used both in the law and in common speech, the word *lease* has a somewhat ambiguous meaning. In Chapter 30 we discussed the legal definition, namely that a lease was "an agreement under which temporary exclusive possession of real property *or* possession, use, and enjoyment of personal property are transferred." In other words, a lease can cover real property, such as an apartment, store, or lot, and it can also cover personal property, such as a car, trailer, or television. In Chapter 31 we focused on leases of personal property when we discussed the law of bailments. Bailments must typically have such agreements to define the bailor–bailee relationship. In this chapter, however, we focus on leases of real property. Throughout the chapter we will be referring solely to leases of real property whenever the term *lease* is employed.

Our focus on the real property meaning of the term *lease* requires the use of more specific terms than those used in the general definition. For example, a person who rents the real or personal property of another is termed a **lessee.** A person from whom real or personal property is being rented is termed a **lessor.** However, when the subject matter of a lease is solely real property, more specific terms are used (although *lessor* and *lessee* are accurate still). In particular, a party renting out real property is termed a **landlord.** A renter of real property is referred to as a **tenant.**

As discussed in Chapter 30, the tenant who has a leasehold is entitled to exclusive possession of the premises against the whole world, including the owner. Such exclusivity distinguishes a tenant from other individuals with similar rights. For example, a **lodger** is an occupant of premises but has only the use of them, not their exclusive possession.

Lessee: person who rents real or personal property of another

Lessor: party from whom real or personal property is being rented

Landlord: owner of real property being rented

Tenant: person renting real property

Lodger: occupant allowed only use of premises

> When Mom and Dad brought Granddad home to stay with us, he was 84. They had found him wandering the streets late at night a couple of times. He said he was looking for Grandma, but she had died of cancer several years before. Granddad stayed in the spare bedroom. He would wander the house and yard and eat with us. Mom was always cleaning up his room just the way she did mine. Granddad would get mad when she had put something up where he couldn't find it. He didn't want Mom to work on his room. Mom would just say that he was lodging with us, not leasing, so she could clean anywhere she chose and he couldn't keep her out.
>
> *Life and the Law*

Business Invitees: persons invited onto premises of another to conduct commercial transactions

Licensees: persons with privilege of entry onto another's real property

Trespassers: persons who willfully enter property of another without consent

A tenant is also distinguishable from business invitees, licensees, and, certainly, trespassers. **Business invitees** are persons who are impliedly invited onto the premises of another to conduct commercial transactions (a Christmas shopper at a toy store, for example). **Licensees** are persons who are afforded the privilege of entering onto another's real property through the possessor's explicit or implied promise. A UPS deliverer is a good example of a licensee. Finally, **trespassers,** persons who willfully enter the property of another without consent, are easily distinguishable from leasehold tenants. Note that the property holder's duty (and, therefore, potential liability) varies according to these types. For example, the property holder is only required to refrain from doing intentional harm to a trespasser (such as setting traps) but must warn a licensee of known dangers (such as hidden pits). Business invitees must be provided with safe premises on which to conduct business with the property holder. So businesspersons are charged with conducting reasonable inspections of their stores to ensure that no harm comes to their customers while therein.

Bearing in mind this more specific idea of a lease and its parties, we now need to discuss the four principal types of leaseholds that can be created by a lease.

What Types of Leaseholds Can Be Created by a Lease of Real Property?

Generally, the types of leaseholds can be categorized by the time allocated for the tenancy. The four principal types are the periodic tenancy, the tenancy for years, the tenancy at will, and the tenancy at sufferance.

The Periodic Tenancy

The periodic tenancy is the most common. When you rent an apartment from someone on a month-to-month or week-to-week basis, you are a tenant in a periodic tenancy. At law, the definition of **periodic tenancy,** although relatively imprecise, generally requires that a tenancy (also known as a tenancy from year to year) be a leasehold that continues for successive like intervals subject only to termination by proper notice from one of the parties. At common law, subject to change by the terms of the lease, the rent was due at the end of each such period, be it monthly, weekly, daily, or whatever.

Periodic Tenancy: leasehold that continues for successive like intervals

The timing of the termination notice is important in a periodic tenancy. Unless the lease provides differently (for example, by requiring "30 days' notice"), a full period must elapse between the time of notice and the effective date of termination for any period less than year to year. This means that if you wanted out of a monthly periodic leasehold on January 1, you would have to give notice before the preceding December 1. If you gave notice on December 1 or afterward, you could not terminate the leasehold before February 1. For periodic tenancies of a year or longer, from three months' notice up to a full year's notice is required, depending on the law in the jurisdiction. Again, all of this can be changed in the lease agreement.

The Tenancy for Years

The name given to this type of tenancy is misleading. A **tenancy for years** should instead be called a "tenancy of fixed duration," as that is all it is. The duration can be any length of time as long as it is definite. The tenancy for years automatically terminates when the set length of time has run. No notice is required. According to the Statute of Frauds, the lease for the tenancy for years must be in writing if the duration is for a year or more. An oral lease is enforceable for durations of less than a year. However, oral leases are best

Tenancy for Years: leasehold of fixed duration

avoided. In most states, ownership to the intended tenant, not just exclusive possession, is conveyed by a tenancy for years that has been set up to run for 100 years or more.

HYPOTHETICAL CASE

> The McKlernon family owned a large acreage in Pennsboro, Missouri. When the McKlernons were approached by the Mount Etna Development Corporation with plans to build a regional mall on the site, they agreed to lease their land for 99 years. Under the laws of the state, if they had agreed to a longer lease, they would have passed ownership of the acreage to the corporation.

Note that some states hold that a periodic tenancy is created if a landlord permits a tenant for years to remain in possession after the lease has ended. Other states hold that this action creates a tenancy at will as described below.

The Tenancy at Will

Tenancy at Will: leasehold of indefinite duration created by law when tenant holds over with permission

A **tenancy at will** is a leasehold that permits the exclusive possession of real property for an indefinite duration. Two characteristics distinguish this type of tenancy from the other types. First, its termination is subject to the current will of its parties instead of being determined by a fixed length or a repeating term specified in a lease. Proper notice of the impending termination of the tenancy at will may have to be provided to the other party, however. State statutes or common law usually set the notice requirement anywhere from no advance notice to 30 days' notice in writing. Due to the undetermined length of the tenancy at will, there is no requirement that the lease be in writing.

The second distinguishing characteristic of a tenancy at will is that the tenant remains on the property with the owner's permission. The tenancy therefore ends with a change in ownership. This is important in many situations, as a periodic tenancy and a tenancy for years continue to bind new owners.

HYPOTHETICAL CASE

> Avalone wanted to sell her apartment house to a firm involved in redeveloping the neighborhood in which the house was situated. To make the house more marketable, she did not renew the tenancies for years as they expired. If the tenants wanted to stay, they could, but only under a tenancy at will, which would not burden any new ownership. Therefore, should the redevelopers purchase the building, they could move all such tenants out simply by giving proper written notice and then waiting for the two-week notice period required by state statute to run.

Tenancy at Sufferance: leasehold of indefinite duration created by law when tenant wrongfully retains possession of premises

The Tenancy at Sufferance

A **tenancy at sufferance** is a leasehold that is created by law whenever a periodic tenant or a tenant for years wrongfully retains possession of the premises after the lease has expired. A tenant at sufferance is liable for rent for the time involved and is not entitled to any form of notice before **eviction** (the act of removing a tenant from possession of the premises). However, should the landlord accept rent from a tenant at sufferance who remains in possession, either a tenancy at will or a periodic tenancy will be created, depending on state law.

Eviction: act of removing tenant from possession of premises

What Are the Rights and Duties of the Landlord and the Tenant?

The presumption at the heart of landlord–tenant law is that the two parties will negotiate all the necessary terms for the leasehold. If they do so, the resulting lease defines the rights and duties of both. A sample lease is shown in Figure 32–1.

Generally, such leases will be interpreted according to the law of contracts. However, because of the archaic nature of real property law, the wording of a lease is more likely than the wording of a contract to be given its technical legal meaning and to be so applied by a court. By definition, for example, labeling a term of the lease a **condition** makes the validity of the lease contingent on the term so labeled. Breach a condition and the lease is at an end. If, instead, a lease term is labeled a **covenant,** a breach of that term, again by definition, will give only the injured party the right to sue for the damages caused by the breach, leaving the lease still in effect. It should be no surprise, therefore, that whenever a tenant accepts the lease offered by the landlord, the tenant will find that most of the requirements placed on him or her are labeled conditions and that most of the requirements placed on the landlord are labeled covenants.

Condition: term of lease upon which validity of lease is contingent

Covenant: term of lease the violation of which gives injured party right to sue for damages

HYPOTHETICAL CASE

Willy Wildebeard leased a home from Pristine Homes, Inc. A condition in Willy's lease was that he would not practice any profession or maintain any business on the premises of the home (see clause 2 in Figure 32–1). A month after moving in, Willy opened a motorcycle repair shop in the garage of the home. He frequently took motorcycle parts into the spare bedroom for storage. Tracking in oil and grease from the shop soon ruined the carpets and stained walls and fixtures. When Pristine Homes found out what Willy was doing, it evicted him and sued for damages to the premises. This action was possible because Willy's conduct had violated the lease condition and thereby rendered the leasehold null and void. Had the term been merely a covenant, the lease would have remained in effect. Willy would then have been able to stay on as a tenant, and Pristine Homes would have been able to sue him solely for damages.

Realize, however, that no matter how often landlords and tenants are advised to conclude a detailed, well-negotiated lease, the courts are too often confronted by the contrary. When this happens, that is, when a lease is not negotiated or when terms are omitted from a lease, the law imposes its own list of rights and duties on the parties. A discussion of these follows.

Figure 32–1

—PRISTINE HOMES-

—PRISTINE HOMES-

—PRISTINE HOMES-

IF IT'S PRISTINE, IT'S CLEAN

LEASE OF REAL PROPERTY

This lease, entered into on the 31st day of May, 19**, is by and between Pristine Homes, Inc., herein referred to as "Landlord," and Willy Wildebeard, "Tenant."

Hereby the Landlord leases to Tenant the home and grounds at 1313 North Parade Street, Hohumshire, Vermont, for the term of one year. Said term shall commence on the 1st day of June, 19**, and terminate on the 31st day of May 19**, unless Tenant holds over.

Tenant agrees to the following conditions:

1. To pay Landlord a rent of $10,400, $1,600 of which shall be due on the first of June, 19**, and the remainder shall be paid in $800 increments on the first of each of the remaining 11 months in the term of the lease.

2. Not to maintain any business or practice any profession on the premises during the term of this lease or any period thereafter.

3. That, in the event Tenant holds over, Tenant shall be obligated to pay rent at the rate of $1,600 per month.

4. That Tenant will provide Landlord with 30 days' notice of termination should Tenant hold over.

5. That, at the termination of this lease, Tenant will return to Landlord possession of the premises peaceably and in as good a condition as they were received absent reasonable wear and tear.

6. That Tenant will not waste the premises or assign or sublet or permit anyone else to occupy the premises without the written permission of the Landlord.

7. That Tenant will provide reasonable access for Landlord for the purpose of making inspections, rendering repairs and improvements, and showing the premises to prospective tenants or buyers.

Landlord agrees to provide habitable premises for the possession and use of the Tenant as a residence.

The Terms of this Lease shall be binding upon the heirs, administrators, and executors of the Landlord and Tenant.

In Witness Hereof:

_____   _____
Willy Wildebeard   Priscilla Pristine as President,
                                          Pristine Homes, Inc.

The Landlord's Rights and Duties

The landlord–tenant relationship is typically based on an essential exchange: possession of the premises in return for rent. However, unless agreement to the contrary is reached, the responsibilities of the parties go deeper than just this simple bargain.

The first and foremost duty of the landlord is to provide possession of suitable premises. Where the premises are to be used for human housing, they should be in a condition fit for living. Ensuring this was at one time left up to the tenant and the market. If a tenant did not find the premises in proper condition, he or she could look elsewhere before finalizing the lease. Such is not the case today in most jurisdictions. Today even small cities have housing codes that set minimum standards for rental properties offered for human habitation. Such codes generally require certification by a qualified governmental inspector before occupancy can begin. The inspector seeks to ensure that rental properties are free from structural problems, leaky roofs, improper wiring, improperly vented fixtures and gas appliances, and security and health problems. In addition, although at one time landlords were not liable for injuries sustained on leased premises, today courts often hold them accountable. This is especially likely if the injuries are sustained in the common areas, such as stairwells or elevators, or result from negligently made repairs or hidden defects that the landlord should have been aware of but did not disclose to the tenant.

The landlord also has the duty to pay the property taxes on leased property, be it apartments or rental homes. However, the terms of a long-term commercial lease often obligate the tenant to pay these taxes. An apartment dweller, on the other hand, pays them indirectly by way of rental payments.

To balance out these duties, the landlord has two fundamental rights. The first is simply the right to be paid rent. The second is the right to regain the possession of the real property upon the termination of the lease or upon its violation by the tenant. Often the tenant has improved the premises. As we discussed in Chapter 30, improvements that are fixtures, except for trade fixtures, belong to the landlord. Given a violation of a lease condition, such as a failure to pay the rent, the landlord can evict the tenant. Realize, however, that the landlord does not take matters into her or his own hands and personally throw the tenant out. The sheriff or a suitable official stand-in will carry out the eviction upon petition to and order of the proper court.

The Tenant's Rights and Duties

The tenant's primary duty is the payment of rent. The payment must be tendered in a timely fashion and in the medium agreed to, be it money from the tenant's income, a part of the harvest from the land, or a percentage of the gross receipts from a concert.

Beyond paying rent, the tenant must bear the responsibility for taking reasonable care of the premises. The tenant must make minor repairs, such as fixing a leaky faucet or replacing light bulbs or fuses. For a major problem, such as a hole in the roof or a worn-out combustion chamber in the furnace, reasonable care comes down to a duty to notify the landlord of the problem. After having given notification, the tenant must take reasonable steps that would prevent avoidable damage. Such things as placing buckets under a leak and taping a cardboard shield over a broken window are the responsibility of the tenant. The idea is to return the premises in basically the same shape they were in when they were received from the landlord. However, the toll taken by reasonable wear and tear does not produce liability for the tenant.

The fundamental right of the tenant is exclusive possession of the premises. "Exclusive possession" means just that. Even the landlord cannot enter the leasehold without the tenant's permission. However, this right has to be balanced by the landlord's need to enter on the premises to make repairs. Should the landlord fail to make proper repairs or provide necessary services (such as heating during the winter), so that the premises are rendered uninhabitable, the tenant may abandon the leasehold and refuse to pay rent. The law terms this a **constructive eviction.** Note that to justify nonpayment of rent, the tenant must truly leave the premises. Otherwise, the leasehold will be held to still be habitable.

Constructive Eviction: failure of landlord to provide services necessary to render premises habitable

HYPOTHETICAL CASE

On one of the hottest days of summer school, the students living in the university's high-rise apartment building woke up to discover that the air-conditioning system was no longer working. The breakdown of the system was caused by a defective part that took three weeks to replace. During this period, the students sweltered in temperatures that remained near 90 degrees even in the "cool" of the night. The only ventilation for the fifteen-story building was provided by small sliding windows in the apartment bathrooms. Near the end of the third week, the topic of constructive eviction came up in a business law class attended by one of the sweltering students. When she suggested that the university had constructively evicted her by not providing air-conditioning, the professor noted that inasmuch as she had remained in residence, a court would hold that the premises were still habitable. Had she left and rented elsewhere, a court would probably have excused her from her lease with the university. She would have also been able to seek damages covering moving expenses and any additional rent she was forced to pay for a leasehold comparable to the university apartment.

The fundamental right of possession is accompanied by a right to use the premises, but only for customary purposes. So, absent some lease provision allowing it, a structure normally used as a residence cannot, for example, be turned into a warehouse for pets.

Finally, unless a lease term prohibits it, the tenant has the right to transfer her or his rights and interests in the leasehold to someone else. Transferring all of these rights and interests to another is termed **assignment of the lease.** Retaining some of these rights and interests while transferring others, is termed **subletting.** A lease assignee becomes directly liable to the landlord for the rent and for the fulfillment of other duties. Even so, the assignor still remains liable under the lease if the assignee fails to fulfill the duties. In a subletting, the sublessor continues to be immediately liable to the landlord under the terms of the lease.

Assignment of the Lease: transfer of all of tenant's rights and interests under a lease to third party

Subletting: transfer of some of tenant's rights and interests in leasehold to third party

**Landlord and Tenant Rights and Duties
(Subject to Actual Lease Terms)**   Figure 32–2

Landlord	Tenant
Duty to deliver suitable premises	Duty to take reasonable care of premises
Duty to pay property taxes on premises	
Right to be paid rent	Duty to pay rent
Right to regain leasehold at end of the lease or upon tenant's breach	Right to exclusive possession of premises
	Right to use premises for customary purposes
	Right to transfer his or her rights and interests in premises to others

Rent, for example, is owed to the sublessor by the sublessee. Should the sublessee fail to pay it, the sublessor (original lessee) is still directly responsible for paying it to the lessor.

How Is a Leasehold Terminated?

We have already discussed several of the ways in which leaseholds come to an end. Periodic tenancies end after proper notice. Tenancies for years end at the expiration of the lease period. Holdover tenants create tenancies at will that may or may not (depending on the jurisdiction) require some period of notice before being terminated. Tenancies at sufferance can be terminated without notice. Violation of a lease condition can also end a tenancy. Any of these eventualities can produce the necessity for eviction if the tenant does not surrender the premises of her or his own accord. Such eviction must be by peaceful means, typically through court suit and subsequent police supervision. Self-help evictions are not permitted in most states. However, landlords can force tenants out through subtler means, for example, the termination of necessary services such as water or heat, though such constructive evictions can have serious consequences for the landlord. Finally, a leasehold may end unexpectedly but without friction, for example, when a tenant who has been transferred out of town to a new job approaches the landlord wanting to end the lease and the landlord agrees to do so. The termination of such a tenant's obligations under the lease is usually accomplished when the landlord retakes possession of the premises.

Regardless of the means involved, it is important to remember that the part of real property law dealing with leaseholds requires a stricter adherence to rules and formalities than does, for example, the law of contracts or sales. For this reason, a written lease thoughtfully negotiated by informed parties is strongly advised.

APPLICATIONS OF
WHAT YOU'VE LEARNED

Vocabulary Development

Fill in the blanks with the appropriate term.

Assignment of the Lease	**Eviction**	**Lodge**	**Tenancy for Years**
Business Invitees	**Landlord**	**Periodic Tenancy**	**Tenant**
Condition	**Lessee**	**Subletting**	**Trespassers**
Constructive Eviction	**Lessor**	**Tenancy at Sufferance**	
Covenant	**Licensees**	**Tenancy at Will**	

1. _____ is a term applied to someone who rents either personal or real property to another.

2. _____ is a term applied to someone who rents real property to another.

3. A tenancy involving a holdover tenant who has the permission to remain the real property owner is known as a(n) _____.

4. A(n) _____ terminates without notice of any kind after its set term has run.

5. The landlord's failure to provide the necessary heat in the winter can be a basis for a(n) _____.

6. The breach of a(n) _____ of a lease gives the injured party the right to sue for damages.

Problems

1. Which of the following are business invitees, which are licensees, and which are trespassers? What duty do you owe to each of these types of persons?

   a. A young boy cutting across your vacant lot without your knowledge on his way home from school.

   b. A pizza deliverer bringing your anchovy deluxe to the door of your house.

   c. A hunter on your land without permission.

   d. A utility company employee checking the electric meter on the side of your house.

   e. A customer of your restaurant while parking in your parking lot.

   f. A person invited to your spouse's Tupperware party in your house.

2. Flaire Cambell majored in engineering at Central State University. During her last year of school, she leased an apartment from Lagree. Her lease was a month-to-month periodic tenancy. Flaire moved out of her apartment on May 31, the day before her graduation. She mailed notice of her termination to Lagree immediately after the graduation ceremonies. Her rent was $325 per month. How much money does she owe Lagree for unpaid rent?

3. You invite your apartment mate's parents to visit for a surprise birthday party for their child. Unfortunately, the father is injured when he falls after his foot catches in the ragged rug that covers the stairwell. Who is liable? Who would have been liable if he had slipped on a throw rug you had on the apartment's hardwood floor?

4. It is the middle of a cold January in Yukon City, Montana. The average daytime high since the beginning of the new year has been just a little over freezing. You return home from work to find that you can see your breath inside your apartment. You check to see whether you've left a window open, then realize that the heat is off. You call the landlord and find out that the old fuel oil furnace has broken down. She intends to replace it with a natural gas furnace, but you will be without heat for several weeks. She therefore advises you to buy several electric floor heaters but will not reimburse you for them or for the increased electric bill they will generate. Your budget is extremely tight. What should you do?

Draper and Kramer, Inc. v. Baskin-Robbins, Inc.

690 F. Supp. 728

Test your knowledge of leaseholds on a "hard pact."

Baskin-Robbins, Inc. (BR), entered into a lease of commercial property in a mall in Decatur, Illinois. The lease contained the following term:

> Lessor hereby agrees and covenants that no other premises of the building or group of the buildings, owned or controlled by Lessor, of which the leased premises are a part, shall be leased or used for the business of selling "hand packed ice cream, ice cream cones, or soda fountain items . . . [excepting] co-tenants that have executed leases prior to February 28, 1968.

Several years after Baskin-Robbins entered into this lease, the mall entered into a lease with TCBY Yogurt for the operation of such a store at the mall. When BR learned of the new lease, it contacted TCBY. BR maintained that as TCBY would sell soda fountain items, TCBY would be in violation of the exclusive use clause of BR's lease. Although TCBY conceded that it would sell soda fountain items, it contended that as these items would not be made with ice cream, BR's lease would remain unviolated. BR countered by stating that, whether made with ice cream or yogurt, sodas, sundaes, and cones are still soda fountain items. Eventually, the parties sought the forum of a federal court to resolve the dispute.

Questions

1. Do you feel that our society is well served by allowing such issues to be resolved in our federal court system? Can you think of a better forum? (See the Insight section on alternative means of dispute resolution after you have formulated your answer.)

2. Should "exclusive use" clauses be enforced? What do consumers gain if such clauses are broadly enforced (in this case, if TCBY is precluded from serving soda fountain items)? What do consumers gain if exclusive use clauses are narrowly construed (in this case, if the exclusive use clause merely means that no other store can sell ice cream–based soda fountain items)?

3. How would you decide the issue? How do you think the court resolved it?

The Legal Environment of Business: Insurance

CHAPTERS

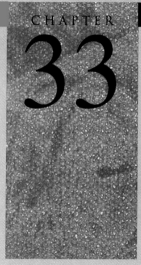

CHAPTER

33

What Is Insurance, and What Types of Risks Can Be Insured Against?

CHAPTER OUTLINE AND OBJECTIVES

After studying this chapter, the student will be able to:

I. Discuss what insurance is and why it is necessary.

II. Define insurable interests.

  a. Insurable interests in property

  b. Insurable interests in life

III. Identify the types of insurance that are available.

  a. Social insurance

  b. Life insurance

  c. Property and casualty insurance

  d. Automobile insurance

  e. Other forms of insurance

IV. Explain how an insurance contract is formed.

  a. Types of insurers

  b. Applicability of contract law

V. Describe how insurance contracts are ended.

VI. Determine from the case of *Lakin* v. *Postal Life and Casualty Company* when a life insurance policy is just an elaborate form of gambling.

What Is Insurance, and Why Is It Necessary?

Indemnify: compensate for loss or damage

Insurance: device transferring risk of loss from specific perils from one person to another

Insurer: party who agrees to accept risk of loss

Insured: party transferring risk of loss to insurer

Premium: consideration paid for insurance protection

Policy: written insurance contract

Face Value: maximum amount that could be paid if harm insured against actually occurs

Beneficiary: third party to whom insurance policy pays upon occurrence of covered loss

Dare we move or breathe, leave the house or children alone, much less drive a vehicle? A trip on the stairs, an inhalation near a broken gas line, a diversion of attention while driving, a match in a small child's hands, all can produce calamitous, life-altering consequences. Such disastrous events can happen to everyone. A person might prepare for them by saving large amounts of cash. However, the typical person can accumulate such amounts only by severe self-deprivation. Thus, preparing for disastrous events on the basis of individual action usually makes little sense.

Collective action, however, can make the problem of preparing for possible disasters as manageable as possible. Many people contributing small amounts can form a resource pool big enough to **indemnify** (compensate for loss or damage) individuals suffering specified large randomly occurring harms. Whether the government, a corporation, or private individuals form the resource pool, the result can be the same.

The primary device used to transfer the risk of loss from specific perils from one person to another is called **insurance.** Insurance comes in many forms and types. It may be granted by the government or some other agency without charge or eligibility criteria. Typically, however, it involves a contract by which an **insurer** (the party who thereby agrees to accept the risk of loss) commits to covering an **insured** (the party who thereby transfers the risk of loss to the insurer) against a certain peril or risk for an amount of consideration called a **premium.** The written insurance contract is called a **policy.** Such a policy usually states a maximum amount that can be paid if the harm insured against actually occurs. This maximum is referred to as the **face value** of the policy. Note that, depending on the type of risk covered by the policy, the compensation for the loss may be paid to a third party, called the **beneficiary,** rather than the insured. This is of course the case when the loss covered is the life of the insured.

Once an insurance contract has been made, the courts treat it as a personal bargain between the insurer and the insured. As a consequence, the insured cannot assign her or his rights under the policy to a third party without the insurer's permission.

Joe ("Crash") Dumi bought a used Corvette from his cousin. Because Crash had a poor rating with the insurance industry due to past problems, he offered his cousin $750 for the six months of automobile insurance coverage left on his cousin's policy on the car. The cousin took the money and wrote out a statement assigning the policy rights to Crash. When Crash lived up to his name and totaled the Corvette a little over two weeks later, he tried to get the insurance company to cover the loss under his cousin's policy. The insurance company refused to do so. Crash's attorney then pointed out to him that insurance policies are not assignable by the insureds. Crash sued his cousin for his $750 payment for the policy and recovered it, but he lost the $17,000 he had in the Corvette.

Insurable Interests

In a similar vein, in order to prevent insurance from being another form of wagering, insurers determine who is eligible to acquire insurance on property or persons by requiring that the insured have an insurable interest in the subject matter of the policy. Having an **insurable interest** means that the insured would suffer some pecuniary (monetary) loss if the insured property were damaged or destroyed or the insured individual died. As mentioned, if such an interest were not required, I could, for example, take out fire insurance on your home. Why? Perhaps because I know that the wiring is bad and will probably start a fire soon. Perhaps because my brother-in-law installed the wiring, and judging from the job he did in my home, I am sure that a fire is imminent in yours. Or perhaps because I intend to torch your home one of these nights. Whatever the motive, such "wagering" through insurance contracts would be highly detrimental to our society.

Insurable Interest: potential pecuniary loss to insured if property is damaged or destroyed or insured dies

Insurable Interests in Property

To be able to collect on a policy covering property, the insured must not only have an insurable interest in the property at the time the policy is taken out but must also have such an interest at the time of loss. Also, it is possible for many persons to have an insurable interest in the same property.

HYPOTHETICAL CASE

Walston Baskit bought a brand-new thresher. Its air-conditioned cab had tinted windows and a built-in CD player and AM/FM stereo. The Pennsboro National Savings Bank held a security interest in the thresher because it had loaned Baskit $87,500 to purchase the machine. Kleen Kut Harvesters, Inc., leased the thresher from Baskit for the month of August so that it could harvest its Kansas crop. Baskit, Pennsboro National, and Kleen Kut all have insurable interests in the thresher, and all of them could purchase insurance on it. If it were destroyed, all three could collect for their individual losses.

Insurable Interests in Life

Unlike property insurance, an insurable interest in life need be shown only when the insurance is taken out—not at the time of loss. As with property insurance, however, many persons can have an insurable interest in one individual's life. Generally, each of us has such an interest in our own life. If we are married, our spouse has an interest in our life. If we have creditors, each of them has an interest in our life. Our business partners or employers have such an interest if they can show that they will suffer financial loss upon our death. However, the law typically disallows children's claims that they have an insurable interest in an elderly parent or sibling.

What Basic Types of Insurance Are Available?

Four basic types of insurance stand out from all the rest. These are (1) social insurance, (2) life insurance, (3) property and casualty insurance, and (4) automobile insurance.

Social Insurance

Many of the more advanced nations around the world, including our own, rely on governmentally funded insurance plans to protect their citizens against the risks of advanced age, unemployment, disability, poverty, and catastrophic medical expenses. In Chapter 34 we will discuss eligibility for and coverage of the US social insurance programs.

Life Insurance

In Chapter 34 we will also deal with the available life insurance coverages, ways to increase coverage for accidental death, and how much can be collected on life insurance policies, by whom, and when.

Property and Casualty Insurance

This category encompasses a broad range of coverages. From fire insurance policies that can be augmented to include storm and earthquake damage to theft and liability policies that provide protection against the frailties of people, property and casualty insurance fills tremendous needs. It will be covered in detail in Chapter 35.

Automobile Insurance

A complex form of property and casualty insurance crucial to our mobile society, automobile insurance requires a detailed discussion. Comprehensive, collision, uninsured motorist, and underinsured motorist coverages and many more are explained in Chapter 35.

Fidelity Insurance:
indemnification coverage for potential losses from dishonesty and laxness in fulfilling obligations owed to insured

Other Forms of Insurance

A less important form of insurance than those listed above, **fidelity insurance** provides protection against forms of dishonesty and laxness in fulfilling obligations owed to the insured.

Insurable Business Risks **Figure 33–1**

Risk	Insurance
Disruption of daily business events due to fire or other peril	Business interruption insurance
Professional negligence	Malpractice insurance
Defective products	Product liability insurance
Employee injury liability	Workers' compensation insurance
Employee dishonesty	Fidelity insurance

HYPOTHETICAL CASE

Although the Mutual Farmer's Association of Pennsboro trusted its employees completely, Bea Kanton, the manager, kept a $100,000 fidelity insurance policy in force. One day in late summer, a farmer came into her office to question some erasures on his grain storage ticket. Because Emma Beason, the secretary-treasurer of the company, was on vacation, Bea had to straighten out the matter herself. When she found the copy of the ticket in the company's files, it became obvious that Emma had altered the amounts on the ticket. Bea spent the next weekend going through the files and discovered that Emma had embezzled over $40,000 from the company in the last two years alone. Although the fidelity insurance would cover the losses, when Emma returned from vacation, she found herself confronting criminal charges.

Another form of insurance of some importance is **marine insurance**. Its coverage indemnifies for losses due to the perils of water transport. Both ships and cargoes are covered by marine insurance.

Marine Insurance: indemnification coverage for potential losses due to perils of water transport

In addition to the types of insurance already mentioned, as many types of insurance are available as insurers see fit to write. The famous insurer of last resort, Lloyd's of London, specializes in **underwriting** (insuring) against all manner of risks, from loss of dexterity in a pianist's fingers to the effects of war. Even so, one type of insurance is not available, namely insurance on the profitability of a business. Insurance companies will not directly insure a person against his or her failure to conduct a commercial operation properly. To do so would rob the businessperson of the fear of failure that promotes success. However, for a list of types of insurance tailored to other business risks see Figure 33–1.

Underwriting: act of insuring

How Is an Insurance Contract Formed?

To answer this question, one must realize first that the principles of contract law apply to the agreements embodied in an insurance policy. Some special rules also apply as well, which we'll cover in a moment. Before we get to them, however, we need to consider the parties offering indemnification, the insurers.

Insurance has always been a lucrative and stable industry. It is well regulated by the insurance commissions of the various states. The companies and associations that hold themselves out as insurers are given publicly available letter rankings after intensive audits of their cash, their management, and the policies they have written. The insurance industry thrives on the large-scale predictability of individually random events ranging from deaths to car crashes. Because of the reliability of statistical projections (referred to as the law of large numbers), profitability is reduced to a question of mathematics and marketing. Consequently, insurers have become the largest of our financial reservoirs.

Types of Insurers

Several types of organizations hold themselves out as potential insurers in today's marketplace. The government, at times in cooperation with the insurance industry, offers types of insurance that would probably be unavailable commercially. These include workers' compensation insurance and retirement insurance. Traditional insurance products such as life and fire insurance are typically offered by stock and mutual insurance companies. Some fraternal organizations also offer such coverages to their members.

Stock Insurance Company: insurer capitalized by investors who expect return on their investment from profits of firm

Mutual Insurance Company: insurer capitalized through premiums of insureds

A **stock insurance company** is one that has been capitalized by investors who expect a return on their money from its profits. A **mutual insurance company** is one that is capitalized through the premiums of the insureds. These premiums are used to meet the administrative expenses of the firm and to form a pool of money from which the resources for indemnifying the policyholders are to be taken. If a mutual insurance company shows a profit, it can be paid back to the policyholders in the form of a nontaxable refund of their premiums.

Applicability of Contract Law

With the exception of the government, which can legislate its own rules, all types of insurers are governed by the law of contracts in the formation, issuance, and application of their insurance contracts. All of the essential elements of contracts that we studied earlier must be present. However, there are some rules and terminology that apply specifically to insurance law.

Agreement and Genuine Assent. The agreement between the parties calling on one party to indemnify the other is typically formed as a result of a detailed examination of both the policy terms and the applicant's level of exposure to risk. The insurance companies, through their agents and their advertising of coverages against various perils, widely extend an *invitation to negotiate* to potential insureds. The wise person considering the purchase of insurance does a great deal of informed comparison shopping of the various policies. Comparison shopping is a near necessity because an insurance agent seldom, if ever, has the authority to alter the terms of a policy so as to tailor it to an individual situation. Instead, the terms are placed before the would-be insureds on a take-it-or-leave-it basis. Taking time to understand the extent of the coverages and the premium structure may save the insured tens of thousands of dollars.

Once the would-be insured finds a suitable policy, she or he must apply for coverage. In other words, the would-be insured becomes the offeror with her or his submission of the application for coverage. The insurer can either accept or reject the offer based on the facts presented by the applicant and, at times, on its own investigation.

HYPOTHETICAL CASE

> Joanna Sturgeon married Bill Prentiss. She was 35 and an executive making in the high five figures with a leading stock brokerage firm. He was 23, just out of graduate school, and an unpublished writer. He stayed home, took care of Joanna's three children by her first marriage, and wrote. Worried about her family's livelihood if she should die, Joanna took out a $5 million life insurance policy. When she applied for the coverage, she answered a detailed set of questions about her health and her ancestral family's medical problems. Before the insurance company would issue the policy, it required Joanna to undergo a series of medical tests, including one for AIDS. Once its investigation was successfully concluded, it accepted Joanna's offer, cashed her premium check, and covered her for the $5 million.

Statements that the applicant makes in her or his offer, such as statements regarding the incidence of cancer in Joanna's family or the presence of safety devices in an automobile or home, may prove extremely significant to the validity of the policy. If such statements are not included in the policy, they are termed **representations**. Statements in the application that are made a part of the issued policy are known as **warranties**. Even if not a part of the policy, an applicant's false representation of a **material fact** (one that, if known, would have caused the insurer not to issue the policy) renders the policy voidable by the insurer. Should it be shown that a warranty is false, whether or not it is material to the issuance and/or believed to be the truth by the applicant, the policy is voidable by the insurer. The same result holds should a material fact not be disclosed when the insurer requests it (this is referred to as **concealment**).

Although the insurance industry normally follows a deliberate and careful approach to risk assumption, it responds quickly to certain insurance needs. In the property and casualty area, for example, agents can enter into temporary oral agreements to extend coverage to those with immediate insurance needs. Let us say that you have just purchased your second Rolls-Royce and that you do not want to drive it until it's insured. You can call your agent from the dealership and secure temporary insurance merely through the agent's say-so over the phone. The policy goes into effect at once, but the agent will confirm the transaction by issuing a written voucher of insurance called a **binder.** This will satisfy the legal requirement for a writing. As you might expect, the insurance company reserves the right to cancel any such agreement upon review. However, you will be covered for any loss insured against until the cancellation occurs.

Consideration. Mutual consideration in the forms of a premium and the indemnification it buys binds both parties to the insurance contract. Although certain large insurance premiums can be paid in installments, payment is usually due in advance of the coverage period. This is especially true for automobile

Representations: statements in application that are not made part of issued policy

Warranties: statements in application that are made part of issued policy

Material Fact: event or circumstance that, if known, would have caused insurer not to issue policy

Concealment: failure to disclose material fact in application

Binder: written voucher of insurance

insurance. Also, certain eventualities can compel the return of premiums or the reduction of the coverage bargained for. For example, when it is discovered that a person lied about his or her age in purchasing life insurance coverage, the policy's payoff is typically reduced to the amount of insurance that the premium would have purchased had the true age of the insured been known.

Form of the Contract.   Insurance policies must be in writing. Insurance laws uniformly require this. State insurance statutes also typically require that significant terms not be hidden in lengthy paragraphs of verbiage or at least that they be highlighted by color or large print. Failure to follow such statutory requirements usually results in the voiding of the hidden terms by the courts. Another rule working in favor of the insured is that any ambiguity in the policy is construed against the drafting party.

HYPOTHETICAL CASE

Edith Walker's life came to a tragic ending one summer night as she staggered on her way home and fell into the path of an oncoming car. She was highly inebriated according to a test of her blood alcohol content. The Pennsboro Life Insurance Company refused to pay on its $100,000 policy on Ms. Walker because the policy specifically excluded payment when "death occurs as a result of alcoholism." The local chapter of Alcoholics Anonymous (AA), ironically named as the beneficiary of Ms. Walker's policy, brought suit, claiming that one incident involving drunkenness did not constitute the disease of alcoholism. The court agreed and construed the ambiguous term against its maker. As a consequence, Pennsboro Life had to pay AA the $100,000 face value.

Capacity of the Parties.   As discussed in principle back in Chapter 10, the insane, habitual drunkards, and minors are held to be without capacity to enter into insurance contracts. Minors in particular are able to avoid most such contracts with the notable exception of life insurance.

How Are Insurance Contracts Ended?

In general, insurance policies end either through expiration of the coverage period or by action of a party or parties to the contract. For example, in the case of property or casualty insurance, even a substantial payout for damage does not end the policy. Homeowner's or automobile insurance policies cover the subject properties until they are canceled or the coverage period expires.

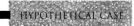
HYPOTHETICAL CASE

Travis Lear's recreational vehicle was vandalized during a stopover in a desert campground. The insurance company paid $7,230 to have it put back into shape. Leaving the repair garage, Trav ran over a high curb and bent the frame. The insurance policy was still in force, so the insurance company paid another $4,800 to correct the problem. Lear's insurance remained in effect even after the second incident as neither party sought to cancel it and the coverage period had not expired.

Cancellation, unlike expiration, usually requires notice. The length of time required depends on the type of insurance and varies widely. Should the coverage period paid for extend beyond the effective date of cancellation, the insured generally has the right to a refund.

APPLICATIONS OF
WHAT YOU'VE LEARNED

Vocabulary Development

Fill in the blanks with the appropriate term.

Beneficiary	**Indemnify**	**Marine Insurance**	**Premium**
Binder	**Insurable Interest**	**Material Fact**	**Representations**
Concealment	**Insurance**	**Mutual Insurance**	**Stock Insurance Company**
Face Value	**Insured**	**Company**	**Underwriting**
Fidelity Insurance	**Insurer**	**Policy**	**Warranties**

1. _____ would cover losses I incurred when a trusted employee embezzled money from my business.

2. The consideration I pay for insurance is called the _____.

3. The party to whom the insurer will pay upon the covered loss is termed the _____.

4. _____ is another term for the act of insuring.

5. _____ are statements of facts, that I make in the application for insurance that become part of the written insurance contract.

6. The failure to disclose a material fact to a potential insurer is termed _____.

7. The written insurance contract is termed a(n) _____.

Problems

1. While Angela and John were married, Angela took out a $500,000 life insurance policy on John. Even after their bitterly contested divorce, she kept the policy in effect with regular premium payments. Six months after their divorce, John died a violent death under suspicious circumstances. However, nothing could be proven against Angela. Will she collect on the policy? Why or why not?

2. During their marriage, Angela and John owned a large yacht on which Angela had also taken out insurance. As a part of the divorce settlement, John received the full ownership of the yacht. As with the life insurance, Angela had kept up her payments on the yacht insurance. In fact, John died in an explosion that destroyed the yacht. Will Angela collect on the yacht's insurance policy? Why or why not?

3. Which of the following are generally not insurable risks?

   a. Atie Ate, the renowned concert pianist, wants to insure her fingers for $1 million against any accident or disease that would prevent her from performing during the next five years.

   b. Jim Hofta wants to take out life insurance on himself that would pay the face amount of the policy to him if he lives to the age of 65.

   c. Sandy Andreas wants to take out earthquake insurance on the parking lot of her business.

   d. Sandy Andreas wants to take out life insurance on Kay Junn, the chef she has just employed to cook in her new restaurant.

   e. Sandy Andreas wants to take out insurance to cover the risk that she will not make enough money in the restaurant to cover the mortgage payments on the property.

4. In the final estimate, which policy should cost less in covering identical risks—the policy of a mutual insurance company or the policy of a stock insurance company? Why?

5. Cindy Swanson, the famous child star, was beset by financial problems as she neared 18 years of age. Realizing that she had paid in thousands of dollars to her insurance companies over the last decade, she decided, as a minor, to avoid the policies and demand the return of the premiums. When she totaled it up, she found that she had paid in $32,000 for homeowner's insurance on her Beverly Hills townhouse and $45,000 for her life insurance coverage. How much is she likely to get back? Why?

ACTUAL CASE STUDY

Lakin v. Postal Life and Casualty Insurance Company

316 S.W.2d 542

Test your skill in discerning when it is insurance and when it is just gambling.

Lakin took out a life insurance policy on Hankinson, who Lakin claimed was his business partner, and was listed as the beneficiary of the policy. Lakin faithfully paid the policy premiums. When Hankinson died and the insurance company refused to pay, Lakin brought suit for the amount due under the policy's terms. The evidence revealed that Hankinson had not paid in any capital or contributed

any expertise to the alleged partnership. In addition, Hankinson was not permitted to issue partnership checks or to hire or fire employees. Finally, upon Hankinson's death no settlement of his alleged partnership share had been made.

Questions

1. Upon what basis should the court make its decision?

2. What, if anything, should Hankinson receive from the insurance company?

CHAPTER

34

How Do Life Insurance and Social Insurance Protect Us?

CHAPTER OUTLINE AND OBJECTIVES

After studying this chapter, the student will be able to:

I. Discuss how life and social insurance protect us.

II. Identify the terms found in a typical life insurance policy.

    a. Exclusions

    b. Days of grace

    c. Double indemnity and disability coverages

    d. Insurance of insurability

    e. New forms of coverage

III. Evaluate the available types of life insurance policies.

    a. Term insurance

    b. Fund accumulation policies

    c. Beneficiaries under the various policy types

IV. Explain the significance of the available types of social insurance

    a. Eligibility for social insurance benefits

    b. The securing of benefits by eligible parties

V. Evaluate the difference between law and justice in *Lincoln National Life Insurance Company* v. *Johnson*, the case of the legally insane beneficiary who stood to recover on a life insurance policy after killing the insured.

How Are We Protected by Life Insurance and Social Insurance?

We begin our in-depth look at the various types of insurance with the ones that protect us against the gravest risks, that is, the loss of life, limb, and vitality. Although our society gives lip service to the idea that every life is priceless, in actuality we each have a dollar value to the people who depend on us in some way. To most of these people, be they family, employers, or members of a public that we serve, the loss of our productivity and our accumulation of capital would make a monetary difference. Without us, our spouses and children might not be well supported, our employers might not be able to produce or sell as good a product, the services offered by our society might be less adequate. Insurance, through its pooling of monetary resources and its payout of such resources as needed, helps alleviate losses of these kinds.

Life Insurance: indemnification for loss due to death of person whose life is insured

In particular, **life insurance** provides a contractual means for transferring the potential loss due to the death of a certain individual to an insurer who will pay a prearranged amount of money to a named beneficiary upon that occurrence.

Social Insurance: indemnification against forced retirement, disability, severe illness, unemployment, and other risks

Social insurance provides similar protection against forced retirement, disability, severe illness, unemployment, and other risks. Without such protection, members of our society would be far less likely to take the financial and personal risks that are the lifeblood of progress. However, because of the enormousness of the potential losses, only the government has been able to bring together the pool of resources necessary to offer social insurance protection to the general public.

What Terms Are Found in a Typical Life Insurance Policy?

A large number of insurers offer policies to cover the most serious of all risks, the loss of life. The life insurance contract is based on the representations and warranties made by the insured and on the tests and investigations performed by the insurer. The insurance company evaluates this information to determine the premium that it demands for the face value of the life insurance policy.

Exclusions

Exclusions: terms eliminating coverage in certain situations

That evaluation is also reflected in the **exclusions,** terms eliminating coverage in certain situations, found in life insurance policies. "War clauses," for example, exclude coverage when the person whose life is insured is involved in armed hostilities. Other possible exclusions include:

Death of the insured resulting from piloting or being a passenger on an airplane.
The execution by act of law of the person whose life is insured.
Suicide of the insured. However, most policies set a time limit on this provision. Usually, the insurer must pay if the suicide occurs more than two years after the issuance of the policy. If the suicide occurs before the time limit has run, the insurer merely has to return the premiums paid.

Murder of the insured by the beneficiary. Note, however, that this applies solely to murder, not to some other form of criminal involvement in the insured's death.

Benjamin Fishery was doing 75 miles per hour when his car left the road, burst through a hedge, and slammed into a tree in the yard of Peter and Mary Martin. When the Martins ran out to help, Ben was climbing out of the car with hardly a scratch on him (the air bag on the driver's side having saved his life). Unfortunately, Ben's wife was dead on arrival at a local hospital. The state highway patrol arrived at the scene of the accident almost immediately and arrested Ben for driving while intoxicated. His blood alcohol content was almost double the legal limit. He was later convicted of both the DWI charge and manslaughter, for which he received a total of six months in jail. Nonetheless, Ben recovered $250,000 under his wife's life insurance policy.

Various other exclusions exist. These are generally tailored to hazardous occupations that insureds reveal in their answers to preissuance questionnaires. However, fraud or misrepresentation in supplying answers to these questionnaires may result in the mistaken issuance of policies. As mentioned in Chapter 33, the insurer has the right to void a policy based on erroneous material representations or warranties by the applicant. Even so, most policies contain a term, called an **incontestable clause,** that puts a time limit on the exercise of this right. A limit of one or two years from the issuance date of the policy is common. Beyond that time, if the insurer has not voided coverage, the policy is in full force regardless of any misrepresentation, fraud, or concealment by the applicant unless it is discovered that the applicant has lied about her or his age. In that case the face amount of the policy is adjusted to the face amount that the premium would have bought had the correct age been known.

Incontestable Clause: policy term placing time limit on insurer's right to avoid due to improper information in application

When Connie Stinson took out a life insurance policy from a Pennsboro insurance company, she either concealed from the company that she had had cancer, was a heavy smoker, had been treated several times for alcoholism, and was a licensed pilot or she gave the company inaccurate information regarding these matters. Two years and one day after the policy was issued, Connie committed suicide by crashing her twin-engine plane into a mountainside. Because of the incontestable clause, the insurance company could not void the policy on the ground of suicide and had to pay the full face value of the policy, $1 million, into her estate.

Days of Grace

Another term of considerable importance to an insured relates to the **days of grace.** This is the period, usually a month, during which an overdue life insurance

Days of Grace: time period during which overdue life insurance premium can be paid to keep policy in force

Lapses: terminates

premium can be paid to keep the policy in force. The payment can be rendered even if the insured has died in the interim. If it is not rendered, the policy **lapses** (terminates).

Double Indemnity and Disability Coverages

In today's information-rich world, life expectancy tables, often developed and maintained by insurance companies, affect our expectations of personal longevity. Such expectations are often a major factor in determining the amount of insurance coverage we buy on our lives. Obviously, if we live a long life, our employment income is likely to be sufficient to put our children through school and send them out on their own, to put away savings for retirement, and so on. After all that has been achieved, the need for a payout to our survivors upon our death is minimal. Many people therefore insure themselves with that final, minimal need in mind. But what if accident prevents them from living out their natural span of days? How can their families replace the income lost for this reason? A partial solution to this problem is a coverage that can be placed in a life insurance policy for a relatively small increase in the premium. This coverage is referred to as **double indemnity.** It causes the insurer to pay twice (or three or four times for triple or quadruple indemnity, respectively) the face amount upon the accidental death of the person on whose life the insurance is being carried.

Double Indemnity: Policy term obligating insurer to pay twice face value upon accidental death

Disability Coverage: coverage indemnifying for permanent inability to work

Disability coverage protects against a devastating potential consequence of accident and disease, namely a permanent inability to work. Innovative life insurance policies provide for the payment of a regular income supplement upon the certification of such an inability by physicians. Earlier policies provided for the cancellation of further premium payment obligations upon the occurrence of an inability to work.

Insurance of Insurability

Insurance of Insurability: policy term allowing insurance coverage without physical exam

A common term in a life insurance policy that is obtained by agreeing to a slightly higher premium is **insurance of insurability.** Such coverage allows the insured to purchase new amounts of life insurance coverage or to continue current amounts without being required to pass a physical examination or other test.

New Forms of Coverage

Innovative coverages are constantly being developed and offered to potential insureds. Life insurance that pays upon the diagnosis of a terminal illness, not upon its conclusion, is one of these coverages. Also, as discussed in the next section, various new types of policies are frequently brought out to respond to changes in parallel markets for investment funds. One way or another, the insurance industry tries to remain competitive and to fill the needs that brought it into being.

What Types of Life Insurance Policies Are Available?

Whatever the changes in its name or its packaging, there is still one basic type of life insurance. Simply put, it is the type based on a contract whereby a premium is paid for a period of coverage at a certain dollar level of indemnification. Upon the end of the period of coverage contracted for or upon the payout of the face value due to the death of the party whose life is insured, the contract comes to an end. Such pure life insurance, without any frills involving savings plans or other marketing gimmicks, is referred to as **term insurance.**

Term Insurance: simplest policy, with premium paid for certain face value of coverage

HYPOTHETICAL CASE

Bixler bought a $50,000 term life insurance policy on herself through the university where she taught. She paid $35 per month during the academic year for the coverage. At the end of the year the coverage ended. As the $35 per month had gone strictly for the purchase of insurance, she had not built up any savings during the year. She noted that her premium would rise to $37 per month if she took out the same amount of insurance next year as her age had increased and along with it the statistical probability of her death.

Term Insurance

Term insurance policies can be set up with one or two basic forms of payment. In return for a constant face value, **level term** life insurance policies require the payment of a set premium throughout the period that the insurance is in force. In return for a steadily decreasing face value, **decreasing term** policies require the payment of a premium that is smaller than the level term premium for the same initial face amount but like the level term premium is constant throughout the time that the insurance is in force. This cheaper form of insurance often comes closer than level term insurance to satisfying the requirements of insureds whose need for a large face value declines as they grow older, as their mortgages are paid off, and as their children go out on their own.

Level Term: policy requiring payment of set premium for constant face value

Decreasing Term: policy requiring payment of constant premium for steadily decreasing face value

Term insurance's simple function causes it to pop up frequently in our everyday lives. For example, the **travel insurance** policy bought to potentially indemnify for the loss of the insured's life during a trip is term insurance. So too is the **group insurance** policy offered to each member of a body of people with some common characteristic, such as all the employees of a state university or all dentists, all veterans, or all senior citizens. Finally, **credit insurance** policies to pay off the lender if the debtor dies are also term insurance.

Travel Insurance: policy covering life of insured during a trip

Group Insurance: policy offered to each member of body of people with some common characteristics

Credit Insurance: policy to pay off lender whenever debtor dies

Fund Accumulation Policies

Many types of policies other than term insurance flood the life insurance market. Almost all of these types of policies have a built-in savings function that is made possible by the regularity with which the insureds must make their payments to keep the insurance coverage in force. These payments (inaccurately called

Figure 34–1   **Common Types of Life Insurance Policies**

Term	Fund accumulation
Level term	Whole life
Decreasing term	Endowment
Travel insurance	
Group insurance	
Credit insurance	

Whole Life: type of life insurance paying accumulated funds and face value on death of insured

Cash Value: interest and principal in accumulation fund of life insurance policy

Endowment: type of life insurance paying face value to insured if alive after certain time

premiums) are split by the insurer into two amounts. One amount (the true premium) pays for the insurance, and the other goes into an accumulation fund.

A major type of policy with accumulation funds is the whole life policy. **Whole life** insurance policies pay a moderate interest rate on the accumulated funds. The interest and principal in the fund account are referred to as the **cash value** of the policy. This cash value may be borrowed against by the insured, but the insured, absurd as it may seem, must pay interest, usually at a lower than market rate, on this loaned amount of his or her own money. Upon the death of the insured, the insurer must pay the beneficiary the policy's face amount plus the cash value (less any loan amount outstanding).

Endowment life insurance is another type of fund accumulation policy. Under its terms the insured typically pays a very high "premium" for insurance coverage and the right to receive the face value, if still alive, at retirement or the end of a certain period. This type of policy makes sense to individuals who might need a large lump sum of money at a particular time in life, say to buy a retirement home in the Sun Belt.

The interest paid by the insurers on the funds accumulated in these types of policies is typically significantly lower than that available through other investment means. Consequently, financial advisers regularly tout the advantages of buying term insurance and investing the difference. Nonetheless, the forced regularity of the savings causes many to avail themselves of these types of insurance.

Newer types of fund accumulation policies have recently been developed. Some allow the insured to control how the accumulated funds are invested; others guarantee minimum returns on the funds. Regardless, fund accumulation policies remain popular among insureds and lucrative for insurers.

Beneficiaries under the Various Policy Types

As discussed in Chapter 33, the beneficiary is the individual named to receive the payout from an insurance policy. With the possible exception of the insured under an endowment policy who lives long enough to receive its benefits, all life insurance policies pay off to someone other than the person whose life is insured. This person may be a family member, a business associate, or an estate. As long as the required insurable interest can be shown by the person taking out the insurance, that person can name any potential recipient for the funds. Two or more beneficiaries can be named to receive equal shares. On the other hand,

Types of Social Insurance   **Figure 34–2**

```
S   O   D   U   H
U   L   I   N   E
R   D   S   E   A
V   A   A   M   L
I       B   P   T
V   G   I   L   H
O   E   L   O
R       I   Y
S       T   M
        Y   E
            N
            T
```

primary and contingent beneficiaries may be preferred. A **primary beneficiary** (the person named first in priority to receive the whole policy payout) must still be alive when the person whose life is insured dies. The **contingent beneficiary** is the person named to receive the policy payout should the primary beneficiary die first.

One way or another, it is the prerogative of the person who has taken out the policy to name the beneficiary and to change the beneficiary upon suitable notice in writing to the insurer.

Primary Beneficiary: person named to receive policy payout if alive when insured dies

Contingent Beneficiary: person named to receive policy payout should primary beneficiary die before insured

What Types of Social Insurance Are Available?

The federal Social Security Act of 1935, as amended, provides for most of the social insurance we are familiar with in this country. Old-Age, Survivors, Disability, and Health Insurance (labeled OASDHI by the Social Security Administration) coverages are available to those eligible (See Figure 34–2 for an acronym that helps in remembering the social insurance coverages that are available.) Also provided is unemployment coverage, which the states administer in compliance with the Federal Unemployment Tax Act (FUTA).

These coverages are based on a pool of funds collected by taxing employees and employers. Of the first $50,000 earned annually by the employee, 6.2 percent is used to support the Old-Age, Survivors, and Diability Insurance programs and 1.45 percent is used to support Medicare, for a total of 7.65 percent of wages. On $50,000 this amounts to $3,825. The employer is taxed an equal amount. Taken together, the tax rate used to generate the funds that support these programs totals 15.3 percent.

Eligibility for Social Insurance Benefits

To be fully insured and therefore eligible to receive OASDHI benefits, a person must have recorded proof with the Social Security Administration that she or he

Quarters: three-month periods in which worker earned at least approximately $600, used in determining eligibility for certain social insurance programs

Medicare: program helping eligible individuals pay for hospital, physician, and other health care expenses

worked at least a set number of **quarters** (three-month periods in which the person earned at least approximately $600). Up to four quarters can be awarded in each year. Retirement benefit eligibility requires 40 quarters of credit. Disability and Survivors' benefit eligibility is determined on a sliding scale requiring from as few as 6 quarters at age 28 to as many as 40 quarters at age 62. To be eligible to receive its benefits, **Medicare** (a program that helps eligible individuals pay for hospital, physician, and other health care expenses) only requires that the recipient be 65 or older or be eligible for disability payments under OASDHI. Finally, although unemployment program eligibility varies somewhat from state to state, almost all states require that the recipient be totally out of work for a set period, be registered with the state, and be actively looking for employment and ready, willing, and able to work if suitable work is found. For work to be "suitable," it must be within a reasonable distance from the worker's residence and, even though for lower pay, in a field in which the worker has experience or training.

The Securing of Benefits by Eligible Parties

The steps that must be taken to secure benefits vary from program to program. Any eligible party 62 years of age or older may receive her or his retirement benefits by simply applying for them. The full benefit amount, however, is payable when the retirement benefits are requested at age 65 and not before. The closer to age 62 the benefits are requested, the lower the amount of the monthly check. Note that up to age 70 the retirement benefits of persons making more than a set amount of outside income are reduced.

Survivors' benefits can be obtained by persons related to a deceased worker (who, to render the possible recipient eligible, must have had over six quarters of coverage in the three years prior to her or his death) in the following ways:

By being the worker's parent over 62 years of age and dependent on the worker for support.

By being the worker's surviving spouse and at least 60 years old (or at least 50 if disabled) or being of any age if caring for a disabled child or any child under 18.

By being the worker's dependent child.

Disability benefits are payable to fully insured individuals with an appropriate disability who are under 65 years of age and have worked 20 quarters within the 10 years preceding the disability.

Under the Medicare program, *health insurance benefits* to cover hospital, physician, and other health care expenses flow to persons over 65: such benefits flow under the Medicaid program to persons under 65 who lack the financial ability to pay for health costs. If Medicare is not applied for within the three-month period before or after the insured's 65th birthday, a considerable wait for benefits will ensue. Medicaid requires only proof of a current level of indigency. The Medicaid rolls are currently approaching 30 million persons.

Finally, *unemployment benefits* are available to eligible parties upon filing. However, depending on the applicable state rules, these benefits may be reduced or denied if the worker:

Quit her or his job without just cause (for example, unsafe working conditions provide such cause).

Turns down or doesn't even try to acquire suitable work.

Is a full-time student.

Lies about job skills.

Was fired due to criminal or other improper conduct.

Lost his or her job due to participation in a strike or other labor dispute.

Is receiving a pension or Social Security retirement benefits.

The various forms of social insurance discussed above reflect the fact that we are all a part of the same society and therefore responsible to one another for one another. From the humblest castoffs who find their residence in our streets to the residents of our grandest mansions, our differences from one another are not great enough to justify denying the needs of the former for the purpose of indulging the wants of the latter.

APPLICATIONS OF WHAT YOU'VE LEARNED

Vocabulary Development

Fill in the blanks with the appropriate term.

Cash Value
Contingent Beneficiary
Credit Insurance
Days of Grace
Decreasing Term
Disability Coverage
Double Indemnity
Endowment
Exclusions
Group Insurance
Incontestable Clause
Insurance of Insurability
Lapses
Level Term
Life Insurance
Medicare
Primary Beneficiary
Quarter
Social Insurance
Term Insurance
Travel Insurance
Whole Life

1. _____ is offered to a certain class of similarly situated individuals.

2. _____ eliminate coverage in certain situations, for example, the coverage of a life insurance policy if the policyholder dies during air travel.

3. Providing insurance that covers hospital, physician, and other health care costs, _____ is a program that has been set up under the Social Security Act.

4. A(n) _____ is a period in which a worker earned at least a certain amount. The accumulated number of these periods is used in determining eligibility for certain social insurance programs.

5. The _____ is the person named to receive the payout from a life insurance policy as long as she or he is alive at the time of the insured's death.

6. A(n) _____ insurance policy requires higher than usual premiums but pays out the face value if the person whose life is insured lives for a certain term or past a certain age.

7. The period during which paying a delinquent premium can keep a life insurance policy in force is called the _____.

8. A(n) _____ term in a life insurance policy requires that the insurer pay twice the face value upon the accidental death of the person whose life is insured.

9. A term in a life insurance policy that disallows the insurer from voiding the policy because of inaccurate statements made in the application is referred to as a(n) _____.

10. The accumulated funds under a whole life insurance policy that are payable along with the face value of the policy are referred to as the _____ of the policy.

Problems

1. Some people, notably extremely rich individuals and individuals without dependents, maintain that they do not need life insurance coverage. Evaluate the positions taken by such people. Are there other kinds of people who might make this claim?

2. Assume that Andrew Jackson Borden's life insurance policy contains all of the exclusions from coverage discussed in the chapter. Would the insurance company be allowed to avoid paying if he died in any of the following ways?

   a. He was hatcheted to death by his beneficiary, Lisbeth Andrews Borden.

   b. He died in combat in the Far East.

   c. He died in an auto accident caused by his being intoxicated.

   d. He committed suicide barely a month after taking out the policy. (Would your answer change if the suicide occurred three years after he took out the policy? Why?)

3. On December 13, 19**, while returning home from a long sales trip, Blaine Thomas died in an automobile accident. He was buried a few days later. Ten days after his death his wife, Olive, found that the last premium on his life insurance policy was due December 12 but had gone un-

paid. The policy was for $250,000 with a triple indemnity clause. What other clause in the policy should Olive look for? If she finds that clause and places the policy back in force, how much should the insurer pay the beneficiary?

4. If you were going to take out a life insurance policy, which would you be more likely to use, term insurance or a fund accumulation policy? State your reasoning.

5. Which of the following facts will prevent applicant Herb Hoover from receiving unemployment benefits?

   a. In his application he lied in claiming that he was a musician by trade.

   b. He was dismissed from his previous job due to an economic downturn.

   c. He was dismissed from his previous job because his employer relocated to Mexico.

   d. Because the pay was only 75 percent of his previous wage, he turned down suitable work arranged for him by the unemployment bureau.

   e. He was dismissed because he participated in a work stoppage at his previous employer's factory.

ACTUAL CASE STUDY

Lincoln National Life Insurance Company v. Johnson

669 F. Supp. 201

Consider the case of a dead insured and the legally insane beneficiary who killed him, yet stood to recover on the deceased's insurance policy.

The insured, Russell Johnson, was allegedly murdered by his son and beneficiary, Kurt Johnson. After Kurt was found not guilty by reason of insanity, the insurer deposited his proceeds from the policy into a special account to be paid as directed

by the court. Kurt's guardian (appointed for him because Kurt was confined to a state mental hospital after the verdict in the murder case) filed a claim for the deposited funds on Kurt's behalf. There is a long-standing policy in Illinois law that someone should not profit from his or her intentionally committed wrongful act.

Questions

1. Would it be just for Kurt to recover in this case? Would letting him recover encourage others similarly situated to follow his example? What policy device would prevent this problem?

2. As a matter of law, will Kurt recover in this case? Should a beneficiary who killed the insured in self-defense be able to recover?

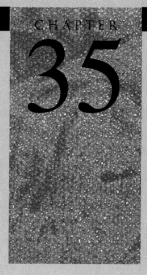

CHAPTER

35 Why Do We Need Property and Casualty Insurance, and What Specific Coverages Make Auto Insurance So Necessary?

CHAPTER OUTLINE AND OBJECTIVES

After studying this chapter, the student will be able to:

I.   Identify the types of protection offered by property and casualty insurance.

II. Discuss the coverages and terms offered in a fire insurance policy.

    a. Basic policy and riders

    b. Recovery requirements

    c. Coinsurance

III. Explain the usefulness of marine and inland marine insurance.

IV. Evaluate the need for liability insurance.

    a. Advantages of the all-risk policy

    b. Fidelity insurance

VI. Discuss the available coverages under a typical automobile insurance policy.

    a. Liability coverage

    b. Medical payments coverage

    c. Collision, comprehensive, and uninsured and underinsured motorist coverage

    d. No-fault insurance systems

VII. Consider, using *Hall* v. *Wilkerson* as the basis for discussion, the effects of alcohol, not on a driver's performance, but on whether the driver is insured.

What Types of Protection Are Offered by Property and Casualty Insurance?

A lot can be inferred from the words *property and casualty,* which are generally used to designate the types of insurance considered in this chapter. First of all, property insurance is obviously intended to protect property, both real and personal, from perils that might befall it. Fire, criminal action, earthquake, and storm can all be insured against under the terms of property insurance. Casualty insurance, on the other hand, protects the overall worth of the insured from liability for accidentally or negligently inflicted losses on the property or person of another. Some policies, especially automobile insurance policies, incorporate both property and casualty provisions. In a nutshell, property and casualty insurance affords protection from the harmful and potentially ruinous consequences of the acts of God and people.

What Coverages and Terms Are Offered in a Fire Insurance Policy?

Fire insurance is a fundamental type of property insurance. The basic fire insurance policy provides for indemnification from losses to property resulting from fire, from damage done to property in getting it out of harm's way of a fire, and from lightning strike. For a homeowner, the property referred to in such a policy includes the dwelling, such other structures as a garage and a storage shed, and the personal property contained therein.

Basic Policy and Riders

Riders: terms that modify standard forms to fit specific situations

Extended Coverage Rider: policy term used to add protection against perils not covered in basic policy

To be certain that the coverage provided by a fire insurance policy is appropriate and fair, each state requires its own standard form for the basic fire insurance policy. Generally, these forms protect property only from the potential losses from fire mentioned above. In each instance, however, the basic form can be modified by riders.

Riders (also called endorsements), are terms that tailor standard forms to fit specific situations. An **extended coverage rider,** for example, is used in many states to add protection against a variety of perils not covered in a basic policy. High winds, riots, aircraft and vehicle impacts, smoke, explosions, hail damage, and other sources of loss are covered by this rider.

HYPOTHETICAL CASE

Corrigan lived directly under the approach to Runway 9 at the International Airport in Pennsboro. Concerned about the constant traffic some 2,500 feet above his chimney, he added an extended coverage rider to his fire insurance policy. Less than three weeks later, a very large tire from a jumbo jet's landing gear fell through his roof. Luckily, no one was at home at the time. Due to the newly added rider, the insurer paid the $28,000 in repair costs for the home. The insurer then sought to recover its money from the airline.

Recovery Requirements

In most forms of property insurance, a **claim** (assertion of an insured's right to indemnification) will be paid if the insurer receives proper notice and proof of the loss sustained by the insured. Depending on the circumstances, the notice must be given immediately or within a reasonable time of the loss. Immediate notice of a fire, for example, provides the insurer with enough time to investigate the occurence while the embers are still warm. For many types of losses, written notice is required. Proof of loss, on the other hand, can typically be given within several months of the incident and still be effective. Such "proof" requires a sworn statement providing detailed information, such as the time and cause of the loss and the extent of the loss in both property and personal injuries. It also requires a listing of witnesses and of other insurance that might be in force and usable to help indemnify the loss. Proper compliance with the notice and proof of loss requirements greatly heightens the chances of a smooth and reasonably quick recovery process.

Under a typical fire insurance policy, the steps necessary to bring about recovery have been augmented somewhat. Proof of loss must include a showing that the fire was actual, hostile, and the proximate cause of the damage. Considering the last first, you might recall that we dealt with the concept of proximate cause back in Chapter 6. Applying that concept here means that the insured is required to show that the fire was the indispensable and immediate factor causing the harm. Generally, courts accept without question that a hostile fire is the proximate cause of accompanying losses caused by burning, smoke, scorching, water and other extinguishing efforts, and removal of endangered property.

What, then, is "hostile" fire? To begin with, a **hostile fire** is a fire that erupts someplace where the insured does not intend it to burn. **A friendly fire** is a fire that burns where the insured intends it to burn. If your furniture is scorched from being too close to the fire in the fireplace, you cannot recover for that loss under a standard fire insurance policy because the fire is still friendly. However, if a live coal escapes from the fireplace and sets a curtain on fire, you can recover for that loss because the fire has escaped from its friendly confines and become hostile.

Finally, an "actual" fire requires more than just an overabundance of heat. Some flame is necessary to meet this third requirement for recovery.

Once a properly documented claim has been submitted to the insurer, the insured can look forward to indemnification. Most property insurance policies, however, provide the insurer with the luxury of choice as to the form of indemnification. For example, instead of paying for the loss, the insurer can have the damaged property repaired or replaced. If the insurer chooses to pay, the policy may provide that only the **actual cash value** (the original price less a reduction for time in use) of the property is recoverable. Due to inflation, this amount is far less than it would cost to replace most goods in today's market. Therefore, for additional premiums, insurance companies offer indemnification at replacement cost values.

In situations involving casualty insurance, the insurance company, after having paid, will be **subrogated** (substituted for another in pursuing a claim or right) for the insured if some third party is at fault. It will then be able to sue the third party on its own. In the situation described above, for example, Corrigan's insurance company will be able to pursue recovery against the airline.

Claim: assertion of insured's right to indemnification

Hostile Fire: fire that burns where insured does not intend it to burn

Friendly Fire: fire that burns where insured intends it to burn

Actual Cash Value: original price less reduction for time in use

Subrogated: substituted for another party in pursuing a claim or right

Figure 35–1   **Typical Steps in the Recovery of a Fire Insurance Claim**

1. The insured must first give the insurance company prompt notice of loss and later provide the insurance company with proof of loss.
2. Notice and proof allow the insurance company first to investigate in order to establish that the fire was actual, hostile, and the proximate cause of the claimed damage and then to verify the claimed extent of the loss.
3. The insurance company determines whether to repair/replace the damaged property or to pay for the loss.
4. The insurance company settles the insured's claim.

Coinsurance

Coinsurance: contract by which policyholder becomes partially self-insuring

Containing the costs of various forms of insurance has been high on the list of many insureds for some years. A principal means of doing so in the fire insurance area is through the use of coinsurance. **Coinsurance** is a contractual means by which the policyholder becomes self-insuring for a certain percentage of the protected property's worth. A typical coinsurance clause requires the insured to keep a policy in force with a face value of 75 percent of the protected property's worth. If the insured does so, the insurer will pay all losses up to that amount in full. This means that the insured will have to suffer financial loss only if more than 75 percent of the protected property's worth is destroyed. In the worst possible case, that is, a total loss, the insured will lose 25 percent of the worth of the protected property and will be compensated by the insurance company for the other 75 percent. However, as fire departments almost always respond quickly enough to prevent a total structural loss, this eventuality seldom occurs.

Should the insured fail to keep up with inflating property values by not increasing the face value of her or his fire insurance accordingly, the insurance company will determine how much it will pay by multiplying the dollar amount of the losses by a fraction whose numerator is the current policy face amount and whose denominator is what the policy face amount should have been.

R. A. R. Enterprises owned a large warehouse that it insured against loss by fire. To keep its costs low, it agreed to have a 75 percent coinsurance term placed in the policy. When the policy was taken out, the warehouse was valued at $100,000. Therefore, R. A. R. purchased a policy with a face value of $75,000. In the next seven years, the value of the building doubled, to $200,000. However, R. A. R. did not increase the face value of its policy. Consequently, when a fire caused a $50,000 loss, the fire insurance company paid only $25,000. This equals the $50,000 loss taken multiplied by $75,000/$150,000, that is, the current policy face value divided by the policy face value that R. A. R. should have carried to live up to its end of the coinsurance deal ($150,000 equals 75 percent of $200,000).

If coinsurance terms are complied with, premiums are kept reasonably well below what they would be if the full value of property were insured. If coinsurance terms are not complied with, that is, if the face value of coinsurance policies is not increased as the value of the coinsured property increases, the amount of any consequently uncovered loss will usually cancel out any short-term savings on premiums.

What Is the Usefulness of Marine and Inland Marine Insurance?

Marine insurance is another form of property insurance. We discussed it briefly in Chapter 33. It indemnifies for losses due to the perils of water transport, and it covers ships and cargoes. **Inland marine insurance** was developed to protect personal property from the perils of land transport. Over the years several modifications were made in the basic inland marine policy. The most significant modification offered coverage of personal property, not just in transit, but at any time. Today an inland marine policy can cover all of the insured's personal property or can be tailored to cover only specific, scheduled property of the insured (detailed on a list provided by the insured to the insurer). Finally, although originally available only to property owners, a form of inland marine insurance is now offered to such bailees as common carriers and repair shops.

Inland Marine Insurance: protects personal property from the perils of land transport

Why Carry Liability Insurance?

It is popularly believed that we live in an extremely litigious (prone to legal disputes) society. Many find confirmation for this belief in the sheer number of lawyers who make a living off our courtroom confrontations (or our desire to avoid them). Confirmation is also available in the high premiums that insurance companies charge for providing a certain type of indemnification to professional-sand other insureds. These insureds are worried about their potential legal responsibility for injuries that they might unintentionally inflict on the person or property of others. The insurance they require is termed **liability insurance.** For insureds ranging from doctors to businesspeople to homeowners to operators of motor vehicles, liability insurance (often labeled malpractice insurance when used to cover professionals) and its cost are facts of life.

Liability Insurance: indemnification against potential legal responsibility for injuries insured might unintentionally inflict on person or property of others

HYPOTHETICAL CASE

J. J. Eric turned 16 on the last day of 1990. His parents taught him to drive shortly thereafter. After they were assured of his ability, they gave him primary use of one of the family's three vehicles, a 1988 Mercury Cougar. The state they all lived in required by law that each driver maintain $10,000 of liability coverage in his or her automobile insurance policy. This was because many drivers at fault in accidents were found to be without financial reserves to pay the damages they owed for the harm they had caused. The Erics made a practice of having 10 times the liability

continued on page 484

concluded
coverage that the state required. They did so to avoid being wiped out by a large damage recovery against them for being at fault in an automobile accident. Unfortunately, the driving history of many younger drivers meant that when the Erics placed such liability coverage on JJ, the insurance company more than tripled the amount of their premium.

Advantages of the All-Risk Policy

All-Risk Policy: contract for indemnification incorporating liability, fire, theft, and property insurance coverages

Instead of contracting for liability, fire, theft, and property insurance separately, many insureds take out one policy that has all of these coverages. That policy is known as an **all-risk policy.** It is also known as a "homeowner's policy" or as "comprehensive insurance." Such a policy includes not only fire insurance but also the extended coverage provided in many riders to the standard fire policy. The amount of the personal property insurance is usually set at a percentage of the amount for which the dwelling is covered. Typically, this insurance is floating coverage on the household's personal property wherever it is located at the time of the loss (on vacation, at school, etc.).

Buying the all-risk policy is usually more expensive than buying each coverage separately, and the all-risk policy does have exclusions, regardless of its name. For example, the liability coverage usually excludes coverage when the insured is driving an auto, boating, or flying or harms someone intentionally or faces strictly business losses. (It will, however, cover such forms of liability as that owed to a guest who slips on the rug and fractures a vertebra. Offsetting the exclusions and the increased cost is the peace of mind that comes with buying a policy tailored to cover the greatest and most significant number of risks to the insured. Also, some provisions are included that may not appear in individually negotiated insurance policies. For example, "living expense coverage," which is used to pay for living quarters while repairs are made to the dwelling (usually up to one-fifth of the face amount), is automatically available with a standard all-risk policy, as is "medical expense coverage" for those injured on the insured's premises or by acts of the insured off his or her premises even though the insured is without legal responsibility for the harm done.

Fidelity Insurance

As mentioned in Chapter 33, fidelity insurance makes it possible to insure against embezzlement, fraud, theft, and other criminal conduct by employees that might cause severe harm to an otherwise profitable business. Having such insurance helps in a number of ways that go beyond merely providing the reassurance of promised indemnification. Insurance companies offering fidelity insurance often evaluate the security measures and other safeguards being employed to forestall criminal conduct by insiders of the business. If such an evaluation discloses weaknesses, the insurer will require that these be corrected in return for continuing indemnification. Regardless, like the other types of coverage that we have discussed in this chapter, fidelity insurance can provide an indispensable safety net to those wise enough to employ it.

Automobile Insurance Coverages   **Figure 35–2**

Liability: For bodily injury, death, or property claims against the insured.

Medical payments coverage: For medical treatment of the insured and the insured's passengers for injuries received while riding in or on or getting in or out of the insured's vehicle.

Collision coverage: Indemnifies the insured from losses to the insured's vehicle due to its running into another object or overturning.

Comprehensive coverage: Indemnifies for losses to the insured's vehicle due to causes other than those covered by collision coverage (for example, hail, theft, or vandalism).

Uninsured and underinsured motorist coverages: Allows collection, from the insured's insurer, of bodily injury and wrongful death damages (not property damage) inflicted on the insured by an uninsured or underinsured motorist who is at fault in the accident.

What Coverages Are Available under a Typical Automobile Insurance Policy?

Now we turn our attention to automobile insurance, a type of insurance that is not only in all likelihood indispensable but is also legally required in most states. As you may have inferred from earlier discussions in this chapter, this particular type of insurance is best obtained in policies that deal with it exclusively. This is mainly due to the complexity of its coverages and to the support network necessary to fairly review automobile claims so as to contain their costs. Realize that each policy can have liability, medical, property, and other coverages specifically tailored to cover the risks of the road and the driver assuming them (see Figure 35–2). To properly understand an automobile policy, each of these coverages has to be examined in some detail.

Liability Coverage

The most important kind of indemnification in automobile insurance, and the one that most states require of licensed drivers, is for liability. A typical liability term obligates the insurer to indemnify the insured up to the policy limits "for any bodily injury, death, or property damage claims for which the insured becomes legally responsible to third parties as a result of an auto accident." The bodily injury liability limit is usually stated in a way indicating the limit that the insurer will pay to each bodily injured party and the limit that it will pay for all bodily injury victims in the accident. The property damage limit is the maximum amount that the insurer will pay to indemnify the insured for property damage that results from the accident. Obviously, the higher the liability limits, the higher the premium.

Regardless of the amount of liability coverage obtained, the insureds can contract to extend that coverage to household members or drivers operating with the permission of any one of the insureds. This is done by what is referred to as an **omnibus clause.**

Because of its potential liability, the insurer typically contracts for the responsibility of either defending or settling the case. This duty (which includes

Omnibus Clause: contract provision extending liability coverage beyond insured to household members or permitted drivers

While her attention was diverted, Nikki Prince negligently ran a red light and crashed her car into a small van. The van's driver, Bill Washam, was killed. His three passengers were injured. After the impact, the two vehicles' momentum carried them into the front area of a convenience store. Several witnesses at the scene left their names with investigating officers. Their statements all clearly indicated Nikki's fault and Washam's blamelessness. The bodily injury liability limits of Nikki's automotive policy were $200,000 for each injured or deceased person and $500,000 for all such claims stemming from one accident. The policy also indemnified for up to $100,000 in property damage. Because of the evidence, the insurance company entered into negotiations to settle the claims. Washam's family sought $1 million for his wrongful death but agreed to accept $350,000. The claims of the other injured individuals were settled for a total of $150,000. The total property damage equaled $125,000. The insurer paid only $200,000 of the $350,000 because of the per person limit on liability, but it paid all of the other bodily injury claims as each was less than $200,000 and the total of all such claims paid for the accident was less than $500,000. The insurance company paid $100,000 of the $125,000 property damage, again because of the limits set on its indemnification. As Nikki had no other liability insurance that would protect her save for an all-risk policy that specifically excluded liability from the operation of automobiles, the unpaid amounts on the property damage and death claims would have to be collected from her personal wealth

the payment of attorney's fees, bond premiums, etc.) ends at the discretion of the insurer when the limit of liability has been paid or tendered. A settlement negotiated by the insured is invalid unless directly authorized or ratified by the insurer.

Note that if Nikki had had a passenger who was injured, that party might have been able to sue her for negligence. Standing in the way of such a suit, however, might be one of many **guest statutes.** On the books in many states, these statutes prohibit such suits by nonpaying passengers unless the driver was grossly negligent or intentionally caused the accident. Gross negligence goes beyond what Nikki displayed in the above incident by negligently running a red light. It is best illustrated by driving while intoxicated or operating a vehicle in a known unsafe condition.

Guest Statutes: laws prohibiting suits by nonpaying passengers against driver unless latter was grossly negligent or intentionally caused accident

Medical Payments Coverage

Medical claims of the parties in the insured's motor vehicle in an accident such as Nikki's might go uncompensated without **medical payments coverage.** Such coverage indemnifies the insured and any person who is injured while entering, leaving, or riding in or on the insured's vehicle. The guest statutes do not bar collecting on this coverage. Limits are usually expressed in a "per person" figure (10,000 per person is a typical coverage), but usually no limit per accident is established.

Medical Payments Coverage: indemnifies for losses sustained by insured and any other person injured while entering, leaving, or riding in or on insured's vehilce

The breadth of medical payments coverage may surprise you. For example, it covers not only medical costs but funeral expenses as well. Also, it follows the insureds even outside their own vehicles. Therefore, whatever the form of the insured's harmful contact with a motor vehicle, the indemnification is available to them.

As a part of her recovery from the accident, Nikki Prince took up bicycle riding. One day, her brakes failed as she cycled down a long hill. At the bottom she slammed into the side of a parked and unoccupied car. Because she had harmful contact with a motor vehicle, the medical payments coverage of her automobile policy paid for her hospitalization, X rays, medicines, and doctor's and dentist's bills.

Collision, Comprehensive, and Uninsured and Underinsured Motorist Coverages

As you have seen, the main focus of an automobile policy is defensive. It is meant, especially through its liability portions, to protect the insured against having to pay for the losses sustained by others due to the insured's operation of a motor vehicle. Add-on coverages such as medical payments coverage help compensate the insured for his or her personal losses. Similarly, collision and comprehensive coverages are both intended to protect the insured from damage to the insured's own vehicle.

Collision Coverage. **Collision coverage** indemnifies the insured for losses to the insured's vehicle due to its running into another object (be it another car, a post, a garage wall, a bridge, or you-name-it) or overturning. The coverage payout is usually based on actual cash value, reduced by whatever deductible ($500 is common) the insured might have selected. In return for reduced premiums, the deductible places the burden on the insured for most, if not all, of the losses sustained in minor mishaps.

Comprehensive Coverage. **Comprehensive coverage** indemnifies for damage to the insured's vehicle stemming from causes other than that covered by collision insurance. Theft, hail, vandalism, the chipping or breakage of glass, all and more are insured against by comprehensive coverage. Like collision coverage, this coverage is usually subject to a deductible from the payout based on actual cash value.

Uninsured and Underinsured Motorist Coverage. Despite the various **financial responsibility laws** (which require that drivers show proof of insurance or other ability to pay a liability judgment), many drivers are uninsured. **Uninsured motorist coverage,** which is available for an increased premium, allows an insured to collect bodily injury and wrongful death damages (not property damages) from her or his insurer if the driver causing the harm does not have insurance. The coverage even applies to hit-and-run accidents in which that driver cannot be found. As with liability coverage, per person and per accident limits are set for uninsured motorist coverage.

Underinsured motorist coverage has become available in recent years because many motorists maintain only the minimum legally required liability coverage (typically $10,000 per person/$25,000 per accident). Therefore, the injured party must look to the negligent driver's personal assets for any substantial recovery. When these are insufficient to cover the loss, **underinsured motorist coverage** allows the insured to collect from her or his own insurer the unrecoverable

Collision Coverage: indemnifies for losses to insured's vehicle due to its running into another object or overturning

Comprehensive Coverage: indemnifies for damage to insured's vehicle stemming from causes other than impact with object or upset

Financial Responsibility Laws: statutes requiring that drivers have proof of insurance or other ability to pay liability judgment

Uninsured Motorist Coverage: allows insured to collect bodily injury and wrongful death damages from own insurer if party at fault has no insurance

Underinsured Motorist Coverage: allows insured to collect against own insurer for bodily injury and wrongful death damages exceeding other party's insurance coverage and personal worth

amount of the damages for bodily injury and wrongful death up to certain per person and per accident limits.

No-Fault Insurance Systems

No-Fault Insurance Systems: legal framework under which insurer pays for insured's loss regardless of which party was to blame for accident

Although their actual details vary greatly from state to state, **no-fault insurance systems** attempt to cut down on the litigation burden facing our courts by requiring that, within certain loss limits and regardless of who is at fault, the parties involved in an automobile accident be indemnified by their own insurers. Should the amount of damage exceed the loss limits, the old fault rules and system come into play.

APPLICATIONS OF WHAT YOU'VE LEARNED

Vocabulary Development

Fill in the blanks with the appropriate term.

Actual Cash Value	**Extended Coverage**	**Inland Marine**	**Omnibus Clause**
All-Risk Policy	**Rider**	**Insurance**	**Riders**
Claim	**Financial Responsibility**	**Liability Insurance**	**Subrogated**
Coinsurance	**Laws**	**Medical Payments**	**Underinsured Motorist**
Collision Coverage	**Friendly Fire**	**Coverage**	**Coverage**
Comprehensive	**Guest Statutes**	**No-Fault Insurance**	**Uninsured Motorist**
Coverage	**Hostile Fire**	**System**	**Coverage**

1. _____ will not pay as long as the party who was at fault in the auto accident has liability insurance.

2. A(n) _____ indemnifies against fire, theft, windstorm, and other perils often covered in individual policies.

3. A(n) _____ is a legal framework covering automobile insurance under which each insured's insurer indemnifies her or him for losses regardless of who is to blame.

4. _____ indemnifies the insured

for losses that occur when his or her own vehicle overturns or is run into another object.

5. _____ prohibit suit by vehicle passengers against drivers unless the drivers are grossly negligent or willfully cause the harm in question.

6. A(n) _____ is a burning in its intended place.

7. _____ requires that the insured be partially self-insuring for certain indemnifiable losses.

Problems

1. How does automobile insurance encompass both property and casualty insurance?

2. Which of the following losses would not be indemnified under the basic fire insurance policy?

   a. Lightning damage to a main dwelling.

   b. Tornado damage to a main dwelling.

   c. Lightning damage to a garage or an outbuilding.

   d. Damage done to a TV set because it is dropped while being rescued from a hostile fire in the main dwelling.

   e. Charring of a coat that has been placed too close to the fireplace.

   f. Hail damage to the shingles on a house roof.

3. To cover its fire station, the city of Pennsboro bought a fire insurance policy with an 80 percent coinsurance clause. When the insurance was taken out, the building was valued at $100,000 and the required face value was $80,000. As time passed, the value of the building increased to $200,000. Then one day, while the fire department was out fighting a blaze, an unknown arsonist set fire to the station.

   a. Presume that Pennsboro had just increased the face value of the insurance policy to $160,000. If the station were a total loss, how much would the insurer pay? How much would the city be responsible for?

   b. If, instead of being a total loss, the damage came to $160,000, how much would the insurer pay if the face value of the policy on the $200,000 station was $160,000? How much would the city be responsible for?

   c. Presume that Pennsboro did not increase the face value of the policy since it was taken out. If the station were a total loss, how much would the insurer pay? How much would the city be responsible for?

4. Which of the following would not be covered by a general (no specific list of insured property required) inland marine insurance policy?

   a. Your watch that is stolen from the repair shop.

   b. Your house window that is damaged by an unclaimed baseball.

   c. Your television set that is dropped while being moved to the bedroom.

5. Which of the following risks would not be covered by the typical all-risk (homeowner's) policy described in the chapter?

   a. A fire that destroys much of the family room.

   b. The insured's camcorder, which is stolen from her while she is on vacation.

   c. The liability incurred by the insured when she playfully pushed a friend off a boat dock while on vacation. (The tide was out, the water level lower than she expected. He broke an arm and sustained a concussion.)

6. Bodily injury liability, property damage liability, medical payments, collision, comprehensive, uninsured motorist, and underinsured motorist coverages are often found in automobile insurance policies. Identify which of these coverages would indemnify the following losses:

   a. Hospital and doctor costs for injuries sustained in an auto accident by the passenger of the negligent insured.

   b. Medical costs for an insured who is hit by a car while roller-skating.

   c. The pain, suffering, lost wages, and medical expenses of the vehicle driver who was injured in an auto accident negligently caused by the insured.

   d. Damage to the insured's vehicle sustained when the insured failed to make a curve, causing the vehicle to crash into a large oak tree.

   e. Damage to the insured's vehicle caused by someone running a sharp metal object along the fender.

   f. Damage to the insured's vehicle and injuries to the insured sustained in a crash with a vehicle driven by a person without financial resources or automobile insurance.

Hall v. Wilkerson

926 F.2d 311

See the potential effect on insurability of alcohol consumption by the driver of a borrowed car.

After having consumed a large quantity of beer, Wayne Wilkerson was involved in a one-vehicle accident in which his passengers, Susan Kilmer and Richard Schoch, were seriously injured. He was driving Gwendolyn Hall's car. Hall's insurance policy read, "WHO IS AN INSURED (under this policy)?" The policy answered its own question as follows: "For YOUR car—YOU, any RELATIVE, and anyone else using YOUR CAR if the use is (or is reasonably believed to be with YOUR PERMISSION, are INSUREDS."

Hall and Wilkerson were not related, and when Hall granted Wilkerson permission to use the car, she specifically told him that there were to be no drugs in the car and that "alcohol is a drug like any other drug."

Hall's insurance company and the injured parties come before the court seeking a declaration of whether or not Wilkerson was an insured at the time of the accident.

Questions

1. Should the policyholder have the power to eliminate insurance coverage by imposing conditions on permission to drive as Hall did here? (For example, what if Hall granted Wilkerson permission to drive on the condition that he neither damage the car nor involve it in an accident?)

2. If Wilkerson is not an insured, the injured parties lose a major source of funding to pay for the expenses of recovering from their injuries. This may prevent them from receiving treatment that would enable them to engage in gainful employment and/or force them into conditions of financial hardship. On the other hand, holding that they are unable to recover because Wilkerson is not an insured may send a warning to others to be careful about the persons from whom they accept rides under similar circumstances. From a societal standpoint, which alternative do you think is the wiser?

3. How do you think the court held?

PART

X

Other Legal Areas with a Significant Impact on Business

CHAPTERS

CHAPTER

36

How Do the Consumer Protection Laws Affect Business?

CHAPTER OUTLINE AND OBJECTIVES

After studying this chapter, the student will be able to:

I. Discuss what consumer law is and why it has become necessary.
    a. The pre-consumer law era's legal approach
    b. Governmental intervention in the consumer's behalf
    c. The extent of current consumer protection laws

II. Describe how consumer law protects us from substandard or defective products.
    a. Warranties and other remedies for individuals
    b. Governmental actions

III. Describe how consumer law protects us from improper product promotions.
    a. Schemes involving use of the mails
    b. Improper advertising and labeling
    c. Improper sales methods
    d. Improper practices in used and new automobile sales
    e. Price-fixing

IV. Describe how consumer law protects us from improper product financing.
    a. Truth in Lending Act requirements
    b. Creditworthiness

V. Describe how consumer law protects us from improper debt collection.
    a. Billing disputes
    b. Collection practices

VI. Evaluate, by reading the case of *Suits* v. *Little Motor* Company, what it means to receive a mileage disclosure statement indicating that a used car's mileage was "unknown."

What Is Consumer Law, and Why Has It Become Necessary?

Consumer Law: body of legal standards protecting buyers of goods used primarily for personal, family, or household purposes

Consumers: buyers of goods used primarily for personal, family, or household purposes

Caveat Emptor: Latin for "let the buyer beware"

In the last four decades a new category of law has appeared on the legal scene. Labeled **consumer law,** it is comprised of statutes and common law precedents that protect **consumers**—those who purchase goods that are to be used primarily for personal, household, or family purposes.

The Pre–Consumer Law Legal Approach

Consumer law significantly altered the hands-off approach that for centuries dominated the legal system's attitude toward consumer protection. A Latin expression, **caveat emptor** (let the buyer beware), concisely states this aloof position. For its validity, caveat emptor relied on two premises. The first was that consumers had enough information and ability to pick out the safe and useful products they needed. Therefore, only in the most exceptional cases would the law concern itself if consumers did not receive the benefit they expected from their bargain or were injured by a defective product. The second premise was that through competition the market mechanism would ultimately provide worthy products for the least cost.

Unfortunately for hapless consumers over the decades, both of these premises were naively conceived and, in reality, an avoidance of a responsibility that the courts did not want to assume. What was true but unacknowledged for centuries has become blatantly obvious in the modern era. Products today are far more complex than they ever were; defects are far less detectable. Companies that were once independent and proud of their reputations and products have dissolved into the fog of conglomerate ownership. Able to tap the power of pooled resources and thereby to create product demand through mass marketing, sellers became and remain far less dependent on consumer satisfaction and the disappearing market mechanism for their success. Manufacturers once located reasonably near their consumers and oriented to serving regional markets are now located in other countries, practically unreachable by the legal process that misled, dissatisfied, or injured consumers might initiate.

Governmental Intervention in the Consumer's Behalf

Because of the imbalance in favor of the forces of production and marketing, the government gradually intervened to assist the consumer. In recognition of the inadequacy of the older laws in the area of consumer protection, new legislation was passed. In addition, new agencies were created or existing agencies were given new consumer protection tasks. The Federal Trade Commission (FTC) provides a good example of this transitional process.

The FTC was created in 1914 to assist in the enforcement of federal laws against concentrations of economic power. A part of its job was, to quote the

Federal Trade Commission Act, "to protect against unfair methods of competition." For nearly the first half-century of its existence, the FTC did just that: protected against unfair competition. However, odd as it may seem, the FTC decided that this protection was meant to be afforded only to competitors. This meant that if the entire garment industry decided to label "100 percent wool" a sweater that was in reality 50 percent wool, 50 percent synthetic material, it would be within the bounds of the FTC Act. The FTC would act against competitors who did not label their garments accordingly. Unlike the favored competitors who had to rely on the government to protect them, consumers were left behind the imaginary shield of caveat emptor. Finally, however, in the late 1950s through the 1960s, reacting to scandals, public indignation, and legislative mandates, the FTC shifted its emphasis to protection of the consumer, and it did so with a vengeance. In fact, the FTC decided that its function was to defend the "most vulnerable consumer." In other words, the FTC now sought to protect the little old lady who allows the patronizing young salesman to talk her into putting overpriced siding on her home and the young child whose attention advertising focused on the secret prize in the box of sugar-laden breakfast cereal. In response, industry and the advertising agencies claimed that they were being overregulated. Ultimately, the Reagan administration came to power with a popular mandate to change the situation. That administration reoriented the FTC to its current posture of protecting the "reasonable consumer" instead of the most vulnerable consumer. The reasonable consumer would not buy siding primarily because of the salesperson or breakfast cereal because of the hidden toy. People foolish enough to do so deserved the lesson they got, and their government was not going to protect them or redress their losses. Caveat emptor.

The recent turn of events at the FTC is typical of what has happened in other areas of consumer law. Nevertheless, the laws that resulted from the "buyer's revolt" of the 1960s are still a shell of potentially effective protection around the end-use purchaser of goods and services that we term a consumer. (Note that in almost every instance the consumer referred to in these laws is a natural person. No protection is afforded artificial persons such as corporations.

The Extent of Current Consumer Protection Laws

Today "consumer law" is a hodgepodge of statutes and rules that many governmental bodies apply to correct many separate and distinct problems. Figure 36–1, however, groups the problem areas into a reasonably understandable pattern. As shown in that figure, consumer law can be fairly well divided according to areas of application. The areas to which it is applied include product standards, product promotions, and product financing. (The remainder of this chapter is organized along the same lines as the figure.) Figure 36–1 also lists some of the laws and agencies that deal with the various problem areas.

Figure 36–1

Problem Areas and the Consumer-Oriented Agencies and Laws Directed at Their Solution

Protected Area	By Agency and/or Act
Product standards (in general)	Consumer Product Safety Commission and UCC Warranty law
Motor vehicles	National Highway Traffic Safety Commission
Mobile homes	Department of Housing and Urban Development
Food, drugs, and cosmetics	Food and Drug Administration
Product promotions	
Mail fraud	US Postal Service
Mail order	Federal Trade Commission
Deceptive advertising	Federal Trade Commission
Door-to-door sales	Federal Trade Commission
Labeling	
Food, drugs and cosmetics	Food and Drug Administration
Others	Federal Trade Commission
Unordered merchandise	Federal Trade Commission
Bait and switch schemes	Federal Trade Commission
Used car sales	Federal Trade Commission
Price-fixing	Antitrust Division of the US Department of Justice
Product financing	
Credit costs	Truth in Lending Act
Creditworthiness	
Credit reports	Fair Credit Reporting Act
Discrimination by sex, race, marital status, age, religion, national origin	Equal Credit Opportunity Act
Unauthorized use of another's credit card or creditworthiness	Truth in Lending Act
Collection	
Billing errors/disputes	Fair Credit Billing Act
Improper collection tactics	Fair Debt Collection Practices Act

How Does Consumer-Oriented Law Protect Us from Substandard or Defective Products?

The laws that shield consumers from substandard or defective products are for the most part applied after the fact. Except for the careful drug screening of the Food and Drug Administration (FDA), the current consumer protection schemes require that someone or many someones be injured before anything is done. It is interesting to note that the FDA is often under fire from consumers for being too slow in approving drugs for general use even though premature approval might result in severe bodily harm or death to some.

After injury has been inflicted by a substandard or defective product, remedial action may come as a result of individual initiative, such as a lawsuit for a violation of the warranties we discussed in Chapter 17 (good title, merchant-ability, and fitness for a particular purpose), or as a result of an initiative taken on behalf of society by an agency authorized to do so.

Warranties and Other Remedies for Individuals

A cornerstone of consumer law is the ability of the injured individual to recover directly through lawsuit for the harm done to her or him by a defective product. Otherwise, the injured individual would be at the mercy of politically controllable government bureaucrats.

As noted in our previous discussion, the reach and coverage of warranties (especially of merchantability and fitness for a particular purpose) have been extended considerably in recent years. These extensions, to allow more ultimate users of products more rights to sue and recover for harm done to them by defects in the product, have been supplemented by the Magnuson-Moss Warranty Act (also discussed in Chapter 17). This act promotes the providing of adequate information on warranties to consumers and curtails the ability of issuers of warranties to disclaim them.

In Chapter 6 we discussed an important change in the law that enhanced the ability of an injured consumer to recover in the face of long odds. That change made it easier for the injured consumer to present a satisfactory case. To be specific, until the last few years, if you were injured by a defective product your only way to collect was by producing enough evidence to prove the manufac-turer's negligence. Due mainly to the complexity of modern products and to the fact that the evidence was initially in the manufacturer's hands, often proved to be a difficult, expensive, and unsuccessful proposition. As just mentioned, however, the law has changed to help the injured party. Today that person does not have to show that the product was defective because of the manufacturer's or seller's violation of the duty of due care. Instead, it is enough to show that:

1. The injury came from the use of the product in the manner intended.
2. There was an unreasonably dangerous defective condition.
3. The defendant was engaged in the business of manufacturing or selling the product.
4. The product had not been substantially altered by the time of the injury.

So a person injured while using his lawn mower to trim his hedge (a case that was litigated) could not recover. However, the family members injured in a crash caused by the deployment of their car's air bags when their car hit a pothole in a bridge were able to recover.

Of course, the manufacturer or seller can still use its superior resources and its superior access to information to counter the plaintiff's case. This is often done. However, the new rules help balance the scales of justice somewhat.

The success of these warranty and product liability changes in the law (see Chapter 17 for full coverage of these topics) can be measured by the thunderings of makers of proven defective products against the "injustice" of requiring that they pay for the harm they have caused.

Governmental Actions

Involving Most Consumer Products.   In 1972, in an effort to consolidate control over the many agencies and laws regulating consumer product safety, the federal government created the Consumer Product Safety Commission (CPSC). It was given jurisdiction over all consumer products except such items as motor vehicles, drugs, cosmetics, food, airplanes, and boats. (The exceptions fall under the regulatory control of other agencies.) Although the basic goal of the CPSC was to bring about the use of safer products by providing information on defective designs to manufacturers and consumers alike, it was also given the power to set safety standards and to ban unsafe products from the marketplace.

To facilitate the accomplishment of its mission, the CPSC receives reports from hospitals across the nation on product-caused injuries. It also requires that a maker or distributor report defects that it finds in its product. If the CPSC determines from these data that a product is hazardous, it may require that the consumers of the product be notified and that those responsible for the condition repair, replace, or refund the purchase price of the product. Indications that the CPSC is considering action often prompt offending manufacturers or distributors to recall their products "voluntarily."

Involving Motor Vehicles and Mobile Homes.   The power to order recalls of products posing a threat to public safety has been placed in the hands of the National Highway Traffic Safety Administration (NHTSA). This federal agency was created in 1966. Since then, congressional mandates and executive orders have altered its powers and direction many times. These constant changes have prevented the NHTSA from getting on with its business. Lobbying by the auto industry has been especially effective in delaying needed enforcement of safety standards. In some cases, this lobbying has had disastrous consequences. For example, in early 1977 holes were drilled in a particular school bus frame for the attachment of the fuel tank safety shields mandated by new federal rules. No shields were put in place, however. Thanks to lobbying by Henry Ford III and Lee Iacocca in early 1972, the date for implementing the standards was moved back from that year to April 1977. The bus ultimately came to be owned by a church in Kentucky. One day a group of the church's young people set out in it for a holiday at a nearby theme park. During the return trip, it was struck nearly head-on by a drunken driver. The impact ignited fuel in the gas tank located behind the front entry door. Over 20 of the youths in the bus were burned alive or died of smoke inhalation. An autopsy revealed that none of them died of injuries due to the collision. The driver of the small pickup that struck the bus was convicted of multiple counts of manslaughter. Ford Motor Company acted quickly to settle with survivors and relatives of the deceased for an estimated $40 million. Two families refused to settle, believing that they should publicize the unsafe condition of similar school buses. The story was ultimately carried by *People* magazine. A marker noting the Covington, Kentucky, bus disaster is located on the interstate highway where the collision occurred.

Safety standards for mobile homes fall under the authority of the Department of Housing and Urban Development (HUD). Over the years HUD has issued requirements on heating systems, insulation, and other items used in the construction of such properties.

Involving Food, Drugs, Cosmetics, and Other Consumer Items.   It is vital that the goods we consume or come into intimate contact with not be **adulterated** (below minimum purity and quality standards). The FDA and the US Department of Agriculture (USDA) share the main responsibility for seeing that adulterated goods do not reach the public. Both the FDA and the USDA conduct inspections of production facilities to ensure that food, drugs, and cosmetics are fit for human consumption and use. The USDA conducts poultry and meat inspections, while the FDA covers most of the remaining food, drug, and cosmetic products. The FDA also makes rules for properly labeling nutritional makeup, weight, and quantity of food items and the names and addresses of food producers, packagers, and marketers.

Adulterated: below minimum purity and quality standards

As mentioned, the FDA conducts a time-consuming and meticulous screening to ensure that only drugs with reasonably safe side effects are made available in our marketplace. This screening is often controversial. In 1962 the new drug thalidomide was being sold on the European market. Used to relieve nausea in pregnant women, the drug had no reported side effects. Yet Dr. Frances Kelsey, an FDA researcher, was suspicious. She had noted that after using the drug, some British women reported a numbness in their hands and feet. Other reported side effects reinforced her suspicions. As a consequence, when asked to approve the use of thalidomide in the United States, she refused to do so. Months passed, then a year. During that time, her persistent "no" brought a storm of pressure from superiors at the FDA and from the drug's importers, the William S. Merell Company of Cincinnati, Ohio. Then, after 14 months, Dr. Kelsey's suspicions were confirmed. Dr. Helen Taussig, famous for her work with children's illnesses, reported that thalidomide had quietly been withdrawn from the West German market because hundreds of babies had been born with horrible malformations due to its use. Among the most monstrous of the defects included children (approximately 10,000 all told) born with shortened and seallike limbs, deformities of the eyes and ears, and open gastrointestinal tracts. Sadly, even though thalidomide had not been approved in the United States, over 20,000 American women had been given samples of the drug. Typically, they had not been told of its experimental status and a number of them bore malformed children. Dr. Kelsey was ultimately praised by a Congress for her courage that doubtlessly contained more than a few members who had pressed for the legitimization of thalidomide, and President John Fitzgerald Kennedy ultimately awarded her the distinguished service medal for her devotion to the good of the people.

How Does Consumer Law Protect Us from Various Improper Product Promotional Schemes?

Regretfully, laws available to protect consumers never seem to keep up with the schemes to part them from their dollars. Nevertheless, as indicated in Figure 36–1, several laws intended to thwart such schemes are worthy of note.

Schemes Involving Use of the Mails

Mail Fraud: use of mails to execute fraudulent scheme

Use of the mails to execute a fraudulent scheme is known as **mail fraud.** Postal laws provide a broad umbrella of protection to consumers who are contacted by letter or other posting in order to improperly induce them to part with their money. A conviction of mail fraud, however, requires a measure of proof often difficult to obtain, especially given the volume of the cases reported to the US Postal Service. As a consequence, most investigations are conducted by mail and are ended with the alleged offender's promise to clean up the questionable practice.

In addition to offering protection against clearly fraudulent practices, postal laws (in conjunction with FTC rules) provide consumers with powers to aid the government in countering questionable uses of the mails. One such use is sending the consumer unordered merchandise and then billing the consumer for the merchandise. Sending and billing for unordered merchandise are now illegal. The consumer is allowed to keep such merchandise as a gift or to dispose of it in any way that he or she sees fit. In addition, the sender of unordered merchandise is required to send a statement of these rights to the person receiving it.

The FTC has acted to ensure that goods ordered by mail are shipped promptly. Under the FTC rule on the subject, the seller must either ship orders within the time promised in the seller's ads or, if no time is mentioned, within 30 days of receiving the consumer's order. If the seller cannot meet this shipment schedule, the consumer must be offered the option of canceling for a prompt refund or of waiting until the product is available.

Improper Advertising and Labeling

The FTC also attempts to ensure that false and deceptive advertising does not mar a consumer's choices of products to fulfill her or his needs. Overreaching claims, for example the claim that a mouthwash either prevented or cured sore throats, can be removed from publication. The FTC can even order **corrective advertising,** if necessary, to correct a misrepresentation whose effects linger past the time in which the improper ad claim is made.

Corrective Advertising: legally mandated media exposure to correct lingering effect of misrepresentation

The FTC and the FDA, acting under the Fair Packaging and Labeling Act of 1966, combine to protect consumers against improper descriptions of merchandise contained on the item itself or on its enclosure. Warning labels, misuse of such descriptive terms as *jumbo* or *giant* in reference to size, packaging whose size misleads as to the volume of contents, and requirements for accurate and meaningful descriptions of the nutritional contents of foodstuffs are all focal points of regulation in this area.

Improper Sales Methods

Aware that a salesperson working door-to-door often had an overwhelming advantage over his or her customer, the FTC established rules governing such a **home solicitation sale.** Generally, a salesperson of this kind, if properly trained, could overcome every consumer argument from "I want to shop around" to "I can't afford it right now." (The typical response to the former argument is to produce some recent ads of competitive products showing that their price is higher. The typical response to the latter argument is to propose a financing plan with low monthly payments: "Well, can you afford $7.50 a month for this fine tire washer? Of course. You pay that much for lunch. Just sign here, and it's yours.")

Home Solicitation Sale: sale by person working door-to-door

The home solicitation rules apply to sales over $25 made to a consumer in most places other than the seller's regular place of business. From apartments to homes to motel rooms rented by the seller to product parties held in another person's dwelling, the rules require that the seller inform the consumer of his or her right to cancel the transaction by placing notice to that effect in the mail by midnight of the third business day after the sale. The rules do not apply to sales made solely by mail or phone; or to insurance, real estate, or securities sales; or to the provision of emergency home repairs.

HYPOTHETICAL CASE

Matt Teast saw a TV ad for Poverty Stricken Painters. It described a sale of art works at incredibly low prices that was to be held at a local motel's convention hall. Matt attended and bought two paintings for a total of $247. The seller was required by law to notify Matt that he had three business days to consider the transaction and could cancel it by mailing a cancellation form by midnight of the third day if he so desired.

Bait and switch sales are also a concern of the FTC. To carry out a bait and switch scheme, a store advertises an item at a very low price (the bait) but understocks the item or leaves it out of stock. When a prospective purchaser inquires, a salesperson talks the prospective purchaser into a higher-priced, more profitable, item (the switch).

Bait and Switch Sale: sale opportunity created by advertising low-priced lure, then refocusing consumer on another good

The FTC passed a rule to control the use of such schemes. The rule prohibits advertising containing offers to sell a product that are not bona fide. Yet recent case histories show that many of the best retail establishments in the United States still use such schemes to develop consumer leads, evidently preferring to pay a fine rather than abandon a lucrative but illegal method of doing business. Actions by a seller that are indicative of a bait and switch scheme include salespeople running down the advertised product, being unable to deliver it within a reasonable time, and failing to have enough of it in stock at every outlet mentioned in the advertising campaign.

Improper Practices in Used and New Automobile Sales

Because of the heavy volume of complaints about used car sales techniques, the FTC placed its buyer's guide rule into effect in 1985. This rule requires used car dealers to provide prospective purchasers with a variety of information by placing a window sticker (called a buyer's guide) on each car offered for sale. The most important parts of the guide warn the consumer to disregard oral promises and list the extent of express and implied warranties. The guide also suggests that would-be purchasers have the car inspected by their own mechanic before closing the deal.

A common problem in used car sales is odometer tampering. A federal statute, the Motor Vehicle information and Cost Savings Act, prohibits individuals from altering or disconnecting a vehicle's odometer so that it shows an improper reading except to repair or replace the odometer. In such cases a notice showing the date of the repair or replacement and the true mileage at that time must be affixed to the driver's door frame.

New Car Sales and the "Lemon Laws." Americans, they say, have a love affair with their cars. Never is this bond stronger and at no time are expectations higher than when a new car is purchased. But what if the honeymoon between the purchaser and the shiny, chromed, four-wheeled purchase is marred by a defect that the dealer cannot repair? A used car is bought with the unavoidable suspicion that there must be some reason why its previous owner parted with it, some defect not worth correcting. Not so with a new car. It is expected to be worry-free and reliable, at least in the short term. If there are minor defects in its thousands of parts assembled by hundreds of relatively uninterested individuals, these should be easily correctable. When the new car does not live up to the high expectations of its purchaser, when it cannot be placed in letter-perfect condition no matter how many trips the purchaser makes to the dealership, Americans term it a *lemon.* Well over half of our states have now passed statutes called, as you might suspect, **lemon laws,** to deal with this situation. Such laws vary, but basically if a dealership is unable to repair a defect that significantly affects the value or use of a newly purchased car in a certain number of trips (typically four), the car owner can petition for a new car or the return of the purchase price.

Lemon Laws: statutes giving rights to consumer if dealer is unable to repair defects in new car

Price-Fixing

Often retailers, manufacturers, or other distributors of products band together to maintain prices at a certain level. Such price-fixing is illegal, and the agreements supporting it are void and unenforceable. Price-fixing and other manipulations of the market mechanism will be dealt with in Chapter 38.

How Does Consumer Law Protect Us from Various Improper Product Financing Schemes?

The final area of protection afforded consumers concerns the financing of their purchases. Consumers often fixate on the price of the purchase and the attributes of the product while ignoring the terms of the financing arrangement. All too often, it is the superficial examination of those terms that causes regrets. As a consequence, Congress passed the Truth in Lending Act (TILA).

Truth in Lending Act Requirements

TILA requires that lenders disclose two items of primary importance to a borrower who wants to shop around for credit. First, lenders must disclose the actual **finance charge** for the loan. This is the dollars and cents amount that the borrower would pay for the use of the money over the term of the loan. Second, lenders must disclose the **annual percentage rate** (APR) being charged. Armed with these two indexes, a consumer sensitive to the difference credit terms make can shop for those of greatest benefit.

Finance Charge: amount borrower is to pay for use of money

Annual Percentage Rate: comparative interest percentage for loan given on basis of one-year term

Note that TILA also requires the disclosure of the number, amount, and due dates of all payments as well as the existence and amount of any balloon payment. Note too that it applies both to the loan of money and to the purchase of services or goods on credit.

Leasing. Leasing, a means of temporarily acquiring the possession and use of consumer products, has become a more and more popular alternative to purchasing. As a consequence, the Uniform Commercial Code was augmented by Article 2A on leasing, and Congress passed the Consumer Leasing Act. Like TILA, this act requires the disclosure of significant terms to the consumer. This is done in the hope that the consumer will shop around. The act applies only to personal property leased for more than four months for household, family, or personal use. It does not cover business leases, leases of real property, and leases for terms shorter than four months. It requires, among other things, disclosure of the full lease cost and of the lessee's various responsibilities for the upkeep of the leased property. If there is a large **balloon payment** (final payoff amount due in payment sequence), it must be no more than three times the average monthly payment.

Balloon Payment: final payoff amount due in payment sequence

Creditworthiness

Being able to compare terms for financing or leasing personal property is important only if you have the credit standing needed to enter into such arrangements. Various measures have therefore been passed by the federal government to ensure fair access to credit.

Equal Credit Opportunity Act. As noted in Chapter 23, this act is the linchpin of consumer rights in the area of credit. All regular providers of credit, including banks, credit card issuers, stores, credit unions, and many others, must comply with it. Violators of the act's requirements may be sued in federal district court for actual damages plus court costs, attorney's fees, and punitive damages. In general, the act forbids discrimination against applicants for credit on the basis of their race, religion, national origin, sex, marital status, age, or whether they receive public assistance.

Fair Credit Reporting Act. As mentioned, an applicant who is denied credit must be given the reason for the rejection within 60 days. The applicant can then determine whether or not the rejection was based on incorrect information. Right or wrong, credit bureaus or agencies often supply the crucial information that lenders act on. Congress determined that consumers had a right to know the contents of the files kept on them by such reporting institutions. Consequently, it passed the Fair Credit Reporting Act. Under the act a consumer can discover all such information (except medical reports), its sources, and the recipients of credit reports within the last six months. If informed of alleged inaccuracies by a consumer, the credit agency must investigate. If the information in its records is inaccurate, it must make the appropriate correction. If it refuses to correct what the consumer maintains is incorrect, the consumer can place his or her version in its file to be sent out with future requests for information.

Unauthorized Credit Card Use. Losing a credit card or having a credit card stolen could be disastrous for the cardholder had Congress not provided protection against these contingencies in TILA. In effect, Congress made the card issuer responsible for any charges on the card after the issuer had been notified of potential unauthorized use. The notice can be conveyed by any effective means, including telephone. But even without notice, the cardholder is liable for only the first $50 of unauthorized charges. TILA also prohibits issuers from sending out unsolicited credit cards unless these are just replacements for cards already in use.

How Does Consumer Law Protect Us from Various Improper Debt Collection Schemes?

Can a credit card company ruin your credit standing by reporting your refusal to pay for a defective good charged on your credit card as an overdue payment? Can a debt collector tell others that you owe money or use postcards in requesting payment? Can a creditor get you to agree in advance to allow deductions from your paycheck to pay off a debt if you default on it? As you may suspect (or hope), the answer to all of these questions is no. Consumer law greatly curtails the abuses once allowed in collecting outstanding accounts.

Billing Disputes

The Fair Credit Billing Act (FCBA) is one of the reasons why the answer to these questions is no. It allows a consumer to dispute an error in billing from a creditor by following a congressionally mandated procedure. First, the consumer must notify the creditor of a billing error within 60 days. The notice must contain an explanation of the consumer's claim. The creditor then has 30 days to acknowledge the receipt of notice and 90 days to investigate and, hopefully, correct the mistake. If the creditor believes the bill to be correct, it must explain why.

Purchase of Unsatisfactory Goods or Services.   When a consumer is not satisfied with a good or service received in a transaction in which a credit card has been used for payment, it is extremely upsetting to have the credit card issuer demanding payment regardless. In addition, the poor quality of the good or service may indicate that the company from which it was obtained is going out of business. This means that the money paid to the credit card issuer may not be recoverable in a suit against that company. As a consequence of these factors, the FCBA set down the following rules:

In situations in which a purchase of over $50 in unsatisfactory goods or services is charged on a credit card and the purchase occurs within the cardholder's state or within 100 miles of the cardholder's mailing address, the consumer may withhold payment.

However, the seller of the goods or services must be given a chance to correct the problem.

If the seller fails to correct the problem, the cardholder may use that fact as a defense should the credit card issuer bring suit for collection.

The creditor is forbidden to give a cardholder a bad credit report for using his or her rights under the FCBA.

Collection Practices

In our society, owing money is not a crime nor is being delinquent in repaying it. The debtor's prisons were abolished long ago (even in England the imprisonment of debtors was outlawed by the Debtor's Act of 1869) and the emphasis then shifted to enabling debtors to again become productive members of society.

As a continuation of that thrust, Congress has acted to constrain the activities of **collection agencies** (which are in the business of collecting debts for others) by passing the Fair Debt Collection Practices Act (FDCPA). This act makes it illegal to:

Collection Agencies: those in business of collecting debts for others

Use harassing or abusive techniques to collect a debt—no threats of violence, no profane language, no publishing of lists of those who refuse to pay (this applies only to those who collect debts for others, so a bad check or a failure to pay may be posted by the actual creditor), no harassing phone calls or repeated ringings of the debtor's number, no communicating at an inconvenient place or time, and no calls to the debtor at work if the collector knows that the employer does not allow such calls.

Inform others that the debtor owes money or use methods of communication, such as postcards, that achieve the same effect.

Communicate with the debtor directly once notified that the debtor has an attorney (thereafter, communications can be conducted only with the attorney) or once notified in writing that the debtor refuses to pay the debt (thereafter, the only communications permitted are those that notify the debtor of specific actions taken by the creditor).

Should these or other tenets of the FDCPA be violated, the collection agency can be sued for damages (actual and punitive) and attorney's fees.

As mentioned, the FDCPA covers only collection agencies. Other laws, however, forbid creditors themselves from utilizing many devices that they once had at their disposal. Chief among these are such clauses, often included in the credit contracts themselves, as **confessions of judgment.** By such confessions of judgment, consumers at one time gave up their rights to a court hearing when sued for defaulting on a debt. The creditor could proceed directly to executing the unpaid debt against the debtor's resources without direct court oversight. **Assignment of wages** clauses were also notorious at one time. In these clauses, debtors allowed deductions from their paychecks to be sent directly to the creditor if they defaulted on a loan. Such deductions are still allowed, but only if the consumer can cancel them at any time, something that creditors formerly did not allow.

All of these laws and many laws at the state and agency levels of government, developed primarily in the last half-century, have provided consumers with the expectation, if not the reality, of fair treatment. To be effective, however, consumer law, like the market with which it interacts, has to be constantly in a process of evaluation and change. If it ceases to evolve, its effect and the efforts of those who brought it to reality will be lost.

Confessions of Judgment: contract clause in which debtor relinquishes right to court hearing on default

Assignment of Wages: contract clause in which debtor agrees to payroll deduction for loan payoff on default

APPLICATIONS OF WHAT YOU'VE LEARNED

Vocabulary Development

Fill in the blanks with the appropriate term.

Adulterated	Bait and Switch Sale	Confessions of Judgment	Finance Charge
Annual Percentage Rate (APR)	Balloon Payment	Consumer Law	Home Solicitation Sale
	Caveat Emptor	Consumers	Lemon Law
Assignment of Wages	Collection Agency	Corrective Advertising	Mail Fraud

1. Di Nette bought some kitchen furniture on credit. She paid off the loan in 13 installments. The first 12 were $20 each, and the last was $55. The $55 installment was a(n) _____.

2. Dee Sieved bought a new car. It quickly developed freakish electrical problems that the dealership could not fix. After four trips to the repair shop, she invoked her rights under the state's

_____ and got back her purchase price.

3. The government ordered a shipment of a popular antidepressant removed from the market due to its high level of impurities. The drug was

_____.

4. Because Faye Sawd did not have enough cash to

purchase the car she wanted, she financed it. Because her credit was extremely poor, the lender charged her a high rate of interest. The car, which was priced at $72,000, would cost her a total of $91,000 by the time she made her last payment. The $19,000 difference is known as the _____.

5. Everett Blud founded a business to collect unpaid debts for creditors. The business, known as Blud's Hounds, was a(n)_____.

6. _____, a Latin phrase, means "let the buyer beware."

Problems

1. Which of the following consumers is worthy of the FTC's protection under its current standards?

a. An 85-year-old widower who buys a "ticket to heaven" for $7,500 from the Reverend Bill Gates, a TV evangelist.

b. An accountant who, because he lacks any knowledge about cars, pays for a change of spark plugs in his diesel-engined car.

c. A young child who, while watching Saturday morning TV, is urged to call a 1-900 number ($17.50 the first minute and $5 each minute thereafter) so that she can talk firsthand to her favorite cartoon character.

2. Match the problem with the likely remedy under the consumer laws by placing the letter of the remedy in the blank.

Your new car develops a significant defect that cannot be repaired after four visits to a dealer.

_____

The goods you ordered by mail are out of stock and cannot be sent within 30 days.

_____

You receive an unordered set of the works of the great composer Beethoven on compact discs through the mail. Later you are billed for the CDs.

_____

You are denied credit because you are divorced._____

a. You can bring suit for actual and punitive damages plus attorney's fees.

b. You can keep the goods as a gift or dispose of them as you choose.

c. You can cancel and receive your full purchase price back or wait for them to become available.

d. You can have the purchase price refunded or receive a new one.

ACTUAL CASE STUDY

Suits v. Little Motor Company

642 F. 2D 883

Put yourself in the shoes of a customer faced with a loophole in the mileage disclosure statute.

The mileage disclosure form presented by Little Motor to Brenda Suits upon her purchase of a used car stated that the actual mileage reading was unknown. The odometer then showed a reading of 000,073 for the 10-year-old car. Brenda brought a suit for damages under the Motor Vehicle Information and Cost Savings Act. Evidence submitted at the trial shows that when Little Motor

bought the car from a Chevrolet dealership, it was presented with a mileage disclosure statement showing that the actual mileage was 100,073. As was normal practice, however, Little Motor requested that the statement be sent to it by mail. Thus, it could sell the car before the statement arrived, as it had done, and simply list the mileage as unknown. The key to recovery for Brenda is whether or not this circumvention of the rules reflects an intent to deceive. Little Motor's representative has pointed out in his defense that any buyer of a 10-year-old car in the shape and with the odometer reading of the one under consideration knows that the odometer has turned over 100,000 miles.

Question

1. What type of consumer should we endeavor to protect in this situation, the most vulnerable one or a reasonable one? Should the standard change with the situation?

2. How valid is Little Motor's defense as to what the 000,073 reading means? Could that reading imply something else?

3. Should the court rule in Brenda's favor? Why or why not?

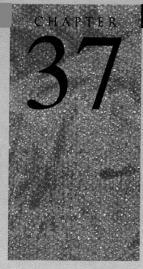

CHAPTER

37

How Does Environmental Law Affect Business?

CHAPTER OUTLINE AND OBJECTIVES

After studying this chapter, the student will be able to:

I. Discuss what environmental law is and how it developed.
   a. The abuse of public goods
   b. The promise of the Environmental Protection Agency
II. Identify the most important federal statutes governing the use of the environment.
   a. National Environmental Policy Act
   b. Clean Air Act
   c. Clean Water Act
   d. Solid Waste Disposal Act and amendments
   e. Toxic Substances Control Act
   f. The Superfund as created by the Comprehensive Environmental Response Compensation and Liability Act of 1980.
   g. Other statutes providing environmental protection
III. Analyze the case of *Procter & Gamble* v. *City of Chicago*, which considered the predicament of a company whose laundry detergent contained an element outlawed by the city of Chicago because of its contribution to water pollution.

Some Significant Environmental Disasters of Recent Times

Love Canal, Niagara Falls, N.Y. For two decades (1930s to early 1950s), the Hooker Chemical and Plastics Corporation used the old canal bed as a dumping ground for its residues. In 1953 the bed was filled in and a school and housing subdivision were built thereon. In 1971, when toxic chemicals began leaking through the clay cap sealing the dumping site, it was realized that the extremely high incidence of birth defects, miscarriages, liver cancers, and seizures in the area's children might have a determinable cause. Love Canal was ultimately declared a disaster area, and approximately 1,000 families were relocated. The Hooker Corporation declared that it was not responsible. After an extensive cleanup, houses in the Love Canal area were allowed to be put up for sale in 1990.

Bhopal, India In the early morning hours of December 3, 1984, methyl isocyanate, a gas used in insecticide manufacture at the Union Carbide plant escaped from an underground tank. Within 40 minutes, it had spread over an area occupied by some 200,000 of Bhopal's citizens. Over 3,500 men, women, and children died in their sleep. Tens of thousands of others awoke gasping for breath, vomiting, and frothing at the mouth. Many of these survivors were stricken by blindness. The corpses of animals and birds killed by the deadly gas littered the streets. Union Carbide's chairman, William Anderson, was arrested and charged with criminal conspiracy in the matter. In 1989 the company agreed to pay some $470 million in damages to the survivors.

Chernobyl, Union of Soviet Socialist Republics (now located in the Ukraine) On April 26, 1986, a nuclear reactor exploded during an experiment. A steam-generated explosion then blew the top off the reactor. Yet a third explosion, this time of chemicals, followed. As a result of the explosions, 31 persons were killed outright or shortly thereafter. Among them were several engineers who, knowing that their exposure to the intense radiation would kill them, went into the contaminated area and took measures that prevented the other reactors at the site from blowing up. The force of the explosions and fires carried the radiation into the upper atmosphere and thereby across much of the Northern Hemisphere. Several million persons living north and west of the reactor were the most exposed to this radiation, and subsequent reports indicated that this population experienced a significantly higher incidence of leukemia, thyroid cancer, and other illnesses related to such exposure.

On Bligh Reef, off the Pacific Coast of Alaska Near midnight of March 12, 1989, the *Exxon Valdez* was navigated too close to the submerged rocks bordering the shipping channels and ran aground at a speed of over 12 knots. The crash gutted the tanker hull in eight places, sending millions of gallons of oil into the waters of Prince William Sound. Equipment dispatched to the scene by Alyeska (the company formed by the seven major oil companies profiting from the Alaska oil fields) arrived approximately 12 hours later and proved incapable of handling even a small percentage of the spill. (Alyeska had previously stated to the Alaskan state government that it could reach any spill within five hours with sufficient equipment to deal with it.) Eventually, over 1,100 miles of shoreline were coated by the oil. To clean up the mess, Exxon hired over 12,000 individuals, many of whom had been thrown out of fisheries jobs due to the spill. The *Exxon Valdez* was ultimately refloated, repaired, renamed, and placed back in service. The disaster killed over 35,000 birds, over 1,000 otters, and innumerable fish. It was pointed out that the use of double-bottomed hulls on oil transport ships, which the Department of the Interior had proposed years earlier, might have prevented the disaster. However, our representatives in Congress had ignored the proposal due to pressure and contributions from the oil companies.

What Is Environmental Law, and How Did It Develop?

As discussed in Chapter 30, the position of our culture as embedded in our common law is that things can and should be treated as the sole property of one or more individuals to the exclusion of others. The legally recognized bundle of ownership rights of real or personal property includes the latitude to harm or destroy the land, buildings, or other things subject to those rights. This latitude to harm or destroy property (for example by denuding it of its trees, stripping it of its topsoil, coating it with chemicals to grow crops or grass, or leaking sewage into the potable water) was not accompanied by a common law duty to treat property as a good steward. The common law's restrictions on the misuse of property were almost nonexistent. In the common law, the tort of **nuisance** came and comes closest to providing some parameters. A nuisance is something that annoys or disturbs a party's possession of her or his property by rendering the property's ordinary use or enjoyment physically uncomfortable or impossible. Excessive odors, smoke, or vibration have all been held to be nuisances. However, the use of nuisance law could not check the most dangerous forms of environmental pollution.

Nuisance: use or misuse of property that unreasonably interferes with use of other property

The Abuse of Public Goods

When you add the impact of our society's concept of a public good to the scarcity of legal weapons to stop pollution, you are at the philosophical headwaters of our environmental problem. This is because the term **public good** is used to identify a common resource whose access and use should be available to all. Air and water are the most important public goods. Certainly, we should all have the access necessary to breathe air and drink water. However, the same access has also been held to allow all of us to use air and water to dispose of our wastes. For example, each of us takes oxygen from the air and gives back the waste product of carbon dioxide (even though the United States currently "produces" less than 80 percent of the oxygen we use and the carbon dioxide poses severe problems in some parts of our country). In addition, almost every US community carries off human excretions with water and then dumps that water in various stages of impurity into our country's streams and lakes. Our industries continue to dump ton upon ton of wastes, many of them toxic, into the air and water, as they have done for well over a century. Like the bullet shot into the air to celebrate New Year's, these wastes have to fall to earth somewhere. As they accumulate in the ground, the water, and food chains, they may bring birth defects and diseases such as cancer. As a consequence, effectively beginning a little over two decades ago, we have sought to regulate but certainly not eliminate these discharges. **Environmental law** is the name that we apply to such attempts to control activities that have a potentially harmful effect on the land, air, and water resources that support the

Public Good: resource to which all should have access and use

Environmental Law: legal controls to prevent harmful effects on our planet's life-support systems

existence of life on this planet. Figure 37–1 lists common environmental problems and the statutes relevant to them.

The Promise of the Environmental Protection Agency

As with consumer law, the initial attempts at environmental law were isolated and often misdirected. Unlike consumer law, however, environmental policy and regulatory efforts were, for the most part, placed under the control of a central coordinating body, the Environmental Protection Agency (EPA). The EPA was established in 1970 under an executive reorganization plan. Congress gave it the mission of (1) setting up national standards for allowable pollution of the air, the water, and the remainder of the life-supporting environment and (2) working with other governmental entities, especially the states, to see that those standards were enforced. To achieve its mission, the EPA was given the power to monitor and direct the enforcement of the main federal antipollution statutes.

What Are the Most Important Federal Statutes Governing the Use of the Environment?

National Environmental Policy Act

Easily one of the most important of the federal statutes governing the use of the environment is the one that created the mechanism for setting the policy used to coordinate activities under all the other federal statutes of this kind. That statute, the National Environmental Policy Act (NEPA), went into effect in 1970. It created the Council on Environmental Quality (CEQ). The council gathers data on the environment, reviews the effectiveness of current environmental policies, recommends appropriate changes in those policies, and submits annual reports on the condition of the environment. It is important to realize that the CEQ's function is advisory. It does not set detailed pollution standards. It cannot stop projects harmful to the environment. It lacks enforcement powers. However, it does stand sentry duty to ensure that the president and Congress are aware of the status both of ongoing environmental issues and of environmental issues that are in the making.

The CEQ can fulfill this latter, early warning duty because of an innovative requirement that Congress placed in the NEPA section immediately following the one in which it created the CEQ. This second section of the act requires that every proposal for legislation or other federal action significantly affecting the quality of the environment be accompanied by an **environmental impact statement** (EIS). According to the rules that the CEQ established for such a statement, an EIS must contain, among other items, a detailed account of:

Environmental Impact Statement: required statement on environmental consequences of significant action by federal government

1. The purpose of and need for the proposed project.
2. Reasonable alternatives to the project.

| Environmental Problems and Relevant Statutes | Figure 37–1 |

Problem	Statute
Noise pollution	Noise Control Act and Quiet Communities Act
Wildlife eradication	Endangered Species Act and other acts related to conservation of birds, fishes, and other wildlife
Water pollution:	
Discharge of pollutants into waterways	National Pollutant Discharge Elimination System (permit required)
Discharge of pollutants into the oceans	Marine Protection, Research, and Sanctuaries Act (permit required)
Spills of hazardous substances into the oceans, on Continental Shelf, or within 12-mile limit	Clean Water Act
Threats to clean drinking water	Safe Drinking Water Act
Destruction of wetlands	Permit required under Clean Water Act (US Army Corps of Engineers issues as warranted)
Discharge of high-temperature water into watercourse (thermal pollution)	Clean Water Act
Air Pollution	
Poor air quality	National Ambient Air Quality Standards established under Clean Air Act
Threats to pure air areas	Clean Air Act
Stationary point sources of pollution	Clean Air Act requires pollution control equipment for established and new point sources
Motor vehicle emissions	Clean Air Act authorizes EPA to set vehicle emission standards and select available fuels
Toxic air pollutants	Clean Air Act requires EPA to maintain list and requires public notice of releases by air polluters
Land pollution	
Chemical use	Insecticide, Fungicide, and Rodenticide Act requires registration
	Toxic Substances Control Act requires testing new chemicals and reporting of their effects on human health
Discharge of hazardous waste	Resource Conservation and Recovery Act, Superfund (Comprehensive Environmental Response, Compensation, and Liability Act), and Nuclear Waste Policy Act

3. A description of the current environment of the area on which the project would have an impact.
4. A description of the environmental consequences of the project, including its unavoidable adverse effects, the irreversible and irretrievable resource commitments that it would require, and the relationship between its environmental impact and the maintenance and enhancement of long-term productivity.
5. The agencies to which the EIS was distributed and the names and qualifications of those who prepared it.

Again, the idea behind the EIS, and for that matter, the NEPA, was to provide advance notice of proposed actions and fundamental knowledge of their environmental consequences to interested and would-be-affected parties. It was hoped that the open debate resulting from this publicity would ensure a wise decision.

That hope was ill founded. After the passage of the National Environmental Policy Act, challenges immediately arose. Federal agencies attempted to bypass the EIS requirement by saying that the action in question was not "significant." If an EIS was filed, it was often incomplete because federal agencies included only data on project alternatives that they could bring about. Gradually, these loopholes were closed. However, it was soon noted that even if an EIS covered all of the policy alternatives, the agency involved could simply ignore the EIS evaluations and do what it sought to do in the beginning, regardless of the environmental consequences. In short, the EIS was reduced to a formality that had to be observed before the agency went ahead and did what it had originally intended to do. For example, the Nuclear Regulatory Commission (NRC) issued a construction permit for a nuclear electric generation plant, ignoring the EIS conclusion that the facility would be unnecessary and hazardous. A group of citizens then brought suit to have the action overturned. The US Court of Appeals ruled that the NRC had made an arbitrary and capricious error of judgment in issuing the permit and ordered the action stopped. The US Supreme Court heard the case on appeal and overturned the appellate court's ruling. In *Vermont Yankee Nuclear Power Corp.* v. *Natural Resources Defense Council,* it held that although the NEPA did set forth significant goals for the nation, the EIS was basically a procedural requirement and its conclusions were therefore not binding on agencies. Therefore, an agency could choose an alternative different from the one deemed most advisable in an EIS that the agency itself had developed.

Later decisions by the US Supreme Court reaffirmed these views. In cases decided in the early 1990s, the Court held that it was enough to simply consider environmental concerns and that such concerns were not necessarily determinative or decisive regardless of the degree of their detrimental impact.

Whatever the current state of the NEPA and the EIS, there are many other statutes that are meant to protect the environment. These include the Clean Air Act, the Clean Water Act, the Solid Waste Disposal Act, and the Toxic Substances Control Act. We will discuss each of these in turn. Before we do that, however, realize that all of these acts allow private suits to be filed against both private polluters and regulatory agencies to ensure adherence to their provisions. This potential for private action, even when agencies may have been politically neutralized and kept from fulfilling their duty to protect the average citizen from

Top States in Annual Release of Toxic (Poisonous) Wastes	Figure 37–2

Louisiana	230,000 tons
Texas	205,000
Tennessee	108,000
Ohio	86,000

Source: Latest Environmental Protection Agency reports covering discharges into the air, into the water, underground, and onto the land.

environmental threats (see Figure 37–2 for some idea of the magnitude of these threats), is often considered the only saving grace of the entire environmental program.

Clean Air Act

Originally enacted in 1955, the Clean Air Act (CAA) has been significantly amended three times. After some initial mistakes in approach (for example, prescribing one minimum air standard for the entire country, which caused heavily polluting industries to avoid paying fines by moving their facilities to some of the country's cleanest air environments and thereby destroying them), the EPA has allowed for different air quality standards for different situations.

Primary standards for air quality, for example, are general standards that must be met to protect the public's health. **Secondary standards** are those that must be met to preserve the public welfare in the form of animal and plant life and visibility. Stationary and mobile sources of pollution, such as smokestacks and motor vehicles, respectively, are required to reduce their emissions to meet the standards of the geographic region that surrounds them. The standards imposed on sources of pollution emitting hazardous substances are harsher than those imposed on average sources of pollution.

Primary Standards: general levels of quality needed to protect public's health

Secondary Standards: levels of quality set to preserve public welfare

State cooperation is the key to the achievement of the EPA's air quality objectives. States are required to divide their total area into manageable air quality control regions (AQCRs) and to have state implementation plans (SIPs) in place to achieve air quality standards as necessary. These SIPs must contain the steps that the state will take to clean up **nonattainment regions** (those whose level of a particular pollutant exceeds the allowable limit) and to maintain **nondeterioration regions** (those whose level of a particular pollutant falls below a predetermined level). As it is possible for the same AQCR to be a nonattainment region for one pollutant and a nondeterioration region for another, the SIPs tend to be very complex.

Nonattainment Regions: regions whose level of particular pollutant exceeds the allowable limit

Nondeterioration Regions: regions whose level of particular pollutant is below a predetermined level

For applicants that want to initiate or increase their operations in a nonattainment region, the law is not an insurmountable obstacle. A permit will be issued if the applicant promises to use technology that will result in the smallest possible amount of new emissions and promises to offset any emission increase by reducing the same pollutant emissions from its other facilities in the region by the amount that the new facility will increase them. However, the permit will not be issued unless the applicant's other facilities are meeting the SIP.

In nondeterioration regions, where the air is cleaner than the EPA and SIP standards require it to be, the best available mechanisms must be installed to prevent significant deterioration. Preconstruction reviews must be carried out by the state and reported to the EPA before projects can go forward.

Recently, the sanctions that can be imposed on violators of the CAA were increased. This was done because many businesses found it more economical to pay the fines instead of installing the corrective equipment. Now businesses that fail to comply with the EPA and SIP standards may be fined an amount equal to the cost of installing equipment that fulfills the SIP requirements. The new penalty structure comes just in time to help in implementing new programs that seek to reduce cancer-causing emissions, acid rain, and ozone-depleting pollution.

Clean Water Act

The federal government began its regulation of dumping into our navigable waterways in 1890. The Rivers and Harbors Act of that year empowered the US Army Corps of Engineers to control through permits the release of materials hazardous to water transport. In the early 1960s, after the publication of Rachel Carson's *Silent Spring* spurred environmental consciousness in this country, the focus of the act was altered somewhat. Instead of being used to protect surface vessels from the release into the watercourse of large obstacles to their passage, it was used to require permits of those who treated the waterways as a cheap means for disposing of chemicals and other pollutants. Even so, the Rivers and Harbors Act was merely a stopgap method of curtailing the degradation of our streams and lakes.

Finally, in 1970, the passage of the Water Pollution and Control Act coupled with the formation of the EPA put in place an overall scheme for the regulation of such pollution. The act has been significantly amended twice—first by the Clean Water Act of 1977 (CWA), which put in place an all-encompassing, detailed regulatory plan and then by the Water Quality Act of 1987.

The CWA requires a permit for every point source, such as a pipe or ditch, from which waste is discharged into water. Such permits are available through the National Pollutant Discharge Elimination System (created in 1972 to replace the permit system of the Rivers and Harbors Act). As with the Clean Air Act, the main burden of this system's administrative enforcement is placed on the states.

Effluent: liquid waste

To obtain a permit, a polluter must meet **effluent** (liquid waste) limitations on the amount and type of wastes that can be discharged. The EPA administrator, however, has the power to grant variances to these limitations. The limitations themselves are based on the use of one of two technological levels of filtration equipment. The first, least expensive, and least effective level is referred to as "the best practicable control technology" (BPT) available. The second, most expensive, most effective level, and the level most lobbied against, is labeled "the best available technology economically achievable" (BAT). Originally, all dischargers were to be using at least the BPT by 1977 and the BAT by 1987. Congress, however, has made a habit of extending the deadlines; for example, the 1987 Amendments moved the BPT deadline to 1989 and the BAT deadline to 1991. As of 1994, neither the BPT nor the BAT had been fully implemented.

Solid Waste Disposal Act

Originally passed in 1965 to assist the states in dealing with solid wastes, the Solid Waste Disposal Act contained only guidelines for establishing programs that promised solutions. Even as amended in 1970 by the Resource Recovery Act, it did not require proper waste disposal. Instead, it offered grants for the study and development of a variety of waste treatment and recycling programs. Not until several high-profile news stories (for example, the stories on the Love Canal and Times Beach) connecting toxic waste disposal with such problems as cancer and birth defects was legislation passed whose scope and sanctions offered any chance of solving waste disposal problems.

The Resource Conservation and Recovery Act of 1976 and the Hazardous and Solid Waste Amendments Act.

The first attempt at such legislation, the Resource Conservation and Recovery Act of 1976 (RCRA), has not met with resounding success due mainly to the lack of sufficient EPA staff to administer it properly. The main thrust of the act, which amended the Solid Waste Disposal Act, requires the development and implementation of solid waste management plans at the state level in accordance with EPA guidelines. If a state does not produce a satisfactory plan, the EPA can impose a plan of its own. To meet with the EPA's satisfaction, such plans must allocate disposal responsibilities among the various governmental levels of the state, must establish a coordinated strategy for regional planning to control solid wastes, must eliminate or improve open dumps, and must gradually redirect nonhazardous wastes into "sanitary" landfills or recycling programs. As mentioned, implementation of the RCRA has been slow. Today, almost two decades after its passage, states are just beginning to implement such plans.

A more immediate threat and greater media attention have fostered significantly speedier action in response to other portions of the RCRA, namely its requirements for the identification and tracking of **hazardous wastes.** These are wastes that pose a substantial present or future danger to human health or the human environment if improperly managed. All of the businesses that handle hazardous waste—from the businesses that create it, called **generators,** to the businesses that transport, store, and dispose of it—are required by the RCRA to document the waste's travels. Failure to follow the RCRA procedures can result in significant fines and/or imprisonment even for company officers and stockholders if they are personally involved in the violations. By the latter part of the 1980s, amendments to the RCRA, mainly by the Hazardous and Solid Waste Amendments Act (HASWA), had empowered the EPA to determine whether any land-based disposal of any hazardous waste should be permitted. In addition, landfills were required to utilize double liners and to monitor groundwater and the

Hazardous Wastes: substances posing danger to human environment if improperly managed

Generators: creators of hazardous waste

air for dangerous emissions. Finally, the amendments to the RCRA gave greater power to citizens to sue to be sure that the act was being enforced.

Toxic Substances Control Act

In 1976 Congress passed the Toxic Substances Control Act (TSCA) to identify and help control the manufacture and distribution of chemicals that might generate hazardous waste. Under the terms of the act, 90 days before beginning the production of a new chemical, manufacturers are required to provide the EPA with information on the chemical's name, identity, intended use, and adverse effects. The EPA then examines the test data on the chemical to be certain that its risk is not too great. If the test data are insufficient, the EPA may order further testing. If an unreasonable risk is present, the EPA may stop production or use, or both. The act also mandates that records of detrimental health effects be kept for three decades and that records of environmental damage be kept for five years.

All of the information relating to health and safety aspects of the chemical's use that is required by the act may be made public. Trade secrets and confidential financial data may not, however.

The Superfund

No matter how many programs are established to control the current dumping of hazardous wastes, we are still burdened with a legacy of literally thousands of hazardous waste sites, known and unknown, that came into existence before the establishment of these programs. If such sites are determined to be a threat to human health and environment, something must be done about them quickly. Lawsuits or appeals to legislatures cannot provide the immediately necessary actions. With this in mind, Congress set up the **Superfund** or Hazardous Substances Response Trust Fund to pay for the cleanup of such sites. Thereafter, legal procedure is used to seek reimbursement of the Superfund by the parties responsible for their existence.

Superfund: Hazardous Substances Response Trust Fund

The Superfund was created by the Comprehensive Environmental Response, Compensation, and Liability Act of 1980 (CERCLA). CERCLA made the owners and operators of hazardous waste sites as well as the generators and other handlers of hazardous waste strictly liable for the reimbursement mentioned above. This strict liability was imposed jointly and severally, depending on the number of responsible parties reachable in the reimbursement action. In addition, EPA authorities were given the power to obtain disclosure of a company's complete financial position. This enabled the EPA to know the extent of an offender's ability to pay the cleanup costs. A company's failure to properly respond to EPA requests for financial data can result in fines of up to $25,000 per day. If necessary, EPA personnel can enter the premises of a company under investigation to take samples of suspicious substances and discharges, conduct inspections, and copy any and all the company's records.

After 45 years of use, Knoxius Chemical Company decided to get rid of its production facility in Chicago. The facility was owned by Knoxius's subsidiary, Springtime Manufacturing. It had been used to make chemical products running the gamut from Agent Orange to hexachlorophene. Unfortunately, most of the toxic by-products of these operations had been stored in several large warehouses at the site. As a consequence of potential cleanup costs estimated to be in the tens of millions of dollars, Knoxius could not find a buyer for the property. Finally, the legal staff proposed and management accepted a plan to dissolve the subsidiary and to give the property in question to the First Fundamental Walk of Truth Gospel Temple, a nondenominational church on the side of Chicago opposite from the site. The church gladly accepted the gift, and Knoxius then dissolved Springtime and ceased all of its Illinois operations. Within two years, the church was held strictly liable for $37 million in fees for cleanup of the site. Unable to pay the fees or to pay attorneys for attempting to make Knoxius pay them, the church simply disbanded, leaving the Superfund without reimbursement.

Other Statutes Providing Environmental Protection

The Insecticide, Fungicide, and Rodenticide Act of 1947 as augmented by the Environmental Pesticides Control Act of 1972 imposes a regulatory scheme requiring the registration and labeling of pesticides and their classification into general or restricted use categories. Restricted use pesticides can be used only by or under the supervision of qualified applicators.

Another problem needing regulation surfaced in the late 1980s when medical waste (used needles, swabs, tissue samples, etc.) and other hazardous materials began to come ashore on Long Island beaches and elsewhere. As a consequence, Congress passed acts that placed controls on previously ignored practices whose adverse effect on the environment had long been a matter of common knowledge. The Ocean Dumping Ban Act, Shore Protection Act, and Medical Waste Tracking Act came into force in 1988.

Finally, Congress gave us the Noise Control Act of 1972. Under its provisions, the EPA is required to identify and regulate major noise sources. Federal rules in this area preempt contrary state and local laws whose standards are more lenient but allow state and local requirements that pose stricter standards.

In 1987 the city of Pennsboro passed an ordinance prohibiting the emanation of excessive noise from a structure after 11 PM (midnight on weekends). Police officers who could hear such sounds at curbside by rolling down their patrol car windows were authorized to cite violators. The ordinance was amended in the early 1990s to provide protection against vehicular speaker systems.

Figure 37–3 provides, for quick reference, a listing of governmental abbreviations pertaining to environmental law.

Figure 37–3   **Acronym Anonymity**

Acronym	Government Term
AQCR	Air Quality Control Region
BAT	Best Available Technology
BPT	Best Practical Technology
CEQ	Council on Environmental Quality
CERCLA	Comprehensive Environmental Response, Compensation, and Liability Act
CAA	Clean Air Act
CWA	Clean Water Act
EIS	Environmental Impact Statement
EPA	Environmental Protection Agency
HASWA	Hazardous and Solid Waste Amendments Act
NEPA	National Environmental Policy Act
NRC	Nuclear Regulatory Commission
RCRA	Resource Conservation and Recovery Act
SIP	State Implementation Plan
TSCA	Toxic Substances Control Act

APPLICATIONS OF WHAT YOU'VE LEARNED

Vocabulary Development

Fill in the blanks with the appropriate term.

Effluent	**Generators**	**Nondeterioration Regions**	**Public Good**
Environmental Impact	**Hazardous Wastes**	**Nuisance**	**Secondary Standards**
Statement	**Nonattainment Regions**	**Primary Standards**	**Superfund**
Environmental Law			

1. A(n) _____ provides advance notice of federal projects that might significantly affect the environment.

2. An area whose air pollution exceeds federal allowable limits is termed a(n) _____.

3. A(n) _____ is a creator of hazardous waste.

4. A resource to which all citizens should have access and use is termed a(n) _____.

5. Pollution levels set to preserve the public welfare are termed _____.

Problems

1. What ethical justification is there for allowing society to determine what uses can be made of the air, land, and water? What ethical justification is there for individuals to assume that they have the right to use a public good as they see fit?

2. What public goods other than the air, land, and water might become important in the future?

3. Do you think that the EPA can be efficiently and effectively managed? Why or why not?

4. How did the initial implementation of the Clean Air Act contribute to the deterioration of some of the cleanest air in the country? How are the purer air areas (nondeterioration regions) protected today?

5. Do the taxpayers always have to pay for Superfund expenditures on toxic waste cleanups?

ACTUAL CASE STUDY

Procter and Gamble v. The City of Chicago

509 F.2d 69

Let's see what happened when a major American city's concern for the environment conflicted with a major American company's concern for its market.

The Chicago City Council outlawed by ordinance the sale of detergents containing phosphorus. It did so because it believed that eliminating phosphorus was one of the keys to obtaining clean water in the Chicago area. Procter & Gamble sued for relief in federal court, alleging that the ordinance passed by the council violated the US Constitution by putting an undue burden on interstate commerce.

Questions

1. Should the states and cities have the leeway to protect the environment by means of their own statutes or ordinances? What problems would you anticipate if such leeway were granted?

2. Does the Chicago ordinance put an undue burden on interstate commerce?

3. How should the court rule here? Are there any perspectives other than those advanced in the positions of the opposing sides?

How Do the Antitrust Laws Affect Business?

CHAPTER OUTLINE AND OBJECTIVES

After studying this chapter, the student will be able to:

I. Describe why antitrust law was developed.

II. Explain the regulatory framework established by the Sherman, Clayton, and other federal antitrust statutes.

  a. Sherman Act

  b. Rule of reason versus per se application of antitrust law

  c. Federal Trade Commission Act

  d. Clayton Act

  e. Robinson-Patman Act

  f. Celler-Kefauver Amendments

  g. Hart-Scott-Rodino Antitrust Improvements Act

III. Recognize the potential violations of the antitrust laws of which businesspeople should be most aware.

  a. Violations among competitors selling competing products (horizontal constraints).

  b. Violations among competitors selling the same product (vertical constraints).

IV. Determine what approach should be taken when, as in the case of *Missouri* v. *National Organization for Women*, a group organized for political purposes uses an economic boycott as a weapon to achieve its ends.

Why Was Antitrust Law Developed?

A good introduction to the topic of antitrust law comes from the text of a recent interview with a widely read legal scholar and professor:

"What is the greatest enemy of business in this country?" Right off the top, I must tell you that this is a trick question. You might answer "the government" or "governmental regulation." As you may suspect, that answer is anticipated and wrong. If you keep trying you might eventually come up with the correct answer: *"Competition!"* Competition is the greatest enemy of business in this country. Government regulation may be a harassment and otherwise a bother, but only in the rarest of cases does it put someone out of business, whereas competition does that to many businesses every day. The statutes and regulations to which we give the relatively obscure label "antitrust law" in this country are really our attempt to preserve competition and thereby keep businesses subservient to consumers through the market mechanism. Recent federal administrations have deemphasized such laws along with other governmental regulation while encouraging bigness as a remedy for foreign competition and declining productivity. It hasn't worked, and now our even bigger companies are getting their socks blown off by companies one-thousandth their size because those smaller outfits are far more competitive. It's sad, but we're about to relearn the lesson our forebears learned a century ago, a lesson about economic concentrations and bigness and how they threaten our way of life. Concisely put, the lesson is that without competition our way of life is doomed. This simple truth is dearly bought each and every time it is learned.

Left alone, businesses act to eliminate competition. Thus, some governmental supervision is necessary to preserve free markets. Adam Smith recognized the need for such supervision and warned against what would happen without it. As is all too often the case, Smith's statements and the historical experiences confirming his position were ignored. Within a century of its founding, the United States confronted a challenge in which vast portions of its most important markets were being consolidated under the control of an elite group of businessmen. Railroads, banks, petroleum, and many other industries were being monopolized. Nowhere was this trend more evident than in the petroleum industry. There John D. Rockefeller accomplished a near miracle by bringing under one umbrella of control some of the most independent capitalists in the country, men who had truly earned their "wildcatter" nickname. Rockefeller did this through a legal holding device called a trust. A **trust** is a separate entity created by law to which ownership of property can be transferred, after which the property is managed by designated individuals in accordance with the wishes of the transferor. In essence, a controlling interest in the stock of companies once in competition with one another was transferred to the trust. The few parties in charge of the trust, called the **trustees,** would then use their power to eliminate competition by fixing prices, territories, and so on. In essence, the bigger the trust, the greater the corner on the market obtained by its members and thus the greater their profits.

By the late 1880s the abuses of the market system caused by the trusts jeopardized the welfare of the country. Congress, reacting to the concerns of the

Trust: legal entity capable of owning and utilizing property according to direction of its creators

Trustees: parties in charge of trust

electorate, passed the Sherman Antitrust Act in 1890. It thereby began a century of governmental defense of competition at the federal level. Unfortunately for those called on to enforce it, this initial antitrust act was written in such broad and absolute terms that it seemed to throw out the good with the bad.

What Regulatory Framework Was Established by the Sherman, Clayton, and Other Federal Antitrust Statutes?

Sherman Act

The Sherman Act was passed in the white heat of antitrust fever. As a consequence, it rings with the absolutism that has damned many like efforts to legislate hard-and-fast rules in black and white without the necessary gray of exceptions. Read through the portions of sections 1 and 2 of the act below from the standpoint of a prosecutor charged with its enforcement, and see if you can understand why the wording presented so many problems.

Section 1

Every contract, combination in the form of trust or otherwise, or conspiracy, in restraint of trade or commerce . . . is hereby declared to be illegal. Every person who shall make any contract, or engage in any combination or conspiracy hereby declared to be illegal shall be deemed guilty of a misdemeanor.

Section 2

Every person who shall monopolize, or attempt to monopolize, or combine or conspire with any other person or persons, to monopolize any part of the trade or commerce . . . shall be deemed guilty of a misdemeanor.

If I'm building one house a month between early spring and late fall this year and I contract with you to supply the lumber for all of them, have I violated the act's section 1? After all, I might be able to get a better price for the lumber if I took separate bids for each one. Have you also violated section 1 by agreeing to sell the lumber to me?

If I have the option to buy the world's only titanium mine and have access to a trade secret that will allow me to produce a computer chip 1,000 times faster than any on the market today, but it can be made only from titanium, will I be prosecuted for an attempt to monopolize under section 2?

Exactly what is an attempt to monopolize anyway? What is a restraint of trade? Congress did not answer these questions or many others that arose, either in the act or in its legislative history. Instead, such questions were left to the courts to answer. Thus, businesspeople were given no clue as to whether today's accepted business practice would result in their prosecution tomorrow for a crime neither they nor their prosecutors could accurately define beforehand.

In addition, the sanctions imposed by the act were severe. Although a violation was only a misdemeanor at criminal law (today the amended act makes a violation a felony), the act authorized civil suits against violators for

Treble Damages: judgment award set at three times dollar value of actual harm

treble damages (three time actual damages) plus reasonable attorney's fees. Finally, the courts could issue injunctions to stop any improper practice and could hold in contempt those who disobeyed such injunctions.

Rule of Reason versus Per Se Application of Antitrust Law

The ambiguity of the Sherman Act caused two approaches to develop as to how to apply it and the other antitrust statutes that followed it. The first approach was articulated by the US Supreme Court in deciding the case of *United States* v. *Standard Oil of New Jersey Trust* in 1910. In that landmark decision, which resulted in the breakup of John D. Rockefeller's instrument of control over the petroleum industry, the Court set down the **rule of reason.** This rule was founded on the Court's observation that every contract restrains trade in one way or another. Rather than declare all such agreements illegal as a consequence, the Court decreed that the courts had to examine each from the standpoint of reasonability to see whether it acted to eliminate competition or to promote it. This approach removed from the Sherman Act the absolutism that had paralyzed prosecutors. However, it also retained the uncertainty of not being able to know whether an activity was illegal under the antitrust laws until this was determined at trial.

Rule of Reason: doctrine requiring that results of certain conduct be evaluated to determine whether conduct is illegal

The second approach identified categories of conduct that would be considered illegal under the antitrust laws regardless of their justification or reasonableness. These categories, which included price-fixing and other collusive violations, were held to be **illegal per se.** This means that a price-fixing agreement is illegal even if it results in lower prices than would have existed without it.

Illegal per Se: doctrine holding certain conduct illegal regardless of its results

The rule of reason approach gave the courts a great deal of power in interpreting the Sherman Act. Before long, their exercise of that power, for example in holding unions to be unreasonable restraints of trade, bothered Congress and caused it to move to rein them in. The Federal Trade Commission Act and the Clayton Act, both passed in 1914, were the results.

Federal Trade Commission Act

The Federal Trade Commission (FTC) Act attempted to end the uncertainty about just what was and what was not an illegal restraint of trade. The act created the FTC and empowered it to eliminate such "unfair methods of competition" in the United States. The FTC was thereby to achieve administratively what the courts and Congress had failed to achieve. First of all, this required defining what was not permissive behavior under the antitrust laws. In addition, the FTC was to assist the Antitrust Division of the US Department of Justice in enforcing the antitrust laws.

Clayton Act

Hot on the heels of the FTC Act came the Clayton Act. Unlike the FTC Act, under which clarification of the antitrust acts by the FTC had to wait for its formation and for the slowly grinding gears of its administrative process, the Clayton Act as passed contained clear answers to many of the questions regarding the antitrust acts that had arisen in the past. It also reversed or endorsed several court decisions regarding improper behavior under the antitrust laws that had placed in question the Congressional intention behind those laws. For example the Clayton Act, made price discrimination favoring one competitor over another illegal. It also:

Prohibited **tie-in sales** (sales in which a seller allows a buyer to purchase one product only if the buyer purchases another as well), if they tend to substantially reduce competition.

Prohibited a director of one company from sitting on the board of its competitor.

Prohibited **exclusive-dealing agreements** (agreements whereby a retailer agrees with a supplier not to sell a product that competes with the supplier's product).

Prohibited a **merger** (the absorption of one company by another) of competing companies if the effect of the merger is to substantially lessen competition.

Most members of the business community received with gratitude the immediate clarification of antitrust law offered by the Clayton Act. The FTC eventually produced regulations and other material that further clarified both Sherman and Clayton. Nonetheless, a little over 20 years after the passage of the FTC and Clayton's acts, Congress legislated another act to expand and update them.

Tie-In Sales: agreement by which, in order to buy desired good, buyer must also purchase another

Exclusive-Dealing Agreement: stipulation whereby retailer will not sell good that competes with supplier's product

Merger: absorption of one company by another

Robinson-Patman Act

The Robinson-Patman Act, passed in 1936, attempted to straighten out various misconceptions on price discrimination that stemmed from wording in the Clayton Act. According to Robinson-Patman, it is "unlawful to discriminate in price between different purchasers of commodities of like grade and quality." However, such discrimination is held to be lawful only if its effect is to harm competition on one of various levels in the distribution chain or if it tends to create a monopoly. The act also provides defenses to accusations of price discrimination. These defenses include passing on a manufacturer's savings in production costs due to a relatively large order, savings in shipping costs due to a buyer's location, and price cuts necessary to meet a competitor's prices. Although not considered very successful in its clarification mission, the act has been used to get rid of several improper practices that we will touch on later in the chapter.

Celler-Kefauver Amendments

Predictably, business quickly found a way around the Clayton Act's prohibition of stock mergers. Instead, firms merged by a purchase of assets, which perhaps violated the spirit of the act but was in the clear as far as prosecution was concerned. Mergers of manufacturers, suppliers, and retailers in a product chain also occurred. As Clayton prohibited only mergers between competitors, it was impotent to stop such mergers. It was also impotent to stop "conglomerate" mergers, that is, mergers between businesses in unrelated areas of commerce. The Celler-Kefauver Amendments therefore made it illegal to acquire stock or assets of another commercial entity where "the effect of such acquisition may be substantially to lessen competition, or to tend to create a monopoly." This broad wording produced uncertainty among companies considering merging. To resolve it, many of them sought some premerger indication from the Justice Department as to whether they might be prosecuted for uniting with another commercial entity. To resolve such doubts, the Justice Department publishes and updates *Merger Guidelines,* a detailed guidebook that indicates when proposed mergers will be challenged by legal action.

Hart-Scott-Rodino Antitrust Improvements Act

Shock waves were sent through the business community when Senator Gary Hart of Colorado proposed changes in the antitrust laws that would have allowed the government to break up any four or fewer companies who together owned two-thirds of any relevant market. Although Hart's proposal died a quick death, the legislation that resulted from the upheaval did take two relatively major steps forward. First, the Hart-Scott-Rodino Antitrust Improvements Act authorized state attorneys general to initiate suit against antitrust violators when citizens of their state were injured. Secondly, the act placed a 30-day advance merger notification requirement into law.

All of these acts and amendments have been instrumental in making antitrust law what it is today. You need to know them in detail for your own protection. Before we examine these laws closely, however, take a look at Figure 38–1 to see whether your area of business might be exempted from their coverage.

Of Which Potential Violations of the Antitrust Laws Should Businesspeople Be Most Aware?

For self-protection, a businessperson today must be sensitive to conduct that could be construed as a violation of the antitrust laws. Either to a victim of the violations of others or to an unwitting perpetrator, being able to identify potential antitrust problems can be crucial to the success and longevity of a business. Consequently, the remainder of this chapter covers the most likely violations in enough depth to allow such identification.

Interbrand Competition: rivalry between individuals selling different products

Horizontal Constraints: interbrand restraints on trade

For the sake of analysis, these violations are best divided into two categories. The first category comprises violations that interfere with **interbrand competition,** which involves individuals who should be working against each other to sell competing products from different producers (see Figure 38–2). Such violations we label **horizontal constraints** because they typically involve sellers at the same level of commerce (for example, a salesperson selling Gotcha Pagers conspiring

**Current Exemptions from the Provisions
of the Antitrust Laws**

Figure 38–1

Exempt Area	Regulator, if Any
Baseball	None as yet. The national pastime remains immune.
Trucking, airlines, railroads, and ships at sea	Although the trucking and airline industries were formerly regulated by the Interstate Commerce Commission (ICC) and the Federal Aviation Administration (FAA), respectively, their deregulation in the last decade left their long-standing exemption in doubt. Railroads are still regulated by the ICC, and the Maritime Administration regulates oceangoing American vessels.
Farming and fishing cooperatives and similar enterprises	Department of Agriculture and Department of the Interior
Insurance companies	Insurance commissioners of the various states
Radio and television broadcasting	Federal Communications Commission, which grants monopoly rights to broadcast over certain frequencies.
Banks and similar financial institutions	Can be chartered at the state or federal level. At the state level, they are regulated by various state agencies; at the federal level, the Federal Reserve Board exercises primary control over them.
Stock exchanges	Securities and Exchange Commission
Labor unions	Department of Labor and National Labor Relations Board

Intrabrand Competitors for the Breakfast Cereal Market

Figure 38–2

Figure 38–3   **Intrabrand Competition for the Breakfast Cereal Market**

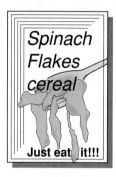

Sept. 9, 1993
Pennsboro Leader Ad Supplement
Page 6

NOW at Anton's Super Store
No coupon required.

Spinach Flakes cereal

Just eat it!!!

2– 72 oz. boxes ONLY $7.99!

Sept. 9, 1993
Pennsboro Leader Ad Supplement
Page 7

Special at Mom and Pop's Grocery
No coupon required.

Spinach Flakes cereal

Just eat it!!!

2– 72 oz. boxes ONLY $8.49!

Intrabrand Competition: rivalry between entities selling same product

Vertical Constraints: intrabrand restraints on trade

to fix prices with a salesperson selling Nokayama Pagers). The second category comprises violations that interfere with **intrabrand competition,** which involves individuals who should be competing to sell the same product (see Figure 38–3). Such violations we label **vertical constraints** because they involve relations between parties that are up and down the chain of distribution of the product in question (for example, a salesperson from the local store selling Gotcha Pagers conspiring to fix prices with a Gotcha factory representative selling Gotcha Pagers).

Violations among Competitors Selling Competing Products (Horizontal Constraints)

Monopolizing.   To be held guilty of this cornerstone of antitrust prohibitions set down in the Sherman Act's section 2 ("Every person who shall monopolize . . . shall be deemed guilty"), a firm must be shown to have **monopoly power** (in essence, the ability to control prices) and to have exhibited **monopolizing conduct** (behavior indicating that it achieved or abused its position of market dominance by improper methods).

Monopoly Power: seller's ability to control market

Monopolizing Conduct: firm's abuse of dominant market position

Market power.   As mentioned, when a business or some other entity no longer finds the prices it can charge dictated by a competitive market but is instead able to set its prices almost at will, it has market power. Until the mid-1970s the various state bar associations sent out suggested fee schedules to their members. If a member violated such a schedule, the bar association could prosecute the member for a breach of the code of ethics and have the member disbarred. Finally, in a 1975 case, the US Supreme Court held that these practices were a violation of the antitrust law (*Goldfarb* v. *Virginia State Bar Association,* 421 U.S. 773).

Currently, in order to determine whether a business has monopoly power allowing it to exercise a significant control over prices, courts focus on the answers to two questions: What is the relevant market in which to consider questions of monopolization, and what is the market share of the business/defendant within the relevant market? In the antitrust case law, the phrase **relevant market** means the total demand for the product or service allegedly being monopolized and those interchangeable with it as determined within the geographic area in question. So if charges were directed against a power lawn mower manufacturer for trying to monopolize, the court would first have to determine the relevant market. To do so, the court would begin with the sales of the defendant's mowers within the geographic area in question. Next it would add the sales of reasonably interchangeable products—other power lawn mowers, push lawn mowers, garden tractors with mower attachments, and the like—within the same area. Then it would divide the defendant's sales by the total sales in the relevant market to determine the defendant's **market share** (the percentage of the relevant market under the defendant's control). Once this percentage has been arrived at, it is matched to a "market power" scale provided by Judges Learned Hand and Augustus Hand in deciding the mid-1940s antitrust case against the Aluminum Company of America (Alcoa). To quote their opinion in that case: "That percentage we have already mentioned—over 90— . . . is enough to constitute a monopoly; it is doubtful whether 60 or 64 percent would be enough; and certainly 33 percent is not." (*United States* v. *Aluminum Company of America,* 148 F.2d 416).

Relevant Market: demand for interchangeable products within geographic area

Market Share: percentage of relevant market belonging to one entity

With these percentage guidelines in mind, courts and businesses alike can determine whether monopolizing power (indicated by a market share of more than 90 percent according to the above) exists with reasonable certainty. As the market share slides toward the 33 percent level, so too does the possibility that such power will not be held to exist. In addition, as mentioned, a business cannot be held guilty of a violation of the act merely for holding such power. The business must also exhibit monopolizing conduct.

Monopolizing conduct. Common sense tells us that we do not want to punish someone who obtains a monopoly position by working hard and offering the best product at the lowest price. Most people feel that businesses with a large market share should be punished only if they achieve or maintain that position by using underhanded methods to eliminate or forestall competition. The monopolies granted inventors under our patent laws testify to the wisdom of this view. The Sherman Act, however, did not recognize any such exception. "Every person who shall monopolize . . . shall be guilty." Judicial interpretation eventually read "reason" into the application of the act, and businesspeople were therefore no longer threatened with prosecution for superior work, efficiency, skill, risk taking, and so on.

Instead, the focus shifted to whether or not the possessor of monopoly power had acquired it by means of monopolizing conduct. In deciding the *Standard Oil of New Jersey Trust* case, the US Supreme Court gave us a good description of such conduct by reciting some activities of that trust's founders.

> It suffices to say that such [monopolizing conduct] may be grouped under the following heads: Rebates, preferences, and other discriminatory practices in favor of the combination by railroad companies; restraint and monopolization by control of pipe lines, and unfair practices against competing pipe lines; contracts with competitors in restraint of trade; unfair methods of competition such as local price cutting at the points where necessary to suppress competition; espionage of the business of competitors, the operation of bogus independent companies, and the payment of rebates on oil, with the like intent; the division of the United States into districts, and the limiting of the operations of the various subsidiary corporations as to such districts so that competition in the sale of petroleum products between such corporations had been entirely eliminated and destroyed; and finally reference was made to what was alleged to be the "enormous and unreasonable profits" earned by the Standard Oil Trust and the Standard Oil Company as a result of the alleged monopoly.
>
> *Standard Oil Co.* v. *United States,* 221 U.S. 1

So, through the decisions cited above, the courts gradually evolved a position that a showing of monopoly power and a history of monopolizing conduct are required to place a defendant in jeopardy of being convicted of monopolization.

Attempting to Monopolize.   As far as attempts to monopolize are concerned, the prosecution must show that the defendant utilized established market power improperly in an "attempt" to consolidate market control. Without market power behind it, such an attempt is not considered a violation of the Sherman Act.

As discussed, proposed consolidations of competing companies that might substantially lessen competition "in any line of commerce in any section of the country" (to quote section 7 of the Clayton Act) will be fought by the Justice Department. Such resistance to mergers and similar business activities that might create a company with too much market power stems from the Sherman Act prohibition of "attempts to monopolize."

Conspiracy.   Unlike monopolization or attempts to monopolize, which present prosecutors with significant problems of proof because of the relative ambiguity of the rule of reason approach, conspiracies between competitors either to restrain trade (section 1 of the Sherman Act) or to monopolize (section 2) are per se violations. The primary example of such conspiracies is price-fixing.

Price-Fixing.   The getting together of competitors to fix prices is the most clearly acknowledged antitrust offense. Price-fixing was made a per se violation by the 1927 Supreme Court decision in *United States* v. *Trenton Potteries*. Significantly, the *Trenton Potteries* case acknowledged that joining with your competitors to set prices is illegal *even if prices fall as a result.*

In fact, a number of America's largest corporations have faced the near disastrous consequences of a conviction for this offense. In the 1960s, for example, high executives of General Electric and Westinghouse got together to fix prices on the turbines used by electric utilities to generate power. Before the prosecutions were over, nearly 50 of these executives were found guilty. Although fewer than one-fifth of those found guilty served prison sentences, the careers of almost all of them were greatly harmed. In addition, the two companies involved were hit by fines and by treble-damage awards to parties injured by the price gouging. The fines totaled only approximately $2 million, but the treble-damage awards totaled over $400 million. Since this substantial amount was in 1960s dollars, it would easily be the equivalent of $1.5 billion today.

Conscious Parallelism.   A common practice today in areas of our economy in which only a few companies control most of the market (a condition referred to as **oligopoly**) is for all of them to follow the pricing policies of the largest of these companies. This practice is labeled **conscious parallelism.** If the members of the oligopoly set prices independently of one another, the behavior is legal. However, if there is evidence of collusion other than the obvious patterning of prices, the behavior can be prosecuted as a per se violation of the antitrust laws. Even circumstantial evidence is allowed to indicate wrongdoing. As one court said:

> [We are not] so naive as to believe that a formal signed-and-sealed contract or written resolution would conceivably be adopted at a meeting of price-fixing conspirators in this day and age. In fact, the typical price-fixing agreement is usually accomplished in a contrary manner . . . A knowing wink can mean more than words . . . It is not necessary to find an express agreement, either oral or written, in order to find a conspiracy, but it is sufficient that a concert of action be contemplated and that defendants conform to the arrangement . . . Thus not only action but even a lack of action may be enough from which to infer a combination or conspiracy.

United States v. *Esco Corporation,* 340 F.2d 1000

Oligopoly: economic condition in which only a few companies control most of the market

Conscious Parallelism: oligopolists following price leadership of one of their group

In short, if a business is a member of an oligopoly, it must be extremely careful about the factors it considers in setting its prices and about its contacts with the other members about prices. Any evidence of collusion other than parallel prices can be suasive in a resulting criminal case.

Boycotts.   When competitors refuse to deal with **(boycott)** suppliers or customers unless transactions are concluded on terms that the competitors have mutually agreed to observe, a violation of the antitrust acts has occurred. Generally, such violations are considered illegal per se.

Boycott: refusal to deal

Territorial and Customer Allocations.   Per se violations are almost always produced by conspiracies of competitors to divide territories or customers among themselves. The exclusive dealing zones so created represent a restraint of trade.

Violations among Competitors Selling the Same Product (Vertical Constraints)

Resale Price Maintenance.   Among firms competing to sell the same product, resale price maintenance is a violation as serious as price-fixing between sellers of competing products. The phrase **resale price maintenance** refers to the

Resale Price Maintenance: efforts of manufacturer or distributor to control price of product at commercial level other than its own.

efforts of a manufacturer or distributor to control the price at which a product is marketed at a commercial level other than its own. For example, when a manufacturer tries to force retailers of its product to maintain a set price on that product, the manufacturer's efforts are referred to as resale price maintenance. Whether their purpose is to keep the price artificially low to preclude or injure competition or artificially high to ensure maximum profits, contracts to maintain prices of goods in such circumstances are illegal per se. The obvious loophole in this rule is the situation in which no contract is involved. Indeed, the Colgate Company tested that point in the early part of this century when it informed its resellers that if they failed to follow a suggested price list for Colgate products, they would no longer be able to buy them. Because no contract was involved, the US Supreme Court held that the Colgate plan was legal.

However, should there be more to such an action than a mere refusal to deal, a contract may be found and a conviction will result. Such a case occurred when, subsequent to the Supreme Court decision upholding the Colgate plan, a company instituted a plan in which it refused to deal with any resellers of its products that would not follow its suggested price list but promised to reinstate such disenfran-chised resellers if they changed their minds. This was too much for the Supreme Court. It found the condition of reinstatement to be like a contract and held that the company had committed a per se violation (resale price maintenance) of the antitrust laws.

This single Court-approved position—"If you sell my goods below my suggested price, I'll not sell any more of them to you,"—has come to be known as the Colgate line. Businesspeople step over it at their peril.

As you might suspect, rather than do that, some have tried to sidestep it. One attempt at this was through the use of the consignment. Under such an arrange-ment, the possession of goods belonging to one party (the consignor) is trans-ferred to another party (the consignee) by whom they are to be sold. The ownership remains with the consignor, who, to avoid taking a loss, can rightfully set the lowest allowable sales price for the goods. The consignee usually gets a percentage commission on the actual sales price. Consignment law was in place long before the antitrust laws, and its terms seemed a ready-made haven for those who wanted to circumvent the loss of control over price brought on by those laws. Nonetheless, the Supreme Court would have none of it. It held that if the substance of the transaction was an attempt at resale price maintenance, the transaction was illegal per se even if its form was similar to that of a consignment. It is important to note that, not wishing to destroy the consignment device, the Court held that such transactions were illegal only when conducted on a "large scale." However, it did not go on to provide firm guidance as to what a large scale was.

Price Discrimination. As mentioned, the amended Clayton Act outlawed certain forms of price discrimination. Specifically outlawed by various pieces of legislation were selling below cost or discriminating in price between geographic areas in order to destroy competition, receiving the benefits of price discrimina-tion, and hiding price discrimination behind discount or commission schedules, service contracts, or preferential payment plans.

The various pieces of legislation also endorsed certain defenses to charges of price discrimination. These included:

Differences in costs of manufacture—larger orders usually have a smaller unit cost than smaller orders as the setup costs are usually the same for both but are allocated to more units in larger orders than in smaller orders.

Differences in costs of delivery—shipping costs are usually greater for smaller orders than for larger orders due to the greater handling requirements of smaller orders.

Necessity for meeting competition—a good faith response (not below cost) to meet a price established by the competition is defensible.

Allocation of Territories and Customers. Although antitrust violations stemming from assignments of the territory or customers of a particular product were once treated as per se violations of the antitrust laws, the Supreme Court decreed in 1977 that they would thereafter be evaluated by the rule of reason. To quote the court in that decision: "The market impact of vertical restrictions is complex because of their potential for a simultaneous reduction of intrabrand competition and stimulation of interbrand competition." (*Continental T.V.* v. *GTE Sylvania,* 433 U.S. 36).

It was this complexity that caused the Court to opt for a rule of reason evaluation. Among the many factors that can be cited are distance between retailers, flexibility of consumer travel, capitalization of the various entities involved, and shipping costs.

Exclusive Dealing. Section 3 of the Clayton Act makes it illegal to condition a sale on the agreement of the buyer not to sell a competitor's products if such an agreement substantially lessens competition. The courts have interpreted this prohibition to be effective against any party with considerable market power that demands such an arrangement of a buyer. The degree of market power necessary to allow a substantial lessening of competition is generally determined by a product-by-product analysis similar to the use of the rule of reason.

Tie-In Sales. As defined previously, a tie-in sale occurs when a seller will agree to sell one product only if the buyer will agree to buy another product. Such sales are treated as being illegal per se whenever the seller has considerable market power. Otherwise, the tie-in sale can still be evaluated under the rule of reason test. Note that franchisers are afforded some protection by the Lanham (trademark) Act. As such businesses are often built around a particular mark, franchisers may utilize tie-in sales (for example, sales requiring that franchises purchase particular ingredients and a particular monitoring device to ensure the production of uniform Bunnyburgers) to fulfill the Lanham Act's requirements that they protect the quality of their trademarked goods.

Vertical Mergers. Finally, the business manager needs to be especially wary of the vertical merger. All too often, manufacturers buy members of their distribution chain at the wholesale or retail level, or both. Section 7 of the Clayton

Act makes such combinations illegal primarily if they tend to create a situation in which a great deal of the market is under one control, that of the merged companies. Obviously, if a manufacturer of, say, skimobiles merged with a company that owned 80 percent of a region's retail outlets for such vehicles, the resulting combination could reduce dramatically a competitor's chances of success in that region. On the other hand, if the same manufacturer instead merged with a company that owned only 10 percent or less of the retail outlets, the merger would be allowed without any thought of prosecuting its participants.

APPLICATIONS OF WHAT YOU'VE LEARNED

Vocabulary Development

Fill in the blanks with the appropriate term.

Boycott	Interbrand Competition	Oligopoly	Tie-In Sales
Conscious Parallelism	Intrabrand Competition	Relevant Market	Treble Damages
Exclusive-Dealing Agreement	Market Share	Resale Price Maintenance	Trust
Horizontal Constraints	Merger	Rule of Reason	Trustees
Illegal per Se	Monopolizing Conduct		Vertical Constraints
	Monopoly Power		

1. A refusal to deal is also termed a(n)_____.

2. A(n)_____ is a legal entity capable of holding ownership of property that is to be managed according to the dictates of the entity's creator.

3. The _____ requires that the effect of certain restraints on trade be evaluated before they are considered illegal.

4. The absorption of one company by another is termed a(n) _____.

5. Competition between individuals selling the same product is termed _____.

6. _____ is a practice in which the members of an oligopoly follow the price leadership of one of their members.

7. An activity denoted as _____ will be held unlawful regardless of its results.

Problems

1. What problems were caused by the manner in which the Sherman Act was drafted? How could these problems have been avoided?

2. What do you think is the most significant sanction available under the antitrust laws? Why?

3. Many believe that the rule of reason test is unfair. Why would anyone take this position? Can you recommend a better test?

4. Of the various possible antitrust violations, which one has affected you as a consumer the most? Which one has affected you as an actual or potential competitor the most? Can you identify possible violations that exist in the marketplace around you right now that have gone unprosecuted?

5. Could access to national TV advertising be viewed as a restraint on trade due to its cost and thereby its obvious slant in favor of large companies? Why or why not?

ACTUAL CASE STUDY

Missouri v. National Organization for Women

620 F.2D 1301

Consider a different twist on a boycott.

The National Organization for Women (NOW) boycotted commercial entities in the states that had not ratified the Equal Rights Amendment to the US Constitution. Missouri, one such state, sued NOW for its alleged illegal boycott under the antitrust laws.

Questions

1. Is this a type of boycott that the antitrust laws are or should be concerned with? How would you distinguish it from others?

2. By which standard are boycotts usually judged—the rule of reason standard or the per se illegality standard?

3. Which of these standards would you recommend for use in this case?

CHAPTER

39

How Does the Regulation of the Sale of Stocks, Bonds, and Other Securities Affect Business?

CHAPTER OUTLINE AND OBJECTIVES

After studying this chapter, the student will be able to:

I. Discuss why laws regulating the issuance and exchange of securities are necessary.

II. Explain the breadth of the coverage of our securities laws.
   a. State laws
   b. Federal regulation of securities in interstate commerce.

III. Identify the circumstances under which a security issue can be exempted from the registration requirements of the Securities Act.
   a. Securities issued by governmental entities and not-for-profit organizations
   b. Short-term commercial paper
   c. Private placements
   d. Small public offering
   e. Intrastate offering

IV. Recognize the protection that the securities laws provide for the stock trader.
   a. Against insider trading
   b. Against fraud and manipulation

V. Apply your study of securities regulation by analyzing the case of the *Securities and Exchange Commission* v. *W. J. Howey Co.*

Why Are Laws Regulating the Issuance and Exchange of Securities Necessary?

On October 29, 1929, the death knell of the post–World War I prosperity in the United States tolled on Wall Street. On that "black Tuesday" the stock market went into cardiac arrest. The New York Stock Exchange, the financial heart of the country, had been in questionable condition for some time. Its prices were artificially inflated by easy credit (many investors paid only 10 percent of the purchase price of their shares with their own money and the rest with money typically borrowed from brokerage houses) and debased by an ethic that tolerated fraud and unfair advantage. Even so, the stock market carried the faith and hopes of investors throughout the country, from churches to colleges to widows to banks. So on that day nearly three-quarters of a century ago, the very foundation of an entire nation was shattered.

Very few escaped the tragedy. One man who did managed to do so by observing that stock speculation had got out of hand and then acting quickly on that observation. That man was Joseph P. Kennedy, one of the wealthiest and most active investors of the time. Legend has it that during a taxi ride only a few weeks before the Great Crash, Kennedy unexpectedly received stock tips from the driver. Thinking about it afterward, he realized that, if the market was being guided by such flows of information at such a level much like a horse race, it was time to get out. He did so and saved the fortune that, years later, would help make his son president of the United States.

The effects of the Crash were devastating. By 1932, when the economy was at its worst, US Steel and General Motors stock were selling at less than one-tenth their pre-Crash prices. (The Dow Jones Industrial Average plummeted from around 500 pre-Crash to bottom out at 42.) The steel industry as a whole was operating at under 20 percent of capacity. Its customers did not need much steel as demand for their products had fallen drastically. The American Locomotive Company, maker of over 600 train engines per year before the Crash, sold one in 1932. The gross national product of the United States fell from over $100 billion to around $40 billion. Over 5,000 banks failed, obliterating the life savings of their depositors (at that time no federal deposit insurance was available). Nonfarm unemployment soared to over 25 percent (leaving over 30 million men, women, and children without any supporting income whatsoever). Hundreds of thousands of evictions from homes followed hard on the heels of the wave of unemployment.

These pervasive effects of the unprecedented fall in the prices of an unregulated market in securities fostered a widespread demand for the installation of protective controls by the federal government. Soon after taking office, President Franklin Delano Roosevelt responded to that demand by seeing that the Securities Act of 1933 and the Securities Exchange Act of 1934 were put into law. These two acts established the Securities and Exchange Commission (SEC) and gave it the power to regulate the issuance, marketing, and reselling of investment securities. As the first head of the SEC, Roosevelt appointed the same Joseph P. Kennedy we spoke of earlier. When asked why, Roosevelt responded that Kennedy knew all the loopholes in the current laws and therefore could close them. A prosperous post-World War II economy free of severe problems attributable to stock market machinations was to show that Roosevelt was correct in his assessment.

What Is the Breadth of the Coverage of Our Securities Laws?

State Laws

Although the most comprehensive regulation of securities now originates at the federal level, the states also have a tradition of regulation in this area. The federal securities laws are directed at interstate transactions; the state securities laws are intended to control intrastate transactions. The state laws are referred to as **blue-sky laws**. (Some say that this label originated in the stock sellers' practice of praising each offering to the blue sky, while others trace its origin to the idea that the purpose of the laws was to prevent stock purchases that were the equivalent of investing in a few square feet of the blue sky.) As you might suspect, these laws vary greatly in the controls they place on the transfer of securities and in the powers they grant holders of securities. Midwestern states, owing to the frequent perpetration of fraudulent schemes on farmers, have some of the strictest laws of this kind. Generally, these laws set down registration requirements and, perhaps most important, the latitude of action that the company management is allowed without having to seek the approval of the stockholder-owners. Because of a firm's ability to choose its state of incorporation and where it wants to do business (and, by these choices, the state securities laws that will be applied to it), these state laws do not provide as much true protection as is found in the federal statutes and regulations.

Blue-Sky Laws: state laws regulating securities

Federal Regulation of Securities in Interstate Commerce

The federal requirements with regard to securities, primarily SEC regulations, set up a generally applicable and comprehensive scheme of regulation. The scope of the regulation extends to all transactions, from issuance to every resale, in "securities" in interstate commerce.

Definition of Security. Although the Securities Act of 1933 provides a detailed definition of the term *security*, our courts have developed a much more condensed and workable one. In particular, the Supreme Court considers a **security** to be an investment contract whereby investors provide the capital and share in the earnings generated through the management and control of the promoters.

Security: contract whereby investors provide capital to be managed for profit by others

> Blately built a 33-unit condominium development on the beach in Nag's Head, North Carolina. He then sold the units to prospective investors. A part of each sales contract involved Blately's employment to manage the upkeep of the development and the marketing of the condominiums as seasonal rentals for vacationers. The proceeds of the rentals were to be used to pay for Blately's management and to pay a return to the owners. A federal court held that the ownership interests in the condominiums were in fact securities and therefore subject to SEC requirements.

Once something has been determined to be a security, it becomes subject to the requirements of the federal statutes. These statutes and the SEC rules and regulations that implement them depend on disclosure of all relevant information on the corporation and the security issue to prevent improper advantage of the average investor from being taken. Broadly speaking, the Securities Act of 1933 covers the initial offering of a security on the public market, while the Securities Exchange Act of 1934 covers the public trading of a security after issuance. This section of the chapter and the one that follows (on exemptions from the coverage of the Securities Act of 1933) are devoted to the 1933 Act; the final section is on the 1934 Act.

As far as issuing securities is concerned, note, first and foremost, that the SEC does not review a prospective offering for its worth. The SEC merely requires that information about the offering be truthfully rendered and properly distributed to would-be investors. It is up to the investors to evaluate the offering. Therefore, the main enforcement emphasis under the 1933 Act is on the veracity and completeness of the information given to prospective investors.

As a mechanism for providing this crucial information, all securities (unless exempted by statute) must be registered with the SEC prior to being issued. (Such registration does not relieve them of the requirements of any pertinent state statute, however.) In particular, a **registration statement** must be filed with the SEC before a single share can be sold. This statement consists of detailed information on the company's financial status, its history, its management's experience, the reason for and risks of a particular offering, and a variety of other information. A significant portion of the information contained in the registration statement must be made available to a prospective buyer of any portion of the issue. This information is published in what is called a **prospectus**, which also contains an invitation to buy. The prospectus must be approved by the SEC. Should false information be contained in the prospectus or other documents filed with the SEC, the company, its officers and directors, and the lawyers and accountants who compiled those documents could be subject to personal liability in a civil suit for the losses suffered by investors. If the information was willfully falsified, criminal charges could be brought, with conviction resulting in a fine of up to $10,000 or imprisonment of up to five years, or both.

Complying with the SEC procedure for issuing a security is both complex and

Registration Statement: informational filing with SEC on security issue

Prospectus: SEC-required document containing investment information and invitation to buy

expensive. As a consequence, many companies attempt to qualify their issues under one or another of the exemptions from the requirements of the 1933 Act.

Under What Circumstances Can a Security Issue Be Exempted from the Registration Requirements of the Securities Act?

If you are a businessperson looking for an exemption as a way around the $75,000 to $150,000 outlay necessary to register a security issue properly, you need to recognize two things: first, it is true that many stock issues do go unregistered as a result of the exemptions we are going to discuss, but second, the improper or unwise bypassing of registration often comes back to haunt those involved. So evaluate your options carefully.

The exemptions themselves range from those that are clear-cut, relatively risk-free, and easy to comply with to those that are difficult to comply with and laden with the constant risk of blowing up in the issuer's face. The remainder of this section discusses the most common of these exemptions in order of their increasing risk and complexity.

Securities Issued by Government Entities and Not-for-Profit Organizations

States, counties, cities, and their authorized agencies can offer securities issues without registering them. Corporations organized for educational, health, recreational, or charitable purposes are also exempt from registering their securities.

HYPOTHETICAL CASE

The Pennsboro Turnpike and Intercounty Airport Authority issued and sold $30 million in bonds to finance the construction of a new airport terminal and runway system. In conjunction with that project, the Pennsboro Hospital, a nonprofit organization, issued $5 million in bonds to finance the acquisition of three Medevac helicopters and the construction of hangar and maintenance facilities at the new airport. Neither issue had to be registered with the SEC.

Short-Term Commercial Paper

As long as it is not advertised for sale to the public, a business may issue any form of commercial paper for financing. The only requirements are that the note, draft, or whatever must be due within nine months and arise out of a current business transaction.

> In order to purchase two new cabs for its fleet to be stationed at the new airport, the Pennsboro Independent Cab Company issued a 180-day promissory note in favor of the Pennsboro Bank. No registration was required.

Private Placements

In 1982, in what was labeled Regulation D, the Reagan administration carved out a number of new exemptions to the SEC registration requirements. These exemptions are intended to legitimize the general category of private offerings of securities.

There are three main exemptions under Regulation D. The first and broadest allows an issuer to sell up to $500,000 worth of securities in a year to an unlimited number of investors without being required to provide those investors with any information whatsoever. Realize, however, that, as mentioned, this does not exempt the issuer from the requirements of the states involved. In addition, as with the other exemptions under Regulation D, the issuer must refrain from public advertising of the offering, must provide notice of a Regulation D offering to the SEC, and must mark the stock certificates as being **restricted securities**. This means that the shares cannot be resold without registration unless the resale is another exempt transaction.

The other two exemptions allow a much greater amount of securities to be issued. The key to having a security issue fall under one of these exemptions is to be very careful that the offering is directed to appropriate investors.

Who are these appropriate investors? Regulation D divides them into two categories: accredited investors and investors who are capable of evaluating the risks of the issue on their own (nonaccredited investors). If a nonaccredited investor is involved, it is up to the issuer who is claiming the exemption to be able to prove that the investor was indeed capable of understanding the risk involved. This becomes a rather formidable task if the investor is claiming just the opposite and has the losses to back up that claim.

Therefore, the first category, the accredited investor, represents the intended, truly safe haven for the private placement. According to Regulation D, an **accredited investor** is one of the following:

Any bank, investment company, insurance company, or employee benefit plan.
Any business development company.
Any charitable or educational institution with assets greater than $5 million.
Any director, executive officer, or general partner of the issuer.
Any person who purchases at least $150,000 of the offering as long as the amount purchased does not exceed 20 percent of that person's net worth.
Any person with a net worth of over $1 million.
Any person with an annual income greater than $200,000.

Restricted Securities: shares that cannot be resold without registration or exemption

Accredited Investor: capital source specified in Regulation D as having the ability to evaluate securities offering

So, hopefully, after finding interested and accredited investors as defined above, the issuer can avail itself of either of the other two exemptions under Regulation D.

The first of these two exemptions allows up to $5 million in securities in a 12-month period to be sold to an unlimited number of accredited investors and not more than 35 other purchasers. The latter purchasers, however, must receive a registration statement.

The second exemption is the more important. It allows an issuer to sell an unlimited number of securities to any number of accredited investors and no more than 35 nonaccredited purchasers. Again, it is extremely important that the nonaccredited purchasers to whom securities are sold be capable of evaluating the risks involved. This is the exemption that covers the vast majority of the billions and billions of dollars of private placements made each year.

Small Public Offerings

Available to companies that wish to offer $1,500,000 or less of securities to the general public within a 12-month period, the small public offering exemption provided by Regulation A is frequently used. It requires the filing of an offering statement in the closest SEC regional office at least 10 days before the planned offering. An **offering statement** is a document that includes financial statements and other information contained in a typical prospectus. Unlike the financial statements provided for a full registration, however, this information does not have to be professionally audited. Once the SEC is satisfied with the offering statement, the securities can be sold. However, a copy of the offering statement must be provided to purchasers and the issuer is exposed to liability based on the information contained in (or omitted from) that document.

Offering Statement: SEC document with investment information required under Regulation A

Intrastate Offerings

As we have discussed in relation to other federal agencies, under the Interstate Commerce Clause of the federal constitution, an action that affects only *intra*state commerce cannot be regulated by the federal government. However, given past US Supreme Court interpretations of that clause, it is possible that no stock issue can be considered truly intrastate. To clarify matters for those who would nonetheless try for such an exemption, the SEC passed a rule detailing what it would allow as an intrastate offering.

In particular, the rule provides that to be eligible to make an intrastate securities offering, the issuer must be incorporated in the state and have at least 80 percent of its gross revenues originate there. Once the issue has been sold, it will continue to be considered intrastate only if no resales are made to nonstate residents within nine months. It is this last requirement that causes so many corporations to shy away from this exemption. Even having buyers sign agreements that they will not resell any shares for nine months has proven ineffective

| Exemptions from Registration | Figure 39–1 |

The Protection of Regulation	Offerings exempted from Registration
■ Most stock offerings	■ Securities issued by government entities and not-for-profit organizations ■ Short-term commercial paper ■ Private placements ■ Small public offerings ■ Intrastate offerings

in the past. Consequently, the risk of ultimately losing the intrastate exemption, as well as the fines and other potential liabilities that might result, causes most issuers to choose another exemption if one is available.

Although the above list of exemptions is tempting to young companies that need capital and not the added expense of registration, it is important to remember that at some point most unregistered securities will be made available to the general public. At that time, whoever wishes to sell them will have to bear the expense of registration. Also, if a company is to tap the immense source of capital that the national stock markets offer, at some point it will have to "go public" and register its stock. Once the company's stock is publicly traded or is otherwise subjected to scrutiny, the Securities Exchange Act of 1934 comes into play.

What Protection Is Provided by the Securities Laws for the Stock Trader?

Unless exempted, all securities that are traded on a national exchange or over-the-counter must be registered with the SEC in accordance with the Securities Exchange Act. In addition, any company with over 500 shareholders and over $1 million in assets must provide detailed information about the company and its financial position to its shareholders and the SEC. This information must be updated frequently (usually quarterly). Because of experience with past manipulative schemes, the SEC has also implemented several rules to alert traders—and thereby, hopefully, to protect them—to significant changes in a reporting company's financial circumstances.

Rules Governing Insider Trading

Insiders: persons privy to confidential information pertaining to corporate activities

Many observers of the market situation that precipitated the 1929 crash identified lack of regulation of the actions of **insiders** (officers, directors, major stockholders, and others privy to confidential information pertaining to corporate activities)

as a major cause of the financial disaster. As a consequence, Congress placed two sections in the Securities Exchange Act to correct the situation. The first, section 16(a), requires a monthly disclosure of any change in the ownership position of an officer or a director of a corporation or any stockholder with more than 10 percent of any class of the corporation's stock. The second, section 16(b), makes these same parties automatically liable to the corporation for any so-called "short swing" profits, that is, profits they made by buying any corporate stock and then selling that stock within six months of its purchase.

Kendra Brian held an outside director's position on the board of Pennsboro Motors Corporation (PMC). Although she had not attended the last two quarterly board meetings due to illness, Kendra believed strongly in PMC and the employment opportunities it offered to members of the Pennsboro community. As a consequence, she purchased 1,000 shares of PMC stock at $14 per share in late August. Two months later, after PMC announced a merger with Giant Motors Corporation, the price of PMC stock shot up to $32 per share. Kendra immediately sold her 1,000 shares at a profit of $18,000. Under section 16(b), whether or not she knew about the merger beforehand, her profit is recoverable by the corporation or by a stockholder suit on its behalf brought in federal court.

Another federal statute that affects insider trading is the Insider Trading Sanctions Act of 1984. Under its provisions, a person profiting or avoiding loss by trading on the basis of material nonpublic information about a security can be made to pay as damages to the corporation involved three times the amount of that profit or the amount of the loss avoided. In addition, criminal liability in the form of a fine ranging up to $100,000 can be imposed. Individuals who provide inside information that others use for trading purposes, even if they do not trade themselves, may also be held liable.

Although she did not trade in the security herself, Heather LaSulle, a stockbroker with a large, nationally known firm, was held liable for the profits made by several of her customers who acted on inside information that she provided.

Various publications provide information on legitimate insider trading that they obtain from SEC reports to the general investment community. An old saw about the value of such activity as an investment indicator is that insiders may sell for a variety of reasons (they need money for the children's education, they need money for medical expenses, the corporation has fallen on hard times, etc.) but that they buy for one reason only, because of confidence in the potential of the stock price to go higher.

Rules Against Fraud and Manipulation

Section 10(b) of the 1934 Act makes it illegal for any person to use a manipulative or deceptive device in a manner prohibited by SEC rules. This mirrored a basic common law prohibition to the same effect but left the door wide open for the SEC to carry the matter further by outlawing any specific manipulative or fraudulent conduct it considered especially improper. The SEC ultimately responded by producing Rule 10(b)–5. The applicability of the rule is extremely broad, as is obvious from its text:

> It shall be unlawful for any person, directly or indirectly, by use of any means or instrumentality of interstate commerce, or of the mails, or of any facility of any national exchange:
>
> to employ any device, scheme or artifice to defraud,
> to make any untrue statement of a material fact or to omit to state a material fact necessary in order to make the statements made, in the light of the circumstances under which they were made, not misleading, or
> to engage in any act, practice or course of business which operates or would operate as a fraud or deceit upon any person in connection with the purchase or sale of any security.

Notice especially that application of the rule is not limited to securities registered with the SEC or to companies of a certain size. It simply requires the involvement of "any means or instrumentality of interstate commerce, ... the mails, or ... any national exchange ... with the purchase or sale of any security." In addition to enforcement actions brought by the SEC, the courts allow private parties to bring civil damage suits for 10(b)–5 violations. As a result, the rule has been used by and against a wide spectrum of parties. The most pertinent outcomes of all this use include the following:

Individuals who received tips from insiders have been held liable for their trading profits.

Consultants, lawyers, accountants, and other professionals who legitimately acquired insider information due to a confidential relationship with the corporation have been held liable for the use of that information and for improperly revealing it or failing to disclose it as appropriate under the circumstances.

Traditional insiders have been held liable for trading in securities of their corporation before fully disclosing significant information to the public.

Rule 10(b)–5 and other, more specialized rules provide a working shield against improper acts that might rob the investor of the confidence necessary to make our capital markets work.

Vocabulary Development

Fill in the blanks with the appropriate term.

Accredited Investor
Blue-Sky Laws
Insiders
Offering Statement

Prospectus
Registration Statement
Restricted Security
Security

1. An exempted security that must be registered or exempted again before it can be resold is termed a(n) _____.

2. A document that must be given to every buyer of a Regulation A offering is the _____.

3. A(n) _____ is an investment whose profit is a function of the management of others.

4. A state's regulation of securities is handled through the application of the state's _____.

5. Prior to purchase, each potential investor is provided with pertinent financial information and an invitation to buy in the form of a(n) _____.

Problems

1. In the last few years, US Senators and financiers have predicted an abrupt collapse of our economy through either depression or hyperinflation. What would you do to secure food, clothing, and shelter if, in the next week, you lost your job, your currency became worthless, and the financial institutions closed, thereby denying you access to your savings, your stored valuables, and so on?

2. George Armstrong purchased a franchise in a new fast-food restaurant chain famous for its grilled buffalo burgers. The franchise cost over $2.5 million. Later Armstrong found that financial data and information on supply problems had been withheld from him. When his restaurant lost money for four consecutive years, he brought suit against the franchiser. Armstrong based his suit on the claim that a franchise was a security. Was Armstrong correct in his assessment?

3. You are the president of Pennsboro Polished Pots (PPP). As you need capital to expand, you plan to sell an issue of $25 million in equity securities in a private placement. Which of the following potential investors would be considered an accredited investor?
   a. The Palatial, an insurance company.
   b. George Patton, a vice president of PPP with annual income of just under $145,000.
   c. The Pennsboro Hospital, which has assets of more than $15 million.
   d. Doug MacArthur, an insurance salesman with annual income of just under $225,000.
   e. The Pennsboro Bank with assets of over $135 million.
   f. Debra Eisenreich, a retired army officer with assets of $1,250,000 and liabilities of $300,000.

4. You are considering making an investment, but you need more information about the various securities that your broker has recommended to you. A friend has suggested that you check the local library for data furnished the SEC by the issuer of each. On which of the following would such information be available?
   a. A city of Pennsboro bond issue of $1 million.
   b. A $1 million note due in a year and issued by the Pennsboro Hospital.
   c. A $1 million stock issue available for sale only within the state of Missouri from the Hindleg Corporation, which is headquartered in its state of incorporation, Delaware.

5. By what ethical theory can you justify holding insiders liable for short-swing profits, even if they acted only on information available to the general public?

ACTUAL CASE STUDY

Securities and Exchange Commission v. W. J. Howey Co.

66 S. Ct. 1100

Now, see how flexible the definition of security *is.*

When the Howey Company of Florida needed money, it simply sold off parts of the citrus grove it owned. As a part of the sale, however, every purchaser was also required to enter into a service contract with Howey-in-the-Hills, Inc., which was owned by the owners of the Howey Company. The land purchase contract did not allow the purchasers to work the land or sell crops grown thereon. Everything of that nature was reserved to Howey-in-the-Hills by the service contract. The purchasers did receive a share of the profits from those crops.

Because of complaints, the SEC brought suit, claiming that the sales of land and service were actually securities and, as such, should have been registered.

Questions

1. What is the definition of a *security* under the securities acts?

2. Can you distinguish the Howey-in-the-Hills situation from that of a typical franchise arrangement?

3. Should the contracts of sale and service have been registered as securities?

40

How Does International Law Affect Business?

CHAPTER OUTLINE AND OBJECTIVES

After studying this chapter, the student will be able to:

I. Discuss why agreements to govern international business are necessary.
   a. International Convention for the Protection of Industrial Property
   b. General Agreement on Tariffs and Trade
   c. North American Free Trade Agreement

II. Explain how firms become involved in the international marketplace and what constraints are placed on them by our laws.
   a. Traditional means of doing international business
   b. Legal constraints

III. Evaluate how the disputes that arise in international transactions are handled.

IV. Discuss the suit victims of the Bhopal disaster brought against Union Carbide and the potential civil and criminal liability of Union Carbide executives for the Bhopal disaster.

Why Are Agreements Controlling International Trade Necessary?

Today we are all a part of a huge international marketplace in products, services, and labor. Given the current level of our country's negative trade balances and the rate at which manufacturing jobs are disappearing from our country, whether this is or will be advantageous to the welfare of our country's citizens is debatable. However, the reality of the international marketplace cannot be denied. For those who urge our increased participation in that marketplace, a stable system of rules that both reduces the risk and increases the volume of international trade is mandatory. Even from the perspective of those who resist our participation, such a system is necessary to prevent us from being drawn into a conflict that might arise from a ruleless and chaotic international environment.

So, whether to enhance trade or inhibit conflict, most parties agree on the necessity of having in place a stable system of rules that govern international commerce. In fact, some believe that as a result of growing supranational economic ties and resulting identities of concerns among businesses in various countries, nation-states will wither away (an outcome predicted in diverse sources, including Marxist-Leninist philosophy). Regardless of the long-term result, immediate necessity has caused our country and other advanced nations to enter into a variety of agreements to regulate international commerce. Figure 40–1 contains summary descriptions of the most significant agreements of this kind. Two such agreements worthy of special note are discussed below.

International Convention for the Protection of Industrial Property

Convention: international agreement or compact

One of the most important concerns of those who cast their products onto the international marketplace is the potential for loss of patents, copyrights, trademarks, and brand names. This potential exists because in many foreign countries the first one to register such property becomes its owner. As a consequence, the United States has become a signatory of the International Convention for the Protection of Industrial Property (ICPIP). Under the terms of that **convention** (an international agreement or compact), registration in the originator's country is effective as registration in all of the signatory countries. This eliminates the sometimes insurmountable and often impractical need to register the patent, copyright, mark, or brand name in each of the signatory countries.

General Agreement on Tariffs and Trade

Tariffs: fees levied by governments on imported goods

The General Agreement on Tariffs and Trade (GATT), which is perhaps the most important international collaboration affecting commerce, was begun in 1947. The main thrust of this series of economic treaties was and is to eliminate the protections that many nations afford their domestic industries through **tariffs** (fees levied by governments on imported goods) and other barriers to commercial

**Significant Organizations and Agreements
Affecting International Commerce**

Figure 40–1

Organization or Agreement	Function
International Court of Justice	Established by League of Nations to resolve international disputes of all types in accordance with international law; jurisdiction extends only over cases voluntarily submitted to it
International Maritime Organization	Works to promote safety and efficiency in maritime operations and to eradicate unnecessary restrictions on waterborne trade
International Monetary Fund	Provides conditional loans to help member nations overcome their financial problems and stabilize their overall currency exchange rates
North American Free Trade Agreement	Provides for the reduction or elimination of tariffs on various goods traded between the United States, Mexico, and Canada
Permanent Arbitration Court	Provides forum for nonjudicial resolution of international disputes that parties voluntarily submit to it
World Bank (International Bank for Reconstruction and Development)	Promotes investment in member nations, especially in technology, industry, and agriculture.
World Intellectual Property Organization	Promotes establishment of legal provisions for worldwide protection of intellectual property.

exchange between countries. These barriers range from the US ban on tuna from countries whose tuna fishing methods slaughter dolphins to the quotas on grain imports that protect the politically potent French farmers, "Trade wars" between countries, which are fought by escalating and broadening trade restrictions on the opposing country's goods, are violations of the GATT. So too are instances of favoritism shown toward a particular trading partner at the expense of others. If a country reduces trade barriers on particular goods for one country, it must do so for all of the countries covered by the GATT.

Rounds of talks to foster progress in the overall reduction of trade barriers under the GATT have been conducted periodically since 1947. However, thanks to dramatic changes recently proposed through the initiative of the GATT director general, the specifics of the GATT are currently the focal points of the most intense scrutiny and debate that they have ever received. These changes would have a considerable effect on competition in textiles, farming, banking, computer software, and other industries.

North American Free Trade Agreement

Announced jointly by its three participants—Canada, Mexico, and the United States—in August 1992, the North American Free Trade Agreement (NAFTA) was ratified over a year later. Over 365 million people and nearly $7 trillion in markets were joined by the main agreement and by several side pacts on matters pertaining to labor law and the environment. NAFTA's main provisions include:

The elimination of tariffs on farm goods over the next decade and a half.

The phasing out over the next decade of tariffs on automobiles that have over 60 percent of their value produced in the free trade zone.

The ending of limits on bank ownership within the next decade.

An easing of restrictions on the flow of business professionals among the three participating countries. However, general barriers to immigration from Mexico into the United States would remain in place.

How Do Firms Become Involved in the International Marketplace, and What Constraints Are Placed on Them by Our Laws?

Traditional Means of Doing International Business

Importing: bringing foreign goods into home marketplace

Once a domestic firm determines that it wants to participate in international commerce, it must choose the appropriate means. Among the choices for firms that want to become involved with **importing** (bringing foreign goods into the domestic marketplace for sale) are the following:

1. They may buy the goods from their overseas producers and sell the goods here.

HYPOTHETICAL CASE

Shoez, Inc., a national discounter of athletic shoes, purchased 3,000 pairs of the new French soccer shoe to resell to its customers in this country and Canada.

2. They may agree to act as an agent for a foreign firm and sell that firm's goods here for a fee.

HYPOTHETICAL CASE

R. A. R., Inc., a small midwestern electronics firm, agreed to act as agent for a Malaysian firm that made electronic growth stimulators for plants. R. A. R.'s payment was 30 percent of the sales price.

3. They may merge with a foreign firm, through either a stock or asset acquisition, to become a part of a unified, multinational concern.

Desolation, Inc., a California firm famous for its adventure-laden backpack trips into the Mount Saint Helens area, merged with a Japanese company specializing in worldwide tours to disaster areas. The Japanese company had previously merged with firms similar to Desolation throughout the world to form a unique multinational firm.

Joint Venture: firms participating in specifically limited transaction for profit

4. They may agree to participate in a **joint venture** (two or more firms participating in a specifically limited transaction for profit) with a foreign firm.

A Russian car company in Novosibirsk agreed to join with an American go-cart manufacturer to produce a motor car for sale in the American market. The car, known as the NovGo, was billed as a luxury, road-legal dune buggy and sold remarkably well.

5. They may acquire a franchise from a foreign firm (a method that is gaining in popularity).

Mall Pluggers, Inc., a New Jersey corporation known for developing successful small chain stores for regional malls, bought a franchise offered by Koala Country, an Australian company famous for its marketing of unusual Australian artifacts and crafts.

Export: sale of domestic products in foreign markets

When the situation is reversed, with domestic firms wishing to **export** (sell domestic products in foreign markets), the choices are fundamentally the same:

1. They may simply sell their goods to firms in foreign markets, which will then resell them.
2. They may sell their products through agents in foreign markets.
3. They may merge with a foreign firm that will sell their products in its market.
4. They may participate in a joint venture.
5. If appropriate, they may franchise their mark and managerial plans to foreign owner/operators.
6. If national laws permit, they may establish a wholly owned subsidiary in a foreign country. Figure 40–2 depicts the various means of exporting and importing.

Legal Constraints

Doing business in the international arena often involves dealing with levels of risk and uncertainty previously unencountered by a domestic US firm. Thus, the

Figure 40–2   **Domestic Firms' Methods of Importing and Exporting Goods**

Exporting

Exporting Methods
- Sell their goods to firms in foreign markets who will then resell them.
- Sell their products through agents in the foreign markets.
- Merge with a firm in the foreign market.
- Participate in a joint venture.
- Franchise their mark and managerial plans to foreign owner/operators.
- Establish, if national laws permit, a wholly owned subsidiary in the foreign country.

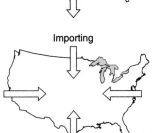

Importing

Importing Methods
- Purchase foreign goods and market them in the United States.
- Act as agent to sell foreign goods in United States market.
- Merge with foreign supplier and sell its goods in United States market.
- Enter into joint venture with foreign firm to sell goods in United States market.
- Become franchisee of foreign franchisor and sell its products in United States market.

management of such a firm must make doubly certain that it is on a firm foundation of legality with regard to the laws of its home country. Unfortunately, some of our country's laws are confusing and even place our businesspeople at an unfair disadvantage when they are dealing in the international sphere.

The Antitrust Laws. Both section 1 and section 2 of the Sherman Antitrust Act apply to trade or commerce with foreign nations. So contracts, combinations, or conspiracies restraining such trade or persons monopolizing, attempting to do so, or conspiring to do so are subject to prosecution and civil suit. Even if the activity occurs in a foreign country, as long as it substantially affects the foreign or interstate commerce of the United States, it is prosecutable here as an antitrust violation. Price-fixing and tie-in sales remain per se violations even when conducted overseas. Foreign territorial allocations between competitors are also illegal under our antitrust laws. Even citizens of foreign countries and their governmental entities have the right to sue our citizens in our courts for damages resulting from violations of our antitrust laws. At the furthest extreme, foreign persons with significant ties to the US economy have brought suits against other foreign persons with such ties under our antitrust law provisions and in our courts.

As a consequence, a wise businessperson gives as much consideration to the antitrust laws in making international business decisions as in making domestic business decisions. Certain protections are available, however. **Export trading companies,** a status authorized under federal law for firms that conduct exclusively international trade and derive most of their revenue from the export of US-produced goods and services, can request special protection from antitrust actions. Such protection, if granted, comes in the form of a **certificate of review** issued by the secretary of commerce with the assent of the US attorney general. According to section 306 of the Export Trading Company Act, this document confers a general exemption from "criminal or civil action . . . brought under the

Export Trading Companies: firms specializing in export of US products

Certificate of Review: document conferring exempted status from antitrust laws.

antitrust laws against a person to whom a certificate of review is issued" for any conduct that is specified in the certificate or complies with it. The act also notes some exceptions to the certificate's protection.

Foreign Corrupt Practices Act. In 1977 Congress passed the Foreign Corrupt Practices Act (FCPA). This act was intended to enforce our domestic concept of ethical business conduct against US businesspeople overseas. Instance after instance of bribery, illegal by our standards but legal in the country in which it occurred, was brought to the attention of Congress. In response, Congress passed the FCPA, which made the perpetrators of such activities both criminally and civilly liable. Even as amended in 1988 to diminish its effect, the act remains a major handicap to US businesspeople trying to secure contracts in arenas in which other competitors are not so encumbered.

Antidiscrimination. Is it illegal under US laws to discriminate in your employment overseas by hiring merely US citizens, or Christians instead of Moslems, or minority whites instead of majority blacks? Our antidiscrimination laws, specifically Title VII of the Civil Rights Act of 1964, might be read as prohibiting such practices "in trade ... among the several states or between a state and anyplace outside it." However, the federal courts have recently held that such antidiscrimination laws apply solely within the United States, even if the parties discriminated against on foreign soil are US citizens. In so interpreting our antidiscrimination laws, the courts concluded that any contrary interpretation might force our corporations to give up trying to compete in a foreign market due to the legal necessity of hiring foreign nationals almost exclusively.

Export and Import Controls. Although the US Constitution proscribes export taxes, quotas can be imposed on all conceivable types of exports, from timber products to airplanes. The Export Administration Act of 1979 specifically restricts the export of our technology, and other acts inhibit the transfer of military know-how, especially in the field of nuclear and biological weapons. Finally, trade with certain nations (Cuba, Vietnam, and others) is completely prohibited. The US Department of Commerce and reputable export trading companies are the primary sources of information in these areas.

As far as imports are concerned, beyond the normal risks of doing business in the international financial environment (see the discussion of letters of credit in Chapter 18), the cost of such goods is increased by tariffs, as mentioned, and such goods are also subject to quotas and other restrictions. Importers must be especially careful not to participate in any dumping schemes. **Dumping** is the sale on the US market of imported goods at a price below their fair value (that value is usually the price of the goods in the producing country). As a penalty, an extra tariff may be imposed retroactively on goods dumped on the US market. This tariff may be assessed against the US company involved in the dumping scheme, leaving that company to seek reimbursement from the foreign company supplying the dumped goods.

Dumping: sale of imported goods at price below fair value.

How Are Disputes Handled That Arise in International Transactions?

Arbitration: process involving use of neutral, nonjudicial third party to decide dispute

Dispute resolution in international business dealings is traditionally handled in one of two ways: arbitration or resort to courts. **Arbitration** uses a neutral third party (the arbitrator) who hears both sides of the dispute and then renders a decision. This method is being used increasingly because of its swiftness of action and relatively low expense and because it enables the parties to choose someone with expertise in the field of conflict to resolve their dispute. With foresight, a well-drafted commercial arbitration clause can be placed in international sales contracts. Various professional groups of commercial arbitrators are available to render decisions and can be preselected in such clauses. Finally, note that the valid decisions of commercial arbitrators are enforceable against the losing parties in the courts of most countries.

Where the parties to an international trade agreement fail to agree to a valid commercial arbitration clause, a court is the only legitimate remaining resort. In such a situation, the major questions to be answered are which court (forum) will try the case and what laws will be used. At times, choice of forum and choice of law clauses are included in trade agreements. When this is done, the courts of most nations will uphold the choice. (Note that the latest United Nations Convention on Contracts for the International Sale of Goods, which is somewhat similar to the Uniform Commercial Code and was ratified by the United States in 1986, is viewed by many as a suitable choice.) However, when no choice is indicated, it becomes a question of finding a court with proper jurisdiction over both parties. This often turns out to be a US court, especially if the offending party is a US corporation. In such a situation, the defense raised most often is forum non conveniens, which means that the court claiming jurisdiction is so inconvenient to one of the parties as to prevent a fair trial of the case and that the case could be better tried in another forum.

When residents of Costa Rica brought suit in a Texas court against Dow Chemical, Shell Oil, and other corporations for sterility and other serious medical problems allegedly caused by spraying the fields on which they worked with a pesticide banned in the United States, the defendants asserted a defense of forum non conveniens. The Texas high court, however, disallowed the defense and allowed the case to proceed, commenting that to do otherwise might mean a denial of the plaintiffs' rights.

Unless a contract clause directs otherwise, after a court with appropriate jurisdiction has been found, that forum's choice of law rules will be used to pick the appropriate laws to be used to resolve the issues of the case. Once a court with suitable jurisdiction has rendered a decision, the question of how to enforce that decision has to be faced. By the international law principle of **comity,** other nations should defer to that court's decision, if the laws of the nation in which the case was decided are consistent with the laws of the court called on to enforce the decision.

Comity: principle requiring deference to decision of another nation's courts

An Argentine company contracted to buy compact discs from a California manufacturer. When the agreement broke down, the buyer sued the seller in an Argentine court and was awarded $1.5 million in damages. Because the seller's property was located in California, the Argentine company filed the damage award with that state's courts and sought enforcement. If the California court determines that the award was reached using principles of law consistent with our own, the principle of comity requires the court to enforce the decision.

Regardless of the actual choice made between arbitration and court resolution of problems arising out of an international trade agreement, such a choice should be made and clearly included in the contract. No matter how strong the goodwill of the parties to such an agreement, the sheer number of potential problems ensures that issues requiring resolution by such a means will probably arise. The wise businessperson will plan for this eventuality.

Vocabulary Development

Fill in the blanks with the appropriate term.

Arbitration
Certificate of Review
Comity
Convention
Dumping

Export
Export Trading Companies
Importing
Joint Venture
Tariff

1. A document granting joint ventures special protection from antitrust actions is termed a(n) _____..

2. A(n) _____ is a fee paid for importing various items into a country.

3. A(n) _____ is another name for an international treaty or understanding.

4. Selling imports on our domestic market at a price set below their fair value is referred to as _____.

5. _____ is a process by which a dispute is resolved by placing it before an objective nonjudicial third party.

Problems

1. Should the United States continue to participate in the GATT process or in free trade agreements that result in the loss of many jobs? Why or why not?

2. Should the Foreign Corrupt Practices Act be repealed? Why or why not?

3. The East Wind Bicycle Company, a US firm, and the Yokosuka Cycle Corporation conspire to fix prices and allocate territories in Taiwan. Can a Taiwanese company sue East Wind for a violation of our antitrust laws in our courts? Can the same Taiwanese company use our courts to sue Yokosuka Cycle for such violations in our courts?

ACTUAL CASE STUDY

Insight into the shortcomings of existing modes of dispute resolution in the international arena can be gained by considering the case of the victims of the Bhopal tragedy and the near failure of efforts to afford those victims relief. As mentioned in Chapter 37, in 1984 cyanide gas leaking from a Union Carbide plant killed over 3,500 people and injured 200,000 or more in Bhopal, India. On behalf of the victims, the Indian government eventually brought suit in the United States against the parent company. In 1989 the action was settled for $470 million. This result was endorsed by the Supreme Court of India. However, a new administration took power in India shortly thereafter and moved to reopen the civil case as well as to extradite several Union Carbide executives and try them on criminal charges.

Questions

1. What arguments can be made for allowing the new Indian government to act in this fashion?

2. Should the United States allow the extradition of the Union Carbide executives to face trial in India? (Consider other countries that might request extradition of American executives should we follow such a policy.)

3. Should our own environmental, worker safety, and other standards apply to the employees of our companies overseas?

4. What could be done to ensure fairness and conclusiveness in international legal cases?

CHAPTER

41

How Can Divorce or Death Affect a Business?

CHAPTER OUTLINE AND OBJECTIVES

After studying this chapter, the student will be able to:

I. Explain what potential problems the owner's death or divorce pose for a business.

II. Describe what a divorce is and what its legal consequences are.

    a. Marriage

    b. Divorce

III. Explain the legal effects of an individual's death.

    a. Distributions guided by a will

    b. Distributions without a will

    c. Estate distribution procedure

    d. Trusts

IV. Discuss the potential effects of redistributions of assets due to death or divorce on your own situation by answering the questions at the end of the chapter.

What Potential Problems for a Business Are Posed by the Owner's Death or Divorce?

Back when we were comparing the various forms of organization for an ongoing business, we noted that many higher-caliber professional managers shy away from working for sole proprietorships or partnerships because of the dependence of such businesses on the talents and longevity of one or a few individuals. Should these individuals move on or for personal reasons be unable to focus on the business, everyone involved with the business is adversely affected. More importantly, the business may come to a crashing end. Even the corporate form can suffer from such extramarket problems. However, the loss of one individual's contributions to a typical corporation is much less likely to have a debilitating overall effect. In general, the more sophisticated the business form, the more it relies on an institutionalized way of doing business rather than on personal performance. Therefore, the effects of one individual's divorce or death are unlikely to be of major consequence. Nonetheless, regardless of the form of business involved, it is important for a businessperson to know what to expect from these potential upheavals in the lives of key personnel. This chapter is therefore devoted to providing some knowledge about the consequences of divorce and death and the devices used to circumvent their effects. We'll begin with divorce.

What Exactly Is a Divorce, and What Are Its Legal Consequences?

Marriage

Marriage: legal status of man and woman united as husband and wife by law for life or until divorced

A good way to begin answering these questions is to first realize that a **marriage** is typically defined as the legal status of a man and a woman united by law for life or until divorced. Many couples are actually wed under two authorities, the law and their religion. The parties' moral commitment to the union often stems from their religion; the parties' legal commitment, formed for the convenience of society in determining responsibility for such outcomes of the relationship as children and debts, originates in the law.

On the early frontier of our nation, however, the legal authority to bind a marriage was often practically unavailable. As a consequence, the concept of common-law marriage was utilized to affix responsibility for children, debts, and the like. A union was legally recognized as a **common-law marriage** whenever two single people of opposite sex lived together, held themselves out as husband and wife, and shared property in common over an extended period (typically 5–10 years).

Common-Law Marriage: status of husband and wife afforded without license

Whatever its origin, a marriage recognized by the law is considered a result of a legally binding contract. The contract is made when one person proposes a marital union to a member of the opposite sex and the other person accepts. (If both parties later mutually agree to call off their plans to marry, the marriage contract is termed **annulled** and is considered legally void. Marriages can also be annulled if they were concluded on fraudulent grounds relating to pregnancy status, history of previous marriage, disease, childbearing ability or desire, and age.)

Annulled: voided

Divorce

The key point as far as our analysis is concerned is that the legal system makes its own determination, independent of religious authority, of whether or not a marriage existed. Therefore, although different religions may have various procedures for effectively ending a sanctified union, the **divorce** we are worried about is defined as the total dissolution of a legally recognized marriage relationship upon the order of a court of law.

Divorce: dissolution of legally recognized marriage relationship upon order of court of law

In recent years, the availability of no-fault divorce has made this legal determination that a marriage has ended much easier to obtain. Under **no-fault divorce** rules, the spouse that originates the petition for divorce no longer has to accuse the other spouse of some form of misconduct (fault) such as adultery, alcoholism, drug addiction, felony conviction, impotence, or cruelty. Instead, it is enough to show the court that one or both of the marital partners want to end the relationship. The matters that then concern the court are the amount of **alimony** (maintenance payments by a wage-earning spouse to support a non-wage-earning spouse during separation or after divorce), child custody, the amount of child support, and, most important for business, how the property is to be divided. These determinations form the basis for the court decree ending the marriage unless they are resolved by a **prenuptial agreement** (a contract formed in consideration of marriage that specifies the financial rights of both parties in such situations as divorce), other agreements, or the common sense of the parties. Unfortunately, in the vast majority of cases all of these are in short supply.

No-Fault Divorce: marital dissolution afforded without showing of misconduct

Alimony: maintenance payments by wage-earning spouse to support non-wage-earning spouse during separation or after divorce

Prenuptial Agreement: contract formed in consideration of marriage specifying rights of husband and wife during and/or upon conclusion of marital relationship

Sometimes, however, a couple who **separated** (lived in separate quarters) before divorce have negotiated a separation agreement covering some of the matters that concern the court. If such a couple cannot agree to a final division of rights and responsibilities, the court may use this agreement as the foundation upon which its divorce decree is built. Other inputs used by the court are the wishes of the parties, precedent, tradition, and equity.

Separated: condition of marital partners living in separate quarters

Regardless of how the court makes its determinations, its main focus in a divorce proceeding is on an immediate and permanent settlement of the matter at hand. This means that the court decree may endanger the longevity of a business owned by one or both of the parties. Financial demands or the property settlement imposed by the decree on one or both of the parties may force the sale of the business or a significant portion of its assets. If both parties were involved in the business, the divorce usually spells the end of the contributions of one or the other to its success. The smaller the business and the less complex its organizational form, the greater the overall effect of such changes. In one way or another, divorce is often not only a serious hurdle for the parties immediately involved, but also for those who watch from the near sidelines of friendship and identical financial interest.

What Are the Legal Effects of an Individual's Death?

Death is another extrabusiness event that can greatly affect a firm's success. If a sole proprietor dies, the business typically dies with him or her. If a partner answers the last roll call, the partnership is dissolved and perhaps put under financial stress to pay off the deceased's interest. Even a corporation may be affected by the consequences of a death, for example, the shifting of an ownership block, reorganization, or a period of flux before resulting changes are implemented. Regardless of the size and complexity of the firm involved, knowledge of the legal procedure followed upon a person's death can help reduce the uncertainty that follows a death and can provide some insight into measures that could soften the blow of the loss.

As with divorce, when a person dies, the legal system is called on to resolve the fundamental legal issues that result. Applicable law and the wishes of the decedent, if the latter are legitimately available, are the basic materials from which this resolution is formulated.

The legal procedure involved begins with a determination of whether the decedent died with a valid will.

Distributions Guided by a Will

Will: person's directions for property distribution upon death

Testate: status of person who dies leaving valid will

Intestate: status of person who dies without leaving valid will

Testator: male maker of will

Testatrix: female maker of will

A **will** is a person's expression of how his or her property is to be distributed upon death. (If a person dies without a will, statutes control the distribution of that person's estate.) A person who dies leaving a valid will dies **testate;** a person who dies without leaving a valid will dies **intestate.** As a will can be altered almost anytime during the lifetime of its maker (who it labeled the **testator** if male, the **testatrix** if female), the law has imposed strict requirements to prevent forgeries of wills and to resolve conflicts that develop between different versions of wills. A sample will appears in Figure 41–1.

To be valid a will must:

Reflect the true intent of the deceased unaffected by duress, fraud, or undue influence.

Be in writing (although a few states allow oral wills—see below).

Be signed by the maker in front of at least two witnesses (more witnesses are required in certain states). These witnesses must be disinterested adults who have been told that they are observing such a signing.

Be the informed result of the action of a maker with legal capacity.

Not be revoked by a later will's explicit statement to that effect or by the action of statutes that terminate its effectiveness due to marriage, birth of offspring, or divorce.

Nuncupative Will: oral will

As mentioned, some states recognize orally made wills, which are legally termed **nuncupative wills.** However, strict limits are set on the amount of property that such wills can affect. These limits generally allow a nuncupative will to affect the distribution of only personal property up to $1,000 in value. The one state that allows all property to be disposed of by such a will requires that the

The Last Will and Testament of Gerinald Lucius Snootweld III   **Figure 41–1**

I, GERINALD LUCIUS SNOOTWELD THE THIRD, of the City of Pennsboro, County of Lawrence, State of Missouri, being of sound mind and memory hereby revoke all previous wills and codicils and make, declare, and publish this document as my last Will and Testament.

FIRST: I order that, after my death, my debts and the expenses of my funeral be paid without undue delay out of my estate.

SECOND: I hereby nominate and appoint my spouse, Frances Baines Tyler-Snootweld, as my executrix of this will. If she is not able or willing to act in such a fashion, I nominate and appoint my son, Gerinald Lucius Snootweld the Fourth, as executor. I direct that neither of these individuals be required to provide security in the form of a bond or otherwise to guarantee their proper performance of their duties as executrix or executor.

THIRD: I hereby give my entire estate to my spouse except for the following:

My Academy uniforms and saber; to be given to Gerinald L. Snootweld the Fourth.

My furnishings in my Manhattan apartment; to be given to my faithful secretary, Desiree Williams.

My 1993 stretch Lincoln limousine; to be given to my driver, Samuel Morris.

In the event that any of the individuals named in this third proviso predecease me, I hereby give that individual's property to my spouse.

IN WITNESS WHEREOF, I, Gerinald Lucius Snootweld the Third, sign my name to this document, my last will and testament, on January 3rd, 1995.

Signature

We, the undersigned, do hereby testify that the foregoing instrument was duly signed and declared by the testator, Gerinald Lucius Snootweld III, to be his will on January 3rd, 1995. In addition, we attest that the testator to the best of our knowledge is of legal age and sound mind and memory and is under no constraint or undue influence. On this day, January 3rd, 1995, we so indicate by our signatures below.

---
of 1717 West 13th, Pennsboro, MO 65708

---
of Barleycorn Drive, Pennsboro, MO 65708

---
of Union Pacific Highway, Pennsboro, MO 65708

---

will be made during the decedent's last illness. **Holographic wills** (those written in the decedent's own hand, which are typically signed but unwitnessed) are accepted by approximately half of the states.

Holographic Will: will written in decedent's own hand

Because a will goes into effect only upon the death of its maker, it is alterable until that time. Alterations to a will are best placed in the form of formal written documents called **codicils**. Witnesses to a codicil are required. In the states that allow holographic wills, alterations to such wills may be handwritten (signature required) by the maker.

Codicil: formal written alteration to will

Per Capita: property equally split among living lineal descendants

Per Stirpes: property that deceased parent would have received split equally among lineal descendants

Community Property: rights of spouses to assets acquired during marriage

Where the testator or testatrix decides to leave property to his or her lineal descendants, the division is typically made either per capita or per stirpes. **Per capita** means that the living lineal descendants split the property equally. **Per stirpes** means that the lineal descendants split equally what a deceased parent would have received. Per stirpes and per capita divisions are illustrated in Figure 41–2.

Even if a valid will is left behind, the wishes of the decedent may not be carried out in full. This is due to the impact of statutes allowing a surviving spouse to elect to take the share that would have been afforded him or her if the decedent had died intestate. This share (generally one-third to one-half) can be taken instead of the share allocated to the surviving spouse under the terms of the decedent's will. In certain states (Arizona, California, Idaho, Louisiana, Nevada, New Mexico, Texas, Washington, and Wisconsin), the surviving spouse can elect to take a fraction (usually one-half or one-third) of the deceased's share of the **community property** (assets acquired during a marriage) instead of the share allocated to her or him in the will.

Distributions without a Will

If a person dies without a valid will, the property remaining after valid claims against the estate have been paid is distributed in accordance with the laws of intestate succession. These laws vary significantly from state to state. However, a general idea of their approach can be obtained from those of the state of Hawaii. Under the laws of the Aloha State, if a person dies intestate and:

With no spouse but children surviving, the children inherit equal shares in the real and personal property.

With a spouse and one or more children or children's children surviving, the spouse gets one-half of the real and personal property and the children share equally in the remainder. If a child is deceased but has surviving children, those children share equally in the deceased child's share.

With a spouse and no children or children's children surviving, the spouse gets one-half of the real and personal property and the deceased's parents receive the remainder. If the deceased's parents are not alive, the deceased's brothers and sisters receive equal shares in the remainder.

With no spouse, no children, and no children's children surviving, the deceased's parents each receive one-half of the real and personal property or, if only one parent survives, he or she receives it all. If both of the deceased's parents are dead, the brothers and sisters of the deceased share equally. (The children of deceased brothers or sisters share in their place.)

Escheats: reverts

With no inheritors, the property of the deceased **escheats** (reverts) to the state.

Estate Distribution Procedure

Whether a person dies testate or intestate, there is an orderly procedure that must be followed to properly distribute the deceased's assets. This procedure is begun by offering proof of death to the appropriate court (most often referred to as a probate court) in the deceased's state. This proof may be in the form of a death

Per Stirpes and Per Capita Divisions of an Estate

Figure 41–2

Division of a $1,800,000 Estate per stirpes

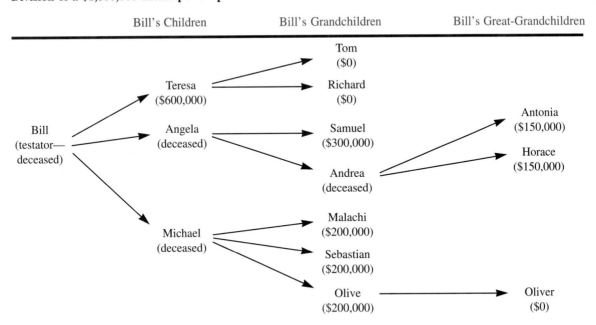

Division of a $1,800,000 estate per capita—the 10 lineal living descendants all share equally

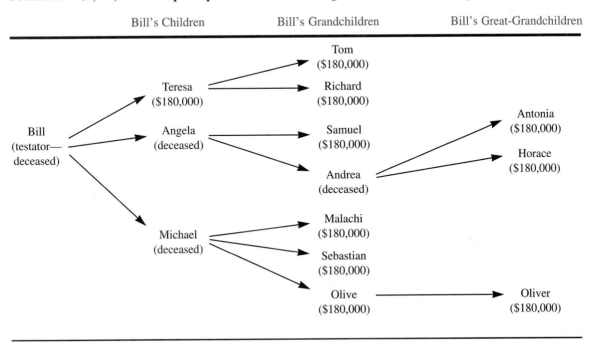

certificate, official notification of death from an armed service, or even testimony of the deceased's presence in a disaster that resulted in unidentifiable or irretrievable bodies. In this last case, the court can take judicial notice of the situation and issue a declaration of death.

If a person simply vanishes without a trace, after several years he or she can be declared dead under the Enoch Arden laws (named for a poem by Tennyson about a seaman who returns home after a long absence to find his "widow" married to another). Almost without exception, the time required under such laws is either five or seven years.

Once proof of death has been established, the court selects or endorses an individual to handle the estate. This appointee is labeled an **executor** (male) or **executrix** (female) if there is a will. If the deceased died intestate, the appointee is labeled an **administrator** or **administratrix.** This person must perform many important duties, and she or he can be held liable if they are improperly executed. The duties include:

Assembling, preserving, inventorying, and appraising the assets of the estate.
Giving public notice of the estate and of the necessity for filing claims against it within the statutory period (typically six months).
Paying valid claims against and debts of the estate (including income and estate taxes).
Distributing the remainder of the estate according to the will, directions of the court, or applicable statute.

This procedure can take several months beyond the six-month filing period, especially if the validity of the will is challenged (referred to as contesting the will) or if the meaning of some of the will is unclear. A lawyer's professional help is almost always required in such matters.

Trusts

The unsettling effect of death on a business can often be softened by the wise use of trusts. We first encountered this legal device back in Chapter 38's discussion of antitrust law. Therein we defined a *trust* as a separate legal entity to which the ownership of property (real or personal) can be transferred. A trust is managed by a designated individual (the trustee) in accordance with the wishes of the transferor. The trustee has the legal title to the trust property and must utilize it properly in order to accomplish the trust's objectives.

The creator of a trust is known as the **settlor.** The party (or parties) for whose benefit the trust is managed in accordance with the settlor's wishes is labeled the **beneficiary** (beneficiaries). The trustee has a fiduciary duty to the beneficiary and cannot cause the beneficiary to acquire liability to third parties through the trust management. In addition, the trust does not usually terminate at the death of the trustee. Another person is simply appointed to fulfill the trustee's role, and the operation of the trust continues.

A trust may be created during the lifetime of the settlor, in which case it is known as an **inter vivos trust.** A trust created after the death of the settlor in

Executor: testate deceased's personal male representative to oversee settlement of estate

Executrix: testate deceased's personal female representative to oversee settlement of estate

Administrator: male appointee of court to oversee settlement of intestate deceased's estate

Administratrix: female appointee of court to oversee settlement of intestate deceased's estate

Settlor: creator of trust

Beneficiary: party (or parties) for whose benefit trust is managed

Inter Vivos Trust: trust created during lifetime of settlor

accordance with her or his will is labeled a **testamentary trust.** Trusts are also named for their purpose. For example, a trust created for the fulfillment of an altruistic purpose is known as a **charitable trust.** Such a trust is created in almost the same way as a trust serving a private purpose (which is known as a private trust). Another kind of trust, known as a **spendthrift trust,** protects the beneficiary's interest in the trust property from claims by the beneficiary's creditors. For a spendthrift trust to be valid, the beneficiary must relinquish all control over the trust property. In addition, the creditors can satisfy their claims out of any trust income the beneficiary is paid.

These types of trusts are usually created by a written or oral statement in which the terms are expressly stated by the settlor. As a consequence, they are known as express trusts. The law, however, also makes provision for two types of implied trusts. The first of these types is known as a **resulting trust.** When the person intended to receive the benefit of an express trust cannot do so, the trust property is presumed by law to be held in trust for its original owner.

Testamentary Trust: trust created after death of settlor in accordance with her or his will

Charitable Trust: trust created for altruistic or humanitarian purpose

Spendthrift Trust: trust to protect beneficiary's interest in trust property from beneficiary's creditors

Resulting Trust: trust in favor of original owners of trust property where trust benefit cannot be conferred

 HYPOTHETICAL CASE

Ashton formed a charitable trust to raise money to install air conditioners at the local high school. She transferred to the trust several items of property that were to be sold for the cause. Unfortunately, the school building burned before that purpose could be fulfilled. A resulting trust with Ashton as its beneficiary was therefore formed at law around the transferred property.

The other type of implied trust is known as a **constructive trust.** Such a trust is created to require a person holding property to transfer it to another because retention of the property would be a wrongful and unjust enrichment of the holder. Property obtained through fraud, duress, or like means is deemed to be held by the wrongdoer in constructive trust for the person wronged.

Although knowing about implied trusts can at times render considerable help, the real benefit of knowing about trusts comes from realizing that proper use of a private, express trust can enable the owner/manager of a business to survive many a twist of fortune and that careful wording of the trustee's instructions can go a long way toward preserving a successful way of doing business even after the owner/manager's death. The wisdom of acquiring a skilled lawyer's professional help in setting up such devices cannot be overemphasized.

Constructive Trust: trust to remedy wrongful transfer of property where beneficiary is true owner

Vocabulary Development

Fill in the blanks with the appropriate term.

Administrator	Community Property	Intestate	Settlor
Administratrix	Constructive Trust	Marriage	Spendthrift Trust
Alimony	Divorce	No-Fault Divorce	Testamentary Trust
Annulled	Escheats	Nuncupative Will	Testate
Beneficiary	Executor	Prenuptial Agreement	Testator
Charitable Trust	Executrix	Resulting Trust	Testatrix
Codicils	Holographic Will	Separated	Will
Common-Law Marriage	Inter Vivos Trust		

1. A(n) _____ consists of the orally expressed wishes of a deceased as to how her or his property is to be distributed.

2. Marital partners living apart are termed _____ at law.

3. A marital dissolution that does not require assessment of fault is known as a(n) _____.

4. A(n) _____ is the transfer of property by will to an individual who is to manage it for the benefit of another.

5. A person who dies without leaving a valid will is said to have died _____.

6. The creator of a trust is labeled a(n) _____ at law.

7. Formal written alterations to a will are called _____.

Problems

1. In your view, which ethical system or systems justify divorce? Which do not?

2. Ethically, how would you support the development of the no-fault divorce? Do you regard no-fault divorce as a personal threat or a personal asset?

3. Is the need for preventing forgeries strong enough to justify the law's requirements that for validity a will must be formally written and executed before witnesses? Who benefits from these requirements?

4. Angus McElroy died testate. His will allocated all of his property to his three children on the condition that they support his wife, Agnes, during her lifetime. Agnes feels that she has been cheated by the will. What are her rights in the matter?

THE LAST EXCERCISE

Take a moment and focus your newly acquired perspective on yourself. Here are some questions, some of which may not be applicable to you at present but might be in the future, to ask now and at intervals throughout your life:

How would my divorce, my parents' divorce, or the divorce of any of my children affect my resources? What planning can I do to soften the effects of such a blow?

How would my death affect the people around me at work and in the home? How would the death of my boss, parents, spouse, or others affect me and the people around me at work and in the home? What provisions can I make for such an eventuality?

How would I be affected by the termination of my job or the termination of the company for which I work? What short- and long-term plans can I lay to alleviate the effects of either or both of those occurrences?

GLOSSARY

A

abandoned property   Property whose owner has given up all intention of maintaining rights or interests in it.

acceleration clause   A clause allowing the obligee to declare the full amount of an obligation due and payable upon the occurrence of a particular event, such as a failure to make a payment.

acceptance   A sign by the offeree indicating that she or he will be bound by the terms of the offeror's offer; in sales law, acceptance occurs when the buyer, after a reasonable opportunity to inspect goods, signifies to the seller that the goods are fine, performs an act inconsistent with the seller's continued ownership of the goods, or simply fails to reject the goods; in commercial paper law, acceptance is an assurance that the drawee will be liable on and pay a draft according to its terms.

accession   The acquisition of property by a natural increase of property already owned, such as by an animal having offspring.

accord and satisfaction   A legal maneuver involving the discharge of a party (satisfaction) from a previous contractual obligation by his or her fulfillment of the terms in a new contract (the accord).

accredited investor   A firm or an individual falling into one of several categories identified by the Securities and Exchange Commission as comprising investors that do not need the protection of registration in a prospective sale of securities.

act   A movement directed by the actor's will.

actual cash value   The amount of indemnification due for property loss; that amount is equal to the original price less a reduction for time in use.

actual cause   The harm-causing factor without which the injury could not have occurred.

actual damages (also referred to as compensatory damages)   A monetary amount intended to compensate for the real harm done.

actus reus   The physical behavior that, if it occurs along with the mental state required by statute, constitutes a crime.

adequate assurance of performance   An action satisfactorily indicating intent to fulfill a contract.

administrator   A male individual selected or endorsed by the court to handle the estate of an individual who died intestate.

administratrix   A female individual selected or endorsed by the court to handle the estate of an individual who died intestate.

adulterated   Below minimum purity and quality standards.

affirmative action plans   Plans that specify methods and time frames in which actions will be taken to eliminate the adverse impact on certain subgroups, such as women or racial minorities, of employers' past discriminatory practices.

after-acquired property clause   A term in a security agreement under which property acquired after the agreement has been made can replace the collateral identified in the agreement subject to the lien set up by the agreement.

agency   A legal relationship whereby one party (the principal) gives the power to legally bind him or her to another party (the agent).

agency by estoppel   A court-ordered status whereby individuals are prohibited from denying that an agency existed and thus are responsible for legal obligations created as a result of the agency.

agency coupled with an interest An agency that is irrevocable by the principal because the agent holds an interest in the subject property above and beyond the expectation of payment for agency services.

agent A person authorized to bind another legally.

agreement not to compete Typically, a term in an employment contract that limits a worker's ability to enter into competition with his or her former employer for a reasonable period after termination of the employment relationship.

alienate To transfer title to property by sale, gift, will, etc.

alien corporation A corporation organized outside the United States.

alimony Maintenance payments by a wage-earning spouse to support a non-wage-earning spouse during separation or after divorce.

all-risk policy (also known as a homeowner's policy) An insurance policy containing coverages for a wide range of risks, including liability, fire, theft, and property loss.

alternative payees Persons named as payees on a piece of commercial paper, each of whom has a full right to all of the funds to be paid.

annual percentage rate The interest rate for a loan expressed as a yearly figure.

annulled A marital contract that has been voided by mutual agreement or by discovery that it was based on fraudulent grounds relating to pregnancy status, history of previous marriage, disease, childbearing ability or desire, or age.

answer The defendant's response to a civil complaint.

antedated An instrument issued bearing a past date.

anticipatory breach A declaration by a party, made before the actual beginning of performance, that she or he will not perform her or his contractual obligations.

apparent authority Seeming but not actual authority to legally bind another to contracts.

appeal A complaint to a higher court of an error of law made during the conduct of a case.

appellate courts An upper level of courts established to review the decisions reached in lower-level courts in order to maintain fairness and uniformity in the application of the law.

appellate jurisdiction The power to review cases for errors of law.

arbitration A dispute-resolving procedure that uses a neutral third party (the arbitrator) who hears the opposing sides and then renders a decision.

arraignment A court proceeding at which a person who has been taken into official custody is informed of the charge or charges against her or him and is allowed to plead.

arrest The taking of a suspect into custody to answer a criminal charge.

arrest warrant An order that a person be arrested by competent authorities.

arson The willful and malicious burning of a structure.

articles of incorporation A written application for corporate status that is filed with the appropriate government entity.

articles of partnership A partnership agreement (in accordance with Uniform Partnership Act terminology).

artisan A person skilled in a trade or craft requiring manual dexterity.

artisan's lien A possessory security interest against personal property for unpaid-for improvements thereon.

assault An intentional tort that results when the defendant willfully places an individual in reasonable fear of a harmful or offensive touching.

assignee The party to whom contractual rights are assigned.

assignment A transfer of rights from the original parties to a contract to others who were not original parties.

assignment of a lease A transfer by a tenant of all his or her rights and interests in the leased premises to someone else.

assignment of wages A clause in a loan contract by which a debtor agrees to have deductions from his or her paychecks sent directly to a creditor upon the debtor's default on the loan.

assignor The party who assigns his or her contractual rights to another.

assumption of risk A defense to tort liability based on the injured party's knowledge and assumption of the specific risk of injury involved.

attach   To seize.

attachment   The point in a loan transaction when the creditor (who may be a lender of money or a seller of the collateral) acquires a legally enforceable right to take the collateral and sell it to satisfy the debt.

auction   An authorized party's public sale of property to the highest bidder.

auction sale without reserve   An auction at which the auctioneer cannot withdraw goods after he or she asks for bids on them.

auction sale with reserve   An auction at which the auctioneer is able to withdraw goods at any time before she or he announces completion of their sale.

avoid   To cancel a contract.

B

bail   The property or bond posted with the court to ensure an accused's later appearance.

bailees   Individuals to whom goods are bailed.

bailment   The legal relationship created by the acquisition of possession of another's personal property subject to an agreement to return it or deliver it to a third party.

bailors   Individuals who bail goods.

bait and switch scheme   An illegal sales gimmick whereby a seller lures a buyer with an extremely low price on an understocked, underfeatured item, then switches the buyer to a far more expensive product.

balloon payment   An installment loan's final payoff amount typically considerably larger than a normal installment and due at the regular time for payment.

bankruptcy   A federal statutory procedure by which debtors' eligible assets are utilized to discharge them from some, if not all, of their obligations.

bankruptcy debtor   Any individual or business (except those considered special cases, such as banks, savings and loans, building and loans, railroads, and insurance companies) that claims the protection of the bankruptcy laws.

bankruptcy insider   A person with a close relationship to the bankruptcy debtor, such as a relative or partner.

bankruptcy trustee   An individual selected to administer the debtor's estate in bankruptcy.

barter   The bargained-for exchange of goods and services without the use of money.

battery   An intentional tort that results when the defendant willfully touches someone in a harmful or offensive way.

bearer   A person in possession of a valid legal instrument that does not specifically identify its owner.

bearer paper   Commercial paper payable to its possessor and found in one of two forms: (1) issued payable to cash, bearer, or the equivalent and without any indorsements or (2) issued payable to cash or to the order of someone but with the last indorsement blank.

beneficiary   A party (or parties) for whose benefit a trust is managed in accordance with the settlor's wishes; in insurance law, a party named in an insurance policy to whom compensation for a loss is to be paid.

best evidence rule   A rule that allows only original or firsthand evidence to be placed before the court.

bilateral contract   A contract whose parties assume a mutuality of obligations to fulfill their promises.

bill of exchange   Historically, a paper ordering the transfer of precious metal from one party to another; in current commercial paper law, synonymous with a draft.

bill of lading   A document that states the terms of a shipping contract for consigned goods, contains a description of those goods, and details who has the right to demand them by presenting the document upon their arrival at their destination.

binder   A written voucher of insurance.

blank indorsement   A signature on the reverse of a commercial paper instrument unaccompanied by any designation of a person who is to receive the payoff on the instrument.

blue laws   Laws that regulate the making or performing of contractual obligations on Sunday.

blue-sky laws   State laws intended to control intrastate security transactions.

board of directors   The group charged with the management of a corporation.

bonds   A certificate or some other evidence of debt requiring that the issuer/borrower repay the amount borrowed or principal plus interest according to a fixed schedule.

boycott   A refusal to do business with a particular person or firm.

breach of contract   An unexcused failure to perform according to the terms of a contract.

breach of the peace   A violation or disturbance of public tranquillity and order.

bribery   Offering, giving, receiving, or soliciting something of value in return for influence on how an official carries out a public or legal duty.

bulk transfer   A trading away of a major part of a commercial enterprises's inventory, supplies, and/or equipment in a transaction that does not occur during the ordinary course of doing business.

business invitees   Those who are impliedly invited onto the premises of another in order to conduct commercial transactions.

business judgment rule   A rule whose effect is to immunize management from liability resulting from business decisions made within the power and authority granted corporate officers in the corporate charter and state statutes.

business law   The relatively specific group of laws that regulate the establishment, operation, and termination of commercial enterprises.

business trust   A business form, popular in some northeastern states, in which selected trustees manage property (signed over to the trust by its owners) so as to provide income or other forms of return to the trust's beneficiaries.

bylaws   The rules governing the internal organization of a corporation and management of the corporation's proceeds.

C

carrier's lien   A possessory security interest in cargo for unpaid shipping charges.

cashier's check   A commercial paper instrument on which a bank is both the drawer and the drawee and which can be issued payable to the purchaser of the instrument or to any party the purchaser desires.

cash value   The interest and principal in the savings fund of a whole life insurance policy or a similar life insurance policy.

causa mortis gift   A gift given in anticipation of death.

caveat emptor   A Latin phrase meaning "let the buyer beware."

certificate of deposit (often called a CD)   A bank's written acknowledgment of the receipt of money coupled with a promise to pay it back, usually with interest, on the due date.

certificate of limited partnership   A document filed in the appropriate governmental office to give third parties notice that a business is operating as a limited partnership.

certificate of review   A document that confers a general exemption from "criminal or civil action . . . brought under the antitrust laws against a person to whom a certificate of review is issued "for any conduct specified in the certificate or complying with it (Export Trading Company Act, sect. 306).

certified check   A check of a depositor in a bank on which the bank has indicated, by the word *accepted* or *certified* accompanied by the signature of a bank official and the date, its warranty that sufficient funds are available for payment.

charitable trust   A trust created for the fulfillment of an altruistic or humanitarian purpose.

charter   A certificate of incorporation issued by a properly empowered governmental entity that thereby officially creates the separate legal person termed a corporation.

check   An unconditional written directive to a bank to pay deposited funds on demand to the order of an individual named on the instrument or to the bearer.

civil case   A lawsuit to resolve a dispute between private citizens.

claim   The assertion of an insured's right to indemnification.

close corporation   A corporation whose stock-based control is held by a single individual or a tight-knit group of individuals.

codicils   Formal, written, and witnessed alterations of a will.

coinsurance   A contractual means by which a policyholder becomes self-insuring for a certain percentage of the worth of insured property.

collateral   Property subject to a creditor's claims.

collection agencies   Organizations that collect debts for others.

collective bargaining   Negotiations over the conditions and terms of employment between representatives of a work force and its employer.

collision coverage   An automobile insurance coverage that indemnifies the insured from losses to the insured's vehicle due to its running into another object or overturning.

comakers   Two or more promisors on a promissory note.

comity   A principle of international law requiring that other nations should defer to and enforce the decision of a foreign court if the laws of the nation in which the case was decided are consistent with their own laws.

commercial paper   A written promise or order to pay a sum of money.

common carriers   Businesses that hold themselves out to the general public to transport goods for a fee.

common law   The customary law of a region.

common-law marriage   Where recognized by law, a marital union created whenever two single people of opposite sex lived together, held themselves out as husband and wife, and shared property in common over an extended period (typically 5–10 years).

common stock   A type of stock that gives its owner the right to vote in corporate elections and a proportionate share in distributed corporate profits.

community property   Assets acquired during a marriage by the marital partners.

comparative negligence   A defense that does not deny all recovery when the party injured in an accident was somewhat negligent but instead allows recovery according to the relative degree of fault of the parties to the accident.

compensatory damages   See "actual damages."

complaint   A document filed in a civil case with the clerk of a court with original jurisdiction over a litigable matter in which the injured party's version of the facts of the case is stated, the court's

jurisdiction over the case is shown, and a request or "prayer" for relief is made.

complete performance   A contractual result whereby all of the parties to a contract perform every promise made in the contract.

comprehensive coverage   An automobile insurance coverage that indemnifies the insured for damage to his or her vehicle stemming from causes other than those covered by collision insurance, such as theft, hail, vandalism, or the chipping or breakage of glass.

computer crime   The destruction or wrongful use of a computer or the data it contains.

concealment   The failure to disclose a material fact when requested to do so by the insurer.

condition   In real property law, a term upon which the validity of a lease is contingent.

condition concurrent   A contractual term requiring that both parties to a contract perform some or all of its obligations at the same time.

condition precedent   A contractual term specifying an event that must occur before an obligation to perform is placed on one or all the parties to a contract.

condition subsequent   A contractual term specifying an event whose occurrence will extinguish an obligation to perform.

confession of judgment   A consumer's relinquishment of his or her right to a court hearing when he or she is sued for defaulting on the payment of a debt.

confidential relationships (also termed fiduciary relationships)   Relationships that the law recognizes as being founded on trust.

conforming goods   Goods that fulfill the seller's obligations under a contract with the buyer.

confusion   The blending of indistinguishable goods of two or more owners so that each owner's share cannot be identified.

conscious parallelism   A practice followed by the members of oligopolies whereby all of the members follow the pricing policies of the largest member.

consent   A willing and knowledgeable assent.

consequential damages   Damages reasonably foreseeable as being caused by a particular breach of contract.

consideration   What an offeror demands and, in most situations, must receive in return for making his or her offer a promise legally binding against him or her.

consignment   A bailment of goods to a common carrier for shipment.

constitution   The fundamental law of the land.

constitutional law   The text of a constitution and the laws and judicial rulings that interpret and apply it.

constructive delivery   A symbolic act indicating the delivery of a gift.

constructive eviction   A landlord's failure to make necessary repairs or provide necessary services that renders the premises of a lease uninhabitable.

constructive trust   A trust created to require a person holding property to transfer it to another because retention of the property would wrongfully and unjustly enrich the holder.

consumer goods   Items purchased primarily for personal, family, or household purposes.

consumer law   A growing field of the law comprising statutes and common law precedents that protect purchasers of goods that are to be used primarily for personal, household, or family purposes.

consumer products   Items of tangible personal property that are used for personal, family, or household purposes.

consumers   Purchasers of goods that are to be used primarily for personal, household, or family purposes.

contingent beneficiary   The person named to receive a policy payout should the primary beneficiary die before the insured.

contract   An agreement between two or more parties that creates an obligation.

contract carriers   Companies that hire out to transport goods only for those with whom they care to do business.

contract to sell   An agreement involving future goods.

contractual capacity   The ability to appreciate the consequences of entering into a contract.

contributory negligence   A defense that disallows any recovery for an injury if the injured party's negligence contributed to the injury.

convention   In international law, an international agreement or compact.

convertible bond   A type of bond that is exchangeable for a set amount of stock at the option of the bond's creditor.

copyright   An exclusive right to the publishing, printing, copying, reprinting, and selling of the tangible expression of an author's or artist's creativity.

corporation   A legal entity created through statutory authority to be a separate, artificial person distinct from the operation or project of the business that the entity is organized to conduct.

corrective advertising   A sanction of the Federal Trade Commission invoked to counteract the lingering effects of an improper advertising claim.

cost-plus contract   A contract whose terms require the purchaser to pay the developer the amount of money it costs to create a product plus a certain percentage of that amount.

counterclaim   A claim based on the incident at hand that the defendant in a civil case makes against the plaintiff.

counteroffer   A response to an offer that alters the terms of the offer.

course of dealings   Understandings developed by the parties to a contract in their previous transactions.

court of record   A legal forum in which an exact account of what went on at trial is kept so as to allow appeals.

courts of equity   Courts that were empowered to fashion remedies that courts of law could not fashion and then to issue injunctions enforcing those remedies on the parties involved.

courts of law   Courts holding formal proceedings in which they apply powers given them by the political authority in order to resolve disputes of the people.

covenant   A term in a lease whose breach will give the injured party only the right to sue for the damages caused by the breach, leaving the lease still in effect.

credit insurance   A term insurance policy that is intended to pay off a particular lender should the debtor die.

creditor beneficiary   A third party to a contract to whom payment of some debt or other obligation is expressly directed by the contractual party owing that debt.

credit rating   An evaluation of a person's ability to repay debts.

crime   A specific behavior that is an offense against the public good, the commission of which is punishable by the government.

criminal case   A prosecution of an individual charged with an offense against society as defined in its law code.

cross-claim   A claim that a defendant in a civil case makes against another defendant.

cross-examination   Examination of a witness concerning the testimony that the witness gave under direct examination by the opposing side.

cumulative preferred stock   A type of preferred stock whose owners must receive all unpaid preferred stock dividends before the owners of common stock receive any dividends.

cumulative voting   A method of voting for directors in corporate elections that increases the likelihood of minority representation on corporate boards.

D

damages   monetary compensation awarded by the court to the injured party in a lawsuit.

days of grace   A period, usually one month, during which an overdue premium can be paid to keep a life insurance policy in force.

debenture   A bond that is issued without any security.

debt financing   The borrowing of money to capitalize a business.

decreasing term   A term life insurance policy requiring the payment of a constant premium (smaller than the premium paid for level term insurance for the same initial face value) throughout the time that the policy is in force in return for a steadily decreasing face value.

decree   A judgment of a court of equity.

deed   A formal written instrument utilized to transfer title to real property.

de facto corporation   A corporation whose status as such may be challenged by the state in which the

corporation's good faith but erroneous attempt to incorporate was made.

defamation   The damaging of another's reputation by the making of false statements.

defamation per se   A category of defamatory statements so obviously harmful that the plaintiff does not have to prove damages to be able to recover for them at law; this category includes statements falsely accusing someone of having a communicable disease, of committing a criminal offense, or of being unable to perform the duties of an office, employment, or profession.

defendant   The person accused of wrongdoing in a criminal case; the person named in a civil complaint as the party causing the injury.

defense of self or others   A defense to criminal charges if the defendant reasonably believed that there was danger of severe bodily harm or death from an unprovoked attack and that the attack could be repelled only if the defendant used enough force.

de jure corporation   A corporation that is considered a separate legal entity by the law and whose status as such cannot be challenged by either private citizens or the state of incorporation.

delegation   A transfer of contractual duties.

demand note   A note that becomes due and payable whenever the payee or a subsequent owner presents it for payment.

depository bank   The first bank to which a commercial paper instrument is transferred for collection.

design patent   A statutorily granted monopoly to protect the unique configuration or appearance of the surface or components of an object.

destination term   A sales contract term that requires the seller of goods to be responsible for the delivery of the goods to their destination.

direct examination   The initial examination of a witness by the side that calls him or her.

directors   The stockholder representatives charged with overall responsibility for the management of a corporation.

disability coverage   A life insurance policy term that protects against a potentially devastating consequence of accident and disease, namely a total permanent inability to work.

disaffirm   To avoid.

discharge   To free from a legal obligation.

discounted   In commercial paper law, an instrument sold at less than the face amount.

discrimination in employment.   Hiring, promoting, or discharging on the basis of race, color, sex, religion, or national origin; these practices were made illegal by the Civil Rights Act of 1964.

dishonored   A draft on which the drawee refused to pay.

disparagement of reputation   The making of false statements about the reputation of a business or about the quality of its products.

dissolution of partnership   Under the Uniform Partnership Act, a change whereby any partner ceases to be associated with the carrying on of a partnership's business.

dividends   A stockholder's proportionate share in the distribution of corporate profits.

divorce   The total dissolution of a legally recognized marriage relationship upon the order of a court of law.

doctrine of incorporation   A contractual doctrine that disregards the legal effect of oral bargains struck before a contract has been reduced to writing.

documents of title   Legal instruments that evidence the power of the person who has them in her or his possession to control the instruments themselves and the goods they cover.

domestic corporation   A corporation doing business in the state under whose laws it was organized.

donee   The intended recipient of a gift.

donee beneficiary   A third party who receives her or his rights under a contract as a gift from a party or parties to the contract.

donor   The person or other entity giving a gift.

dormant partners   Individuals who are actual partners but are not acknowledged publicly as partners and do not actively participate in the management of the partnership.

double indemnity   A term in a life insurance policy that requires the insurer to pay twice (or three or four times for triple or quadruple indemnity, respectively) the face value of the policy upon the accidental death of the person on whose life the insurance is being carried.

draft   An unconditional written order to a person to pay money, usually to a third party.

drafts   Creates a document or an initial written version of a legal device.

drawee   The party directed in a draft to pay a sum of money to someone's order.

drawer   The person who issues the order to pay found in a draft.

due process   The right of involved parties to receive notice of the charges or matters to be resolved at an upcoming hearing or trial and to present evidence, confront witnesses, and otherwise represent themselves at that proceeding.

dumping   The sale on the US market of imported goods at a price set below their fair value (usually the price of the goods in the producing country).

duress   At contract law, a wrongful threat that denies a person of her or his free will to contract.

E

easement   The right to use the land of another.

effluent   Liquid waste.

egoism   An ethical system under which a person's actions are determined by their consequences for his or her self-interest (see "psychological egoism" and "hedonism").

electronic fund transfers   The use of communication and computer technology as a substitute for commercial paper instruments.

embezzlement   The wrongful conversion to his or her personal use of property entrusted to an individual by another.

eminent domain   The right of governments to take private land for a bona fide public use.

employee   The party in the employment relationship who is being paid by another to do work.

employer   The party in the employment relationship who is paying another to do work.

employment   A relationship in which one party (the employer) pays another party (the employee) to do work under the control and direction of the paying party.

encumber   To subject property to the legal claim of someone other than the owner.

endowment life insurance   A type of accumulation fund policy under which the insured typically pays a very high "premium" for insurance coverage and the right to receive the face value, if still living, at retirement or the end of a certain period.

enjoyment   The exercise of a right.

entrapment   A defense to criminal charges that requires showing that government officers or agents induced the defendant to commit a crime not already contemplated by her or him.

environmental impact statement (EIS)   A detailed report required of a federal agency with control over a proposed action that would significantly affect the environment.

environmental law   The name applied to statutory- and common law-based attempts to control actions with a potentially harmful effect on the land, air, and water resources that support the existence of life on this planet.

equipment   Goods used primarily in an ongoing business.

equity   Basic fairness.

equity financing   The selling of stock of various kinds to individuals who want to become part owners of a business or to increase the amount of their existing ownership in the business.

escheat   The right of the state to property without existing claimants.

estate   The real and personal property interest of a party.

ethical systems   Codes of conduct.

eviction   The act of removing a tenant from the possession of premises.

exclusions   Terms in an insurance contract that eliminate coverage in certain situations.

exclusive-dealing agreements   Contracts under which a retailer agrees with a supplier not to sell a product that competes with the supplier's product.

executed contract   A contract that has been fully performed by all of its parties.

executive branch   The division of government with the power to investigate violations of the law and to prosecute the alleged violators.

executor   A male individual selected or endorsed by the court to handle the estate of a decedent who died testate.

executory contract   A contract in which some performance, regardless of how slight, has yet to be rendered.

executrix   A female individual selected or endorsed by the court to handle the estate of a decedent who died testate.

exemplary damages (punitive damages in some jurisdictions)   A monetary award arbitrarily set by the jury that bears little, if any, direct relationship to the amount of the plaintiff's actual injuries but is instead aimed at making an example of or punishing (thus punitive) the defendant.

export   Sell domestic products in foreign markets.

export trading companies   Firms that exclusively conduct international trade and derive most of their revenue from the export of goods and services produced in the United States.

express contract   A contract whose terms are set down in a clear-cut fashion either orally or in writing.

express warranty   An oral or written term or its equivalent in a sales agreement in which a promisor makes some statement of assurance about the good being sold.

extended coverage rider   A policy endorsement used in many states to add protection against a variety of perils not covered in a basic fire policy.

extortion   The use of threats of injury to a victim's person, family, property, or reputation to get consent to take the victim's property.

extraordinary care   A standard of responsibility that holds the bailee liable for any and all loss or damage that is not solely attributable to unforeseeable acts of God or war.

extreme duress   A real defense to the collection of commercial paper based on the fact that the paper was issued to avert a threat to inflict death or severe bodily harm on the issuer's immediate family or to destroy the issuer's home.

F

face value   The maximum amount that can be paid under a policy if the harm insured against actually occurs.

fair use doctrine   A tenet of copyright law that permits the unauthorized reproduction of copyrighted material if such reproduction is done reasonably so as not to injure the rights of the copyright holder.

farm products   Livestock, crops, and supplies used or produced in farming operations that are in the farmer's possession.

felony   A crime severe enough to be punishable by death or imprisonment for a year or longer.

fictitious payee rule   A tenet of commercial paper law providing that, if an employee tricks her or his employer into issuing an instrument in payment of a nonexisting obligation, the loss is to be taken by the employer and not by the payor bank.

fidelity insurance   A type of insurance that provides protection against certain forms of dishonesty and against laxness in fulfilling obligations owed to the insured.

fiduciary duty   In partnership law, a duty requiring that the partner put the partnership's interest above her or his own.

fiduciary relationships   See "confidential relationships."

finance charge   The actual cost of a loan expressed in dollars and cents.

financial responsibility laws   Statutes requiring that drivers have insurance or other ability to pay a liability judgment.

financing statement   A brief documentation of the existence of a security interest filed with the appropriate governmental office so as to perfect a creditor's security interest in collateral.

fixtures   Tangible, movable, things that become permanently attached to land or buildings.

forbearance   The refraining by a person from doing something that the person has a legitimate right to do.

foreign corporation   A corporation doing business in any state other than the one in which it was organized.

forgery   The false making or altering of a written document so as to create or change the legal effect of the document with an intent to defraud.

franchise   A business arrangement in which of a trademark, trade name, or copyright is licensed to a business for its use in selling goods or services and the business is provided with a detailed and well-tested system for conducting its operations.

franchisee   The recipient and capitalizer of a franchise.

franchisor   The provider of a franchise.

fraud   In contract law, an untrue or reckless statement of a material fact made by one party to induce another party to enter into a contract.

fraud in the execution   A real defense to the collection of commercial paper based on the fact that the issuer did not realize that she or he was issuing commercial paper.

fraud in the inducement   A personal defense to the collection of commercial paper based on the fact that the issuer was deceived or defrauded into issuing the commercial paper.

fraudulent transfer   A shifting of a bankruptcy debtor's assets made with the intent to defraud, hinder, or delay creditors.

friendly fire   A fire burning where it was intended to burn.

fringe benefits   Forms of payment not directly related to work performance, such as pensions, vacation time, and free insurance.

full warranty   The seller's promise to cover the labor and material costs necessary to completely fix a product.

fungible goods   Goods one unit of which is acknowledged by trade usage to be identical with any other unit.

future goods   Goods not in existence or identified to the contract at the time of the contracting.

G

gambling   Paying something of value to win a prize in a game of pure chance.

garnishment   A court order compelling the payment into the court of an individual's wages or other financial resources held by a third party so as to satisfy a judgment.

general partners   Partners who engage in the management of a partnership and are fully, personally liable for its obligations.

general partnership   An association of two or more persons, each of whom is fully, personally liable for all of the association's financial obligations, to carry on as co-owners a business for profit.

general power of attorney   A written agency authorization that allows the agent to do anything legally necessary to conduct the principal's affairs.

generators   Entities that create hazardous waste.

gift   A transfer of property, voluntarily and without consideration, by one party to another.

good faith   Honesty in fact or subjective honesty.

goods   Things that are movable when they are identified as the subject matter of a sales agreement; in secured transactions, things that are tangible and movable when the security interest attaches.

grand jury   A "jury of inquiry" with powers to develop evidence and indict alleged violators of the criminal law.

grantee   A transferee of property.

grantor   A transferor of property.

gratuitous agency   An agency arrangement under which the principal is not obligated to pay for the agent's services.

gratuitous bailment   A bailment for the sole benefit of one of its parties.

gross negligence   Intentional reckless disregard of duty with knowledge of the harmful consequences.

group insurance   A term insurance policy offered to each member of a body of people with some common characteristic.

guarantor   A person who agrees to be secondarily liable for the payment of a debt or the performance of an obligation.

guardian   An individual who has been given the responsibility for taking care of a legally incapacitated party.

guest statutes   Laws that prohibit injury suits by nonpaying passengers against the driver of a vehicle in which they were riding unless the injury resulted from the driver's gross negligence or intentional behavior.

H

habitual drunkard   Someone who exhibits an involuntary tendency to become intoxicated as often as the temptation to do so is presented.

hazardous wastes   Wastes that pose a substantial present or future danger to human health or the environment if they are improperly managed.

hearsay   Evidence stemming not from the personal knowledge of the witness but from what the witness heard another say.

hedonism   An ethical system under which persons act to satisfy their senses of taste, touch, smell, sight, and hearing.

historical school   A legal philosophy based on the belief that legal systems develop according to each nation's historical experiences.

holder   A person possessing an instrument issued or indorsed to her or him or made payable to the bearer.

holder in due course   A holder who gives value for a piece of commercial paper in good faith without any notice of defect or dishonor.

holder through a holder in due course   A holder of an instrument who cannot become an HDC on his or her own but who acquires the rights of an HDC by acquiring the instrument after an HDC has held it.

holographic wills   Wills that are written in the decedent's own hand and are typically signed but unwitnessed.

home solicitation sales   Sales over $25 made to consumers in places that are generally not the seller's regular places of business.

horizontal constraints   Illegal restraints on competition that typically involve sellers at the same level of commerce.

hostile fire   A fire that erupts someplace where the insured intends it not to be.

hotelkeeper (also occasionally labeled innkeeper by the law)   A party who operates an establishment that holds overnight accommodations out to the public for hire.

hotelkeeper's lien   A possessory security interest that a hotelkeeper acquires in a guest's property as compensation for unpaid-for lodging.

hung jury   A jury that cannot reach agreement on a verdict.

I

identified (to the contract)   The selection of specific goods as the subject matter of a deal.

illegal per se   Under the antitrust laws, conduct that is considered illegal regardless of its justification or reasonableness.

impeachment cases   Trials of government officials for misconduct in office.

implied contract   A contract whose terms have not been stated and must therefore be determined from the surrounding circumstances or a foreign pattern of dealings.

implied warranties   Guarantees imposed on sales agreements by law.

importing   Bringing foreign goods into the domestic marketplace for sale.

imposter rule   A tenet of commercial paper law stating that if a party has been duped into issuing an instrument to a person whom the issuer has misidentified, the loss from the resulting forgery falls on the careless issuer.

incidental beneficiaries   The unintended recipients of a contract's direct or indirect benefits.

incidental damages   Damages awarded by a court to cover the costs expended by an innocent party to stem the loss from an injury; damages that are foreseeable but indirect losses to the injured party.

incontestable clause   A life insurance contract term that puts a time limit on the insurer's right to void a policy because of fraud or misrepresentations by the insured.

incorporators   The individuals who sign the articles of incorporation.

indemnify   To compensate for loss or damage.

independent contractor   Someone who contracts to do a job for another but performs the work entailed in his or her own way and is not subject to the direction and control of the person with whom he contracted to do the job.

indictment   A grand jury's official accusation of an individual for criminal conduct.

indorse   To sign the reverse of a piece of commercial paper.

information   An accusation brought by a responsible public officer (the state attorney general or the local prosecutor) against a defendant.

infractions   Minor criminal offenses such as littering or improper parking.

infringement   Violation of the rights of a holder of a patent, copyright, or trademark.

infringes   Exercises without authority any of a patent, copyright, or trademark holder's granted rights in his or her invention.

injunction   A court order directing that some action be taken or halted.

inland marine insurance   Insurance of personal property against the perils of land transport.

in pari delicto   A Latin phrase meaning "of equal guilt."

insanity defense   A defense to criminal charges that requires showing that the defendant was suffering from a mental disease or defect that prevented him or her from behaving rationally.

inside directors   Individuals who are employees, officers, or major stockholders of the corporation of which they are directors.

insiders   Officers, directors, major stockholders, and others who are privy to confidential information pertaining to a corporation's activities.

insolvent   The condition of being unable to meet debts when they come due.

installment note   A note that requires a series of payments of principal and interest until a debt has been paid off.

insurable interest   A property right in goods whose potential loss can be indemnified.

insurance   The primary device used to transfer the risk of loss from specific perils from one person to another person or a group.

insurance of insurability   A life insurance policy coverage that allows the purchase of new amounts of life insurance coverage or the continuation of current coverage levels without being required to pass a physical examination or other test.

insured   The party who transfers the risk of loss to the insurer.

insurer   The party who agrees to accept the risk of loss from another.

intangible property   Something that is the evidence of value.

intentional tort   A personal injury or wrong willfully inflicted by the tortfeasor to harm another's person or property.

interbrand competition   A struggle between firms working against each other to sell distinct competing products from different producers.

interstate commerce   Trade and other commercial activity between or among the citizens of different states or the states themselves.

inter vivos (between the living) **gift**   An absolute, nonconditional gift.

inter vivos trust   A trust created during the lifetime of the settlor.

intestate   The legal condition of a person who dies without leaving a valid will.

intrabrand competition   A struggle between firms working against each other to sell the same product.

intrastate commerce   Trade and other commercial activity conducted wholly within one state.

inventory   Goods bought for sale or lease.

invitation to negotiate   A solicitation of offers.

involuntary bailment   A bailment created by the law to cover situations in which personal property inadvertently ends up in the hands of a stranger.

involuntary bankruptcy   A bankruptcy proceeding initiated with a petition filed by a debtor's creditors.

irresistible impulse (also known as a temporary mental defect)   A defense to criminal charges that requires showing that, because of a mental disease or defect, the defendant was temporarily unable to resist an impulse to commit a criminal act.

issuing a bad check   The crime of writing a check on an account knowing that the funds in the account are insufficient to cover it and that the financial institution on which it is written will probably not pay it; doing this becomes a crime when the financial institution does indeed fail to pay it.

J

jointly and severally liable   The status of individuals who may be held responsible individually or as co-obligors for some form of legal liability.

jointly liable   The status of individuals who are held to be co-obligors for some form of legal ability.

joint payees   Payees named on a piece of commercial paper who have equal rights in the funds to be paid.

joint tenancy   A form of property ownership involving two or more parties, each of whom is legally considered to own all of the subject property.

joint venture   The participation of two or more firms in a specifically limited transaction for profit.

Judeo-Christian ethics   A religion-based ethical system requiring certain behavior regardless of consequences.

judicial branch   The division of government to which the power to conduct trials and pronounce judgment is given.

jurisdiction   The power of a court or other official body to hear and decide cases.

jurisprudence   Legal philosophy.

jury   A panel of citizens whose role is to assess evidence properly introduced in court in order to advise a judge on what the actual facts of a case are.

justice   In jurisprudence, the evenhanded administration of the laws; the title given to judges who sit on state or federal supreme courts.

juveniles   Individuals who are under the age of full responsibility for their criminal acts (generally set at 18 years).

K

Kantian ethical system   A system of ethics that endorses a possible action only if the principle behind it could be made a universal law without producing an illogical or self-defeating situation.

knowingly   A requirement of certain criminal statutes that the act in question be performed by the defendant with knowledge that a particular harm is likely to occur.

L

landlord   A party renting real property.

lapses   Terminates.

larceny   The unauthorized taking and carrying away of another's goods or money.

law The rules of conduct that a political authority will enforce.

lease The agreement under which the exclusive possession of real property or the possession, use, and enjoyment of personal property are temporarily transferred.

leasehold A legal estate composed of the right to the exclusive possession of the subject premises for a certain term.

legal realism A school of jurisprudence that holds that the law should reflect the most desirable real-life practices in use in a particular area.

legislative branch The division of government to which the power to make laws is given.

lemon laws Statutes requiring a dealership to provide the owner of a newly purchased car with a new car or to return the purchase price if the dealership is unable to repair a defect that significantly affects the value or use of the newly purchased car in a certain number of attempts (typically four).

lessee A person who rents the real or personal property of another.

lessor A person from whom real or personal property is being rented.

letter of credit A promise by a person (typically a financial institution such as a bank) that it will honor and pay drafts drawn in compliance with its terms.

level term Life insurance policies requiring the payment of a set premium throughout the period that they are in force in return for a constant face value.

liability insurance Coverage of insureds for their potential legal responsibility for injures that they might unintentionally inflict on the person or property of others.

libel The communication of false statements in a reasonably permanent form such as in writing or on videotape.

licensees Persons who are afforded the privilege of entering onto another's real property through the explicit or implied permission of the possessor.

lien A claim on property for payment of a debt.

life insurance A contractual means for transferring the potential loss due to the death of a certain individual to an insurer who will pay a prearranged amount of money to a named beneficiary upon that occurrence.

limited liability Liability for the obligations of a business that extends only to the amount of someone's investment in the business.

limited liability corporation (LLC) A form of corporate entity available in some states that combines the advantages of the limited partnership and the S corporation while eliminating their usual restrictions (such as the limits set on the number of owners and the prohibition of managing by owners with limited liability).

limited partnership A partnership composed of one or more general partners with full personal liability and one or more limited partners whose liability for the obligations of the partnership extends only to the amount of their investment in it.

limited power of attorney A written agency authorization that allows the agent to carry out only specific transactions or to act as agent for only a set period.

limited warranty A written warranty that meets some but not all of the requirements of a full warranty.

liquidated damages A realistic approximation of the damages that should be awarded by a court in the event of a breach of contract.

liquidation A sale for cash.

litigants The parties who engage in a lawsuit.

lodger An occupant of premises who has only their use, not their exclusive possession.

lost property Property that has been involuntarily parted with due to the negligence or inadvertence of its true owner.

M

mail fraud A crime committed by using the mails to execute a fraudulent scheme.

majority A legal status afforded to those who are at or beyond a set legal age.

maker The promisor on a promissory note.

mala in se crime A crime that is inherently and essentially evil in its nature and consequences.

mala prohibita crime A crime that is not inherently evil but is considered wrong only because it has been defined as such by a legislature.

malice   A wrong, evil, or corrupt motive.

marine insurance   A form of insurance whose coverage indemnifies for losses due to the perils of water transport.

market share   The percentage of the relevant market under the defendant's control.

marriage   The legal status of a man and a woman who are united by law for life or until divorced.

material fact   In contract law, a fact crucial to a party's decision as to entering into a contract; in insurance law, a fact that, if correctly known, would have caused the insurer not to issue a policy.

material term   An essential element of a contract.

mechanic's lien   An encumbrance against real property for unpaid bills for labor and supplies used in improvements thereon.

medical payments coverage   An automobile policy coverage that indemnifies against medical expenses the insured and any person who is injured while entering, leaving, or riding in or on the insured's vehicle.

Medicare   A social benefit program that helps eligible individuals pay for hospital and doctor expenses.

mens rea   The mental state that, along with the required physical behavior, defines a criminal act.

merchant   A person who deals in goods of the kind involved in a transaction or a person who by his occupation holds himself out as having the knowledge or skill peculiar to the practices or goods involved in a transaction or a person to whom such knowledge or skill may be attributed by his employment of an agent, broker, or other intermediary who by his occupation holds himself out as having such knowledge or skill.

merger   In antitrust law, the absorption of one company by another.

midnight deadline   Midnight of the banking day following the day a commercial paper instrument is received.

minimum wage   A statutorily set floor under hourly wages.

minor   A legal status afforded to those who are under a set age.

misdemeanor   A crime that is punishable by a relatively minor fine and/or imprisonment for less than a year.

mislaid property   Property whose owner consciously laid it aside with the intent to retrieve it later but which now cannot be found.

mistake   A defense to criminal charges when, because of honest error by the defendant, the required criminal mental state is negated.

mitigation   A duty upon the party injured by a breach of contract to minimize the harm done.

money   The medium of exchange that any government has officially adopted as part of its currency.

monogamy   The condition of having only one spouse.

monopolizing conduct   Behavior indicating that a dominant market firm achieved and/or abused its position by improper methods.

monopoly   Control over the production of a good or the provision of a service held by one person or one firm.

monopoly power   The ability to control the marketplace.

mortgage   A device that transfers the right to have the real property subject to it sold to satisfy an unpaid debt.

mortgagee   The creditor in a mortgage transaction.

mortgagor   The debtor in a mortgage transaction.

motion for judgment on the pleadings   A pretrial motion contending that there are no factual issues to be resolved in a full trial and consequently that the judge should just decide which laws to apply to the facts agreed to in the pleadings and enter judgment accordingly.

motive   The reason for acting in a particular manner.

mutual benefit bailment   A bailment in which both the bailor and the bailee are intended to receive payment of some kind.

mutual insurance company   An insurance company that is capitalized through the premiums of its insureds.

mutual mistake   A mistake made by both or all parties to a contract.

mutual rescission   A discharge of contractual obligations that is brought about when the parties to a contract agree to return and return whatever (or the equivalent value of whatever) they have received under the contract.

mutuum   A loan for consumption.

N

natural law school   A legal philosophy based on the belief that an ideal legal system was implanted in the reason of human beings before they were ruined by passion, greed, and the like.

negligence   Acting in a way that violates the duty of due care that a reasonable person owes to others.

negotiable instrument   A writing signed by its maker or drawer that is unconditionally payable on demand or at a specific time to order or to bearer in a sum certain in money.

negotiation   A transfer of commercial paper as a result of which the transferee becomes a holder, a holder in due course, or a holder through a holder in due course.

no-fault divorce   A legal means of ending a marriage that no longer requires the spouse who originates the petition for divorce to accuse the other spouse of some form of misconduct (fault) such as adultery, alcoholism, drug addiction, felony conviction, impotence, or cruelty.

no-fault insurance systems   State laws requiring that, within certain loss limits and regardless of who is at fault, the parties involved in an automobile accident be indemnified by their own insurers.

nominal damages   A token monetary award to acknowledge that the rights of the plaintiff have been violated, but with little resultant harm.

nominal partners   Individuals who are not actually partners but hold themselves out as such or allow themselves to be held out as such.

nonattainment regions   Areas whose level of a particular pollutant exceeds the minimum legal standard.

nonconforming goods   Goods that deviate from the specifications of·the buyer or are defective in some way.

nondeterioration regions   Areas whose level of a particular pollutant is below the minimum standard.

not-for-profit corporation   A corporation created to achieve educational, charitable, or other ends without any return to its investors.

novation   A legal maneuver whereby a contracting party secures a release by substituting someone else to perform her or his contractual obligations.

novel   A previously unknown idea, typically one representing a "burst of genius."

nuisance   Something that annoys or disturbs a party's possession of her or his property by rendering the property's ordinary use or enjoyment physically uncomfortable or impossible.

nuncupative wills   Wills that are orally made.

O

objective standard   A criterion used to determine whether contractual intent is present; the basis for the criterion is whether a reasonable person observing the contractual negotiations impartially would have concluded from the conduct of the parties that such intent was present.

obligee   The person to whom an obligor is obliged.

obligor   The person who is obligated to fulfill a contractual promise.

obvious   Plainly evident to a person with average skill in the particular field involved.

offer   A proposed bargain or exchange.

offeree   The person to whom an offer is made.

offering statement   A document, required to be filed in a Securities and Exchange Commission office for small public offerings, that contains financial statements (not professionally audited) and other information included in a typical prospectus.

offeror   The person who makes an offer.

oligopoly   An economic condition in which only a few companies control most of the market.

omnibus clause   An automobile policy term by which the insured can extend coverage to household members or to drivers operating with the permission of any of the insureds.

open price term   An omission from a sales contract of specification of the consideration due for goods.

option contract   A contract that binds the offeror to his or her promise to keep an offer open for a set period of time.

order of relief   A court declaration that a debtor is in a state of bankruptcy liquidation.

order paper   Commercial paper payable to or at the direction of the party named in the special indorsement at the end of its indorsement chain and found in only one of two forms: (1) either it has been issued to a specific party and has not yet been indorsed, or (2) regardless of whether it was issued to cash or to a specific person, it has a special indorsement at the end of its indorsement chain.

ordinary care   Reasonable care under the circumstances.

ordinary duress   A personal defense to commercial paper based on the fact that it was issued due to economic threats or legitimate threats of criminal prosecution.

original jurisdiction   The power to determine the facts of the matter and make the initial determination of the law to be used to decide a case.

output contract   A contract under which a product maker contracts to sell all of his or her production during a set period to another party to the contract.

outside directors   Individuals without a significant financial interest in the corporation of which they are directors.

overboard   A statute whose application is so inclusive that it would make a large number of actions criminal.

overdraft   The amount of a check in excess of the deposited funds.

P

parole   The conditional release of a criminal before the required term of imprisonment has been completed.

parol evidence rule   A contractual doctrine that disallows any oral (parol) testimony contradicting, adding to, or modifying a written contract.

participating preferred stock   A type of stock whose owners are entitled to receive a share of the monies for common stock dividends left over after the dividends on preferred stock have been paid.

partition   The dividing of property held in tenancy or of the value received for such property.

partnership at will   A partnership that any partner may dissolve at any time without incurring any liability for doing so.

partnership by estoppel   Not an actual partnership but a legal device created to make individuals who have alleged nonexistent partnerships or their own nonexistent membership in existing partnerships responsible for the losses that innocent individuals have incurred as a consequence of such allegations.

past consideration   Nonbinding consideration given without expectation of or demand for a binding promise in return.

patent   A nonrenewable legal monopoly over the right to make, use, or sell a device.

pawn   A pledge.

payee   The party named in commercial paper to receive the funds or to have the power to order them paid to someone else.

payor bank   The bank by which an item is payable as drawn or accepted.

per capita   A means of dividing up the property in a decedent's estate under which the decedent's living lineal descendants split the property equally.

perfection   In a loan transaction, the next stage after attachment by which a secured party obtains a set priority in relation to other creditors in the collateral.

perfect tender   The tender of delivery of goods and the goods so tendered that conform to the contract in all respects.

periodic tenancy (also known as a tenancy from year to year)   A leasehold that continues for successive like intervals of time subject only to termination by proper notice from one of the parties.

personal defenses   Defenses to the collection of commercial paper that are good only against mere holders and assignees.

personal property   All things that are not real property.

per stirpes   A means of dividing up the property in a decedent's estate under which the living lineal descendants of a deceased parent split equally what the deceased parent would have received.

piercing the corporate veil   The court-ordered stripping away of the protection of limited liability normally afforded to corporate owners.

plaintiff   A person who initiates a lawsuit by filing a complaint.

plea bargain   An agreement by which the defendant agrees to plead guilty in exchange for a reduced charge or for the prosecutor's recommendation of a lighter sentence.

pleadings Formal written statements, such as the complaint and answer, exchanged between the parties prior to trial.

pledge The transfer of possession of a debtor's personal property to a creditor who has the right to sell it upon default to pay off an obligation of its owner.

policy A written contract of insurance.

possession The ability to exercise control over something to the exclusion of all others.

postdated An instrument issued bearing a future date.

power of attorney A written authorization of agency.

precedent The rule of law to be applied to a particular legal issue.

preferential transfer A payment by an insolvent debtor giving the payee creditor more than that person would have received in a Chapter 7 bankruptcy proceeding.

preferred stock A type of stock whose dividend amount is usually set and whose dividends are paid in full before any dividends are paid on common stock.

preliminary hearing An official proceeding at which the evidence against the accused is presented so as to allow the court to determine whether the state should be allowed to proceed with a trial.

premises The real property subject to the legal action at hand.

premium The amount of consideration that an insurer is paid for assuming a particular risk.

prenuptial agreement A contract formed in consideration of marriage that specifies the financial rights of both parties in such situations as divorce.

pretrial conference A conference at which the judge and the attorneys for all parties meet and try to get the parties to settle their problems without a formal trial.

price The cost in money or value paid for a good or service; in sales law, the consideration required to be transferred in exchange for goods.

prima facie evidence Proof sufficient on its face to serve as the basis for a factual presumption.

primary beneficiary The person named first in priority to receive the payout of an insurance policy.

primary liability The unconditional responsibility to pay a commercial paper instrument whenever the instrument is due.

primary standards General standards of air quality that must be met to protect public health.

principal In commercial paper law, the face amount of a note; in agency law, the person authorizing another to act in her or his stead.

private carriers Companies that transport in their own vehicles their own goods or goods they have sold or leased.

private corporation A corporate entity set up, funded, and run by private individuals to achieve private ends.

privity The mutual relationship between buyer and seller based on the establishment of a bargain.

probable cause Reasonable legal grounds for the action in question.

probate court A specialized court that is responsible for administering wills and estates.

probation The release of a party convicted and sentenced for a crime on the condition that the sentence will not be executed as long as the party abides by the terms of the release set by the court.

profit The right to take from the soil of the land of another.

promisee The person to whom a contractual promise is made.

promise to perform a preexisting duty A promise to do something that the promisor is already legally obligated to do.

promisor The person who makes a contractual promise.

promissory estoppel A doctrine of contract law the prevents a promisor from stating that he or she did not receive consideration for his or her promise.

promissory note A written promise by one party to pay money to the order of another party.

promoters Individuals who advocate a business idea and its corporate form to potential investors.

promotion The advocacy to potential investors of a business idea and its corporate form.

property   The rights and interests that each of us can have in things.

prospectus   A document on a stock issue (containing information relevant to the purchase of the stock and an invitation to buy it) that must be approved by the Securities and Exchange Commission and be made available to prospective buyers of any portion of the issue.

proximate cause   A harm-causing factor for which the defendant is legally responsible because the harm caused is within the factor's range of foreseeable consequences.

proxy   An authorization by which a shareholder allows someone else to cast his or her vote in a corporate election.

psychological egoism   An ethical system under which an individual acts primarily because of the impact that her or his behavior will have on others.

public corporation   A corporate organization set up by a local or state government or the federal government to accomplish a governmental purpose.

public good   A common resource to which all should have access and use.

puffing   A salesperson's exaggerated statement of opinion.

punitive damages   See "exemplary damages."

purchase   The transmittal of property from one person to another by voluntary agreement and action based on consideration.

purchase money security interest   A security interest acquired by a party, be it a lender or a seller, that provides the value needed to purchase specific consumer goods.

Q

qualified indorsement   A signature on the reverse of a piece of commercial paper accompanied by the phrase "without recourse" or another phrase of similar effect.

quarters   A qualifying term for social benefits defined as a period in which a worker earned at least approximately $600.

quasi contract (also referred to as an implied-at-law contract)   Not actually a contract, but a remedy that the courts utilize to return value to someone who has enriched another person in the absence of an express or implied contract between them.

quitclaim deed   A deed that merely passes whatever claim or interest the grantor may have or might receive in the real property.

quota   A certain number of employee positions that an employer has set aside to be filled exclusively by a subgroup on which the employer's previous discrimination in employment has had an adverse impact.

R

ratification   The display of a willingness to be bound by a contract's terms.

ratified   In agency law, expressly or impliedly approved by accepting the benefits of an unauthorized act.

ratifies   In commercial paper law, approves or confirms.

reaffirmation agreement   A bankruptcy debtor's agreement made before the completion of the bankruptcy procedure, to pay off a specific debt even after it has been discharged.

real (also called universal) **defenses**   Defenses that will prevent holders, HDCs, HHDCs, and, of course, mere assignees from collecting on a check, draft, or other piece of commercial paper.

real estate   Land and the things permanently attached to land.

real property   Land, buildings, and items permanently attached to the land and buildings.

recklessness   Acting without consideration of the high risk that harm will result from doing so.

reference to standard form contract   A contract composed solely of a list of items signed by the contracting parties that is used to fill in the blanks of a predetermined prototype contract.

registered agent   A person named to represent a corporation in receiving binding service of process.

registration statement   A document that consists of detailed information on the financial status of a company, its history, its management's experience, the reasons for and risks of a particular offering, and a variety of other information; the document must be filed with the Securities and Exchange

Commission before a single share of the offering can be sold.

rejection   The expression of a lack of interest in an offer.

relevant market   The total demand for the product or service allegedly being monopolized and those products or services interchangeable with it as determined within the effective geographic area in question.

rent   To pay consideration for the right to use or occupy premises; in addition, the consideration paid for this right.

renunciation   The abandonment of a right without transferring it to another.

representations   Statements that the applicant for insurance makes in her or his offer but that are not included in the policy.

repudiation   An express statement or clear implication that a party to a contract is not going to perform.

requirements contract   A contract that obligates one party to the contract to buy all it needs of a particular good from another party to the contract during a set period.

resale price maintenance   The efforts of a manufacturer or distributor to control the price at which a good is marketed at a commercial level other than its own.

rescind   To cancel any current or future effect of a contract and to take all possible steps to return the contract's parties to their precontractual positions.

respondeat superior (let the master answer)   The rule of law placing vicarious liability on the employer or principal.

restricted securities   A designation meaning that the subject shares cannot be resold without registration unless the resale is an exempt transaction.

restrictive indorsement   A signature on the reverse of a piece of commercial paper accompanied by wording that curtails or restricts the transferee's rights.

resulting trust   A trust implied at law when the person intended to receive the benefit of an express trust cannot do so; under such a trust the trust property is presumed by law to be held in trust for its original owner(s).

reverse discrimination   Government-endorsed favorable hiring, promoting, or discharging based on the otherwise prohibited categories of sex, race, color, etc.

revocation   The recalling or taking back of an offer by the offeror prior to acceptance.

riders (also called endorsements)   Terms that modify or tailor standard insurance forms to fit specific situations.

right of survivorship   A rule of property law providing that when a joint tenant of a property dies, the entire ownership of the subject property remains with the surviving tenants and is not subject to the claims of the deceased's family or estate.

right-to-work laws   Laws prohibiting collective bargaining agreements from requiring union membership as a condition of employment.

robbery   The taking of goods or money in the possession of another, from his person or his immediate presence, by the use of force or fear.

royalty   Compensation for the use of property.

rule of reason   A Supreme Court decree that certain prosecutions brought under the Sherman Act had to be judged by the courts from a reasonability standpoint to see whether alleged illegal acts eliminated or promoted competition.

S

sale   The passing of title to goods from a seller to a buyer for a price.

sale on approval   A transaction in which the buyer is allowed to return the goods purchased within a reasonable period even if they conform to the contract.

sale or return   A transaction in which goods sold primarily for resale may be returned even if they conform to the contract.

satisfactory performance   A contractual result that requires the obligor to satisfy the obligee's personal tastes in order to render a proper performance.

scope of authority   The parameters of power that a principal grants an agent.

S corporation   A corporation that is organized in the same manner as a normal corporation except for the fact that its profits and losses are taxed directly to its stockholders.

secondary boycott A boycott by third parties who agree to cease doing business with a firm with which a union is involved in a dispute.

secondary liability The legal responsibility to pay a commercial paper instrument whenever the party primarily liable does not do so.

secondary standards Standards of air quality that must be met to preserve the welfare of the public in the form of animal and plant life and visibility.

secret partners Individuals who are working general partners but are not publicly known as such.

secured loan A debt transaction in which the creditor is given a security interest in specific property of the debtor for utilization in the event of the debtor's default.

security Sufficient assurance that a loan will be repaid; in security regulation law, an investment contract whereby investors provide the necessary capital and share in the earnings generated through the promoters' management and control.

security agreement The written agreement by which the owner of collateral creates a creditor's security interest in the collateral.

security interest A property right that allows its holder legal recourse against specific property.

separated The condition of marital partners who live in separate quarters.

service of process An official presentation of the summons and complaint to a defendant.

settlor The creator of a trust.

severally liable The status of a person who is individually responsible for a legal obligation.

severalty Ownership by only one person, the simplest and most common form of ownership.

shareholders The owners of a corporation.

shipment term A sales contract term that requires the seller to turn over the goods sold to a carrier for delivery to the buyer.

sight draft A draft payable on demand or "at sight."

silent partners Individuals who are properly and publicly acknowledged as partners but who do not participate actively in management of the partnership.

slander The communication of false statements in a temporary form (typically, this is done orally).

social insurance A form of insurance that provides protection against the realities of forced retirement, disability, severe illness, unemployment, and other risks.

sole proprietorship A business owned by one person who is fully, personally liable for all of its obligations.

special indorsement A signature on the reverse of a commercial paper instrument along with a statement naming the indorsee and directing payment of the instrument to that party.

specific performance A contractual remedy by which the court orders that a contract be fulfilled by a particular party.

spendthrift trust A kind of trust that protects the beneficiary's interest in the trust property from claims by the beneficiary's creditors.

stale check A check that is presented for payment over six months after the date of issue indicated on its face.

stare decisis The policy of enforcing established precedents so as to ensure fairness to all similarly situated parties.

statute of frauds A statute requiring that, in order to be enforceable, a written version of an alleged contract, signed by the party against whom enforcement is sought, be produced in court.

statute of limitations A statute that limits the time available to bring suit or to initiate a prosecution.

statutes Legislatively created laws.

stay A suspension or halt.

stock Certificates or shares of ownership in a corporation.

stock insurance company A firm that has been capitalized by investors who expect a return on their money from its profits.

stop-payment order A directive to the drawee institution not to transfer funds in accordance with the terms of a previously issued draft.

strict liability A legal doctrine that holds the defendant liable for harm resulting from certain types of conduct or activity regardless of how much care the defendant took to prevent the harm from occurring.

strike A concerted employee refusal to work for an employer.

subject matter The good or service involved in a contract.

subletting A transfer by a tenant of some of her or his rights and interests under a lease.

subrogated Substituted for another in the pursuit of a claim or right against a third party.

subscription agreement A written contract by which a potential investor agrees to buy a certain amount of a corporation's stock if and when the stock is issued.

substantial performance A contractual result whereby a party exhibits a good faith effort that meets contractual expectations except for minor details.

sum certain An amount clearly ascertainable from the face of a piece of commercial paper.

summons A court order that the defendant appear and respond to a civil complaint or criminal charge within a given period.

Superfund The federally created Hazardous Substance Response Trust Fund, which was set up to pay for irrecoverable cleanup costs at hazardous waste sites.

surety A person who agrees to be primarily liable for the payment of a debt (or the performance of an obligation) of another.

T

tariffs Fees levied by governments on imported goods.

tax lien An encumbrance against property subject to taxation for an unpaid levy.

tenancy at sufferance A leasehold terminable without notice, that is created by law whenever a periodic tenant or a tenant for years wrongfully retains possession of the premises after the lease has expired.

tenancy at will A leasehold that permits the exclusive possession of real property for an indefinite duration.

tenancy for years A leasehold for any fixed duration, such as days, weeks, months, or years.

tenancy in partnership A co-ownership in partnership property set up in Section 24 of the Uniform Partnership Act by which each partner is given an equal right with the other partners to possess specific partnership property for partnership purposes.

tenant A renter of real property.

tenant in common A co-owner of undivided property who may transfer her or his ownership interest without the permission of the other co-owners.

tenants by the entirety A husband and wife whom the common law treats as tenants who each own all of the subject property in the same manner as joint tenants with the right of survivorship but with the additional proviso that the creditors of one spouse cannot satisfy their claims by reaching the property held by both spouses in this tenancy.

tender of delivery An offer to turn over goods to a buyer.

tender of performance A ready, willing, and able offer to perform in accordance with the terms of a contract.

terminable at will In labor law, a relationship that may be ended by either party at any time without notice and without producing a litigable cause of action unless a fixed term is contracted for.

termination statement A document filed in the same governmental office as the foregoing financing statement giving notice that the property used as collateral is no longer encumbered.

term insurance A life insurance policy containing only coverage on the life of the insured.

testamentary trust A trust created after the death of the settlor in accordance with her or his will.

testate The legal condition of a person who dies leaving a valid will.

testator The male maker of a will.

testatrix The female maker of a will.

third-party beneficiary A party outside a contract to whom the parties to the contract may intend benefits to flow.

third-party complaint A procedural device that makes a party not previously involved a part of a civil suit.

tie-in sale   A transaction wherein a seller allows a buyer to have one product only if the buyer purchases another as well.

time draft   A draft due after a certain period, such as a number of days or months.

time note   A note payable at a set future date.

title   The formal ultimate legal right to ownership of property.

tortfeasor   The person who commits a tort.

tortious bailment   A bailment created by the law to cover situations in which personal property wrongfully comes into a person's hands.

torts   Personal injuries or wrongs for which the law provides remedies.

trade acceptance   A draft drawn by a seller on a buyer as drawee that the buyer accepts upon receipt of a satisfactory shipment of goods.

trade fixtures   Items attached to another's realty by a renter to facilitate a business that the renter is conducting on the realty.

trademark   The identifying symbol, word(s), or design by which a business distinguishes its products to consumers.

trade usage   An understanding or pattern of dealing established in the area of commerce under consideration.

transcript   A verbatim record of what went on during a trial.

traveler's check   A commercial paper instrument, sold to a user by a financial institution acting as both drawer and drawee, that requires the user's signature before the issuer and then again before the payee as authentication to enable cashing.

travel insurance   Term insurance intended to indemnify for the loss of life of the insured on a trip by plane or some other mode of travel.

treason   The levying of war against the United States or adherence to its enemies by giving them aid and comfort.

treble damages   A damage award available in certain types of cases that is equal to three times the actual damages.

trespassers   Persons who willfully enter the property of another without consent.

trial court   The court in which a case is fully heard for the first time.

trial jury   A group of persons selected according to law to impartially determine the factual questions of a case from the evidence allowed before them in court.

trials   Formal proceedings for the examination and determination of legal issues.

trust   A separate entity created by law to which the ownership of property can be transferred so that the property can then be managed by designated individuals in accordance with the wishes of the transferor.

trustees   The parties in charge of a trust.

U

ultra vires   Any action taken by a corporation that is outside its legitimate powers.

unconscionable contract   A contract entered into as a result of the greatly unequal bargaining power of its parties; the stronger party makes a take-it-or-leave-it offer to which the weaker party has no viable market alternative.

underinsured motorist coverage   A coverage available under an automobile insurance policy that allows an insured to collect against her or his insurer for the irrecoverable amount of the damages for bodily injury and wrongful death up to certain per person and per accident limits.

underwriting   Insuring various risks.

undisclosed principal   A principal involved in an agency arrangement in which the agent acts under a contract that forbids revealing that he or she is acting for a principal.

undue influence   A condition in which the dominating party in a confidential relationship is able to compel the dominated party to enter into a contract that benefits the former.

unfair labor practices   Certain forms of conduct by a union or an employer that were made illegal by the National Labor Relations Act.

Uniform Commercial Code   A set of laws governing areas of trade and business regulated by the states.

unilateral contract   A contract by which one party to a contract is obligated to fulfill a contractual promise only if another party to the contract performs.

unilateral mistake   A mistake made by only one of the parties to a contract.

uninsured motorist coverage   A coverage available under an automobile insurance policy that allows an insured to collect bodily injury and wrongful death damages (not property damages) from her or his insurer if the driver causing the harm does not have insurance.

unsecured loan   A loan transaction that does not provide the creditor with an interest in specific property of the debtor, thereby leaving the creditor, in the event of default, with the sole alternative of proceeding against the debtor's general asset position.

use   The enjoyment of things by their employment.

useful   The requirement that a patentable invention have a utility that will reward society for the granting of patent rights to its inventor.

usury   The charging of an interest rate for the loan of money that exceeds the legal limit.

utilitarianism   An ethical system under which an action is deemed proper if it produces the greatest good for the greatest number of the people affected by it.

utility patent   A 17-year monopoly statutorily granted to protect a novel and useful invention.

V

valid contract   A contract that is legally binding and enforceable.

valid title   A legally enforceable title.

value (under the UCC)   A contractual consideration, a past indebtedness, or a credit extension.

verdict   A statement of whatever conclusions a jury has reached on the questions of fact.

vertical constraints   Illegal restraints on competition that typically involves parties in the same distribution chain.

vicarious liability   A legal doctrine that imposes responsibility on one party for the actionable conduct of another party on the basis of an existing relationship between the two parties.

vocational rehabilitation   Training that is provided to injured employees so that they will be able to assume another type of job.

voidable contract   A contract whose legal effect may be canceled by one or more of its parties.

voidable title   A title that may be terminated at the option of one of its parties.

void contract   A contract that has no legal effect.

void title   A nonexistent title.

W

warehouseman's lien   A possessory security interest in stored items for unpaid storage costs.

warranties   Statements made by an applicant for insurance in her or his offer that become a part of the issued policy.

warranty   A guarantee under the law of sales that is used to describe the product, and its quality and performance.

warranty deed   A deed that not only conveys title from the grantor (the transferor of the property) but also contains several warranties for the benefit of the grantee (the transferee of the property).

warranty of fitness for a particular purpose   An implied warranty imposed on any seller who knows or should know the buyer's intended use for the goods sold and upon whose skill or judgment the buyer is relying for the supply of suitable goods.

warranty of good title   An implied warranty imposed on the seller of goods that guarantees that the title transferred to the buyer is valid and that the transfer is rightful.

warranty of merchantability   A guarantee that the goods sold are fit for their ordinary intended use.

white-collar crime   Embezzlement and similar criminal activities by well-respected agents and executives.

whole life insurance policies   Policies that offer a savings feature and pay a moderate interest rate on the funds accumulated from their premiums.

will   A person's expression of how his or her property is to be distributed upon his or her death.

winding up (of partnership)   The concluding of the partnership's business (no new contracts can be entered into except as necessary to fulfill existing obligations) and the selling of the partnership's property.

writ of certiorari   An order compelling a lower court to turn over the record of a case to an appellate court for review.

writ of execution   A court order to compel a party subject to a court judgment to comply with it.

A

abatement of nuisance: eliminación de an estorbo

abstract of title: resumen de título

acceptance: aceptación

accession: accesion

accommodation paper: documento de favor

accord and satisfaction: acuerdo y satisfacción

Act of State: Acto de Gobierno

adjudicate: juzgar, adjudicar

administrator: administrador

adverse possession: posesión adversa

affirm: affirmar

affirmative action: acción affirmativo

agent: agente

allege: alegar

allegation: alegato

answer: contestación

anticipatory breach: infraccion anticipador

appelle: apelado

arbitrate: arbitrar

assignee: cesionario

assignment: cesion

assignor: cedente

B

bailee: depositario

bailment: deposito, entrega

bailor: depositante

bankruptcy: bancarrota

bearer: portador

beneficiary: beneficiario

bid: oferta

bill of lading: conocimiento de embarque

Blue Sky Laws: el nombre popular de leyes estatales hechos a proteger a inversionistas en la venta de valores

brief: breve, escrito

bulk transfer: transferencia a granel

burden of proof: carga de la prueba

C

case law: leye de causas, precedentes

cashier's check: cheque de caja, cheque bancario

cause of action: derecho de acción

caveat emptor: tenga cuidado el comprador

caveat venditor: tenga cuidado el vendedor

certification: certificación

certified check: cheque certificado

check: cheque

C.I.F.:   costo, seguro y flete

civil action: acción civil

class action: litigio entablado en representación de un grupo

C.O.D. "Cash on Delivery":   entrega contra pago

code: codigo

codicil: codicilo, cambio a un testamento

common carrier: transportador público

compensatory (see damages):   compensatario

complaint: queja, demanda

composition with creditors: concordato con acreedores

condition: condición

condition precedent: condición precedente

condition subsequent: condición subsigiente

conditional gift: regalo condicional

consignee: consignatario

consignment: consignación

consignor: consignador

contract: contracto

conversion: conversión

corporation: corporacion, sociedad automoma

counterclaim: contrademanda

counteroffer: contraoferta

custody: custodia

D

D/B/A: Haciendo negocio como

damages: danos y perjucios

debtor: deudor

deceit: engaño

decision: decisión

deed: escritura, titulo

defendant: accusado, demandado

defraud: estafar

deliver: entregar

de novo, trail: jucio de nuevo

deposition: deposición

derivative action: accion derivado de an accionista a beneficio de la corporación

dictum: opinión expresado por un tribunal

directed verdict: veredicto dirigido por el juez

discharge in bankruptcy: extinción de una obligacion en bancarrota

dismiss: despedir, rechazar

donee: donatario

donor: donante

dower: los bienes del esposo fallecido que le corresponden a las viuda

draft: letra de cambio

drawee: girado

duress: por cumpulsion

E

easement: servidumbre

en banc: en el tribunal

equity: equidad, valor liquido

equity of redemption: derecho de rescate de una propiedad hipotecada

estoppel: impedimento por actas propios

ex ship: enviar al gasto y riesgo del venededor

exculpatory clause: clausa exculpatoria

executor: albacea

executory: por complirse

executrix: albacea

F

F.A.S.:   Franco Muelle

felony: felonia, crimen

fiduciary: fiduciario

financing statement: declaracion de seguridad

fixture: instalación fijo

F.O.B.:   libre a bordo

fungible goods: bienes fungibles

G

garnishment: embargo

gift: un regalo

good faith: buena fe

guarantor: garante

guaranty: garantia

H

heirs: herederos

holder in due course: tenedor de buena fe

I

illusory: illusorio

implied warranty: garantia implicita

incapacity: incapacidad

independent contractor: contratista independiente

indorsement: endorso

injunction: interdicto judicial

inpersonam: contra la persona

insolvency: insolvencia

in status quo: en stata quo

instrument: instrumento

J

jointly: conjuntamente

jointly and severally: conjuntamente y independientemente, solidariamente

joint tenancy: tenencia conjunta

judgment: jucio

judgment N.O.V.:   sentencia contraria al veredicto

jurisdiction: jurisdicción

L

law merchant: derecho commercial

lease: contrato de arrendamiento

legal: legal

lien: gravamen, carga

litigant: litigante

M

magistrate: juez, magistrado

mechanic's lien: gravamen de constructor

mens rea: intención criminal

minitrail: mini jucio

minor: menor

misdemeanor: delito, ofensa menor

mistrial: jucio nulo

mitigation of damages: mitigación de danos

mortgage: hipoteca

N

necessaries: necesarios

negligence: negligencia

negotiable: negociable

negotiable instrument: instrumento negociable

negotiation: negociación

no arrival, no sale: sino llegan los bienes, no hay pago por ellos

nolo contendere: no contestare

non compos mentis: incapacitado mentalmente

novation: novación

O

oath: juramento

obligee: obligante

obligor: obligado

objection: objeción

offer: oferta

offeree: quien recibe una oferta

offeror: oferente

opinion: opinión

option: opción

ordinance: ordenanza

P

parol evidence: prueba extrínseca

partners: socios

payee: tenedor, beneficiaro de pago

per curiam: por el tribunal

perjury: perjurio

petition (bankruptcy):   petición de bancarrota

plaintiff: demandante

plea: alegato

polygraph: aparato para detectar mentiras

positive law: ley positiva

post dated check: cheque posfechado

power of attorney: poder actual

precedent: precedente

privity: relacion juridica o contractual

probate: validacion de testamento

promisee: a quien se promete

promisor: prometedor

promissory estoppel: impedimento promisorio

promoters: promotores

prospectus: prospecto

proximate cause: causa immediata

Q

quasi contract: cuasicontracto

R

ratification: ratificacion

rebuttal: refutación

recorder: registrador, grabador

redemption: redención

remand: devolver

remedy: remedio

res: asunto

respondent: respondiente

S

satisfaction: satisfación

scienter: a sabiendas

security agreement: accuerdo de seguridad

shareholder: accionista

sovereign immunity: inmunidad soberana

specific performance: ejecucion de lo estipulado en un contrato

stated capital: dicha capital

stare decisis: acaturse a los precedentas judiciales

status quo: el estado de las cosas en un momento dado

stockholder: accionista

subpoena: citacion

summary judgment: sentencia sumaria

summons: emplazamiento

T

testimony: testimonio

tort: daño legal

tortious: dañoso

trail: jucio

transcript: transcripción

treble damages: danos triplcados

trustee in bankruptcy: sindico concursal

U

unliquidated debt: deuda no liquidado

Ultra Vires Act: acta fuera de la facultad de una corporacion

usury: usura

V

venue: lugar de jurisdicción

verdict: verdicto

versus: contra

void: nulo

voidable: anulable

W

waive: renunciar

waiver: renuncia

warranty: garantia

whistleblowing: un empleado quo informa sobre actividades ilicitas en su empresa

writ: orden judicial

writ of certiorari: auto de avocación

writ of executional (or garnishment): ejecutoria, mandamiento de ejecución

Constitution of the United States

THE CONSTITUTION OF THE UNITED STATES OF AMERICA

PREAMBLE

We the People of the United States, in Order to form a more perfect Union, establish Justice, insure domestic Tranquility, provide for the common defense, promote the general Welfare, and secure the Blessings of Liberty to ourselves and our Posterity, do ordain and establish this Constitution for the United States of America.

ARTICLE I

Section 1 All legislative Powers herein granted shall be vested in a Congress of the United States, which shall consist of a Senate and House of Representatives.

Section 2 The House of Representatives shall be composed of Members chosen every second Year by the People of the several States, and the Electors in each State shall have the Qualifications requisite for Electors of the most numerous Branch of the State Legislature.

No Person shall be a Representative who shall not have attained to the age of twenty five Years, and been seven Years a Citizen of the United States, and who shall not, when elected, be an Inhabitant of that State in which he shall be chosen.

Representatives and direct Taxes shall be apportioned among the several States which may be included within this Union, according to their respective Numbers, which shall be determined by adding to the whole Number of free Persons, including those bound to Service for a Term of Years, and excluding Indians not taxed, three fifths of all other Persons.[1] The actual Enumeration shall be made within three Years after the first Meeting of the Congress of the United States, and within every subsequent Term of ten Years, in such Manner as they shall by Law direct. The Number of Representatives shall not exceed one for every thirty Thousand, but each State shall have at Least one Representative, and until such enumeration shall be made, the State of New Hampshire shall be entitled to choose three,

Massachusetts eight, Rhode-Island and Providence Plantations one, Connecticut five, New York six, New Jersey four, Pennsylvania eight, Delaware one, Maryland six, Virginia ten, North Carolina five, South Carolina five, and Georgia three.

When vacancies happen in the Representation from any State, the Executive Authority thereof shall issue Writs of Election to fill such Vacancies.

The House of Representatives shall chuse their Speaker and other Officers; and shall have the sole Power of Impeachment.

Section 3 The Senate of the United States shall be composed of two Senators from each State, chosen by the Legislature thereof,[2] for six Years; and each Senator shall have one Vote.

Immediately after they shall be assembled in Consequence of the first Election, they shall be divided as equally as may be into three Classes. The Seats of the Senators of the first Class shall be vacated at the Expiration of the second Year, of the second Class at the Expiration of the fourth Year, and of the third Class at the Expiration of the sixth Year, so that one third may be chosen every second Year; and if Vacancies happen by Resignation, or otherwise, during the Recess of the Legislature of any State, the Executive thereof may make temporary Appointments until the next Meeting of the Legislature, which shall then fill such Vacancies.[3]

No Person shall be a Senator who shall not have attained to the Age of thirty Years, and been nine Years a Citizen of the United States, and who shall not, when elected, be an Inhabitant of that State for which he shall be chosen.

The Vice President of the United States shall be President of the Senate, but shall have no Vote, unless they be equally divided.

The Senate shall chuse their other Officers, and also a President pro tempore, in the Absence of the Vice President, or when he shall exercise the Office of President of the United States.

---

[1]Changed by the Fourteenth Amendment.

[2]Changed by the Seventeenth Amendment.
[3]Changed by the Seventeenth Amendment.

The Senate shall have the sole Power to try all Impeachments. When sitting for that Purpose, they shall be on Oath or Affirmation. When the President of the United States is tried, the Chief Justice shall preside: And no Person shall be convicted without the Concurrence of two thirds of the Members present.

Judgment in Cases of Impeachment shall not extend further than to removal from Office, and disqualification to hold and enjoy any Office of honor, Trust or Profit under the United States: but the Party convicted shall nevertheless be liable and subject to Indictment, Trial, Judgment and Punishment, according to Law.

Section 4   The Times, Places and Manner of holding Elections for Senators and Representatives, shall be prescribed in each State by the Legislature thereof; but the Congress may at any time by Law make or alter such Regulations, except as to the Places of chusing Senators.

The Congress shall assemble at least once in every Year, and such Meeting shall be on the first Monday in December, unless they shall by Law appoint a different Day.[4]

Section 5   Each House shall be the Judge of the Elections, Returns and Qualifications of its own Members, and a Majority of each shall constitute a Quorum to do Business; but a smaller Number may adjourn from day to day, and may be authorized to compel the Attendance of absent Members, in such Manner, and under such Penalties as each House may provide.

Each House may determine the Rules of its Proceedings, punish its Members for disorderly Behaviour, and with the Concurrence of two thirds, expel a Member.

Each House shall keep a Journal of its Proceedings, and from time to time publish the same, excepting such Parts as may in their Judgment require Secrecy; and the Yeas and Nays of the Members of either House on any question shall, at the Desire of one fifth of those Present, be entered on the Journal.

Neither House, during the Session of Congress, shall, without the Consent of the other, adjourn for more than three days, nor to any other Place than that in which the two Houses shall be sitting.

Section 6   The Senators and Representatives shall receive a Compensation for their Services, to be ascertained by Law, and paid out of the Treasury of the United States. They shall in all Cases, except Treason, Felony and Breach of the Peace, be privileged from Arrest during their Attendance at the Session of their respective Houses, and in going to and returning from the same; and for any Speech or Debate in either House, they shall not be questioned in any other Place.

No Senator or Representative shall, during the Time for which he was elected, be appointed to any civil Office under the Authority of the United States, which shall have been created, or the Emoluments whereof shall have been encreased during such time; and no Person holding any Office under the United States, shall be a Member of either House during his Continuance in Office.

Section 7   All Bills for raising Revenue shall originate in the House of Representatives; but the Senate may propose or concur with Amendments as on other Bills.

Every Bill which shall have passed the House of Representatives and the Senate, shall, before it becomes a Law, be presented to the President of the United States; If he approves he shall sign it, but if not he shall return it, with his Objections to that House in which it shall have originated, who shall enter the Objections at large on their Journal, and proceed to reconsider it. If after such Reconsideration two thirds of that House shall agree to pass the Bill, it shall be sent, together with the Objections, to the other House, by which it shall likewise be reconsidered, and if approved by two thirds of that House, it shall become a Law. But in all such Cases the Votes of both Houses shall be determined by Yeas and Nays, and the Names of the Persons voting for and against the Bill shall be entered on the Journal of each House respectively. If any Bill shall not be returned by the President within ten Days (Sundays excepted) after it shall have been presented to him, the Same shall be a Law, in like Manner as if he had signed it, unless the Congress by their Adjournment prevent its Return, in which Case it shall not be a Law.

Every Order, Resolution, or Vote to which the Concurrence of the Senate and House of Representatives may be necessary (except on a question of Adjournment) shall be presented to the President of the United States; and before the Same shall take Effect, shall be approved by him, or being disapproved by him, shall be repassed by two thirds of the Senate and House of Representatives, according to the Rules and Limitations prescribed in the Case of a Bill.

Section 8   The Congress shall have Power To lay and collect Taxes, Duties, Imposts and Excises, to pay the Debts and provide for the common Defence and general Welfare of the United States; but all Duties, Imposts and Excises shall be uniform throughout the United States.

To borrow Money on the credit of the United States;

To regulate Commerce with foreign Nations, and among the several States, and with the Indian Tribes;

To establish an uniform Rule of Naturalization, and uniform Laws on the subject of Bankruptcies throughout the United States;

To coin Money, regulate the Value thereof, and of foreign Coin, and fix the Standard of Weights and Measures;

To provide for the Punishment of counterfeiting the Securities and current Coin of the United States;

To establish Post Offices and post Roads;

To promote the Progress of Science and useful Arts, by securing for limited Times to Authors and Inventors

---

[4]Changed by the Twentieth Amendment.

the exclusive Right to their respective Writings and Discoveries;

To constitute Tribunals inferior to the supreme Court;

To define and punish Piracies and Felonies committed on the high Seas, and Offences against the Law of Nations;

To declare War, grant Letters of Marque and Reprisal, and make Rules concerning Captures on Land and Water;

To raise and support Armies, but no Appropriation of Money to that Use shall be for a longer Term than two Years;

To provide and maintain a Navy;

To make Rules for the Government and Regulation of the land and naval Forces;

To provide for calling forth the Militia to execute the Laws of the Union, suppress Insurrections and repel Invasions;

To provide for organizing, arming, and disciplining, the Militia, and for governing such Part of them as may be employed in the Service of the United States, reserving to the States respectively, the Appointment of the Officers, and the Authority of training the Militia according to the discipline prescribed by Congress;

To exercise exclusive Legislation in all Cases whatsoever, over such District (not exceeding ten Miles square) as may, by Cession of particular States, and the Acceptance of Congress, become the Seat of the Government of the United States, and to exercise like Authority over all Places purchased by the Consent of the Legislature of the State in which the Same shall be, for the Erection of Forts, Magazines, Arsenals, dock-Yards, and other needful Buildings;—And

To make all Laws which shall be necessary and proper for carrying into Execution the foregoing Powers, and all other Powers vested by this Constitution in the Government of the United States, or in any Department or Officer thereof.

Section 9   The Migration or Importation of such Persons as any of the States now existing shall think proper to admit, shall not be prohibited by the Congress prior to the Year one thousand eight hundred and eight, but a Tax or duty may be imposed on such Importation, not exceeding ten dollars for each Person.

The Privilege of the Writ of Habeas Corpus shall not be suspended, unless when in Cases of Rebellion or Invasion the public Safety may require it.

No Bill of Attainder or ex post facto Law shall be passed.

No Capitation, or other direct, Tax shall be laid, unless in Proportion to the Census of Enumeration herein before directed to be taken.[5]

No Tax or Duty shall be laid on Articles exported from any State.

No Preference shall be given by any Regulation of Commerce or Revenue to the Ports of one State over those of another: nor shall Vessels bound to, or from, one State, be obliged to enter, clear, or pay Duties in another.

No Money shall be drawn from the Treasury, but in Consequence of Appropriations made by Law; and a regular Statement and Account of the Receipts and Expenditures of all public Money shall be published from time to time.

No Title of Nobility shall be granted by the United States: And no Person holding any Office of Profit or Trust under them, shall, without the Consent of the Congress, accept of any present, Emolument, Office, or Title, of any kind whatever, from any King, Prince, or foreign State.

Section 10   No State shall enter into any Treaty, Alliance, or Confederation; grant Letters of Marque and Reprisal; coin Money; emit Bills of Credit; make any Thing but gold and silver coin a Tender in Payment of Debts; pass any Bill of Attainder, ex post facto Law, or Law impairing the Obligation of Contracts, or grant any Title of Nobility.

No State shall, without the Consent of the Congress, lay any Imposts or Duties on Imports or Exports, except what may be absolutely necessary for executing its inspection Laws: and the net Produce of all Duties and Imposts, laid by any State on Imports or Exports, shall be for the Use of the Treasury of the United States; and all such Laws shall be subject to the Revision and Controul of the Congress.

No State shall, without the consent of Congress, lay any Duty of Tonnage, keep Troops, or Ships of War in time of Peace, enter into any Agreement or Compact with another State, or with a foreign Power, or engage in War, unless actually invaded, or in such imminent Danger as will not admit of delay.

ARTICLE II

Section 1   The executive Power shall be vested in a President of the United States of America. He shall hold his Office during the Term of four Years, and, together with the Vice President, chosen for the same Term, be elected, as follows

Each state shall appoint, in such Manner as the Legislature thereof may direct, a Number of Electors, equal to the whole Number of Senators and Representatives to which the State may be entitled in Congress: but no Senator or Representative, or Person holding an Office of Trust or Profit under the United States, shall be appointed an Elector.

The Electors shall meet in their respective States, and vote by Ballot for two Persons, of whom one at least shall not be an inhabitant of the same State with themselves.

---

[5]Changed by the Sixteenth Amendment.

And they shall make a List of all the Persons voted for, and of the Number of Votes for each; which List they shall sign and certify, and transmit sealed to the Seat of the Government of the United States, directed to the President of the Senate. The President of the Senate shall, in the Presence of the Senate and House of Representatives, open all the Certificates, and the Votes shall then be counted. The Person having the greatest Number of Votes shall be the President, if such Number be a Majority of the whole Number of Electors appointed; and if there be more than one who have such Majority, and have an equal Number of Votes, then the House of Representatives shall immediately chuse by Ballot one of them for President; and if no Person have a Majority, then from the five highest on the List the said House shall in like Manner chuse the President. But in chusing the President, the Votes shall be taken by States, the Representation from each State having one Vote; A quorum for this purpose shall consist of a Member or Members from two thirds of the States, and a Majority of all the States shall be necessary to a Choice. In every Case, after the Choice of the President, the Person having the greatest Number of Votes of the Electors shall be the Vice President. But if there should remain two or more who have equal Votes, the Senate shall chuse from them by Ballot the Vice President.[6]

The Congress may determine the Time of chusing the Electors, and the Day on which they shall give their Votes; which Day shall be the same throughout the United States.

No Person except a natural born Citizen, or a Citizen of the United States, at the time of the Adoption of this Constitution, shall be eligible to the Office of President; neither shall any Person be eligible to that Office who shall not have attained to the Age of thirty five Years, and been fourteen Years a Resident within the United States.

In Case of the Removal of the President from Office, or of his Death, Resignation, or Inability to discharge the Powers and Duties of the said Office, the Same shall devolve on the Vice President, and the Congress may by Law provide for the Case of Removal, Death, Resignation or Inability, both of the President and Vice President, declaring what Officer shall then act as President, and such Officer shall act accordingly, until the Disability be removed, or a President shall be elected.[7]

The President shall, at stated Times, receive for his Services, a Compensation, which shall neither be increased nor diminished during the Period for which he shall have been elected, and he shall not receive within that Period any other Emolument from the United States, or any of them.

---

[6]Changed by the Twelfth Amendment.

[7]Changed by the Twenty-fifth Amendment.

Before he enter on the Execution of his Office, he shall take the following Oath or Affirmation:—"I do solemnly swear (or affirm) that I will faithfully execute the Office of President of the United States, and will to the best of my Ability, preserve, protect, and defend the Constitution of the United States."

Section 2   The President shall be Commander in Chief of the Army and Navy of the United States, and of the Militia of the several States, when called into the actual Service of the United States; he may require the Opinion, in writing, of the principal Officer in each of the executive Departments, upon any Subject relating to the Duties of their respective Offices, and he shall have Power to grant Reprieves and Pardons for Offences against the United States, except in Cases of Impeachment.

He shall have Power, by and with the Advice and Consent of the Senate, to make Treaties, provided two thirds of the Senators present concur; and he shall nominate, and by and with the Advice and Consent of the Senate, shall appoint Ambassadors, other public Ministers and Consuls, Judges of the supreme Court, and all other Officers of the United States, whose Appointments are not herein otherwise provided for, and which shall be established by Law; but the Congress may by Law vest the Appointment of such inferior Officers, as they think proper, in the President alone, in the Courts of Law, or in the Heads of Departments.

The President shall have Power to fill up all Vacancies that may happen during the Recess of the Senate, by granting Commissions which shall expire at the End of their next Session.

Section 3   He shall from time to time give to the Congress Information of the State of the Union, and recommend to their Consideration such Measures as he shall judge necessary and expedient; he may, on extraordinary Occasions, convene both Houses, or either of them, and in Case of Disagreement between them, with Respect to the Time of Adjournment, he may adjourn them to such Time as he shall think proper; he shall receive Ambassadors and other public Ministers; he shall take Care that the Laws be faithfully executed, and shall Commission all the Officers of the United States.

Section 4   The President, Vice President and all civil Officers of the United States, shall be removed from Office on Impeachment for, and Conviction of, Treason, Bribery, or other high Crimes and Misdemeanors.

ARTICLE III

Section 1   The judicial Power of the United States, shall be vested in one supreme Court, and in such inferior Courts as the Congress may from time to time ordain and establish. The Judges, both of the supreme and inferior Courts, shall hold their Offices during good Behaviour, and shall, at stated Times, receive for their Services, a Compensation, which shall not be diminished during their Continuance in Office.

Section 2   The judicial Power shall extend to all Cases, in Law and Equity, arising under this Constitution, the Laws of the United States, and Treaties made, or which shall be made, under their Authority;—to all Cases affecting Ambassadors, other public Ministers and Consuls;—to all Cases of admiralty and maritime Jurisdiction;—to Controversies to which the United States shall be a party;—to Controversies between two or more States;—between a State and Citizens of another State;[8]—between Citizens of different States;—between Citizens of the same State claiming Lands under Grants of different States, and between a State, or the Citizens thereof, and foreign States, Citizens or Subjects.

In all Cases affecting Ambassadors, other public Ministers and Consuls, and those in which a State shall be Party, the supreme Court shall have original Jurisdiction. In all the other Cases before mentioned, the supreme Court shall have appellate Jurisdiction, both as to Law and Fact, with such Exceptions, and under such Regulations as the Congress shall make.

The Trial of all Crimes, except in Cases of Impeachment, shall be by Jury: and such Trial shall be held in the State where the said Crimes shall have been committed; but when not committed within any State, the Trial shall be at such Place or Places as the Congress may by Law have directed.

Section 3   Treason against the United States, shall consist only in levying War against them, or in adhering to their Enemies, giving them Aid and Comfort. No Person shall be convicted of Treason unless on the Testimony of two Witnesses to the same overt Act, or on Confession in open Court.

The Congress shall have Power to declare the Punishment of Treason, but no Attainder of Treason shall work Corruption of Blood, or Forfeiture except during the Life of the Person attainted.

ARTICLE IV

Section 1   Full Faith and Credit shall be given in each State to the public Acts, Records, and judicial Proceedings of every other State. And the Congress may by general Laws prescribe the Manner in which such Acts, Records and Proceedings shall be proved, and the Effect thereof.

Section 2   The Citizens of each State shall be entitled to all Privileges and Immunities of Citizens in the several States.

A Person charged in any State with Treason, Felony, or other Crime, who shall flee from Justice, and be found in another State, shall on Demand of the executive Authority of the State from which he fled, be delivered up, to be removed to the State having Jurisdiction of the Crime.

No Person held to Service or Labour in one State, under the Laws thereof, escaping into another, shall, in Consequence of any Law or Regulation therein, be discharged from such Service or Labour, but shall be delivered up on Claim of the Party to whom such Service or Labour may be due.[9]

Section 3   New States may be admitted by the Congress into this Union; but no new State shall be formed or erected within the Jurisdiction of any other State; nor any State be formed by the Junction of two or more States, or Parts of States, without the Consent of the Legislatures of the States concerned as well as of the Congress.

The Congress shall have Power to dispose of and make all needful Rules and Regulations respecting the Territory or other Property belonging to the United States; and nothing in this Constitution shall be so construed as to Prejudice any Claims of the United States, or of any particular State.

Section 4   The United States shall guarantee to every State in this Union a Republican Form of Government, and shall protect each of them against Invasion; and on Application of the Legislature, or of the Executive (when the Legislature cannot be convened) against domestic Violence.

ARTICLE V

The Congress, whenever two thirds of both Houses shall deem it necessary, shall propose Amendments to this Constitution, or, on the Application of the Legislatures of two thirds of the several States, shall call a Convention for proposing Amendments, which, in either Case, shall be valid to all Intents and Purposes, as Part of this Constitution, when ratified by the legislatures of three fourths of the several States, or by Conventions in three fourths thereof, as the one or the other Mode of Ratification may be proposed by the Congress; Provided that no Amendment which may be made prior to the Year One thousand eight hundred and eight shall in any Manner affect the first and fourth Clauses in the Ninth Section of the first Article; and that no State, without its Consent, shall be deprived of its equal Suffrage in the Senate.

ARTICLE VI

All Debts contracted and Engagements entered into, before the Adoption of this Constitution, shall be as valid against the United States under this Constitution, as under the Confederation.

The Constitution, and the Laws of the United States which shall be made in Pursuance thereof; and all Treaties made, or which shall be made, under the Authority of the United States, shall be the supreme Law of the Land; and

---

[8]Changed by the Eleventh Amendment.

[9]Changed by the Thirteenth Amendment.

the Judges in every State shall be bound thereby, any Thing in the Constitution or Laws of any State to the Contrary notwithstanding.

The Senators and Representatives before mentioned, and the Members of the several State Legislatures, and all executive and judicial Officers, both of the United States and of the several States, shall be bound by Oath or Affirmation, to support this Constitution; but no religious Test shall ever be required as a Qualification to any Office or public Trust under the United States.

ARTICLE VII

The Ratification of the Conventions of nine States, shall be sufficient for the Establishment of this Constitution between the States so ratifying the Same.

Done in Convention by the Unanimous Consent of the States present the Seventeenth Day of September in the Year of our Lord one thousand seven hundred and eighty seven and of the Independance of the United States of America the Twelfth. In witness whereof We have hereunto subscribed our Names.

AMENDMENTS

[The first 10 amendments are known as the "Bill of Rights."]

Amendment I (Ratified 1791)

Congress shall make no law respecting an establishment of religion, or prohibiting the free exercise thereof; or abridging the freedom of speech, or of the press; or the right of the people peaceably to assemble, and to petition the Government for a redress of grievances.

Amendment 2 (Ratified 1791)

A well regulated Militia, being necessary to the security of a free State, the right of the people to keep and bear Arms, shall not be infringed.

Amendment 3 (Ratified 1791)

No Soldier shall, in time of peace be quartered in any house, without the consent of the Owner, nor in time of war, but in a manner to be prescribed by law.

Amendment 4 (Ratified 1791)

The right of the people to be secure in their persons, houses, papers, and effects, against unreasonable searches and seizures, shall not be violated, and no Warrants shall issue, but upon probable cause, supported by Oath or affirmation, and particularly describing the place to be searched, and the persons or things to be seized.

Amendment 5 (Ratified 1791)

No person shall be held to answer for a capital, or otherwise infamous crime, unless on a presentment or indictment of a Grand Jury, except in cases arising in the land or naval forces, or in the Militia, when in actual service in time of War or public danger; nor shall any person be subject for the same offence to be twice put in jeopardy of life or limb; nor shall be compelled in any criminal case to be a witness against himself, nor be deprived of life, liberty, or property, without due process of law; nor shall private property be taken for public use, without just compensation.

Amendment 6 (Ratified 1791)

In all criminal prosecutions, the accused shall enjoy the right to a speedy and public trial, by an impartial jury of the State and district wherein the crime shall have been committed, which district shall have been previously ascertained by law, and to be informed of the nature and cause of the accusation; to be confronted with the witnesses against him; to have compulsory process for obtaining Witnesses in his favor, and to have assistance of counsel for his defence.

Amendment 7 (Ratified 1791)

In Suits at common law, where the value in controversy shall exceed twenty dollars, the right of trial by jury shall be preserved, and no fact tried by a jury, shall be otherwise re-examined in any Court of the United States, than according to the rules of the common law.

Amendment 8 (Ratified 1791)

Excessive bail shall not be required, nor excessive fines imposed, nor cruel and unusual punishments inflicted.

Amendment 9 (Ratified 1791)

The enumeration in the Constitution, of certain rights, shall not be construed to deny or disparage others retained by the people.

Amendment 10 (Ratified 1791)

The powers not delegated to the United States by the Constitution, nor prohibited by it to the States, are reserved to the States respectively, or to the people.

Amendment 11 (Ratified 1795)

The Judicial power of the United States shall not be construed to extend to any suit in law or equity, commenced or prosecuted against one of the United States by Citizens of another State, or by Citizens or Subjects of any Foreign State.

Amendment 12 (Ratified 1804)

The Electors shall meet in their respective states, and vote by ballot for President and Vice-President, one of whom, at least, shall not be an inhabitant of the same state with themselves; they shall name in their ballots the person voted for as President, and in distinct ballots the person voted for as Vice-President, and they shall make distinct lists of all persons voted for as President, and of all persons voted for as Vice-President, and of the number of votes for each, which lists they shall sign and certify, and transmit sealed to the seat of the government of the United States, directed to the President of the Senate;—The President of the Senate shall, in the presence of the Senate and House of Representatives, open all the certificates and the votes shall then be counted;—The person having the greatest number of votes for President, shall be the President, if such number be a majority of the whole number of Electors appointed; and if no person have such majority, then from the persons having the highest numbers not exceeding three on the list of those voted for as President, the House of Representatives shall choose immediately, by ballot, the President. But in choosing the President, the votes shall be taken by states, the representation from each state having one vote; a quorum for this purpose shall consist of a member or members from two-thirds of the states, and a majority of all the states shall be necessary to a choice. And if the House of Representatives shall not choose a President whenever the right of choice shall devolve upon them, before the fourth day of March next following, then the Vice-President shall act as president, as in the case of the death or other constitutional disability of the President.[10]—The person having the greatest number of votes as Vice-President, shall be the Vice-President, if such number be a majority of the whole number of Electors appointed, and if no person have a majority, then from the two highest numbers on the list, the Senate shall choose the Vice-President; a quorum for the purpose shall consist of two-thirds of the whole number of Senators, and a majority of the whole number shall be necessary to a choice. But no person constitutionally ineligible to the office of President shall be eligible to that of Vice-President of the United States.

Amendment 13 (Ratified 1865)

Section 1   Neither slavery nor involuntary servitude, except as a punishment for crime whereof the party shall have been duly convicted, shall exist within the United States, or any place subject to their jurisdiction.

Section 2   Congress shall have power to enforce this article by appropriate legislation.

Amendment 14 (Ratified 1868)

Section 1   All persons born or naturalized in the United States, and subject to the jurisdiction thereof, are citizens of the United States and of the State wherein they reside. No State shall make or enforce any law which shall abridge the privileges or immunities of citizens of the United States; nor shall any State deprive any person of life, liberty, or property, without due process of law; nor deny to any person within its jurisdiction the equal protection of the laws.

Section 2   Representatives shall be apportioned among the several States according to their respective numbers, counting the whole number of persons in each State, excluding Indians not taxed. But when the right to vote at any election for the choice of electors for President and Vice President of the United States, Representatives in Congress, the Executive and Judicial officers of a State, or the members of the Legislature thereof, is denied to any of the male inhabitants of such State, being twenty-one[11] years of age, and citizens of the United States, or in any way abridged except for participation in rebellion, or other crime, the basis of representation therein shall be reduced in the proportion which the number of such male citizens shall bear to the whole number of male citizens twenty-one years of age in such State.

Section 3   No person shall be a Senator or Representative in Congress, or elector of President and Vice President, or hold any office, civil or military, under the United States, or under any State, who, having previously taken an oath, as a member of Congress, or as an officer of the United States, or as a member of any State legislature, or as an executive or judicial officer of any State, to support the Constitution of the United States, shall have engaged in insurrection or rebellion against the same, or given aid or comfort to the enemies thereof. But Congress may by a vote of two-thirds of each House, remove such disability.

Section 4   The validity of the public debt of the United States, authorized by law, including debts incurred for payment of pensions and bounties for services in suppressing insurrection or rebellion, shall not be questioned. But neither the United States nor any State shall

---

[10]Changed by the Twentieth Amendment.

[11]Changed by the Twenty-sixth Amendment.

assume or pay any debt or obligation incurred in aid of insurrection or rebellion against the United States, or any claim for the loss or emancipation of any slave; but all such debts, obligations and claims shall be held illegal and void.

Section 5   The Congress shall have power to enforce, by appropriate legislation, the provisions of this article.

Amendment 15 (Ratified 1870)

Section 1   The right of citizens of the United States to vote shall not be denied or abridged by the United States or by any State on account of race, color, or previous condition of servitude.

Section 2   The Congress shall have power to enforce this article by appropriate legislation.

Amendment 16 (Ratified 1913)

The Congress shall have power to lay and collect taxes on incomes, from whatever source derived, without apportionment among the several States, and without regard to any census or enumeration.

Amendment 17 (Ratified 1913)

The Senate of the United States shall be composed of two Senators from each State, elected by the people thereof, for six years; and each Senator shall have one vote. The electors in each State shall have the qualifications requisite for electors of the most numerous branch of the State legislatures.

When vacancies happen in the representation of any State in the Senate, the executive authority of such State shall issue writs of election to fill such vacancies: *Provided,* That the legislature of any State may empower the executive thereof to make temporary appointments until the people fill the vacancies by election as the legislature may direct.

This amendment shall not be so construed as to affect the election or term of any Senator chosen before it becomes valid as part of the Constitution.

Amendment 18 (Ratified 1919; Repealed 1933)

Section 1   After one year from the ratification of this article the manufacture, sale, or transportation of intoxicating liquors within, the importation thereof into, or the exportation thereof from the United States and all territory subject to the jurisdiction thereof for beverage purposes is hereby prohibited.

Section 2   The Congress and the several States shall have concurrent power to enforce this article by appropriate legislation.

Section 3   This article shall be inoperative unless it shall have been ratified as an amendment to the Constitution by the legislatures of the several States, as provided in the Constitution, within seven years from the date of the submission hereof to the States by the Congress.[12]

Amendment 19 (Ratified 1920)

The right of citizens of the United States to vote shall not be denied or abridged by the United States or by any State on account of sex.

Congress shall have power to enforce this article by appropriate legislation.

Amendment 20 (Ratified 1933)

Section 1   The terms of the President and Vice President shall end at noon on the 20th day of January, and the terms of Senators and Representatives at noon on the 3d day of January, of the years in which such terms would have ended if this article had not been ratified; and the terms of their successors shall then begin.

Section 2   The Congress shall assemble at least once in every year, and such meeting shall begin at noon on the 3d day of January, unless they shall by law appoint a different day.

Section 3   If, at the time fixed for the beginning of the term of the President, the President elect shall have died, the Vice President elect shall become President. If a President shall not have been chosen before the time fixed for the beginning of his term, or if the President elect shall have failed to qualify, then the Vice President elect shall act as President until a President shall have qualified; and the Congress may by law provide for the case wherein neither a President elect nor a Vice President elect shall have qualified, declaring who shall then act as President, or the manner in which one who is to act shall be selected, and such person shall act accordingly until a President or Vice President shall have qualified.

Section 4   The Congress may by law provide for the case of the death of any of the persons from whom the House of Representatives may choose a President whenever the right of choice shall have devolved upon them, and for the case of the death of any of the persons from whom the Senate may choose a Vice President whenever the right of choice shall have devolved upon them.

Section 5   Sections 1 and 2 shall take effect on the 15th day of October following the ratification of this article.

---

[12]Repealed by the Twenty-first Amendment.

Section 6   This article shall be inoperative unless it shall have been ratified as an amendment to the Constitution by the legislatures of three-fourths of the several States within seven years from the date of its submission.

Amendment 21 (Ratified 1933)

Section 1   The eighteenth article of amendment to the Constitution of the United States is hereby repealed.

Section 2   The transportation or importation into any State, Territory, or possession of the United States for delivery or use therein of intoxicating liquors, in violation of the laws thereof, is hereby prohibited.

Section 3   This article shall be inoperative unless it shall have been ratified as an amendment to the Constitution by conventions in the several States, as provided in the Constitution, within seven years from the date of the submission hereof to the States by the Congress.

Amendment 22 (Ratified 1951)

Section 1   No person shall be elected to the office of the President more than twice, and no person who has held the office of President, or acted as President, for more than two years of a term to which some other person was elected President shall be elected to the office of the President more than once. But this Article shall not apply to any person holding the office of President when this Article was proposed by the Congress, and shall not prevent any person who may be holding the office of President, or acting as President, during the term within which this Article becomes operative from holding the office of President or acting as President during the remainder of such term.

Section 2   This Article shall be inoperative unless it shall have been ratified as an amendment to the Constitution by the legislatures of three-fourths of the several States within seven years from the date of its submission to the States by the Congress.

Amendment 23 (Ratified 1961)

Section 1   The District constituting the seat of Government of the United States shall appoint in such manner as the Congress may direct:

A number of electors of President and Vice President equal to the whole number of Senators and Representatives in Congress to which the District would be entitled if it were a State, but in no event more than the least populous State; they shall be in addition to those appointed by the States, but they shall be considered, for the purposes of the election of President and Vice President, to be electors appointed by a State; and they shall meet in the District and perform such duties as provided by the twelfth article of amendment.

Section 2   The Congress shall have power to enforce this article by appropriate legislation.

Amendment 24 (Ratified 1964)

Section 1   The right of citizens of the United States to vote in any primary or other election for President or Vice President, for electors for President or Vice President, or for Senator or Representative in Congress, shall not be denied or abridged by the United States or any State by reason of failure to pay any poll tax or other tax.

Section 2   The Congress shall have power to enforce this article by appropriate legislation.

Amendment 25 (Ratified 1967)

Section 1   In case of the removal of the President from office or of his death or resignation, the Vice President shall become President.

Section 2   Whenever there is a vacancy in the office of the Vice President, the President shall nominate a Vice President who shall take office upon confirmation by a majority vote of both Houses of Congress.

Section 3   Whenever the President transmits to the President pro tempore of the Senate and the Speaker of the House of Representatives his written declaration that he is unable to discharge the powers and duties of his office, and until he transmits to them a written declaration to the contrary, such powers and duties shall be discharged by the Vice President as Acting President.

Section 4   Whenever the Vice President and a majority of either the principal officers of the executive departments or of such other body as Congress may by law provide, transmit to the President pro tempore of the Senate and the Speaker of the House of Representatives their written declaration that the President is unable to discharge the powers and duties of his office, the Vice President shall immediately assume the powers and duties of the office as Acting President.

Thereafter, when the President transmits to the President pro tempore of the Senate and the Speaker of the House of Representatives his written declaration that no inability exists, he shall resume the powers and duties of his office unless the Vice President and a majority of either the principal officers of the executive department or of such other body as Congress may by law provide, transmit within four days to the President pro tempore of the Senate and the Speaker of the House of Representatives their written declaration that the President is unable to discharge the powers and duties of his office. Thereupon Congress shall decide the issue, assembling within forty-eight hours for that purpose if not in session. If the Congress, within twenty-one days after receipt of the latter written declaration, or, if Congress is not in

session, within twenty-one days after Congress is required to assemble, determines by two-thirds vote of both
Houses that the President is unable to discharge the
powers and duties of his office, the Vice President shall
continue to discharge the same as Acting President;
otherwise, the President shall resume the powers and
duties of his office.

Amendment 26 (Ratified 1971)

Section 1   The right of citizens of the United States, who
are eighteen years of age or older, to vote shall not be
denied or abridged by the United States or by any State on
account of age.

Section 2   The Congress shall have power to enforce
this article by appropriate legislation.

Amendment 27 (Ratified 1992)

No law, varying the compensation for the services of the
Senators and Representatives, shall take effect, until an
election of Representatives shall have intervened.